Unicode Explained

Other resources from O'Reilly

Related titles   CJKV Information Processing   Mastering Regular
Fonts and Encodings   Expressions
Java Internationalization   SVG Essentials
Java I/O   XML in a Nutshell

oreilly.com   *oreilly.com* is more than a complete catalog of O'Reilly books. You'll also find links to news, events, articles, weblogs, sample chapters, and code examples.

oreillynet.com is the essential portal for developers interested in open and emerging technologies, including new platforms, programming languages, and operating systems.

Conferences   O'Reilly brings diverse innovators together to nurture the ideas that spark revolutionary industries. We specialize in documenting the latest tools and systems, translating the innovator's knowledge into useful skills for those in the trenches. Visit *conferences.oreilly.com* for our upcoming events.

Safari Bookshelf (*safari.oreilly.com*) is the premier online reference library for programmers and IT professionals. Conduct searches across more than 1,000 books. Subscribers can zero in on answers to time-critical questions in a matter of seconds. Read the books on your Bookshelf from cover to cover or simply flip to the page you need. Try it today for free.

Unicode Explained

Jukka K. Korpela

O'REILLY®

Beijing · Cambridge · Farnham · Köln · Sebastopol · Tokyo

Unicode Explained
by Jukka K. Korpela

Copyright © 2006 O'Reilly Media. All rights reserved.
Printed in the United States of America.

Published by O'Reilly Media, Inc., 1005 Gravenstein Highway North, Sebastopol, CA 95472.

O'Reilly books may be purchased for educational, business, or sales promotional use. Online editions are also available for most titles (*http://safari.oreilly.com*). For more information, contact our corporate/institutional sales department:(800) 998-9938 or *corporate@oreilly.com* .

Editor: Simon St. Laurent	**Indexer:** Joe Wizda	
Production Editor: Adam Witwer	**Cover Designer:** Karen Montgomery	
Copyeditor: Linley Dolby	**Interior Designer:** David Futato	
	Illustrators: Robert Romano and Jessamyn Read	

June 2006: First Edition.

Revision History for the First Edition:
2006-06-07   First release
2014-03-14   Second release

See *http://oreilly.com/catalog/errata.csp?isbn=9780596101213* for release details.

Nutshell Handbook, the Nutshell Handbook logo, and the O'Reilly logo are registered trademarks of O'Reilly Media, Inc. *Unicode Explained*, the image of a long-tailed glossy starling, and related trade dress are trademarks of O'Reilly Media, Inc.

Unicode® is a trademark of the Unicode Consortium

Many of the designations uses by manufacturers and sellers to distinguish their products are claimed as trademarks. Where those designations appear in this book, and O'Reilly Media, Inc. was aware of a trademark claim, the designations have been printed in caps or initial caps

While every precaution has been taken in the preparation of this book, the publisher and authors assume no responsibility for errors or omissions, or for damages resulting from the use of the information contained herein.

ISBN: 978-0-596-10121-3

[LSI]

1394569157

Table of Contents

Part II.   A Systematic Look at Unicode

Part III.   Advanced Unicode Topics

Preface

Characters often seem simple on the surface, but they are at the heart of a wide variety of data communications and data processing problems, including text processing, typesetting, styling text, text databases, and the transmission of textual information.

Computers were invented just for computing. For quite some time, they were so expensive that their use was limited to the most important numerical calculations that would have been impossible otherwise. Text was used mainly to add legends and headings to numeric output, often using a very limited character repertoire, maybe even lacking lowercase letters. As the cost of computing has dropped, computers have become extensively used for human communication in text format. Most people think of computers as communicators rather than calculators. People want to communicate in different languages, and we also use notation systems that may require rich repertoires of characters.

Unicode was developed to help make this both possible and smooth. Unicode was first defined in the early 1990s, but its use has progressed fairly slowly. Modern computers often use Unicode internally, but applications and users still tend to work with older character codes, which are often very limited. It has been rather complicated to work with Unicode in text processing, for example. At long last, however, these problems are becoming easier to solve. Information technology is becoming really multinational, supporting different languages, writing systems, and conventions. IT products need to be at least potentially suitable for use in different cultural environments, or "localizable." Unicode itself is just part of the technical basis for all this, but it is an indispensable part.

The technological basis of using Unicode, though still imperfect, is much better than most people's capabilities for making use of it. Even computer professionals often don't know how to work with large repertoires of characters. The bottleneck is lack of a basic knowledge and skills, not a lack of hardware or software.

The concept of a character is one of the most difficult basic concepts in information technology, yet fundamental to text processing, databases, the Web, XML-based markup, internationalization, and other areas. People who encounter Unicode when studying such topics often run into serious difficulties. They mostly find material that assumes that the reader already knows what Unicode is. It might be even worse: it is very easy to find incorrect or seriously confusing information about Unicode and characters, even in new books. People find themselves in a maze of twisty little passages of characters, fonts, encodings, and related concepts.

This book guides you through the Unicode and character world. It explains how to identify and classify characters—whether common, uncommon, or exotic—and to type them, to use their properties, and to process character data in a robust manner. It helps you to live in a world with several character encodings.

Audience

Readers of this book are expected to be familiar with computers and how computers work, broadly speaking. They are not expected to know computer programming, though many readers will use the contents in system design and programming.

This book is intended for people with different backgrounds and needs, including:

- An end user of multilingual or specialized text-related applications. For example, anyone who works with texts containing mathematical or special symbols, or uses a multilingual database. These readers should probably explore Chapters 1 through 3 first, practice with that content, and then read Chapters 7 and 8.

- An IT professional who needs to understand Unicode and work with it. The need might arise from text data conversion tasks, from creating internationalized software or web sites, or from system design or programming in an environment that uses Unicode.

- An IT teacher who needs a better understanding of character code issues, both to understand the subject area better and to disseminate correct information. There is rather little about character codes in curricula, and this is largely a chicken-and-egg problem: there are no good textbooks, and teachers themselves don't know the topic well enough. The first three chapters of the book could provide the foundation for a course, optionally coupled with other chapters relevant to a particular curriculum.

- An IT student, hobbyist, or professional who keeps hearing about Unicode and needs to work with technologies that use Unicode, such as XML.

Assumptions and Approach

Previous knowledge about character codes is not assumed. If you already know about them, you may need to change your mental model a bit.

This book starts at the ordinary computer user's level. Thus, it unavoidably contains explanations that look trivial to some readers. However, these discussions might help in explaining things to others when needed. The book also contains practical instructions on actually working with "special" characters, and an IT professional might find this irrelevant. However, studying such issues and practicing with them will help a lot in creating a background for more technical work with the infrastructures of character usage.

In explaining practical ways of doing things, this book often uses Microsoft Windows and Microsoft Office programs as examples. This is because so many people use such software and need to know how to use Unicode in them. Moreover, even if you personally prefer other software, odds are good that you need to work with Windows and Office at times. Information on using Unicode in some other environments can be found in the following:

- Markus Kuhn: "UTF-8 and Unicode FAQ for Unix/Linux," which is available at *http://www.cl.cam.ac.uk/~mgk25/unicode.html*
- Tom Gewecke: "Unleash Your Multilingual Mac," which is available at *http://hometown.aol.com/tg3907/mlingos9.html*

After the first three chapters, this book gets more technical, and many of the issues discussed are abstract and even formal. Therefore, understanding most of the material in the initial chapters is essential for the rest. To most people, it is very difficult to read about abstract things if you lack a concrete background that lets you map the abstract concepts and rules to specific practice.

This book explores Unicode processing generally, but cannot go into great detail on all parts of the Unicode character space. For much more information on ideographic characters and processing of East Asian languages, see Ken Lunde's *CJKV Information Processing* (O'Reilly).

Except for the last chapter (Chapter 11), this book does not assume that the reader knows about computer programming. However, some references to programming are made throughout the book.

Contents of This Book

The book has three parts:

Part I

Chapters 1 through 3 provide a self-contained tutorial presentation of Unicode and character data. It is aimed at anyone who has a basic understanding of computing, and introduces characters in information technology, with some historical background. Although much of this part is well-known to many IT professionals, it provides a consistent terminology that could give professionals (and especially teachers) a model for talking to laymen about characters.

Part II

Chapters 4 through 6 give detailed information about using Unicode and other character codes. These chapters are especially aimed at computer science students and teachers, information technology professionals, and people involved in linguistic data processing and databases containing string data. Together with the first part, this covers what every IT professional should know about characters. It explains the principles and methods of defining character codes, describes some of the widely used codes, presents code conversion techniques, and takes a detailed look at Unicode. This includes properties and classification of characters, collation and sorting, line breaking rules, and Unicode encodings.

Part III

Chapters 7 through 11 discuss relatively independent topics, to be read according to each reader's specific needs. They are topics that are important and even crucial to many, but not necessary to all. For example, if you need to author or administer multilingual web sites, you should read the section on characters in HTML and XHTML. To be honest, I would suggest that most people need to read it at least twice. Character code problems are intrinsically difficult, and very widely misunderstood. It takes time to digest the concepts and principles before you can really start working with the algorithms and tools.

The chapters can be characterized as follows:

Chapter 1, *Characters as Data*

This chapter describes, at a general level but exemplified by simple and typical cases, how computers represent and process characters. It defines fundamental concepts like character set, code position, encoding, glyph, and font. At this point, Unicode is the only character set discussed, to avoid confusion. To make the discussion more concrete and motivating, some features of writing systems are described. The historical development of character codes is presented to the extent that is necessary for understanding why even apparently simple characters, such as dashes and é, still cause problems. The use of different encodings is illustrated by examples of viewing email messages and web pages, using commands to select the encoding if needed. The basic methods for finding, installing, and selecting fonts are described.

Chapter 2, *Writing Characters*

This is a practical presentation of some common methods of entering characters, including keyboard variation, special keys, changing keyboard settings, virtual keyboards, character maps, automatic "correction" of character sequences, program commands, and different escape notations. It is largely a collection of recipes, useful, for example, to people who work daily with texts containing "difficult" characters. For this reason, some quick reference tables for very commonly needed characters are presented. However, it is also relevant to IT specialists who need to understand the possible input methods when designing applications and systems. The examples used are mostly from MS Windows and MS Office environments but various alternatives (such as "Unicode editors") are also discussed. HTML and XML character reference and entity reference techniques are presented as well. The chapter ends with an exercise for writing some specialized texts using some of the techniques presented.

Chapter 3, *Character Sets and Encodings*

This chapter describes some very widely used character codes and encodings, mainly ASCII, ISO-8859-1 and other ISO-8859 standards, Windows Latin 1 and relatives, and UTF-8. (However, the semantics of characters are described in Chapter 8.) Some less common encodings such as DOS code pages are described in order to give some basics for working with legacy data and legacy systems. A few widely used multibyte encodings for East Asian languages are briefly described, too. The section describes how conversions between the encodings can be performed, either with the functions of commonly used programs or separate converters. It also discusses practical feasibility of the character sets in different contexts, such as email, Internet discussion forums, and document interchange. MIME is presented to the extent needed for dealing with the charset issue.

Chapter 4, *The Structure of Unicode*

An in-depth presentation of the fundamentals of Unicode, including design principles, coding space, and special terminology. The nature of Unicode as an umbrella standard based on a large number of older standards is explained, as well as its relationship to ISO 10646. The unification principle as well as criticism of it is described.

Chapter 5, *Properties of Characters*

This chapter describes the various properties defined for characters in the Unicode standard and their relationship with some programming concepts. This is, in part, a companion to the much more formal definitions in the standard itself. In particular, compatibility, decompositions, collation, sorting, directionality, and line-breaking properties as well as Unicode normalization forms are described.

Chapter 6, *Unicode Encodings*

This chapter describes UTF-8 and other Unicode encodings in detail, including the algorithmic descriptions and the practical considerations on choosing an encoding.

Chapter 7, *Characters and Languages*

The chapter describes some IT-related requirements of different languages and writing systems, such as how to deal with right-to-left writing. This includes conversions between writing systems (transliteration or transcription). The interaction between encoding, language, and font settings is described. Moreover, language codes, language metadata, and language markup are described, illustrated with XML examples.

Chapter 8, *Character Usage*

This chapter consists of sections devoted to different character blocks and collections that are practically important especially in the Western world. The first section is more generic and discusses the relationship of character standards, orthography, and typography. (Even in purely English-language text, typographically correct punctuation requires characters beyond ASCII.) The chapter contains detailed information about the semantics and usage of individual characters, although the level of detail depends greatly on the importance of the character. All the major blocks are briefly characterized to give an overview, but the emphasis is on ASCII, different Latin supplements, general punctuation, and mathematical and technical symbols.

Chapter 9, *The Character Level and Above*

Characters form but one "protocol level," above which there are higher levels such as markup level, record structure level, and application level. This chapter provides guidelines for the coding of information at different levels when there is choice, such as using markup versus character difference (largely still an open problem despite the efforts of the W3C and the Unicode Consortium). This is particularly important for processing of legacy data and for avoiding overly fine distinctions at the character level. The chapter ends with a section on media types for text and the difference between plain text, other subtypes of text, and application types such as text-processing formats.

Chapter 10, *Characters in Internet Protocols*

This chapter describes how character encoding information is transmitted using Internet protocols, including MIME and HTTP, and how content negotiation works on the Web (for the purposes of negotiating on character encoding). This constitutes a basis for a presentation of some fundamentals of multilingual web authoring at the technical level. Moreover, the use of characters in the protocols themselves, such as Internet message headers and URLs, is described, with focus on the partial shift from pure ASCII to Unicode. In particular, the technical basis of Internationalized Domain Names and Internationalized URLs is described.

Chapter 11, *Characters in Programming*

This chapter presents a number of ways to represent character and string data in different programming languages, such as FORTRAN, C, C#, Perl, ECMAScript, and Java™, as well as other computer languages such as XML and CSS. It emphasizes both the differences and similarities, which are illustrated with sample programs to perform simple manipulation of string data. The chapter is especially intended for people who teach programming but also for people who study or practice programming in an environment where character data is essential. Programs that cannot distinguish, for example, between an empty string, a space character, the NUL character, and the digit zero will have large problems in a Unicode environment. The chapter also examines requirements for modern processing of character data, including the principle of being prepared to handle a large character repertoire and that of separating internal encoding from input and output encodings. The International Components for Unicode (ICU) activity and its results are described. The chapter also contains a section on Common Locale Data Repository (CLDR) and its future use in disciplined programming. This largely goes beyond the character concept but is motivated by the use of Unicode in CLDR and by the organizational connection with the Unicode Consortium.

Appendix, *Tables for Writing Characters*

The Appendix provides some commonly needed information useful for entering characters. It includes tables of key sequences, as well as a mapping chart from the Symbol font to Unicode.

Self-Assessment Test

To estimate your progress in knowledge about Unicode, you can perform the following self-assessment test. Read the following statements and comment on each of them with one of the following alternatives (using whatever symbols you find convenient, such as those in parentheses): "I do not understand what the statement says" (??), "I know what it says but I do not know whether it is true" (?), "true" (+), and false (−). Moreover, for any "true" or "false" answer, consider what you would present as an argument in a discussion in which someone says you're wrong.

At any point in reading the book, and especially when you think you have learned enough, reread the statements and perform the test again. You might regard the following as a spoiler, so it has been written backward so that you can hopefully ignore it at this point if you like. It reveals what the test is about: .elpoep ot siht nialpxe ot deen thgim uoy dna ,gnorw era yeht yhw wonk ot laitnesse si ti ecnis ,hguoht ,siht gniwonk htiw deifsitas eb ton dluohs uoY .eslaf lla era yeht tub ,skoob ecnerefer ni neve edam ylnommoc era stnemetats ehT

1. Unicode is a 16-bit character code.
2. Unicode contains all the characters used in the languages of the world.
3. Unicode is meant to replace all the other character codes.
4. Unicode cannot be used in real applications now; it is just a future plan.
5. Using Unicode, the size of a text file gets doubled.
6. We don't need Unicode if we write only in English.
7. Unicode consists of 256 code pages.

Conventions Used in This Book

The following typographical conventions are used in this book:

Italic

Indicates new terms, URLs, email addresses, filenames, and file extensions.

`Constant width`

Indicates computer code in a broad sense. This includes commands, options, switches, variables, attributes, keys, functions, types, classes, namespaces, methods, modules, properties (does *not* include Unicode "properties"), parameters, values, objects, events, event handlers, XML tags, HTML tags, macros, the contents of files, and the output from commands.

`Constant width bold`

Shows commands or other text that should be typed literally by the user.

`Constant width italic`

Shows text that should be replaced with user-supplied values or by values determined by context.

This icon signifies a tip, suggestion, or general note.

This icon indicates a warning or caution.

The following special notations are used in this book to refer to characters:

"*x*"
> Refers to character *x* by showing it within double quotation marks. For clarity, characters that might be confused with other characters in the text—i.e., letters a–z, A–Z, and some common punctuation, such as hyphens (-), commas (,), and periods (.) —are enclosed in quotation marks.

U+nnnn
> Refers to a character (or a code point) by its Unicode number. The number *nnnn* is written in hexadecimal notation, usually in four digits using leading zeros if needed.

Web sites and pages are mentioned in this book to help the reader locate online information that might be useful. Normally both the address (URL) and the name (title, heading) of a page are mentioned. Some addresses are relatively complicated, but you can probably locate the pages easily by using your favorite search engine to find a page by its name, typically by typing it inside quotation marks. This may also help if the page cannot be found by its address; it may have moved elsewhere, so the name may work.

Using Code Examples

This book is here to help you get your job done. In general, you may use the code in this book in your programs and documentation. You do not need to contact us for permission unless you're reproducing a significant portion of the code. For example, writing a program that uses several chunks of code from this book does not require permission. Selling or distributing a CD-ROM of examples from O'Reilly books does require permission. Answering a question by citing this book and quoting example code does not require permission. Incorporating a significant amount of example code from this book into your product's documentation does require permission.

We appreciate, but do not require, attribution. An attribution usually includes the title, author, publisher, and ISBN. For example: "*Unicode Explained* by Jukka K. Korpela. Copyright 2006 O'Reilly Media, Inc., 0-596-10121-X."

If you feel your use of code examples falls outside fair use or the permission given above, feel free to contact us at *permissions@oreilly.com*.

Safari® Enabled

 When you see a Safari® Enabled icon on the cover of your favorite technology book, that means the book is available online through the O'Reilly Network Safari Bookshelf.

Safari offers a solution that's better than e-books. It's a virtual library that lets you easily search thousands of top tech books, cut and paste code samples, download chapters, and find quick answers when you need the most accurate, current information. Try it for free at *http://safari.oreilly.com*.

How to Contact Us

Please address comments and questions concerning this book to the publisher:

O'Reilly Media, Inc.
1005 Gravenstein Highway North
Sebastopol, CA 95472
800-998-9938 (in the United States or Canada)
707-829-0515 (international or local)
707 829-0104 (fax)

We have a web page for this book, where we list errata, examples, and any additional information. You can access this page at:

http://www.oreilly.com/catalog/unicode

To comment or ask technical questions about this book, send email to:

bookquestions@oreilly.com

For more information about our books, conferences, Resource Centers, and the O'Reilly Network, see our web site at:

http://www.oreilly.com

Acknowledgments

The presentation of problems, solutions, and ideas owes much to people with whom I have been in contact in character-related matters through years, such as (roughly in chronological order by their influence) Timo Kiravuo, Alan J. Flavell, Arjun Ray, Roman Czyborra, Bob Bemer, and Erkki I. Kolehmainen.

The reviewers, Andreas Prilop, John Cowan, and Jori Mäntysalo gave a very substantial amount of valuable input, both on content and on presentation. Simon St.Laurent has had an active and supportive role through the entire process as an editor.

PART I

Working with Characters

This part describes the fundamentals of representing character data in computers, including Unicode and other important character codes. It also discusses several practical ways of writing Unicode characters.

CHAPTER 1

Characters as Data

Computers were originally built to process numbers. Over the last few decades, they've become increasingly better at handling text as well, but the transition from human scribbling and beautiful typography to bits and bytes has been complicated. Going from a paper document to a computerized representation of that document means learning about how the computer handles text, and requires learning about characters, character codes, fonts, and encodings. Unicode provides a set of solutions for some of these problems, while retaining presentation flexibility for making text look as we feel it should.

Introduction to Characters and Unicode

Computer programs use two basic data types in most of their processing: characters and numbers. These basic types are combined in various ways to create strings, arrays, records, and other data structures. (Inside the computer, characters are numbers, but the ways that these numbers are handled is very different from numbers meant for calculation.)

Early computers were largely oriented toward numerical computation. However, characters were used early on in administrative data processing, where names, addresses, and other data needed to be stored and printed as strings. Text processing on computers became more common much later, when computers had become so affordable that they replaced typewriters. At present, most text documents are produced and processed using computers.

Originally, character data on computers had limited types and uses. For economic and technical reasons, the repertoire of characters was very small, not much more than the letters, digits, and basic punctuation used in normal English. This constitutes but a tiny fraction of the different characters used in the world's writing systems—about 100 characters out of literally myriads (tens of thousands) of characters. Thus, there was a growing need for a possibility of presenting and handling a large character repertoire on computers; Unicode is the fundamental answer to that.

Why Unicode?

Since you are reading this book, I assume you already have sufficient motivation to learn about Unicode. Nevertheless, a short presentation follows that explains the benefits of Unicode.

Computers internally work on numbers. This means that characters need to be coded as numbers. A typical arrangement is to use numbers from 0 to 255, because that range fits into a basic unit of data storage and transfer, called a *(8-bit) byte* or *octet*.

When you define how those numbers correspond to characters, you define a *character code*. There are quite a number of character codes defined and used in the world. Most of them have the same assignments for numbers 0 to 127, used for characters that appear in English as well as in many other languages: the letters a–z plus their uppercase equivalents, the digits 0–9, and a few punctuation marks. Many of the code numbers in this so-called ASCII set of characters are used for various technical purposes.

For French texts, for example, you need additional characters such as accented letters (é, ô, etc.). These can be provided by using code numbers in the range 128–255 in addition to the ASCII range, and this gives room for letters used in most other Western European languages as well. Thus, you can use a single character code, called Latin 1, even for a text containing a mixture of English, French, Spanish, and German, because these languages all use the Latin characters with relatively few additions.

However, you quickly run out of numbers if you try to cover too many languages within 256 characters. For this reason, different character codes were developed. For example, Latin 1 is for Western European languages, Latin 2 for several languages spoken in Central and Eastern Europe, and additional character codes exist for Greek, Cyrillic, Arabic, etc. When only one language is used, you can usually pick up a suitable character code and use it. In fact, someone probably did that for you when designing the particular computer system (including software) that you use. You may have used a particular character code for years without knowing anything about it.

Character codes that use only the code numbers from 0 to 255 are called *8-bit codes*, since such code numbers can be represented using 8 bits.

Things change when you need to combine languages in one document and the languages are fundamentally different in their use of characters. In an English-German or French-Spanish glossary, for example, you can use Latin 1. In English-Greek data, you can use one of the character codes developed for Greek, since these codes contain the ASCII characters. But what about French-Greek? That's not possible the same way, since the character codes discussed above do not support such a combination. A code either has Latin accented letters in the "upper half" (the range of 128–255), or it has Greek letters (α, β, γ, etc.) there. It would be impractical, and often impossible, to define 256-character codes for all the possible language combinations.

As you probably know, the number of characters needed for Chinese and Japanese is very large. They just would not fit into a set with only 256 characters. Therefore, different strategies are used. For example, 2 bytes (octets) instead of one might be used for one character. This would give 65,536 possible numbers for a character. On the other hand, the character codes developed for the needs of East Asian languages do not contain all the characters used in the world.

The solution to such problems, and many other problems in the world of growing information exchange, is the introduction of a character code that gives every character of every language a unique number. This number does not depend on the language used in the text, the font used to display the character, the software, the operating system, or the device. It is universal and kept unchanged. The range of possible numbers is set sufficiently high to cover all the current and future needs of all languages.

The solution is called *Unicode*, and it gives anyone the opportunity to say, "I want this character displayed and the number is…" and have herself understood by all systems that support Unicode. This does not always guarantee a success in displaying the character, due to lack of a suitable font, but such technical problems are manageable.

Much widely used software, including Microsoft Windows, Mac OS X, and Linux, has supported Unicode for years. However, to use Unicode, all the relevant components must be "Unicode enabled." For example, although Windows "knows Unicode," an application program used on a Windows system might not. Moreover, the display or printing of characters often fails since fonts (software for drawing characters) are still incomplete in covering the set of Unicode characters. This is changing as more complete fonts become available and as programs become more clever in their ability to use characters from different fonts.

Unicode Can Be Easy

Unicode is both very easy and very complicated. The fundamental principles are simple and natural, as the explanation above hopefully illustrated. The actual typing and viewing of Unicode characters can also be easy, when modern tools are used. As we get to complicated issues like sorting Unicode strings or controlling line breaking, you will find some challenges. But this book starts from simple principles and usage.

For example, an average PC running the Windows XP system has a universal tool for typing any Unicode character, assuming that it is contained in some font installed on the system. The tool is called the *Character Map*, or CharMap for short. Figure 1-1 shows the user interface of this program. The program can be launched from the Start menu, although you may need to look for it among "System tools" or something like that. You can select a collection of characters from a menu, and then click on a character to select it. The selected characters can be copied onto the clipboard with a single click, and you can then paste them (e.g., with Ctrl-V) where you like.

There are many other similar tools, often with advanced character search features. There are also ways to configure your keyboard on the fly so that keys and key combinations produce characters that you need frequently.

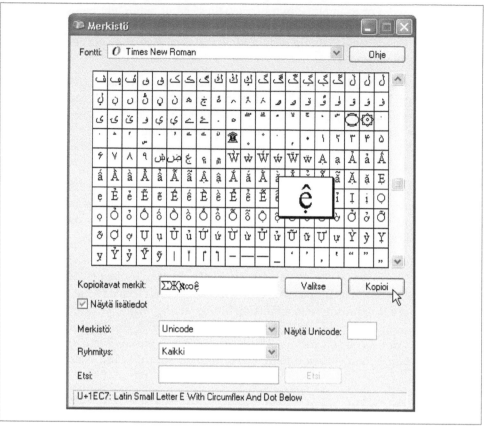

Figure 1-1. Character Map, part of Windows XP, lets you type any Unicode character

What's in a Character?

We use characters daily: we type them, and we read them on screen or on paper. We use text-processing programs routinely, much like people used to use typewriters, pens, or other writing tools. How could characters create problems?

Why Do We Need to Know About Characters?

If English is your native language, you are accustomed to using a small set of characters, consisting of the letters A–Z and a–z, digits 0–9, and a few punctuation characters. Most novels, newspaper articles, and memos contain no other characters. Since you seem to be able to type these characters directly on a keyboard, why should you learn more about characters and get confused? To be honest, character issues *are* confusing.

Suppose you use a computer only to write and edit texts in English, perhaps as a secretary or a technical editor. You still have reasons to know about characters:

- Computer technology has caused a decline in *typography*, and you can make a positive impression by using correct punctuation instead of typewriter-style punctuation. If you use a text-processing program, it probably takes care of using "smart" quotation marks instead of "straight" quotes, but you need to learn how to produce dashes —like this—and how to prevent bad line breaks.

- Normal English texts may contain special characters occasionally. Someone may spell Caesar as Cæsar, or use a word like fiancé, rôle, or garçon the French way, or use the per mille sign ‰ or the euro sign €. Michael Everson writes: "Despite unfounded but widespread belief to the contrary (based doubtless on the prevalence of ASCII), diacritics (usually French ones) are often found in naturalized English words. Examples are: à la carte, abbé, Ægean, archæology, belovèd, café, décor, détente, éclair, façade, fête, naïve, naïvety (but cf. non-naturalized naïveté), noël, œsophagus, résumé, vicuña" (*http://www.evertype.com/alphabets/english.pdf*). You may regard some of these spellings as foreign or obsolete, but people may still use them in English. There are often good reasons to change the spelling to something simpler, but not knowing how to produce the characters is not a good reason.

- Your text may contain *foreign names* with some strange characters. Although it is common to simplify the spelling, you can stand out positively by doing things correctly. Suppose that someone's surname is Hämäläinen and she works in an important international position. She is probably accustomed to seeing her name written as Hamalainen or Haemaelaeinen. But wouldn't she be delighted if someone were polite enough and competent enough to spell her name right, just for a change? However, she might not like it if someone tried to do so and failed, producing Hmlinen or H{m{l{inen.

- You might even be asked to include *quotations* in a foreign language. You might even need to work with a document in a foreign language, because someone has to do that and this is your day for being that someone. In that case, you may need to use foreign punctuation as well and to find a way to enter foreign characters efficiently, in addition to just knowing a universal clumsy way of entering any character.

- Texts increasingly contain technical and scientific special *notations*. Even casual memos and messages may need to mention μm (micrometer) or to use the almost equals sign ≈ or the male sign ♂. In scientific or technical texts, mathematical formulas are often quite crucial and need to be exactly right, down to the choice of each special symbol. The world is getting more technical and symbolic. Even nontechnical texts like bridge columns contain special symbols, such as ♠.

In *multilingual applications*, characters and their codes are a major issue. Even a web site with two or more languages or a bilingual dictionary can be regarded as multilingual applications, and they create the problem of representing the characters of both or all languages. For example, people using French and people using Russian on computers probably work with their own tools, settings, and conventions, but if you need to create a document that is bilingual in French and Russian, you need to make sure you can work with both Latin letters with diacritic marks and Cyrillic letters. In effect, you would need to use Unicode, one way or another.

If you are a *computer professional*, you need to be prepared to handle data-processing problems that may involve characters of any kind. Someday someone will ask you to work with a system for processing data in a strange language or with strange symbols in it, perhaps even in a writing system where text runs right to left. It will be very difficult if you have no background in working with such issues. Most people need quite some time to digest character problems and techniques. You may find that, with something you thought you knew for years, you have completely misunderstood some basics.

Even if you process only "normal" text, character code standards and specifications are more important than they used to be. Modularity of software requires that you isolate character-level processing from other levels. You should not test for a character variable's value being equal to 32 to test whether it is a space character. Often, even a more sensible test, against the character constant ' ', is suboptimal, and using a built-in function like isspace is better, since it takes care of other space-like characters as well. Tools developed for such operations are increasingly based on general specification in character standards, especially the Unicode standard. They are supposed to define, in a systematic and all-compassing way, the fundamental properties of characters, like being space-like, or being a letter, or allowing a line break before or after a character. To use such definitions and software modules that implement them, you don't need to know every detail, but you need to know the principles and the ways to get at the details when needed.

In addition, if you design or develop programs, databases, or systems, you will find that it is extremely difficult to adapt them to processing different character sets, if they were not designed to work that way. If the software is full of code that relies on using 1 byte (octet, 8-bit entity) for one character, it may need an almost complete rewrite if it needs to be modified to process Chinese text as well.

Characters as Units of Text

A character is a basic (or "atomic") unit of written text. A piece of text is a sequence of characters, also called a string. This does not necessarily mean that text is always displayed so that its characters appear linearly one after another, although this is what happens for English text, if we ignore the issue of division into lines. In other writing systems, consecutive characters may be combined into one glyph in complex ways. However, the text is still *logically* a sequence of characters.

Characters as abstractions

To store, process, and transfer data in digital form, we need an abstract concept of a character. It would not be feasible to store the specific appearance of each written character. Instead, we store information that tells which character it is, independent of the specific visual shape it has. If we wish to affect the way in which our characters are displayed and printed, we use special formatting commands or other tools.

The abstract concept of character is essential in Unicode, in all digital processing of character data, and even in writing itself. The meaning of a piece of text does not change if you change its font, the specific design of its characters. To put it a bit differently, the style and taste—and even the effect—of text might change, but we have an intuitive understanding of something invariant behind such variation. For example, "A," "A," "*A*," and "**A**" are instances of the same character. Since you know the Latin alphabet, you should have no difficulty with this. You might find it more difficult to know whether א and א are instances of the same Hebrew character, but people who speak Hebrew are able to recognize that.

Different attempts have been made to describe what characters are. They have even been compared to Platonic forms. The point is that there is so much negative in the concept: it is largely defined by saying what a character is *not*. In a sense, we extract properties and concrete features, until there's very little left—something that could be called the idea of a particular character. Dan Connolly has written in his classical treatise "'Character Set' Considered Harmful": "Note that by the term character, we do not mean a glyph, a name, a phoneme, nor a bit combination. A character is simply an atomic unit of communication. It is typically a symbol whose various representations are understood to mean the same thing by a community of people."

This raises the question of what to do if different people recognize things differently. In some languages, "v" and "w" have been treated as typographic variants of a single character; other languages treat them as completely distinct letters. In such situations, Unicode normally defines separate characters.

To clarify the abstract nature of characters, a Unicode character, or a character defined by some other standard:

- Normally has no particular stylistic appearance but may vary between broad limits, as long as the designs can be recognized as the same character
- Is essentially black and white, though a character as a whole could be colored with any other two colors (making, for example, the ♥ character appear in red), using methods external to character standards
- Has an official name (as described later) but no fixed name across languages, and not necessarily any commonly known name in a particular language
- Has no fixed pronunciation, except for some specifically phonetic characters; however, there are of course correspondences between letters and sounds, even across languages that use the same basic writing system
- May have very specific usage as a special symbol (e.g., © is just a copyright symbol) or a broad range of different uses (e.g., / can be a separator of a kind, a mathematical operator, or something else)

Variation of appearance or different characters?

Problems arise when the concept of an abstract character has to be applied to concrete situations. We know what the letter "A" is, but is it the same as the lowercase letter "a"?

That is, is the difference between them just variation in appearance, the same way as the letter "A" in the Times font differs from the letter "A" in the Arial font? In fact, the lowercase letters are a medieval invention, created by people who wrote text by hand and needed forms that are more convenient for that.

We could have defined "A" and "a" as just visual variants of the same abstract character, but we didn't. Quite early in the history of computers, this decision was made. It has far-reaching implications. If you wish to process input data so that upper- and lowercase letters are equivalent, to make things easier to people who type the data, you need to do something special to take care of that.

To take things a bit further, consider the Latin letter "A" and its relationship to the corresponding Cyrillic letter and the corresponding Greek letter, capital alpha. All three letters look the same in most fonts, and they share a common origin. Yet they belong to different alphabets: the Latin alphabet A, B, C, D..., which we use in English and many other languages, the Cyrillic alphabet А, Б, В, Г..., which is used in Russian and many Eastern European languages, and the Greek alphabet Α, Β, Γ, Δ... (alpha, beta, gamma, delta...).

It would have been possible to identify the Latin "A" and its Cyrillic and Greek counterparts. However, it was decided to keep them separate. Generally, Unicode (and character standards in general) do not unify characters across writing system boundaries. We might take this just as a fact of life and live with it. But we might also look at its reasonableness. Consider the operation of converting text from upper- to lowercase. The Latin letter "A" should become "a," whereas the Greek letter alpha "Α" should become α. It would be impossible to do this automatically if it were impossible to tell, from the internal digital representation, whether the original data contains the Latin "A" or the Greek "A."

Writing systems were invented by people, and characters are creations of mankind, not nature. Thus, the identity of abstract characters is in a sense just a decision made by some people. However, it is usually an informed decision.

Variation in shape turned into a character difference

In many cases, stylistic variation in drawing or printing a character has been "frozen" so that a variant obtains a specific shape and meaning. The ancient Romans used the letter "V" both as a consonant and as vowel. Later, it appeared in different variants, such as a rounded one, like our "U." People started using the original version and different curved variants in different contexts. As such usage became systematic, consistent, and common, the letter "U" was born.

Therefore, we now have the independent characters "V" and "U." They are, in turn, written with stylistic variation, though now the general idea is that the variation should not obscure the difference between these two characters. Yet, you might still see "V" used for "U" for stylistic reasons, especially to imitate ancient inscriptions (SENATVS POPVLVSQVE ROMANVS).

The letters "U" and "V" have later given birth to new characters that have originally been formed as their typographic variants, as well as the letter "W," originally a digraph (VV).

Special forms of this letter have been recognized as separate characters, such as the modifier letter small w, ʷ. The story goes on. In different areas that need new symbols, characters are created as variants or modifications of old characters. This seems to suit the human mind better than the invention of new character shapes from scratch.

Characters and "abstract characters"

The Unicode standard defines different meanings for the term *character*. The first one is: "The smallest component of written language that has semantic value; refers to the abstract meaning and/or shape, rather than a specific shape (see also *glyph*), though in code tables some form of visual representation is essential for the reader's understanding." The second meaning is that "character" is a synonym for "abstract character," which is defined as "a unit of information used for the organization, control, or representation of textual data."

Thus, the difference seems to be that an abstract character may have a control purpose only. Control purposes include line breaks, for example. In more common terminology, "character" in Unicode often means a printable (graphic) character, whereas "abstract character" means what is commonly called just "character," which includes printable and control characters.

On the other hand, the Unicode standard also uses the expression "abstract character" to refer to a symbol that may be perceived by users as a character ("user character"), although it cannot be represented as a single Unicode character (also known as encoded character or coded character). In particular, a symbol with special marks (diacritic marks) on it, such as ó, cannot always be represented as one character in Unicode but may be a sequence of two or more characters.

The expression "semantic value" is somewhat misleading in this context. A character such as a letter can hardly be described as having a meaning (semantic value) in itself. It would be better to say that a character has a *recognized identity* and it may be sometimes used as meaningful in itself (as a symbol or as a one-letter word) but more often as a component of a string that has a meaning. Moreover, the "smallest component" part is somewhat vague. A character such as ú (letter u with an acute accent), which belongs to Unicode, can often be regarded as consisting of smaller components: a letter and a diacritic (acute accent). In fact, in Unicode, the character ú may be regarded *either* as a character on its own or as a combination: as two successive characters, letter "u" and a combining acute accent.

The intuitive concept of character varies by language and cultural background. If you know the letter ä mainly from J. R. R. Tolkien's books, you might regard it just as letter "a" with a special mark that indicates that it is to be pronounced separately. You might even regard the two dots just as optional decoration, as in "naïve" if spelled in the French way. If your native language were Finnish, you would certainly treat ä as a completely separate character, and you would have learned at school that it has its own position in alphabetic order (a, b, c,…x, y, z, å, ä, ö). Similarly, in Swedish, the words "här" ("here"), "har" ("has"), and "hår" ("hair") must be kept clearly separate. To a German, ä is different from "a," but it is treated as primarily equivalent to "a" in alphabetic order and is in a sense a variant of "a" ("a Umlaut").

Unicode, aiming at universality, generally recognizes written forms as separate characters, if at least one language or commonly used notation system makes a difference. Thus, "a" and ä are treated as distinct. If you wish to handle them as equivalent, you need to program code that treats them that way.

Characters and other units of text

Although a character is a natural "atom" of text in data processing, it does not always correspond to people's intuitive idea of the basic constituents of text. Looking at text in English, we might occasionally ask ourselves whether the ligature fi is two characters or one. In other writing systems, similar questions arise more often. Unicode takes a liberal approach to identifying a complex character in many cases. You can represent fi as one character or (more often) as two characters, "f" and "i." As mentioned above, similar principles apply to letters with diacritic marks.

People who speak languages with many diacritic marks or ligatures may regard a symbol like fi or ú as a single character, even though they are often coded as sequences of characters. In some cases, it would not even be possible to code the symbol as a single character in Unicode, since Unicode does not contain all the combinations and ligatures that can be formed.

Moreover, although characters might be written separately, as in "ch," their combination might be understood as a single entity by some people. In English, "ch" denotes a particular sound and has thus some identity of its own. Some other languages treat the combination as an inseparable unit even in alphabetic order: in a dictionary, words would appear in an order like car, czar, char. Such treatment has become less common, though, since it is somewhat more difficult to implement in automated processing. Unicode treats "ch" as two characters but recognizes that it *might* constitute a unit in ordering.

Partly for such reasons, the ordering of characters is rather complex. Unicode does not prescribe a single ordering of characters and strings. Rather, it defines a basic (default) ordering that can be used as basis for defining language-dependent and even application-specific orderings.

Characters Versus Images

Characters are normally represented in graphic form, as something that can be called an image. However, there is a fundamental difference between an image and a character. An image can be a particular rendering of a character, much like a spoken word is a particular presentation of an element of a language. Moreover, most images are not renderings of characters at all.

Character code standards mostly identify a symbol as a character only if it is actually used in texts—e.g., in books, magazines, newspapers, and electronic documents. Characters that are normally used only in product labels and other specialized contexts are often borderline cases. However, they are often identified as characters if they are used in conjunction with symbols that are undeniably characters.

A typical example is the estimated symbol ℮, a stylized variant of the letter "e." It is not used in normal texts, but only in European packaging to claim conformance to certain standards in specifying a quantity. However, it is identified as a character, partly because it is used in packages in relation to text characters—e.g., in "℮ 200 g" (indicating that the mass of the product is 200 grams, within tolerances defined in specific regulation).

On the other hand, logos and identifying symbols are not treated as characters, even though they might be accompanied by texts. By its nature, a logo consists of a name or abbreviation in a particular graphic style. Hence, it would be unnatural to encode it as a character or sequence of characters, although we might use a string of characters as a *replacement* for a logo (e.g., when a document containing a logo needs to be converted to plain text and the logo conveys essential information).

Similarly, most of the various political, ideological, or religious symbols are treated as graphic symbols that are not characters. They are not normally used in texts. Their shape may vary, but not as part of font variation. However, for various reasons, some graphic symbols have been defined as characters in some character codes, contrary to these principles. Unicode therefore contains them as characters, so that existing texts using such characters can be encoded.

 Generally, a graphic symbol is encoded as a character in Unicode, if there is need for exchanging it in digital form in plain text. Decisions on this are sometimes difficult and may be affected by tradition.

The distinction between a character and an image is often a practical decision to be made by the author or editor of a document. In many cases, you have a choice between a character and an image. For example, suppose that you are designing a user interface for a document, program, or web page and you need graphic symbols for "Next" and "Previous." It may often be best to use words, but let us assume that you want to use arrows pointing to the left and to the right. Beware that even at this fairly abstract level, the decision is not culturally neutral: it implies left-to-right writing direction.

In Unicode, there is a largish block of arrow characters. Among them, a few like ← and → are widely available in commonly used fonts. However, they are not very prominent graphically, even if shown in bold, in large font, and in color. Their graphic design is character-like, not iconic. Some other characters in the Arrows block of Unicode look more solid, but they are not as common in fonts. For buttons or links, specially designed images may thus work better. On the other hand, in running texts, the arrow characters often work well. If you wish to make references to other entries in an encyclopedia by using arrows, then "→foobar" works better than a word preceded by a distinctive graphic.

Generally, when deciding between the use of characters and the use of an image for presenting a graphic symbol, the following items should be considered:

- Are there some Unicode characters that could be used, and are they suitable both by their defined semantics and by their typical graphic appearance?
- Is it possible that the document will be rendered so that images are not displayed? If yes, is it possible to specify a textual alternative to the image (such as the `alt` attribute in HTML markup)?
- How safely would the character work, given all the possible problems with encodings, fonts, etc.?
- Is it acceptable, and perhaps desirable, that the symbol changes size, shape, or color when text font size, face, or color is changed?
- Is it possible that the data will be processed as a character string—e.g., stored in a database or used in a search string?

For example, suppose we write about music and wish to refer to F-sharp and B-flat using the conventional musical symbols: F♯, B♭. The Unicode approach would use the special characters: music sharp sign ♯ and music flat sign ♭. However, these characters, although part of Unicode since Version 1.1, are poorly supported in fonts. Even though you could find them in some fonts at your disposal, their appearance might not fit into your typographic design. You might end up using the number sign # and the letter "b" as replacements. In web authoring for example, you might decide that although B♭ would be technically quite correct (using a so-called character reference to include the flat sign), it is safer to create a small image, say *flat.gif*, and embed it with markup like B<img src="flat.gif" alt="-flat">. This means that the flat symbol remains in constant size if the text size is changed, but this is usually tolerable.

Sometimes character-looking symbols are not characters. Microsoft Word by default changes the three-character sequence "-->" into a kind of arrow symbol (→). However, this arrow is different from any Unicode character: it is just a glyph in the Wingdings font. It is therefore something between a character and an image; as so many compromises, it combines the drawbacks of the alternatives.

Processing of Characters

The previous discussion mentioned that characters can be processed and used in many ways that are not possible (or practical), if information is represented as images, sounds, or in another nontext format. This includes:

- Searching for occurrences of a word or other fragment of text, using either a simple search string or a text pattern
- Performing automatic replacements, such as substituting a string for another in all occurrences
- Indexing the data for efficiency of searching and for creating an alphabetic index or concordance (list of occurrences of words)
- Sorting text data—e.g., for presentation in alphabetic order

- Copying text from an application or data format to another, often via a clipboard
- Modifying text as in a text editor or text-processing application, by deleting, inserting, and replacing characters
- Selecting parts of text by user actions, such as painting or keyboard commands
- Recognizing constructs like words, syllables, morphemes (components of a word with a meaning), and sentences
- Computing statistics on the use of characters, words, phrases, etc.
- Spelling and grammar checks
- Automatic or computer-aided translation
- Presenting texts in audible form, via speech synthesis, which is more natural these days than you might expect from many science fiction films

Even the display of characters on screen or paper involves processing:

- Choice of font, which can be a complex process
- Application of bolding, italics, and other features, if requested
- Selection of contextual forms for characters
- Recognition of character sequences that should or could be rendered using ligatures or other special methods
- Formation of characters with diacritic marks, often requiring complex algorithms
- Adjusting spacing between characters and words, perhaps for justification of lines
- Breaking text into lines, perhaps using hyphenation

In particular, suppose that some document exists on paper only, or as a scanned image only. The above lists of possibilities can be consulted when estimating whether the text should be converted into text format. The conversion may require quite a bit of work, including the identification of special characters occurring in the documents.

Sometimes the benefits of text format turn into drawbacks, or they are regarded as problems. If you send a contract by email and ask the recipient to print, sign, and send it, can you be sure that he does not edit the text before printing, without your noticing? Ease of copying text can be a problem, if it is used to violate your copyright. For such reasons, plain text and even other text forms are sometimes avoided. Perhaps even a printing possibility is undesirable. Some data formats, such as PDF, can be locked, or protected against copying and modification and printing—though in a relative sense only.

Giving Identity to Characters

To represent characters in digital form, we need to encode them using bits, but first we need something to encode. We need a *collection of characters* that are distinguishable from each other. We do not define characters individually but as parts of a collection. The Latin letter "A" is defined, among other things, by designating it as distinct from lowercase "a" or from any Greek or Cyrillic letter.

A character is also described by its *meaning*, or semantics. However, we must be careful about this. A character is usually just an atom of text and normally lacks a meaning in the sense that words or some parts of words have meanings. In the word "singing," the stem "sing" and the suffix "-ing" have meanings, but it would not be natural to say that the letter "g" has a meaning, in any comparable sense.

The meaning of letter "g" is basically that it is one of the (lowercase) Latin letters, used to write words in some writing systems. Its pronunciation may vary (even within one language—compare "get" with "gem"), although it might be possible to indicate some typical phonetic values. Generally, definitions of letters in character standards are independent of pronunciation issues, except for some characters specifically designed for such usage (e.g., characters in the International Phonetic Alphabet, IPA).

As we get to more technical characters, such as the plus sign + or the copyright symbol © or the smiling face ☺, we find characters that can be described as having a meaning of their own. They might even correspond to words, such as "plus" and "copyright."

Definitions of characters in standards

The definition of a character in a standard needs to be unambiguous and definitive, not just loose prose. Old character standards tried avoiding the problem of definition by simply showing the character, assigning a number to it, and possibly naming it. This has turned out to be insufficient for many purposes. How could you tell from just seeing an "A" whether it is meant to be the Latin letter only, or also the Greek or Cyrillic letter?

The most important character standard in the modern world is *Unicode*, so let us take a look at its way of defining characters. Unicode identifies a character by:

- Showing a representative *glyph* for the character—i.e., one specific but typical visual form that the character may have

- Assigning a unique *number* to it; this number will never be changed

- Assigning a unique *Unicode name* for it; this will never be changed either, even if it is found misleading or originally mistyped, and it is best to regard it as a *mnemonic identifier* rather than a name in a normal sense

- Specifying a set of *properties* for it in a rigorous, formalized manner; they describe, for example, the general class (letter, digit, punctuation, etc.) of the character, its uppercase equivalent when applicable, etc.

- Making *annotations*—i.e., prose descriptions that clarify the meaning, often comparing the character with other characters, presenting alternate names for it, and sometimes even describing possible variation in the visual appearance

For example, the plus sign is defined in Unicode as follows:

- The representative glyph looks much like +.

- The number is 2B, often written as 002B for uniformity, in hexadecimal (base 16) notation, which means 43 in decimal (base 10).

- The name is PLUS SIGN.
- The general category is "Sm," which is short for "Symbol, Math." Line breaking is permitted after the character. There are several other formalized properties as well; we will discuss the various properties in detail in Chapter 5.
- There are no annotations for this character.

Annotations used to emphasize differences

The plus sign is not easily confused with any other character, and it has no widely used alternate names in English. Therefore, no annotations were deemed necessary. For the comma character "," character number 002C, for example, there is an annotation that says that the character has the alternative name "decimal separator." This does not mean that the decimal separator should be a comma (although most languages in fact use a comma for that). It just means that in some contexts some people call the comma "decimal separator." This effectively identifies a comma used as a decimal separator with the character number 002C, as opposed to treating it as a separate though similar character. On the other hand, the annotations related to the comma character also contain notes that refer to "Arabic comma," "single low-9 quotation mark," and "ideographic comma" as separate characters. This can be read as a warning against confusing the comma with those visually similar characters. For example, some languages use a single low-9 quotation mark as an opening quote in some contexts (e.g., in German: ‚gut'); without a warning, you might be inclined to think that it's just a special use for the comma.

The representative glyphs

The definitions of characters in Unicode are logical and do not imply any particular presentation of a character, either internally (in digital form, as bits) or visibly on paper or screen. However, a representative glyph is given to clarify the identity of a character.

The Unicode standard explicitly says that the representative glyph is not a prescriptive form of the character, but it lets a "knowledgeable user" recognize the character.

The glyphs used in Unicode code charts tend to be neutral and generic rather than typographically well-designed. They typically lack artistic ambitions, and they have been designed so that differences with other characters have been emphasized. That is, glyphs for characters that are often rather similar in practice, especially if we consider variation across fonts, have usually been designed to be sufficiently different from each other.

The number and the Unicode name as identifiers

The number assigned can be regarded as identification only, although in practice, it is used as a basis for the digital representation. The Unicode name is an alternative, more mnemonic identifier. As a mental exercise, consider the possibility of sending information by telephone so that you utter the names of Unicode characters, in order to express something complicated like a foreign word or a formula. If both participants have access to information about Unicode characters, the communication can be completely successful even though no visible characters are sent and no digital encoding is used.

Thus, when characters are represented in digital form, each character is internally a number, an integer. Numbers in turn are represented as sequences of bits, but this is a different level. When a file contains the string "Hello" (without the quotation marks), it really contains five numbers corresponding to the characters. In most character codes, this is the sequence 72, 101, 108, 108, 111.

A character code can assign numbers to characters arbitrarily, but once assigned in a specification, they should not be changed. In practice, the assignments have been made in a partly systematic way, so that related characters often have consecutive numbers.

Many modern standards, specifications, and instructions identify characters by their Unicode numbers to achieve unambiguity. Previously, documents on matters like mathematical or technical notations or transliteration of texts used to specify the symbols to be used just by showing them as visual forms, as ink on paper. This turned out to be particularly problematic in the computer era, when different people interpreted such signs differently, resulting in incompatible encoding of data.

Suppose that you specify, for example, that in some notation, the double prime character ("), with Unicode number 2033 in hexadecimal, be used (say, to denote seconds as a subdivision of a degree when expressing angles). Actually, the Unicode number alone would suffice, but mentioning the name makes the specification more readable. In principle, you do not even need to write the character itself, though usually it helps. By identifying the Unicode number, you have achieved several things:

- You have unambiguously *identified* the character you mean. People may still decide to use some similar character instead, if they have difficulty typing the right character. Yet, it is clear which is the right character; others are various replacements.

- You have given a number that can be used as an *index* to large collections of information about the character, such as varying visual shapes for it, its defined properties, fonts containing it, definitions of meaning, and comments on scope of usage.

- The number can be used for *typing* the character by anyone who knows a general input method for Unicode characters in a particular environment. Typical word processors have at least one mechanism that produces a specific character, if you just specify its Unicode number.

Thus, anyone who participates in creating or clarifying notational specifications should know the principles of Unicode and should promote the use of Unicode numbers for characters. You should probably expect resistance, since it is not quite easy to see the benefits.

Unicode is more explicit

Older character standards, such as ASCII and the ISO 8859 family of standards, contain substantially less information about characters. They rely on the names of characters and the representative glyphs—and intuitive understanding related to the traditions of using characters. The same applies to the ISO 10646 standard, which is the official international standard that corresponds to Unicode. This means that we have two standards that are fully in accordance, ISO 10646 and the Unicode standard, but the latter contains a lot of additional information. Moreover, the Unicode standard is freely available on the World Wide Web, which is why people speak about Unicode and not ISO 10646, except in official standards and related documents.

The collection of all Unicode (or ISO 10646) characters is sometimes called the Universal Character Set (UCS). This expression is used especially in formal contexts, when one needs to refer to ISO 10646 and does not want to mention Unicode. In normal prose, we usually refer just to Unicode characters.

Spelling of names and the U+nnnn convention

The Unicode names of characters are written in all uppercase in the Unicode standard, but this is just a convention. In fact, the standard itself spells the names in all lowercase in some contexts. Uppercasing is often used to indicate (or hint) that a character is referred to by its Unicode name. However, in this book, we use normal (mixed) case for the names, except in some quotations.

We will use the conventional style of mentioning a Unicode character by its code number in hexadecimal (base 16) and prefixed with U+—e.g., U+002B. We could use just the number, but then you might not always know whether we use a number for such identification or just as a number.

This notation is used with at least four hexadecimal digits, so there are often leading zeros. All characters in the so-called Basic Multilingual Plane (BMP) can be expressed in four digits, but some newer characters need more.

We will normally mention first the Unicode name, then the code, often with a glyph between them. Thus, while you might see a Unicode character mentioned as U+002B PLUS SIGN in many sources, we will mostly say: the plus sign + U+002B.

Unicode Definitions of Characters

The definition of a character in Unicode is given partly in *code charts*, partly in the Unicode Database, which contains large tables of data on characters, by property, to be discussed in Chapter 5. Here we concentrate on the information in the code charts, which are available via *http://www.Unicode.org/charts/*. Each code chart begins with a table of glyphs, followed by notes on each character. The notes vary greatly in length and nature, but they should always be consulted when in doubt about the identity of character. Note that the code charts have been divided into two major groups, "Scripts" (which contains letters, ideographs, and other characters to write different human languages) and "Symbols and Punctuation." There is some overlap, since some blocks of characters belong to both groups.

The description of a character in a code chart consists of the following, where the first three items are given for every character (on one line), and others may or may not be present:

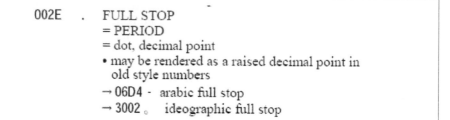

Figure 1-2. Sample description of a character in a Unicode code chart

- Unicode number

- Representative glyph (in normal text size)

- Unicode name, in uppercase; this name is fixed

- Old (Unicode 1.0) name, in uppercase on a line of its own

- Other name(s), preceded by an equals sign = and written in lowercase; these names may be changed

- Comment(s) on usage, preceded by a bullet •

- Cross reference(s) to other characters, preceded by an arrow →; these references often warn against confusing a character with another, similar-looking character

- Information that specifies the character as a decomposable character, using a notation that begins with the symbol ≡ (indicating so-called canonical equivalence) or with the symbol ≈ (indicating weaker correspondence)

Figure 1-2 shows the description of the full stop (period) character in a code chart.

Definitions of Characters Elsewhere

Characters were defined and used long before Unicode. Even in our times, characters are often used without identifying them with a reference to any character code standards. This creates ambiguity and potential diversity when text data is represented in computer-readable form.

For example, the standards that define the SI, the International System of Units (an extension of the metric system), use several special characters such as μ, ×, and Ω. The authoritative formats of the standards are printed documents, and since they do not specify code numbers or Unicode names for the characters, we are left in some uncertainty. Some characters can be identified rather unambiguously, but it is unclear what the "raised dot" character is, for example. This character, used in notations like N·m (for newton meter), is usually interpreted as the middle dot U+00B7, but it can be argued that a more appropriate interpretation is the dot operator U+22C5.

Similarly, the International Phonetic Alphabet (IPA) was originally defined about a century ago. When it later became relevant to use it on computers, the characters had to be identified as Unicode characters. This was far from trivial, since many IPA characters can be regarded as normal Latin letters, or treated as separate symbols.

Even relatively new standards on transliteration or transcription—i.e., on conversions between writing systems—fail to identify all characters unambiguously. For example, many standards and tables for writing Russian words in Latin letters specify that the so-called hard sign, ъ, is to be translated using a special character, but this character is just shown as a glyph on paper. This is subject to different interpretations including the ASCII quotation mark ", the right double quotation mark ", and the double prime ″ (U+2033). The Unicode standard makes, in a code chart, the following note about the modifier letter double prime ″ (U+02BA): "transliteration of tverdyj znak (Cyrillic hard sign: no palatalization)." This might seem to resolve the issue in principle, but in practice, that character is not present in most fonts, and we can also ask whether the Unicode standard is authoritative in transliteration issues. Problems similar to this also exist for some apostrophe-like characters in transliteration systems for Arabic, for example.

What's in a Name?

The names of characters in character standards are assigned identifiers rather than definitions. This is particularly true for Unicode, which now has an absolute principle of name stability. A Unicode name will not be changed even if proved wrong.

Typically, the names are selected so that they contain only letters A–Z, spaces, and hyphens; often the uppercase variant is the reference spelling of a character name.

The same character may have different names in different definitions of character repertoires. Generally, the name is intended to suggest a generic meaning and scope of use. However, the Unicode standard warns (mentioning full stop "." as an example of a character with varying usage):

> A character may have a broader range of use than the most literal interpretation of its name might indicate; the coded representation, name, and representative glyph need to be taken in context when establishing the semantics of a character.

Although the Unicode names can be misleading—a price that we pay for their absolute stability—most of them aren't. The great majority of Unicode names describe the character, and the name is often the only description that the Unicode standard gives about a character individually. Thus, the name should be taken as describing the character, unless there is an annotation that says otherwise.

The Unicode name is in English, in a sense. In many cases, it is normal English, but often the name contains elements from other languages, such as the name in another language but as (somehow) adapted to English spelling.

For many purposes, it would be desirable to refer to characters by some widely understood names, in different languages. There will probably be a registry of such names, though mostly only for those characters that are widely used in each language. It will naturally contain English names as well, partly different for U.S. English and British English. They will of course have much similarity to the Unicode names. The naming is expected to take place in the context of Common Locale Data Repository (CLDR), discussed in Chapter 11.

 Names of characters vary a lot, even within a language. This applies particularly to characters that are widely used in modern notations, but without much tradition, such as the tilde ~ or the commercial at @. Do not assume that people know from the name alone what you mean, even if you speak the same language.

The Unicode standard mentions some colloquial names for characters, even in languages other than English. For the @ character, it mentions that the "common, humorous German slang name" is "Klammeraffe," which means "clinging monkey." Undoubtedly, in some environments, the character might be better known under that name than under any official name. However, you need to be careful in using the alternate names mentioned in the standard. It is better to look for information on actual usage in a language and a subculture. Slang, by its nature, varies by time and people.

When you need to refer to a character and cannot just show it, try to mention commonly known synonyms for it. It is not constructive to say just "use the reverse solidus." Instead, you can say "use the forward slash (that is, solidus), not the backslash (reverse solidus)." Unicode names alone are often rather useless in difficult situations for identifying characters to people who are not familiar with Unicode. The same applies even more to Unicode numbers.

Thus, you are not supposed to use the Unicode names for all characters in all contexts. If you are used to calling the "." character "period," you need not start calling it "full stop." You need not spell out "capital Latin letter A" every time you mention capital (uppercase) "A." However, the Unicode names appear in many contexts, like in character selection menus in editors, so you need to know the idea.

You may wonder why Unicode assigns two immutable identifiers for a character: a number and a name. If each of them is unique and guaranteed to remain unchanged, what do you need the other one for? The short answer is that numbers are the basic identifiers but names are needed too, since they have been used in programs and data to uniquely identify characters. Although it might not be wise to write code that operates on character names that way, it would be unwise to intentionally break all such code now.

Originally, names of characters were meant to act as identifiers across character codes. Different code may assign different numbers to the character ±, but they can be expected to assign the same name, "plus-minus sign," to it, or at least use names that can be recognized as essentially the same. However, this idea never worked well, since the names were in practice not always the same, or even essentially the same. Moreover, Unicode has made the original idea unnecessary, since nowadays the Unicode numbers are widely used to refer to characters across character codes, even when Unicode is not otherwise used for representing characters.

Should We Be Strict About the Meanings of Characters?

People tend to use characters on the basis of their visual appearance. You see a character like ß in some repertoire, and you start using it for the Greek letter beta, if you need it. You see the character ø and you take it as the diameter sign, so you use it in a technical context like "ø = 0.12 m" (saying that the diameter of something is 0.12 meters).

Unicode has strengthened such tendencies. People browse tables or menus of Unicode characters and pick up the first one that looks right for the purpose they have in their mind. Since Unicode has so many more characters than most old standards, there are far more opportunities for getting lost: it is easy to find a Unicode character that more or less looks like the one you need.

Then comes a purist and says that ß is a letter (sharp s) used in German, not any Greek letter, and that ø is a vowel used in some Nordic languages, not a mathematical symbol. Should we care?

Although you might realize the importance of using the right character, not just a right-looking character, you may need to explain the issue to others. Moreover, we often need to make compromises, and then it becomes essential to consider their impact. Reasons for using the right character translate into risks that you need to prepare for, when you cannot use the right character. So here are some basic reasons for being strict:

Some people see the difference
> Although the character looks right to you, a specialist may well see a difference between ß and β (sharp s versus small beta) or between ø and ⌀ (letter "o" with stroke versus diameter sign). When you write a foreign word, anyone who speaks that language as her native language is a specialist compared to you.

Font changes make differences noticeable
> When the font is changed, the difference can become clearly visible. A typical example is that the difference between degree sign ° (as in "50 °F" or "10 °C") and masculine ordinal indicator º (superscript letter "o," used in Spanish) is very small or nonexistent in many fonts, but very clear in many other fonts (e.g., ° versus º). Your text might be rendered in different fonts even though you have carefully selected a particular font. This is particularly true in web authoring and in cooperative authoring.

Conversions operate on characters, not appearance
> Automated editing of text is based on defined properties of characters, not on their appearance. For example, text-editing commands that operate on words will (or at least should) treat ø as a letter, not as a technical symbol. Converting text to uppercase would turn "ß-carotene" into "SS-CAROTENE," since "SS" is the defined uppercase version of ß.

Searching looks for characters, not appearance
> A search function in a program, as well as a database search, works on characters. When asked to find the string "β-carotene" (with beta), they will not find "ß-carotene" (with sharp s). The same applies to pattern matching and replace functions.

Search routines may use some heuristics in their attempt to help users with common errors in using wrong characters, just as they may help with misspellings—as Google might say "did you mean pseudonym?" when you have typed "psuedonym." But don't rely on such features.

Automated processing generally ignores appearance
For example, automatic speech synthesis and automatic translation, works on characters as abstract entities, not on their visual appearance. If your text contains "1º", meant to mean "one degree" but incorrectly uses a masculine ordinal indicator, it might be spelled out as "primero" (Spanish word for "first" in masculine gender). Similarly, it might be translated incorrectly.

Sometimes these considerations do not matter, or—more often—they need to be suppressed in favor of other needs. If you only aim at producing a document to be distributed on paper and you have full control up to and including the print operation, then the appearance is all that matters. But more often than not, documents are stored and sent in digital form. Then you may need to take precautions against wrong processing, perhaps document what you have done, and check things after various conversions and other operations.

Characters differ in the definiteness of their meaning. Some well-known characters like the hyphen - (known formally as hyphen-minus in Unicode) have a wide range of uses, and you may need to use them liberally. Computer programs need to be prepared for handling them accordingly. But other characters have specific semantics. The letter ø and the technical symbol ∅ have limited uses. They should not be confused with each other or used for other purposes without careful consideration.

Ambiguity Among Characters

The identity of characters is defined by the definition of a character repertoire. Thus, it is not an absolute concept but relative to the repertoire; some repertoire might contain a character with mixed usage while another defines distinct characters for the different uses. For instance, the ASCII repertoire has a character called "hyphen." It is also used as a minus sign, as well as a substitute for a dash, since ASCII contains no dashes. Thus, that ASCII character is a generic, multipurpose character, and one can say that in ASCII, hyphen and minus are identical. But in Unicode, there are distinct characters named "hyphen" and "minus sign" (as well as different dash characters). For compatibility, the old ASCII character is preserved in Unicode, too (in the old code position, with the name hyphen-minus).

Similarly, as a matter of definition, Unicode defines characters for micro sign, n-ary product, etc., as distinct from the Greek letters (small mu, capital pi, etc.) from which they originate. This is a logical distinction and does not necessarily imply that different glyphs are used. The distinction is important, for example, when textual data in digital form is processed by a program (which "sees" the code values, through some encoding, and not the glyphs at all). Note that Unicode does not make any distinction, for example, between the Greek small letter pi (π), and the mathematical symbol pi denoting the well-known constant 3.14159... (i.e., there is no separate symbol for the latter). For the ohm sign (Ω), there is a specific character (in the Symbols Area), but it is defined as being canonical equivalent to Greek capital letter omega (Ω)—i.e., there are two separate characters but they are equivalent. On the other hand, Unicode makes a distinction between Greek capital letter pi (Π) and the mathematical symbol n-ary product (∏), so that they are not equivalent.

If you think this doesn't sound quite logical, you are not the only one to think so. The point is that for symbols resembling Greek letters and used in various contexts, there are three possibilities in Unicode:

- The symbol is regarded as identical to the Greek letter (just as its particular usage).
- The symbol is included as a separate character, but it is defined as equivalent to the Greek letter. There are two kinds of equivalence: canonical and compatibility.
- The symbol is regarded as a completely separate character.

You need to check the Unicode references for information about each individual symbol. As a rough rule of thumb about symbols looking like Greek letters, mathematical operators (like summation) exist as independent characters whereas symbols of quantities and units (like pi and ohm) are identical to Greek letters or equivalent to them.

How Do I Find My Character?

Suppose you have been requested to convert some printed or handwritten text into a digital format. (At the end of this chapter, we have such an exercise.) For English text with no special characters, you might be able to use a scanner. But what would you do with characters that the scanner does not recognize reliably?

Such problems are fairly common. For example, you might need to check the spelling of a foreign name from a printed reference book, or you might need to quote some printed material. Even standards on various notations often fail to specify the characters unambiguously: the authoritative format of a standard is usually a printed publication, and all you have got there is ink on paper, glyphs.

The recognition of a character from its glyph can be quite difficult, and it may require both factual and cultural knowledge about the subject area and the text. You also need technical information on character standards, since you ultimately need to identify glyphs as appearances of characters defined in the standards.

Looking for characters through lists or code charts is a rather hopeless task. The amount of characters is huge, and many characters look very similar to each other. For example, how can you know whether a glyph on paper is letter "a" with a caron (ǎ) or letter "a" with a breve (ă)? Thus, you first need some information or guess on the nature of a character. If you know or suspect that the character appears in a Romanian name, you have a good starting point, since the character repertoire used in Romanian can be found in a suitable reference. Similarly, if you know that a glyph like ₣ is a currency symbol, you have almost identified it.

The following list suggests some general online resources for identifying characters:

"Where is my Character?" (http://www.Unicode.org/standard/where/)
An explanatory document by the Unicode Consortium. It explains some problems caused by the variation of shapes of characters.

Unicode Code Charts (http://www.Unicode.org/charts/)
This is official information and covers all Unicode characters. It is organized first by division into "Scripts" (writing systems for human languages, containing letters, syllables, and word signs) and "Symbols and Punctuation." These parts are further divided into large categories such as "European Alphabets." Figure 1-3 illustrates the appearance of the main page of the Code Charts.

Fileformat.info, section Unicode (http://www.fileformat.info/info/Unicode/)
This contains data taken from the Unicode site and organized for viewing in different ways. It also contains information on Unicode support in different fonts. As you get down to information on individual characters, their properties are displayed in a compact format, which is great when you are ready to use it.

Database of characters at the EKI (http://www.eki.ee/letter/)
Although not as exhaustive in character repertoire as the above, this database lets you search for characters in a few ways and shows some essential extra information on usage: it lists languages that use a character and character encodings (charsets) that contain it. Although these lists are not complete, they are often helpful. For example, they tell that letter "a" with a caron (ǎ, U+01CE) is used in Yoruba and in Romanization of Bulgarian and Chinese, whereas the letter "a" with a breve (ă, U+0103) is used in Romanian and Vietnamese and Romanization of Khmer, as shown in Figure 1-4. However, the information is not always completely reliable; in particular, the character used when writing Bulgarian as Romanized—i.e., in Latin letters—is not "a" with a caron but "a" with a breve, according to standards.

Which Characters Does Each Language Use?

For details on the use of characters in different languages, you need to consult grammar guides and textbooks on the languages themselves. However, there is an extensive compilation of basic information in *The World's Writing Systems* by Peter T. Daniels and William Bright (Oxford University Press). There is brief description of character usage in a few languages in *The Chicago Manual of Style*, 15th Edition (The University of Chicago Press). Online, you can find "The Alphabets of Europe," by Michael Everson, at *http://www.evertype.com/alphabets/*. It is extensive and based on detailed research, although it partly applies different criteria to different languages: for some languages, it includes only the basic modern alphabet; for others, it lists historical characters and other

European Alphabets	African Scripts	Indic Scripts	East Asian Scripts	Central Asian Scripts
(see also **Comb. Marks**)	*Ethiopic*	Bengali	*Han Ideographs*	Kharoshthi
Armenian	Ethiopic	Devanagari	Unified CJK Ideographs (5MB)	Mongolian

Figure 1-3. Part of the interface to online Unicode code charts

characters that are not used in normal writing. The CLDR database, discussed in Chapter 11, contains information on the use of letters in different languages.

Variation of Writing Systems

The most widely used writing systems, or scripts, can be classified as follows:

Alphabetic scripts
> Denote sounds with letters, though usually not in a strict one-to-one manner. Examples: Latin, Greek, and Cyrillic scripts, each of which exists in different versions.

Consonant scripts, or abjads
> Basically denote consonants, leaving vowels to be inferred; however, consonant scripts may have letters for long vowels, and in some situations even short vowels are written using small signs attached to consonants. Examples: Hebrew and Arabic scripts.

Abugida scripts
> These use consonant letters that imply a particular vowel after the consonant, when used in the base form. Alternatives with other vowels or without any vowel are indicated by additional marks. Many South and Southeast Asian scripts belong to this category—e.g., the Devanagari script used for many Indic languages.

Syllabic scripts
> Use basically one character for each syllable. Examples: the Hiragana and Katakana scripts, used for Japanese.

Ideographic scripts
> Use basically one character for one (short) word. The most widely known ideographic script is Han, often known as Chinese script, though it is also used (in part) for other languages as well, especially Japanese and Korean, and therefore often called "CJK."

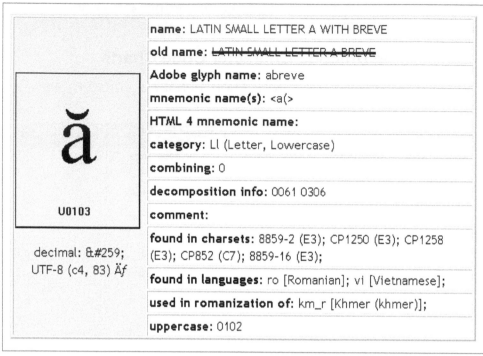

	name: LATIN SMALL LETTER A WITH BREVE
	old name: ~~LATIN SMALL LETTER A BREVE~~
	Adobe glyph name: abreve
	mnemonic name(s): <a(>
	HTML 4 mnemonic name:
	category: Ll (Letter, Lowercase)
	combining: 0
	decomposition info: 0061 0306
U0103	**comment:**
	found in charsets: 8859-2 (E3); CP1250 (E3); CP1258 (E3); CP852 (C7); 8859-16 (E3);
decimal: ă **UTF-8 (c4, 83)** Äƒ	**found in languages:** ro [Romanian]; vi [Vietnamese];
	used in romanization of: km_r [Khmer (khmer)];
	uppercase: 0102

Figure 1-4. Sample information on a character in the eki.ee database

Consonantal writing may sound impossible, because it introduces so much ambiguity. However, although an individual written form of a word is often ambiguous, the ambiguities are usually resolved easily from the context by a person who understands the language well. Moreover, languages written with a consonantal script typically have a structure that makes this easier than for English, for example. When vowels are mainly used to express variations of a common theme expressed by a word root, consisting of a pattern described by a combination of consonants, the vowels can usually be inferred from the grammatical context.

The word "script" is often used in character code contexts instead of "writing system." It is important to distinguish it from the use of the word "script" to denote a programming concept—a certain type of a computer program, such as a Perl script.

Some scripts, such as the Latin script, are written with spaces between words, and a space is normally a permissible line break point. Hyphenation may introduce other break points. Other scripts may permit line breaks more freely.

The Latin script and many other scripts are written left to right, with lines proceeding from top to bottom. These are not universal properties of human writing, and even the Latin script is historically based on a script that was written right to left. Unicode addresses the problem of left-to-right versus right-to-left writing in two ways: by defining inherent directionality for characters and by defining control characters for affecting writing di-

Figure 1-5. The four contextual forms of the Arabic letter "ba"

rection. For example, Hebrew and Arabic letters have inherent right-to-left directionality. Special methods are needed when text in such letters contains names or quotations that have the opposite directionality, or vice versa.

In Latin scripts, each character is normally displayed as a separate image on screen or paper, though the spacing between characters may vary. In other scripts, the formatting of texts for visual presentation can be essentially more difficult: the shape of a character may depend on context; adjacent characters can be written together (using a ligature or using cursive writing where characters join smoothly); and a character might be displayed as an auxiliary symbol above, below, before, or behind another character.

Glyphs and Fonts

It is important to distinguish the character concept from the glyph concept. A glyph is a presentation of a particular shape a character may have when rendered or displayed. It has even been said that any character is an abstract idea, whereas glyphs for the character are its different visible manifestations.

Each character we use in English normally has the same basic shape, and glyphs for it differ in typographic design only. It is obvious that "T" in the Times font represents the same character as "T" in the Arial font, for example. However, the letter "a" has two rather different shapes (compare "a" in normal Times font and "*a*" in Times italic). When you write literally by hand, you may draw characters differently in different positions of a word. For example, a word-final "s" may be quite different than a word-initial "s." In typewritten or typeset text, or in text displayed or printed on computers, such distinctions are not made, even in so-called handwriting-style fonts.

In Greek writing, a word-final sigma (ς) is rather different from a normal small sigma (σ), although they are logically the same character. The first and last letter of the word σοφός (sophos, "wise") are the same but are written differently. However, since this is a special case, character codes usually solve this by encoding them as two separate characters, and Unicode follows suit, even without defining any equivalence between them.

In other writing systems, the variation can be much bigger, especially if the writing systems imitate handwriting. In Arabic, letters have two or four *contextual forms*, which can be quite different from each other. Figure 1-5 shows the four forms of an Arabic letter, usually called "ba" or more exactly bā', though the Unicode name is Arabic letter beh (U+02BE). The forms are (from right to left!) for use as isolated, at the start of a word, in the middle of a word, and at the end of a word. As you can see, for example, the word-final form (on the left) has a part that helps in joining the character with the previous character. Each of these forms, in turn, can appear differently in different fonts.

In the ISO-8859-6 character code (Latin/Arabic), for example, each Arabic letter has one code position only. This leaves it to rendering engines to determine the context (position within a word) and to use the correct contextual form. Unicode, on the other hand, contains both such characters (effectively, taken from ISO-8859-6) and each of the contextual forms as a separately coded character. This lets you write Arabic so that the rendering process can be very simple, at the cost of extra work in writing. However, even using Unicode, you are normally supposed to use the more abstract Arabic letters.

It is ultimately a matter of definition whether two graphic presentations are glyphs for the same character or distinct characters. However, it is normally not an individual's decision but a collective agreement. The definition of a character repertoire specifies the "identity" of characters, among other things. One could define a repertoire where uppercase "Z" and lowercase "z" are just two glyphs for the same character. On the other hand, one could define that italic "Z" is a character different from normal "Z," not just a different glyph for it.

In fact, in Unicode for example there are several characters that could be regarded as typographic variants of letters only, but for various reasons, Unicode defines them as separate characters. For example, mathematicians use a variant of letter "N" to denote the set of natural numbers (0, 1, 2,...), and this variant is defined as being a separate character (double-struck capital N, ℕ, U+2115) in Unicode.

The design of glyphs has several aspects, both practical and esthetic. For a review of a major company's description of its principles and practices, see Microsoft's "Character design standards" on its typography pages at *http://www.microsoft.com/typography/*.

Some discussions, such as ISO 9541-1 and ISO/EC TR 15285, make a further distinction between "glyph image," which is an actual appearance of a glyph, and "glyph," which is a more abstract notion. In such an approach, "glyph" is close to the concept of "character," except that a glyph may present a combination of several characters. Thus, in that approach, the characters "f" and "i" might be represented using an abstract glyph that combines the two characters into a ligature fi, which itself might have different physical manifestations. Such approaches need to be treated as different from the issue of treating ligatures as (compatibility) characters.

Allowed Variation of Glyphs

When a character repertoire is defined (e.g., in a standard), some particular glyph is often used to describe the appearance of each character, but this should be taken as an example only. The Unicode standard specifically says the glyphs used for a character can be quite different from the "representative glyph," but within cultural conventions:

> Consistency with the representative glyph does not require that the images be identical or even graphically similar; rather, it means that both images are generally recognized to be representations of the same character. Representing the character U+0061 Latin small letter a by the glyph "X" would violate its character identity.

Thus, the definition of a character repertoire is not a matter of just listing glyphs. In fact, it's the exception rather than the rule that a character repertoire definition explicitly says something about the meaning and use of a character. For example, the description of the dollar sign $ says that the character may have one or two vertical bars, to make it clear that such variation does not change the character's identity. On the other hand, the pound sign £ has one crossbar, in contrast with the lira sign ₤, which is identified as a separate character.

Fonts and Their Properties

A font contains a repertoire of glyphs. In a more technical sense, as the implementation of a font, a font is an organized set of glyphs. The glyphs may have names that identify them; this is the way used in PostScript fonts. More often, glyphs are identified by their numbers, which typically correspond to code positions of the characters (presented by the glyphs). Thus, a font in that sense is character-code dependent. An expression like *Unicode font* refers to such issues of basic structure and does not imply that the font contains glyphs for all Unicode characters. In fact, such comprehensive fonts are very rare at present.

A font may contain the same glyph for distinct characters. For example, although characters such as Latin uppercase "A," Cyrillic uppercase "A," and Greek uppercase alpha are regarded as distinct characters (with distinct code values) in Unicode, a font might contain just one "A" that is used to present all of them. In fact, this applies to most fonts. On the other hand, a font may contain alternative glyphs for a character, for use in different contexts.

Fonts have names, which are often trademarks. The name of a font can be a single word like "Times" or it may consist of two or more words, such as "Times New Roman." It is not uncommon to see fonts that are very similar to each other but have completely different names such as "Helvetica" and "Arial."

Fonts can be classified in many ways, and this belongs to typography rather than our topic. However, some basic classifications as indicated in Table 1-1 are relevant for our purposes, since they appear in program settings for selecting fonts for displaying characters. For example, a program may have one choice of a font for serif font, another choice for sans serif font. These font classes are distinguished by the presence or absence (in French, "sans" means "without") of short strokes that terminate the lines of many letters. Usually there is also the difference that in a sans serif font, the lines of letters have (almost) equal thickness, whereas in a serif font, the thickness varies (e.g., the vertical line of "T" is thicker than the horizontal line).

Table 1-1. Some basic classes of fonts

Class of fonts	Characteristics	Sample font(s)
Serif	Widely used for copy text in books	Times, Georgia
Sans serif	Often used on screen and for small print	Arial, Verdana
Monospace	Equal-width characters, often used for code	Courier New

Class of fonts	Characteristics	Sample font(s)
Cursive	Letters join to each other as in handwriting	Cooper Blklt BT
Fantasy	Exotic, artistic (font)	Comic Sans MS

The attribute "proportional" refers to any font where the width of character varies, as opposed to monospace fonts. Monospace fonts are often used for computer code, and sometimes to imitate old typewriter text. To be exact, there can be variation in width even in a monospace font: some Unicode characters are defined to be invisible, so they need to have a width of zero, and some characters such as fixed-width spaces have a specific width by definition.

There are many online services for viewing samples of fonts and for identifying the font of some text you have seen. They often tell how to download or buy the fonts, too. See, for example, *http://www.identifont.com* and *http://www.linotype.com*.

Typographers often use the term *typeface* to denote the basic design of glyphs, reserving the word "font" for particular implementations and variants. For example, the Times typeface is available as normal (regular), as bold, as italic, and bold italic, as well as in different sizes. Variants of a typeface in different sizes may differ in their details—i.e., they are not just formed from a basic size by simple scaling.

Font Variation Versus Characters

As mentioned above, variants such as normal, bold, and italic do not normally constitute a character difference. That is, a normal "A" is the same character as a bold "**A**" or an italic "*A*." Neither does changing the typeface change the identity of a character, as a rule. However, some Unicode characters have been defined essentially as variants of other characters, although this difference could have been made at the font level only. Such characters are defined in the Unicode standard as having *compatibility decompositions*, using notations as in Figure 1-6. The symbol ≈ stands for compatibility equivalence, and <font> indicates font variation—similar to what you could achieve using the font element in HTML, but here <font> is just a general notation, not markup. The <font> notation in the Unicode standard does not specify what kind of a font is to be used, and as you can see from the descriptions of U+210C and U+210D, <font> can mean quite different things for different characters. For example, U+210E is essentially "h" in italics, but in the Unicode standard, this is just implicit in its representative glyph.

Fonts in Implementations

The implementation of fonts is relevant to our topic, since it affects the practical availability of characters. If a character is only available in a font that is poorly implemented, we may need to look for other approaches. For example, high-quality printing may require the use of certain font technologies.

The most important font technologies at present are:

```
210C  ℌ  BLACK-LETTER CAPITAL H
         = Hilbert space
         ≈ <font> 0048 H  latin capital letter h
210D  ℍ  DOUBLE-STRUCK CAPITAL H
         ≈ <font> 0048 H  latin capital letter h
210E  ℎ  PLANCK CONSTANT
         ≈ <font> 0068 h  latin small letter h
```

Figure 1-6. Some descriptions of characters in the Letterlike Symbols block in the Unicode standard

Bitmap fonts

Also known as raster fonts, system fonts, or screen fonts, these fonts essentially present a character as a matrix or raster of pixels, or bits indicating the presence or absence of a pixel. Bitmap fonts are more or less obsolete, though they are still used as "system fonts," often in window titles and dialog boxes.

PostScript Type 1

This technology, developed by Adobe, is widely used in the print industry and in desktop publishing. On your PC, you may find Type 1 fonts, too.

TrueType

This technology was developed by Apple, and then licensed to Microsoft. Probably most fonts on your PC are TrueType fonts (with filenames ending in *.ttf*).

OpenType

This is a new technology developed jointly by Microsoft and Adobe. It is Unicode oriented and more platform-independent than older technologies.

Fonts other than bitmap fonts are effectively computer programs of a kind, controlling the drawing of lines that constitute a glyph. Fonts are generally protected by copyright laws, although the scope and terms of protection vary by country.

If you use Windows, you will probably benefit from downloading and installing the software from *http://www.microsoft.com/typography/TrueTypeProperty21.mspx*, "Font properties extension." It enhances the functionality of Windows so that when you open the Fonts folder (via Start → Control Panel), you can right-click on the icon of a font file and select Properties to get rather detailed information on the font. However, the amount of information depends on the technology of the font. Figure 1-7 shows some properties of a TrueType font. The properties include the ranges of Unicode characters that the font supports. Beware, however, that such support is not always exhaustive; it may lack some characters of the range, especially if the Unicode standard has been extended since the creation of the font. (The figure contains some Finnish words, too. Such things may happen if you install a program that uses English on an operating system that uses a different language in its interface.)

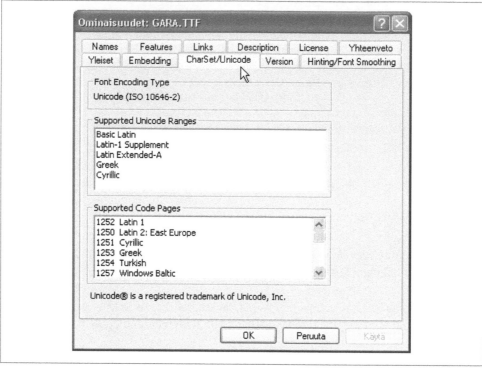

Figure 1-7. Properties of a font (Garamond), as viewed with the Font properties extension

Failures to Display a Character

In addition to the fact that the appearance of a character may vary, it is quite possible that some program fails to display a character at all. Perhaps the program cannot interpret the character encoding of the data, either because it was not properly informed about the encoding or because it has not been programmed to handle the particular encoding.

Even if a program recognizes some data as denoting a character, it may well be unable to display it since it lacks a glyph for it. Often it will help if the user manually checks the font settings, perhaps trying to find a rich enough font. Advanced programs could be expected to do this automatically and even to pick up glyphs from different fonts, but such expectations are often unrealistic at present. However, it is quite possible that no such font can be found. As an important detail, the possibility of seeing, for example, Greek characters on some Windows systems depends on whether "multilingual support" has been installed.

A well-designed program will in some appropriate way indicate its inability to display a character. For example, a small rectangular box, the size of a character, could be used to indicate that there is a character that was recognized but cannot be displayed. Some programs use a question mark, but this is risky—how is the reader expected to distinguish such usage from the real "?" character? Advanced browsers may display a symbol that indicates the general class (e.g., Latin letter or mathematical symbol) of the character.

Font Embedding

To overcome a situation in which a recipient of a document might not have a font needed for the characters in it, techniques have been developed for embedding fonts into documents themselves. This is quite different from what word processors normally do with fonts: they include information about fonts (by font name), not fonts themselves.

Font embedding does not normally mean the inclusion of an entire font but only an extract from the font data, as needed for a particular document. The technique may prevent the recipient from using the embedded font for anything but viewing the particular document. This makes font designers more willing to allow embedding.

Another reason for font embedding is the desire to have a document presented exactly as designed. If you create a document using fonts that you like and send it, the recipient's program may well be capable of displaying all the characters but by using different fonts, in part. Usually if you specify a font that is not present in the recipient's system, the program used for viewing the document will use its default font instead. This might be regarded as a serious problem especially by visual designers.

The Font properties extension that was illustrated in Figure 1-7 gives access to information about font embedding possibilities, in the Embedding pane. If embedding is allowed for a TrueType font, you can, for example, set Microsoft Word to embed the font. For this, you would select Tools → Settings → Save, and then check the box about font embedding. Remember to reset this setting after saving the document, since otherwise Word will keep embedding all TrueType fonts, which is generally unnecessary.

For the Web, Microsoft has developed the Web Embedding Fonts Tool (WEFT) for use with HTML and CSS. However, it has not gained much popularity, partly due to its relative complexity. Instead, the usual approach is to use the PDF format, since common PDF creation tools allow easy font embedding. In addition to commercial products such as Adobe Acrobat, there are free tools like PDFCreator, which adds a "virtual printer" to your system. You can then use the Print command in various programs to generate a PDF version of a document, and in this context, you can check settings that make the tool embed the fonts you have used.

Font embedding has its drawbacks, too. Often it would be desirable for the user to change the font for legibility, but font embedding has more or less been designed to prevent this. A special character may look odd to a user, who might well recognize it if he could view it using some font he knows well. The PDF format does not allow easy font resizing, which would be crucial to many people. Therefore, it is best to distribute your material in alternative formats in accordance with recipients' choices, such as Microsoft Word, RTF, HTML, or PDF.

Definitions of Character Repertoires

The implementation of Unicode support is a long and mostly gradual process. Unicode can be supported by programs on any operating systems, although some systems may allow much easier implementation than others; this mainly depends on whether the system uses Unicode internally so that support to Unicode is built in.

Even in circumstances where Unicode is supported in principle, the support usually does not cover all Unicode characters. For example, an available font may cover some part of Unicode that is only practically important in some area. When text data produced in one program is to be processed in another, we should be prepared for difficulties with any unusual characters. For data transfer, it is essential to know which Unicode characters the recipient is able to handle.

Thus, although Unicode contains a huge number of characters, not all of them can be used safely. Among the 100,000 or so characters, usually only a small subset can be used in a particular application and context without a serious risk of distorting information.

Formally Defined Repertoires

Each character code, by itself, defines a character repertoire: the collection of characters that can be represented in the code. In addition to this, subsets of such collections can be defined.

A character repertoire is any collection of characters, without implying any particular implementation even at the level of code numbers. However, in practice, the simplest way to define a character repertoire is to use Unicode as the basis and simply list the code numbers. Such a definition specifies a *closed collection*, which does not change if the Unicode standard is enhanced. In contrast, by listing a set of Unicode blocks you define an *open collection*, which is fixed at any given moment of time but will automatically expand if new characters are added to any of those blocks in a revision of the Unicode standard.

For example, there are three Multilingual European Subsets (MES-1, MES-2, MES-3), defined in a CEN Workshop Agreement, CWA 13873. Among them, MES-2 is the most important. It is a closed collection, covering Latin, Greek, and Cyrillic scripts. The CWA is available at *http://www.evertype.com/standards/iso10646/pdf/cwa13873.pdf* or via *http://www.cenorm.be/cenorm/businessdomains/businessdomains/isss/cwa/*.

Practical Repertoires

In addition to international standards, there are company policies that define various subsets of the character repertoire. A practically important one, especially in regards to support in widely used fonts, is Microsoft's "Windows Glyph List 4" (WGL4), also known as "PanEuropean" character set, listed on the page "Using special characters from Windows Glyph List 4 (WGL4) in HTML" at *http://www.alanwood.net/demos/wgl4.html*.

Contrary to what you might expect, the characters in it have not all been included in MES-2.

In data-processing contexts, a character can be considered "safe" if it is certain or very probable that it will be correctly transmitted and presented to the recipient. In a broader sense, being safe entails more: the sender should be sure of the character he means, and the recipient should understand it correctly. Mostly, however, we consider the technical problems: difficulties in presenting the character in a digital form, in sending it over network connections and possibly to a different program and operating environment, and in rendering it visually. Nowadays, it's usually the last phase that poses most problems.

From a practical point of view, we can distinguish the following repertoires of characters. Each repertoire listed here contains all the previous repertoires. The list can be useful when you design an application, or instructions on writing things, or a computer language. When selecting which repertoire you use or support, it is advisable to proceed slowly in the list and consider whether the usefulness of extra characters outweighs the risks. The names used for the repertoires here are practical descriptions, not official names. They make liberal use of encoding names, which will be described in more detail in Chapter 3.

ASCII name characters: English letters A–Z and a–z and digits 0–9
These are the safest characters and often the only characters you can use in names or *identifiers* in a computer language. Often a few extra characters like underline _, hyphen - and full stop "." are allowed, too. Be careful with any extra characters when selecting a name for a file, a username, or a data item name. The naming rules you have learned in some context may not apply in others. For example, Unicode names for characters use just letters A–Z without case distinction, digits 0–9, space, and hyphen (hyphen-minus, to be exact).

*The invariant subset of ASCII: the above, plus characters ! " % & ' ( ) * + , - . / : ; < = > ? and the space character*
This can be described as the rock-bottom repertoire of characters in data processing. However, in different transfer and transformations, even these characters may get changed somehow. A common example is the ampersand &, which often needs to be written in some special way (e.g., as & in HTML and XML).

The full ASCII repertoire: the above, plus characters # $ @ [\ ] ^ _ ` { | } and ~
This repertoire, called Basic Latin in Unicode, usually works well across programs, computer platforms, and network connections. The characters listed here work mostly just as well as the other ASCII characters, but some standards allow national variation that may make them unsafe. Moreover, producing some of these characters can be a nontrivial task on a non-U.S. keyboard.

The ISO Latin 1 repertoire consists of the above plus 96 additional characters, such as à, é, Ô, £, §, µ, ©, and ¥
This repertoire is also called ISO 8859-1, and it will be described in more detail in Chapter 3 and Chapter 8. It is sufficient for writing most Western European languages, except for some typographic issues. It is widely available in the Western world, but

not necessarily elsewhere. Some characters in it still cause problems to some Mac users.

The Windows Latin 1 repertoire, which adds the dashes "–" and "—" as well as English (curly) quotation marks and apostrophe, and a few other characters

This repertoire is generally available on Windows systems and on most other systems as well. The extra characters usually need to be produced using special key combinations or other tools such as word processor functions. Due to character code differences between systems, the extra characters are generally not safe in email, for example.

The WGL4 repertoire

Although the repertoire has been defined by a private company and not in any standard, the characters in it are standard and rather widely available in environments other than Windows, too. The repertoire has a total of 652 characters. In addition to the characters mentioned above, it contains additional Latin letters, the basic characters used in modern Greek, a repertoire of Cyrillic letters sufficient for several languages, a mixed collection of mathematical and other symbols, and some line drawing characters.

The Unicode 2.0 repertoire

There is quite a jump from the WGL4 repertoire to the Unicode 2.0 repertoire, but there are few intermediate general purpose repertoires. Since Unicode is an evolving standard, there are considerable differences between its versions. For example, a font that purportedly supports "full Unicode" might actually support just Unicode 2.0. Newer versions are much more extensive. At the time Unicode 4.1 was published (March 2005), no widely used font supported essentially more than Unicode 2.0 (published in July 1996).

The full Unicode repertoire(s)

Unicode as currently defined is very large, but anything beyond Unicode 2.0 (except for the euro sign €, defined in 2.1) is rather unsafe. Experimental use, as well as use for well-defined limited applications, can be possible and interesting. When designing such use, select and document clearly the Unicode version you need. In the future, things can be expected to change, as font support to (at least) Unicode 4.1 will be shipped with important operating systems.

To illustrate the repertoire of characters that is reasonably "safe" in many situations, Table 1-2 shows all WGL4 characters. This is just an overview. Many of the characters cannot be identified by their shape only. The classification of the characters used in the table is a practical one, rather than formal.

Table 1-2. WGL4 characters

Classification	Characters
Basic Latin letters	ABCDEFGHIJKLMNOPQRSTUVWXYZabcdefghijklmnopqrstu vwxyz
Variants of Latin letters	ª º ƒ

Classification	Characters
Ligatures	fi fl
Added Latin letters	ÆæŒœØøÐđÐðÞþßŊŋ
Latin letters with diacritics	ÀÁÂÃÄÅÇÈÉÊËÌÍÎÏÑÒÓÔÕÖÙÚÛÜÝàáâãäåçèéêëìíîïñòóôõöù úûüýÿÃāĂăĄąĆćĈĉĊċČčĎďĒēĔĕĖėĘęĚěĜĝĞğĠġĤĥĦħĨĩĪĪ ĮįİıĲĳĴĵĶķĹĺĻļĽĽŁłŃńŅņŇňŊnŌōŎŏŐőŔŕŖŗŘřŚśŜŝŞşŠšŢţŤťŦŧ ŨũŪūŬŭŮůŰűŲųŴŵŶŷŸŹźŻżŽžÅåÆæØøŴwŴŵŴŵŴŵŶŷ
Greek characters	ΑΒΓΔΕΖΗΘΙΚΛΜΝΞΟΠΡΣΤΥΦΧΨΩΆΈΉΊΌΎΏΪΫαβγδεζηθικλμ νξοπρςστυφχψωάέήίόύώϊϋΐΰ·͂
Cyrillic letters	АБВГДЕЖЗИЙКЛМНОПРСТУФХЦЧШЩЪЫЬЭЮЯЁЂЃЄЅІЇЈ ЉЊЋЌЎЏабвгдежзийклмнопрстуфхцчшщъыьэюяёђѓєѕіїј љ њћќўџґ
Digits	0123456789[123]
Fractions	½ ¼ ¾ ⅛ ⅜ ⅝ ⅞
Punctuation	, : ; . ! ¡ ? ¿ " « » ‹ › " " „ ' ' ' … - – — _ † ‡ • ‰ ′ ″ ‼ ‾ ⁄
Space characters	space (U+0040), no-break space (U+00A0)
Parentheses	( ) [ ] { }
Multiple-use characters	# % & * - / \ @ ^ _ ` | ¦ ~ § ‾ ¶ · °
Spacing modifier letters	ˊ ˋ ˆ ˜ ¸ ˆ ˇ ˘ ˙ ˚ ˛ ˝
Currency symbols	$ ¢ £ ¤ ¥ ₣ £ ₧ €
Letterlike symbols	© ® ℅ ℓ № ™ µ Ω e
Arrows	← ↑ → ↓ ↔ ↕ ↨
Mathematical operators	+ − ± × ÷ < = > ≈ ≠ ≡ ≤ ≥ ¬ ∂ Δ ∏ ∑ ∕ • √ ∞ ∟ ∩ ∫
Miscellaneous technical	⌐ ⌐ ⌠ ⌡
Box drawing	─ │ ┌ ┐ └ ┘ ├ ┤ ┬ ┴ ┼ ═ ║ ╒ ╓ ╔ ╕ ╖ ╗ ╘ ╙ ╚ ╛ ╜ ╝ ╞ ╟ ╠ ╡ ╢ ╣ ╤ ╥ ╦ ╧ ╨ ╩ ╪ ╫ ╬
Block elements	▪ ▫ ▬ ▭ ▮ ▯ ░ ▒ ▓ █ ▲ ► ▼ ◄
Geometric shapes	■ □ ▪ ▫ ▬ ● ○ ◘ ◙ ◦ ◊
Miscellaneous symbols	☺ ☻ ☼ ♀ ♂ ♠ ♣ ♥ ♦ ♪ ♫

Numbering Characters

Definitions in character standards assign a number to each character. The numbers are unique in each standard, but different standards assign the numbers differently. Some commonly used standards are mutually compatible, in part: the numbers of characters in ASCII (ranging from 0 to 127) are the same as in the ISO 8859 standards, and the numbers of characters in ISO 8859-1 (ranging from 0 to 255) are the same as in Unicode.

The numbers are nonnegative integers 0, 1, 2,…, but are not necessarily consecutive; there can be gaps in the assignment. For example, in ISO 8859 standards, numbers in the range 128 to 159 are unassigned; more specifically, they are reserved for control purposes, leaving it up to other standards to define them. Unicode contains a lot of gaps, due to the coding structure, partly in order to leave space for future extensions.

It might sound natural to use the first few code numbers for digits 0, 1,…, but character standards use different assignments. Don't expect to find much logic in it. The code number of a character should be treated as fairly arbitrary, but fixed.

The number assigned to a character in a character standard has many different names: *code number*, *code position*, *code value*, *code element*, *code point*, *code set value*, as well as simply *code*. In the Unicode standard, the term "code point" is used both about a number and about a location in the coding space where a character could reside. Some code points are allocated for characters, a few have been explicitly designated as not corresponding to characters (now or ever), and most code points are still not assigned in any way.

Since characters are internally represented by their code numbers, a character can also be treated as an integer. In fact, many old programming languages lack a data type for characters and use an integer type instead. However, the code numbers are usually not used in arithmetic operations, since they mostly lack numeric meaning. If a character's number is smaller than another character's number, this by no means implies a corresponding relation in alphabetic order. For some small regions of code numbers, the order actually corresponds to alphabetic order, though.

For example, in Unicode, the numbers for the characters "a," 0 (digit zero), ! (exclamation mark), ä (letter a with umlaut), and ‰ (per mille sign) are 97, 48, 33, 228, and 8240 in decimal notation. More often, hexadecimal notation is used: 61, 30, 21, E4, and 2030. The code number assignments are essentially arbitrary: the code number has no relationship with the meaning of a character.

Normally, you do not need to memorize the numbers; you check them from suitable references. However, if you use some code numbers frequently, you will probably learn to remember some of them by heart. This explains the sarcastic saying: "Real Programmers might or might not know their spouse's name. They do, however, know the entire ASCII (or EBCDIC) code table."

Hexadecimal Notation

As mentioned above, character numbers are usually specified in hexadecimal notation, or *hex notation*. The phrase *hexadecimal number* is often used, but in fact, it is just a convention for writing numbers. The hexadecimal notation FF denotes the same number as the decimal notation 255.

In hexadecimal notation, letters "A" through "F" (or "a" through "f") are used to denote numbers from 10 to 15 (10 to 15 in decimal notation). The number denoted by a two-digit hexadecimal notation is the value of the first digit times 16 plus the value of the second digit. For example, hexadecimal 2E means $2 \times 16 + 14 = 46$ in decimal. Similarly, the four-digit hexadecimal notation 215A means $2 \times 16^3 + 1 \times 16^2 + 5 \times 16 + 10 = 8{,}538$ in decimal. The largest four-digit hexadecimal number is FFFF, which is 65,535 in decimal.

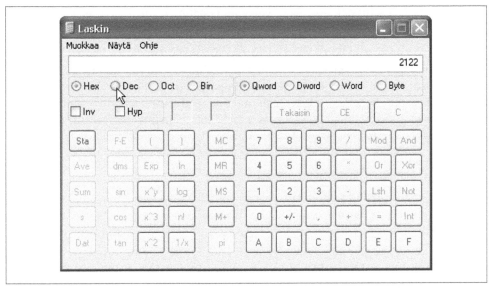

Figure 1-8. The Calculator in Windows XP, in Scientific mode

It is usually evident from context whether a number is presented as hexadecimal or decimal. In particular, Unicode code numbers written as U+*nnnn* are always in hexadecimal. When necessary, some special convention is used to indicate the base. In plain text, it is common to use a "0x" (digit zero, letter "x") prefix for hexadecimal numbers, such as in "0x215A." In mathematical notations, the base is often written (in decimal) as a subscript, as in $215A_{16}$ or $8{,}538_{10}$.

It is easy but boring to convert between decimal and hexadecimal, so we mostly use computers for that. In Windows, the Calculator program can be used for such conversions, when set in "scientific" mode. As shown on Figure 1-8, you can, for example, set the Calculator to hexadecimal mode, enter a number, and click on "Dec" to get the value in decimal.

The reason for using hexadecimal notation in character code issues is that Unicode and other standards use that notation. This in turn reflects the design decisions of using 8-bit bytes and grouping characters into 256-character sets. For example, the Unicode number U+205F denotes the character in relative position 5F inside the set U+2000..U+20FF. Such handy things are not possible if decimal numbers are used.

Another reason is that it is trivial and fast to convert between hexadecimal and binary, and computers internally use binary. Each hexadecimal digit corresponds to 4 bits: 0 = 0000, 1 = 0001, 2 = 0010, 3 = 0011,..., E = 1110, F = 1111.

Numbers as Indexes

We can regard a character code as a row of boxes, each capable of containing one character. In many widely used old character codes, the sequence has 256 boxes. In Unicode, the sequence is about a million boxes long. Although Unicode is often presented as a set of code tables (arrays), each consisting of 256 elements, its fundamental structure is essentially linear.

The code numbers are ordinal numbers, or indexes, of the boxes, starting from zero. They can also be understood as indexes to tables of properties of characters. Thus, to find out whether a particular character is a letter in the most general sense, you would conceptually use the character's code number to access a table that contains information about the general category of each character. Actual implementations do not necessarily use such table lookup techniques, but the idea illustrates the point of using code numbers.

There are some things to note on this model, however:

- Not all boxes contain a character. That is, not all code points correspond to a character. In Unicode, *most* code points are currently unassigned, and some have been explicitly defined as "noncharacters"—i.e., as not corresponding to any character, ever.

- Not all characters have a box of their own, or a code point. Some characters containing a diacritic mark can only be written as decomposed—i.e., as a base character followed by one or more combining diacritic marks. For example, the letter "e" with acute accent, é, has a box of its own; but the Cyrillic letter ю with an acute accent on it (ю́), though used as a character in dictionaries, for example, has no code point —it can only be represented as ю followed by a combining acute accent.

- Although the numbering implies an order, this order is mostly arbitrary and not used much. For instance, if a character's code point is numerically smaller than another character's code point, this implies in general nothing about the mutual order of the characters in alphabetic or sorting order.

Thus, although characters are identified by their code points, which are numbers (unsigned integers), the numeric (arithmetic) value is usually irrelevant. That is, we mostly don't operate on them as numbers, with arithmetic operations. For most purposes, the numbers are just indexes. It is not a pure coincidence, though, that some characters have code points that correspond to their mutual alphabetic order. Many character codes have put letters into alphabetic order, and Unicode has tried to preserve much of that.

Making Use of Character Numbers

There are several ways to use the Unicode number of a character. The methods of writing characters will be discussed in Chapter 2, but here are some possibilities:

- In HTML and XML authoring, you can use a *character reference* of the form &#x*number*;—e.g., ℮. That way, you can include any character, no matter what your keyboard is or what your document's encoding is.

- On Microsoft software that uses the so-called *Uniscribe* input (e.g., many programs under Windows XP), you can type a character's number in hexadecimal, such as 212e, and then type Alt-X and see how the number is replaced by the character.

Figure 1-9. Character insertion window in Microsoft Word lets you select a character by its Unicode number, as one possibility

- You can use the number as an index to information on characters in different tables, databases, and services, including the Unicode standard.

- You can select a character by its number in user interfaces such as the Character Map in Windows, as illustrated earlier in Figure 1-1, or the window that opens in Microsoft Word when you select Insert → Symbol. The latter is illustrated in Figure 1-9, which shows the window in a Finnish version of Word. As you can see, the character name shown is still the Unicode name as such—in this case, ESTIMATED SYMBOL.

Encoding Characters as Octet Sequences

When we need to store character data on a computer, we might consider storing it in an exact visual shape. Some people would call this a very naive idea, but it is in fact quite feasible, even necessary—for some purposes. If you have an old manuscript to be stored digitally, you need to scan it with high resolution and store it in some image format. Sometimes you would do that for individual characters as well. On web pages, for example, it is common to use images containing text for logos, menu items, buttons, etc., in order to produce a particular visual appearance.

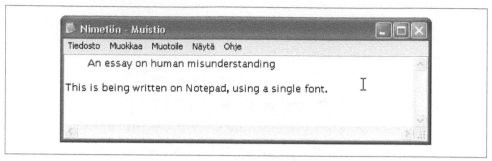

Figure 1-10. Using Windows Notepad, a simple plain text editor

For most processing of texts on computers, however, we need a more abstract presentation. It would be highly impractical to work on scanned images of characters in storing and transferring text, not to mention comparing strings for example. We do not want to do the process of recognizing a character's identity every time we use the character. Instead, we use characters as atoms of information, identified by their code numbers or some other simple way. This is really what "abstract characters" are about.

Plain Text and Other Formats for Text

Plain text is a technical term that refers to data consisting of characters only, with no formatting information such as font face, style, color, or positioning. However, formatting such as line breaks and simple spacing using space characters may be included, to the extent that it can be expressed using control characters only. Moreover, all characters are to be taken as such, without interpreting them as formatting instructions or tags. For example, HTML or XML is not plain text.

Plain text is a format that is readable by human beings when displayed as such. The reader needs to know the human language used in the text, of course. The display of plain text depends on the font that happens to be used. This can often be changed within a program, but such settings change the font of all text. (As an exception, if the font chosen does not contain all the characters used in the text, a clever program might use other fonts as backup for missing characters.)

Plain text is a primitive format, but it is extremely important. In processing texts, the ultimate processing such as searching, comparison, editing, or automatic translation takes place at the plain text level. Databases often use plain text format for strings for simplicity, even though data extracted from them is presented as formatted.

Plain text is universal, since no special software is needed for presenting it, as long as a suitable font can be used. In Windows, you can use Notepad, the very simple editor, to write and display plain text, as illustrated in Figure 1-10. There are many plain text editors, some of which contain fairly sophisticated processing tools. However, their character repertoire is often very small.

Plain text is commonly used, and normally should be used, in email, Internet discussion forums, simple textual documents (like *readme.txt* files shipped with software), and many

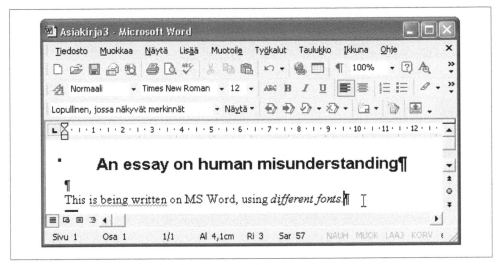

Figure 1-11. Using Microsoft Word, a text-processing program

other purposes. For example, the RFC (Request for Comments) series of documents, describing the standards, protocols, and practices on the Internet, have ASCII plain text as their format.

The phrase "ASCII file" or "ASCII text" is often used to denote plain text in general, even in contexts where ASCII is obviously not used and could not be used. This is because ASCII has been used so long and so widely, and quite often "ASCII" is mentioned as an opposed to anything that is not plain text (e.g., "ASCII" versus "binary" transfer).

Text-processing programs such as Microsoft Word normally process and store text data in a format that is somehow "enhanced" with formatting and other information. This includes the use of different fonts for different pieces of text, specific positioning and spacing, and invisible metadata ("data about data") such as author name, program version, and revision history. Figure 1-11 illustrates the use of Microsoft Word.

If you create a file containing just the word "Hello" using a plain text editor, the file size will be five octets, or maybe 10 octets, depending on encoding. If you do the same using a text-processing program such Microsoft Word, you might get, for example, a file size of 24 kilobytes (24,576 octets), because a text-processing program inserts a lot of basic information in its internal format, in addition to the text itself and some information about its appearance (font face and size). This means that if you accidentally open a Word file in a plain text editor or process it with a program prepared to deal with plain text only, you get a mess. This is illustrated in Figure 1-12, which contains a Word document with just the text "This is a simple document." written into it, opened in Notepad.

Similar considerations apply to widely used document formats such as *PDF* (Portable Document Format). There are also intermediate formats, which contain text and formatting information, such as *RTF* (Rich Text Format). It was designed for purposes like exchanging text data between different text-processing programs.

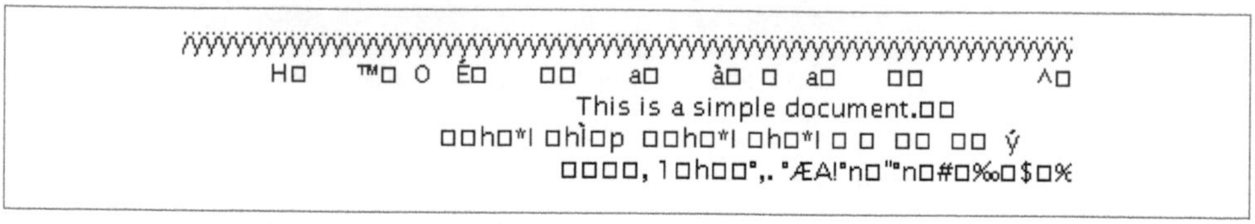

Figure 1-12. Part of a Word document accidentally opened in Notepad

If you are not familiar with the idea of formats like plain text, Word format (often called ".*doc* format" due to the common filename extension), and RTF, you could launch your favorite text-processing program. Write a short document and save it, and then use the "Save As" option in the "File" menu (or equivalent), and study and test the alternative save formats you find there. Save the document in each format in the same folder, and then view the contents of the folder, with file sizes displayed. You might then see what happens if you open each format in a text editor like Notepad, just to get a general idea. Such exercises will prepare you to deal with requests like "Please send your proposal in RTF format." This will also aid you in recognizing situations like receiving an RTF file when you have asked for something else.

Bytes and Octets

In computers and in data transmission between them—i.e., in digital data processing and transfer—data is internally presented as octets, as a rule. An *octet* is a small unit of data with a numerical value between 0 and 255, inclusively. The numerical values are presented in the normal (decimal) notation here, but other presentations are widely used too, especially octal (base 8) or hexadecimal (base 16) notation. The hexadecimal values of octets thus range from 0 to FF.

Internally, an octet consists of 8 bits—hence the name, from Latin octo "eight." A *bit*, or binary digit, is a unit of information indicating one of two alternatives, commonly denoted with the digits 0 and 1 in writing but internally represented by some small physical entity that has two distinguishable states, such as the presence or absence of a small hole or magnetization. The digits 0 and 1 that symbolize the values are also called bits (0 bit, 1 bit). When a bit has the value 1, we often say that the bit has been set.

In character code contexts, we rarely need to go into bit level. We can think of an octet as a small integer, usually without thinking how it is internally represented. However, in some contexts the concept of *most significant bit* (MSB), also called *first bit* or *sign bit* is relevant. If the most significant bit of an octet is set (1), then in terms of numerical values of octets, the value is greater than 127 (i.e., in the range 128–255). In various contexts, such octets are sometimes interpreted as *negative* numbers, and this may cause problems, unless caution is taken.

The word "byte" is more common than "octet," but the octet is a more definite concept. A *byte* is a sequence of bits of a known length and processed as a unit. Nowadays it is almost universal to use 8-bit bytes, and therefore a distinction between a byte and an octet is seldom made. However, in character code standards and related texts, the term octet is normally used.

There is nothing in an octet that tells how it is to be interpreted. It is just a bit pattern, a sequence of eight 0s or 1s, with no indication of whether it represents an integer, a character, a truth value, or something else. For example, the octet with value 33 in decimal, 00010001 in binary (as bits), could represent the exclamation sign character !, or it could mean just the number 33 in some numeric data. It could well be just part of the internal representation of a number or a character. Information about the interpretation needs to be kept elsewhere, or implied by the definition of some data structure or file format.

Character Encodings

A character encoding can be defined as a method (algorithm) for presenting characters in digital form as sequences of octets. We can also say that an encoding maps code numbers of characters into octet sequences. The difference between these definitions is whether we conceptually start from characters as such or from characters that already have code numbers assigned to them.

There are hundreds of encodings, and many of them have different names. There is a standardized procedure for registering an encoding, and this means that a primary name is assigned to it, and possibly some alias names. For example, ASCII, US-ASCII, ANSI_X3.4-1986, and ISO646-US are different names for an encoding. There are also many unregistered encodings and names that are used widely. The Windows Latin 1 encoding, which is very common in the Western world, has only one registered name, windows-1252, but it is often declared as cp-1252 or cp1252.

The case of letters is not significant in character encoding names. Thus, "ASCII" and "Ascii" are equivalent. Hyphens, on the other hand, are significant in the names.

Single-Octet Encodings

For a character repertoire that contains at most 256 characters, there is a simple and obvious way of encoding it: assign a number in the range 0–255 to each character and use an octet with that value to represent that character. Such encodings, called single-octet or 8-bit encodings, are widely used and will remain important. There is still a large amount of software that assumes that each character is represented as one octet.

Various historical reasons dictate the assignments of numbers to characters in a single-octet encoding. Usually letters A–Z are in alphabetic order and digits are in numeric order, but the assignments are otherwise more or less arbitrary. Besides, any extra Latin letters, as used in many languages, are most probably assigned to whatever positions that were "free" in some sense. Thus, if you compare characters by their code numbers in a single-octet encoding, you will generally not get the right alphabetic ordering by the rules of, for example, French or German.

Multi-Octet Encodings

As you may guess, the next simpler idea of using *two* octets for a single character has been invented, formalized, and used. It is not as common as you might suspect, though.

A simple two-octet encoding is sufficient for a character repertoire that contains at most 65,536 characters. An octet pair (m,n) represents the character with number $256 \times m + n$. Alternatively, we can say that the number is represented by its 16-bit binary form. This makes processing easy, but there are two fundamental problems with the idea:

- Each character requires two octets, which is rather uneconomical if the text mostly consists of characters that could be presented in a single-octet encoding.

- Unicode is no longer limited to the code number range 0..65,536, so extra methods would anyway be needed to represent characters outside it.

Thus, encodings that use a *variable* number of octets per character are more common. The most widely used among such encodings is *UTF-8* (UTF stands for Unicode Transformation Format), which uses one to four octets per character. For those writing in English, the good news is that UTF-8 represents each ASCII character as one octet, so there is no increase in data size unless you use characters outside ASCII.

If you accidentally view an UTF-8 encoded document in a program that interprets the data as ASCII or windows-1252 encoded, you will notice no difference as long as the data contains ASCII only. In fact, any ASCII data can trivially be declared as UTF-8 encoded as well. If the data contains characters other than ASCII, they would in this case be displayed each as two or more characters, which have no direct relationship with the real character in the data. This is because consecutive octets would be interpreted as each indicating a character, instead of being treated according to the encoding as a unit.

The "Character Set" Confusion

Character encodings are often called *character sets*, and the abbreviation *charset* is used in Internet protocols to denote a character encoding. This is confusing because people often understand "set" as "repertoire." However, *character set* means a very specific *internal representation* of characters, and for the same repertoire, several different "character sets" can be used. A character set implicitly defines a repertoire, though: the collection of characters that can be represented using the character set.

It is advisable to avoid the phrase "character set" when possible. The term *character code* can be used instead when referring to a collection of characters and their code numbers. The term *character encoding* is suitable when referring to a particular representation.

For example, the word "ASCII" can mean a certain collection of characters, or that collection along with their code numbers 0–127 as assigned in the ASCII standard, or even more concretely, those code numbers (and hence the characters) represented using an 8-bit byte for each character.

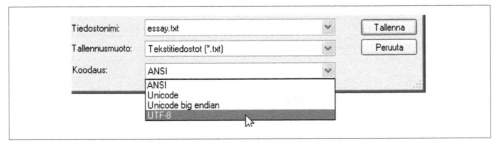

Figure 1-13. An extract from a Save As dialog in Notepad

Working with Encodings

When you use characters on a computer, some software will internally encode them in binary format. Most users never need to know the details of this, still less need to actually handle the encoding process, but it is essential to know that there are different encodings, with different properties. In transferring data between applications and computers, you may need to change the encoding or select a suitable encoding.

Selecting the Encoding When Saving

Text editors and many other programs typically have a File menu, with a Save function for storing data onto disk. Normally, this function uses the file format and the character encoding that is typical of the program. However, there is usually also a Save As function, which lets the user select the format and encoding. This function is often used because it lets you save an edited document under a different filename.

The Save As function is often the simplest way to *convert* between different encodings (and file formats). You simply open a file and save it differently. For example, suppose you have used Notepad to create a plain text file. If you use, for example, an English version of Windows, the default encoding that Notepad uses is Windows Latin 1. Now suppose that a friend has asked you to send your text in the UTF-8 encoding for some reason. You simply open your file in Notepad, select File → Save As and then choose the UTF-8 encoding from the menu of encodings, as shown in Figure 1-13. It illustrates the three basic things you can (and need to) specify in Save As dialogs: the filename, the file format, and the encoding.

The list of possible encodings in a Save As dialog varies greatly, and the names of the encodings are not always official names. For example, in Microsoft products, "ANSI" often appears as denoting the character code that the system uses as its normal 8-bit code, such as the Windows Latin 1 encoding, which should be called "windows-1252." The word "Unicode" may denote different encodings used for Unicode, typically UTF-16. Use the UTF-8 encoding for Unicode text, unless you have a good reason for doing otherwise.

When using a text-processing program, the situation is usually different. There is a file format menu in the Save As dialog but often no encoding menu. The reason is that in text processing, the overall format is crucial, and the encoding is often coupled with the format.

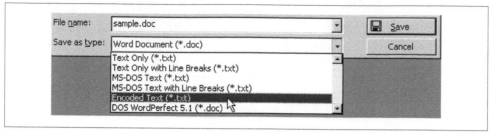

Figure 1-14. An extract from a Save As dialog in Microsoft Word

In Microsoft Word, for example, the list of formats may contain alternatives as shown in Figure 1-14, with options corresponding to the internal formats of different programs and some plain text formats. Here, too, it may require some guesswork or study to identify what the options really mean. On Windows systems, "*.txt" is associated with several different encodings, and "*.ans" refers to ANSI (e.g., windows-1252). The notation "*.asc" may suggest ASCII encoding, but in fact it refers to an old DOS encoding, a *code page*, which is a single-octet encoding and may vary from one system to another.

Having selected a plain text (*.txt*) format, modern versions of Microsoft Word ask you to specify the encoding in another dialog. In older versions, this happens if you select the "Encoded text" format. In this mode, the default is "Windows" or, more explicitly, something like "Western European (Windows)," which means windows-1252. The dialog is shown in Figure 1-15. The user has typed in the text "This is a sample document—with special characters like ♣ and Ω." When saving as windows-1252, Microsoft Word is about to quietly change the em dash "—" to hyphen "-" (for some odd reason) and to omit the two special characters, but it issues a warning about them. If you would like to have them saved, you would need to select an encoding that makes this possible, such as UTF-8.

In Save As dialogs, there are often additional settings that affect *line break* conventions, which are discussed in Chapter 8. These conventions specify which control characters are used to separate lines of text, as well as the method of presenting paragraphs internally. Microsoft Word stores a paragraph as one long line and splits it to separate lines as needed for display. It is often desirable to split a paragraph into lines of reasonable length (e.g., at most 80 characters) when saving as plain text.

How Encodings Should Be Detected

Character encodings are of crucial importance, but most people—including most computer professionals—need not know the technicalities of encodings. To view an email message or a web page that is UTF-8 or ISO 8859-2 encoded, you need not know how characters are encoded in them. Instead, you need a program that understands the encodings, and perhaps you need to tell it to use a particular encoding.

The correct interpretation and processing of character data of course requires knowledge (or correct guess) about the encoding used. For email, the encoding should be specified (by the email program) in so-called MIME headers, unless ASCII, the default encoding,

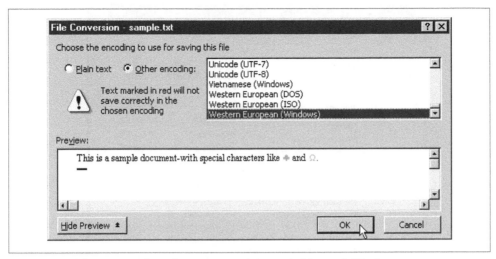

Figure 1-15. Selecting encoding when saving as plain text in Microsoft Word

is used. For HTML documents, such information should be sent by the web server along with the document itself, using HTTP headers, which resemble MIME headers. The headers are normally invisible to users but processed by a program, such as an email reader or web browser. Using special tools, the headers can be made visible for an analysis.

Thus, when everything works well, you need not see MIME or HTTP headers or care about them. But if things look odd, you may need inspect them or at least force a program make a particular guess on the character encoding. In some situations, you might have some prose description of the data format, such as an email sender's note like "the attached file is in ISO-8859-2." Beware that people don't always use the right terms in such notes.

Previously the ASCII encoding was usually implied by default, and it is still very common to do so. Nowadays ISO-8859-1, which can be regarded as an extension of ASCII, is often the practical default. The current trend is to avoid giving such a special position to ISO-8859-1 among the variety of encodings. In XML, the default encoding is UTF-8.

To summarize, the character encoding of input data can be deduced from:

- An explicit indication of the encoding—e.g., in protocol headers
- An explicit or implicit agreement on using a particular encoding by default in a certain context
- A private agreement or note about the encoding in a particular case
- Guesswork based on the context or inspection of the data using different guesses

In Chapter 3, we will discuss some commonly used encodings and their typical scope of use. This will help you in the guesswork. For example, if you get an email message from Poland and it contains some Polish names that look misspelled, the odds are good that the

Figure 1-16. Fixing the display of an email message by setting the character encoding manually

message is in fact in ISO-8859-2 or windows-1250 encoding, since these are very common in Poland.

Setting the Encoding Manually

Suppose you get email from abroad and it contains some strange characters in names or in other text. Figure 1-16 shows an example of a received email message, as displayed by the Mozilla Thunderbird email program. The message is meant to contain French words like "Rhône" and "moiré" but is displayed incorrectly, with Greek letters in place of accented Latin letters. The sender may have seen text all right, but something went wrong, and the error is not the recipient's email program. The reason is that the message was incorrectly sent with a message header that claims that it is encoded in ISO-8859-7, as we can see by selecting View → Character Encoding. Clicking on "Western (ISO-8859-1)" fixes the display.

Setting the encoding manually in the recipient's email program does not always help. For example, if a message has incorrect information about encoding, it may be converted to another encoding before it reaches the recipient. Since the information is wrong, the conversion goes all wrong too, and special repair might be needed.

Sending Unicode Email

Before sending Unicode email, make sure the recipient is willing to receive Unicode-encoded messages and knows what that means. Although most users have email programs that are capable of displaying such messages, the user may need to change settings (especially font settings) to see them properly. Moreover, on programs that cannot handle Unicode, the message would look more or less like garbage.

It's a good idea to test things by sending email to yourself. There are things that can go wrong in that simple case, and it's best that only you see your own initial mistakes. However, many problems will not be detected that way. If possible, find someone who works in a different environment (say, Mac or Unix, if you are using Windows) and uses a different email program, and exchange some test messages with Unicode characters in them.

There are basically three ways to send Unicode text by email:

- As an attachment—e.g., in Microsoft Word format. This is usually no different from using a "normal," non-Unicode attachment. The recipient needs to know what to do with the attachment. Beware that attachments are often frowned upon for security reasons, and they might even be filtered out by firewalls.

- In HTML format, typically as generated by an email program. Effectively, the program would convert "special" characters to HTML character references. This is what typically happens when you try to compose an email message with special characters in Outlook Express. Although this may solve some problems, it also causes some. HTML format messages cannot be read by all programs, and they may affect the classification of your message as unsolicited bulk email, or "spam."

- As plain text, with message headers that specify the encoding (as explained in detail in Chapter 10). This is a simple and clean approach. It's very easy on Mozilla Thunderbird, for example. If you don't have that program on your system, you can download it from the *http://www.mozilla.org* site.

Figure 1-17 shows a dialog that appears when you have composed a Unicode email message in Thunderbird. The program asks for permission to send the message as UTF-8 encoded, which is just fine. In composing a message, you can use, for example, the Character Map program when using Windows, as explained in "Introduction to Characters and Unicode" earlier in this chapter.

Sent this way, the email message is *plain text*, effectively just a sequence of characters as Unicode code points, though with headers that specify the encoding. This means, in particular, that there is *no font information* included. It is up to the receiving email program to use the font(s) it has been set to use. The recipient needs to have some font that contains the character you have included, but she does not need to have the same font as you. This is essential for communication between people who work on different platforms, often with quite different choices of fonts.

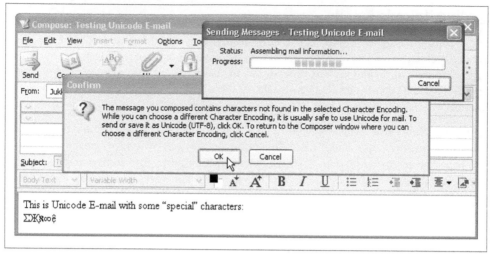

Figure 1-17. Sending Unicode email in Thunderbird

Outlook Express (OE) may automatically convert the message into HTML format, if your text contains characters outside the repertoire that OE normally supports. To prevent this, go to the settings for outgoing mail in the Tools menu, and check that the plain text format is selected. Note that there are separate settings for outgoing email and for outgoing newsgroup (Usenet) messages. Check also the options for text format in the settings: make sure "MIME" is checked, and select "no encoding" instead of an encoding like Quoted Printable or Base64. When you then send email with special characters, OE asks how to send the message; select sending as Unicode. As you see, OE is less convenient for getting started with Unicode email than Thunderbird but once you've found the right settings, OE works well for Unicode.

Viewing Web Pages in Different Encodings

A web page author can specify the character encoding of her page in several ways, discussed in Chapter 10. Normally, your web browser recognizes the encoding and uses it to interpret and display the page. However, sometimes an author fails to use any of those ways or specifies a wrong encoding. Then the user may need to select the encoding, perhaps with trial and error, until the page becomes legible.

Your browser might not be prepared to handle all encodings. For Internet Explorer in particular, there is a set of updates available from the Windows Update site *http:// windowsupdate.microsoft.com*. In addition to updates that fix security problems, the site contains optional updates that add some encodings to the capabilities of Internet Explorer (IE). The site *http://www.mauvecloud.net/charsets/* contains pages for testing browser support to encodings.

If you visit web pages in many languages, you will probably encounter some pages that are not displayed correctly due to encoding mismatches. For example, you might visit a

Hungarian page and see most characters correctly but some letters all wrong. If you have problems with finding such problems, try the index *http://www.dmoz.org/World/*, which contains links to collections of web pages in different languages; the link names are in the language itself.

The explanation is probably that the web server has not sent any information about the encoding. In Hungary, web browsers are probably configured to use ISO-8859-2 in such cases, and users do not observe any problem. However, your browser might use ISO-8859-1 by default, and this makes a difference for a handful of characters. For example, the octet that denotes ű (u with double acute accent) according to ISO-8859-2 will be treated as û (u with circumflex) according to ISO-8859-1.

What you can do as a user is to tell your browser to use an encoding that differs from the browser default:

- On IE, select View → Encoding, and then the appropriate encoding. Use the "More" option when needed. In the example, you would select "Central European (ISO)," which is what Microsoft calls ISO-8859-2.

- On Firefox, select View → Character Encoding, and choose the suitable encoding directly or via "More Encodings," as illustrated in Figure 1-18. Firefox classifies, for example, ISO-8859-2 as "East European" and calls it "Central European (ISO-8859-2)."

Often you can fix the display of a web page rather easily, since you can guess the encoding. This requires some experience, though. For example, Hungarian pages are most probably in ISO-8859-2 or in windows-1250 encoding; but for Russian pages, there are a few encodings (in the Cyrillic group) you might need to try.

Common Confusion: Encoding Versus Language

Quite often the choice of a character repertoire, code, or encoding is presented as the choice of a *language*. Programs typically confuse their users quite a lot in this area.

On the Opera browser (available from *http://www.opera.com*), for example, the keyboard shortcut Alt-P (or the command Tools → Preferences) and the choice of the "General" pane takes you to settings titled "Languages," as shown in Figure 1-19. The pane contains settings for three quite independent things:

- The user interface language—i.e., the names of menus and options in the browser itself, quite independently of any particular page content.

- The language preferences sent by the browser. You can specify an ordered sequence of languages, to be used in the (rare) cases where a web page is served in different language versions using a particular protocol.

- The default encoding, to be used when a web page fails to specify its encoding in any explicit manner. The encoding windows-1252 is suitable here if you mainly view

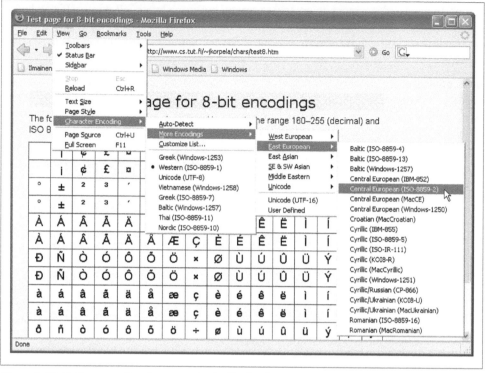

Figure 1-18. Setting encoding for a page in the Firefox browser

pages in English and other Western European languages. However, the encoding itself is a technical setting and does not depend on any language settings.

All these settings are useful, but lumping them together into one pane called "Languages" is misleading.

A language setting is quite distinct from character issues, although naturally each language has its own requirements for character repertoire. Even more seriously, programs and their documentation very often confuse the above-mentioned issues with the selection of a *font*.

Working with Fonts

In a word processor like Microsoft Word, it is deceptively simple to change the overall font, or the font of some particular piece of text. You can paint a piece of text with the mouse and select a font for it from a drop-down menu. In web authoring, it is not much more difficult, especially if you use authoring software that resembles a word processor. However, things become difficult if the chosen font does not contain all the characters you need.

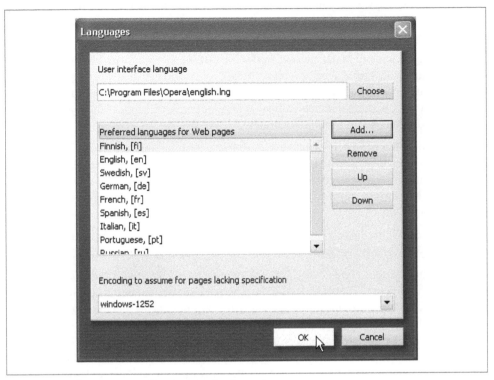

Figure 1-19. The "Languages" settings in the Opera browser

 Each computer system is shipped with some repertoire of fonts, which may be insufficient for working with a large character repertoire even if the system is basically "Unicode enabled."

Installing Additional Support

For example, a typical Windows system might not have any font that is rich enough to present all the characters you need. Unfortunately, Windows has often been preinstalled without full "multilingual support." You may therefore need to install additional fonts.

On Windows XP, you would do this as follows:

1. Select Start → Control Panel → Regional Options and Language Options.

2. In the "Languages" tab, there are checkboxes for two groups of languages, "complex scripts and right-to-left languages" and "East Asian languages." Check either or both of them to install optional fonts and system support for these languages. You will be informed about disk requirements and asked to confirm. You might be prompted to insert the Windows CD-ROM or point to a network location where the files are located.

On older Windows systems, you may need to select Control Panel → Add/Remove Programs, click on Multilanguage Support, and then Details. Make sure a checkmark appears beside the language or languages you want to use, and then click on OK.

There is support to many languages available, for different versions of Windows, in the Windows Update site *http://windowsupdate.microsoft.com*. The site also contains important security updates. However, even if your computer has been configured to download and install security updates automatically, this does not cover the extra language support. You need to download and install it separately.

If you have installed MS Office, you have probably got some important additional fonts, such as Arial Unicode MS, which is not a complete Unicode font, but is rather extensive (though it exists in different versions). However, it is possible that this font was not included when MS Office was installed; you may need to install it separately from the MS Office CD then.

There are some additional instructions for installing fonts in a few environments on the page "Display Problems?" at *http://www.Unicode.org/help/display_problems.html*.

As a quick check, access *http://www.Unicode.org/standard/WhatIsUnicode.html*, which contains the document "What is Unicode?" in English but also, under the heading "Translations," links to versions of the document in many other languages. Do the link texts look meaningful (though perhaps all Greek or all Hebrew to you), or are there boxes or question marks that look like symbols of unrepresentable characters? This test is best carried out using a Mozilla or Opera browser rather than Internet Explorer 6, which will only use characters in the currently selected font. Note that it is rare, these days, to be able to see *all* the link texts there properly, since some of them contain characters that are not present in relatively large fonts. Figure 1-20 shows the test page viewed on Opera, on a system where the font support is relatively good.

Of course, installing additional fonts and language support on your computer does not make documents created by you behave any better on other computers. If you had to install something extra in order to type some Chinese, the odds are that if you send a Chinese document you composed to your neighbor, he might not see it properly without installing something extra, too. We cannot expect all, or even most, computers to be able to display the full Unicode repertoire, or even anything close to it.

The situation is expected to change in time in the sense that new systems will have a few *complete* Unicode fonts installed. Additional fonts may still be needed for typographic reasons. In general, any font that has a large character repertoire cannot be typographically optimal for any particular writing system. The font needs to have many characters that are distinguishable from each other, and this imposes restrictions on the design of characters.

Font Support in Web Browsers

There is a major difference between Internet Explorer (at least up to Version 6) and more modern browsers. IE basically uses a single font for a piece of text, as specified on the page itself or in the browser settings. If the text contains a character that is not present in

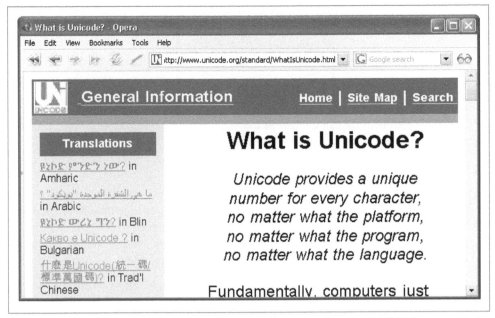

Figure 1-20. A page with links containing characters from several languages, therefore suitable for testing font support

Figure 1-21. A word with a special character in Internet Explorer

the font, IE shows just a small rectangular box to indicate the lack of glyph, as shown in Figure 1-21. Firefox, for example, is capable of picking up glyphs from different fonts, if the primary font is not sufficient for all characters.

When a browser, or other program, uses glyphs from different fonts, the situation is not as happy as you might think. The problem is that a font typically has a distinctive style and flavor, and mixing fonts often produces typographically poor results. This is illustrated in Figure 1-22, where a Romanian word containing letter "t" with comma below is rendered using a different font for that character. (In practice, the letter "t" with a comma below is almost always replaced by the letter "t" with a cedilla, which is much better supported in fonts, making it possible to present words like "Constanța" in a typographically suitable way.)

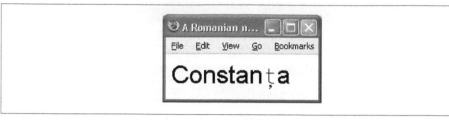

Figure 1-22. A word with a special character in Firefox

Font Substitution: a Solution and a Problem

The font problem discussed above appears in contexts other than web pages, too. In composing a text in a word processor, you may have decided (or someone may have decided for you) on the fonts to be used. It may well happen that you need a character that does not appear in the font you use, and you need to pick it up from another font. A program might do this for you, by automatically switching to a substitute font.

The presentation of special symbols like ⌘ in a different font need not have drastic effects, though it may cause uneven line spacing. Font changes inside a word are often much worse. Thus, it is best to design the use of fonts so that the primary font is sufficient at least for all *letters* that might be needed. Sometimes, however, it is feasible to use a reasonably similar font as a secondary font—e.g., Arial Unicode MS as a "backup font" for Arial.

When using fonts like Arial Unicode MS or Geneva as "backup fonts," you might run into problems with *italicized* or **bold** text. The reason is that some fonts exist in one version only, not in italics or bold versions. Many programs still display them in italics or in bold by "faking" the typographic features by modifying the shapes of characters. However, some programs don't do this, and those that do may produce typographically poor results. Thus, try to limit the use of "backup fonts" to nonstylized copy text.

When deciding on a font, you should use some test files that contain both typical text and some less typical "exotic" characters that may appear in actual documents. The Common Locale Data Repository (CLDR), discussed in Chapter 11, contains lists of "exemplary characters" for different languages. These lists include both characters normally used in the language and characters that often appear in names in texts in that language, due to cultural connections. For example, text in Spanish may well contain names in Portuguese or French. Therefore, a good test file for Spanish contains more than just Spanish characters.

Moreover, depending on the topic areas of texts, various special symbols will be needed. If you design the use of fonts in a publication on technology, you should probably pay attention to the availability of technical symbols such as µ and ø in the fonts. That way, you can avoid embarrassing problems that you might encounter when you have selected a font but later find out that it lacks some essential characters. For example, the site *http://www.fileformat.info/info/Unicode/char/* contains tools for finding fonts (within some

DIAMETER SIGN (U+2300) Font Support

This is a list of fonts that support Unicode Character 'DIAMETER SIGN' (U+2300).

This only includes fonts installed on this server. If you want to see if one of the fonts on your machine has support, try the Custom Font Report tool.

If you are a font author and would like your font listed here, please let me know.

Font	
Arial Unicode MS	view
CaslonRoman	view
Code2000	view

Figure 1-23. Information on font support for a character

repertoire of fonts) that support a particular character. Figure 1-23 shows an example of such information, which indicates here that support for the diameter sign is rather limited, despite the rather common use of this character in technical contexts. Among the fonts listed, Arial Unicode MS is the most realistic alternative, since it is shipped with MS Office products, though not always installed along with them.

The font problems are one reason why the common use of "Lorem ipsum" texts (i.e., meaningless pig latin texts) in visual design is not such a good idea. Those texts seldom contain anything but the basic Latin letters and a few punctuation characters. It is safer to play with more realistic texts with a richer character repertoire. This does not mean that you need to reject all fonts that do not contain all the characters you might imaginably need in the texts. Rather, the suggested testing ensures that the most important characters work well, and you can prepare for eventual problems with less common characters.

Printer Fonts

When a document is printed, the fonts used in it may need to be replaced by printer fonts. It may well happen that the document looks fine on screen but some characters are lost or distorted in printing. The situation may vary by printer. A printer may use a font shipped with the printer itself (on ROM), or a font that has been separately installed into it, or a downloaded font—i.e., a font sent by the program to the printer.

 It often happens that a document with special characters looks good on screen, but some characters are wrong when the document is printed.

Therefore, you may need to test your fonts especially before making an important decision on using particular fonts in publications. Make sure that your test file is extensive enough to cover even less common characters. Typical printer test pages contain a relatively limited repertoire of characters.

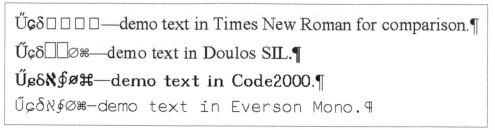

Figure 1-24. Text samples in some large-repertoire fonts

Finding Fonts

Typographically good fonts are usually commercial products, sold either as such or packaged into text-processing, publishing, or other programs. However, there are some fonts with large character repertoires available as freeware or shareware, and they can be useful for special applications or as general "backup fonts." The following fonts are illustrated in Figure 1-24; the rectangular boxes indicate a lack of glyph in the font.

Doulos SIL (http://scripts.sil.org/DoulosSILfont)
> A free font family that contains a large repertoire that is suitable for almost any text based on a Latin or Cyrillic script. It also contains a rich set of phonetic symbols and is therefore useful for linguistics.

Code2000, Code2001, Code2002 (http://home.att.net/~jameskass/)
> Large shareware fonts. Often used as ultimate backup due to coverage, but not typographically for normal use.

Everson Mono (http://www.evertype.com/emono/)
> A simple, monospace font, which is legible even in rather small size. Shareware.

For many additional fonts, please refer to *http://www.alanwood.net/Unicode/fonts.html.*

Installing new fonts is typically easy. On Windows, having downloaded a font, you can open the Control Panel via the Start menu, open the Fonts folder, and select File → Install New Font. Then find the folder where you downloaded the font, and the font will appear in a menu, to be selected for installation. After installation, you can check that the font is available, by opening a program's font menu.

Fonts in Web Authoring

Originally, web pages had no font information; each browser used its own font. Soon after, `<font>` tags were introduced and gained popularity among web authors. This meant a seemingly simple way to specify a font: `<font face="Arial">Hello world</font>`, or perhaps with `face="Arial,Helvetica,Geneva"` to provide a list of alternatives, because not all browsers have a font named Arial. However, this approach is inflexible and makes things difficult to modify and maintain.

The more modern approach is to specify font usage separately from the HTML markup through the use of *Cascading Style Sheets* (CSS). For example, you could specify the font for an entire page in CSS as follows: body { font-family: Arial, Helvetica, Geneva; }. Modern browsers effectively turn <font> tags into CSS rules internally.

The fallback problem

Since many fonts used on computers have rather small character repertoires, the question arises what to do if your document contains more or less "unusual" characters. You might wish to use, say, the Arial font in general, but you may need other fonts for some special characters.

Recommendations by the World Wide Web Consortium (W3C) suggest that an author include a *generic font name* as the last name in a font list. These names (serif, sans-serif, monospace, cursive, and fantasy) correspond to broad classes of fonts. The idea is that normally the font list consists of fonts of the same class, and the last item there would effectively tell the browser to use *some* font of the class, if it cannot find any of the specific fonts listed. A typical example would thus be body { font-family: Arial, Helvetica, Geneva, sans-serif; }.

In principle, generic font family names are supposed to be mapped to *typical* fonts in a category. Thus, sans-serif would not mean any sans-serif font that a browser may have but the most typical representative of the class of sans-serif fonts. However, typical fonts tend to be old fonts, and old fonts tend to have relatively small character repertoires.

The CSS font model (font-matching algorithm) is based on the idea of determining (at the conceptual level at least) the font *individually* for each character. If none of the fonts declared contains a glyph for the character, the browser is supposed to use a browser-dependent default list of fonts. This is how, for example, the Opera and Firefox browsers work. The problem is with IE, which more or less just uses the declared font-family value and picks up the first font there that is available on the system, without checking whether it contains all the characters that appear in the text.

This means that with the above-mentioned CSS rule, a piece of text containing, for example, the diameter sign ⌀ (U+2600) will contain a small rectangle in place of the character on IE. The browser sees the name Arial in the font list and uses it, since a font with that name exists. Characters not present in that font will then be replaced by a symbol for missing character. On Opera and Firefox, the lack of character is detected and the list of fonts is scanned further. Here, Helvetica and Geneva are probably not of use, whereas the font used as a generic sans-serif font might contain the character. Even if it does not, the browser proceeds to its internal list of fallback fonts. In effect, if *any* font on the system contains the character, it will be shown. This often results in a typographically poor rendering, but at least the character is displayed.

The practical conclusion is that for web authoring, the font names in a font-family list should be chosen so that each of them contains all the characters that appear in the text of an element. At least as long as IE Version 6 is widely used, we should avoid relying on the defined fallback mechanism.

Generally, if a document or part of a document contains characters that do not appear in commonly available fonts, there are two things you can do. You can specify no font, leaving it to users to select the best font on their browsers they can. Or, according to another school of thought, you can try and identify some fonts so that any of them alone is sufficient for all of your characters. This typically means declarations like font-family: Arial Unicode MS, Lucida Sans Unicode. The choice of fonts cannot be an exact science, since fonts with the same exact name (such as Arial Unicode MS) often exist in different versions, with different character repertoires.

Effects of browser settings

As a user of a browser such as Opera or Firefox, you can affect the default fonts used by the browser. You can define what fonts the generic font names serif, sans-serif, etc. map to. You can also specify which default font is used for texts for which no font suggestion is made on a page. The latter possibility exists on IE as well, and it typically contains settings for different *writing systems*. That is, you can select one font for texts in Latin letters, another font for texts in Cyrillic letters, etc. The details can be somewhat obscure and depend on the browser, but the point is that there can be three kinds of "default fonts" in a browser:

- The font used (when possible) for a character for which no font information is given on a web page. This font typically depends on the writing system that the character belongs to. Note that a web page very often specifies the overall font to be used, and in that case, this setting has no effect.
- The font used when a page specifies a generic font name.
- The internal list of fonts to be used when everything else fails. Typically, this cannot be changed in normal browser settings but only through a configuration file.

For example, in Firefox, you can select Tools → Options → General → Languages to enter a "Fonts & Colors" settings window as in Figure 1-25. It lets you specify, for different writing systems, whether a sans serif or a serif font is used by default and what the default serif, sans serif, and monospace (teletype) fonts are, as well as default font size. The effect of these settings is somewhat complicated, since browsers may recognize the script (writing system) of text from some technical matters, not from the text itself.

The "Fonts for" menu in Figure 1-25 has the options shown in Figure 1-26. You should be mildly surprised at seeing a mixture of names, some of which seem to refer to scripts, some not. Unicode is of course not a script, and Western, Central European, Baltic, and Turkish refer to character codes rather than scripts. The logic of deciding what such names really mean varies by browser, but at the implementation level, the assignments are for *languages* in Firefox. It uses various methods to deduce or guess the language. Here "Unicode" refers to anything that does not fall into any other category.

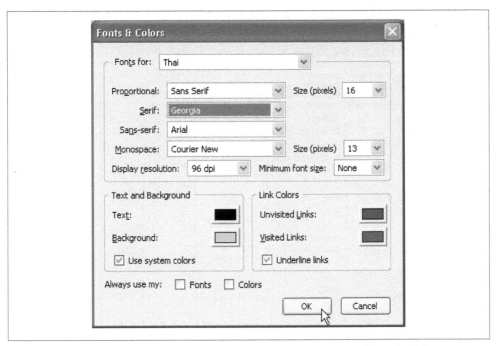

Figure 1-25. In the Firefox browser, the default fonts can be specified as different for different scripts; here they are set for the Thai script

Summaries

The following summaries use very concise language, and they are hardly understandable in isolation. However, having read the text of this chapter, you may find them useful and return to them later. The terminology related to characters varies quite a lot, so the summaries help in checking out how this book names things.

Summary of Definitions

Following is a list of terms you may come across:

Character
    A basic unit of textual information, as abstract concept, as opposed to stylistic and typographic variation between shapes that can be identified as the same character.

Character code
    A mapping, often presented in tabular form, that defines a one-to-one correspondence between characters in a character repertoire and a set of nonnegative integers.

Character encoding
    A method (algorithm) for presenting characters in digital form by mapping sequences of code numbers of characters into sequences of octets. Encodings have names, which can be registered.

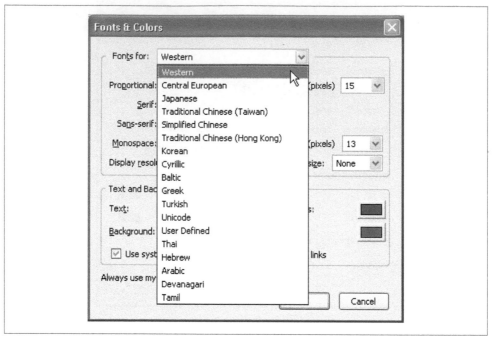

Figure 1-26. Menu of contexts for font settings in a version of Firefox

Code number

The integer assigned to a character in a character code. Synonyms: code position, code value, code element, code point, code set value, code.

Character repertoire

A collection of distinct characters. No specific internal presentation in computers or data transfer is assumed. The repertoire per se does not even define an ordering for the characters; ordering for sorting and other purposes is to be specified separately. A character repertoire is usually defined by specifying names of characters and a sample (or reference) presentation of characters in visible form.

Glyph

A basic unit of visual rendering of characters—i.e., a particular visible presentation of a character, or part of character, or pair or sequence of characters.

Octet

A sequence of eight binary digits (0 and 1) treated as a unit.

Summary of Concept Levels

We can consider a character, say @, at different conceptual levels, or levels of abstraction:

Character as an abstraction

The idea of a particular character, in the mind of an individual and in social usage. For example, whatever @ suggests to you, or your friends, or people in your country.

Character as defined in a specification

A particular definition of a character, aimed at making the idea explicit and communicable. The definition can show some glyph(s) for the character, name it (e.g., "commercial at"), describe it verbally, and list its properties in some general framework.

Coded character

A character as defined in a specification together with its code number in some system of such numbers. In most systems, the number of @ is 40 in hexadecimal. The number can be used as a concise way of referring to the characters, often using some special notation like 0x40 or U+0040.

Encoded representation

A particular internal representation of the code number of a character, and hence of the character. This depends on the encoding used. For the @ character, the representation could be the octet 40 (hex) alone—i.e., the bit sequence 00001000. In another encoding, however, it could consist of two octets, 00 and 40.

Glyph

A rendering of a character—e.g., @ or @ or @.

CHAPTER 2

Writing Characters

The practical difficulties of producing characters on normal computer keyboards are among the most serious obstacles to more widespread use of rich character repertoires. Most modern computers have rather good Unicode support, but people don't make use of it, because they simply don't know how to type special characters.

This chapter presents some common methods of entering characters. It is largely a collection of recipes, useful to people who work daily with texts containing "difficult" characters. Appendix A gives a quick reference for commonly needed characters.

The topic is also relevant to IT specialists who need to understand the possible input methods when designing applications and systems. The same applies to giving instructions on data entry, or simply asking someone to send you in writing (on paper or in digital form) something that contains characters that are "special" to him. It is not sufficient to know some way of typing characters, since users may not have the same methods at their disposal, or they might find it too awkward.

Method Varieties

There is no single answer to a question like "How do I write the character…?" The methods vary by program and equipment. In any given situation, there are usually several ways to write a character.

When you give individual instructions to someone, or you are solving your own problem with typing characters, you should normally try to find one way to input the characters, preferably the most convenient one. However, as usual, convenience is relative. It does not pay off to find a clever way of producing a character if you need it only once and you already know a general, if clumsy, way to input that character. When you give general instructions to many people, especially to people who work in different environments, you should try to explain a few alternatives. It is quite probable that different people need or like different methods.

A Simple Way or a Universal Way?

There are many different methods for typing characters, often available in parallel. Some of them are very general, allowing even the insertion of any Unicode character. Some methods have been tailored for very special purposes, perhaps even for the entry of one particular character that would otherwise be difficult to produce. This chapter aims at clarifying things by explaining typical approaches. The multitude of methods can be divided into a few basic categories, to make things more understandable.

When you select methods to be explained to users of an application, it is usually best to aim at *systematic* ways rather than the fastest ways. That is, opt for a method that works for all the characters needed rather than an eclectic combination of tricks. The same may apply to your own use, e.g., when you need to type particular characters frequently.

Appendix A contains a collection of methods for some commonly needed characters. For casual use, pick up whatever works for you and suits you. For more regular use, it is better to analyze the needs and to make some choices.

Suppose, for example, that in some application or document, the only special characters needed are superscript two ² and the less-than-or-equal-to sign ≤. In a Windows XP environment, the former can be typed rather fast as b2 Alt-X, whereas the latter can be typed with fewer keystrokes: Alt-8804. Understanding and remembering two different methods might be an unnecessary burden. So instead of optimizing each case separately, it might be best to teach (or learn) a single systematic method: either b2 Alt-X and 2264 Alt-X, or Alt-0178 and Alt-8804. On the other hand, if the application is widely used or the document is large, it might pay off to spend some time in customizing things to achieve something more natural. For example, MS Word can be rather easily configured to automatically turn ^2 into ² and <= into ≤.

An Overview of Methods

For practical reasons, the methods presented in this chapter are mostly from MS Windows and MS Office environments, but various alternatives (such as Unicode editors) are also discussed. The HTML and XML character reference and entity reference techniques are presented as well. The chapter ends with an exercise for writing some specialized texts using some of the techniques presented.

To illustrate the variation in the ways of writing characters, Table 2-1 shows some ways of writing the copyright sign ©, U+00A9. In each program or other environment, there might be several ways to write this. We have omitted the most obvious way, using a keyboard key for the character, since © is hardly ever found on keyboards. Each of the ways will be discussed in more detail in this chapter.

Table 2-1. Typical methods of writing special characters

Program or context	Method	Remarks
Windows Notepad	Alt-0169	169 is decimal code for ©
Win XP WordPad	a9 Alt-X	Uses Uniscribe
Mozilla Thunderbird	Insert → Characters...	→ Common symbols, select ©
Microsoft Word	(c)	Word converts to ©
XML	&#xa9;	Character reference
XML	&#169;	Character reference using decimal notation
HTML	&copy;	Entity reference
CSS	\a9	Has a trailing space
TeX or LaTeX	\copyright	\symbol{'251} works, too

The methods can be classified roughly as follows:

Key combinations

These use keyboard keys, often with modifier keys like Alt and often referring to characters by their code numbers. After using a combination, you see the desired character appear.

Character sequences

These resemble key combinations, but a sequence of characters produced using keyboard keys appears in the data (file) as such. It will only later be rendered as the intended character—by a web browser, for example.

Command menus

You select a command and subcommand from a program's menu. Such tools are almost self-documenting but often very limited, letting you produce just a few commonly used characters. Typically, these commands can also be invoked using keyboard shortcuts.

Selection from a table

You invoke a function of a program—e.g., using a menu command—and a window containing a table of characters appears on the screen. By clicking on a character, you select it. So-called *virtual keyboards* can, in part, be regarded as a special case of this, though the characters appear there in a keyboard setup and not in a rectangular grid.

Choosing Fonts

Some methods of typing characters produce just an abstract character; others include font information. For example, when using Notepad, no font information is included, though whenever someone looks at the characters, some font needs to be used. Databases normally contain character data as coded characters only, with no font information. In MS Word, fonts are an integral part of the content, although the use of fonts can be controlled in a disciplined way by using styles in Word.

Tšaikovski

Figure 2-1. A character from a different font can be a disturbance

In any case, when text data is to be presented visibly, font issues are essential. You do not need to worry about it in database design and data entry, but when printing out strings from a database, a font or fonts need to be selected at some point. In web design, for example, we can choose to leave the font selection to browsers and users, but font problems still need to be anticipated. You do not want to create a document that most people will not see correctly.

The larger the number of different characters, the more you have problems with typographic quality, for several reasons:

- The character requirements reduce the number of fonts that can be chosen. Many typographically ambitious fonts have fairly small repertoires of characters, and many large fonts are typographically rather questionable.

- If you use characters from different fonts, the results are often poor, at least if you are not careful. In Figure 2-1, the "s" with caron (š) is disturbingly different from the general style of letters, because it is a "loan-character" from another font.

- A large repertoire often contains characters that can easily be confused with each other. Their design in a font should thus be sufficiently different. This may exclude an otherwise excellent font, or it may lead you into mixing fonts.

The moral is that you should look out for typographic discrepancies, when you enter characters. If possible, use the same font throughout. If you need to use characters from different fonts, try to use some rather large font as a backup, such as Arial Unicode MS or Lucida Sans Unicode when the basic font is a sans-serif font, and Times New Roman or Code2000 for serif fonts. Such large fonts tend to be relatively neutral in typographic design, so they can work reasonably in the midst of text in another font of the same class.

 When designing a publication or series and selecting fonts for it, try to analyze the repertoire of characters that will be used. Consider especially the potential needs for additional letters in foreign words, special (e.g., mathematical) symbols, and different types of punctuation.

The following true story illustrates the risks of insufficient analysis. A public institution was redesigning the format of its printed serial publication, and this included the choice of a new font. Among other things, the publication discussed orthographic questions such as the difference between the hyphen "-" and the en dash "–" and the importance of choosing correctly between the two. The embarrassing thing was that the chosen font made a very small difference between the two characters.

Typographers and designers often used "Lorem ipsum" texts in sample documents. *Lorem ipsum* is a piece of text that looks like Latin to a person who does not know Latin too well, and it contains only basic Latin letters and a few punctuation marks. This implies that it is not suitable for considering how real-world texts appear in the chosen font. Therefore, it is better to design your own sample text and use it. Its content should depend on the nature of the real texts that will be used, but the following short sample text can be suitable as a starting point for typical non-specialized texts in English (see Table 2-6 at the end of this chapter for more specialized samples):

> The quick brown fox jumps over the lazy dog. 1234567890.
> THE QUICK BROWN FOX JUMPS OVER THE LAZY DOG.
> "You 'quote' inside quoted text this way—in U.S. style."
> 'You "quote" inside quoted text this way – in British style.'
> His fiancée Märtha visited Rhône.
> áà éè íì óò úù âêîôû æœ äëïöüÿ āēīōū ǎěǐǒǔ åø çñß

It is not rare to see fonts that look good for normal mixed-case text but poor for all-caps text. Similarly, letters with diacritic marks can cause surprises: the accents might look like just thrown in, instead of sitting nicely near the base character. Consider the importance of using typographically suitable dashes and quotation marks, too. The last line of the sample lists letters that relatively often appear in foreign names in English texts, according to one version of the Common Locale Data Repository (CLDR).

Keyboard Variation and Settings

Understanding the effects of keyboard variation is essential, because you may need to work with different keyboards, or you may need to write instructions for people who use different keyboards. If you design computer applications for a potentially worldwide market, you need to make them work in wide range of environments. Even a simple form on a web page might be a computer application in this sense.

Typing Characters—Just Pressing a Key?

Typing characters on a computer may appear deceptively simple: you press a key labeled "A," and the character "A" appears on the screen. Well, you actually get uppercase "A" or lowercase "a" depending on whether you used the Shift key or not, but that's common knowledge. You also expect "A" to be included into a disk file when you save what you are typing, you expect "A" to appear on paper if you print your text, and you expect "A" to be sent if you send your text by email or something like that. Moreover, you expect the recipient to see an "A."

It has hopefully become clear from the previous discussion that the representation of a character in computer storage or disk or in data transfer may vary a lot. You have probably realized that especially if it's not the common "A" but something more special, like an "A" with an accent—say, À—strange things might happen, especially if data is not accompanied with adequate information about its encoding.

You might still be too confident. You probably expect that on your system at least things are simpler than that. If you use your very own very personal computer and press the key labeled "A" on its keyboard, then shouldn't it be evident that in its storage and processor, on its disk, and on its screen it's invariably "A"? Can't you just ignore its internal character code and character encoding? Well, probably yes—with "A." Don't be so sure about À, for instance. On a typical PC, for example, try this: create a file containing À in Notepad and then open the command-line interface (DOS prompt) and display the file using the type command. Instead of À, you will see the graphic element ∟, or something else, depending on your computer's settings.

When you press a key on your keyboard, the keyboard sends the code of a character to the processor. The processor then, in addition to storing the data internally somewhere, normally sends it to the display device. Now, the keyboard settings and the display settings might be different from what you expect. Even if a key is labeled, say, Ä, it might send something other than the code of Ä in the character code used in your computer. Similarly, the display device, upon receiving such a code, might be set to display something different. Such mismatches are usually undesirable, but they are definitely possible.

Keyboard Limitations and Variation

Typical computer keyboards do not contain enough keys even for all characters in an 8-bit character code with 256 code positions. If your computer uses internally, say, the ISO Latin 1 character repertoire, you probably won't find keys for all the 191 characters in it on your keyboard. Many characters can be produced by using auxiliary keys, such as Shift and Alt, that extend the repertoire of characters. However, you cannot type, for example, the yen sign ¥ or the plus-minus sign ± on a normal U.S. keyboard in any *obvious* way.

Different keyboards are manufactured and used, often according to the needs of particular languages. For example, keyboards used in Sweden often have a key for the å character but seldom a key for ñ; in Spain, the opposite is true. For an illustration of the variation, as well as to see what layout might be used in some environments, visit *http://www.microsoft.com/globaldev/reference/keyboards.aspx*, an interactive Windows Layouts page by Microsoft. Using it requires Internet Explorer with JavaScript enabled. For an example of its presentation style, see Figure 2-2.

Practical considerations limit the number of characters that have a key of their own or appear as engraved on a key at all. For the Unicode character repertoire, it would of course be quite impossible to have a key for each character. This is one reason why it is important to identify which characters are commonly used in a writing system and in a language. Among all the Unicode characters, only a small part can be directly assigned to keys.

Auxiliary Keys

Some keyboard key combinations, typically involving the use of an *Alt* or *AltGr* key or some other auxiliary key, are often automatically processed by converting them to special characters. For example, pressing the "E" key while keeping AltGr pressed down might produce the euro sign, €. This usually takes place at a low, device-oriented level, in software called the keyboard driver. In that case, normal programs would have all their input from the keyboard processed that way. The practical impact is that on a given system, these methods usually work across programs, unless some program specifically overrides such functionality for its own purposes.

Notations that refer to the use of auxiliary keys vary a lot. O'Reilly books use the style AltGr-M (and similarly Alt-M, Ctrl-M, Shift-M, etc.). Another common style is AltGr+M, and sometimes you'll see AltGr M.

The well-known Shift key is an auxiliary key, too. It is used to modify the meaning of another key, e.g., by changing a letter to uppercase or turning a digit key to a special character key.

The effects of auxiliary keys depend on the program used, and even on its settings—and on the keyboard and its settings. The effects are often user-modifiable. For example, producing the euro sign using the method described at the beginning of this section requires a special "euro update" on old Windows systems. Some confusion was caused when people said, e.g., "to type the euro, use AltGr-E" as general, unqualified advice. A keyboard might even not have an AltGr key, and if it does, the key that produces the euro sign varies by country.

On many keyboards, especially in Europe, there is an Alt key to the left of the spacebar and an AltGr key to the right of it, and these keys have different functionality. On U.S. keyboards, there is usually an Alt key on each side of the spacebar. The reason why European keyboards usually have an AltGr key is because it makes it easy to type the additional characters needed in many languages.

Generally, using the AltGr key corresponds to using the Alt key and the Ctrl key simultaneously; AltGr is the same as Alt-Ctrl. Thus, if your keyboard has no AltGr key, you might still be able to type the micro sign µ, for example, by pressing Alt-Ctrl-M. However, this depends on keyboard and program settings.

Some keyboards have two different Ctrl keys as well, so that the left Ctrl key works the usual way, and the right Ctrl key is yet another key for producing alternate graphic characters.

The name AltGr is short for "alternate graphic," and it is mostly used to create additional *characters*, whereas the Alt key is typically used for keyboard access to *command* menus, as an alternative to using a mouse. The AltGr key creates a new layer of possible characters that normal keys can produce, but usually this layer is not very densely populated. Moreover, the use of AltGr is partly handled at application program level, not in keyboard drivers; thus, in a particular system, AltGr-R might produce the registered sign ® in one program, but do nothing in another. To see the AltGr assignments in your copy of MS Word, search for "Alt Gr" in its Help system.

Typical usage includes AltGr-M to produce the micro sign µ. The connection between the normal character in a key and the alternate character is not obvious, but it is usually somehow natural. The AltGr settings vary greatly by the needs of different languages and cultural environments. A few examples:

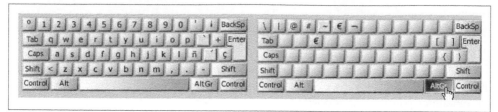

Figure 2-2. Spanish keyboard in two states, normal and AltGr state

- On a British (U.K.) keyboard, AltGr-A produces á, and similarly for e, i, o, and u. Alt-$ produces €.

- On a Canadian Multilingual keyboard, AltGr is used to type several characters, such as < and >, which cannot be typed directly, since keys have been allocated to some accented letters. AltGr is also used for typing French quotation marks (guillemets).

- On a Greek keyboard, AltGr is used to type several special symbols, e.g., AltGr-ρ produces ®; AltGr-υ produces ¥; and Alt--, ±.

- On a Romanian keyboard, which has some keys reserved for letters with diacritic marks, the AltGr key is used to type some characters like \ and |. There are also some AltGr combinations for characters that do not appear in Romanian but in neighboring languages, e.g., ß and đ.

- On a Spanish keyboard, as shown in Figure 2-2 (captured using Microsoft's online service "Keyboard Layouts"), you need the AltGr key to type some common characters, like @.

Key caps may have additional engravings that act as hints and reminders on the alternate graphic characters. For example, the "E" or $ key may have € engraved onto it.

Dead Keys

For languages that use diacritic marks extensively, it is natural to try to accommodate letters with diacritic marks into the keyboard. This is possible for many languages that use a small set of such letters, perhaps just two or three—e.g., ä, ö, and ü in German. However, if there are many different combinations of a letter and diacritic marks, it is more practical to include keys that correspond to the diacritic marks.

Many keyboard designs contain auxiliary keys for typing characters with diacritic marks. The key might have the characters ´ and ` (acute accent and grave accent) engraved onto it, for example. Hitting such a key has no visible effect as such, but when followed by a letter, it might add an accent on the letter. Thus, on a Spanish keyboard, as was illustrated in Figure 2-2, you would press the ´ key, and then the "O" key to type ó.

Such an auxiliary key is often called a *dead key*, since just pressing it causes nothing; it works only in combination with some other key. You press it before pressing a letter key, not simultaneously. A more official name for a dead key is *modifier key*.

A dead key itself may be affected by a Shift key. Thus, Shift-´ followed by "a" might produce à, and Shift-´ Shift-A would then produce À. Moreover, even AltGr might affect a dead key. On a normal Finnish keyboard, there is a dead key with the dieresis (¨) and the circumflex (^) above it (i.e., as "upper case," to be generated using the Shift key) and the tilde (~) below or left to it. This means that on such a keyboard, the AltGr key is needed for producing a letter with tilde.

The use of dead keys has essential limitations. Usually the diacritics cannot be freely combined with letters. For example, if I use a Finnish keyboard and hit the acute key (´), and then the "C" key, I do not get a c with acute (ć) but the acute accent character followed by the letter (´c). The dead keys work within some repertoire and encoding and settings, not as a general tool.

On keyboards with dead keys, characters that can be directly typed on a U.S. keyboard may cause difficulties. For example, if the tilde ~ key is a dead key (to make it easier to type ã, õ, etc.), then you cannot always type the tilde itself directly. If you try to type a string like "~abc", it will be converted to ãbc. The solution is to press the spacebar after pressing the tilde key. This might be seen as putting the tilde on a space character. This illustrates why even ASCII characters such as the tilde can be difficult to produce.

Keyboard solutions are not always systematic. They may result from combinations of different ways of supporting diacritic marks. For example, a typical French keyboard has separate keys for those accented characters that are used in French (e.g., à), but in order to write the accents as characters, you need special methods, such as AltGr-è followed by a space to produce the grave accent `.

Virtual Keyboards

In several systems, including MS Windows, it is possible to switch between different keyboard settings. This means that the effects of different keys do not necessarily correspond to the engravings in the key caps but to some other assignments. This way you can turn your keyboard to French, Greek, Russian, or another language just by clicking on an icon at the bottom of the screen and selecting a setting from a menu, as shown in Figure 2-3. What you need to do is to enable the "language support" you need. It is called language support, but the relevant part is keyboard settings. We will not go into details here, since the techniques depend on the version of Windows.

MS Windows has some keyboard shortcuts for switching between different keyboard layouts. If you right-click on the language indicator in the toolbar, you can access settings that control such shortcuts. They typically involve the Alt and Shift keys. It is convenient to be able to switch between two layouts simply by pressing Alt and Shift simultaneously, if you know how this works. It is less convenient to do such things by mistake and find yourself using an odd-behaving keyboard where, for example, pressing the "-" key produces "/" and you have no idea how to fix that. Therefore, avoid installing keyboard layout options on other people's computers without informing them.

Figure 2-3. Changing keyboard settings from Finnish (code FI) to Spanish (code ES)

For example, if you write in English but frequently need Greek letters, you can install Greek keyboard settings. You would then learn how to switch between the settings—for example, by using Alt and Shift keys. To type the letter pi (π), you would do the switch, press the "P" key, and switch back to your normal keyboard settings.

If you mainly write in English but occasionally need to type names in Western European languages, with accented characters, you may find the *U.S. International* keyboard setting suitable. You would install and use it like any other keyboard layout: go to the Regional and Language Options control panel, and select the Languages tab, then click the Details button and the Add button in the next dialog. Finally, you'll see the Add Input Language dialog box, where you can check the Keyboard/Layout box and choose United States-International. This keyboard differs from the common U.S. keyboard settings in a few ways, which let you type almost all ISO Latin-1 characters:

- The grave accent key ` in the upper left corner acts as a dead key for typing letters with grave accent (à, è, etc.); used with the Shift key, this key acts as a dead key for typing letters with tilde (ã, ñ, etc.).

- The apostrophe key ' acts as a dead key for typing letters with an acute accent (e.g., á); used with the Shift, it works similarly for the dieresis (e.g., ä).

- Used with the Shift key, the 6 key acts as a dead key for the circumflex (e.g., â).

- The Alt key on the right acts as AltGr, which can be used to produce a large number of characters, as shown in Figure 2-4.

- There are additional characters that you can produce using both the AltGr key and the Shift key together with a normal key.

A Keyboard on Screen

It would be nice if we could modify the keycaps dynamically using, for example, LED displays in them. Changing keyboard settings would change the appearance of the keyboard. Although this idea is old and technically possible, it is not economically feasible. Instead, "virtual keyboards" can be used.

This means that an image of a keyboard is visible on the screen. It helps the user type characters in two alternative ways:

Figure 2-4. Characters available using the right Alt key (Alt Gr) in the U.S. International keyboard layout

- By clicking on keys in the virtual keyboard
- By using the visible information to see the current assignments of the keys of the physical keyboard

For the Office software on Windows systems, there is a free add-in available for this: Microsoft Visual Keyboard, *http://office.microsoft.com/downloads/2002/VkeyInst.aspx*. Using it, you select the keyboard settings as illustrated above, and you use, for example, Microsoft Office Tools under the Start menu to get a virtual keyboard on the screen. You can select between a large number of national settings, or even define new keyboard settings.

Figure 2-5 shows how you could position a virtual keyboard over a MS Word window; you can put it anywhere you like. Using a normal U.S. or Western European qwerty keyboard, you can type Greek rather easily. Many key assignments are rather natural: a = α, b = β, d = δ, etc. For the less natural correspondences, the virtual keyboard is a quick reference and reminder. In general, the relationship between a physical keyboard and virtual keyboard can be much less intuitive than it is here.

Virtual Keys for Character Input in Forms

When we need just a few characters in addition to those that can be typed on a normal keyboard, virtual keys can be quite handy. This means that we have images of keys on screen in an input form, as shown in Figure 2-6. The user is expected to use the physical keyboard for most of the input, but if the keyboard does not contain the ä and ö keys, the user can instead click on the virtual keys. This is really just a virtual keyboard with a very small set of keys.

The virtual key approach is especially suitable for situations in which the input is in a language that needs few extra characters in addition to basic Latin letters (or other set of characters that users are expected to have in their keyboards). This has many benefits:

- The user interface is intuitive: it is rather obvious what the user needs to do.
- The choices are limited to a relevant number of characters. This makes things easier than the use of general purpose methods, which may require selections from large and confusing repertoires.

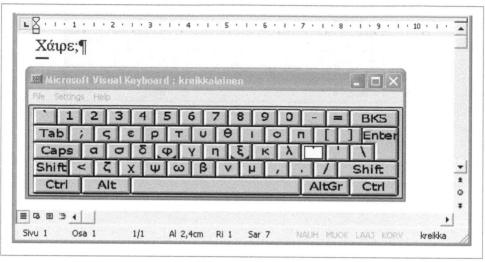

Figure 2-5. Working with the Greek virtual keyboard

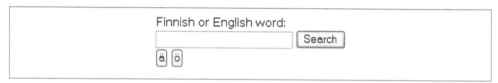

Figure 2-6. An input form with two virtual keys

- Character selection errors are reduced, since the user does not have to choose between, say, ă and å, as in more general methods. A particular language or other context seldom contains both characters.

The virtual key idea is easy and quick to implement. Thus, it can be applied even on an individual basis, to create a convenient input form for someone's personal needs and preferences. On the other hand, this approach is normally *application dependent*: the method needs to be implemented separately for each data entry form. For implementation issues, see "Character Input and Output" in Chapter 11.

Along similar lines, we could use virtual keys that correspond to writing several characters. If user input is expected to contain some fixed strings rather often, a form designer can set up keys (buttons) that add those strings. This is particularly useful if the strings contain characters that cannot be directly typed on users' keyboards.

Program Commands

We often need program-specific ways of entering characters from a keyboard, either because there is no key for a character we need or there is but it does not work. The program involved might be part of system software, or it might be an application program. We describe here some typical cases.

Copying via the Clipboard

In typical computer systems, you can copy data from one program to another through an internal storage area called the clipboard. On Windows, you can usually highlight text with the mouse or select a piece of text otherwise, and then press Ctrl-C to copy, click on a location in another window, and press Ctrl-V to paste a copy of the text there. This also works inside a program of course, so you can use it to create copies of a character or a string.

This feature is well known by most users and often very convenient, though it cannot be the primary method of writing text. You can however copy characters from web pages or from text documents specifically designed for use as "cliptext."

Often this technique has the property of *copying text formatting* along with the text. If you copy bold 16-point Verdana text from Excel to Word, you get 16-point Verdana text, not text in the normal font as defined by your Word settings or template. This might be desirable, but more often, it is a problem. Moreover, constructs like hypertext links may get copied along with the text. To make sure that only the plain text is inserted, you can first paste the text in Notepad, select it again there, press Ctrl-C, and paste in the desired destination.

Menu Commands

Programs may have command menus for inserting characters, so that characters are identified by some names or glyphs. At the simplest, you just select a command and a subcommand from a menu. Usually it is more complicated, to allow the insertion of more characters that can conveniently be included into a command menu.

Insertion menu in Thunderbird

In Mozilla Thunderbird, when composing an email message, you can select Insert → Characters and symbols. This opens a small window, as in Figure 2-7. There, you can select a class of characters by clicking on one of the radio buttons. This affects the drop-down menu under the buttons. For example, when Common Symbols is selected, the Character drop-down menu contains a collection of Latin 1 special characters (other than letters), such as © and ±.

Such an input method is intuitively easy and can be found and used by a user even without any documentation. On the other hand, it is rather clumsy, since any insertion requires several steps.

Symbol (character) insertion menu in MS Word

In MS Word, you can use the command Insert → Symbol to invoke an auxiliary window, which has two modes of operation. In the default mode, Symbols, you can select a char-

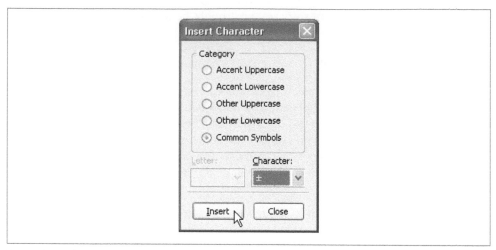

Figure 2-7. Character insertion window in Thunderbird

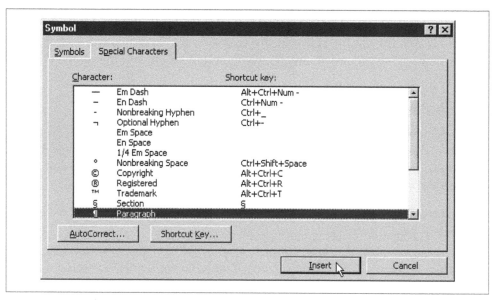

Figure 2-8. Special Characters insertion window in MS Word

acter from a table, as explained in the section "Character Maps" later in this chapter. You enter the second mode by clicking on Special Characters. There, you can pick up a character from a short list, as shown in Figure 2-8. The list also contains information about shortcut keys for the characters, so it can be used to check such things. Among the characters that have no default shortcut keys, the fixed-width spaces (em space, en space, and 1/4 em space = four-per-em space) work with a few fonts only.

Construct	Unicode	Show ¶	Example	Normal view	Method
horizontal tab	U+0009	→	foo → bar	foo bar	Alt-09
optional break		⬚	foo/⬚bar	foo/bar	Insert menu
non break indicator		▯	foo▯bar	foobar	Insert menu
space	U+0020	·	foo·bar	foo bar	SP (space bar)
em space	U+2003	○	foo ○ bar	foo bar	Insert menu
en space	U+2002	○	foo○bar	foo bar	Insert menu
¼ em space	U+2005	⏐	foo⏐bar	foo bar	Insert menu
no-break space	U+00A0	○	foo○bar	foo bar	Ctrl-Shift-SP
optional hyphen		¬	foo¬bar	foobar	Ctrl--
nonbreaking hyphen		–	foo–bar	foo-bar	Ctrl-Shift--
paragraph mark		¶	foo¶ bar	foo bar	(enter key)
table cell		¤	foo¤	foo	

Figure 2-9. Formatting characters and markers in MS Word

Some of the symbols that you can add via the Special Characters menu (or corresponding shortcuts) are really just *internal markers* used by MS Word. Either they do not correspond to any Unicode character or they involve using Unicode characters in an abnormal way. For example, Optional Hyphen, which is invisible but indicates an allowed hyphenation point in a word, is not what you might expect, the soft hyphen (U+00AD) is a marker recognize by MS Word. We will return to this in Chapter 8.

The Show Formatting (Show ¶) tool

In MS Word, there is a special mode of viewing a document on screen so that some formatting characters and markers appear as visible symbols, as *formatting marks*—e.g., paragraph breaks as ¶ symbols. The mode works independently on the input method that has been used. It is useful, for example, when checking which spaces are no-break spaces, since they will appear as small rings (resembling the degree sign ° but larger). The formatting marks do not appear in printed copies.

You can select a view with formatting marks by clicking the ¶ icon in the toolbar. Clicking the icon again changes the view to normal. If this icon is not present, you can use a menu command like View → Show Paragraph Marks instead.

The detailed look varies by the version of MS Word, but it resembles the one shown in Figure 2-9. The columns in it indicate the name of the character or other construct; its Unicode code number, if any; its display in "Show Formatting" mode; an example of such appearance in text context; the same text in normal view; and a method for typing in the construct. "Insert menu" refers to the Special Characters insertion menu. Table cells are created using special commands in MS Word. The issue is mentioned here because making paragraph marks visible also makes a ¤ symbol appear at the end of the content of each table cell.

Sometimes you might wish to view some of the formatting indicators but not all. This can be achieved by choosing Tools → Options, and then selecting the View pane, shown in

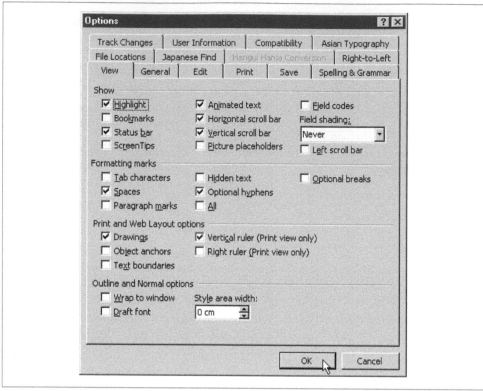

Figure 2-10. Setting the display of formatting marks in MS Word

Figure 2-10. Some settings under "Formatting marks" affect several marks; e.g., "Optional breaks" makes line break prohibitions visible, too. Clicking the ¶ icon in the toolbar corresponds to checking "All" in this dialog.

Methods Using the Alt Key on Windows

There are several ways to type a character on Windows if you know the code number. Not all of the ways work in all contexts, and they differ from each other so that they are easily confused with each other. Table 2-2 summarizes the methods, and then each method is explained in detail. The example characters, for which key sequences are given in columns "Ex. 1" and "Ex. 2," are the copyright sign © (U+00A9) and the ohm sign Ω (U+2126). The expression "New Windows software" refers to programs such as WordPad and MS Word on Windows XP and newer.

Table 2-2. General methods for character input on Windows

Method	Ex. 1	Ex. 2	Description	Applicability
Alt-0*n*	Alt-0169		Uses decimal number	Windows in general
Alt-*n* (*n*≤255)	Alt-184		Code page dependent	Windows in general
Alt-*n* (*n*>255)		Alt-8486	Unicode, decimal	New Windows software
n Alt-X	a9 Alt-X	2126 Alt-X	Unicode, hexadecimal	New Windows software
Alt-+*n*	Alt-+a9	Alt-+2126	Unicode, hexadecimal	New Windows (often)

The Alt-0n method

On Windows systems, you can (usually—some application programs may override this) produce any character in the 8-bit Windows character set (such as Windows Latin 1) as follows:

1. Press down the Alt key and keep it down. (Use the Alt key, not AltGr.)
2. Using the separate numeric keypad (not the numbers above the letter keys!), type the number of the character *in decimal and with a leading zero*. You do not see anything happen on screen when you do this.
3. Release the Alt key. The character now appears.

The code values for which this works are in the range 32–255 (decimal). For instance, to produce the letter Ä (which has code 196 in decimal), you would hold Alt down, type 0196, and then release Alt. Upon releasing Alt, the character should appear on the screen.

In MS Word, the method works only if Num Lock is set (by pressing the Num Lock key in the numeric keypad).

Portable computers often lack a numeric keypad. They usually have a key combination (explained in the manual) that makes some normal keys simulate a numeric keypad. Typically, the same combination turns the situation back to normal.

This method is often referred to as Alt-0*nnn* to emphasize that you normally type four digits starting with zero, but we use the shorter notation Alt-0*n*. It is quite possible to use less than four digits when the number is small; for example, Alt-092 produces a \. However, characters with such small code numbers can usually be typed more directly.

The codes are interpreted according to the *Windows character code*, which may vary by country and language version as well as keyboard settings. In the Western world, the code is normally windows-1252, also known as Windows Latin 1. This means, as will be explained in Chapter 3, that code numbers 32–126 and 160–255 (decimal) are the same as in Unicode. However, if you, for example, set your keyboard layout to Russian, the meanings change: they refer to windows-1251 (Windows Cyrillic). Then, for example, Alt-0169 still produces ©, since the copyright sign has the same position in windows-1251 as in windows-1252, but Alt-0233 produces й and not é as with English keyboard settings.

The code page–specific Alt-n method

If you use the method described in the previous section but omit the leading zero—i.e., use Alt-*n*—the effect is different. That way, you insert the character that occupies code position *n* in the DOS character code! More generally, the character inserted is the one in that position in the *code page* in use. Code pages have the same assignments for code numbers 30–126 as Unicode but differ from Unicode and from other code pages in other positions.

Code pages will be discussed in Chapter 3. For a quick reference to the character assignments in code pages, see *http://www.fileformat.info/info/charset/codepage.htm*.

Briefly, a code page is an 8-bit encoding that is used in some contexts in Windows environments—a holdover from DOS systems. You can find out your system code page number by giving the command **chcp** on the command prompt (DOS prompt). Normally, your computer uses the code page defined by the manufacturer according to the market area, called the *OEM code page* (OEM stands for original equipment manufacturer).

For example, Alt-196 might insert a graphic character, box drawings light horizontal ─ (U+2500). To get the copyright sign, you would use Alt-184, if your system's current code page is 850, which is common in Western Europe. In that code page, the code of the copyright sign is 184 in decimal (B8 in hexadecimal). Code page 437, which is common in the U.S., does not contain the copyright sign at all. On the other hand, it contains some Greek letters and additional mathematical symbols, such as ≤.

There are variations in the behavior of various Windows programs in this area. Using DOS codes and this input method is best avoided, although it would save a little typing. It is very easy to get confused with the methods and the numbers.

It may happen that if you type, for example, Alt-1 or Alt-3, you get graphic characters like ☺ and ♥. This is because some code page versions have allocated graphic characters to code positions 0–31 (decimal), although these positions are normally reserved for control characters. Though occasionally handy, such methods cannot be relied on, since they depend on the code page, its version, and the program.

The Unicode-based Alt-n method

In some programs on modern Windows systems, you can use Alt-*n* for $n > 255$ to produce the Unicode character with code number *n* in decimal. Thus, the method is:

1. Press and hold the Alt key.
2. Type the decimal number *n* using the numeric keypad. Nothing visible happens yet.
3. Release the Alt key. The character with Unicode number *n* now appears.

This works in programs such as WordPad and Word on Windows XP. In many other programs—e.g., in Notepad or in form field input in Internet Explorer—the method does not work. If you try it, the value *n* is mapped to a value in the range 0–255 (using division by 256 and taking the remainder) and it has a code page–specific effect as above.

Characters that belong to Windows Latin 1 but not to ISO Latin 1 thus have two alternative sequences. For example, the em dash, —, can be typed as Alt-0151 or as Alt-8211.

This method is relatively fast but requires you to type the decimal code number "in blind," i.e., without seeing what you have typed. The next method is different.

The Alt-X method

This method, too, works only in some programs on modern Windows systems. Like the Unicode-based Alt-*n* method, it uses so-called Uniscribe program code for handling the keyboard, and only a few programs use Uniscribe so far.

The method consists of the following:

1. Type the hexadecimal Unicode code number of the character you want. You can use the normal keyboard. (You can alternatively use the numeric keypad for digits 0–9, if the Num Lock mode is set.)

2. Press Alt-X, i.e., hold down the Alt button and press the "X" button. The number now turns to the character.

The method also works for any string of hexadecimal digits in a document, not just a string you have directly typed. If an existing document contains, say, the string 101, you can click on the position right after the last digit and press Alt-X. The string then turns to the character ā (U+0101). If the hexadecimal string is preceded by U+ (or u+), those characters, too, disappear in the process.

The method applies to the *maximal* sequence of hexadecimal digits before the point where Alt-X is typed. If you would like to write bā, you cannot just type b101 Alt-X, since the letter "b" is a hexadecimal digit, so you would get the character U+B101. Instead, you can type a space before the digits 101, apply Alt-X, and then remove the extra space.

The method works in the other direction, too: when the preceding character is not a hexadecimal digit, pressing Alt-X turns the character to its hexadecimal Unicode number. However, the effect is not always directly reversible. If you have typed "8−" (digit eight and minus sign) and then press Alt-X, you get 82212. Pressing Alt-X would turn this five-digit string to the character U+82212. If such a problem appears, insert a space temporarily.

Program-specific keyboard command assignments may mask out the possibility of using this method. It is therefore not a good idea to define a text-processing macro with an invocation that starts with Alt-X.

The Alt-+n method

This method is similar to the *n* Alt-X method in the sense that it uses hexadecimal Unicode numbers and works on modern Windows systems. However, this method has some specific features:

- It works in most programs and contexts, including Notepad, form fields in web browsers, Unicode email, etc.

- It has limitations due to Alt key assignments in programs.
- It depends on system configuration, so it might not work by default.

To use this method, proceed as follows:

1. Press and hold the Alt key.
2. Press the + key in the numeric keypad. (Think of it as indicating that the following number is to be treated as hexadecimal.)
3. Type the hexadecimal number *n* using either normal keys or (for digits 0 to 9) the numeric keypad. Nothing visible happens yet.
4. Release the Alt key. The character with Unicode number *n* now appears.

If this does not work (and you are using a relatively modern Windows version, such as Windows XP), it is because your system has been configured not to use this input method. This can be changed through the Windows registry settings, using the registry editor (regedit). If you are not familiar with registry settings, try to find someone who knows them and can fix your settings. In HKEY_Current_User → Control Panel → Input Method, set EnableHexNumpad to 1 (one). If the variable does not exist, add it there and set its type to REG_SZ. Now you must reboot the system. This inconvenience is probably partly intentional: the method is still experimental and lacks support.

Using the Alt key together with normal keys (outside the numeric keypad) often conflicts with keyboard shortcuts in programs, such as Alt-F for opening a File menu. This may cause limitations for characters with letters in their hexadecimal code number.

Ctrl-Q and Other Methods in Emacs

In the Emacs editor, which is popular especially on Unix-type systems, you can produce any ISO Latin 1 character by typing first Ctrl-Q, and then the character's code as a three-digit *octal* (base 8) number. To produce Ä, you would type Ctrl-Q followed by the three digits 304 (and expect the Ä character to appear on screen). This method is often referred to as C-Q-*nnn*.

There are additional ways of entering many ISO Latin 1 characters in Emacs. You can for example use the M-x iso-accents-mode command (where M-x means meta-X, which can typically be produced by pressing first the Esc key, and then the X key). It sets Emacs to a mode of operation where several ASCII characters are converted to diacritic marks when typed *before* a letter. For example, typing 'e would produce e with an acute accent, é.

Character Maps

A character map as an input method is an array of images of characters where you can click on an image and have the character inserted into your data. A click might immediately insert the character in the current point of insertion in some window. More often, a click selects the character, and then you click on a button to do something with it. A character map acts as a *selection table*, a menu arranged as a table.

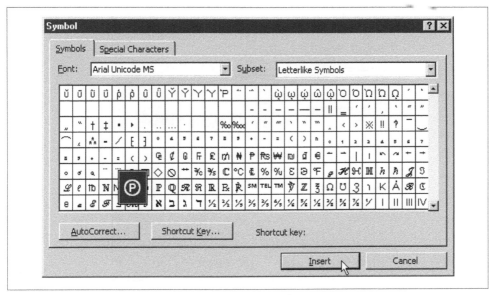

Figure 2-11. Character map in an old version of MS Word

Different programs have different character maps, ranging from a simple one (typically containing just 256 positions) to a full Unicode table with many extra features. Of course, only a small range—e.g., 80 positions—of Unicode characters can be visible at any given moment.

Old Windows systems have a rather primitive character map, which you can launch by selecting Start → Programs → Utilities → System utilities → Character Map. On newer systems, the character map is much more powerful, but the method of starting it is equally clumsy and hard to find if you did not know about it.

Character Map in MS Word

Let us first consider the character map in MS Word in an old Windows system. The system's character map being primitive, Word offers more. As mentioned before, you launch the map using the command Insert → Symbol to invoke an auxiliary window, where the initial pane Symbols contains a map, as in Figure 2-11.

Newer systems have more powerful character maps, but even the old interface has the basic functionality you need to insert any Unicode character:

1. Select a font from the Font menu. This is essential because the map usually shows only those characters that appear in the chosen font. Arial Unicode MS contains a relatively large subset of Unicode.

2. Select a subset of Unicode from the next menu. For example, if you are looking for the sound recording copyright symbol, consisting of a "P" in a circle, you can expect to find it in the Letterlike Symbols set. The subsets are mostly Unicode blocks

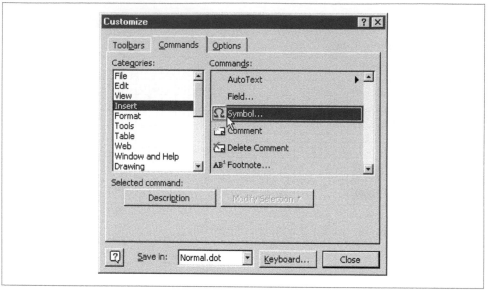

Figure 2-12. Customizing MS Word with an Insert Symbol button

(explained in Chapter 8), but beware that in non-English versions of Word, some of the names of the subsets can be thoroughly misleading.

3. Find the character and click on it; a larger version of the character shows up.

4. If you wish to make it easier to type the character in the future click on the Shortcut Key button. See "Replacements on the Fly" later in this chapter.

5. Click on the Insert button.

6. You can now close the Symbol window, but it might be better to just iconize it, so that you can easily get it back when needed.

You may wish to enhance the user interface with a button that opens the Symbol window. It is a bit faster to click on it than to use the commands. The button has the icon Ω by default, and you add it to the row of buttons using Word's normal customization tools. (You would select Tools → Customize and then, in the situation shown in Figure 2-12, select Commands pane, the Insert category and then the Symbol command, then you'd drag and drop the Ω button into the toolbar.)

Using a character map like the one shown in Figure 2-11, you have to select characters mainly on the basis of their appearance. This can be deceptive because Unicode often contains a number of characters that can easily be confused with the character you are looking for. The Unicode subset is often useful in guessing the nature of a character.

In newer versions of Word, the character map has more features, as illustrated in Figure 2-13. It has the same basic features as the older version but in addition, it includes:

• A collection of recently used characters, in a row

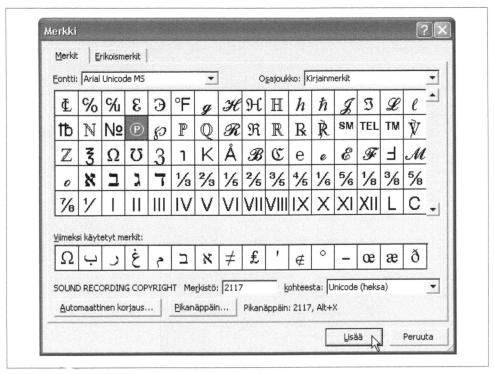

Figure 2-13. Character map in Word 2002 on Windows XP

- The Unicode name of the character, in uppercase
- The Unicode number, in hexadecimal, e.g., 2117
- A shortcut for the character, such as "2117, Alt+X" (corresponding to 2117 Alt-X in our notation)

You can also use the box where the Unicode number is shown as an input area. If you type a hexadecimal number there, Word will find the character for you. It will appear in the context of characters near to it in Unicode. This can be useful if you have some idea of the number of the character you are looking for.

As described in Chapter 1, the Unicode names of characters can be misleading, but mostly they aren't; "sound recording copyright" is a very descriptive name, for example.

Windows Character Map

As mentioned above, all Windows systems have a character map that you can launch in Windows via the Start menu, but the functionality of the map varies by Windows version. It generally differs from the character map in MS Word, partly due to different usage. When using Word, you directly insert characters into your document. When using the Windows character map, you add characters to the *clipboard*. Then you can paste them wherever you like—e.g., by using Ctrl-V.

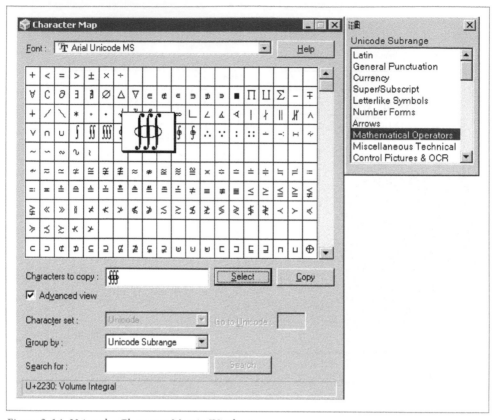

Figure 2-14. Using the Character Map in Windows

Having launched the character map, the simple way to pick up characters is to find them from the array of characters. For this, you may need to select, from a menu, a font that contains the character you need. In Figure 2-14, the font is Arial Unicode MS, and the user is picking up a mathematical operator. If you do not see all the information as in the figure, click on the "Advanced view" checkbox and select "Unicode Subrange" from the "Group by" drop-down menu. (The user interface is somewhat odd: the checkbox acts as a button with immediate action, changing the view.)

If you are looking for a character such as a Latin letter with a diacritic mark, you can easily scroll down the character array to find it because most such characters appear near the start of the character array, either among the characters that are immediately visible or a little later.

You can double-click on a character in the array to copy it to the clipboard. You need not use the buttons in the interface for this.

You can select several characters in succession. They will all be copied to the clipboard as one string, as shown in a box in the Character Map window.

In general, when you need characters that are not near the start of the Unicode code order, you can benefit a lot from other features in the Character Map:

- If you know the Unicode number of the character you are looking for, type it (in hexadecimal) into the Show Unicode box. The character will then appear in the upper-left corner of the character array.

- If you know an essential part of the Unicode name of the character, type it into the Find box and click the Find button. Characters that match your search will appear in the character array.

- If you wish to search by general category, select Unicode Subrange from the "Group by" menu. This is an odd way of reaching a useful feature: an auxiliary window will appear on the right (as in Figure 2-14), with names of character categories. By clicking on a category name, you get that category into the character array.

- Alternatively, you can make a selection from the "Character set" menu. The default selection is Unicode, but you can choose a set of characters that corresponds to some widely used non-Unicode character encoding, such as Windows: Cyrillic, if you are primarily interested in Cyrillic letters, or Windows: Turkish, if you need to type some Turkish names.

Replacements on the Fly

A program may process your input so that it is immediately changed as you type. This is usually based on assumptions on what people really want to type but cannot type directly, due to keyboard limitations. Sometimes such features are very convenient, sometimes really frustrating, if the user does not know how to override or undo their effects.

Default Replacements in MS Word

Word processors often modify user input so that when you have typed, for example, the three characters (c), the program changes that string, both internally and visibly, to the single character ©. This substitution is often convenient, especially if you can add your own rules for modifications. On the other hand, it causes unpleasant surprises and problems when you actually meant what you wrote—e.g., you wanted to write letter "c" in parentheses.

 Use Ctrl-Z as the immediate cure to an undesired on-the-fly conversion in MS Word. If you are uncertain of what happened, use Edit → Undo instead (since Word will show which operation will be undone).

In MS Word, there are several automatic conversions like the one described above. They can be modified: you can remove conversions that you regard as annoying, and you can add conversions of your own.

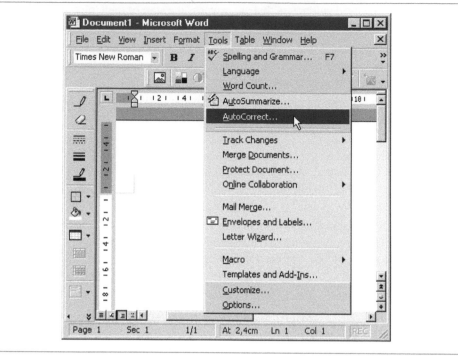

Figure 2-15. The Tools menu in MS Word

Viewing and changing the rules

There are many different settings in MS Word, and their organization is not always what we might expect. In the Tools menu, as shown in Figure 2-15, the Customize and Options commands lead to various settings, but the automatic replacements are found via the command AutoCorrect. Having selected the command, you get a new window, where the first pane is as in Figure 2-16.

In addition to some settings related to the case of letters, the AutoCorrect pane contains a table of replacements. It has default rules, such as replacing (c) with ©, and you can click on a rule and then click the Delete button to remove it. You can add your own rules. In Figure 2-16, the user has typed ^2 into the Replace box and ² into the With box, and by clicking on Add, she will add a rule that makes it easier to type superscript 2.

You can enter special characters in the With box using the methods explained above, such as the Windows Character Map. It can be a bit awkward, but once you have gone through it, you have an input method that you have designed for yourself. Beware, however, that the replacement is (in general) performed only when the string to be replaced appears as a "word," i.e., surrounded by spaces or other whitespace characters. Thus, you may need to type a space and delete it later.

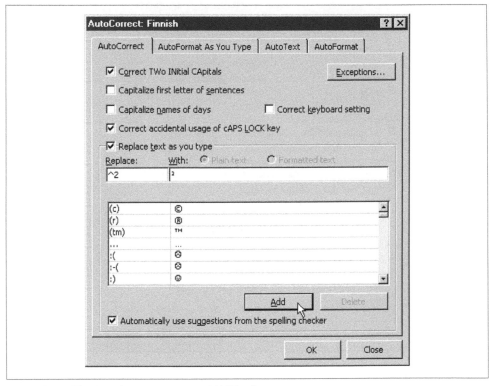

Figure 2-16. The AutoCorrect settings in MS Word

Language dependency

The settings for replacements are language-dependent in the sense that they depend on the *language of the text* as guessed by Word or as explicitly told to it. As a reminder of this, the settings have the current language name in the window's title bar (see Figure 2-16). In particular, check the language setting if you have changed the keyboard settings, since setting the keyboard layout often changes the assumed language of text in Word.

Thus, you could set things up so that when typing in English, the two hyphens in "foo--bar" get converted to an em dash, producing "foo—bar," but two consecutive hyphens are preserved when typing in French.

This not quite as comfortable as it may seem, since Word is not perfect in guessing the language, and human beings are not perfect in remembering to check such things. Moreover, things get a bit awkward if you would like to have certain replacements applied regardless of language. You need to copy these replacements into the settings for all languages.

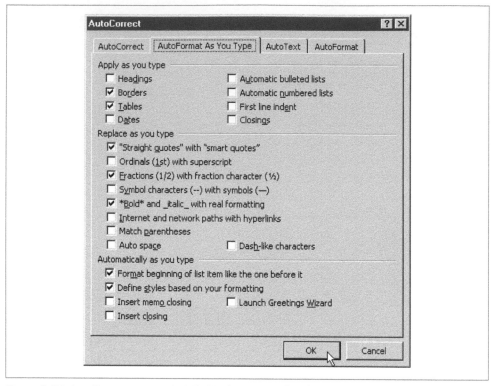

Figure 2-17. AutoFormat settings in MS Word: contextual replacements

Autoformatting in MS Word

In the AutoCorrect window, there are some other panes as well. One of them is related to character processing: the AutoFormat pane, as shown in Figure 2-17. The settings vary by Word version, but the general idea is the same: automatic replacements that are not all just simple string replacement but involve some contextual analysis. You can select which replacements are enabled by checking or unchecking the checkboxes.

Some of the AutoFormat settings are actually simple string replacements, but one setting (like "Ordinals (1st) with superscript") can correspond to a collection of settings (e.g., 1st, 2nd, etc.).

Even the setting that is described as replacing -- with – actually does other things as well; it replaces the following:

- A single hyphen with an en dash, if the hyphen is preceded by a space: **-foo** becomes –foo

- Two consecutive hyphens with an en dash, if the hyphens are preceded by a space: **foo -- bar** becomes foo – bar (helping to write British-style dashes)

- Two consecutive hyphens with an em dash, if not preceded by a space: **foo--bar** becomes foo—bar

---

Example: quotation marks

Language-dependency is essential for quotation marks. Their use varies greatly by language. Here are some examples:

- "foo" (U.S. English style)
- « foo » (French style)
- „foo" (German style)
- "foo" (Swedish style; note that the quotes are identical)

Normally, you can just type text, and Word converts, say, your input **"foo"** (typed using the normal key for ASCII quotation mark) to a language-specific form. However, this requires that Word knows or guesses right the language you use. Therefore, it is a good idea to check first, when starting to create a document, that Word has the right idea of language. Normally the language indicator appears on the bottom row of Word's window. You can click on it to change the language, or you can use Tools → Language.

Whether this happens depends on whether the checkbox about replacing "Straight quotes" with "smart quotes" has been checked in the AutoFormat settings (see Figure 2-17). Thus, the setting has a more general meaning than its name suggests.

MS Word does not know the British English style of using single quotation marks for normal quotations. However, you can simply use the key for ASCII apostrophe, and Word will convert your input **'foo'** to 'foo' when in English mode.

The automatic conversion of ASCII quotes to language-dependent quotes might fail to work, for example, if your version of Word does not support a particular language or the feature has been disabled. You can type the correct quotation marks manually. Appendix A contains some quick references for this. For example, Ctrl-' " (control-apostrophe followed by quotation mark) creates a right double quotation mark, ".

Defining Your Own Shortcuts

Shortcuts are key combinations using Alt, AltGr, or Ctrl for special purposes, such as typing special characters. They differ from the replacements discussed above, since the replacements modify the data that has been typed. In practice, however, the two methods serve similar purposes and can be used as alternatives. For example, MS Word may by default replace the character sequence (r) with the character ®, but in many situations, you can also write ® by pressing AltGr-R (or Alt-Ctrl-R).

In MS Word, you can locate a character in the Character Map and then click on the Shortcut Key button to enter a dialog in which you can define a shortcut for the character. (See Figure 2-11.) By default, this definition will be saved into the *Normal.dot* file, so it can be used whenever you later edit documents based on that template. In Figure 2-18, the user has entered the dialog and typed Alt-P (echoed in a text box as Alt+P), because that's the shortcut he wants to use for the character he selected.

Using this dialog, there are a few things to note:

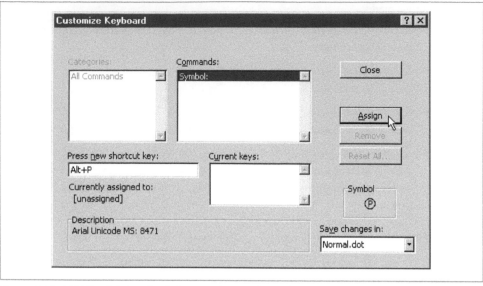

Figure 2-18. MS Word dialog for defining a shortcut for a character

- Use this technique primarily for characters that will be needed often and that are difficult to type using other methods.

- Select a shortcut that has some connection with the character. For example, Alt-P for a circled P is easy to remember. See Table 2-3 for some additional ideas. You cannot use normal keys as such; you need to involve Ctrl, Alt, or AltGr (and optionally Shift). However, as a second key, you can use a normal key as such (example: Ctrl-/ a).

- Check that you are not going to override any existing shortcut you may need. The existing setting, if any, can be seen under the text "Currently assigned to."

- Check that you are defining a shortcut for the right character (shown under Symbol).

- Remember to click on Assign before clicking on Close.

- After defining the shortcut, check immediately that it works in the desired way. You will be in a good position to fix things if needed; later, you might not remember what you were really about to do.

- It is a good idea to write down the assignments you have defined. You can, however, check them later: select the character from the map and enter the dialog, and look under "Current keys."

- As the plural "Current keys" suggests, you can define several alternative shortcuts for a character. This can be a good idea especially if you are designing a working environment for other people, who might not understand and remember quite clearly whether they need to use Alt-P, AltGr-P, or Ctrl-P. However, there is then a risk of overriding some shortcut definitions they might need. If you use the Ctrl key, you probably will not mask out any useful existing assignment in MS Word.

Table 2-3. Possible ideas for shortcuts

Shortcut	Meaning	Context for use
Ctrl-/ L	Ł (L with stroke, U+0141)	Polish names
Ctrl-. e	ė (e with dot above, U+0117)	Lithuanian names
Ctrl-- -	→ (right arrow, U+2192)	Mathematical texts, references
Alt-Ctrl-2	² (superscript two, U+00B2)	General text containing, for example, m²
Alt-S c	♣ (black club suit, U+2663)	Bridge column
AltGr-S	š (s with caron, U+0161)	Czech names
Alt-f	♀ (female sign, U+2640)	Biological texts

Special Techniques

General techniques that let you type any Unicode character are often impractical when you need to write a large number of characters of some particular kind. More specialized techniques are often more convenient. Moreover, some characters cannot be written just by selecting a character from a map, since they need to be represented as combinations of two (or more) Unicode characters.

Combining Diacritic Marks

Unicode has a special concept of combining diacritic marks, which will be described in detail in Chapter 8. Here, we discuss its relevance to typing characters.

A combining diacritic mark is a Unicode character that is not meant to be shown as such but only in conjunction with another character, a base character. For example, a combining acute accent, U+0301, has really no independent appearance, but when combined with the Latin small letter "u" U+0075 as a base character, it produces ú. By definition, the two-character sequence U+0075 U+0301 is *canonically equivalent* to Latin small letter "u" with acute accent U+00FA. The latter is an example of a *precomposed* character, which means that a base character and some diacritic mark(s) have been combined and the combination is defined as a separate Unicode character.

There is not much point in typing ú in a manner based on that equivalence, since there are ways that are more practical. It is possible, though, in programs that have sufficiently good Unicode support, and it can be useful as an exercise. Try this in MS Word, for example:

1. Press the "u" key.
2. Type **301 Alt-X**. You should now see the "u" change to ú.
3. You can now type Alt-X to check what you have got; it should show u301, indicating that you really have "u" followed by a combining acute accent. If you had typed ú as a single character, Alt-X would give you 00FA, which is the code of that character.

Canonical equivalence does not mean identity. The character ú (U+00FA) is still distinct from the character sequence U+0075 U+0301, for example, in string matching, unless measures have been taken to deal with the equivalence. Moreover, even the rendering may differ. If you look carefully, you may notice that the accent in ú (U+00FA) is different from the accent in ú (U+0075 U+0301). This is because the former has probably been specifically designed by the typographer who created the font, while the latter is often the result of "mechanical" composition by a program.

This probably sounds confusing, but it has practical applications. Although you don't want to use this method to type ú, for example, what would you do if requested to produce the Cyrillic letter yu, ю, with an acute accent on it? Such a character does not exist in Unicode as precomposed—i.e., in a code position of its own. It exists in Unicode only in the sense that it can be expressed as ю followed by a combining acute accent.

To produce ю́, you would type ю and then use one of the ways discussed to add U+0301 —for example, 301 Alt-X. The visual appearance of the combined character might not be ideal, but there is little you can do about it. Many programs use rather simplistic methods to create characters with diacritic marks.

There are many potential combinations of characters with diacritic marks, and only a small percentage of them have been included in Unicode as characters. The rest are mostly very rare characters, such as special symbols used in mathematics. Some human languages use such combinations, though.

For example, letter ī̀—i.e., "i" with both a macron (a horizontal line above) and a grave accent—does not exist in Unicode as such. It can be expressed in several ways: "i" followed by a combining macron and a combining grave in some order, or as ī followed by a combining grave, or as ì followed by a combining macron. This multitude causes some problems, and there are techniques in Unicode to reduce the variation by so-called normalization. If you need to produce the character only on paper or screen, you can try the different methods (using a large font to see the differences) and use the combination that produces the typographically best result. This often heavily depends on the font.

In Unicode, a combining diacritic mark always appears *after* the character that it relates to. This is different from the use of dead keys for typing letters with diacritic marks: you press the dead key before the letter key.

Spacing Between Characters

Spacing between characters is mostly a typographic issue and, as such, is outside the scope of this book. We will however consider some Unicode approaches to spacing, emphasizing their limited usefulness as compared with other tools. Basically, you use tools like commands in a layout or publishing program to control character spacing.

In Unicode, there are some *fixed-width space* characters, which will be discussed in Chapter 8. Contrary to normal spaces, which are usually flexible (can be expanded or shrunk in formatting), fixed-width spaces have a more or less fixed width.

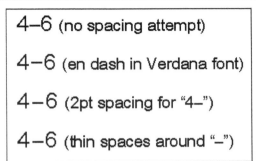

Figure 2-19. Different methods for adding spacing around a dash

Consider the typographic problem with an expression like 4–6 (four, en dash, six, meaning "from four to six"). In most fonts, the en dash will (almost) touch both digits, creating a somewhat unpleasant appearance. We could write "4 – 6" using spaces around the en dash, but this would violate orthographic rules, and it would also create too much spacing, as a rule. There are different approaches to the problem:

- Use a font where the problem does not appear. This might mean using a different font for the en dash than for the text around it. Naturally, this is a tricky way, and it does not work if you cannot really control fonts.

- Use the tools of a typesetting or other program to adjust character spacing. Even in MS Word, you can do that. Select the characters 4–, and then choose Format → Font → Character Spacing, and set Spacing to Expanded by, say, 1pt or 2pt. The setting affects the spacing *after* each character in the selected area. (In HTML or XML authoring, you might use CSS, specifically the letter-spacing property, to affect spacing in a similar manner.)

- Insert suitable fixed-width spaces, such as thin spaces (U+2009), before and after the en dash. You could also try a hair space (U+200A), but it is probably too narrow (perhaps just one pixel wide).

The last approach is the only one that operates at the character level only, so it belongs to our topic. However, it is usually not the best way. It gives rather coarse control, at least if the typesetting program does not let you modify the widths of the fixed-width spaces. Moreover, it works for some fonts only. (If you enter fixed-width spaces and the current font does not contain them, your program might insert the space in some other font, often causing odd effects.) On the positive side, it expresses the spacing request at the character level and can thus be used even in plain text.

The three approaches are illustrated in Figure 2-19. The basic font there is Arial Unicode MS, which contains the thin space character.

Inputting East Asian Characters

You may wonder how people type Chinese/Japanese/Korean (CJK) characters on a computer, given the fact that there are thousands of such characters. Using a general character map is rather impractical, since it is very difficult to find CJK characters there.

Some techniques are based on the phonetic values of characters: using Latin letters, you type a string that corresponds to the pronunciation, and a program shows you a menu of alternative characters to select from. Other techniques work on the graphic elements of characters, such as the number of strokes or the radical (root symbol). A program might even recognize characters as drawn using a mouse.

There are several *Input Method Editors (IME)* available from different sources. These utilities combine many alternative methods of CJK character input, as illustrated in the document *http://www.microsoft.com/globaldev/handson/user/IME_Paper.mspx*.

If you use Microsoft products, you can download and install support to one or more of the East Asian writing systems: Chinese Traditional, Chinese Simplified, Japanese, and Korean. Along with the support, you get an IME. Since the choice and installation heavily depends on a particular system (including version of Windows) and on whether MS Office is used or not, we just refer to information available via *http://www.alanwood.net/unicode/utilities_editors.html*. Be aware that because of the number of CJK characters, the packages are rather large.

Escape Sequences

Characters can often be written using various "escape" notations. This rather vague term means notations that are later converted to (or just displayed as) characters according to some specific rules. The rules are applied by a program like a text formatter or web browser, and the rules depend on the context. They may belong to a markup, programming, or other computer language. (Programming language–related issues will be discussed in Chapter 11.) If different computer languages have similar conventions in this respect, a language designer may have picked up a notation from another language, or it might be a coincidence.

The phrase "escape sequence," or even "escape" for short, is rather widespread, and it reflects the general idea of escaping from the limitations of a character repertoire or device or protocol or something else. These notations should not be confused with the use of the ESC (escape) control code in ASCII and other character codes. Especially in old text, "escape sequence" may mean a sequence of characters starting with ESC and typically used for controlling a device. The "escape sequences" discussed here are strings of printable characters used in text, and we will emphasize this by using the term "escape notation."

Examples of Escape Notations

Table 2-4 illustrates the use of escape notations in some markup and other computer languages. It shows examples of notations for the character Ä (A with dieresis, U+00C4) and the string "−8 °C" (minus sign, digit eight, no-break space, degree sign, letter C). Often a computer language has several alternative escape notations for a character; shown is just one of the possibilities. The principles of the notations will be explained in some detail after the table. As you see, the notations are partly similar, partly quite different. Once you know a few of them, learning new ones will be easy, as long as you manage to keep the different systems as separate in your mind.

Table 2-4. Escape notations in computer languages

Language or notation	Code for Ä	Code for −8 °C
CSS	\c4	\2013 8\a0 \b0 C
HTML	&Auml;	−8 °C
PostScript	\304	(-8 \260C)
RTF	\'c4	\u8722\'2d8\~\'b0C
TeX	\"A	$-$8~\char'0260 C
XML (and HTML)	&#xc4;	–8 °C

As you can see, the notations typically involve some (semi-)mnemonic name or the code number of the character, in some number system. The ISO 8859-1 code number for our example character Ä is 196 in decimal, 304 in octal, and C4 in hexadecimal. The notations contain some method of indicating that the letters or digits are not to be taken as such but as part of a special notation denoting a character. Often some specific character such as the backslash \ is used as an "escape character." This implies that such a character cannot be used as such in the language or format but must itself be "escaped." For example, to include the backslash itself in a string constant in C, you need to write it twice (\\).

In cases like these, the character itself does not occur in a file (such as an HTML document or a TeX source file). Instead, the file contains the "escape" notation as a character sequence, which will then be interpreted in a specific way by programs like a web browser or a TeX program. We can in a sense regard the "escape notations" as encodings used in specific contexts upon specific agreements.

CSS

CSS (Cascading Style Sheets) is a language for suggesting presentational features for an HTML or XML document. It does not have much use for string constants, but in principle, so-called generated content strings may contain arbitrary Unicode data. The convention is that within a string constant, \n means the character with hexadecimal Unicode number n. This works well when the number is followed by a character that cannot be part of a hexadecimal number. There are special conventions that help in other cases: a \n construct is treated as terminated after six consecutive hexadecimal digits, and a space immediately following a \n construct is ignored. By these rules, the string 1–5 (containing an en dash, U+2013) can be written as a CSS constant in two ways: "1\0020135" or "1\2013 5".

PostScript

PostScript is a page description language defined by Adobe. PostScript format can be viewed on screen, too, using tools like GhostScript software. More than markup, PostScript is a powerful (and complex) programming language. Normally PostScript code is generated from other formats with automatic tools, but sometimes people edit the resulting code for fine-tuning of visual appearance or small changes to the content.

PostScript contains a large collection of names for glyphs. The names are mnemonic and relatively long, such as Adieresis for Ä. Some character databases mention, along with other information about characters, the PostScript names, also known as "Adobe names." However, the names refer to glyphs, not characters. You would not use Adieresis in a PostScript file to get Ä printed; instead, you would use \304.

Adobe's information on PostScript, including the PostScript reference manual, can be found at *http://www.adobe.com/products/postscript/resources.html*.

RTF

Rich Text Format (RTF) was designed for information interchange between text-processing programs, preserving much of the formatting of text. Such programs typically have a "Save As RTF" function, and they can open RTF files and automatically convert them to the program's internal format. RTF contains much more than plain text, but often conversion to RTF format loses some information, if advanced or specialized tools have been used in text processing. RTF is favored by some organizations for security reasons: RTF does not contain macros, so RTF files, unlike MS Word files, cannot contain macro viruses.

RTF should not be confused with the general concept of "rich text," which may mean almost any data format that allows some formatting of texts, such as italics and bolding.

RTF markup is verbose and confusing to a human reader, since it is meant to be read by programs primarily. In addition to notations for characters as discussed here, RTF contains quite a lot of commands merged with text content. The RTF format is, however, a text format, defined as the Internet media type text/rtf and usually containing ASCII characters only. (The media type application/rtf is used, too.)

The meanings of notations like 'c4 depend on the encoding used. However, an RTF file may contain commands that specify the encoding, making the document more portable.

In the example \u8722\'2d8\~\'b0C, the notation \u8722 refers to the minus sign character (U+2212) by its code number in decimal. The notations \'2d and \'b0 refer to the hyphen-minus (U+002D) and the degree sign (U+00B0) by their two-digit hexadecimal codes, whereas \~ is a special notation that denotes the no-break space. The hyphen-minus character appears in the notation for fallback behavior: it is the character to be rendered if the preceding character cannot be displayed.

For more information on RTF, consult *RTF Pocket Guide* by O'Reilly or the extensive web site, *http://interglacial.com/rtf/*.

TeX

In TeX typesetting systems (including LaTeX, AMSTeX, etc.), there are different ways of producing characters, possibly depending on the "packages" used. Examples of ways to produce Ä include: \"A, \symbol{196}, \char'0304, and \capitaldieresis{A}. For a large list of such notations, consult *The Comprehensive LaTex Symbol List*, *http://www.ctan.org/texarchive/info/symbols/comprehensive*.

Notations for Human Readers

There are also "escape notations" that are to be interpreted by human readers directly. For example, when sending email, you might use A" (letter A followed by a quotation mark) as a surrogate for Ä (letter A with dieresis), or you might use AE instead of Ä. The reader is assumed to understand that, for example, A" on a display actually means Ä. Quite often, the purpose is to use ASCII characters only, so that the typing, transmission, and display of the characters is "safe."

However, such notations typically make texts rather messy. The name Hämäläinen does not look too good or readable when written as Ha"ma"la"inen or Haemaelaeinen. Such usage is based on special (though often implicit) conventions and can cause a lot of confusion when there is no mutual agreement on the conventions. Many different and mutually incompatible conventions are used. For example, to denote letter "a" with an acute accent, á, a convention might use the apostrophe, a', or the solidus, a/, or the acute accent, a´, or something else.

Some notations are rather evident, such as using a^ to denote â. The character ^ has no normal use in words, so the most plausible explanation is that the writer meant to indicate that a circumflex should appear above the preceding letter. But quotation marks, apostrophes, and even acute and grave accents could sometimes be mistaken for punctuation marks.

There is an old (1992) proposal by K. Simonsen, "Character Mnemonics & Character Sets," published as RFC 1345, that lists a large number of "escape notations" for characters. They are very short, typically two characters—e.g., "Co" for ©, "A:" for Ä, and "th" for þ (thorn). Naturally, there's the problem that the reader must know whether, for example, "th" is to be understood that way or as two letters t and h. So the system is primarily for referring to characters, but under suitable circumstances, it could also be used for actually writing texts, when the ambiguities can somehow be removed by additional conventions or by context. RFC 1345 is old and not approved by any authority, but if you need, for some applications, an "escape scheme," you might consider using those notations instead of reinventing the wheel. RFCs are available via *http://www.rfc-editor.org/*.

Explanations to Human Readers

Extending the meaning of "escape sequence" even further—and probably beyond what many experts find reasonable—let us consider the common problem of explaining verbally which character you mean. This may happen when you cannot show the character (e.g., when spelling out a foreign name over the phone) or when showing the character is not sufficient. Here we are not primarily interested in using characters in running text but in specifying which character is being discussed.

As an example, consider a situation where you need to mention the Cyrillic letter Я in a situation where you can safely use only ASCII (e.g., email, or a Usenet discussion). There are various ways to try to describe the character:

The Russian letter that looks like a mirrored "R"
> Such descriptions of the shape of a character might do their job in some cases, but they don't work well in general. The shape of a character may vary, and different people interpret shapes differently. For example, the letter Ч looks like a chair to some people, while some might describe it as digit 4, etc.

U+042F
> This is the other extreme: a unique code-like notation, which is just fine when understood, but rather useless to most readers.

Я
> This is code-like too. It might, however, be understood by people who know HTML authoring but have never heard of the U+... notation.

Cyrillic capital letter ya
> This is better, and when understood as a Unicode name, it is unique and immutable. However, such names are not always intuitively understandable, even to people who know the character itself. For example, due to differences in English and French transliteration of Russian, the phrase "Cyrillic capital letter che" might be understood either as meaning Ч or as meaning Ш.

The character you can see at http://www.fileformat.info/info/unicode/char/042f/
> This would mean a reference to a web page that contains information on the character, including a glyph of it as a largish image. If you use it in an email message, the recipient is usually able to just click on the address to visit the page. Unfortunately, for many purposes, the content of online services that could be used for such references tends to be rather technical in nature. The formal information might even confuse the reader.

A combination of some of the above
> This is usually the best strategy. The methods used will vary by the audience and by the character. An explanation such as "Cyrillic capital letter ya (in Unicode: U+042F)" might work reasonably well.

Sometimes you need to avoid common phrases in order to be unambiguous. It is common to say "double slash" in English, when you mean two consecutive slash characters, //.

However, such wording is potentially ambiguous, since Unicode contains the double solidus operator // (U+2AFD) as a separate, independent character. Unicode contains hundreds of characters with the word "double" in their name. Thus, a wording like "two slashes" is safer. Since even this might be misunderstood as referring to one character, the expression "two slash characters" is even safer.

HTML, SGML, and XML Notations for Characters

HTML is the markup language in which web pages are usually written. It is formally a special case of SGML or XML, which are generic markup languages. These languages have special notations that you can use for writing characters, if it is for some reason difficult or impossible to use the characters themselves.

Character and entity references in web authoring

If you use a "Save as HTML" or "Save as Web page" command or something similar in a word processor, it is quite possible that some characters in your text get stored as entity references or as character references. For example, you have typed é but the program stores it as é or as é. Web-authoring programs often do the same.

There is nothing wrong with this per se (in most cases; some programs generate incorrect character references, though). Web browsers can deal with such references. Many web page editors can interpret them as well. But if you wish to edit the document later using a program like Notepad, you will see the references, and things can get really awkward if you need to work with data like résumé a lot. Depending on the software you use, the references might appear as such, or interpreted and displayed as the characters they denote.

Some programs have options that control whether and how Unicode characters are replaced by entity or character references. Moreover, they may have options for setting the encoding of the HTML document, and this may affect the situation.

For example, suppose you use OpenOffice to create a document with é and a Chinese character, and then use File → Save and select HTML format. With default settings, the program saves é as é and the Chinese character as a character reference like 不. The latter part is understandable, since the default encoding in HTML documents created with OpenOffice is windows-1252, which contains no Chinese characters. There is no good explanation for using é, though. If you set the encoding to utf-8 (via Tools → Options → Load and Save → HTML Compatibility), then the Chinese character is saved as such, UTF-8 encoded. The é entity reference still appears. It is of course a correct notation, but it makes HTML source harder to read.

Thus, one of the reasons for using references is that the document's encoding might not allow all characters to be represented as such, and character references offer a universal way to overcome such limitations. But programs might also use such output form for no good reason.

If you represent all non-ASCII characters using entity references or character references, you can use ASCII only in an HTML document. The data will be "7-bit safe"—i.e., it can even be sent over a connection that does something nasty to octets with the most significant bit set. This is seldom relevant these days, but many tutorials have taught that entity and character references are safer than using the actual characters, and people tend to believe such things.

Exceptionally, such issues might still be relevant, if you work, say, in a Mac environment and upload your documents to a server that runs Unix. It might then happen that the software you use for uploading performs a wrong character encoding conversion, or doesn't do a conversion when it should. But if you have used only ASCII characters (and wrote, for example, accented letters using entity references), then no such conversion is needed, and no conceivable conversion will harm you either, since conversions would leave ASCII characters intact.

The Free Recode program available from *http://recode.progiciels-bpi.ca* can perform an impressive amount of code conversions, including conversions that replace references by characters or vice versa. Beware that it uses rather odd terminology: it refers to "HTML charsets" when it actually means HTML format. Normally "charset" means character encoding, at the character level, without any notion of entity references or character references.

The role and use of character and entity references

Entity references like é and *character references* like é are actually quite distinct concepts, though commonly confused with each other in HTML tutorials—and even in specifications! What they share is that they relate to *markup languages*, namely SGML, XML, and languages defined with them, such as HTML. The references do not belong to Unicode at all, though they usually make use of Unicode code numbers. Rather, they are at a "higher level."

Thus, the references make sense only in contexts where markup is used and interpreted. For example, they do not work in normal email, though they may work if email is sent and interpreted in HTML format. However, references might at times appear otherwise too, due to programming errors, or sometimes intentionally. For example, in some situations, Internet Explorer represents characters in user input in forms as character references. However, by the specifications, a browser should send form data as plain text, not in HTML format in any way. On some web-based discussion forums, you might be able to type a character reference and have it displayed to your readers as the character you mean. Technically, this is easily achieved in the design of forum software: it just needs to pass the reference through as such.

Definition: character reference

Generally, in any SGML-based system, or *SGML application* as the jargon goes, a character reference of the form &#*number*; can be used. It refers to the character that occupies code position *n* in the character code defined for the SGML application in question. This is actually very simple: you specify a character by its index (position, number). In SGML terminology, the character code that determines the interpretation of a character reference is called, quite confusingly, the *document character set*. It need not have anything to do with the character encoding in which the document is written.

Originally, SGML used decimal numbers in character references. Later, the hexadecimal alternative was added, and it uses letter "x" (or "X") in front of the digits: &#x*number*;. Thus, Ä is equivalent to Ä.

For HTML, the document character set is Unicode (or, to be exact, a subset thereof, depending on HTML version). A most essential point is that for HTML, the document character set is completely independent of the encoding of the document! Some early browsers (Netscape 4) got this wrong.

XML, which can be regarded as a lightweight derivative of SGML, has a very similar character reference concept. XML fixes the document character set to Unicode. It also simplifies the syntax by making the trailing semicolon (which is optional in some situations in SGML) an obligatory part of a character reference.

Definition: entity reference

Entity references such as © in HTML can be regarded as symbolic names defined for some characters. Contrary to popular belief, entity references are not less system-dependent than character references like ©. It's rather the opposite. The entity references in HTML are *defined* by equating them with character references, using XML declarations like:

```
<!ENTITY copy   "&#169;">
```

Entity references in SGML and XML correspond to *macro invocations* in many programming and command languages. You define an entity with a declaration (e.g., the sample above) and you use ("call") the entity by prefixing its name with an ampersand. An SGML or XML processor, including web browsers, simply substitutes internally the defining string © for a reference—in this case, ©. In the general case, the definition of an entity could be a long string, even the content of an external file.

Entity references in HTML

The HTML language (including XHTML) has a finite set of predefined entities, and they are all defined in terms of character references. This is a special case, but it has made people understand entity references just as names for characters. Even HTML specifications call them *character entity references* as opposed to *numeric character references*.

Moreover, although HTML was formally defined as an application of SGML, web browsers never supported the general mechanisms for declaring and using entities. Thus, in practice, entities exist only in the sense that you can use the predefined entities. To the extent that web browsers support XHTML—i.e., XML-based versions of HTML—the situation is different: new entities can be declared.

By SGML rules, the trailing semicolon in entity references may be omitted, if the next character is non-alphanumeric (e.g., a space). However, popular browsers often get this wrong, so € is much safer than &euro without the semicolon. Moreover, in XML, and therefore in XHTML, the semicolon is required.

The entity references in HTML are officially defined in the HTML specifications; for example, see *http://www.w3.org/TR/xhtml1/dtds.html#h-A2*. There are also some more readable presentations, such as *http://www.htmlhelp.com/reference/html40/entities/*. However, there are several reasons why the entity references are not that useful:

- In modern authoring with Unicode-enabled tools, you don't need the entities. You simply write characters themselves and see them as such even in HTML source, and you store and serve your page in UTF-8 encoding, for example.

- Entities exist for a rather haphazard collection of characters.

- The entity names are often just half-mnemonic, or not mnemonic at all. Who could guess that ⟨ means left-pointing angle bracket? What would be your guess on ∋? Part of the quasi-mnemonic nature is caused by the fact that the names have been taken from the SGML standard, which uses entity names with a maximum length of six characters.

Character entities in XML

People often assume that the character entity references known from HTML are automatically available in XML. However, in XML, only a very small set of predefined entities exist, as shown in Table 2-5. Entities have been defined for *markup-significant* characters —i.e., characters that might otherwise be understood as constituting part of markup. If you use the < character in document content, as in the expression "a<b", you need to escape it as < or, equivalently, as < or <. Otherwise, "<b" would be taken as starting a tag. There is actually no need to escape the > character, but an entity has been defined for it for symmetry. The & character, on the other hand, must always be escaped in XML, when it is not meant to start a character reference or an entity reference. The apostrophe and the quotation mark need not be escaped in document content but only in attribute values, where the character would otherwise terminate the value.

Table 2-5. Predefined entities (denoting characters) in XML

Entity reference	Expansion	Character	Unicode name	Need for the entity
&lt;	&#60;	<	Less-than sign	< normally starts a tag
&gt;	&#62;	>	Greater-than sign	For symmetry with <
&amp;	&#38;	&	Ampersand	& normally starts a reference
&apos;	&#39;	'	Apostrophe	Within an attribute value
&quot;	&#34;	"	Quotation mark	Within an attribute value

In XML, any other entities must be defined before use, though you can write the definitions into an external file and refer to the file in an entity declaration.

Specialized Editors

There are many good editors and word processors that can handle Unicode or other large repertoires, many of which are free. The difficult part is to decide which is best for an individual user, or a user community, or purpose. Therefore, the following descriptions are aimed at illustrating some capabilities and features, so that you know what's possible and available.

For information on many other options, see the page "Unicode and Multilingual Editors and Word Processors," *http://www.alanwood.net/unicode/utilities_editors.html*.

BabelPad

BabelPad is a Unicode editor for modern versions of Windows. It is free and available from *http://www.babelstone.co.uk/*. It is relatively easy to get started with, and it has fairly good general tools for entering characters. However, you need to know quite a bit about Unicode to use many of the tools.

BabelPad is illustrated in Figure 2-20. You can use drop-down menus or keyboard shortcuts for the insertion of some characters, but in general you need to use the character map or a character's Unicode number. By clicking on the U+ button in the interface, you can enter a mode in which you can type in the Unicode number. But this is not very convenient for typical work by a secretary or a journalist, for example.

There is a Character Map window, shown in Figure 2-21, that looks rather similar to corresponding utilities in Windows XP and MS Word. However, it has extra features. If you click on a character, and then on the Properties button, you get detailed information on the character, as illustrated in Figure 2-22. The information is technical and formal, you need to understand Unicode properties as explained in Chapter 5 to make the best use of it.

UniPad

UniPad is a Unicode text editor for Windows systems. It uses its own bitmap font, so you can use it independently of the font repertoire in your system. On the other hand, you will not directly see which characters will work in the fonts you have. UniPad is easy to get started with. It is free for very small scale use. It is available from the site *http://www.unipad.org*.

UniPad has onscreen keyboard layouts, or "virtual keyboards," that allow you to type in texts according to keyboard settings that are conventional for a language. Figure 2-23 illustrates such usage. You can also modify the keyboard settings or define your own keyboard layout for such use. Characters can also be selected from a character map.

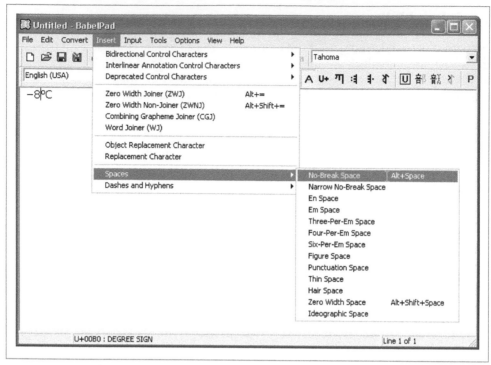

Figure 2-20. Use of BabelPad, here using a command menu to add a character

Exercise

Enter the following text into a document in some way discussed earlier. Create the document in plain text format, Word format, HTML format, or something else. Here the text is printed in large font to make it easier to recognize the characters, but you can use any font size you find suitable. Some characters can be difficult to identify, since identification may require understanding of the specific topic area, languages, and context. On the other hand, this makes the exercise more realistic.

The exercise strings are in Table 2-6, where the first column contains the strings you should write. The second column contains explanations, which might be useful in identifying the characters by cultural connections. If you find an exercise far too difficult, postpone it; after reading Chapter 8, it might be easier. If you find some sample string particularly typical of texts that you work with, consider what method would be the *fastest* one in continuous use. Also consider what would be the *simplest and easiest* way to explain to someone who is almost computer illiterate that she will be able to remember.

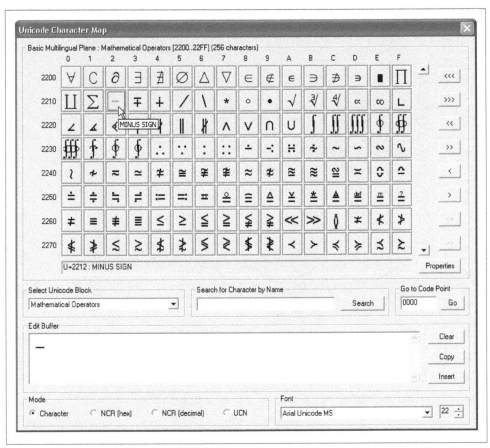

Figure 2-21. The Character Map in BabelPad

Table 2-6. Strings for typing exercises

String	Explanation
naïve	"Naive" in original French spelling
François	French first name
São Paulo	City in Brazil
Salvador Dalí	Spanish painter
¡Viva España!	Long live Spain! (in Spanish)
Carl von Linné, Carolus Linnæus	Swedish and Latin names of the famous biologist
Erdoğan	Turkish family name
Klaipėda	City in Lithuania
Antonín Dvořák, Bohuslav Martinů	Czech composers
Brăila, Constanța	Cities in Romania

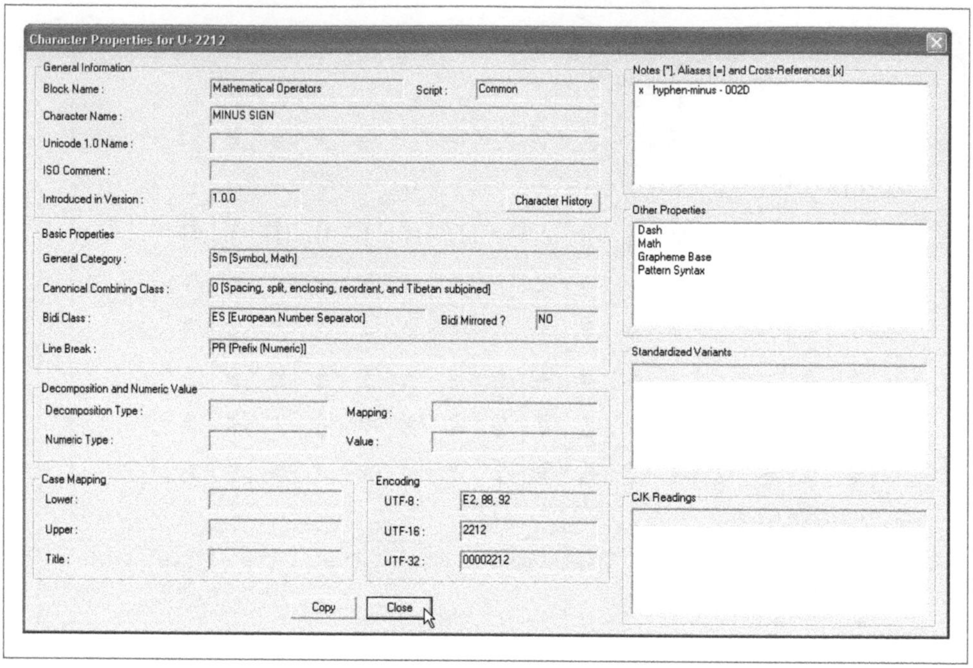

Figure 2-22. Properties of a character as shown by BabelPad

String	Explanation
Nguyễn Văn Thiệu (1923–2001)	Vietnamese general and politician
Anders Ångström	Swedish scientist
Sándor Petőfi	Hungarian poet
Karol Józef Wojtyła	The original name of John Paul II
Latvijas Nacionālā bibliotēka	National Library of Latvia
Żebbuġ	Town in Gozo (Malta)
Lech Wałęsa	Former president of Poland
β-carotene	A chemical compound (provitamin)
γράμμα	Greek word "gramma" in Greek letters
R ≈ 900 μΩ	Resistance is about 900 microhms (micro-ohms)
1.5 ‰	1.5 per mille (per thousand)
2.53 m² ± 0.01 m²	2.53 plus or minus 0.01 square meters
CS ♀ × BA ♂	A crossbreeding formula with symbols for breeds
Er sagte: „Ich weiß nicht."	German text, containing a quotation
[lɪŋˈgwɪstɪk]	Phonetic (IPA) spelling of the word "linguistic"
¬(∃x,y,z,n∈N⁺)(n>2 ∧ xⁿ+yⁿ=zⁿ)	Fermat's last theorem in compact notation

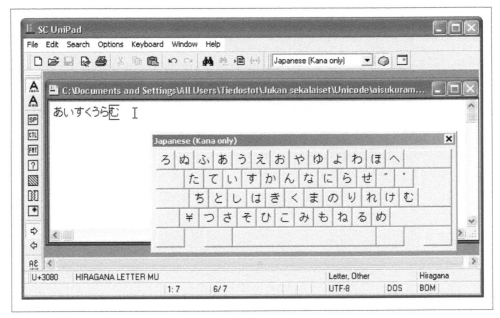

Figure 2-23. Using UniPad to write Japanese in hiragana

As a simple check, change the font of the texts. If you have used a text-processing program, use the Select All function and a font changing command to try a few different fonts. It may happen that some special characters are replaced by symbols of unrepresentable characters (e.g., boxes or question marks). However, if some character is changed to a completely different character, you know that you did something wrong.

CHAPTER 3

Character Sets and Encodings

The world runs on a wide variety of character sets. This chapter describes the many encodings for these sets and lists the characters in them. We also describe how conversions between the encodings can be performed, either with the functions of commonly used programs or separate converters. This chapter also discusses practical use of the character sets in different contexts, such as email, Internet discussion forums, and document interchange.

The use of Unicode does not mean that you need not know anything about encodings. You will inevitably encounter non-Unicode data as well, and you need to work with it, even if this only means converting it into Unicode. Moreover, Unicode itself can be represented in different encodings, such as UTF-8 and UTF-16.

Mostly you don't neeed to know about the details of encodings. You certainly don't have to know the code numbers of characters in each encoding, let alone memorize them. What you need is an overview of the world of encodings, general information about the suitability of each encoding for various purposes, and tools for mapping between encodings.

The presentation of encodings in this chapter is practical rather than historical. For history, one place to refer to is "A Brief History of Character Codes in North America, Europe, and East Asia" at *http://tronweb.super-nova.co.jp/characcodehist.html*.

As explained in Chapter 1, the phrase "character set" is confusing and vague. It is therefore mostly avoided in this book, but you will often see it elsewhere. It may mean any of the following, and often two or three of these at the same time:

- A collection of characters (character repertoire)
- A mapping of characters into the mathematical set of integers (character code)
- A mapping of characters (or their numbers) into sequences of octets (character encoding)

Good Old ASCII

ASCII is still the set of characters that work safely in most text applications and on the Internet. Almost all programming languages, command languages, markup languages,

Internet protocol headers, and many other notation systems still exclusively use ASCII in their basic syntax. They may allow other characters in contexts like quoted strings, but the commands, reserved words, and operators are written using good old ASCII. Moreover, most character codes currently in use can be regarded as extensions of ASCII: they preserve the meaning of code numbers 0 through 127 and add some more.

On the other hand, ASCII has a very small character repertoire. Historically, it was a big improvement over even more restricted character codes, but it was created at a time when bits were very expensive. ASCII was designed to be represented in 7 bits, and many character positions were reserved for control codes such as linefeed (LF) and escape (ESC). Only about a hundred character positions were assigned to printable characters.

Moreover, since the needs of programming were more important than those of text processing, the assignments use positions for many technical characters. Even "smart" quotation marks were omitted; the idea was that the ASCII quotation mark, ", was to be used as a neutral quotation mark.

American Origin

The name ASCII is originally an acronym for "American Standard Code for Information Interchange." The ASCII code was developed in the United States and standardized by ANSI, the American National Standards Institute. The standard is often referred to as ANSI X3.4-1986, but the current version is ANSI INCITS 4-1986 (R2002).

The creation of ASCII started in the late 1950s, and several additions and modifications were made in the 1960s. The 1963 version had several unassigned code positions. The ANSI standard, where those positions were assigned, mainly to accommodate lowercase letters, was approved in 1967/1968, and later modified slightly.

The name *US-ASCII* is also used, and is even the preferred name in some recommendations, to distinguish ASCII proper from different "national variants of ASCII." In principle, the name ASCII is unambiguous, since the "variants" are just different codes with more or less resemblance to ASCII and with names of their own.

Contrary to popular belief, the designers of ASCII did not limit the scope to the English language only. Some characters were included for the purpose of writing accented letters. For example, the tilde ~ character was meant to be used so that it is overprinted on a letter —e.g., writing "n," Backspace, and ~ on paper to produce a character that looks like ñ. This never became popular, and the characters introduced for the purpose were used for other purposes as well, creating a conflict of interests in font design. But ASCII surely *tried* to address the needs of other languages as well.

The ASCII Repertoire

The following presentation contains the printable ASCII characters by their code number (32–126) order, in rows of 16 characters, except for the last one, which has only 15 characters. The first character is the space, which is graphically empty, of course; it is often classified as a graphic character. The font used here is the monospace font used for computer code in this book:

```
  ! " # $ % & ' ( ) * + , - . /
  0 1 2 3 4 5 6 7 8 9 : ; < = > ?
  @ A B C D E F G H I J K L M N O
  P Q R S T U V W X Y Z [ \ ] ^ _
  ` a b c d e f g h i j k l m n o
  p q r s t u v w x y z { | } ~
```

Thus, there are $6 \times 16 - 2 = 94$ graphic characters, if we do not count the space as graphic. They include 26 uppercase letters, 26 lowercase letters, and 10 digits, leaving only 32 code positions for other characters.

The repertoire corresponds rather closely to the characters that can be written on old typewriters and similar devices. This is no coincidence, but intentional design. Only a few extra characters were added, such as the backslash \ (reverse solidus).

The ASCII Encoding

By design, ASCII is a 7-bit character code—i.e., each code number can be represented as an integer in binary notation using 7 bits. In the early days, ASCII data was sometimes packed into 7-bit bytes—e.g., putting 5 bytes into a 36-bit computer "word" (storage unit).

Nowadays, we almost always use an 8-bit byte, or octet, to represent an ASCII character. This leaves 1 bit (normally the most significant bit) unused. It has been used for various purposes—e.g., as a parity check bit, which helps to detect errors in data. In modern protocols and applications, the most significant bit is usually kept as zero. This, too, allows checks of a kind: if a text file purported to contain ASCII data has any octet with the most significant bit set, there is an error of some kind somewhere.

This makes the character encoding used for ASCII really simple: each code number, and hence each character, is represented as an octet with that number as its value, when interpreted as an integer.

ISO 646 and National Variants of ASCII

There are several national variants of ASCII. Technically, each variant is a character code that is defined separately and has its own name. In such variants, some special characters have been replaced by national letters and other symbols. There is great variation here, and even within one country and for one language, there might be different variants. The variants have lost much of their significance because of more modern approaches to encoding characters, but they can still be in use for legacy data and legacy applications.

A large number of the variants have been defined on the basis of the international standard *ISO 646*, issued by the International Organization for Standardization (ISO). ISO 646 has a so-called International Reference Version (IRV), which is equivalent to ASCII; thus, in this context, "International" effectively means "English"! In some contexts, it might be politically correct to refer to ISO 646 IRV instead of ASCII.

ISO 646 defines a character set similar to US-ASCII but with code positions corresponding to US-ASCII characters @, [, \,], {, |, and } as "national use positions." It also gives some liberties with characters #, $, ^, `, and ~. Ecma International has issued the ECMA-6 standard, which is equivalent in content to ISO 646 and is freely available on the Web via *http://www.ecma-international.org*. *Ecma* was originally European Computer Manufacturers' Association, but it is now a worldwide association for standardization, though with some European emphasis.

The ISO 646 standard is cited more officially as ISO/IEC 646, since it is a joint standard approved by ISO and the International Electrotechnical Commission (IEC). A similar note applies to many ISO standards mentioned in this book.

Within the framework of ISO 646, and also outside of it, several "national variants of ASCII" have been defined, assigning different letters and symbols to the "national use" positions. Thus, the characters that appear in those positions—including those in US-ASCII—are more or less "unsafe" in international data transfer, although this problem is losing significance. The trend is towards using the corresponding codes strictly for US-ASCII meanings; national characters are handled otherwise, giving them their own unique and universal code positions in character codes larger than ASCII. However, old software and devices as well as legacy data may still reflect various "national variants of ASCII."

In principle, the phrase "national variant of ASCII" is incorrect. They are character codes that are defined independently, although they have been derived from ASCII. These codes are often registered and named in a manner that reflects the geographic scope. For example, a variant designed for use in Sweden and Finland has the primary name "SEN_850200_B" but also more understandable alias names like "ISO646-SE."

Table 3-1 lists ASCII characters that have been replaced by other characters in some "national variant of ASCII." That is, the code positions of these US-ASCII characters might be occupied by other characters needed for national use. The lists of characters here is not intended to be exhaustive, it just shows some typical examples. The "Code" column specifies the ASCII (and Unicode) code number in hexadecimal.

Table 3-1. ASCII characters that vary in "national variants"

Code	Character	Unicode name	National variants
23	#	Number sign	£ Ù
24	$	Dollar sign	¤
40	@	Commercial at	É § Ä à ³
5B	[	Left square bracket	Ä Æ ° â ¡ ÿ é
5C	\	Reverse solidus	Ö Ø ç Ñ ½ ¥
5D	]	Right square bracket	Å Ü § ê é ¿	
5E	^	Circumflex accent	Ü î
5F	_	Low line	è
60	`	Grave accent	é ä µ ô ù '

Code	Character	Unicode name	National variants
7B	{	Left curly bracket	ä æ é à ° ¨
7C	|	Vertical line	ö ø ù ò ñ f
7D	}	Right curly bracket	å ü è ç ¼
7E	~	Tilde	ü ¯ ß ¨ û ì ´ _

Thus, for example, text containing "foo[1]" might be displayed as "fooälå" when processed by software that assumes that the input is in a national variant of ASCII. Such software has become rare as the use of ISO 8859 and other wider character codes has become common, since almost all characters used in the national variants have been incorporated into an ISO 8859 character code. However, *legacy data* may contain characters that need to be interpreted according to some national variant. If you see a text containing the string "Sch}ler," odds are that } actually means ü. You need information on the legacy codes used in a cultural environment in order to make educated guesses in such situations. For a quick reference to such codes, presented graphically, consult the page *http://kanji.zinbun.kyoto-u.ac.jp/~yasuoka/CJK.html*.

Subsets of ASCII for Safety

Mainly due to the national variants discussed in the previous section, some characters are less "safe" than others—i.e., more often transferred or interpreted incorrectly. In addition to the letters of the English alphabet (A–Z, a–z), the digits (0–9), and the space ( ), only the following characters can be regarded as really "safe" in data transmission:

```
! " % & ' ( ) * + , - . / : ; < = > ?
```

Even these characters might eventually be interpreted wrongly by the recipient. For example, a human reader could see a glyph for & as something other than what it is intended to denote. A program could interpret < as starting some special markup, or ? as a so-called wildcard character, etc.

When you need to *name* things (e.g., files, variables, data fields, etc.), it is often best to use only the characters listed above, even if a wider character repertoire is possible. Naturally, you need to take into account any additional restrictions imposed by the applicable syntax. For example, the rules of a programming language might restrict the character repertoire in identifier names to letters, digits, and one or two other characters. On the other hand, the underscore (low line) character _ is often usable in names, and it normally works reliably.

The Misnomer "8-bit ASCII"

The phrase "8-bit ASCII" is used surprisingly often. It follows from the discussion in the previous section that in reality ASCII is strictly and unambiguously a 7-bit code in the sense that all code positions are in the range 0–127. It can be, and it usually is, represented using 8-bit bytes, but with the first bit always zero, or used for other purposes so that it is not part of the encoded form of a character.

The misnomer "8-bit ASCII" most often denotes windows-1252, the 8-bit code defined by Microsoft for use in the Western world. More generally, 8-bit ASCII is used to refer to various character codes, which are extensions of ASCII and mutually more or less incompatible. The character repertoire in such a code contains ASCII as a subset, the code numbers are in the range 0–256, and the code numbers of ASCII characters equal their ASCII codes.

ISO 8859 Codes

ISO 8859—or more formally, ISO/IEC 8859—is a family of character code standards. They were largely developed by Ecma, which distributes ECMA standards that are equivalent to ISO 8859 standards. ISO 8859 standards are largely oriented toward languages of European origin.

ISO 8859 codes are widely used on different platforms and in different contexts. For example, on the Web, ISO 8859-1 was long treated as the default encoding. On Windows, ISO 8859 as such is not used that much, but the corresponding, somewhat extended Windows encodings are common. In Unix and Linux, ISO 8859 is very common.

Each ISO 8859 standard tries to address the needs of one or more specific languages and cultural environment, within the fairly narrow framework of 8-bit structure. This means that in most cases, you cannot represent multilingual text using any single ISO 8859 encoding.

ISO 8859-1 (ISO Latin 1)

The international standard ISO 8859-1 defines a character repertoire identified as *Latin alphabet No. 1*, commonly called *ISO Latin 1*, as well as a character code for it. The repertoire contains the ASCII repertoire as a subset, and the code numbers for those characters are the same as in ASCII. The standard also specifies an encoding, which is similar to that of ASCII: each code number is presented simply as one octet.

In addition to the ASCII characters, ISO Latin 1 contains various accented characters and other letters needed for writing languages of Western and Northern Europe, and some special characters. These characters occupy code positions 160–255, and they are, in code number order and rendered in a monospace font:

```
  ¡ ¢ £ ¤ ¥ ¦ § ¨ © ª « ¬ ® ¯
° ± ² ³ ´ µ ¶ · ¸ ¹ º » ¼ ½ ¾ ¿
À Á Â Ã Ä Å Æ Ç È É Ê Ë Ì Í Î Ï
Ð Ñ Ò Ó Ô Õ Ö × Ø Ù Ú Û Ü Ý Þ ß
à á â ã ä å æ ç è é ê ë ì í î ï
ð ñ ò ó ô õ ö ÷ ø ù ú û ü ý þ ÿ
```

On the first row, the first character is the so-called *no-break space*, which corresponds to the ASCII space character but disallows line breaks in text formatting. The third-to-last character on the first row is the *soft hyphen* character, which either has no graphic appearance or looks the same as the ASCII hyphen character.

The standard mentions that ISO 8859-1 was designed to cover the needs of the following languages: Danish, Dutch, English, Faeroese, Finnish, French, German, Icelandic, Irish, Italian, Norwegian, Portuguese, Spanish, and Swedish. It also covers Albanian and some non-European languages, such as Indonesian/Malay, Tagalog, Swahili, and Afrikaans.

Names of Encodings

A character encoding may have several names, even several official names. This is illustrated in Table 3-2, which summarizes some names of ISO 8859-1. Names of encodings are often written with a hyphen instead of space—e.g., *ISO-8859-1*—or sometimes with an underscore (low line)—e.g., *ISO_8859-1*. This is because in Internet protocols (see Chapter 10), the character encoding needs to be specified by a name that does not contain spaces. However, each context has its own rules for accepted names. Generally, encoding names are case insensitive: iso-8859-1 is the same as ISO-8859-1.

Table 3-2. Names of the ISO 8859-1 standard and encoding

Name	Context of use
ISO/IEC 8859-1:1998	Official name of a particular version of the standard
ISO/IEC 8859-1	Official name of the standard in general
ISO 8859-1	Commonly used name of the standard and the encoding
ISO-8859-1	Preferred MIME name of the encoding (e.g., in Internet headers)
ISO_8859-1	An alternate MIME name (among others)
ISO8859-1	Unofficial, unregistered name used in some contexts
Latin alphabet No. 1	Official name of the character repertoire (in the standard)
Latin 1	Common name of the encoding and repertoire
ISO Latin 1	Another common name, to distinguish from Windows Latin 1
West European (ISO)	A name for the encoding, used in some software

Other ISO 8859 Codes

ISO 8859-1 is a member of the ISO 8859 family of character codes, which extends the ASCII repertoire in different ways with different special characters, for the purposes of different languages and cultures. Just as ISO 8859-1 contains ASCII characters and a collection of characters needed in languages of Western and Northern Europe, there is ISO 8859-2 alias ISO Latin 2 constructed similarly for languages of Central/Eastern Europe, etc. The ISO 8859 character codes are isomorphic in the following sense: code positions 0–127 contain the same characters as in ASCII, positions 128–159 are unused (reserved for control characters), and positions 160–255 are the varying part (often called "the upper half"), used differently in different members of the ISO 8859 family.

The ISO 8859 character codes use the obvious encoding: each code position is represented as one octet. Such encodings have several alternative names in the official registry of character encodings, but the preferred ones are of the form ISO-8859-*n*.

Although ISO 8859-1 has been a de facto default encoding in many contexts, it has in principle no special role. ISO 8859-15 alias ISO Latin 9 was expected to replace ISO 8859-1 to a great extent, since it contains the politically important symbol for euro (€), but it has gained relatively little practical use. Old software does not recognize it, and new software supports Unicode encodings, which give a much wider repertoire of characters.

Table 3-3 lists the ISO 8859 alphabets. Note that ISO 8859-n is Latin alphabet no. n (or ISO Latin n for short) for n = 1, 2 ,3, 4, but this correspondence is broken for the other Latin alphabets. For eventual new approved or proposed ISO 8859 standards, check the page *http://anubis.dkuug.dk/jtc1/sc2/* (official home of ISO/IEC JTC 1/SC 2, the international standardization subcommittee for coded character sets).

Table 3-3. ISO 8859 character codes

Standard	Name of alphabet	Characterization	ECMA
ISO 8859-1	Latin alphabet No. 1	"Western," "West European"	94
ISO 8859-2	Latin alphabet No. 2	"Central/East European"	94
ISO 8859-3	Latin alphabet No. 3	(For Maltese and Esperanto)	94
ISO 8859-4	Latin alphabet No. 4	"North European," "Baltic"	94
ISO 8859-5	Latin/Cyrillic alphabet	(For some Slavic languages)	113
ISO 8859-6	Latin/Arabic alphabet	(For the Arabic language)	114
ISO 8859-7	Latin/Greek alphabet	(For modern Greek)	118
ISO 8859-8	Latin/Hebrew alphabet	(For Hebrew and Yiddish)	121
ISO 8859-9	Latin alphabet No. 5	"Turkish"	128
ISO 8859-10	Latin alphabet No. 6	"Nordic" (Sámi, Inuit, Icelandic)	144
ISO 8859-11	Latin/Thai alphabet	(For the Thai language)	
(There is no part 12; it was planned to cover Devanagari, but the idea was abandoned.)			
ISO 8859-13	Latin alphabet No. 7	Baltic Rim	
ISO 8859-14	Latin alphabet No. 8	Celtic	
ISO 8859-15	Latin alphabet No. 9	"Euro" variant of ISO 8859-1	
ISO 8859-16	Latin alphabet No. 10	"South-Eastern European"	

Ecma International has defined ECMA standards that have the same content as some ISO 8859 standards, as indicated in the table. For example, ECMA-94 defines Latin alphabets 1 through 4, equivalent to ISO 8859-1 through ISO 8859-4. The ECMA standards are available via *http://www.ecmainternational.org/publications/standards/Standard.htm*.

For a tabular summary of the coverage of European languages by the different ISO Latin codes, refer to *http://www.cs.tut.fi/~jkorpela/8859.html*. The languages are listed in each standard, but the coverage is somewhat debatable. In particular, ISO Latin codes usually do not contain characters needed for correct *punctuation* of languages, even English.

Windows Latin 1 and Other Windows Codes

The ISO 8859 character codes, which have been defined by international standards, have Microsoft-specific counterparts, which are here called "Windows codes." The main difference is that some code positions are reserved for control characters (and mostly unused) in ISO 8859 but assigned to various printable characters, especially punctuation marks, in Windows codes. Although defined only by a software vendor, the Windows codes are very important due to the market share of Microsoft.

Windows Latin 1

Microsoft defined its own Latin 1 encoding as different from ISO Latin 1, although only in the sense that some positions that are reserved for control codes in ISO Latin 1 (codes 128–159 decimal) are used for printable characters in Windows Latin 1. The main reason was very understandable: the inclusion of typographically correct quotation marks, as in "foo" and 'foo', and em dash (—) and en dash (–). The right single quote is also the typographically correct apostrophe. Some other characters were added as well.

Windows Latin 1 is one of the most commonly used encodings in the world. In most contexts where the default is said to be ISO Latin 1, it's really Windows Latin 1 (sometimes called WinLatin1). For example, if a web document is labeled as ISO-8859-1 but contains octets with values 128–149, browsers will generally display them according to Windows Latin 1. The practical reason is that most often this is what the document's author really meant.

However, the use of octets in the range 128–159 in any data to be processed by a program that expects ISO 8859-1 encoded data is an error, and it might cause problems. The octets might for example be ignored, or be processed in a manner that looks meaningful, or (in rare cases) be interpreted as control characters.

The encoding has been registered under the name windows-1252. In practice, the name cp-1252, or cp1252, was widely used before the registration, and it can still be seen.

Windows Latin 1 is often referred to as the *ANSI character set*, but this is completely misleading. ANSI, the American National Standards Institute, never adopted the set as a standard. Microsoft started using the name because they based the design on a draft for an ANSI standard. Other Windows character codes have also been called "ANSI."

The Windows Latin 1 encoding has existed in somewhat different variants. The main difference in practice is that early versions did not include the euro sign, €. Table 3-4 presents the modern version of the characters in Windows Latin 1 that do not belong to ISO Latin 1. The table is grouped by character semantics and uses Unicode names for the characters. The names used in Microsoft documentation are partly different and vary by document.

Table 3-4. Additional characters in Windows Latin 1

Glyph	Unicode name of character	Code	Win	Comments
–	En dash	U+2013	150	
—	Em dash	U+2014	151	
"	Left double quotation mark	U+201C	147	
"	Right double quotation mark	U+201D	148	
'	Left single quotation mark	U+2018	145	
'	Right single quotation mark	U+2109	146	Also apostrophe
‹	Single left-pointing angle quotation mark	U+2039	139	Left guillemet
›	Single right-pointing angle quotation mark	U+203A	155	Right guillemet
„	Double low-9 quotation mark	U+201E	132	Baseline quote
‚	Single low-9 quotation mark	U+201A	130	
…	Horizontal ellipsis	U+2026	133	
•	Bullet	U+2022	149	
†	Dagger	U+2020	134	
‡	Double dagger	U+2021	135	
˜	Small tilde	U+02DC	152	Diacritic-like
ˆ	Modifier letter circumflex accent	U+02C6	136	Diacritic-like
‰	Per mille sign	U+2030	137	One thousandth
™	Trademark sign	U+2122	153	
ƒ	Latin small letter "f" with hook	U+0192	131	"Florin"
š	Latin small letter "s" with caron	U+0161	154	
Š	Latin capital letter "S" with caron	U+0160	138	
ž	Latin small letter "z" with caron	U+017E	158	Added with euro
Ž	Latin capital letter "Z" with caron	U+017D	142	Added with euro
œ	Latin small ligature oe	U+0153	156	In French
Œ	Latin capital ligature OE	U+0152	140	In French
Ÿ	Latin capital letter "Y" with dieresis	U+0178	159	In French
€	Euro sign	U+20AC	128	Added later

Other Windows Character Codes

Microsoft has also defined other Windows-specific 8-bit character codes that resemble ISO 8859 encodings, such as Windows Latin 2, also known as Windows Central European or Windows East European. They, too, use the range of control codes (128–159) for added punctuation and other characters. In addition to this, the encodings may differ from the corresponding ISO 8859 encoding in other positions. In particular, Windows Latin 2 differs from ISO 8859-2 in several positions.

The Windows codes are widely used as de facto standards in many environments. If you travel to Central/Eastern Europe and use computers there, you will find that they very often have Windows Latin 2 as the default encoding.

The Windows codes are known as windows-1250 through windows-1258 in the official registry of character encodings; these names are often called *MIME names* of encodings, for reasons explained in Chapter 10. Moreover, there is windows-874, which has not been officially registered. In practice, somewhat different names are used, as shown in Table 3-5. Note that the numbering of windows-1250 etc. differs from the numbering of the corresponding ISO 8859 standards. The table also compares the codes with ISO 8859 codes; differences in the range 128–159 are not mentioned here.

Table 3-5. Widely used Windows character codes

MIME	Common name	Compare to	Differences
windows-1250	Windows Central/East Eur.	ISO 8859-2	Differ in some positions
windows-1251	Windows Cyrillic	ISO 8859-5	Different ordering
windows-1252	Windows Latin 1 (West Eur.)	ISO 8859-1	
windows-1253	Windows Greek	ISO 8859-7	Differ in some positions
windows-1254	Windows Turkish	ISO 8859-9	
windows-1255	Windows Hebrew	ISO 8859-8	Some differences
windows-1256	Windows Arabic	ISO 8859-6	Major differences
windows-1257	Windows Baltic	ISO 8859-13	A few differences
windows-1258	Windows Vietnamese	(ISO 8859-1)	Separate design
windows-874	Windows Thai	ISO 8859-11	

The windows-1258 encoding has no direct ISO 8859 counterpart, but its overall design is the same as in ISO 8859-1, with the added characters as in windows-1252 and with some modifications made to meet some needs of the Vietnamese language.

Names like cp1250 or cp-1250 (instead of windows-1250) are often used, but they are not official (registered).

For detailed information, consult Microsoft's documentation "Code pages supported by Windows," *http://www.microsoft.com/globaldev/reference/wincp.mspx*.

Other 8-bit Codes

There is a large number of 8-bit encodings, including HP Roman-8, KOI8-R (for Russian), and many others. A few of them are discussed below.

In general, full conversions between 8-bit character codes are not possible. For example, the Macintosh character repertoire contains the Greek letter pi (π), which does not exist in ISO Latin 1 at all. Naturally, a text can be converted (by a simple program that uses a conversion table) from Macintosh character code to ISO 8859-1 if the text contains only those characters that belong to the ISO Latin 1 character repertoire.

If a document needs to contain, say, both French and Greek (in Greek letters), then no existing 8-bit code would be suitable. Such codes might contain accented characters needed in French, or Greek letters, but not both. It would be impractical to define new codes for every possible combination of characters you might need, and often impossible due to the limitation to a total of 256 code points.

Hence, it is natural to ask whether it should be possible to *switch* between encodings within a file. For example, could you use ISO 8859-1 for the French text, and then switch to ISO 8859-7 for Greek text, and back to ISO 8859-1? Such ideas have been developed, but their use is much more limited than one might think.

The standard ISO 2022 (and the equivalent ECMA-35) defines a general framework for switching between 8-bit codes (and other codes). One of the basic ideas is that code positions 128–159 (decimal) are reserved for use as control codes (*C1 controls*). Some of those codes are used for switching (shifting) purposes, to specify that subsequent data is in a different encoding. Note that the Windows character sets do not fit well into this scheme, since they use codes in that range for printable characters. The standard is rather complex, and only parts of it have been implemented and used. It is used particularly for East Asian languages, such as Japanese, which uses different writing systems. However, even for such purposes, Unicode offers a more uniform approach.

DOS Code Pages

In MS DOS systems, different character codes are used; they are called "code pages." The original American code page was CP 437, which includes some Greek letters, mathematical symbols, and characters that can be used as elements in simple pseudo-graphics. Later, CP 850 became popular, since it contains letters needed for Western European languages —largely the same letters as ISO 8859-1, but in different code positions. Note that DOS code pages are quite different from Windows character codes, although the latter are sometimes referred to by names like cp-1252 (same as windows-1252)! For further confusion, Microsoft now prefers to use the notion *OEM code page* for the DOS character set used in a particular country.

The registered names of DOS code pages as encodings (for use on the Internet) have no space or hyphen: cp437, cp850, etc. They have alias names like IBM437, IBM850, etc., because of the once important role of IBM in the PC market and in development.

In character-encoding menus in Save dialogs, web browsers, etc., you can often see entries like "Cyrillic (DOS)." They refer to DOS code pages designed for particular cultural environment. In that sense, they correspond to the Windows codes mentioned earlier. Otherwise, DOS and Windows code pages can be quite different, in the allocation of code numbers and even in the character repertoire.

Even in modern Windows systems, the command-line user interface (DOS window) still typically uses some DOS code page, so if you try to view a text file there (using the type command, for example), you'll probably get odd results: the data, which is most likely in some Windows encoding, will be interpreted according to another encoding.

DOS code pages should not normally be used for new data, but there is a lot of existing data in such encodings. The main reason for getting acquainted with DOS code pages is finding out how to convert from them to some other encodings. It is not always trivial to identify what the encoding really is, since there are several DOS code pages with similar names and different versions of the code pages.

Detailed information on DOS code pages is available as code page-to-Unicode mapping tables at *http://www.unicode.org/Public/MAPPINGS/VENDORS/MICSFT/PC/*.

The use of the coding space is rather different in the DOS and Windows encodings, except for the range 0 through 7F (hexadecimal), which follows the ASCII tradition. Figure 3-1 shows the "upper halves" of Windows and DOS encodings designed for Central/Eastern Europe. There are differences in the character repertoires—e.g., due to the presence of various drawing characters. Most strikingly, the allocation of characters is almost completely different.

Mac Encodings

On Macintosh (Mac) computers, there has been less variation in character codes than on Windows PCs. However, much like Windows code pages, there are several codes for different languages and language groups. They can now be called "legacy encodings," since the Mac world is moving to Unicode.

The most widely known legacy encoding is *Mac Roman*, which is a combination of ASCII, accented letters, mathematical symbols, and other ingredients. The general idea is similar to that of ISO 8859-1 and windows-1252, but the repertoires are different. At *http://www.unicode.org/Public/MAPPINGS/VENDORS/APPLE/*, you can find cross-mapping tables from Mac Roman as well as other legacy encodings to Unicode.

The original Mac Roman code is presented visually in Figure 3-2. Code positions 0 through 1F (hexadecimal) are not shown there; they (as well as position 7F) are assigned to control characters the same way as in the ASCII context, although partly in a manner different from that used in the ASCII context. As you can see, code positions 20 through 7F (the first six rows in the figure) are the same as in ASCII. The same applies to other legacy encodings, with few exceptions.

As you can see, the Mac Roman character set contains several punctuation marks and mathematical symbols that are not present in ISO 8859-1. On the other hand, it lacks the following ISO 8859-1 characters: multiplication sign ×; superscripts ^{1}, ^{2}, and ^{3}; vulgar fractions ¼, ½, and ¾; broken vertical bar ¦; "y" with acute ý and Ý; Icelandic letters eth (ð, Ð) and thorn (þ, Þ); and the soft hyphen. Moreover, in the modern version, Mac Roman has the euro sign € instead of the currency sign ¤.

Thus, perfect conversion between Mac Roman and ISO 8859-1 (or windows-1252) is generally not possible. It can of course be performed if the text contains only characters that belong to both encodings.

Windows Latin 2 (windows-1250)

€		‚		„	…	†	‡		‰	Š	‹	Ś	Ť	Ž	Ź
	'	'	"	"	•	–	—		™	š	›	ś	ť	ž	ź
	ˇ	˘	Ł	¤	Ą	¦	§	¨	©	Ş	«	¬		®	Ż
°	±	˛	ł	´	µ	¶	·	¸	ą	ş	»	Ľ	˝	ľ	ż
Ŕ	Á	Â	Ă	Ä	Ĺ	Ć	Ç	Č	É	Ę	Ë	Ě	Í	Î	Ď
Đ	Ń	Ň	Ó	Ô	Ő	Ö	×	Ř	Ů	Ú	Ű	Ü	Ý	Ţ	ß
ŕ	á	â	ă	ä	ĺ	ć	ç	č	é	ę	ë	ě	í	î	ď
đ	ń	ň	ó	ô	ő	ö	÷	ř	ů	ú	ű	ü	ý	ţ	˙

DOS Latin 2 (cp852)

Ç	ü	é	â	ä	ů	ć	ç	ł	ë	Ő	ő	î	Ź	Ä	Ć
É	Ĺ	ĺ	ô	ö	Ľ	ľ	Ś	ś	Ö	Ü	Ť	ť	Ł	×	č
á	í	ó	ú	Ą	ą	Ž	ž	Ę	ę	¬	ź	Č	ş	«	»
░	▒	▓	│	┤	Á	Â	Ě	Ş	╣	║	╗	╝	Ż	ż	┐
└	┴	┬	├	─	┼	Ă	ă	╚	╔	╩	╦	╠	═	╬	¤
đ	Đ	Ď	Ë	ď	Ň	Í	Î	ě	┘	┌	█	▄	Ţ	Ů	▀
Ó	ß	Ô	Ń	ń	ň	Š	š	Ŕ	Ú	ŕ	Ű	ý	Ý	ţ	´
	˝	˛	ˇ	˘	§	÷	¸	°	¨	·		ű	Ř	ř	■

Figure 3-1. Windows Latin 2 and DOS Latin 2 (characters in code positions 80 through FF in hexadecimal)

In fact, Mac Roman contains a character in position F0, too (the grayed first cell on the last row of the table in Figure 3-2). It is the stylized apple that is used as the symbol of the Apple company, called "Apple logo." Unicode does not include symbols of companies and trademarks, so the mapping tables map the character to U+F8FF, which is the last code point in the Private Use area, to be used by "private agreement" only.

Modern Mac computers can use a wider character repertoire, but there is still Mac software that is limited to the Mac Roman encoding. This is one of the main reasons for saying that the character repertoire of ISO 8859-1 is not absolutely universally supported yet.

Mac OS X uses Unicode as its primary character code. Legacy encodings are supported either directly, in a limited manner, in some programs, or through the Mac OS Text

	!	"	#	$	%	&	'	(	)	*	+	,	-	.	/
0	1	2	3	4	5	6	7	8	9	:	;	<	=	>	?
@	A	B	C	D	E	F	G	H	I	J	K	L	M	N	O
P	Q	R	S	T	U	V	W	X	Y	Z	[	\	]	^	_
`	a	b	c	d	e	f	g	h	i	j	k	l	m	n	o
p	q	r	s	t	u	v	w	x	y	z	{	|	}	~	
Ä	Å	Ç	É	Ñ	Ö	Ü	á	à	â	ä	ã	å	ç	é	è
ê	ë	í	ì	î	ï	ñ	ó	ò	ô	ö	õ	ú	ù	û	ü
†	°	¢	£	§	•	¶	ß	®	©	™	´	¨	≠	Æ	Ø
∞	±	≤	≥	¥	µ	∂	∑	∏	π	∫	ª	º	Ω	æ	ø
¿	¡	¬	√	ƒ	≈	Δ	«	»	…		À	Ã	Õ	Œ	œ
–	—	"	"	'	'	÷	◊	ÿ	Ÿ	⁄	¤	‹	›	fi	fl
‡	·	‚	„	‰	Â	Ê	Á	Ë	È	Í	Î	Ï	Ì	Ó	Ô
	Ò	Ú	Û	Ù	ı	^	~	¯	˘	˙	˚	¸	˝	˛	ˇ

Figure 3-2. Mac Roman encoding, code positions 20 to FF (hexadecimal)

Encoding Converter or other conversion software. For more information, consult the document "Background information on Unicode mapping tables for Mac OS legacy text encodings," which is available at the following site: *http://www.unicode.org/Public/ MAPPINGS/VENDORS/APPLE/Readme.txt*.

EBCDIC

The EBCDIC code was defined by IBM, and it was once in widespread use on large "mainframe" computers but has lost relative importance. EBCDIC exists in different national variants, and due to its nature as a vendor-defined code, EBCDIC lacked rigorous definitions.

EBCDIC deviates from most 8-bit codes in basic structure. It contains all ASCII characters but in quite different code positions. Another peculiarity is that in EBCDIC, normal letters A–Z do not all appear in consecutive code positions. They are in alphabetic order, but with gaps. The original reason for this was related to punched card technology. EBCDIC has been the most important practical reason why it is incorrect (even in the limited context of the English language) to test for a character being a letter simply by checking that it is in the range A–Z or a–z, in comparison of code numbers.

For example, the CP 037 version of EBCDIC, as defined by the cross mapping table at *http://www.unicode.org/Public/MAPPINGS/VENDORS/MICSFT/EBCDIC/*, is shown in Figure 3-3. Code positions 0 through 3F (hexadecimal) are not shown; they (as well as

	â	ä	à	á	ã	å	ç	ñ	¢	.	<	(	+	|
&	é	ê	ë	è	í	î	ï	ì	ß	!	$	*	)	;	¬
-	/	Â	Ä	À	Á	Ã	Å	Ç	Ñ	¦	,	%	_	>	?
ø	É	Ê	Ë	È	Í	Î	Ï	Ì	`	:	#	@	'	=	"
Ø	a	b	c	d	e	f	g	h	i	«	»	ð	ý	þ	±
°	j	k	l	m	n	o	p	q	r	ª	º	æ	¸	Æ	¤
µ	~	s	t	u	v	w	x	y	z	¡	¿	Ð	Ý	Þ	®
^	£	¥	·	©	§	¶	¼	½	¾	[	]	‾	¨	´	×
{	A	B	C	D	E	F	G	H	I		ô	ö	ò	ó	õ
}	J	K	L	M	N	O	P	Q	R	¹	û	ü	ù	ú	ÿ
\	÷	S	T	U	V	W	X	Y	Z	²	Ô	Ö	Ò	Ó	Õ
0	1	2	3	4	5	6	7	8	9	³	Û	Ü	Ù	Ú	

Figure 3-3. EBCDIC CP 037 characters with code positions 40 to FE (hexadecimal) are the same as the characters of ISO 8859-1, but in a very different order

position FF) are assigned to control characters, though partly in a manner different from that used in the ASCII context. Code positions 40 and 41, appearing as blank here, have been allocated to space U+0020 and no-break space U+00A0, respectively.

The Cyrillic KOI8 Encodings

For languages written in Cyrillic letters, such as Russian and Ukrainian, several 8-bit encodings have been developed. We have already mentioned ISO 8859-5 (Latin/Cyrillic) and windows-1251 (Windows Cyrillic), and there is also DOS Cyrillic and Mac Cyrillic. However, along with windows-1251, the most widely used encoding for Russian is *KOI8-R* (the letter "R" stands for Russian). There are also other versions of KOI8.

The KOI8 encodings assign code positions 0 through 7F as in ASCII and place Cyrillic letters and other characters in the "upper half." As you can see from Figure 3-4, KOI8-R contains a large number of drawing characters. Its repertoire of letters covers only (modern) Russian and a few other languages. In contrast, Windows Cyrillic has many more Cyrillic letters, giving a wider coverage of languages.

Comparing code positions C0 through FF (hexadecimal) in the two encodings—i.e., the last four rows of the tables in Figure 3-4, we notice how they have different schemes for allocating the basic Cyrillic letters. Even if you don't know the Cyrillic alphabet, you probably see that Windows Cyrillic has uppercase letters first, and then lowercase, whereas KOI8-R has them the other way around. In KOI8-R, the letters are not in the Russian alphabetic order but placed so that if the most significant bit of each octet is lost, the text turns into a coarse transliteration with the case of letters reversed: Cyrillic "а" becomes Latin "A," Cyrillic б becomes Latin "B," Cyrillic ц becomes Latin "C," etc.

Windows Cyrillic (windows-1251)

Ђ	Ѓ	,	ѓ	„	…	†	‡	€	‰	Љ	‹	Њ	Ќ	Ћ	Џ
ђ	'	'	"	"	•	–	—		™	љ	›	њ	ќ	ћ	џ
	Ў	ў	Ј	¤	Ґ	¦	§	Ё	©	Є	«	¬		®	Ї
°	±	І	і	ґ	µ	¶	·	ё	№	є	»	ј	Ѕ	ѕ	ї
А	Б	В	Г	Д	Е	Ж	З	И	Й	К	Л	М	Н	О	П
Р	С	Т	У	Ф	Х	Ц	Ч	Ш	Щ	Ъ	Ы	Ь	Э	Ю	Я
а	б	в	г	д	е	ж	з	и	й	к	л	м	н	о	п
р	с	т	у	ф	х	ц	ч	ш	щ	ъ	ы	ь	э	ю	я

KOI8-R

—	│	┌	┐	└	┘	├	┤	┬	┴	┼	▀	▄	█	▌	▐
░	▒	▓	⌠	■	·	√	≈	≤	≥		⌡	°	²	·	÷
═	║	╒	ё	╓	╔	╕	╖	╗	╘	╙	╚	╛	╜	╝	╞
╟	╠	╡	Ё	╢	╣	╤	╥	╦	╧	╨	╩	╪	╫	╬	©
ю	а	б	ц	д	е	ф	г	х	и	й	к	л	м	н	о
п	я	р	с	т	у	ж	в	ь	ы	з	ш	э	щ	ч	ъ
Ю	А	Б	Ц	Д	Е	Ф	Г	Х	И	Й	К	Л	М	Н	О
П	Я	Р	С	Т	У	Ж	В	Ь	Ы	З	Ш	Э	Щ	Ч	Ъ

Figure 3-4. Windows Cyrillic and KOI8-R (code positions 80 through FF hexadecimal)

This implies that if you have Russian text in Windows Cyrillic and your program interprets it according to KOI8-R, or vice versa, words still resemble Russian but in an oddly distorted way. Uppercase becomes lowercase, and vice versa, and with a shift of one position. This is comparable to having "abcdef" munged to "BCDEFG," and such things have actually happened—e.g., in Usenet discussions in the Russian-language *relcom.* * groups, because some people post their messages in KOI8-R, some in Windows Cyrillic, and they might use software that does not include information about the encoding. Modern software can usually handle either encoding, but only if the encoding is properly declared. The situation is not as bad as you might guess, since nowadays most people post in KOI8-R in those groups. If your software does not use that encoding as the default, you probably need to change its settings in order to read *relcom.* * groups.

This illustrates the point (to be elaborated on in Chapter 10) that the multitude of encodings is not a problem as such, as long as there is adequate information of what the encoding is. It is a better approach than trying to make everyone use the same encoding.

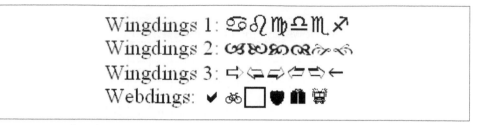

Figure 3-5. Samples of Wingdings fonts

Ad Hoc "8-bit Codes" Defined by Fonts

There is a theoretically quite unsatisfactory, yet widely used method of working with characters: using font settings to extend character repertoire. To take a simple example, use a text-processing program and type the letters abc, and then select them and choose the Symbol font from a font menu. You will probably see the Greek letters αβχ. It seems that this way you can switch between different 8-bit codes, if you have suitable fonts containing various sets of characters. In web authoring, you could achieve a similar effect by using markup like `<font face="Symbol">abc</font>`. (The Appendix contains a table of Symbol font glyphs and their Unicode equivalents.)

This approach may look conceptually simple, and it has often been practically successful, when you just needed some characters on paper, or perhaps on screen. However, it is quite inadequate for any operations where font information may get lost, or ignored. For example, if viewed on a system without the Symbol font, the data in the example in the last paragraph would appear just as "abc." The same happens if the font is changed for some reason, not to mention any operations of saving and sending data as plain text. When data is entered into a database, for example, font information will hardly be saved. A web browser can be configured or instructed to ignore font suggestions on web pages.

Still, the approach can be useful in special circumstances, such as working with some repertoire of uncommon characters. For example, in phonetics, people have often used a special 8-bit font that contains a collection of phonetic (IPA) characters. Although the material is then unreadable without that font (or a comparable tool), things have worked reasonably well within a community that knows what is needed. Similarly, for some languages with a relatively small repertoire of characters, an 8-bit font might be designed and distributed as a quick way of making it possible to use the language

There are some graphic symbols, such as Wingdings symbols, that cannot be effectively used except via a font-based approach. Figure 3-5 shows some symbols that can be produced by applying Wingdings fonts to the text "abcdef." Although some Wingdings symbols have been encoded in Unicode (e.g., as Dingbats), many of them are essentially small decorative drawings rather than characters for writing texts.

Similarly, if you wish to use some "private" characters, such as special characters designed for use within a community, the use of a special font is a simple way to achieve this. If you would use the characters just to create a printed fantasy book, it would not matter that nobody else has your special font. It is possible, but more complicated, to use "private" characters in Unicode: there as a large block of code points reserved for that purpose.

This approach has been used for many languages, especially in circumstances where programs cannot be expected to support anything other than 8-bit encodings. Whenever you see a statement like "you need the … font for viewing this document," the odds are that some strictly font-based approach is used. When Unicode or some other standardized encoding is used, you are not limited to use any particular font; any font that contains the characters will do.

Conceptually, the approach discussed here means that you implicitly define a character by the design of a font. If you put the letter alpha (α) into the code position that is occupied by the letter "a" in ASCII—i.e., 61 (hexadecimal)—you are in the process of defining a character code where that position is allocated for the alpha. However, you rely on the use of a special font, which logically corresponds to a character code conversion.

Unicode and UTF-8

Since the range of code numbers in Unicode is very large, it is useful to have different encodings for different purposes. Some encodings are technically very simple and efficient in terms of internal data processing but wasteful in storage space. Some other encodings aim at compactness, for efficiency in data storage and transfer. Before discussing the encodings, we will consider a general conceptual model, which is aimed at clarifying the different meanings and level of encoding character data.

This discussion deals with Unicode encodings in general terms and in reference to options that you have, as a user, in choosing an encoding. The technical definitions of the encodings (i.e., how data is encoded in detail) are in Chapter 6.

The Conceptual Model: Levels of Coding

In the character context, "coding" or "encoding" of characters can mean different things, at different levels of abstraction. There are several ways to describe the situation, trying to make things clearer and unambiguous. In practice, approaches differ, so sometimes the clarifications end up confusing people. The differences are reflected in terminology. Thus, when reading about characters, you'll see not only unfamiliar words but also words that are familiar to you but have unexpected meanings.

The Internet (IAB) model

Before considering the Unicode model, we consider the superficially simple model that is often called the Internet Architecture Board (IAB) model. It is described in a report of a meeting, published as RFC 2130 (*http://www.rfc-editor.org/rfc/rfc2130.txt*). It has three levels:

Level 1: Coded Character Set
    A collection of abstract characters with code numbers assigned to them

Level 2: Character Encoding Scheme
A mapping from a coded character set (or several such sets) into sequences of octets

Level 3: Transfer Encoding Syntax
A transformation of character data, encoded as a coded character set and possibly as a character encoding scheme too, performed to allow the data to be transmitted

For example, ASCII and Unicode define Coded Character Sets. The Character Encoding Scheme for ASCII uses one octet for each character (and for each code number). For Unicode, there are several possible Character Encodings, such as UTF-8 and UTF-16.

Transfer encoding syntax is something that may or may not be applied. It can consist of an operation that transforms a sequence of octets to another sequence, to be interpreted by different rules. The idea could be, for example, to make sure that all octets used are "safe" in the sense that they can be sent over a connection or a system that may not handle all octets properly. For example, the Base64 transfer encoding uses only a limited repertoire of octets, corresponding to a limited subset of ASCII values.

Evidently, Transfer Encoding Syntax is logically different from the other levels. It is optional, not part of the basic model. The Unicode approach recognizes this, but it also adds two levels: the most abstract level where characters are defined as abstract objects only, without assigning code numbers to them, and an intermediate level, where characters exist as *code units*. A code unit is neither a code number nor a sequence of octets, but at an intermediate abstraction level. The separation of code number from code unit is mostly relevant in Unicode only, but the model itself is of a general nature.

The four-level Unicode model

The Unicode model on character encoding, defined in Unicode Technical Report (UTR) #17 at *http://www.unicode.org/unicode/reports/tr17/*, is summarized in Table 3-6. The last column shows illustrative examples of the way characters (here the Latin "A," in Unicode and UTF-32) could be represented at each level.

Table 3-6. Unicode model of encoding characters

Level of encoding	Explanation	Example
Abstract Character Repertoire	Characters listed and described	"A" (Latin letter A)
Coded Character Set	Characters have code numbers	U+0041
Character Encoding Form	Sequences of code units	00000041
Character Encoding Scheme	Code units mapped to octet strings	00 00 00 41

Thus, to represent the letter "A" in a computer, we logically start by identifying it as an abstract character, as a member of an Abstract Character Repertoire, such as the collection of all Unicode characters. At this level, a character may have a name assigned to it, but its internal representation is in no way fixed.

At the next level, in a Coded Character Set, a code number is assigned to the character according to a character code. The notation U+0041 is, as we have learned, just a way of writing the number 41 (hexadecimal) in a manner that emphasizes its role as a Unicode code number. The code number as such is an abstract mathematical integer.

Next, the code number is mapped to a sequence of code units according to some Character Encoding Form. The size of code units may vary across encodings (7, 8, 16, and 32 bits are typical sizes), but the size is fixed for any particular encoding form. At this level, all characters are of equal size. For Unicode, starting from Version 4.0, the encoding forms are UTF-8, UTF-16, and UTF-32, where the number indicates the number of bits in a code unit. This is sometimes expressed by saying that Unicode is variably an 8-, 16-, or 32-bit code, although it is very easy to misunderstand that. Using UTF-32, for example, U+0041 would map to a 32-bit integer, which we here express as 00000041, to be interpreted in hexadecimal.

The fourth level, Character Encoding Scheme, maps code units to strings of octets. If the encoding form is UTF-32, for example, the encoding scheme maps a 32-bit value to a sequence of four 8-bit values, of octets. This is not a trivial operation, since the order of octets may vary. This reflects different machine architectures, namely different mutual order of octets in a two- or four-octet entity. A 32-bit integer that logically consists of octets o_1, o_2, o_3, and o_4, from most significant to least significant, can be physically represented in the order $o_1o_2o_3o_4$ or in the order $o_4o_3o_2o_1$. To use the usual jargon, "byte order" can be "big endian" versus "little endian." The mapping of code units to octet strings is often called *serialization*.

In practice, Character Encoding Form and Character Encoding Scheme are often not distinguished from each other. A term such as "UTF-16" may refer to a Character Encoding Form only, but it may also refer to a specific Character Encoding Scheme, where the byte order has been fixed.

A mapping of character strings (sequences of abstract characters) to sequences of octets is called a Character Map, or "charmap" for short, in UTR #17. This somewhat odd term thus refers to a mapping that goes from the topmost level, Abstract Character Repertoire, to the bottom level, Character Encoding Scheme. That is, when using this term, we are not interested in what happens at the intermediate level.

A Character Map usually bears the name of a Character Encoding Scheme that determines the mapping in practice. We can more or less identify "Character Map" with "charset" or "character encoding" as understood by nontechnical people. When you select character encoding upon saving a file (e.g., in a Save As dialog), you inevitably fix the representation down to the Character Encoding Scheme.

Transfer Encoding Syntax

In the Unicode view, as mentioned earlier in this chapter, the Transfer Encoding Syntax (TES) is not part of the basic model of character coding. Instead, it is an optional auxiliary transformation. The most common forms of TES are Base64, uuencode (originally developed for Unix), BinHex (developed for Mac), and Quoted Printable (QP).

Transfer encoding helps if you need to send character data from a system to another through a third system that cannot handle 8-bit quantities properly. The third system could even be a mail server that operates on ASCII data only, assuming that every character fits in 7 bits. In some situations, even some ASCII characters might cause problems. In any case, you need a method for encoding octets in a format that can be sent in a safe manner and then restored to the original format by the receiving system.

Thus, the purpose of a TES is to make the data, as an octet string, acceptable to applications and software that might fail to process the original octet string correctly. This especially means avoiding octets that are known or suspected to cause problems.

When you send email on the Internet, for example, your email program may apply some TES on the *outgoing* mail. It may (and indeed should) be capable of interpreting any commonly used TES in *incoming* data. Normally this happens without your knowing. If you are curious, you may view the "raw message source" with some special command (e.g., via File → Properties on Outlook Express). There you can see headers such as:

```
MIME-Version: 1.0
Content-Type: text/plain; charset="iso-8859-1"
Content-Transfer-Encoding: quoted-printable
```

Here, the encoding is iso-8859-1, which means that each character (in the ISO 8859-1 repertoire) is represented as one octet. However, the additional TES modifies this. The QP encoding converts the octet string so that the result contains only a limited repertoire of octets, corresponding to a subset of ASCII. If you view the "raw message source," you will see things such as =E4 where the data contains non-ASCII characters like ä.

Although any TES is normally transparent to users, you may need to get involved in TES issues in email in some cases:

- Some software is unable to handle TES, or conversely requires some TES for some data. This should be rare, but it may happen, especially when you send email so that it will be processed in some special way—e.g., by distribution list software. It would then be your duty to check the settings of your email program, to make sure it does not apply any TES, or applies the required TES. Typically, you would open an Options dialog and find settings for outgoing mail. There you can hopefully switch off or on the setting for Quoted Printable encoding, for example.

- If you process your email using some automated tools, or simply open your mailbox using a simple text editor, you need to be prepared to handling at least some TES. Any automated tool for email processing should use suitable subroutine libraries that take care of TES when needed. However, you might still encounter more or less naïve software that expects message content to be ASCII.

Encodings for Unicode

Originally, before extending the code range past 16 bits, the "native" Unicode encoding was *UCS-2*, which presents each code number as two consecutive octets m and n so that the number equals $256 \times m + n$. This means, to express it in computer jargon, that the code number is presented as a 2-byte integer. According to the Unicode Consortium, the term UCS-2 should now be avoided, as it is associated with the 16-bit limitations.

UTF-32 encodes each code position as a 32-bit binary integer—i.e., as four octets. This is a very obvious and simple encoding. However, it is inefficient in terms of the number of octets needed. If we have normal English text or other text that contains ISO Latin 1 characters only, the length of the Unicode encoded octet sequence is four times the length of the string in ISO 8859-1 encoding. UTF-32 is rarely used, except perhaps in internal operations (since it is very simple for the purposes of string processing).

UTF-16 represents each code position in the BMP (Basic Multilingual Plane) as two octets. Other code positions are presented using so-called surrogate pairs, using some code positions in the BMP reserved for the purpose. This, too, is a very simple encoding when the data contains BMP characters only. For the BMP, it is also efficient in processing in the sense that you can directly address the *n*th character of a string, since all characters occupy the same number of storage locations.

UTF-8 is the most common encoding used for Unicode, especially on the Internet. Using it, code numbers less than 128 (effectively, the ASCII repertoire) are presented "as such," using one octet for each code (character). All other codes are presented, according to a relatively complicated method, so that one code (character) is presented as a sequence of two to six octets, each of which is in the range 128–255. This means that in a sequence of octets, octets in the range 0–127 (bytes with the most significant bit set to 0) directly represent ASCII characters, whereas octets in the range 128–255 (bytes with the most significant bit set to 1) are to be interpreted as multiple-octet encoded presentations of characters.

UTF-8 is efficient in terms of storage required, if the data consists predominantly of ASCII characters with just a few "special characters" in addition to them, and reasonably efficient for dominantly ISO Latin 1 text.

The document "IETF Policy on Character Sets and Languages" (RFC 2277, BCP 18) clearly favors UTF-8. It specifies that new Internet protocols must support UTF-8; they may support other encodings as well.

UTF-7 was designed to deal with situations where data cannot be safely transmitted using arbitrary 8-bit bytes—e.g., on connections that use the first bit of an octet for parity checks, passing just 7 bits through as actual data. In UTF-7, each character code is represented as a sequence of one or more octets in the range 0–127 (bytes with most significant bit set to 0, or 7-bit bytes, hence the name). Most ASCII characters are presented as such, each as one octet, but for obvious reasons some octet values must be reserved for use as "escape" octets, specifying that the octet together with a certain number of subsequent octets forms a multioctet encoded presentation of one character.

As you can see, the number in the names UTF-32, UTF-16, UTF-8, and UTF-7 indicates the size of the code unit in bits.

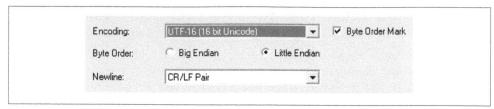

Figure 3-6. Choice of encoding settings in BabelPad

Saving as Unicode

Many programs let you save your data in different encodings. Even the Save As dialog in Notepad has some alternatives, such as "ANSI" (which means windows-1252), "Unicode" (which means UTF-16), "Unicode big-endian" (which means UTF-16 with swapped byte order), and "UTF-8" (which surprisingly means UTF-8).

Advanced software that has been especially designed for multilingual applications typically contains explicit options for setting the encoding. Figure 3-6 illustrates this for BabelPad, the editor discussed in Chapter 1. You can choose UTF-8, UTF-16, or UTF-32 (as Character Encoding Scheme) from a drop-down menu, and then (when applicable) select the byte order. There is also a setting for the newline convention—i.e., which character or characters are used to indicate a line break (see Chapter 8); this is logically distinct from any encoding issues but often presented along with encoding for practical reasons.

On the other hand, many text-processing and other application programs do not let you control the character encoding. They use their built-in settings for that, and might even use a data format of their own that contains information about the encoding.

Encodings for East Asian Language

The languages written in East Asia pose special problems to encoding characters, since the languages use, in part, a very rich character repertoire. Before considering the problems of characters of Chinese origin, we discuss the modern writing system of Vietnamese, which is just about manageable with 8-bit codes.

 These encodings use different approaches to the problem of representing a large repertoire of characters as sequences of octets. We will not consider their technical nature or the choice between them in this book. Consult *CJKV Information Processing* by Ken Lunde (O'Reilly) for detailed information on such matters.

Vietnamese 8-bit Codes

The Vietnamese language is nowadays written in Latin letters but with several diacritic marks, including multiple marks on a single letter. For example, the name of Vietnam in Vietnamese is "Việt Nam" (note that the "e" has both a circumflex above it and a dot below it).

One reason for this is that Vietnamese is a tonal language: the tone (e.g., falling versus rising tone) of a syllable is important and often makes a difference in meaning. Quite often, the tone, indicated by a diacritic mark, is the only thing that distinguishes between words.

In texts in English and other Western languages, it is common to omit all or most of the diacritic marks in Vietnamese names. They are difficult to produce and difficult to preserve in data transmission and processing. However, at least in Vietnamese itself, it would be inappropriate to omit the diacritic marks.

Due to the number of extra characters needed, the ISO 8859 model is not suitable for Vietnamese. There are various 8-bit character codes developed for it; the most common of them are *TCVN*, *VISCII*, *VPN*, and *windows-1258* ("Windows Vietnamese").

VISCII (described in RFC 1456) uses almost all code points in the hexadecimal range 20–FF for printable characters, and it even allocates some points in the 0–1F range to printable characters. Thus, although it has the range 20–7F allocated as in ASCII, it's not a pure extension of ASCII.

Windows-1258 is not very different from ISO-8859-1 but uses some code points for combining diacritic marks. Thus, to write ệ, for example, you would write ê followed by a combining dot below, instead of using a single code point for the character.

Encodings for Chinese

The traditional Chinese writing system uses thousands of ideographic characters. In the 20th century, a simplified version of the writing system was developed in the People's Republic of China, using simpler forms for the characters. It is called "Simplified Chinese" as opposite to "Traditional Chinese." Thus, the difference between the two is in the writing system, rather than the language as a whole, although these alternatives often appear in a menu for language choice.

Either variant of the writing system can be encoded in different ways. For example, in Mozilla, the menu of encodings contains the following options:

- Chinese Simplified (GB18030)
- Chinese Simplified (GB2312)
- Chinese Simplified (GBK)
- Chinese Simplified (HZ)
- Chinese Simplified (ISO-2022-CN)
- Chinese Traditional (Big5)
- Chinese Traditional (Big5-HKSCS)
- Chinese Traditional (EUC-TW)

The names in parentheses refer to specific encodings. The abbreviation "GB" refers to Chinese words that mean Chinese national standard in the People's Republic of China.

The abbreviation "Big5" refers to an agreement on character encoding by five big international companies in the computer industry.

For our purposes in this book, it is sufficient to know that several different encodings for Chinese are in use, and one or another is often strongly preferred by a user or by an organization. The choice may involve political considerations as well. Thus, if you design an application that allows Chinese characters to be entered and shown, it is generally not sufficient to support Unicode alone. You could use some Unicode encoding(s) internally —e.g., in a database—but the input and output operations should be carried out using methods that allow at least some of the specific Chinese encodings to be used as well. This means that the application needs to use character code converters.

Encodings for Japanese

The Japanese language is written using three different types of characters: kanji characters, which are Japanese versions of Chinese characters, and hiragana and katakana, which are much smaller repertoires of characters and are used to describe pronunciation. Although it is possible to represent hiragana or katakana within an 8-bit code, it is usually culturally unacceptable to restrict the writing of Japanese that way. Normally, Japanese is written using a mixture of the three writing systems, and perhaps with additional characters such as Latin letters, too.

Encodings for Japanese include EUC-JP, ISO-2022-JP, and Shift_JIS. The ISO-2022-JP encoding uses the switching mechanism defined in the ISO 2022 standard, effectively using control codes to specify which 8-bit code (representing 256 different characters in the repertoire) is used at each point. Other codes use different approaches to the switching problem. Shift_JIS is also called Shift-JIS or SJIS.

Encodings for Korean

Korean was previously written using characters of Chinese origin; hence the abbreviation "CJK," which refers to Chinese characters in a broad sense, with Chinese, Japanese, and Korean versions. The abbreviation "CJKV" adds the old Vietnamese versions to these.

Nowadays, Korean is mostly written using hangul characters, which were specifically developed for Korean. They constitute a very logical and regular system for writing words phonetically. Hangul has been called an "alphabetic syllabary," since it can be regarded as a system of syllable symbols that consist of letters of an alphabet. The number of letters is comparable in size to the English alphabet, whereas the syllable symbols, as precomposed sequences of letters, constitute a very large set.

If Korean is represented in a form that encodes the letters separately, a program for rendering text needs to recognize how adjacent letters constitute syllables and to show them accordingly. The construction of the written text needs to combine glyphs in specific ways. It is much easier to render Korean text encoded using syllable characters.

Encodings for Korean include EUC-KR, ISO-2022-KR, JOHAB, and UHC.

Converters and Transcoding

As the preceding discussion of some encodings has shown, there are many character codes and encodings in use now and in the future. Unicode is a tool that helps to deal with this complexity, rather than a once and for all solution that replaces all other codes. Even if you use Unicode for everything you can, you still have reasons to know about conversions between encodings:

- Old data often exists in different other encodings ("legacy data")
- Old software, which you may need to use or to interface with, often requires input or writes output in some non-Unicode encoding ("legacy software")
- Other people still use and prefer other encodings, and you may need to cope with that in email, exchange of text files, web page design, etc.

The process of converting character data from one encoding into another was previously often called *recoding*, but nowadays the term *transcoding* is more common. A program or part of program that has been specifically designed to perform *transcodings* can be called a *converter*. Transcoding is often performed by programs that do something quite different as their main job.

Transcoding Tools

For example, a text editor can often read and write data in several encodings, including the possibility of reading data in one encoding and saving it in another, as discussed in Chapter 1. This means that the program has to transcode—i.e., to contain a built-in converter. For an occasional conversion task, the simplest way is usually to open a text file in a suitable editor or word processor and to use the Save As function to save the content under a different filename and with a different encoding. For repeated and often bulky conversions, something more efficient is needed.

When appropriate, a converter can be very simple. Transcoding between 8-bit codes is a matter of mapping each code number to another code number according to a table, and this can be implemented rather efficiently. If you need to write such a converter, the main challenge is to find the relevant mapping table, or tables, from a reliable source. Beware that many codes exist in slightly different versions.

There are cross-mapping tables available at *http://www.unicode.org/Public/MAPPINGS* for transcoding between various encodings and Unicode. They are plain text files but in a format that can easily be read and parsed to construct suitable data structures. For example, the document *http://www.unicode.org/Public/MAPPINGS/VENDORS/MISC/ KOI8-R.TXT*, which is about the Russian KOI8-R encoding, contains lines like the following:

```
0xBF    0x00A9    #    COPYRIGHT SIGN
0xC0    0x044E    #    CYRILLIC SMALL LETTER YU
0xC1    0x0430    #    CYRILLIC SMALL LETTER A
```

This says, for example, that code number BF (in hexadecimal) in KOI8-R denotes the same character as code number 00A9 in Unicode. Anything after the # character in this format is to be treated as comment, and the names of the characters are just for human readers. They are not needed in any way in the transcoding process.

General purpose subroutine libraries often contain transcoding routines. Typically, if you pass a string and the names of two encodings as parameters, you will get the transcoded string as output.

Free Recode

Probably the best known general purpose converter is Free Recode, available from *http://recode.progiciels-bpi.ca/*. It has been designed for use as a so-called filter (in the Unix sense)—i.e., as a program that takes input from the standard input stream (called *stdin* in Unix) and writes the output to the standard output stream (*stdout*). This means that it is typically used as a component of a chain of programs (a *pipe*), where data is processed in phases. In such usage, each component is more or less assumed to work correctly. Therefore, Free Recode plays fast and loose. If the input is correct, so that all data actually represents characters in the source encoding and has a representation in the target encoding, the output is fine. If there are errors in the data—e.g., a character that is unrepresentable in the target encoding—no error message is given, and the output is more or less unpredictable. Moreover, when you pass a filename as an argument to Free Recode, the program performs an "in situ" conversion—i.e., it replaces the old content of the file with the new, transcoded version. It is your responsibility as the user to create a backup copy of the original content if you need to, and usually you do.

Free Recode is available as an executable (*.exe*) file for Windows. When installing it, it is best to add the name of the folder where you put it into the default path. (You do not need to do this if you put the file into the same folder as your data files, but gets rather awkward if you perform many transcodings.) Then you can use Free Recode via the command-line interface (DOS prompt) using a command like:

```
recode cp-437..windows-1252 test.txt
```

This command takes the content of the file *test.txt*, interprets it as CP-437 encoded, and transcodes it into windows-1252. The result overwrites the original content of *test.txt*.

There are several converters available commercially, too. You may find them more suitable, maybe due to a graphic user interface or wider support of different encodings. Searching Google for "character * converter" can be useful in finding them.

The iconv Converter

Unix systems normally contain a converter called *iconv*, which has a simple interface, where you specify the source ("from") encoding after the switch -f, the destination ("to") encoding after the switch -t, and then the source file. The result is written to standard output, which you can direct to a file as usual on Unix. For example:

```
iconv -f iso-8859-1 -t utf-8 demo.txt >demo.utf
```

Check man iconv for more instructions. Beware that your system might have an old version of *iconv*, with rather limited support for different encodings. With some expertise, you could download and install GNU *iconv* to improve the situation. GNU *iconv* contains the *libiconv* library, which you can use when writing programs. For more information, consult *http://www.gnu.org/software/libiconv/*.

Using Character Codes

Several factors affect the choice of character encoding for some particular area of application or purpose. The factors range from the nature of use and technical possibilities and limitations to policy decisions and external requirements. In typical situations, however, the choice is relatively simple.

For example, if you live in Sweden and wish to communicate in Swedish, you normally choose ISO 8859-1 for email, web pages, and plain text files. That's what practically all people in Sweden can work with, and it is reasonably acceptable. There are good reasons for using a larger character repertoire, such as some punctuation marks, but they are probably not good enough to justify the potential risks of using Windows Latin 1 or Unicode. On the other hand, as soon as you really need to include words in, say, Eastern European languages, or technical special symbols, you should probably switch to Unicode, normally using UTF-8 encoding. In that case, you should make a reasonable effort in making sure that the recipients have software that can handle the encoding and the characters you use.

Repertoire Requirements

Each character encoding allows a specific repertoire of characters to be written. Therefore, the set of characters that you need imposes restrictions on the encodings that you can use.

However, as discussed in Chapter 2, in different data formats, there are *escape mechanisms* that let you enter characters that cannot be written directly in the selected encoding. Thus, if you write a web page in English and may occasionally need an omega character Ω, for example, you can use ISO-8859-1 or even ASCII, since you can represent the special character using the entity reference Ω.

Different languages have rather different requirements on the repertoire. In the section "What's in a Character" in Chapter 1, some sources of information on the character requirements of languages were mentioned. The database at *http://www.eki.ee/letter/* can be used to list the characters used in many languages (written in Latin or Cyrillic letters).

The requirements are, however, largely debatable, and they are relative rather than absolute. Does English need é? Most sources don't mention it as a letter of the English alphabet, but it is regarded by many as necessary for correct writing of English texts.

For normal modern English that does not contain special notations, the repertoire of Windows Latin 1 is sufficient, whereas, for example, the ISO Latin 1 repertoire is insufficient (due to the lack of some punctuation marks). This does not mean that you should use the

Windows Latin 1 encoding (windows-1252). You can use UTF-8, or ISO-8859-1, or even ASCII, and accept the consequences.

Encodings and the Internet

Most important, make sure that any Internet-related software that you use to send data *specifies the encoding* correctly in suitable headers. There are two things involved: there must be a header that reflects the actual encoding used and the encoding used must be one that is widely understood by the (potential) recipients' software. You often need to make compromises in regard to the latter aim: you may need to use an encoding that is not yet widely supported to get your message through at all.

In principle, you should first determine the character repertoire you need in a document, database, web page, or other context. Then you should proceed to determining the best possible character code and encoding. In practice, things don't quite work that way. We need to consider some widely recognized encodings and choose between them. Some rules of thumb:

- In email to people that you do not know, use US-ASCII if possible. If not possible, try to analyze whether the recipient(s) can handle some other encoding. When needed, ask for permission to send non-ASCII data as attachments.

- In messages on various international discussion forums, use US-ASCII even if the forum software supports other characters. Check the rules of the forum for other alternatives.

- In email to people in a particular cultural environment, or in discussion forums where a language other than English is used, find out what people mostly do there, and do the same. Usually there is one dominant encoding that you should use.

- On web pages, try to express yourself in ISO-8859-1. For pages in languages other than English, you could often use some widely understood encoding (such as ISO-8859-2 for Central/East European languages). However, UTF-8 is fairly well supported, too, these days. Use UTF-8, if ISO-8859-1 is not practical and there's no particular reason to use one of the 8-bit encodings for different languages.

- In projects and activities where information providers and editors work with different systems and tools, be conservative and try to live with ASCII or ISO 8859-1 or perhaps some other 8-bit code. The reason is that most tools, including simple text editors, can handle such encodings, whereas Unicode encodings often pose problems, and many people do not know how to work with them. Note that some data formats, such as HTML and XML, let you escape from the limitations set by the encoding, and this can be feasible if you need extra characters only rarely.

If you use, say, Outlook Express to send email or to post to Usenet groups, make sure it sends the message in a reasonable form. In particular, make sure it does not send the message as HTML or duplicate it by sending it both as plain text and as HTML (select plain text only). In regard to character encoding, make sure it is something widely understood, such as ASCII, some ISO 8859 encoding, or UTF-8, depending on how large a character repertoire you need.

In particular, avoid sending data in a proprietary encoding (like the Macintosh encoding or a DOS or Windows encoding) to a public network. At the very least, if you do that, make sure that the message heading specifies the encoding! There's nothing wrong with using such an encoding within a single computer or in data transfer between similar computers. But when sent to the Internet, data should be converted to a more widely known encoding by the sending program. If you cannot find a way to configure your program to do that, get another program.

In email programs, there's typically a "Tools" or "Settings" menu, where you can set things like the format and encoding of outgoing messages. The hard part is to understand what the settings and the options are about, but at this point, you should have most if not all the information needed for that. Having checked the settings, you can test them by sending email to yourself and viewing the "hidden data."

The "hidden data" in an email (or Usenet) message consists of the message headers and the message body interpreted as plain text. Normally you see that data as formatted by your email program. This includes interpreting the content according to the specified encoding and displaying some (but usually not all) of the information in the headers, such as the sender's name and email address. There are different ways to view such information, or to view just the headers. The ways are not always easy to find; in Outlook Express for example, you can select the received message and select File → Properties. In Mozilla Thunderbird, you can use View → Message source, and you will see the message headers and raw content in a new window, as illustrated in Figure 3-7. The Content-Type header contains a charset parameter that specifies the encoding. In the absence of such information, the ASCII encoding would be implied.

Encoding in Offline Data

In regard to other forms of transfer of data in digital form, such as diskette or CD-ROM, information about encoding is important, too. The problem is typically handled by guesswork. Often the crucial thing is to know which program was used to generate the data, since the text data might be inside a file in, say, the MS Word format, which can only be read by (a suitable version of) MS Word or by a program that knows its internal data format. That format, once recognized, might contain information that specifies the character encoding used in the text data included; or it might not, in which case one has to ask the sender, or make a guess, or use trial and error—viewing the data using different encodings until something sensible appears.

Make sure you write down the encoding and make information about it available along with the data. This could mean a separate document on a CD-ROM, or a note written with a pen on the CD-ROM or its cover, or a sheet of paper you store and send with the data. This may sound trivial, but it is often neglected. It is best to specify the encoding in two

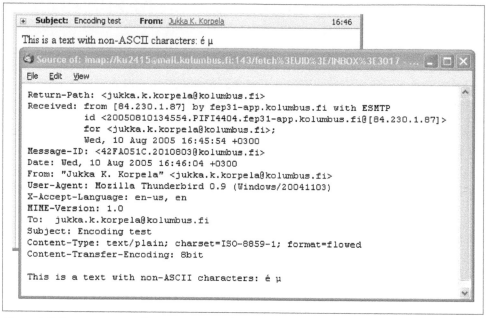

Figure 3-7. Viewing an email message in raw format ("source"), with headers that should indicate the character encoding

ways: by its official name, and by its more widely known informal name. For example: "The files on this diskette are Windows Latin 2 (windows-1250) encoded."

Common Choices of Encoding

Some widely used choices of encoding for different languages are presented in Table 3-7, identified by name of language or a name for a collection of languages, as commonly used in menus in programs.

Table 3-7. Commonly used encodings for some languages

Language(s)	Encodings	Notes
Arabic	iso-8859-6, windows-1256	
Armenian	ARMSCII-8	
Baltic	iso-8859-4, windows-1257	Latvian, Lithuanian
Central European	iso-8859-2, windows-1250	Czech, Polish…
Chinese	gb2312, hz-gb-2312, big5	
Cyrillic	koi8-r, koi8-u, windows-1251	koi8-r: Russian, koi8-u: Ukrainian
Farsi (Persian)	windows-1256, MacFarsi	
Georgian	GEOSTD8	
Greek	iso-8859-7, windows-1253	

Language(s)	Encodings	Notes
Hebrew	iso-8859-8, windows-1255	
Japanese	euc-jp, iso-2022-jp, Shift_JIS	
Korean	euc-kr, iso-2022-kr	
Thai	windows-874, TIS-620	
Turkish	iso-8859-9, windows-1254	
Vietnamese	windows-1258	
Western European	iso-8859-1, windows-1252	English, French, German, Italian...

As you can see, some encodings are intended rather specifically for a single language, while some are for a wide group of languages. This depends mostly on character repertoire requirements rather than language family relationships.

For data that may contain a combination of languages, Unicode encodings are usually the best approach, and often the only possibility. You cannot find any widely understood encoding (other than Unicode encodings) that would let you write a plain text file that contains French and Thai, for example. The encoding that supports French accented letters does not support Thai characters, and vice versa.

Some ISO-8859 encodings and their Windows counterparts have been designed to cover a large set of languages. This especially applies to ISO-8859-1 and windows-1252. Such coverage is possible due to the fact that many European languages use just the basic Latin letters with a small collection of additional letters.

Sources of Information

The following web sites contain useful information on character codes. This means code tables, conversion tables, prose descriptions, usage guidelines, etc.

Czyborra's site (http://czyborra.com)
 A widely known site, which contains good concise descriptions and comments. It is rather old, though, and has not been updated for years.

Fileformat.info on charsets (http://www.fileformat.info/info/charset/)
 This part of the Fileformat.info site contains character tables ("grids") for different encodings, tabular material.

Tex Texin's material (http://www.i18nguy.com/unicode/codepages.html)
 "Character Sets And Code Pages At The Push Of A Button." This might be called a real portal to detailed information on encodings.

Exercises

If possible, carry out the following exercises. If the book has been successful in explaining things, each exercise should take just about 10 to 15 minutes and give you some self-confidence and practice.

Testing encodings

Use an HTML document with an unspecified character encoding containing all octets in the range 160 through 255, like the document that you can copy from *http://www.cs.tut.fi/~jkorpela/chars/test8.htm*. View the document in your web browser, using at least two different 8-bit encodings other than ISO 8859-1. (In Internet Explorer, use View → Encoding.) Analyze which encoding your browser uses by default.

"Deciphering" text

You have got a text file of unknown origin and in unknown encoding but presumably containing text in English. When you view the file in a Windows environment, with Windows Latin 1 as the default encoding, using Notepad, you see the following:

> The letters á and ù are the first and last letter of the Greek alphabet and are often used to symbolize beginning and end. In uppercase, they are Á and Ù; in uppercase with stress mark, they are ¢ and ¿.

Can you deduce what the real encoding is and what the content is?

PART II

A Systematic Look at Unicode

This part gives detailed information about Unicode, its structure and rules, and classifications, and properties of characters. Unicode encodings, such as UTF-8, are also described.

CHAPTER 4

The Structure of Unicode

This chapter is an in-depth presentation of the fundamentals of Unicode, including design principles, coding space, and special terminology. Unicode's nature as an umbrella standard based on a large number of older standards and its relationship to ISO 10646 will be described, examining both the unification principle and criticism of it. However, to divide the complexity to manageable pieces, we postpone the discussion of properties of characters (including, for example, normalization) and the Unicode encodings to the next two chapters.

Design Principles

Here we will start from the proclaimed design principles of Unicode. Later there will be some critical notes and considerations. We will first consider the very general, slogan-like expressions of the goals, and then the more technical principles.

Goals: Universality, Efficiency, Unambiguity

The Unicode standard itself says that it was designed to be universal, efficient, and un-ambiguous. These slogans have real meaning here, but it is important to analyze what they mean and what they do not mean. Let us first see how they are presented in the Unicode standard, and then analyze each item:

> The Unicode Standard was designed to be:
>
> *Universal.* The repertoire must be large enough to encompass all characters that are likely to be used in general text interchange, including those in major international, national, and industry character sets.
>
> *Efficient.* Plain text is simple to parse: software does not have to maintain state or look for special escape sequences, and character synchronization from any point in a character stream is quick and unambiguous. A fixed character code allows for efficient sorting, searching, display, and editing of text.
>
> *Unambiguous.* Any given Unicode code point always represents the same character.

Universality means much more than just creating a superset of sets of characters. Practically all other character codes are limited to the needs of one language or a collection of languages that are similar in their use of characters, such as Western European languages. Unicode needs to encompass a variety of essentially different collections of characters and writing systems. For example, it cannot postulate that all text is written left to right, or that all letters have uppercase and lowercase forms, or that text can be divided into words separated by spaces or other whitespace.

Moreover, Unicode has been designed to be universal *among character codes*. That is, it assigns code points to the characters included in other codes, even if the characters could be treated as variants or combinations of other characters. The reason is that Unicode was also designed for use as an *intermediate code*. You can take character data in any character code and convert it to Unicode without losing information. If you convert it back, you get the exact original data. You can also convert it to a third character code, provided that it is capable of representing all the characters. If the source and destination codes treat, say, £ (pound sign) and ₤ (lira sign) as different, they will appear as different after the conversion that used Unicode as an intermediate code.

Thus, universality implies complexity rather than simplicity. Unicode needs to define properties of characters in a manner that makes explicit many things that we might take for granted—because they are not evident at all across writing systems.

Efficiency refers here to efficient *processing* of data. When all characters have unique identifying numbers, and they are internally represented by those numbers, it is much easier to work with character data than in a system where the same number may mean different characters, depending on encoding or font or other issues. However, efficiency is relative. In particular:

- Efficiency of processing often requires presentation that is wasteful in terms of storage needed (e.g., using four octets for each character). This in turn causes inefficiency in data transfer.

- The representation forms of Unicode are not always efficient in processing. In particular, the common UTF-8 format requires linear processing of the data stream in order to identify characters; it is not possible to jump to the *n*th character in a UTF-8 encoded string.

- Unicode contains a large amount of characters and features that have been included only for compatibility with other standards. This may require preprocessing that deals with compatibility characters and with different Unicode representations of the same character (e.g., letter é as a single character or as two characters).

- For a specific data-processing task, Unicode can be less efficient than other codes. The efficiency goal needs to be understood with the implicit reservation "to the extent possible, given the universality goal."

Unambiguity may look like a self-evident principle, but not all character codes are unambiguous in the Unicode sense. For example, ISO 646 permits variation in some code points, allowing the use of a single code point for either # or £ by special agreement.

Moreover, in Unicode, unambiguity also means unambiguity *across time and versions*: a code point, once assigned, will never be reassigned in a future version.

Sometimes a fourth fundamental principle, *uniformity*, is mentioned. It has been described as a principle of using a fixed-length character code, to allow efficient processing of text. However, as currently defined, Unicode does not use a fixed-length code in a simple sense. In some Unicode encodings, all characters are represented using the same number of octets (or bits), but in many important encodings, such as UTF-8, the lengths may vary.

The 10 Design Principles

The Unicode standard describes "The 10 Unicode Design Principles," where the first two are the same as those quoted in the previous section, universality and efficiency. The unambiguity principle is not included. Obviously, the principles are meant to describe *how* Unicode was designed, whereas the slogan "Universality, Efficiency, Unambiguity" is meant to describe the ultimate *goals*.

The standard admits that there are conflicts between the principles, and it does not specify how the conflicts are resolved. As a whole, the set of principles describe ideas of varying levels (from fundamentals to technicalities), and it should be read critically. It is however important to know the underlying ideas, so we will discuss them briefly:

Universality
> Unicode defines a single repertoire of characters for universal use. (See the previous section for other aspects of universality.)

Efficiency
> Unicode text is simple to process. (See the previous section for the complexity of this issue.)

Characters, not glyphs
> Unicode assigns code points to characters as abstractions, not to visual appearances. Although there are many borderline cases, and although the compatibility characters can be seen as violating this principle, it is still one of the fundamentals of Unicode. The relationship between characters and glyphs is rather simple for languages like English: mostly each character is presented by one glyph, taken from a font that has been chosen. For other languages, the relationship can be much more complex—e.g., routinely combining several characters into one glyph.

Semantics
> Characters have well-defined meanings. In fact, the meanings are often defined rather indirectly or implicitly, if at all—but Unicode is generally much more explicit about meanings than other character code standards, including ISO 10646. When the Unicode standard refers to semantics, it often means (mostly) the properties of characters, such spacing, combinability, and directionality, rather than what the character really means. This is largely intentional: the ultimate meaning may vary by language, context, and usage; think about the various uses of the comma in English and other languages—e.g., as thousands separator or as a decimal separator.

Plain text

Unicode deals with plain text—i.e., strings of characters without formatting or structuring information (except for things like line breaks). In practice, Unicode text is mostly used along with some formatting or structuring information, such as a word processor's formatting commands or some markup; but that is treated as a separate layer in data, above the character level and outside the scope of the Unicode standard.

Logical order

The default representation of Unicode data uses logical order of data, as opposed to approaches that handle writing direction by changing the order of characters. The ordering principles also put all diacritics after the base character to which they are applied, regardless of visual placement. For example, the Greek capital letter omega with tonos has the tonos (stress mark) visually on the left of the omega (Ω), but the decomposed form of this character still consists of omega followed by combining tonos.

Unification

Unicode encodes duplicates of a character as a single code point, if they belong to the same script but different languages. For example, the letter ü denoting a particular vowel in German is treated as the same as the letter ü in Spanish, where it simply indicates that the "u" is pronounced, in a context where it would otherwise be mute.

Dynamic composition

Characters with diacritic marks can be composed dynamically, using characters designated as combining marks. You can take almost any character and combine it with any diacritic; for example, you can create ˜, (comma with tilde) by using the normal comma character and a combining tilde. Therefore, you can write many more characters using Unicode than there are characters in Unicode (i.e., code points allocated to characters)! You can also use multiple combining marks on a character (e.g., you can just make up "a" with both a tilde and an acute accent: ã́), although good rendering of such combinations often requires advanced techniques.

Equivalent sequences

Unicode has a large number of characters that are precomposed forms, such as é. They have decompositions that are declared as equivalent to the precomposed form. An application may still treat the precomposed form and the decomposition differently, since as strings of encoded characters, they are distinct. However, usually such distinctions are not made, and should not be made. The Unicode standard does not declare either the precomposed form or the decomposed form as preferred; they are just two different forms. So-called normalization may make either form preferred in some contexts.

Convertibility

Character data can be accurately converted between Unicode and other character standards and specifications. As explained earlier, this can be regarded as part of the universality principle.

Somewhat surprisingly, the list does not mention *stability* or continuity. Yet, one of the leading principles in Unicode strategy (as described in the goals as "unambiguity") is that a code point assignment once made will never be changed. When a number and a name have been given to a character, they will remain in all future versions, though the properties of the character may be changed.

Another key principle that is not mentioned explicitly is that each character has only one code. As we will see, it is debatable whether Unicode actually follows that principle. Equivalent sequences can even be seen as a strong deviation from the principle.

Unification

Unification means treating different appearances and uses of a symbol as one character rather than several characters. Unicode performs extensive unification, although with many exceptions. In the section "Criticism of Unicode" later in this chapter, we will address the question of whether Unicode has gone too far in unification.

Unification ranges from obvious decisions, like treating the "a" used in English as the same character as the "a" used in French (even though the pronunciation differs) to controversial identification of a Chinese character with a quite different-looking Japanese character because of their common origin. Do not expect to find perfect logic behind the decisions.

Basic decisions on unification in Unicode include the following:

Unification across glyph variation
> Unicode encodes characters, not glyphs. Therefore, the different visual appearances of a symbol are unified to a single character. This is, however, a rather vague formulation. Ultimately, Unicode *defines* what is a character and what is just variation between glyphs. For example, the dollar sign $ is defined so that it may have one vertical stroke or two, depending on the font. There was simply not sufficient reason to treat them as separate symbols. On the other hand, the pound sign £ and the lira sign ₤ are defined as two separate characters, more or less arbitrarily, but basically because sufficiently many people see them as different symbols.

No unification across scripts
> Usually unification has not been applied to characters that look the same, and may have common origin and even similar phonetic value but belong to different writing systems. Thus, Latin letter "O" is treated as distinct from Greek letter "O" (omicron), even though they look the same in most fonts.

Unified diacritics
> Similar-looking diacritic marks used in different languages and with different meanings have generally been unified, even across scripts. Thus, the acute accent used in French (e.g., on the "e" letters in "bébé") is coded as the same as the acute accent used in Polish (e.g., on the "n" letter in "Gdańsk"), even though traditional typography for the languages uses rather different shape for the acute. The acute accent is even unified with the Greek tonos mark (e.g., on first letter in "ώρα"), even though it is

commonly called tonos and not acute and even though its traditional shape is different from both French and Polish style. Often you do not see differences in the shapes of a diacritic because typically each font has a uniform design for a diacritic. However, a diacritic on a Latin letter often looks different from the same diacritic on a non-Latin letter.

The unification applies to the diacritic as a combining mark and as a spacing character (such as acute accent U+00B4, ´) as well as any precomposed letters containing the diacritic (e.g., é as used in French is coded as the same character as é used in Hungarian).

Unification prevented by mapping considerations

Some capital letters have not been unified with each other despite similar or identical appearance, if the corresponding lowercase letters differ. For example, Latin capital letter eth Ð and Latin capital letter "D" with stroke Ð are coded as separate characters, since the corresponding lowercase letters look quite different: ð and đ. Without the difference, it would be impossible to convert text from uppercase to lowercase using simple algorithms.

Unification across different usages

The full stop character "." is used as a period that terminates a sentence, or to indicate an abbreviation, or to act as a decimal separator, to mention a few uses. It is coded as a single Unicode character, with multiple meanings. This is a bit inconvenient if you would like to write, for example, a simple program for recognizing sentences from English text: you cannot just look at the punctuation. On the other hand, people are used to thinking of "." as one character, and it would hardly be possible to make us use different variants of it in different contexts.

Category difference may prevent unification

Sometimes a character difference has been made, even though there is no observable difference in shape, only in meaning. The Latin letter retroflex click ! (U+01C3) has the same glyph as the exclamation mark in practice (and has also been called Latin letter exclamation mark), but it is used in some African languages to denote a click sound (for example, in the name "!kung"). It is therefore classified as a letter, and this is the basic reason for distinguishing it from the exclamation mark.

Limitations due to convertibility

Unification is largely limited by the convertibility principle, which effectively implies that any difference made in some character code must be made in Unicode as well. For example, the micro sign µ would undoubtedly have been unified with the Greek small letter mu, μ, had it not been so that some character codes contain separate positions for them. Unicode needs to allow the distinction to be preserved, even though it defines the micro sign as a compatibility character that is (in a specific sense) equivalent to the letter mu.

Han unification

Ideographic characters used in Chinese, Japanese, Korean, and Vietnamese have been unified across languages to a large extent, even if the shapes of characters may vary significantly. Ideographs have generally been treated as the same for unification, if they share a common origin and the same basic meaning. However, substantial differences in shape may have prevented unification.

Conformance Requirements

The Unicode standard defines conformance criteria. This just means that if some software satisfies them, it can be said to conform to the Unicode standard. This helps other software designers as well as potential customers in evaluating the software. In this context, "software" is to be understood in a wide sense, covering computer programs, parts of programs, complexes of programs, applications, data formats, etc.

For the purposes of conformance requirements, the standard defines some properties of characters as "normative." This means that software that claims conformance to the standard is required to process characters according to those properties, to the extent that it processes them at all. Other properties defined in the standard are called "informative."

Conformance does not require support to all Unicode characters, on display or otherwise. Software that conforms to the Unicode standard may process just a subset of Unicode characters, and this is quite normal because Unicode is an evolving standard: new characters have been added and will be added. We do not want to make conforming software nonconforming just because a rare hieroglyph is added to Unicode.

When some software or data format is described as being based on Unicode or as supporting Unicode, this does not constitute a conformance clause. Quite often, such statements simply mean that the character concept used is that of Unicode. For example, HTML and XML make no claim on Unicode conformance, although they make use of Unicode definitions. Thus, HTML or XML implementations are not required to process characters according to Unicode semantics and rules, though they may do so, for some meanings and rules at least.

Full presentation of the conformance requirements needs many detailed concepts related to character properties. Therefore, it will be given at the end of Chapter 5.

Unicode and ISO 10646

ISO 10646 (officially ISO/IEC 10646) is an international standard, by ISO and IEC. It defines *UCS* (Universal Character Set), which is the same character repertoire as in the Unicode standard, with the same code numbers. ISO 10646 and the Unicode standard are not identical in content but they are fully equivalent in matters covered by both standards. The number of the standard intentionally reminds us of 646, the number of the ISO standard corresponding to ASCII. The rest of the number depends on ISO standard numbering in general.

ISO and IEC are widely recognized international standardization organizations with a broad range of activities, from light bulb standards to general quality control standards. They work on what are regarded as "official standards" especially by governments and officials, although the standards themselves are mostly recommendations, not enforced by law.

The Unicode standard, on the other hand, is a standard defined by the Unicode Consortium, which has a relative focused area of activity. Originally founded for character code standardization, the Consortium has taken new responsibilities, such as creating a common basis for software localization settings. The Unicode standard is sometimes informally cited as "TUS."

Originally, ISO 10646 and the Unicode standard were two different standards created by different organizations, with different objectives. The threat of mutual incompatibility and divergence lead to a decision on full harmonization. The character repertoires were merged into one in 1992. The standards are now in full accordance, and any changes are made in a synchronized way: any change must be approved both by the Unicode Consortium and by the ISO. The harmonization wasn't easy, and it involved changing many character names defined in Version 1.0 of Unicode as different from the ISO 10646 names.

However, full accordance does not mean identity. ISO 10646 is more general (abstract) in nature, whereas Unicode "imposes additional constraints on implementations to ensure that they treat characters uniformly across platforms and applications," as they say in section "Unicode & ISO 10646" of the Unicode FAQ. Moreover, each of the standards contains definitions not present in the other standard. We might say, a bit loosely, that ISO 10646 is more theoretical and the Unicode standard is more practical. ISO 10646 deals with characters, whereas Unicode also describes properties of characters as elements of text, in a manner that affects processing of text.

The ISO 10646 standard has not been put onto the Web. It can be bought in digital (PDF) form via the site *http://www.iso.org*. For practical purposes, the same information is in the Unicode standard. In practice, people usually talk about Unicode rather than ISO 10646, partly because we prefer names to numbers (especially in speech), partly because Unicode is more explicit about the meanings of characters. However, if you write a document for a national standardization body, for example, it is appropriate to cite ISO/IEC 10646 rather than Unicode, although you might mention Unicode in parentheses.

Some ISO standards are divided into "parts," which can in fact be rather independent (though interrelated) standards, such as ISO-8859-1 and ISO-8859-2. The part number is written after the basic number and separated from it with a hyphen. Previously, there were two parts in the ISO 10646 standard: ISO 10646-1 defined the overall structure and the characters in the Basic Multilingual Plane (BMP), whereas ISO 10646-2 defined the other planes (see the section "Coding Space" later in this chapter). However, in 2003, the parts were combined into one.

Full references to ISO standards mention the year of issue of the version of the standard, such as ISO/IEC 10646:2003. The versions do not directly correspond to Unicode versions, since changes that mean a new version of Unicode are often implemented as documents called amendments on the ISO side.

Within the ISO, work on ISO 10646 belongs to the scope of the Joint Technical Committee (JTC) 1, subcommittee (SC) 2, "Coded Character Sets." The word "Joint" refers to the cooperation between the ISO and the IEC. The web site of JTC 1/SC 2 is *http:// std.dkuug.dk/jtc1/sc2/*.

Why Go Beyond 16 Bits?

The original design defined Unicode as a 16-bit code, and you can still find references that describe it that way. A structure of 16-bit codes for all characters internally is very simple and it is in many ways efficient, at least in processing of data, if not always in storage and transmission. It was once regarded as sufficient for all commercially important characters in the world. Thus, there must have been good reasons to go beyond it.

There are several reasons why 16 bits, or 65,536 code positions, were not enough:

- The Chinese-Japanese-Korean (CJK) ideographs, used by a very large number of people, constitute a larger collection than was expected. Although all the commonly used ideographs fit into the 16-bit coding space, there are many characters that are less frequently used, yet should have a code position. Moreover, Japanese and Korean versions of the characters may differ from the Chinese versions to an extent that requires separate codes for them.

- There are many ancient scripts as well as mathematical, scientific, technical, musical, and other special symbols that may need to be coded.

- In order to act as a superset of all character sets, Unicode needs to contain all the characters that have ever been coded in character codes. This means that Unicode needs to have provisions for preserving many distinctions between characters that would be regarded as the same otherwise. It also means that many precomposed characters have to be included. Moreover, no characters will ever be removed from Unicode.

- Allocation of code points to characters, though arbitrary in principle, follows some general rules in practice, leaving much of the coding space unused. Areas and blocks have been reserved for collections of characters, using a unit of 256 characters as minimum amount of allocation. To allow future additions, the allocations must be rather generous.

It would have been possible to deal with all of these problems by using special extension mechanisms such as surrogate pairs. It was ultimately decided, however, that a unified approach is better.

Does Unicode Contain All Characters in the World?

Quite often, Unicode is said to contain all characters used by humans. Although Unicode contains the vast majority of commonly used characters, it is far from all-encompassing. However, we can say that characters that cannot currently be written in Unicode are exceedingly rare, in terms of the number of users at present and the amount of modern printed matter or material in digital form.

The most important kinds of exceptions to the coverage of Unicode are:

- Not all special characters used in science, technology, mathematics, and other areas have been included. New special characters are introduced fairly often, and many of them gain enough usage to justify their inclusion in Unicode.

- Unicode does not contain every Chinese character. A large number of rare characters, used in names, have been omitted from Unicode as well as other character codes.

- There are some individual omissions that are noted from time to time. For example, when analyzing a script, researchers may have misanalyzed its character structure and omitted something that needs to be added later.

- There are small languages that use characters that have not been included in Unicode yet.

- There are many archaic writing systems that have not been included in Unicode yet, such as Egyptian and Mayan hieroglyphs.

The Unicode standard is therefore under continuous development. For example, Version 4.1 of Unicode (March 2005) introduced 1,273 new characters, including some complete (archaic) scripts.

The goal is to include all characters used in *writing*—i.e., in texts—as opposed to all possible graphic symbols. For example, the symbols of card suits are originally not text characters, but they are widely used in texts, such as bridge columns ("a contract of 3♥, with ♣9 lead"), and therefore the symbols are defined as Unicode characters. Many archaic writing systems contain characters that have been or will be included into Unicode due to their use in texts, such as digitized versions of old documents and modern research papers that discuss such documents and their language. On the other hand, characters of the fictional Klingon language are not commonly used in texts, so they have not been included into Unicode so far. The language's fictional nature is no obstacle per se; what matters is actual use in books, magazines, web pages, or elsewhere.

As a different issue, Unicode does not contain and does not aim at containing all characters as separately coded characters with their own code points. Instead, characters with diacritic marks can be represented as a character sequence consisting of a base character and one or more combining diacritic marks.

Identity of Characters

In Chapter 1, we discussed the concept of character and described how Unicode defines particular characters by assigning a code number, a Unicode name, and various properties to it and by showing a representative glyph. Here we consider some of the more technical aspects of defining characters.

Characters as elementary units of text

If we consider normal English text, it looks rather obvious what the elementary units of text are: letters, digits, spaces, punctuation marks, and a few special characters like $.

These units look indivisible, atomic, at any structural level. None of the characters appears to be a composition of other characters, or of any parts.

Things get more complicated in other writing systems, and we need not consider anything more complicated than *accented letters*—e.g., letter e with acute accent, é. Is it a character on its own, or is it a combination of "e" and an acute accent? Unicode codes it in both ways—i.e., allows é to be represented as one character or as two characters. In the latter representation, we are in fact treating the acute accent as a separate character.

However, Unicode does not always consider letters with marks as decomposable into a letter and a mark. For example, the Arabic letter sheen (shin) ش (U+0634) is visually the same as the letter seen (sin) س (U+0633) with a special mark (three dots) on it. Unicode codes them as completely separate, with no mapping between them. This corresponds to the way in which people using the Arabic script understand these letters. Similarly, the letter L with stroke Ł (U+0141) is not decomposable. On the other hand, Unicode defines the Cyrillic letter short i й (U+0439) as decomposable into the Cyrillic letter i и (U+0438) and a diacritic mark (breve), although people who use these letters hardly see things that way.

Different *ligatures* are handled differently, too. The typographic ligature fi can be written as a single character, but it is only a compatibility character. On the other hand, æ is treated as a separate character with no decomposition, although it is historically a ligature and is still used as a typographic alternative to "ae" when writing Latin words.

A *digraph*—i.e., a combination of two characters—can be treated as a basic unit of text, even if its shape is not ligature-like but the two glyphs are clearly distinct. For example, in some languages, the digraph "ch" is treated as a letter, with a position of its own in the alphabet. Even if the digraph is not understood as a letter in every way, it might be treated separately when putting words into a dictionary order. Although this is not the case in English, speakers of English understand "ch" as a combination with a typical phonetic value, so it has more identity than a casual combination of characters has.

As we have already discussed in Chapter 1, Unicode often defines separate characters in situations where there is little or no visible difference. It is a matter of convention, history, and structure of writing systems that we regard the letter "A" as different from the capital Greek letter alpha, which normally looks just the same. As another example, we often treat lowercase and uppercase letters "the same" without even thinking about it; for example, we usually expect searches to be case-insensitive.

Thus, the abstract character concept does not always correspond to the intuitive notion of a character in people's minds. Sometimes it helps to use the phrase *Unicode character* to emphasize that we are referring to a character as coded in Unicode, even if many people would treat it as just a part of a character, or a combination of characters, or "the same" as some other Unicode character.

Unicode numbers

As described in Chapter 1, Unicode assigns two immutable identifiers to a character that has a code point: a number and an alphanumeric string called the Unicode name of the character. For example, $ has the number 24 (hexadecimal) and the name "dollar sign."

The range of possible Unicode numbers has been defined so that the numbers can be expressed using 21 bits—i.e., as strings of 21 zeros and ones representing the number in binary (base 2) notation. However, the full range of numbers representable in 21 bits is not used. Instead, Unicode limits the range to just over one million numbers, as expressed more exactly in Table 4-1 in different number systems. In the Unicode context, we mostly use the base 16 system, which was described in Chapter 1.

Table 4-1. Range of Unicode numbers, expressed using different bases

Number system	Base	Range of possible code numbers in Unicode
Binary	2	0 to 100001111111111111111111
Hexadecimal	16	0 to 10FFFF
Decimal	10	0 to 1,114,111

There are still many documents that describe Unicode as a "16-bit code," but that has not been true for a long time. Neither is Unicode a "32-bit code," although this misconception is less serious. In practice, Unicode code numbers usually appear as represented using units of 8, 16, or 32 bits according to some well-defined scheme. However, if you need to characterize Unicode as an "n-bit code," the best choice for n is 21.

The assignment of numbers to characters is arbitrary in the sense that the number has no relationship with the meaning of the character. For example, digit zero does not have the number 0 but the number 48 (in decimal). This is the same as its number in ASCII and many other character codes, but other than that, there is no way you could have guessed it.

In particular, the Unicode numbers should not be treated as significant in comparing characters. If the number of a character is smaller than the number of another character, this does imply that one is before the other in the alphabet or collating sequence in some language. It happens that the code number of "a" is one less than the code number of "b," but you would get the order quite wrong if you alphabetized, for example, French words on the assumption that the code numbers tell the order. For example, all words beginning with é would be sorted after all words that begin with any unaccented letter, since the code number of é is greater than the code numbers of all basic Latin letters.

 Unicode numbers are identifying labels, permanently attached to characters, rather than numbers in the mathematical sense.

In practice, the allocation of Unicode numbers is not random or arbitrary, even though it may look messy. Characters are organized into *blocks*, and within each block, the allocation usually reflects some traditional order. The allocation is discussed in more detail in the section "Coding Space" later in this chapter.

Unicode names of characters

The Unicode name of a character is defined as follows:

- With the exceptions described below, a character has an explicitly assigned name, which is mentioned in the code charts and in the *UnicodeData.txt* file in the Unicode database. The names are often rather long, such as "LATIN CAPITAL LETTER A WITH GRAVE."

- Unified CJK ideographs have names of the form "CJK UNIFIED IDEOGRAPH-*n*," where *n* is the code number in decimal. For example, the name of U+4E00 is "CJK UNIFIED IDEOGRAPH U-4E00."

- Hangul (Korean) syllable characters U+AC00..U+D7A3 have names that are constructed from their decompositions as defined in the Unicode standard in section 3.12 "Conjoining Jamo Behavior." A character is algorithmically decomposed, and then the short names (as defined in *Jamo.txt*) of the components, such as "P," "WI," and "LH," are concatenated. The result is prefixed with the words "HANGUL SYLLABLE," giving names like "HANGUL SYLLABLE PWILH."

- Control characters have no official name. (They have the text "<control>" in the database in place of a name.)

- Private use characters, unassigned code points, and noncharacter code points have no names in Unicode.

The Unicode names of characters are based on the English language, with many loanwords taken from other languages. Interpreted as an expression in English, the Unicode name of a character is usually descriptive, but it might be uninformative, and sometimes even misleading.

The Unicode name is called the *formal name* in the Unicode standard, to distinguish it from an *alternative name* (alias). Alternative names are mentioned in the code charts, and they also appear in the *NamesList.txt* file in plain text. They are comment-like and can be changed or removed. For example, the Unicode standard once mentioned "hyphus" as an alternative name for hyphen-minus, but this was an attempt at coining a new word rather than be descriptive, and it was silently removed from the standard.

For some characters, a Unicode 1.0 name is mentioned, too, such as "period" for "full stop" and "slash" for "solidus." As the examples show, the Unicode 1.0 names often correspond better to the names normally used in U.S. English. A Unicode 1.0 name is essentially just an alternative name, although it is written in uppercase in the code charts. Formally, it differs from other alternative names by its appearance in the *UnicodeData.txt* file. The Unicode 1.0 names reflect the harmonization of Unicode with ISO 10646: in Version 2.0, Unicode adapted ISO 10646 names for characters if there was a mismatch of names, and the old names were preserved as comments.

The Unicode name proper (the formal name) is fixed partly because it may have been used in programming. It is usually not a good idea to identify characters by their names in program code, but such approaches have been used, especially in old times.

The Unicode names are identifying strings rather than normal text, but for the purposes of reading them aloud, they are English. They contain both English words and words from many other languages, adapted into English orthography. As the names "full stop" and "solidus" indicate, the English language in the names is basically British English. This is reflected in spellings like "centre" and "diaeresis." In this book, the Unicode names are spelled as defined, of course, although words like "dieresis" appear in U.S. English spelling when used in the prose text.

Using the names

Despite many problems with the official (formal) Unicode names of characters, they are very useful. When you need to specify exactly which character you are referring to, it is usually a good idea to mention both its Unicode name and its Unicode number.

When writing for general audience, it might be best to use just commonly used names about characters. For example, if you are giving instructions on using a special symbol in some particular way when using some program, you could just tell people to use #, without mentioning its name. People know it by so many different names that they might get confused, even though they know the character when they see it. If you specify a name, you could list some commonly used names along with the Unicode name. You could tell people to use # (number sign, also known as hash and octothorpe).

When referring to rare characters, names become essential. If you write style instructions for technical papers, for example, just telling people to use ⌀ in some context will not work well. Most of them will think that you mean the character ø that can be conveniently found among the Latin 1 characters. It is better to tell them to use the DIAMETER SIGN ⌀ (U+2300), though they may still need instructions on typing it.

Software tools for selecting characters, such as the characters maps discussed in Chapter 2, often identify characters by their code numbers and Unicode names. This is in many cases insufficient, and it has caused misunderstandings. Some names are misleading or too vague, and some names are theoretical rather than commonly used names. They are often hard to understand to people who do not speak English as their native language. In the future, language-dependent names for characters might be defined in the Common Locale Data Repository (CLDR) discussed in Chapter 11. Meanwhile, most characters have no official or established names in most languages. This is one reason why the Unicode names are used so often.

 Use Unicode names when referring to characters, but do not rely on them alone.

The Unicode names are useful when searching for information, using Google, for example. Most Internet search engines treat all or most non-alphabetic characters as irrelevant (skippable, punctuation) or as special operators. Thus, you cannot search directly for ¶, for example. Instead, you might search for "section sign," once you know the character by its Unicode name. Of course, not all documents that use the character or even those that say something about it, mention it by that name. The alias names mentioned in the Unicode standard are often very useful, too.

Generally, documents that seriously discuss a character can be expected to mention its Unicode name. This implies that as an author, you would do wisely to mention the Unicode name (spelled exactly right), if you write about a character. Mentioning the Unicode number in the U+2300 style is useful, too, since people might use it, too, and have success in searches.

Characters used in character names

The characters that may appear in a Unicode name are:

- Letters A–Z (case insensitively, in practice)
- Digits 0–9
- Space (U+0020)
- Hyphen-minus "-" (U+002D)—i.e., the common hyphen (as in ASCII)

This simple repertoire makes it usually rather straightforward to construct identifiers that correspond to character names, for use in computer programs, database entries, etc. Usually identifier syntax disallows spaces, but you can replace spaces by low line (underscore) "_" characters without ambiguity—e.g., using COMMERCIAL_AT. The hyphen-minus character can be more problematic, if identifier syntax disallows it.

Digits have been avoided in Unicode names; even the digits themselves have names like "digit zero." Some names, however, contain digits, because they have been generated algorithmically, by enumeration (e.g., "Greek vocal notation symbol-1"), or using the code number as part of the name (e.g., "CJK unified ideogram-4E00"). Such names are not very practical, and they have been included just to give every character a formal name. Braille pattern character names contain digits that indicate the positions of dots—e.g., "Braille pattern dots-1245." A few names contain digits because they refer to the shapes of digits—e.g., "double low-9 quotation mark."

Case of letters in names

Technically, the standard defines the letters used in Unicode names as uppercase. No ambiguity can arise, however, from using lowercase. The variation should be considered as typographical only, since the case of letters is not significant in Unicode names. Any processing that takes such a name as input should thus first normalize the spelling to uppercase or lowercase or perform all comparisons in a case-insensitive manner. In a user interface that shows Unicode names, it is probably a good idea to make the case a user-settable option, with uppercase as default.

Notational issues

The number of a character is usually written in hexadecimal notation, using at least four digits—e.g., "0040." It is often preceded by "U+" for clarity—e.g., "U+0040." The "U+" prefix may help both human readers and computer programs to distinguish character numbers from other numbers or digit sequences in a document.

The original idea was to use a special character, multiset union U+228E, ⊎, in front of a code number. This character, consisting of the symbol of union of sets and a plus sign, was meant to symbolize the nature of Unicode as a union of character sets, and more. However, for practical reasons, the symbol was soon replaced by the two ASCII characters "U+."

There is more variation in the writing style of the name. The standard uses mostly all uppercase—e.g., "COMMERCIAL AT." If you use this style in a publication, it is a good idea to try to use a small caps font or a normal font in a smaller size (e.g., COMMERCIAL AT), to avoid making the names all too prominent. Another style, used in the standard for alias names and in annotations, is all lowercase, even for words that are capitalized in normal English, as in "greek question mark."

UCS Sequence Identifiers (USI) and named character sequences

Combining diacritic marks, discussed in Chapter 7, create a general method for forming new characters from a base character (such as "e") and one or more diacritic marks, producing a character like é or ĕ. This creates a new problem of identity: although characters like é and ĕ already exist as separately coded characters in Unicode, most potential combinations do not; should each of them be still regarded as a character, or just as a character sequence? For example, does letter "e" with a combining acute accent and a combining dieresis constitute a single character, or just a sequence of three characters, although rendered using one glyph?

The short answer is that such a sequence is technically a character sequence in Unicode, but it can be regarded as a single character in other contexts and frames of reference. Unicode is capable of representing the character, though as a sequence of Unicode characters and not as a single character.

The general idea is that the existing repertoire of precomposed characters in Unicode will normally not be extended. This saves work and coding space, and it helps to avoid long discussions. After all, commonly used characters with diacritic marks have already been incorporated into Unicode as precomposed characters, so the rest are rather specialized, and few people would be competent in deciding on them.

This has caused some controversy. If you speak a language that needs such a combination, you might be dissatisfied with the statement that it is and will remain a character sequence, not a character. You might want better "characterhood" for the element of your language. Partly for such reasons, the concept of *UCS Sequence Identifier (USI)* was introduced in ISO 10646.

A USI is of the form *<UID1,UID2,...>* where UID1 and so on are short identifiers for characters, usually in the U+*nnnn* notation. For example, <U+012B,U+0300>.

USIs also serve the purpose of assigning distinguishable identity to other sequences, such as the character pair "ch," which may appear as a single unit to many. In some languages, "ch" has both a special pronunciation and a special role in ordering, where it might appear as if it were a letter after "c" (so that words beginning with "ch" are ordered after all other words beginning with "c").

Unicode takes a further step in assigning "characterhood" to character sequences by introducing the notion of a *named character sequence*, defined in Unicode Standard Annex (UAX) #34 at *http://www.unicode.org/reports/tr34/*.

A named character sequence is simply a name for a USI. The name follows the general syntax of Unicode names of characters, though with some special restrictions. For example, the sequence <U012B,U+0300> has the name "Latin small letter i with macron and grave," which looks very much like a Unicode name for a character. Thus, when someone says that such a character (ī̀) should be added into Unicode, one can say: it can be written using existing Unicode characters, and the sequence has even got a name, so you can treat it as a character.

This strategy has not been as successful as you might think. There is a fairly small number of named character sequences currently defined. The registry of definitions for them is the text file *http://www.unicode.org/Public/UNIDATA/NamedSequences.txt*. The approach might still turn out to be useful, especially in giving advice to font designers about sequences that might need a separately designed glyph.

Versions of Unicode

Unicode versions are numbers much the same way as program versions, using a hierarchic number of the form *m.n.p*, where *m* is the *major version* number (which usually remains the same for years), *n* is the *minor version* number, and *p* is the *update version* number. For a detailed description, refer to *http://www.unicode.org/versions/*. The format of citing Unicode and its versions is discussed in Chapter 5.

In practice, the minor version number 0 is often omitted—e.g., "Unicode 4.1" instead of "Unicode 4.1.0." In this book, "Unicode" means Unicode 4.1.0 unless otherwise stated.

Unicode Version 1.0 used somewhat different names for some characters than ISO 10646. In Unicode Version 2.0, the names were made the same as in ISO 10646. However, the Version 1.0 names (such as "period" for "full stop") are still preserved as alternate names, mentioned both in code charts and in the Unicode database.

New versions of Unicode are expected to add new characters mostly, though changes and clarifications are possible. However, there is a firm policy that no characters will be removed, no code numbers changed, and no Unicode names changed. Annotations, including alternate names, and properties of characters may change.

The growth of Unicode is summarized in Table 4-2, which shows the number of characters (code positions assigned to characters, including 65 control characters) and blocks in each version. (Minor versions that did not add any new code position assignments have not been included.) The issue date is specified in year-month notation. The jump in the number of characters in Version 3.1 is mainly caused by the addition of the CJK Unified Ideograms Extension B block (42,711 characters).

Table 4-2. Unicode versions

Version	Issued	Characters	Blocks
1.0	1991-10	7,161	57
1.0.1	1992-06	28,359	59
1.1	1993-06	34,223	63
2.0	1996-07	38,950	67
2.1	1998-05	38,952	67
3.0	1999-09	49,259	86
3.1	2001-03	94,205	95
3.2	2002-03	95,221	107
4.0	2003-04	96,447	122
4.1	2005-03	97,720	142

Version 5.0 is to be published in the third quarter of 2006. Information on it is available at *http://www.unicode.org/versions/Unicode5.0.0/*. It is intended to add 1,365 characters, for the needs of some living languages (e.g., in India), for mathematics, and for academic use, particularly for coding cuneiform and other ancient texts.

Coding Space

Coding space, or "codespace" to use the Unicode standard terminology, is the range of integers that can be used as numbers for characters. In an 8-bit encoding, the coding space is the range from 0 to 255. In Unicode, the coding space ranges from 0 to 10FFFF in hexadecimal, 1,114,111 in decimal. Some numbers in the range correspond to characters, some have been excluded from such usage, and some are currently unassigned.

A *code point*, also called *code position*, is simply a value in the coding space. It may or may not have a character assigned to it.

The way Unicode uses the coding space is, strictly speaking, a technicality that does not affect the identity or properties of any character. In that sense, the allocation is independent of other design decisions. It is surely important to people who develop the Unicode standard, since the amount of characters makes some logical planning and allocation principles necessary. But does it interest others?

Understanding the principles of using the coding space helps in locating characters. Many tables and utilities present Unicode characters as organized according to the coding space structure and usage. Typically, you see blocks of characters, so you need to know what a block is. It also helps to know how blocks are organized internally, though we can list only rather general principles.

Planes

For practical reasons, the coding space has been divided into parts called planes. You can visualize a plane as a huge sheet of paper with 65,536 (256 times 256) squares, each of which might contain a character. Then imagine a pile of 17 such sheets. There you have the Unicode coding space.

Originally, Unicode was designed to be a 16-bit code and ISO 10646 a 32-bit code, divided into 16-bit planes. When they were harmonized, it was decided to use the ISO 10646 approach as the basis. However, an agreement between ISO and the Unicode Consortium guarantees that only the first 17 planes will ever be used. This effectively means that the coding space consists of the numbers that can be expressed in *21 bits*, with the first 5 bits specifying the plane and the rest the position inside a plane.

Until recently, the use of Unicode has mostly been limited to BMP consisting of the range 0..FFFF, corresponding to the original design of Unicode. The other planes are 10000..1FFFF, 20000..2FFFF, etc., up to 100000..10FFFF.

Nowadays, there are many characters allocated on other planes as well, and rarely used characters (such as characters used in extinct writing systems, appearing in historical documents only) are being added to Unicode that way. Thus, Unicode was first theoretically, and then practically extended beyond a limitation to 16 bits (i.e., to code numbers that can be expressed as 16-bit integers).

Currently, and in the foreseeable future, only the first three planes are used for assigning characters in the standard. The big picture is the following, using hexadecimal numbers for the planes (with decimal numbers in parentheses):

- Plane 0, Basic Multilingual Plane (BMP), contains most characters used in modern writing systems (and many from historical systems).
- Plane 1, Supplementary Multilingual Plane (SMP), contains characters used in archaic writing systems as well as various collections of special symbols, including many mathematical symbols.
- Plane 2, Supplementary Ideographic Plane (SIP), contains less-common Chinese-Japanese-Korean (CJK) characters that do not fit into BMP for practical reasons.
- Planes 3 through D (= 13) are currently unassigned—i.e., reserved for eventual future assignments.
- Plane E (= 14) is called Supplementary Special-Purpose Plane (SSPP) and reserved for purposes such as code points for control functions.

- Planes F and 10 (= 15 and 16) are designated for use as Private Use Planes. This means that the standard does not and will not define their use, any more than by saying that they can be used upon private agreements.

Allocation Areas

Between the plane level and the next formally defined levels of allocation—rows and blocks—there is an auxiliary and informal structuring level, allocation areas. The areas are mainly an organizational device for Unicode development, but they may also help you to get an overview of the use of coding space. An area may contain a set of writing systems of similar type or some other large set. The current allocation areas are:

- On plane 0 (BMP):
  — General Scripts (Latin, Greek, Cyrillic, Armenian, and many others)
  — CJK Miscellaneous (different characters used in East Asian scripts)
  — Asian Scripts (Yi script and Korean Hangul)
  — Asian Scripts (Yi script and Korean Hangul)
  — Surrogates (reserved)
  — Private Use (for use by agreements outside the standard)
  — Compatibility and Specials (presentation forms etc., and a few formatting characters and special code points)
- On plane 1 (SMP):
  — General Scripts (various small archaic scripts)
  — Notational Systems (musical, mathematical, and divination symbols)
- On plane 2 (SIP):
  — CJK Unified Ideographs Extension B
  — CJK Compatibility Ideographs Supplement

Rows and Blocks

Each plane contains 65,536 (2^{16}) code points, which can be divided into 256 (2^8) parts called *rows*. The term can be misleading, since such a row is often presented visually as an array (matrix) with 16 rows and 16 columns.

The division of a plane to rows corresponds to splitting the last four hexadecimal digits in a code number into two parts consisting of two hexadecimal digits. For example, U+1234 belongs to row 12 (hexadecimal), where it occupies the relative position 34 (hexadecimal). We can say that for characters in the BMP, the first two of the four hexadecimal digits select the row, and the last two select the position within a row.

We will not use such a row concept much, and it is not very common in the Unicode context. There is a more important concept of a *block*. A block is a contiguous range of code points, which have similar characteristics in some sense and which has a name assigned to it in the Unicode standard. A block may contain code points that are unassigned or designated as noncharacters.

Rows and blocks are two different ways of dividing a plane into parts: a technical (or mathematical) way and a logical way. A block may be just part of a row, and vice versa.

The first block is called "Basic Latin" and it occupies the range U+0000 to U+007F. It has been formed simply because it contains the ASCII characters, with code numbers equaling those in ASCII. The block "Arrows," U+2190 to U+21FF, is much more homogenous: it contains different arrow characters (←, ↕, etc.) and nothing else. The block "Mathematical Operators," U+2200 to U+22FF, contains a mixed collection of operator symbols used in mathematics, but it does not contain *all* such symbols that have been included in Unicode. There are many additional mathematical blocks around the coding space. Unicode blocks are described in more detail in Chapter 8.

Thus, the names of blocks should be understood by implying the word "Some" rather than "The" at the start—for example, the block Currency Symbols is not the block for the currency symbols but a block for some currency symbols. Many currency symbols appear in other blocks, including $ in Basic Latin.

 Although a block may consist of a collection of characters of the same kind, blocks cannot be meaningfully used for classification of characters. Instead, use the General Category property and other formally defined properties (see Chapter 5).

In many cases, a block corresponds to a row in the sense described in the previous paragraphs. For example, the block "Cyrillic" is U+0400 to U+04FF—i.e., row 4 (of plane 0). As the other examples show, however, a block may correspond to a part of a row only. On the other hand, a block may extend over several rows. For example, the block "Mathematical Alphanumeric Symbols," which is a relatively recent addition to Unicode, occupies the range U+1D400 to 1D7FF, therefore spanning rows D4 to D7 of plane 1.

Unicode as Extension of ISO-8859-1

Unicode can be regarded as an extension of practically any character code, in the sense that the Unicode character repertoire contains all characters that appear in at least one character code. However, the code numbers are generally different, of course.

Unicode is an extension of ISO-8859-1 (ISO Latin 1), and thereby an extension of ASCII, in a different, much stronger sense. The code numbers of ISO-8859-1 characters are exactly the same in Unicode as in ISO-8859-1. The range U+0000 to U+00FF has thus been directly copied from ISO-8859-1, although it has been divided into blocks: Basic Latin (U+0000 to U+007F) and Latin-1 Supplement (U+0080 to U+00FF).

Beware that Unicode is not an extension of Windows Latin 1 (windows-1252, often misleadingly called "ANSI") in the same sense. Unicode contains all Windows Latin 1 characters, of course, but characters with numbers 80 to 9F (hexadecimal) in Windows

Latin 1 have quite different numbers in Unicode. They have in fact been scattered around in different blocks, although many of them appear in the General Punctuation block. The reason for this that in Unicode, range U+0080 to U+009F is reserved for control characters, as in ISO-8859-1.

The special role of ISO-8859-1 of course makes many things technically simpler to people and applications for which ISO-8859-1 has been suitable. If they need some additional characters, they can switch to Unicode smoothly, to some extent.

Conversion from ISO-8895-1 to Unicode requires a change in data representation, though. A file of ISO-8859-1 characters consists of 8-bit units, octets, in a manner that is different from Unicode encoding forms. If the data contains ASCII characters only, no change in representation is needed: a file of ASCII characters can be treated as a file of Unicode characters (in the Basic Latin block) in the UTF-8 encoding.

Since ISO-8859-1 is a mixture of rather different characters, the decision to use it as the model for the first two blocks in Unicode has implications for other blocks. The ISO-8859-1 characters do not appear as duplicates in other blocks, even though they would semantically belong there. For example, the plus sign +, once included in ASCII, does not appear in the Mathematical Operators block.

Internal Structure of Blocks

The internal structure of a block is not something that you need to know to use Unicode. Just as numbers of characters are in principle just labels permanently attached to characters, the mutual order and position of characters (by their code numbers) in a block is "arbitrary" in a sense. For example, letters might or might not appear in alphabetic order. Although the standard guarantees that assigned code numbers will never change, it is usually not a good idea to base processing of characters on the mutual relationships of their code numbers.

Unicode blocks are usually shown as arrays with 8 or 16 columns. The code charts in the Unicode standard organize the arrays so that they need to be read by column, if you wish to follow the code number order. For example, Figure 4-1 shows the start of the code chart for the Cyrillic block. Characters U+0400, U+0401, etc., appear in the first column, under the column heading "040." The order looks rather random, if you read the array by row, but if you read by column, and hence by code number order, it has parts where the order corresponds to the alphabetic order in Russian: А, Б, В,....

Each block is meant to contain a collection of characters that belong together in an essential way. Often the collection and its internal order have been taken from an older, 8-bit character code designed for some language or purpose, though with modifications. In this context, official international (ISO) standards have been preferred to vendor-specific codes, even when the latter have been more common in actual use.

For example, the Cyrillic block is based on the ISO 8859-5 code, which we discussed in Chapter 3. Characters in the block have the same relative positions as in ISO 8859-5. However, ISO 8859-5 characters, such as Latin letters, that already exist in Unicode in

	040	041	042	043	044	045	046	047	048	049	04A	04B	04C	04D	04E	04F
0	È	A	Р	a	р	è	Ꙩ	Ψ	Ҁ	Г	Қ	Ұ	I	Ӑ	З	Ӱ
	0400	0410	0420	0430	0440	0450	0460	0470	0480	0490	04A0	04B0	04C0	04D0	04E0	04F0
1	Ё	Б	С	б	с	ё	ѡ	ψ	ҁ	г	қ	ұ	Ж	ӑ	з	ӱ
	0401	0411	0421	0431	0441	0451	0461	0471	0481	0491	04A1	04B1	04C1	04D1	04E1	04F1
2	Ђ	В	Т	в	т	ѓ	Ѣ	Ѳ	҂	Ғ	Ң	Х	ж	Ӓ	Ӣ	Ӳ
	0402	0412	0422	0432	0442	0452	0462	0472	0482	0492	04A2	04B2	04C2	04D2	04E2	04F2

Figure 4-1. Excerpt from the code chart for the Cyrillic block

other blocks were not included in the Cyrillic block. (Many characters in Figure 4-1 look like Latin letters, but they are Cyrillic letters.) This might be described so that the characters in ISO 8859-5 with code numbers A1 to FF were directly copied to Unicode range U+0401 to U+045F, but characters that exist in other blocks (such as Basic Latin and Latin-1 Supplement) were omitted. The rest of the range U+0400 to U+04FF (U+0400 and columns 046 through 04F in the code chart illustrated in Figure 4-1) was used for Cyrillic characters not present in ISO 8859-5.

The omission of already coded characters follows the principle of not coding the same character twice, even though this prevents simple correspondence between other character codes and Unicode. If the Cyrillic block were just a copy of the ISO 8859-5 code table, shifted to a different range, transcoding between ISO 8859-5 and Unicode would be trivial. However, many other things would have become more complex, if such an approach had been taken. For example, all ASCII characters would appear in many copies in different blocks. This would waste coding space and make even simple tests like "is this character 'X'?" more complicated: the data being tested would need to be tested against all the appearances of "X" in different blocks.

This explanation was meant to emphasize that Unicode blocks are not similar or comparable to 8-bit code, even in the relatively common case where a block consists of one "row" of 256 code points and has been defined with some 8-bit code in mind. Using Unicode, you don't switch between blocks by selecting (in some special way) first some block, then another; you just use characters from different blocks.

 Unicode blocks are not "code pages."

Some blocks contain characters from one script (writing systems, see Chapter 7) only, and might be named according to the script, such as "Devanagari." However, in general there is no one-to-one mapping between blocks and scripts. Blocks may contain characters from several scripts, and many scripts have been divided into several blocks.

The block concept and the principle of not coding the same character twice can be illustrated by looking at the block Superscripts and Subscripts. It contains the following code points:

- U+2070 superscript zero
- U+2071 superscript Latin small letter "i"
- U+2072 (reserved, with a cross reference note to U+00B2 superscript two)
- U+2073 (reserved, with a cross reference note to U+00B3 superscript three)
- U+2074 superscript four
- etc., up to U+2079 superscript nine

This looks odd, since we would expect that the superscript digits appear in consecutive code positions. There is a "hole" where we would expect superscript two and superscript three to appear, but the code points are reserved. The reason is that those characters, ² and ³, already exist in the Latin-1 Supplement block. The positions where they would otherwise appear were intentionally left unassigned. This made it explicit that those superscripts do not appear in the block where one might expect to find them, but elsewhere.

So why isn't U+2071 reserved analogously, with reference to U+00B9 superscript one? You don't want to hear the full story, but originally it was reserved, an then allocated to superscript "i" in Unicode Version 3.2 after a long debate. In Unicode terminology, "reserved" means "unassigned (for now)," instead of guaranteeing that the code point will remain unassigned.

Noncharacter Code Points

The last two code points of the BMP, namely U+FFFE and U+FFFF, as well as the corresponding points on other planes, have been explicitly defined as forbidden in Unicode data. By definition, they do not denote any character or control function, and their occurrence in character data may be treated as an error. However, they may appear in a data stream that contains character data; they would then indicate noncharacter data.

The reason for disallowing U+FFFE in any Unicode data is that such a convention helps to detect common errors caused by different byte orders. If a Unicode text file begins with a byte order mark (BOM, U+FEFF), then an attempt to read the file on a system or application that implies the opposite byte order will result in an immediate error. The byte order mark will be read with octets swapped, U+FFFE, and some error recovery can be applied. Byte order is a matter of encoding, to be discussed in Chapter 6. Briefly, byte order specifies the order of octets within a four-octet unit of data.

In a sense, this might be seen as assigning U+FFFE a meaning: it could be interpreted as a "reversed byte order mark," so that an application can simply reverse the order when reading the data. Such things happen when error processing is defined exactly or is obvious from context. An error becomes a feature then.

The code point U+FFFF corresponds to the number −1 when interpreted as a signed integer in two's complement notation. Making it a noncharacter continues an old tradition. Even in the ASCII world, the corresponding code point FF is often treated the same way. Programs that were written to process ASCII data only, but using at least 8-bit storage units, were often made to treat an octet with the first bit set as indicating the absence of character data—e.g., the end of an array of characters or the end of input stream. It was most natural to use an octet with all bits set—FF, for this purpose. In particular, an input routine that returns a character can use U+FFFF as its return value, to indicate that no character was received.

Moreover, code points U+FDD0..U+FDEF have been defined as noncharacters, and applications may use them for different sentinel or indicator purposes. Similarly to U+FFFE and U+FFFF, they should not appear in character data. However, in a program, a function that normally returns a character may return one of these values to signal "no character" and some additional information. These code points can also appear in a data file as long they are not interpreted as characters.

When a program encounters a noncharacter code point in character data, the Unicode standard allows several options:

- It may be treated internally as an indicator or sentinel.
- An error may be signaled.
- It may be ignored.
- It may be removed from the data stream (that the program passes forward).
- It may be treated as an unassigned code point—e.g., so that if a function for getting the value of a property for a character is called with a noncharacter argument, the function would return the same value as for an unassigned code point.

Classification of Code Points

Not all code points in the Unicode coding space correspond to characters. There are the following possibilities:

Assigned
> The code point is assigned to a character. Such an allocation will never be removed or changed, though the properties of the character may be changed. The character might be declared as deprecated, but it will remain a Unicode character. The word "character" is to be interpreted in a broad, Unicode sense: it covers normal characters with graphic appearance, combining diacritic marks (which are normally shown as small marks on a base character), different spaces, formatting characters such as line break indicators, and control characters, to be defined in other standards.

Private use
> The code point is reserved for "private" use—i.e., for use by a specific agreement between interested parties. This, too, is a permanent allocation. Applications may use the code point for their own purposes, such as representing a character that has not been included in Unicode.

Noncharacter

> The code point is designated as not corresponding to any character ever. This is permanent: the code point will never be assigned to a character. For historical reasons, some such code points are called "surrogate" code points.

Unassigned

> The code point is currently unassigned. It may be allocated in the future. Use of the code point for any purpose is unwise: if you use it for private purposes now, it may later become assigned to a character in the Unicode standard. To emphasize this, unassigned code points are called "reserved."

For example, code point U+0021 is assigned to a character, the exclamation mark. Code point U+E000 is reserved for private use; it is the first code point in a large range of private use characters. Code point U+D800 does not correspond to any character; it corresponds to a "high-surrogate" value but does not represent any character. Code point U+0380 is unallocated in Unicode 4.1; it might be assigned to a character later—probably to a Greek character, since it belongs to a block of Greek characters.

Previously, the situation was more complicated due to so-called surrogates. Terminology and concepts around them were confusing, but the surrogate concept has now been moved from the code point level to the encoding level, to be discussed in Chapter 6. The old approach is still reflected in the names "high-surrogate code point" and "low-surrogate code point."

This probably sounds rather confusing. Table 4-3 is meant to illustrate the classification. The column "Category" lists the short symbols of General Category values (to be explained in Chapter 5) for code points that belong to the type.

Table 4-3. Classification of code points

Type	Description	Example	Category
Graphic	A visible character	"A" U+0041	L, M, N, P, S, Zs
Format	Invisible, formatting	Line feed U+000A	Cf, Zl, Zp
Control	Control code, defined elsewhere	Backspace U+0008	Cc
Private use	Use by "private" agreement	U+E000	Co
Surrogate	Reserved, should not appear	U+D800	Cs
Noncharacter	Reserved for noncharacter use	U+FFFF	Cn
Reserved	Unassigned (for now)	U+05FF	Cn

Depending on your viewpoint, you might say that only code points of type "graphic" correspond to characters proper. You might take a broader view and call also "format," "control," and "private use" code points as representing characters. Other code points do not correspond to characters, although reserved code points may do so in future versions.

To illustrate the use of the coding space, Table 4-3 shows the number of code points as defined in the Unicode 4.1 standard and as planned for the Unicode 5.0 standard. The counts are given separately for the Basic Multilingual Plane and other planes.

Table 4-4. Number of different code points in Unicode

Ver. 4.1	5.0 (plan)	Type of code points
51,640	51,980	Assigned graphic characters (BMP)
35	35	Assigned format characters (BMP)
65	65	Assigned control characters (BMP)
6,400	6,400	Private use code points (BMP)
2,048	2,048	Surrogate code points (BMP)
34	34	Noncharacters, other (BMP)
5,314	4,974	Unassigned (reserved) code points (BMP)
45,875	46,904	Assigned graphic characters (supplementary planes)
105	105	Assigned format characters (supplementary planes)
131,068	131,068	Private use code points (supplementary planes)
32	32	Noncharacters (supplementary planes)
871,496	870,467	Unassigned (reserved) code points (supplementary planes)
1,114,112	1,114,112	All code points together

Surrogates

Unicode uses the word "surrogate" in a particular technical meaning. To avoid confusion, it is best to avoid this word in its loose everyday meaning; use words like "replacement" instead if you just want to write about using a character in the role of another character.

Originally, surrogates were invented as a method of overcoming the limitations of the 16-bit coding space. To represent characters outside that space, you would reserve some ranges of 16-bit values, called high and low surrogates, and represent a character as a pair of such values. Naturally, the number of characters that you can represent in the 16-bit coding space itself was decreased, since the high and low surrogates must not be used to represent characters, except in pairs as defined.

In Unicode as defined now, surrogates are not to be used as code points. The ranges allocated for high and low surrogates exist in the coding space, as U+D800..U+DB7F and U+DC00..U+DFFF, but code points in those ranges are not supposed to appear in Unicode data as such. Instead, one particular encoding, UTF-16, uses *code units* (16-bit quantities) with values in the surrogate ranges as a method of *encoding* characters outside the Basic Multilingual Plane.

Thus, when a program reads data in UTF-16 encoding, it needs to interpret any pair of surrogate code units as a single Unicode character. After this interpretation, the data contains the character with its designated code number (> FFFF hexadecimal), with no trace of any surrogates.

If a code point in a surrogate range is encountered in processing Unicode data (assuming it has been decoded from an eventual encoding such as UTF-16), the situation should be handled as an error. If it's not a high surrogate immediately followed by a low surrogate, there might be no way to handle the situation meaningfully, since we cannot know what happened. But if there is a surrogate pair, odds are that the data was in fact UTF-16 encoded and it was not decoded properly, so you might interpret the data according to UTF-16.

When using UTF-8 (8-bit code units) or UTF-32 (32-bit code units), there is no use for surrogates in any sense.

Unassigned Code Points and Private Use

Unassigned code points are simply points that have neither been allocated for any use nor declared as noncharacters or private use points. You might visualize them as white areas on a map, or as unoccupied rooms in the coding space. Programmers often use such "free" positions for their own purposes, but that would be wrong here; the unassigned code points are not free at all. They are reserved for eventual future extensions.

By using unassigned code points, you would violate the Unicode standard. On the practical side, you would take an unnecessary risk. It is quite possible that a future version of Unicode will assign a specific meaning to the code point. This would involve properties that you cannot anticipate.

Even if the characters you need have some planned or proposed area where there might be placed in a future version of Unicode, it would be a serious mistake to use code points in such an area. The Roadmaps to Unicode at *http://www.unicode.org/roadmaps/* show some possible allocations of areas, but they exist for the purposes of planning future versions of Unicode. If you need to use hieroglyphs, for example, you might naively look at the roadmaps and see that the code range U+14000 to U+16BFF has been tentatively allocated for Egyptian and Mayan hieroglyphs, with some more detailed ideas on its internal structure. Using any code point there would be even worse than picking up an unassigned code point at random, since it is probable that some hieroglyphs will be allocated there, and this would almost certainly conflict with the way you would assign characters to code points.

The Unicode standard reserves 6,400 code points in the BMP for so-called private use, for "user-defined characters." This should be more than enough in most cases, but there are 131,068 additional private use code points in other planes. More exactly, the Private Use Area (PUA) consists of the following code points:

- U+E000 to U+F8FF (on plane 0—i.e., BMP)
- U+F0000 to U+FFFFD (on plane F hexadecimal)
- U+100000 to U+10FFFD (on plane 10 hexadecimal—i.e., the last plane)

Here the word "private" has a wider meaning than in common language. For example, two large public institutions could agree on the use of some private use code points for their information interchange. You could use private use code points even in data that you distribute in public, as long as you make it clear that the interpretation and processing of the data requires knowledge about special definitions you have made.

You should not use unassigned code points even for internal purposes like bookkeeping or "sentinels" such as indicators of end of character data or separators between blocks of character data. For such purposes, you can often use code points assigned to control characters or declared as noncharacters.

 Do not use unassigned code points for anything. If you need a code point for a character that cannot be expressed in Unicode (yet), use private use code points.

Unicode Terms

The Unicode standard and related documents contain a large number of special terms, often consisting of common words in highly specialized meanings. In this book, the presentation of the terms has been spread across the material, into contexts where the terms can be illustrated and exemplified. To check the meaning of a particular term, it is therefore simplest to consult the index.

In this section, some special Unicode terms are presented. The terms refer to concepts that don't quite belong to the core of Unicode and don't belong to special sections either.

Deprecated and Obsolete Characters

A *deprecated* character is a character that has been included in Unicode but declared as deprecated in the Unicode standard. This indicates a strong recommendation that the character not be used. It remains in Unicode, though, due to the stability principle. For example, a character may be declared deprecated if it turns out that it was introduced into Unicode in error. There is a machine-readable list of deprecated characters in the document *http://www.unicode.org/Public/UNIDATA/PropList.txt*. In Unicode 4.1, there are few deprecated characters: the combining marks U+0340 and U+0341, the Khmer characters U+17A3 and U+17D3, and the formatting characters U+206A..206F.

In many other standards, the term "deprecated" contains a warning that deprecated constructs may, and probably will, be removed in future versions of the standard. In the Unicode standard, there is no such idea; on the contrary, deprecated characters are guaranteed to remain in the standard.

An *obsolete* character is a character that is not used in new texts anymore but has been included into Unicode due to its historical usage. Obsolete characters are not deprecated, as a rule. It is quite appropriate to use an obsolete character when writing text that discusses old texts that contain the character. For example, Latin small letter long "s," ſ (U+017F), is an obsolete character that was used in Gothic (blackletter) writing instead of "s" in some positions. In a broader sense, a character can be regarded as obsolete if it is no longer used in some language, even if other languages may use it.

These concepts are quite different from concepts like "noncharacter" or "unassigned code point." Deprecated and obsolete characters fall into the category of graphic characters in the basic classification of code points, but they are pragmatically different from normal characters.

Digraphs

A digraph is a combination of two successive characters treated as a unit in some sense, such as "ch" in many languages (e.g., when used to indicate one sound) or "ll" in Spanish, where it denotes a particular sound and might be treated in sorting as if it were a single character. Thus, a digraph is a pragmatic concept, not a formal one, and it is an example of a text element (see next subsection).

Speakers of a language may intuitively understand a digraph as "one character," especially if the ordering rules of the language treat it that way. This is especially true for digraphs that are used as replacements for characters, such as "ae" for ä when writing German (under conditions where one cannot or dare not use ä). From the Unicode perspective, it's still two characters.

However, there are many Unicode characters that are originally digraphs but are now treated as one character. Examples include characters that are completely independent in Unicode, such as small Latin letter ae æ (U+00E6) (even though an English reader may well see it just as a way of writing "ae" together) as well as compatibility characters such as Latin small ligature ij "ij" (U+0133), which decomposes into "i" followed by "j."

Thus, a digraph is normally written as two separate characters in Unicode. Treating them as a unit is up to an application. A digraph may or may not be presented visually as a ligature—i.e., as a single glyph that contains the two characters "melted together."

Similarly, a *trigraph* is a sequence of three characters treated as a unit, as "sch" in German, where it denotes roughly the same sound as the digraph "sh" in English.

Text Elements

The concept of text element is informal: it means a sequence of characters (including the special case of one character) that is treated as a unit in some processing. In typical character input and output, characters are text elements. In layout processes, syllables might be treated as text elements, since line breaks are usually allowed between syllables but not within them. When you form a text concordance (a list of occurrences of words—e.g., in alphabetic order), a word is a text element.

The concept is sometimes confused with a combining character sequence—i.e., a sequence consisting of a base character and one or more combining characters (such as combining accents). Although a combining character sequence could also be a text element, that's casual. A text element is whatever an application regards as a text element.

Unicode Strings

The term "Unicode string" has a more technical meaning than you might expect. It does not refer to a string (sequence) of Unicode characters (code points) but to a sequence of *code units.* Thus, the components of the string are of fixed size in bits (in practice, 8, 16, or 32 bits). In many programming languages, Unicode strings have a code unit size of 16 bits. This does not limit the range of characters, since such a string could be interpreted according to UTF-16.

Thus, a component of a Unicode string need not correspond to a character. A code unit could be part of the representation of a character (say, the second octet of a two-octet representation in UTF-8). Even if a code unit as such represents a code point, it can be a noncharacter or an unassigned code point.

Although a Unicode string is often in some encoding, this is not a requirement. It is possible to consider any sequence of octets as a Unicode string, even if the sequence does not correspond to the rules of any Unicode encoding (in practice, UTF-8 in this case). You could also have a sequence of 16-bit (double byte) code points containing isolated surrogates.

The point here is that "Unicode string" is a technical concept for use in programming, and it is intended to be very simple for such use. A program or function that accepts a Unicode string as input need not check its internal structure and may process in any suitable way. If the output is a Unicode string, it need not correspond to any encoding.

The reason behind this is efficiency. Software designers can make programs check for the integrity of a Unicode string as representing a sequence of characters, but they can do it at the point they prefer.

Guide to the Unicode Standard

The newest version of the Unicode standard itself should be your ultimate reference in matters of Unicode. It is, however, very large and partly very technical and hard to read, though many parts are enjoyable and smoothly written. Perhaps most frustratingly, it is often difficult to find the place or places where some topic is covered; the information might be scattered to different sections of the standard. To help you to find the relevant information and to make use of it, here is a brief guide to the standard.

Accessing the Unicode Versions

The Unicode standard is available online (mostly in PDF format), but not necessarily as a simple consolidated version. You may need to combine information from a major base version with later modifications issued as minor versions. At the time of this writing, the current version is 4.1.0, and its content is defined cumulatively by the following documents:

The Unicode standard, Version 4.0
http://www.unicode.org/versions/Unicode4.0.0/

Unicode 4.0.1, an update to the previous
http://www.unicode.org/versions/Unicode4.0.1/

Unicode 4.1.0, another update (minor version)
    http://www.unicode.org/versions/Unicode4.1.0/

The Unicode database reflects the newest version, but the prose text and code charts may need to be read along with the update documents.

A previous version of the standard, Unicode 3.0, is available online, too, and it might be interesting for comparison: *http://www.unicode.org/unicode/uni2book/u2.html*. There are also many old database files available via *http://www.unicode.org/versions/*.

What Material Constitutes the Unicode Standard?

The Unicode standard is available as a book, though there can be a delay between issuing the standard and printing it. The online version contains PDF documents that correspond to the chapters of the book. But these alone are not self-contained presentations of the standard. There are several points to note. As mentioned earlier in the chapter, there can be incremental updates (minor versions):

- On the Unicode web site, there's a page titled "Updates and Errata," which lists official corrections to the standard. As new versions are issued, corrections are incorporated into them, and the "Updates and Errata" page is effectively cleared. The page is *http://www.unicode.org/errata/*.

- There is a series of documents called "Unicode Technical Reports," some of which are called "Unicode Standard Annexes," (UAX), and regarded as integral part of the standard but published as separate documents. They are available on the CD-ROM that accompanies the book as well as (as possibly updated versions) on the Unicode web site, at *http://www.unicode.org/unicode/reports/*.

- There is the "Unicode Character Database," which defines many properties for characters, in a manner suitable for automated processing. The database and the description of its structure are available via *http://www.unicode.org/ucd/*.

Viewing the Standard Online

As mentioned earlier in the chapter, the online standard is mostly in PDF format. Thus, you need some software that can display PDF files, such as Adobe Reader. The online version cannot be printed using normal methods, so you may still have a reason to buy the printed standard. Copying of texts is possible: using Adobe Reader's text select tools, you can copy text onto the Windows clipboard.

The main table of contents of the online version consists of the following parts:

Front Matter
    This includes a table of contents as in a book, in PDF format, but also "Unicode 4.0 Web Bookmarks," which is a very handy hypertext table of contents. It is in HTML format, with links pointing to locations in the PDF files.

Chapters
    The main text of the standard. See below for an explanation of its structure.

Appendices and Back Matter
Material such as a glossary (in PDF format).

Unicode Standard Annexes
The number of the annexes varies by standard version, since annexes may get incorporated into the main text when creating new versions.

The Unicode Character Database (UCD)
Consists of HTML and plain text files.

Related Links
The links point to additional material on the Unicode site, such as Glossary of Unicode Terms (updated and modified, in HTML format).

The Chapters of the Standard

The breakdown of chapters is as follows:

Chapter 1: Introduction
This is a short chapter, and it gives a good overview of some basic ideas.

Chapter 2: General Structure
This gets more detailed and more technical than the Introduction. It presents the fundamental principles of Unicode, but it is rather hard to read. After finishing this book, though, you can probably understand this chapter.

Chapter 3: Conformance
This is a rather technical chapter, which is important to Unicode implementers. For a "normal" reader, there are some useful explanations of basic concepts like character semantics and code values.

Chapter 4: Character Properties
Describes how the standard defines some general properties for characters, such as General Category (letter, number, separator, etc.) or case mappings (e.g., what character, if any, is the uppercase equivalent of a lowercase letter).

Chapter 5: Implementation Guidelines
As the name says, this is mainly for implementers. But reading 5.1, "Transcoding to Other Standards," can be useful to anyone, and browsing through the headings is a good idea, too. Note in particular that this chapter describes some general principles according to which programs might recognize grapheme, word, line, and sentence boundaries (e.g., to implement a command for moving forward one sentence in text processing). It also explains the problems of sorting and searching, which are more language-dependent than you may have thought.

Chapter 6: Punctuation and Writing Systems
This is the first one of the chapters (6 through 15) that describe the various sets of characters. They contain quite a lot of practical information about the use of various characters and comparisons between characters (e.g., a comparison of different dash-like characters). Note that the sets do not necessarily correspond to blocks. For

example, there are punctuation symbols scattered around into various blocks, in addition to the General Punctuation block. This chapter begins with an overview of writing systems, also known as scripts.

Chapter 7: European Alphabetic Scripts
Latin, Greek, Cyrillic, etc.

Chapter 8: Middle Eastern Scripts
Hebrew, Arabic, Syriac, Thaana.

Chapter 9: South Asian Scripts
Devanagari, Bengali, etc.

Chapter 10: Southeast Asian Scripts
Thai, Lao, etc.

Chapter 11: East Asian Scripts
Han (especially Chinese-Japanese-Korean (CJK) unified ideograms), Hiragana, Katakana, Hangul, Bopomofo, Yi.

Chapter 12: Additional Modern Scripts
Ethiopic, Mongolian, Osmanya, Cherokee, Canadian Aboriginal Syllabics, Deseret, Shavian.

Chapter 13: Archaic Scripts
Ogham, Runic, and other historical scripts.

Chapter 14: Symbols
This includes a rich set of characters used as symbols that are relatively language-independent, such as currency symbols, letterlike operators (which are letters taken into some special use), number forms, mathematical, technical, geometric, and other symbols.

Chapter 15: Special Areas and Format Characters
This chapter discusses codes used for various control purposes, the "private use" area, the "surrogates" area (based on the idea of using two 16-bit values to present one character), and the special code points at the end of the Unicode range (e.g., byte order mark).

Chapter 16: Code Charts
This "chapter" presents the character themselves, and it constitutes about half of the volume. It begins with a short legend and explanations. Then the blocks are presented, in code number order. For most blocks, a chart of (typical) glyphs for the characters in it is given first, followed by a list of the characters, with their code numbers, glyphs, names, and possibly alternate names, references to similar (but distinct) characters, decompositions (compatibility or canonical), and usage notes. These descriptions do not list all the properties of the characters as defined in Unicode; they do not include all the information in the Unicode database.

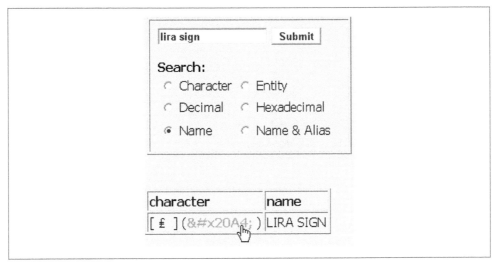

Figure 4-2. A search from the Zvon database by character name has found the character, and a link to information on it is included

Chapter 17: Han Radical-Stroke Index

For the Chinese-origin ideograms. "To expedite locating specific Han ideographic characters within the Unicode Han ideographic set, this chapter contains a radical-stroke index." The Han Radical-Stroke Index itself is available as a separate document.

Thus, Chapters 1 through 5 form the general part. Their essential content is covered in this book. The relevance of the other parts depends on what kinds of characters you work with.

How Do I Find All the Information About a Character?

If you are looking for the most adequate Unicode character for some particular use, there is no simple answer. You might browse through the chart for the block where you expect the character to appear; for example, a mathematical symbol is probably in the Mathematical Symbols block. You can also use more systematic search methods. A few alternatives are described in the following sections.

The Zvon database

If your clue to the character is its name, or its Unicode number, you could use the online Zvon character database: *http://www.zvon.org/other/charSearch/PHP/search.php*. The database, although not authoritative, is based on information at the Unicode site. Beware that the name you have in your mind might not be the one under which the character is known in Unicode—the name might have been assigned to a different character there.

The information in the Zvon database (of which an example is shown in Figure 4-3) is the same as in the Unicode code charts, including the annotations (called "Comment" in

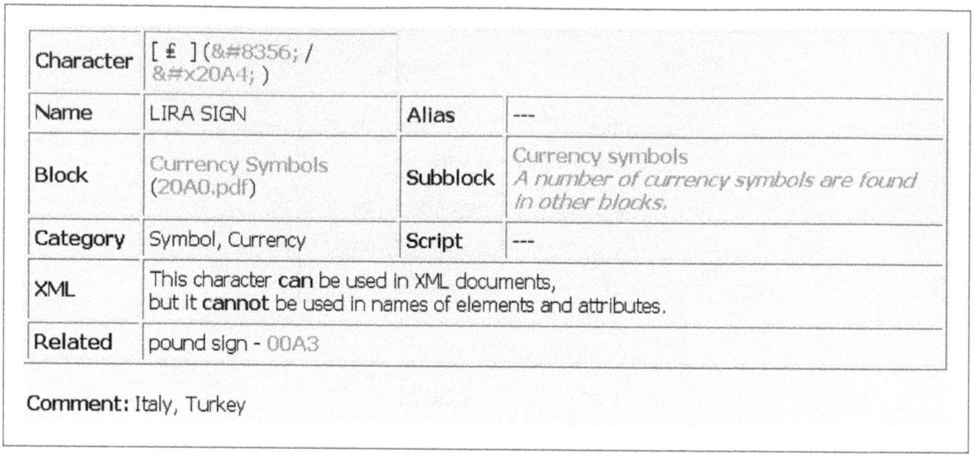

Character	[£] (₤ / ₤)		
Name	LIRA SIGN	Alias	---
Block	Currency Symbols (20A0.pdf)	Subblock	Currency symbols *A number of currency symbols are found in other blocks.*
Category	Symbol, Currency	Script	---
XML	This character **can** be used in XML documents, but it **cannot** be used in names of elements and attributes.		
Related	pound sign - 00A3		

Comment: Italy, Turkey

Figure 4-3. Information on a character in the Zvon database

Zvon), and some additional derived information such as the XML character reference. The information *does not include the notes made in the prose text of the standard.*

Using Unibook

Unibook is software for offline browsing of information about characters, using a graphic user interface, in a Windows environment. It can be downloaded for free from *http://www.unicode.org/unibook/,* and it has detailed instructions for installation and use. It has no technical support, though. Figure 4-4 is a snapshot of using Unibook: the user has searched for "lira sign" (using Ctrl-F to invoke a Find dialog) and has got the character highlighted in its position in a code chart. Clicking on the character causes information to be displayed in a pop-up window, as shown in Figure 4-5.

Using the Unicode standard

Assuming that you know the code number of a character, at least as a tentative answer to the question "Which character should I use?", you can consult the following to see what the Unicode standard says about it:

- Its description in the *code charts.*
- Its properties as defined in the *database.* Note that this means several different properties, defined in different files of the database.
- Any *additional explanations* you might find in the standard, at various places. There is no systematic way to locate such information, but at least you should look at the applicable part in Chapters 6 through 15. They often contain information that is often similar to the general descriptions preceding the code chart (in Chapter 16), just placed elsewhere.

Let us take a simple example: suppose we need all the information on the character U+2206. Since it falls into the range U+2200..U+22FF, we find it in the Mathematical

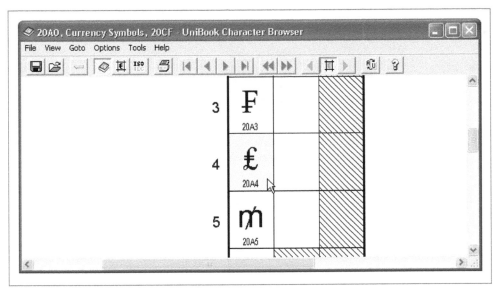

Figure 4-4. Using Unibook, the Unicode character browser

Operators block. This suggests that it is a mathematical symbol in some sense. The formal confirmation for this is that the *Unicodedata.txt* file in the character database contains the following entry for it:

```
2206;INCREMENT;Sm;0;ON;;;;;N;;;;;
```

The file consists of lines, each of which gives information about a character, with information fields separated by semicolons. The fields are summarized in Table 4-5 and described at *http://www.unicode.org/Public/UNIDATA/UCD.html* in more detail. (See also Chapter 5 for a description of the general format of Unicode database fields.) Thus, the example tells that character U+2206:

- Has the name INCREMENT.
- Belongs to general category Sm, which is an "informative" (as opposite to "normative") category. The abbreviation stands for "Symbol, math." Chapter 5 explains what categories mean in general; note that the categories are referred to when defining various properties, such as line breaking properties (UAX #14).
- Belongs to canonical combining class 0, which roughly means just "base character"; see section 4.3 of the standard.
- Belongs to bidirectional category ON, "Other Neutrals."
- Has the Bidi mirrored property value of N, which means "not mirrored."

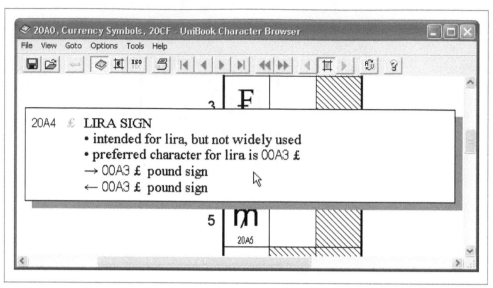

Figure 4-5. Viewing character information in Unibook

Table 4-5. Fields in the Unicodedata.txt file

#	Field name	Default	Meaning of the field
0			Code number of the character (hex.)
1	Name		Unicode name of the character
2	General Category	Cn	Overall classification for the character
3	Canonical Combining Class	0	Used in the Canonical Ordering Algorithm
4	Bidi Class	L,AL,R	Defines the bidirectional behavior
5	Decomposition Mapping	=	Canonical or compatibility decomposition
6	Numeric Value	(none)	Numeric value, if the character is numeric
7	Numeric Value	(none)	Numeric value, if digit but not decimal
8	Numeric Value	(none)	Numeric value, if decimal digit
9	Bidi Mirrored	N	Y (yes), if mirrored in bidirectional text
10	Unicode 1 Name	(none)	Old name, defined in Unicode Version 1.0
11	ISO Comment	(none)	Comment in the ISO 10646 standard
12	Simple Uppercase Mapping	=	Uppercase version as single character
13	Simple Lowercase Mapping	=	Lowercase version as single character
14	Simple Titlecase Mapping	=	Titlecase version as single character

```
2206    Δ    INCREMENT
             = Laplace operator
             = forward difference
             → 0394 Δ  greek capital letter delta
             → 25B3 △  white up-pointing triangle
```

Figure 4-6. Description of character U+2206 in a code chart

 The *Unicodedata.txt* file is a handy reference to some properties of characters. Using a suitable text editor, you can find information on characters
quickly, if you download a copy of the file from *http://www.unicode.org/
Public/UNIDATA/UnicodeData.txt*.

We find additional information on our sample character in the code chart for the Mathematical Operators block, as shown in the extract in Figure 4-6.

The description characterizes some uses of the character by listing "Laplace operator" and
"forward difference" as synonyms for it (in some usage). Obviously, the primary name
suggests the use as an increment symbol in some sense. Note that this does not constitute
an exclusive list of uses for the character by any means, or that it would be obligatory to
use this character for those purposes even when it is available in the repertoire. The actual
usage is a decision made by mathematicians.

The description also clarifies that this is not the same character as Greek letter capital delta
or a white up-pointing triangle (in the Geometric Shapes block). Note that an arrow means
in principle just "cross reference," but quite often its specific purpose is to make it explicit
that two characters are not equal, although they may have identical or similar glyphs.

Then let us check what the corresponding general description in Chapter 12 says. The
relevant part in the standard, section 14.4, contains a clarifying note. It says that the IN-
CREMENT character is one of the mathematical operators derived from Greek characters
that "have been given separate encodings because they are used differently from the corresponding letters." It adds: "These operators may occasionally occur in context with
Greek-letter variables." (In contrast, Unicode 3.0 said that these characters "have been
given separate encodings to match usage in existing standards.") In practice, there are
borderline cases: when a character with the shape of a capital delta occurs in printed form
only, or in an encoding that lacks a code corresponding to U+2206, it can be difficult to
say whether it should be interpreted as the Greek letter (U+0394) or as U+2206. For
example, what about the delta amplitude function or the symbol for the area of a triangle?

There are also dozens of other properties defined for characters than those defined in the
Unicodedata.txt file, as explained in Chapter 5. Although not all properties are practically
relevant for all characters, many of them form part of the meaning of a character in a broad
sense. They affect behavior like line breaking and writing direction. For U+2206, there

are really no surprises in the properties. For example, in line breaking, it behaves the same way as letters, which should be suitable. On the other hand, for the en dash "–" U+2013, for example, the Unicode line breaking rules allow a break after it (e.g., an expression like "5–8" could be broken as "5–" on one line and "8" on the next). In borderline cases at least, such things might matter in the choice of character.

Thus, the identification of a symbol as a particular Unicode character is not really an exact science. There are matters of interpretation, and there is no comprehensive index to all information on a character in the standard.

Additional Reference Material

The Unicode standard and its annexes is partly rather large and complex, and it is not always suitable for quick checks or efficient searches. You may therefore wish to consult other references as well, even though they are not authoritative. To a large extent, other references have been constructed automatically from material issued by the Unicode Consortium, but this does not guarantee that they are error-free; programs have bugs.

Some practical references were listed in Chapter 1. The following online material is more technical or more specialized:

Die Unicode-Datenbank by Jürgen Auer
This site (*http://www.sql-und-xml.de/unicode-database/*) lists Unicode 4.1 characters by block but also by the 30 categories, by additional properties, and by bidirectional value. It also mentions for each character the version of Unicode in which it was introduced, helping to estimate how well it is supported. The explanations are in German, but you can mostly use it without knowing German.

Unicode Charts by Mark Davis
This site (*http://www.macchiato.com/unicode/charts.html*) lists only Unicode 3.0 characters, but it has some useful features. It lets you search for the code of a character by typing or pasting a character into a text box and hitting Enter. You can also view the GIF images of characters instead of the rendering of your browser using some font on your computer.

Unicode Character Properties Excel Workbook
This site (*http://scripts.sil.org/ExcelUnicodeData*) presents the contents of several Unicode database files as a single file that you can open in MS Excel or in Excel Viewer.

DecodeUnicode, a wiki activity
This site (*http://www.decodeunicode.org*) combines data extracted from the Unicode site with additional data contributed to different people using the wiki approach: anyone can write and edit anything. Therefore, the site contains a mixture of descriptive information. The user interface is not intuitive, and much of the material is in German only.

Unicode and Fonts

One of the 10 design principles is that Unicode encodes characters, not glyphs. Thus, Unicode is not about fonts. Although proper presentation of some Unicode text requires a font that contains the characters actually used in the text, any such font will do. You can even use a mixture of fonts. The font selections have to be made outside Unicode.

Unicode as Plain Text

Unicode is basically for plain text, or text as such, without formatting features, structural indicators, or processing commands. Plain text can be characterized as a universal, simple, and portable data format. You can save text data as plain text and expect people to be able to read it after a hundred years, as long as the text is physically preserved. Would you bet on the format used by your favorite word processor to do the same, given the past experience with incompatible data formats?

This doesn't mean that Unicode wants everyone to use plain text. On the contrary, much of work with Unicode has been pragmatically motivated by the advance of markup like XML as well as databases that store text in complex formats. Unicode is used more and more in data formats where characters and strings appear as constituents of higher-level constructs.

Unicode deals (in principle) exclusively with the plain text level of data representation, because it was designed to do just that. *Some* specification must do that, and it would be impractical to let each data format define its own idea of characters. It has turned out to be easier to manage complex things by dividing them into simpler parts, such as levels of data representation.

Plain text is not always quite plain. First, it usually has a division into lines. It may contain spaces, which are not always just plain separators between words but may involve formatting purposes, especially when consecutive spaces or fixed-width spaces are used. There are other deviations from the plain text principle, such as characters for tabbing or affecting ligature behavior. Moreover, some typographic variation can be encoded into the choice of a character.

Font Variants as Characters

Despite the "characters, not glyphs" principle, some Unicode characters are effectively variants of other characters, in the sense of font variation. For example, the character script capital "H" ℋ (U+210B) is equivalent compatibility-wise to Latin capital letter "H" H (U+0048). The equivalence is defined using the notation <font> 0048. This means that it is a font variant of "H" in a sense, but in a rather abstract sense: no specific font is implied, just the general idea of using a script (handwriting) style.

In practice, programs do not select a glyph for the script capital "H" by picking up the glyph for capital "H" from some special handwriting-style font. Instead, they pick up a glyph for U+210B from a font that has a glyph in that position (such as Arial Unicode MS or some other large font).

Apart from such compatibility characters, there is no way to give any font information in Unicode. This is not a flaw but a conscious decision to handle different issues at different levels and in different standards. Plain text can be presented in any suitable font, but if you wish to change font in the midst of text, you are not using just plain text, and you need additional tools (see Chapter 9).

Variation Selectors

A relatively recent addition to the Unicode standard introduced the concept of a Variation Selector, which is an invisible character that is meant to affect the choice of glyph for the preceding character. Thus, a Variation Selector is comparable to font markup or to the choice of font in a word processor, though its effect is generic. It does not specify any particular font but rather the general characteristics of a glyph.

For example, the intersection ∩ (U+2229) is usually presented with a glyph without serifs (i.e., without short lines perpendicular to the two ends below), even if the glyph is from a serif font. You can explicitly request that a glyph variant with such serifs be used by inserting Variation Selector 1 (VS1) U+FE00 after the character U+2229.

The currently available standard variants that can be requested for some characters are listed in *http://www.unicode.org/Public/UNIDATA/StandardizedVariants.html*. They consist of variants of some mathematical operators and some Mongolian characters.

Support for Variation Selectors in current software is very limited. Programs might just treat them as unknown graphic characters, displaying some generic symbol.

Affecting Font Usage

The use of Unicode characters may *indirectly* affect font choices made by programs:

- If the font chosen for text does not contain all the characters in the text, the program may decide to use some other font(s) as fallback. Therefore, some characters may appear in a font different from the surrounding text. A choice between characters that are compatibility equivalent, or even canonically equivalent, can be relevant in this sense. For example, Latin capital letter "A" with ring Å (U+00C5) is probably available in most fonts you might use. If you use the angstrom sign Å (U+212B), which is canonically equivalent to U+00C5, the appearance can be different, since this character appears in some fonts only. Consider this as a problem, not as a formatting tool!

- Some Unicode (control) characters prevent or suggest the use of ligatures or joining behavior—i.e., presenting the surrounding characters together. A program may or may not display characters "f" and "i" in succession using a ligature, if available in the current font. But it must not do that if there is a specific invisible control character between them that prevents a ligature.

Ligatures

A ligature is a visible presentation of two or more characters as a unit. The origin of ligatures is in cursive handwriting, where characters are generally joined together. For printing, ligature types were produced to solve problems in both the visual appearance and in the mechanics of printing. Text does not look good if, for example, the upper part of the "f" is close to dot of the "i" as in "fi," so it can be better to create a type that fuses the two characters together.

In English, we normally use ligatures mostly for "fi," "fl," and "ffl" only, and usually in print only. Many other scripts use ligatures far more often.

Ligatures as discussed here should not be confused with characters that *originate from* ligatures. For example, capital Latin letter "ae" æ (U+00E6) is an independent letter in Norwegian and Danish, although it is originally a ligature of "a" and "e" and is sometimes used just as a typographic variant of "ae" in English when writing Latin words. Unicode recognizes this character as a letter that is not decomposable into anything, although its old name used the phrase "ligature ae." In general, the word "ligature" in a character's name can be misleading.

For most purposes, Unicode treats ligatures as belonging to typographic issues that are not addressed by the Unicode standard. A word containing "fi" may or may not be rendered using a ligature for this character pair, and this does not affect the way in which the word is represented as a sequence of Unicode characters. The ligature behavior can often be affected by the commands and tools of a page layout program. For example, a layout program may present some character combinations as ligatures by default. For example, in computer code represented in monospace font, a ligature "fi" probably looks odd (compare ficora.fi with ficora.fi). You would need to use some program-specific command to prevent such behavior in general or for some selected text.

However, there are some constructs specifically related to ligatures in Unicode:

- For compatibility with other standards, Unicode contains a few ligatures coded as characters. For example, there is Latin small ligature "fi" fi (U+FB00), which is defined as equivalent compatibility-wise to "f" followed by "i." Characters in the Alphabetic Presentation Forms block (U+FB00..U+FB4F) include ligatures for "ff," "fi," "fl," "ffi," and "ffl."

- The character *zero width non-joiner* U+200C, abbreviated ZWNJ, specifically instructs that characters before and after it shall not be joined as a ligature or in a cursive (handwriting-style) connection.

- The character *zero width joiner* U+200D, abbreviated ZWJ, specifically instructs that characters before and after it should be joined as a ligature or in a cursive manner.

The characters ZWNJ and ZWJ are effectively invisible control characters. They are meant to be used for exceptional overrides only. Do not confuse these characters with the word joiner (WJ) character, which relates to line breaking issues; see Chapter 5.

Support for ZWNJ and ZWJ is not common for most scripts. You should not expect to be able to produce, say, an fi ligature that way, though the ZWJ and ZWNJ characters may be effective in scripts where they are really needed, such as the Arabic script. In text formatting, ligatures should normally be generated on other basis, such as program-specific commands or information on the language of the text and typographic conventions for the language.

 In MS Word, you can use the Insert → Symbol function to add special characters that allow or prevent a line break. However, Word uses ZWNJ and ZWJ for this, contrary to their meanings. If text written that way is processed with another application, you should check what happens to these characters.

Vowels as Marks

Several writing systems indicate vowels as marks attached to consonants rather than as separate letters. In Hebrew and Arabic writing, short vowels may be indicated that way, though they are mostly just omitted, to be inferred by the reader.

A different method is applied in writing systems called *abugida* (or sometimes *alphasyllabary*), such as the Devanagari (Devanāgarī) script used for Hindi. The idea is that a basic character alone denotes the consonant sound followed by an implied vowel, namely "a." Other combinations of a consonant and a vowel are indicated by attaching a special mark to the basic character.

For example, the Devanagari letter pa प (U+092A) and the Devanagari vowel letter uu ू (U+0942), when appearing in that order, combine into the appearance पू (read as "puu" or "pū"). If the next character is the Devanagari letter ra र (U+0930), it joins without any break: पूर. It depends on the implementation whether the rendering is achieved by using glyphs that join suitably or by mapping a sequence of characters into a single glyph that represents them as "melted together."

Operations on Glyphs

In Chapter 1, we described the simple idea of characters and glyphs: a character is an abstract entity, though with a general idea of what it looks like, whereas a glyph is a particular appearance of a character. This mental model needs to be broadened, since visible presentation of text may involve much more that just mapping each character to a glyph.

The use of ligatures in presenting texts can be described as *glyph mapping*. If some text contains the abstract characters "f" and "i" in succession, they are first mapped to glyphs for them, and then the adjacent glyphs might be mapped to a ligature glyph.

In some cases, the mapping could be performed at the character level. For example, software for printing text might first map the sequence of "f" and "i" to Latin small ligature "fi" fi (U+FB00), and then map this to a glyph. However, since combined glyphs do not generally have character equivalents, it is best to operate uniformly at the glyph level.

Glyph mapping may involve many other operations, such as:

- Selecting between stylistically different glyphs ("aesthetic variants") for a character, using information expressed outside the plain text
- Selecting an appropriate contextual variant of a glyph—e.g., for Arabic letters, which need to be shown in different glyphs depending on their position in a word

Operations on glyphs are beyond the scope of this book. To get a somewhat more detailed idea of them, in the context of OpenType fonts, see the web page "GSUB - The Glyph Substitution Table" at *http://www.microsoft.com/typography/otspec/gsub.htm*.

Unicode Versus Font Tricks

When you write text in Unicode, you can normally use any font available in the system. Some fonts are "Unicode fonts," some are not, but this refers to technicalities. Even if a font has been designed for rendering data that is represented in an 8-bit encoding, the software you use can probably handle the mappings internally, so that the font can be used for Unicode text as well.

Whether you can vary the font in your text depends on the tools and data formats you use. In plain text, there is no font variation, but word processors work with other formats. They usually have some simple tool for, for example, selecting some words and setting their font to something different than the surrounding text.

However, some special tricks have often been used in an attempt to extend character repertoire by font settings. In Chapter 3, we noted that you could type, on your word processor, the letters "abc" and then select them and use the font-changing command to set the font to Symbol to get "αβχ" (i.e., three Greek lowercase letters). We analyzed this from the viewpoint of character encoding, but here the emphasis is on comparing such tricks with the Unicode approach.

Logically, the Symbol font is a collection of mostly wrong glyphs for characters (e.g., an α glyph for "a"). Of course, the same trick works for Unicode text, too, unless the software you use refuses to perform the illogical move. After all, the Symbol font does not contain the letters "abc," so any request to use it for them should be ignored.

Anyway, using Unicode, such tricks are completely unnecessary and pointlessly risky. A change of font never changes the identity of characters, in the logical sense, so even if you see "αβχ," it's still "abc." This can be checked by changing the font to something else. There's no reason to take the slightest risk of having your data passed through some process that changes the font and distorts what you meant. In Unicode, you simply use the right characters, using some suitable input method. To help you in such a conversion, Appendix A contains a table of Unicode equivalents of Symbol font glyphs.

This should not be confused with font changes needed to make some correctly entered characters visible. For example, if you use any of the methods described in Chapter 2 to enter the Greek letter alpha α, it might still fail to display properly. If the current font does not contain a glyph for alpha, you need to change the font locally (or globally) to something else, such as Arial Unicode MS—but any font containing the alpha will do.

Criticism of Unicode

Unicode has been criticized on several accounts, from very different perspectives. The following discussion tries to summarize most of the arguments and comment on them. The presentation is not apologetic; it will admit that there are good points in the criticism.

Criticism of lack of tools for indicating semantic structures is not discussed here. It is indirectly addressed in section "Why Not Markup in Unicode?" in Chapter 9.

Overall Complexity

Although the basic principles and structure of Unicode are simple, Unicode as a whole is complex, with difficult concepts, definitions, and algorithms. Is it *too* complex?

The writing systems that people use are complex, especially when considered as a collection of systems that may be combined in texts. Some writing systems have myriads of characters; some use diacritic marks extensively; some use contextual forms for characters; and experts on different fields keep inventing new symbolisms. It was possible to make many old character codes much simpler than Unicode just because they ignore most of the reality of different writing systems, languages, and notation systems.

Moreover, Unicode was not created in a vacuum. It was designed to deal with and to interoperate with a multitude of other character codes. The main implication was the introduction of compatibility characters, but this in turn required new concepts, definitions, and techniques such as compatibility decompositions and normalization forms. Another implication is that Unicode tries to preserve some of the internal structure of other codes in its coding system. The most obvious symptom of this is that the very first block in Unicode is the same as the ASCII set, with a mixed collection of characters.

Unicode is complex because it deals with complex phenomena. In fact, much of the other criticism is aimed at Unicode's attempts at simplification of the complexity! But it remains true that if you are willing to limit yourself to one writing system with a fixed repertoire of characters, you could deal with it in a simpler and more efficient way.

Many things could have been done differently, and perhaps in a simpler way. On the other hand, simplicity is relative: when the reality to be dealt with is complex, doing things the simple way in one respect may bounce back elsewhere. Moreover, as support for Unicode becomes more mature, most of the complexity will be hidden from almost all people, behind applications and subroutine libraries.

Inefficiency?

Fairly often, people say that Unicode is too inefficient, since it uses two bytes for each character. We cannot afford doubling the size of each text file, and the duration of any text transfer, can we? There is also a more modern version of this claim, saying that Unicode needs four bytes for a character.

As we have noted, and as will be discussed in detail in Chapter 6, Unicode has several encoding forms. Using UTF-8, for example, the size of a text file remains exactly the same as in ASCII, one octet (byte) per character, as long as the data consists of ASCII characters only. If you use other characters, then you "pay" for them: each of them requires two, three, or four octets.

The inefficiency argument has a point, though. If you have Modern Greek text, for example, you can represent it in some 8-bit encoding, using just one octet per character. In any Unicode encoding, each Greek letter requires at least two octets. For languages like French, the effect is smaller, since the majority of characters used in French are ASCII characters.

In processing character data in Unicode, inefficiency is caused either by the overhead of interpreting an encoding like UTF-8 or by the use of an encoding (such as UCS-2), which is simpler to process but wasteful in terms of storage. Moreover, if you really process character data in a Unicode-conforming way, you need to observe several mandatory rules, due to normative properties of characters. In reality, however, you can process Unicode data without making your application Unicode-conforming.

To summarize, Unicode may imply some inefficiency as compared to simpler character codes, but usually the problem is small when compared with the gain. When the problem becomes important, various compression methods can be used. This may mean either general purpose compression or the special purpose compression schemes described in Chapter 6.

Is It Reasonable to Require Support for 100,000 Characters?

The character repertoire of Unicode is large and expanding, and in most applications, only a small part thereof will be used. Wouldn't it be more reasonable to use, say, a code with 1,000 characters than to use a standard that requires support to 100,000 characters? After all, about 1,000 characters is sufficient for all European languages and the most common symbols.

This criticism is based on a wrong assumption on the impact of the character repertoire. Surely Unicode contains more characters than most people will ever need. Many characters have been included for use in very limited environments, such as a language spoken by a few hundred people in the world, or an extinct language. But the number of characters is a much smaller burden than you might expect.

Software that conforms to the Unicode standard need not be capable of *rendering* all Unicode characters. It need not contain a font that has glyphs for all characters. Not even all the fonts on a system combined need to cover all of Unicode. The conformance requirements in the Unicode standard say that an application may be ignorant of a character, as long as it does not destroy or distort characters that it does not understand.

Unicode-enabled software need not even *recognize* all Unicode characters. You can implement systems that use Unicode but have been designed to process some collection of characters only.

Thus, a program that supports Unicode may well support only a subset of Unicode characters. Upon reading a character outside the subset, it may indicate, in some suitable way showing a question mark in a box, its inability to display the character. It must not, however, simply omit the character or replace it by another character (like "?") when it reads data and passes it to further processing.

The *normative properties* of characters constitute a burden, since an application is required to honor the properties even if it cannot render the characters. This, however, can be handled by using the machine-readable files available from the Unicode Consortium's web site. You are not supposed to hand code the processing of 100,000 different characters. Instead, you use the character's code number as an index to a table of properties, directly or via a system utility.

Cultural Bias

Unicode has often been criticized for being culturally biased so that it favors languages of Western European origin, and specifically English. The history of character codes is largely a story of extensions, starting from a very limited set of characters that were suitable for some technical needs and for coarse writing of English. At each step, care was taken to guarantee efficient processing of already encoded characters, thereby often making the processing of new characters less efficient.

Lack of precomposed characters

Despite the large amount of assigned characters, Unicode does not contain all characters in all languages. Although almost all living languages are covered, some of their characters are covered only indirectly. For example, you cannot express the letter ǐ ("i" with both a macron and a grave accent) as a single character in Unicode. It needs to be represented using combining diacritic marks—e.g., as ī followed by a combining grave accent. You can contrast this with the fact that all characters with diacritic marks as used in Western European languages, such as é and â, are included in Unicode as separate (precomposed) characters.

One could say that Unicode was once open to the inclusion of precomposed characters as needed, but was then closed, after all "important" languages had been covered. The coding space would surely allow the inclusion of many additional precomposed characters to meet the needs of other languages, but a policy decision says otherwise. This means a cultural bias, but the practical importance of the issue is small. Because of the needs of special notations (in mathematics, linguistics, etc.), Unicode needs a general mechanism of using combining diacritic marks. The same mechanism can be used to cover the needs of some natural languages.

East Asian languages

Although most assigned code positions are for characters used in East Asian languages, it has been claimed that Unicode still discriminates against such languages and the CJK (Chinese, Japanese, and Korean) characters. Originally, Unicode was squeezed into 16 bits at the cost of omitting a large number of less important CJK characters and "unifying" different characters into one.

The key issue is *Han unification*—i.e., the treatment of characters of Chinese origin. In a long historical process, those characters had been adopted by other peoples and adapted to their languages. This often involved changes (such as simplification) in the shapes of characters. In defining Unicode, the characters were analyzed, and if, say, a Chinese character and a Japanese (kanji) character were deemed variants of the same character, a single Unicode code point was allocated for it. The general idea was that information about language could be used to decide on the particular shape of the character, and to some extent, this idea really works. In practice, for Japanese text you choose a font that contains Japanese versions of CJK characters, etc. If the same text contains both Japanese and Chinese, font variation or language markup (perhaps resulting in font variation; see Chapter 7) might be used.

However, Han unification has been regarded as an artificial and even barbaric method. We can perhaps understand the feelings of people who say so, if we think about the possibility that, had Unicode been designed in East Asia, perhaps the Latin, Cyrillic, and Greek alphabets would have been unified, making, for example, Latin "b," Cyrillic б, and Greek β just glyph variants of a single Unicode character. After all, they have the same origin, and language information could have been used to select between the glyphs!

The issue of Han unification is not, however, a case of East Asian peoples against the Western world. Many arguments were presented by East Asians *in favor of* the unification. If Unicode contained several clones of many Han symbols, many people would find it less manageable to work with different East Asian languages. The inclusion of unified CJK characters into Unicode does not prevent the addition of language-specific variants in other code positions, but that would work against Unicode principles.

Favoring UTF-8

Several documents specify UTF-8 as the preferred encoding for Unicode, especially in Internet contexts. Technically UTF-8 has many benefits especially for texts that contain mostly basic Latin letters and other ASCII characters, and it works relatively well for the additional Latin letters used in languages of West European origin. For other languages, it does not work that well.

Even for Greek text, UTF-8 uses a lot of space: data size is, roughly speaking, double the size it would need in a suitable 8-bit encoding. The same applies to most languages that are written using a relatively small repertoire of non-Latin letters.

For East Asian texts, it's worse. Some non-Unicode encodings for them are rather efficient, since they have been optimized for such use. For plain text in Chinese, even UTF-16 is more efficient than UTF-8. In UTF-16, all commonly used characters take two octets. In UTF-8, all characters except ASCII characters take *at least* two octets. Moreover, for fast character-by-character processing, UTF-8 needs to be internally transcoded into UTF-16 or some other representation where all or most characters occupy a fixed amount of octets.

Excessive Unification

The unification principles and practices have raised many objections. Unification prevents people from making distinctions that they might wish to make at the level of plain text. In some situations, a distinction could be made, but not reliably.

Problematic unification cases include the following (in addition to Han unification, which was discussed earlier):

- The character ü as an independent letter indicating a particular sound (as in Swedish) versus ü as "u" to which a diacritic mark has been added (as in Spanish). Many people regard these as different characters. In Unicode, you could try to distinguish between the two by using the precomposed character U+007C (Latin small letter "u" with dieresis) in the first case and the two-character sequence U+0075 (Latin small letter "u") U+0308 (combining dieresis) for the latter. However, these are canonically equivalent, and you cannot expect that software conforming to the Unicode standard makes the difference. On the contrary, it normally shouldn't, and it normally doesn't.

- The character æ is a separate letter in Danish and Norwegian. In some other contexts, including some styles of writing Latin words used in English, it is just a ligature of "a" and "e" (as in "Cæsar" for "Caesar"). There is no way to make this distinction in Unicode, although between the lines we can read the idea that ligatures should be handled at other protocol levels, not at the character level (i.e., you would use just "ae" in text and use, for example, styling information to suggest rendering it as a ligature).

- The right single quotation mark, ', is recommended for use as a punctuation apostrophe as well, as in the expressions "don't" or "Jane's." This means that two characters with essentially different meanings have been unified, just because usually the same glyph is used for both. As a consequence, the properties of the character cannot be very descriptive, since they need to take both uses into account. When you set up general rules for processing a character like the single quotation mark, you need to make them such that they are suitable, or at least tolerable, even when the character is actually used as an apostrophe. Note that quotation marks normally surround words or larger expressions, whereas the apostrophe is usually part of a word.

Thus, it is impossible to make, for example, apostrophes look different from right single quotation marks simply by using different code numbers for them and a font in which they are different. According to the Unicode standard, you should code both of them the same way, as U+2019. You would have to use methods above the character level to have them display differently, and this would be too clumsy for many purposes. Yet, people might wish to make the distinction, perhaps because an expression like 'don't' would look better that way.

However, unification can be justified on several grounds:

- It often corresponds to human intuition, since characters that are unified are usually recognized as "basically the same" by people who know them.

- It keeps the number of characters smaller, which helps in coding characters in a practical manner (e.g., keeping common characters in Basic Multilingual Plane if possible).

- It makes it easier for people to recognize which character they wish to use, when they need not look for tiny differences.

- It helps font design, since designers need not think whether very similar characters should have identical glyphs or different glyphs, which are difficult to implement, since they should then be sufficiently different (to avoid making the difference look like an error).

In programming, unification might seem to make things simpler, since there are fewer different characters to be considered. However, it also creates problems. For example, recognizing quotations from a piece of text becomes more difficult, because you cannot know, without extra analysis, that U+2019 is used as a quotation mark and not as an apostrophe.

Semantic Disambiguation Frowned Upon

Unification itself means that in many cases a character has two or more essentially different meanings. In addition, even when different meanings of a graphic symbol have been coded as separate characters, Unicode mostly does this only by defining compatibility characters.

For example, the letter "I" is also used as a Roman numeral that means "one." You are supposed to use the Latin letter capital "I" in that meaning too, in Unicode. Although Unicode also contains the character Roman numeral one I (U+2160), it is equivalent compatibility-wise to normal "I," and it has been included only for compatibility with other character code standards. You are not supposed to use it in new data.

Consider the expression "Charles I." To a human reader, it is usually obvious that "I" is a numeral and shall be read as "the first." To a computer, this is not obvious at all. For example, a speech synthesizer probably reads "I" the way we read the pronoun—i.e., the same way as "eye." There are various ways to address such problems, but they can be complex or have an *ad hoc* nature (e.g., explicit pronunciation instructions), and they are not portable across data formats and applications.

It would be better in many ways if we could disambiguate characters at the character level, by using, for example, Roman numeral one (U+2160) in "Charles I," or by using a separate character, rather than the Greek letter pi, when we mean π as a number (3.14…). Even in cases where such disambiguation is possible in Unicode, it is not recommended in the standard; rather, the standard advises against it. Therefore, we cannot expect most software make any use of it.

The Unicode policy in this issue is understandable, however. Semantic disambiguation at the character level would require a large number of new characters, and most people would probably not want to make the distinctions, or would make mistakes in trying it.

Misleading Names of Characters

Some Unicode names of characters are misleading, misspelled, or even completely wrong, when considered as a descriptive name. This has caused many protests. It is understandable that when you find a character that you know well and you notice an error in its name, you want it to be fixed. Yet, the response is always: Unicode names are fixed and will never be changed.

To take a relatively harmless example, the character U+2118 has been named "script capital p." However, it is neither script nor capital; whether it is a "p" is debatable: it is historically based on the letter, but as a Unicode character, it is defined as a letterlike symbol. By shape, it is a calligraphic variant of lowercase p, ℘. By meaning, it is a conventional symbol for a certain mathematical function. It's thus a character with well-defined semantics, quite independent of the name. The name becomes a problem only if it is taken too seriously.

Some cases are more problematic, however. Some names for characters in scripts that are not well known in the Western world are just wrong: a name might be one that is commonly used to refer to a character in the script, but to another one. To make things worse, some of the bad names have been caused by cultural misunderstandings and by naming a character "from outside"—i.e., by people who do not live in the culture in which the character is used. Some of these names have even been interpreted as insults. Moreover, reluctance to change the names has been interpreted as an even worse insult.

This is an unfortunate situation, but the conclusion is that you should try to avoid getting offended either by the Unicode names or by requests to change them. It is futile to suggest changes to individual names. Suggestions to remove or deprecate the entire system of Unicode names might some day lead to something, but this is not likely.

The alias names for characters, mentioned in the code charts, are often no better than the official Unicode names. For example, the commercial at @ (U+0040) has the annotation "Klammeraffe (common, humorous slang German name)," which is seldom useful to a serious English-speaking person who is uncertain of the character's identity. The solidus / (U+002F) is adequately explained by specifying "slash" as an alternate name, but the further explanation "virgule, shilling (British)" is misleading. The word "virgule" is rare, but "shilling" is worse. The solidus does not mean "shilling," though it was once used in British English to separate the shilling digits from the pence digits, as in 2/6 (two shillings and sixpence) or in 2/- (two shillings). The asterisk * (U+002A) has the annotation "star (on phone keypads)," but the use of the word "star" is not limited to phone contexts, and do we really need to identify all keypad symbols with characters? The capital letter "G" has the annotation "invented circa 300 B.C.E. by Spurius Carvilius Ruga, who added a stroke to the letter C." Interesting as this trivia might be, it is of little value in establishing the identity of the character in the modern world. Besides, it's not necessarily correct; the invention has also been attributed to Appius Claudius.

Thus, the idea that the annotations could be used as boilerplate texts presented to users, when displaying information on characters, is not very feasible. Although the Unicode databases specify many properties of characters, there is no single and uniform source of information on their identity and meaning (usage).

Concepts and Definitions

Although the Unicode standard contains parts that can be regarded as rather complex and theoretical, it has also been criticized for not being theoretical enough. It has been remarked that the fundamental concepts, even the concept of character, have been defined more or less vaguely and even inconsistently. The Unicode standard contains several different ingredients: the prose text, the code charts, the property tables, and different annexes and reports.

For example, Unicode Technical Report #17, "Character Encoding Model," defines "character repertoire" as "an unordered set of abstract characters to be encoded" and adds that the word "abstract" means "that these objects are defined by convention." The question arises then: what is a character that is *not* defined by convention? It seems that the word "abstract" in the Unicode material is just an attribute that has been thrown in for different purposes in different contexts.

In defense of Unicode, it needs to be said that Unicode's starting point was challenging. Many of its compromises, and confusions in terminology, come from several decades of a wilderness of "character sets" or "code pages." Unicode was designed to cover all characters in commonly used character codes, and it was natural to adopt terminology from older standards. Besides, Unicode disambiguates a lot by using terms like octet, code point, glyph, etc., instead of using the word "character" in a wide range of meanings as in ordinary language.

The organization of the Unicode standard has been described as practically confusing, too. Information on characters is partly scattered around the standard. Moreover, the update procedures make it troublesome to find out the exact content of the standard at a given moment of time, if there are any updates since the last major version.

Illogical Division into Blocks

For historical reasons, many Unicode blocks are essentially copies of ranges of characters in other standards. This has led to somewhat strange allocations especially in the first two blocks. Many characters in Basic Latin (ASCII) and Latin-1 Supplement would logically belong to other blocks, such as General Punctuation. Thus, when you try to get an idea of the punctuation characters in Unicode, for example, you need to look at several blocks.

If no previous character codes had been taken into account when defining Unicode, the use of the coding space would undoubtedly be different. It would be based on grouping by usage. The order of blocks would probably be different too. Now the CJK characters, for example, have been distributed into blocks in a manner that looks rather random.

The reasons for making the first two blocks essentially copies of ASCII and ISO 8859-1 are both technical and cultural. Such an assignment helps in efficiency; consider how ASCII characters are representable each as one octet in UTF-8, still keeping UTF-8 simple. They also help in continuity, since people who have worked with ASCII and ISO 8859-1 can find their characters easily.

The evolving nature of Unicode also makes some illogical assignments more or less necessary. New needs have led to allocation of blocks and ranges in a manner that cannot be smoothly integrated with old allocations. All the different extension blocks reflect the gradual incorporation of scripts and characters into Unicode.

Questions and Answers

The Unicode web site contains a Frequently Asked Questions (FAQ) section, divided into topics and categories, at *http://www.unicode.org/faq/*. You will probably find it very useful, especially if you take some time now to have a look at its table of contents, so that you roughly know what you can expect to find there. The following list of questions and answers does not try to compete with the Unicode FAQ. Rather, it discusses some general questions in some depth, partly dealing with same questions as the FAQ, but explaining the answers in a more tutorial-like manner.

Where Can I Find Tools for Using Unicode?

Software tools for Unicode, such as Unicode-capable word processors, editors, subroutine libraries, and converters, exist both as commercial products and as freeware under varying license conditions. Many tools have been developed for a particular environment, such as Windows XP, Macintosh, or Linux, though there are also tools that have been implemented for several environments. You may also encounter more or less obsolete tools that support some old version of Unicode only, although even an old tool might be sufficient for a limited purpose. Thus, there are probably many places to look, and the choice depends on your goals and resources. The Unicode FAQ points to two resources at the Unicode site in its answer to the question:

Useful Resources (http://www.unicode.org/onlinedat/resources.html)
> This link list contains the following parts: Fonts and Keyboards, Linguistics and Script Specialty Sites, Organizations and Other Standards, and Using Unicode. You will find tools for Unicode through the Using Unicode section, though it is rather mixed, and many links point to sites that just exemplify Unicode use.

Unicode Enabled Products (http://www.unicode.org/onlinedat/products.html)
> The page presents a large sample list of products (in a broad sense) that are more or less Unicode-enabled, divided into categories: Databases and Repertoires, Fonts and

Printing Software, Internationalization Libraries, Operating Systems, Programming Languages and IDEs, Search Engines, Standards, Translation Systems, and Other Systems and Products. As you may guess, the list partly exists to demonstrate how widely Unicode can be used. If you intend to create Unicode-enabled software, the International Libraries part is a good start in estimating how to find suitable building blocks.

Although the "Other Systems and Products" part of the latter resource also contains many Unicode editors and word processors, you get a better picture of such software from the resource mentioned in Chapter 2: *http://www.alanwood.net/unicode/utilities.html.*

Why Do People Call Unicode a 16-Bit Code?

Unicode was originally designed to be a 16-bit code, it can be represented in a 16-bit encoding (UTF-16), and all widely used characters are in the BMP range, where code numbers can be presented as 16-bit integers. Before Unicode Version 3.0 (March 2001), all characters were in the BMP, so that although the structure of Unicode allowed a much wider code space, only a 16-bit subspace was in use.

Besides, people read books, articles, and messages that call Unicode a 16-bit code. The idea has the properties of a very successful meme (an idea that people receive and pass forward): within a certain scope (information technology), the idea is simple, easy to understand and remember, and it sounds new and interesting.

Yet it would be incorrect to say that Unicode is a 16-bit code in practice, or for most practical purposes. It's not a 16-bit encoding: Unicode is widely used in an 8-bit encoding, UTF-8. It's not a 16-bit coding space: planes outside the BMP have increasing importance.

How Can I Have a Character Added to Unicode?

If you would like to have a character, or a collection of characters, added to Unicode, you will likely analyze the issue and find out that you can use existing characters. For example, proposals to add new precomposed characters—combinations of a base character and some diacritic(s)—will almost surely be rejected. If you know a character that looks different from any existing Unicode characters, it is probably a variant of an existing character and should be treated that way. It may well be a common character in an uncommon font. If you think your company's symbol counts as a character, the Unicode Consortium will most probably disagree. Ligatures and typographic variants will normally not be accepted either.

If you still think you have a character that needs to be encoded, check the instructions on submitting characters on the Unicode web site. Their basic content is that a proposal must be sent in writing and it must contain:

- At least one image of the proposed character, normally from a printed source (and including several images will help in illustrating the character)

- Substantial documentation that justifies the proposal (explaining, among other things, how the character is used in texts and why it needs to be recognized as different from existing Unicode characters)

- Identification of the sponsor(s), with contact information (postal and email address and phone number)

You should normally first send an informal query on the matter to the public Unicode discussion list (email list), described at *http://www.unicode.org/consortium/distlist.html*. You might take a look at the document registry *http://std.dkuug.dk/jtc1/sc2/wg2/* to see what the proposals look like and how detailed they are.

How Can I Check That I've Understood the Principles?

The principles of Unicode aren't something you need to learn by heart. Rather, you learn them when you read more about Unicode and work with it. Still, it might be a good idea to sit down and check whether you can *write down the 10 principles* of Unicode. Specify each of them for yourself with a word or two that name the principle, and then write a simple sentence that says something about it, maybe just an example. Then check your list against the list given in the section "Design Principles" in this chapter, or against the description in the Unicode standard (in Version 4.1, it's in section 2.2).

As a different test, read the very short description of Unicode, "What is Unicode?" or one of its translations at *http://www.unicode.org/standard/WhatIsUnicode.html*. Read it with a critical mind, and ask yourself the following questions:

- If you had to use the description as a basis when talking about Unicode, could you back up any general statement there with at least one concrete example? (This tests your general understanding of Unicode, not just this chapter.)

- If you had to explain Unicode at elementary school, which parts of the description would you omit?

- The description says that "Unicode provides a unique number for every character." What does "every character" really mean here?

- Name at least three essential problems of using Unicode that are not mentioned in the description.

CHAPTER 5

Properties of Characters

Unicode contains about 100,000 characters and is still growing. To manage the multitude of characters, we need to assign useful classifying and other properties to them. The Unicode standard defines a large number of properties, related to things like decompositions, collation, sorting, directionality, and line breaking, as well as Unicode normalization forms. Some of the properties are answers to simple questions like "Is the character a digit?" or (for letters) "What is the corresponding uppercase letter?" Many properties are more technical and intended for use in formal specifications and in programming.

This chapter concentrates on properties in a rigorous sense: properties defined for characters in the Unicode standard in an exact, objective, formalized manner. All the properties discussed here differ from purely verbal descriptions of characters in the standard, such as the description of possible glyph variation. For example, the description that the ASCII quotation mark " (U+0022) has a vertical glyph is surely relevant, but not formalized. The same applies to other similar notes in the text of the standard and the annotations in the code charts.

The Unicode standard designates some properties as *normative*. Such a property is prescriptive in the sense that if a conforming implementation uses the property, it must do so in accordance with its definition. The non-normative properties are called *informative*. Character properties, even normative properties, are not guaranteed to remain stable, and in practice, some properties have been changed between Unicode versions.

The properties discussed here have different uses:

- They help you to understand correctly the meaning and intended use of a character.
- They specify default processing rules for characters. Programs can and should implement the rules, so that the rules will be overridden only when application-specific reasons make this sensible.
- They are used to construct machine-readable information on characters. You can use such information with viewers that let you search and display it, but also via programs and subroutine libraries, which let you use the information in programs that you design.

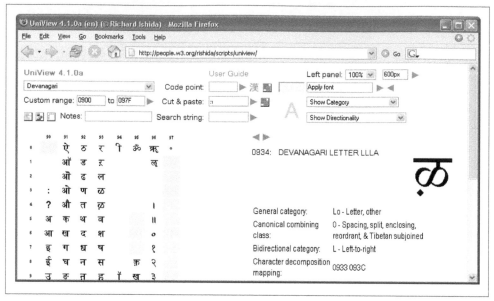

Figure 5-1. *Viewing characters and their properties in Uniview*

Figure 5-1 illustrates the use of an online service, Uniview, for viewing some key properties of characters with a graphic user interface. In the figure, the character itself is shown on the right, with some property values listed under it. Uniview lets you browse and search characters by general category or other properties. Uniview is available at *http://people.w3.org/rishida/scripts/uniview/*.

Character Classification

We will first consider one important property of characters in Unicode, namely General Category (or gc, for short). This will illustrate the definition and usefulness of properties, as well as some problems in defining them.

The Purposes of Classification

Characters can be classified in several ways, for different purposes. The Unicode standard defines a basic classification by assigning the General Category property to each character. Other properties imply classifications that are more specific, such as by the "age" of character—i.e., by the Unicode version in which it was encoded.

The General Category property, defined for all characters, constitutes a fundamental classification into letters, numbers, punctuation, mathematical symbols, etc. For several frequently used characters, this classification is not very natural, since they have multiple uses. For example, the hyphen-minus "-" can be used as punctuation, as a minus sign, or as a special symbol. The reason behind this is the history and design of Unicode: it contains many "legacy characters," which have ambiguous semantics and mixed usage.

The classification is generally useful, though. For example, when writing pattern-matching routines, you often need to work with concepts like "letter" or "digit." Instead of dealing with a huge amount of letters individually, you work with the classification.

The definition of a computer language (e.g., programming, markup, or data description language) typically involves a "name" or "identifier" concept. The rules typically allow an identifier to start with a letter and otherwise contain both letters and digits, and perhaps some special characters like _. Such a rule can be written easily, if we restrict ourselves to ASCII. That means, however, that most people in the world cannot use words of their native language in identifiers. To define a generalized concept of identifier, it is simplest to use the General Category and other properties, rather than list a huge number of characters. We return to this topic in Chapter 11.

If you define things like identifier syntax using the Unicode properties and specify that the newest Unicode version be used, the syntax is automatically updated when Unicode is. This means flexibility, but it also means instability in the sense that strings that were previously not identifiers by the syntax become identifiers later. The opposite is not probable, but possible; most Unicode properties are not guaranteed to remain the same, once defined for a character. For such reasons, definitions of computer languages may fix identifier syntax in a manner that does not depend on Unicode versions, at the cost of making it impossible to use newly added characters in them. For example, in XML, identifier syntax has been fixed to use the properties of characters as defined in Unicode 2.0. Technically, the XML specification does not refer to the properties but explicitly lists its own definitions of character classes (see *http://www.w3.org/TR/RECxml/#CharClasses*), but they are based on Unicode 2.0.

General Category Values

The classification is hierarchical: the General Category property indicates both a major class of a character and a subclass. The property is expressed with a *two-letter code* such as Lu so that:

- The first character is an uppercase letter indicating the major class, which is Letter, Mark, Number, Separator, Other, Punctuation, or Symbol.
- The second character is a lowercase letter that specifies the subclass.

The General Category values are shown in Table 5-1, together with sample characters or code points. Characters in class Mn are nonspacing and combining, and the sample character is shown as combined with a space (see "Diacritic marks" in Chapter 8).

Table 5-1. General Category values

Code	Description	Sample character
Lu	Letter, uppercase	A
Ll	Letter, lowercase	a
Lt	Letter, titlecase	Dž (U+01C5)

Code	Description	Sample character
Lm	Letter, modifier	ʰ (U+02B0)
Lo	Letter, other (including ideographs)	א (alef, U+05D0)
Mn	Mark, nonspacing	̀ (U+0300)
Mc	Mark, spacing combining	ः (U+0903)
Me	Mark, enclosing	(U+06DE) ۞
Nd	Number, decimal digit	1
Nl	Number, letter	IV (U+2163)
No	Number, other	½ (U+00BD)
Zs	Separator, space	(space, U+0020)
Zl	Separator, line	(line separator, U+2028)
Zp	Separator, paragraph	(paragraph separator, U+2029)
Cc	Other, control	(carriage return, U+000D)
Cf	Other, format	(soft hyphen, U+00AD)
Cs	Other, surrogate	(surrogate code points)
Co	Other, private use	(U+E000)
Cn	Other, not assigned (including noncharacters)	(U+FFFF, not a character)
Pc	Punctuation, connector	_ (low line, U+005F)
Pd	Punctuation, dash	- (hyphen-minus, U+002D)
Ps	Punctuation, open	(
Pe	Punctuation, close	)
Pi	Punctuation, initial quote	" (U+201C)
Pf	Punctuation, final quote	" (U+201D)
Po	Punctuation, other	!
Sm	Symbol, math	+
Sc	Symbol, currency	$
Sk	Symbol, modifier	^ (circumflex accent, 0+005E)
So	Symbol, other	©

The names "Punctuation, initial quote" and "Punctuation, final quote" are misleading, since characters in both categories may act as an opening or closing quotation mark, depending on the language. For example, in Swedish, a quotation starts and ends with U+021D (e.g., "Stockholm").

Characters with ambiguous semantics have General Category values that are meant to reflect their typical use in normal text. Thus, for example, hyphen-minus is classified as "Punctuation, dash," although it is often used as a mathematical symbol.

Use of General Category in Programming

To illustrate the use of this property in programming, let us consider the following simple task: read a text file and print all lines that contain an uppercase (capital) letter. Using a modern version of the Perl programming language, with Unicode support, you can do this with a three-liner (which could be written as a one-liner if you like):

```
while(<>) {
    if (m/\p{Lu}/) {
        print; }}
```

This program contains a loop that reads an input line and prints if the condition m/.../ is true—i.e., if a substring of the input line matches the expression between the slashes. The Unicode thing here is the expression, \p{Lu}, which by definition matches any character whose General Property value is Lu. This covers Latin uppercase letters with or without diacritic marks (A, Â, etc.) as well as Greek, Cyrillic, and other uppercase letters. An approach that uses the character properties is of course much simpler than writing program code that tests all the different possibilities separately. Whether the broad concept of "uppercase letter" corresponding to the General Property value Lu is really adequate in a particular situation depends on the context and application.

An Overview of Properties

For overview and quick-reference purposes, we will present an alphabetic table of properties here, followed by a list of explanations of the meanings of the properties. Many of the concepts used there will be explained later, or need to be consulted from the Unicode material, for issues that are too specialized to be discussed in this book.

The word "property" can have several meanings. For example, the shape of a character can be regarded as its property, and so can a statement about its use. However, in Unicode, the word "property" normally refers to *formally defined* properties. Often the definition is given as a table that lists characters and values of the property for each character.

The overall structure is described in the document "Unicode Character Database," *http:// www.unicode.org/Public/UNIDATA/UCD.html*. The Unicode Character Database (UCD) itself is a collection of plain text files in fixed, well-defined formats, which are suitable to automated processing. These files are available at addresses that begin with *http:// www.unicode.org/Public/UNIDATA/*, and they specify the values of properties for each character, either by explicitly assigning a value or by implying a default value.

We have previously mentioned the database file *Unicodedata.txt*, which is important indeed, and a basic file in a sense. However, contrary to what its name may suggest, it does not contain data for all properties. The tendency in the development of the standard has been to divide property definitions into separate files, so that *Unicodedata.txt* contains just some fundamental properties that can be described compactly.

Some properties are *derived* properties, which means that their values have been algorithmically deduced from other properties. Thus, derived properties are logically redundant: anything that you can express with them can be expressed using other properties. Derived properties have been included for convenience, to make some tests, definitions, and operations easier to write. For example, the property Alphabetic is derived, but it corresponds to an intuitive and important concept. It is more natural to say "if a character is alphabetic" than to say the same in terms of more primitive Unicode concepts (different categories of letters and characters comparable to letters). Each property has a set of values, or type, which is one of the following:

- A property name, which may contain spaces; often (especially in programming) the name is written with spaces replaced by low lines (underscores)—e.g., Bidi_Class instead of Bidi Class

- An abbreviation (code), defined in the *PropertyAliases.txt* file in the Unicode database

- A description of the meaning, given in prose, and further refined by rules that refer to the property (e.g., line-breaking rules define what line-breaking properties really mean)

- A status as normative or informative (descriptive)

The enumeration values and the catalog values are short, somewhat mnemonic strings like AL. The same value may have different meanings for different properties, so a value as such is not unique. There are longer, more mnemonic names defined for the values in the *PropertyValueAliases.txt* file. For example, AL has the longer name Arabic_Letter when used as a value of the property Bidi Class and the longer name Alphabetic when used as a value of the property Line Break.

In addition to the properties discussed here, there are many properties defined for Han (Chinese-Japanese-Korean) characters. They are regarded as *provisional*, which means a property "whose values are unapproved and tentative, and which may be incomplete or otherwise not in a usable state." The properties are described in the document "Unihan Database," *http://www.unicode.org/Public/UNIDATA/Unihan.html*.

Summary of Properties

The following list describes briefly all the 88 properties defined in Unicode 4.1.0. For each property, the list specifies the following:

- The abbreviation (short name)

- The long name, as defined in the *PropertyNames.txt* file; for some properties, this is the same as the abbreviation

- The type of the values of the property (yes/no, enumeration, etc.)

- The status as normative or informative; for some properties, the status is "normative or informative," which means that the property is normative for some values, informative for others

- The database file where the property values are specified; to access the file on the Web, prefix the name with *http://www.unicode.org/Public/UNIDATA/*

The list is in alphabetic order by the abbreviation of the property, since the abbreviation is what you normally see in program code, regular expressions, and other compact notations.

age = Age, catalog, normative or informative, DerivedAge.txt
> The number of the Unicode version in which the character was added to Unicode, such as "1.1" or "4.0."

AHex = ASCII Hex Digit, yes/no, normative, PropList.txt
> Indicates whether the character is an ASCII character used in hexadecimal numbers. This means letters "A" to "F" and "a" to "f" and digits "0" to "9."

Alpha = Alphabetic, yes/no, informative, DerivedCoreProperties.txt
> Indicates whether the character is alphabetic—i.e., a letter or comparable to a letter in usage. True for characters with gc value of Lu, Ll, Lt, Lm, Lo, or Nl and additionally for characters with the OAlpha property.

bc = Bidi Class, enumeration, normative, UnicodeData.txt
> The category of the character in the Bidirectional Behavior Algorithm.

Bidi C = Bidi Control, yes/no, normative, PropList.txt
> Indicates whether the character has a special function in the Bidirectional Algorithm.

Bidi M = Bidi Mirrored, yes/no, normative, UnicodeData.txt
> Specifies whether the character shall be represented using a mirrored glyph when it appears in right-to-left text.

blk = Block, catalog, normative, Blocks.txt
> Name of the block to which the character belongs.

bmg = Bidi Mirroring Glyph, string, informative, BidiMirroring.txt
> Suggests a character that can be used to supply a mirrored glyph for this character; see property Bidi M. For example, "(" mirrors ")," and vice versa.

ccc = Canonical Combining Class, number, normative, UnicodeData.txt
> Specifies, with a numeric code, how a diacritic mark is positioned with respect to the base character. This is used in the Canonical Ordering Algorithm and in normalization. The order of the numbers is significant, but not the absolute values.

CE = Composition Exclusion, yes/no, normative, CompositionExclusions.txt
> Specifies whether the character is explicitly excluded from composition when performing Unicode normalization.

cf= Case Folding, string, normative, CaseFolding.txt
> The case-folded (lowercase) form of the character. This is a derived property.

Comp Ex = Full Composition Exclusion, yes/no, normative, DerivedNormalization-Props.txt
> Indicates whether the character is excluded from composition when performing Unicode normalization.

Dash = Dash, yes/no, informative, PropList.txt
>Indicates whether the character is classified as a dash. This includes characters explicitly designated as dashes and their compatibility equivalents.

Dep = Deprecated, yes/no, normative, PropList.txt
>Indicates whether the character is deprecated. Deprecated characters will remain in the standard, but their use is strongly discouraged.

DI = Default Ignorable Code Point, yes/no, normative, DerivedCoreProperties.txt
>Indicates whether the code point should be ignored in automatic processing by default.

Dia = Diacritic, yes/no, informative, PropList.txt
>Indicates whether the character is diacritic—i.e., linguistically modifies another character to which it applies. A diacritic is usually, but not necessarily, a combining character.

dm = Decomposition Mapping, string, normative, UnicodeData.txt and NormalizationCorrections.txt
>The decomposition of the character. The property dt indicates the type of decomposition.

dt = Decomposition Type, enumeration, normative, UnicodeData.txt
>The type of the decomposition (canonical or compatibility) specified by the property dm. The possible values are listed in Table 5-2, later in the chapter.

ea = East Asian Width, enumeration, informative, EastAsianWidth.txt
>The width of the character, in terms of East Asian writing systems that distinguish between full width, half width, and narrow. See UAX #11, "East Asian Width."

Ext = Extender, yes/no, informative, PropList.txt
>Indicates whether the principal function of the character is to extend the value or shape of a preceding alphabetic character.

FC NFKC = FC NFKC Closure, string, normative, DerivedNormalizationProps.txt
>Indicates whether the character requires extra mappings for closure under Case Folding plus Normalization Form KC.

gc = General Category, enumeration, normative, UnicodeData.txt
>The type of the character according to a specific classification, as described in section "Character Classification" later in this chapter.

GCB = Grapheme Cluster Break, enumeration, informative, auxiliary/GraphemeBreakProperty.txt
>Indicates the category of the character for determining grapheme cluster breaks.

Gr Base = Grapheme Base, yes/no, informative, DerivedCoreProperties.txt
>Indicates whether the character is regarded as a base grapheme, for the purposes of determining grapheme cluster boundaries.

Gr Ext = Grapheme Extend, yes/no, informative, DerivedCoreProperties.txt
>Indicates whether the character is regarded as extending grapheme, for the purposes of determining grapheme cluster boundaries.

Gr Link = Grapheme Link, yes/no, normative, PropList.txt
  Indicates whether the character is regarded as grapheme link, for the purposes of determining grapheme cluster boundaries.

Hex = Hex Digit, yes/no, informative, PropList.txt
  Indicates whether the character is used in hexadecimal numbers. This is true for ASCII hexadecimal digits and their fullwidth versions.

hst = Hangul Syllable Type, enumeration, normative, HangulSyllableType.txt
  Type of syllable, for characters that are Hangul (Korean) syllabic characters.

Hyphen = Hyphen, yes/no, informative, PropList.txt
  Indicates whether the character is regarded as a hyphen. This refers to those dashes that are used to mark connections between parts of a word and to the Katakana middle dot.

IDC = ID Continue, yes/no, informative, DerivedCoreProperties.txt
  Indicates whether the character can appear as the second or subsequent character of an identifier.

IDS = ID Start, yes/no, informative, DerivedCoreProperties.txt
  Indicates whether the character can appear as the first character of an identifier. See "Identifier and Pattern Syntax," available at *http://www.unicode.org/reports/tr31/*, and Chapter 11.

IDSB = IDS Binary Operator, yes/no, normative, PropList.txt
  Indicates whether the character is a binary operator in Ideographic Description Sequences.

IDST = IDS Trinary Operator, yes/no, normative, PropList.txt
  Indicates whether the character is a trinary (ternary) operator in Ideographic Description Sequences.

Ideo = Ideographic, yes/no, informative, PropList.txt
  Indicates whether the character is an ideographic CJK (Chinese-Japanese-Korean) character.

isc = ISO Comment, miscellaneous, informative, UnicodeData.txt
  The content of the comment field for the character in the ISO 10646 standard.

jg = Joining Group, enumeration, normative, ArabicShaping.txt
  The group of characters that the character belongs to in cursive joining behavior. For Arabic and Syriac characters.

Join C = Join Control, yes/no, normative, PropList.txt
  Indicates whether the character has specific functions for control of cursive joining and ligation.

jt = Joining Type, enumeration, normative, ArabicShaping.txt
  Type of joining of glyphs: R (right), L (left), D (dual), J (join causing), U (non-joining), or T (transparent). For Arabic and Syriac characters.

lb = Line Break, enumeration, normative or informative, LineBreak.txt
Line-breaking class of the character. Affects whether a line break must, may, or must not appear before or after the character.

lc = Lowercase Mapping, string, informative, UnicodeData.txt and SpecialCasing.txt
The lowercase form of the character.

LOE = Logical Order Exception, yes/no, normative, PropList.txt
Indicates whether the character belongs to the small set of characters that do not use logical order and hence require special handling in most processing.

Lower = Lowercase, yes/no, informative, DerivedCoreProperties.txt
Indicates whether the character is a lowercase letter.

Math = Math, yes/no, informative, DerivedCoreProperties.txt
Indicates whether the character is mathematical. This includes characters with Sm (Symbol, math) as the General Category value, and some other characters.

na = Name, miscellaneous, normative, UnicodeData.txt and Jamo.txt
The Unicode name of the character. Guaranteed to remain stable.

na1 = Unicode 1 Name, miscellaneous, informative, UnicodeData.txt
The old name of the character in Unicode version 1.0, if significantly different from the Unicode name (value of the Name property).

NChar = Noncharacter Code Point, yes/no, normative, PropList.txt
Indicates whether the code point is a noncharacter—i.e., guaranteed to never denote a character.

NFC QC = NFC Quick Check, enumeration, normative, DerivedNormalizationProps.txt
Indicates whether the character can occur in Normalization Form C. Values: N = No, M = Maybe, Y = Yes.

NFD QC = NFD Quick Check, enumeration, normative, DerivedNormalizationProps.txt
Indicates whether the character can occur in Normalization Form D. Values: N = No, Y = Yes.

NFKC QC = NFKC Quick Check, enumeration, normative, DerivedNormalizationProps.txt
Indicates whether the character can occur in Normalization Form KC. Values: N = No, M = Maybe, Y = Yes.

NFKD QC = NFKD Quick Check, enumeration, normative, DerivedNormalizationProps.txt
Indicates whether the character can occur in Normalization Form KD. Values: N = No, Y = Yes.

nt = Numeric Type, enumeration, normative, UnicodeData.txt and Unihan.txt
This property has the value Decimal = De for decimal digits, Digit = Di for other digits, Numeric = Nu for other number denotations (e.g., fractions), and None = None for everything else.

nv = Numeric Value, number, normative, UnicodeData.txt and Unihan.txt
>The numeric value corresponding to the character. This is defined for different digit characters but also characters such as Greek letters, which are used to denote numbers according to a non-positional system. If this field is empty for a character in the database, the value defaults to "Not a Number" (NaN).

OAlpha = Other Alphabetic, yes/no, informative, PropList.txt
>Indicates whether the character is alphabetic but with a General Category value other than Lu, Ll, Lt, Lm, Lo, or Nl. Used to derive the Alphabetic property.

ODI = Other Default Ignorable Code Point, yes/no, normative, PropList.txt
>This property is used to derive the property DI.

OGr Ext = Other Grapheme Extend, yes/no, normative, PropList.txt
>This property is used to derive the property Gr Ext.

OIDC = Other ID Continue, yes/no, normative, PropList.txt
>This property is used to derive the property IDC.

OIDS = Other ID Start, yes/no, normative, PropList.txt
>This property is used to derive the property IDS.

OLower = Other Lowercase, yes/no, informative, PropList.txt
>This property is used to derive the property Lower.

OMath = Other Math, yes/no, informative, PropList.txt
>This property is used to derive the property Math.

OUpper = Other Uppercase, yes/no, informative, PropList.txt
>This property is used to derive the property Upper.

Pat Syn = Pattern Syntax, yes/no, normative, PropList.txt
>Indicates whether the character is or might be used in the pattern syntax for pattern matching as defined in "Identifier and Pattern Syntax," available at *http:// www.unicode.org/reports/tr31/*. See the section "Identifier and Pattern Syntax" in Chapter 11.

Pat WS = Pattern White Space, yes/no, normative, PropList.txt
>Indicates whether the character is treated as whitespace in patterns.

QMark = Quotation Mark, yes/no, informative, PropList.txt
>Indicates whether the character is used as a quotation mark in some language(s).

Radical = Radical, yes/no, normative, PropList.txt
>Indicates whether the character is a radical (in ideographic writing).

SB = Sentence Break, enumeration, informative, auxiliary/SentenceBreakProperty.txt
>Indicates the category of the character for determining sentence breaks.

sc = Script, catalog, informative, Scripts.txt
>The script (writing system) to which the character primarily belongs to, such as "Latin," "Greek," or "Common," which indicates a character that is used in different scripts.

scc = Special Case Condition, string, informative, SpecialCasing.txt
The condition under which a special case-mapping rule is applied. The condition is expressed as a space-separated list of locale IDs or contexts. For example, a value of tr means that the rule is applied for Turkish-language texts only.

SD = Soft Dotted, yes/no, normative, PropList.txt
Indicates whether the character contains a dot that disappears when a diacritic is placed above the character (e.g., "i" and "j" are soft dotted).

sfc = Simple Case Folding, string, normative, CaseFolding.txt
The case-folded (lowercase) form of the character when applying simple folding, which does not change the length of a string (and may thus fail to fold some characters correctly). This is a derived property.

slc = Simple Lowercase Mapping, string, normative, UnicodeData.txt
The lowercase form of the character, if expressible as a single character.

stc = Simple Titlecase Mapping, string, normative, UnicodeData.txt
The titlecase form of the character, if expressible as a single character.

STerm = STerm, yes/no, informative, PropList.txt
Indicates whether the character is used to terminate a sentence.

suc = Simple Uppercase Mapping, string, normative, UnicodeData.txt
The uppercase form of the character, if expressible as a single character.

tc = Titlecase Mapping, string, informative, UnicodeData.txt and SpecialCasing.txt
The titlecase form of the character.

Term = Terminal Punctuation, yes/no, informative, PropList.txt
Indicates whether the character is a punctuation mark that generally marks the end of a textual unit.

uc = Uppercase Mapping, string, informative, UnicodeData.txt and SpecialCasing.txt
The uppercase form of the character.

UIdeo = Unified Ideograph, yes/no, normative, PropList.txt
Indicates whether the character is a unified CJK ideograph. Used in Ideographic Description Sequences.

URS = Unicode Radical Stroke Count, miscellaneous, informative, Unihan.txt
A radical/stroke count quantity describing a Han (CJK) ideograph.

Upper = Uppercase, yes/no, informative, DerivedCoreProperties.txt
Indicates whether the character is an uppercase letter.

VS = Variation Selector, yes/no, normative, PropList.txt
Indicates whether the character qualifies as a Variation Selector used to specify the glyph variant of a graphic character.

WB = Word Break, enumeration, informative, auxiliary/WordBreakProperty.txt file
Indicates the category of the character for determining word breaks.

WSpace = White Space, yes/no, normative, PropList.txt
> Indicates whether the character should be treated by programming languages as a whitespace character when parsing elements. This concept does not match the more restricted whitespace concept in many programming languages, but it is a generalization of that concept to the "Unicode world."

XIDC = XID Continue, yes/no, informative, DerivedCoreProperties.txt
> As IDC, but for a somewhat different definition for "identifier." See Chapter 11.

XIDS = XID Start, yes/no, informative, DerivedCoreProperties.txt
> As IDS, but for a somewhat different definition for "identifier." See Chapter 11.

XO NFC = Expands On NFC, yes/no, normative, DerivedNormalizationProps.txt
> Indicates whether the character expands to more than one character in normalization to C form.

XO NFD = Expands On NFD, yes/no, normative, DerivedNormalizationProps.txt
> Indicates whether the character expands to more than one character in normalization to D form.

XO NFKC = Expands On NFKC, yes/no, normative, DerivedNormalizationProps.txt
> Indicates whether the character expands to more than one character in normalization to KC form.

XO NFKD = Expands On NFKD, yes/no, normative, DerivedNormalizationProps.txt
> Indicates whether the character expands to more than one character in normalization to KD form.

Normative and Informative Properties

The Unicode standard defines somewhat vaguely what it means to designate a property as normative. It does not mean that an implementation must know about the property and use it. But if it does, it must use it as specified in the standard. Thus, an implementation may not interpret the property values as it likes. A non-normative—i.e., informative—property is provided for use on an "as you like" basis: the property and its values have defined meanings and they stay at your disposal, but you may use them for your own purposes as you like.

For example, an implementation may be ignorant of Hebrew and Arabic letters and all directionality problems. But if it processes Hebrew or Arabic in a manner that involves visual presentation, it must apply the directionality principles of Unicode, and this means using the Bidi Class property according to the standard.

Some properties are partly normative, partly informative. The LineBreak property is normative for values that indicate a forced line break, for example, but informative for many other values.

Being normative does not imply a guarantee that the property value will not change in future versions of Unicode. Such changes are expected to be rare, though.

Generally, even a normative property can be overridden by a so-called higher-level protocol (see Chapter 9). For example, the visual rendering of a document must normally obey the normative values of the LineBreak property; line breaks can be prohibited or caused by tools external to plain text, such as stylesheets or explicit formatting instructions. Similarly, you can use informative properties to map lowercase letters to uppercase, yet override the mapping for some characters due to some language-related or even application-specific conventions. Of course, you are supposed to override the properties only if you know what you are doing—i.e., there is a well-defined reason.

A normative property can be designed as *non-overridable*. This means that no modification is allowed at any level. The reason for this is to guarantee that some basic operations are carried out in a guaranteed manner that other software may rely on. In particular, the decomposition properties are non-overridable. When canonical or compatibility decomposition is applied, the program doing so is not allowed to throw in its own decomposition rules or ignore or modify the rules specified in the standard. This means that if your program purports to deliver data in normalized form, you are guaranteeing that Unicode normalization rules and no other have been applied.

Structure of Database Files

As mentioned earlier in this chapter, the Unicode Character Database consists of plain text files, so it does not correspond to how many people understand the word "database." On the other hand, the files can be used to construct a database that can be used with suitable database software for searches, extracts, reports, etc. The files can also be used to generate mapping tables and other data structures needed for creating general purpose subroutines that can be used in programming, so that a programmer can work at a reasonable level of abstraction.

Largely for such purposes, the structure of the files follows some general principles, in addition to specific rules described in each file (in comments) or in the Unicode standard. The principles are:

- The files are in UTF-8 encoding, except *NamesList.txt*, which is ISO-8859-1. However, characters outside the ASCII range (Basic Latin block) appear in comments only, except when noted otherwise in the description of the file. Thus, in most cases, you can view and process the files as if they were ASCII encoded, at least if you ignore the comments.

- A comment starts with # and ends at the end of line. A comment does not belong to the data itself but describes it.

- One line corresponds to one logical record, typically specifying the value of a property for one character.

- Fields of a record are separated by semicolons. In some files, there is a semicolon after the last field, too. When the fields are referred to in text, they are considered as numbered starting from zero—as common in programming, since programming language designers think in terms of displacements from a base address.

- Leading and trailing spaces in a field are not significant.

- The first field of a record usually indicates a code point or code point range. The other fields specify property values for the code point(s).

- Code points are expressed in the usual hexadecimal notation but without the "U+" prefix, using at least four digits for a code number, with leading zeros as necessary.

- A code point range is described by writing two periods (..) between code points— e.g., 0000..007F.

- However, in the *UnicodeData.txt* file, a different method is used to specify values for a range of code points. A notation involving the words First and Last is used so that one line specifies the start and the next line specifies the end of the range. For example, the following two lines there specify that all code points from U+AC00 to U+D7A3 denote Hangul syllable characters, with the same properties as the first and last character of the range: (In such situations, the Unicode names of characters are algorithmically derivable; in this case, the names can be derived from an algorithmic decomposition into Unicode characters with known names.)

```
AC00;<Hangul Syllable, First>;Lo;0;L;;;;;N;;;;;
D7A3;<Hangul Syllable, Last>;Lo;0;L;;;;;N;;;;;
```

- A sequence of consecutive code points is expressed by writing them as separated with space. Thus, 0066 0069 means U+0066 "i" followed by U+0069 "j"—i.e., "ij" without any space.

- A property value may be omitted (still preserving semicolons between fields), thereby implying a default value. If the value is of string type, the default value is the character itself; for example, for case mappings, the default is that a character does not change in the mapping. For other types of values, the default is specified in a comment in the database file.

- Abbreviations and names of properties are written using underline (underscore) instead of a space—e.g., Bidi_Control instead of Bidi Control.

- In a file that may specify different properties for characters, the abbreviation of a property is given in one field, its value in another. For example, the following line (from *DerivedNormalizationProps.txt*) says that for character U+037A, the value of the property FC_NFKC is the two-character sequence U+0020 U+03B9:

```
037A  ; FC_NFKC; 0020 03B9    # Lm  GREEK YPOGEGRAMMENI
```

- In a file that specifies binary (yes/no) properties, the name of a property is given in one field, without a value, implying a "yes" value (True) for the character. For such properties, the value "no" (False) is implied for all characters that are not mentioned. For example, in the *PropList.txt* file, there are only the two lines quoted below that mention the Bidi_Control property (comments omitted from this quotation). This implies that for the two characters U+200E and U+200F and for the five characters U+202A to U+202E, the value of the Bidi Control property is "yes" (True), and for all other characters, it is "no" (False):

```
200E..200F     ; Bidi_Control
202A..202E     ; Bidi_Control
```

Compositions and Decompositions

The 10 design principles of Unicode, presented in Chapter 4, contain one principle on dynamic composition and another principle on equivalent sequences. For example, the letter é can be represented as a single Unicode character, or dynamically composed as a two-character string (letter "e" followed by a combining acute accent). The single character é is said to have a *canonical decomposition* consisting of two characters, and this relationship implies *canonical equivalence*.

Unicode lets you combine a *base character* with an unlimited number of combining diacritic marks. In practice, there's most often just one diacritic, sometimes two, but there is no limit. For example, phonetic or mathematical notations may deploy several diacritic marks on one character. As a base character, you can use any character that does not itself combine with preceding characters and that is neither a control nor a format character.

Unicode would be simpler, if all letters with diacritic marks were represented using dynamic composition. For different practical reasons, another approach was taken, and this implies that we need to deal with precomposed forms and with conversions between them and decomposed forms.

Characters may have decompositions in a different sense, too. Many characters have *compatibility decompositions*. For example, the small Latin ligature "fi," fi, has a compatibility decomposition that consists of the two characters "f" and "i."

The Impact of Diacritic Marks

A diacritic mark is an additional graphic such as an accent (as in è or é) or cedilla (as in ç) attached to a character. It may affect the pronunciation of a character, or the meaning of a word, or both. It appears visually close to the base character, often above or below it, possibly crossing over its line, but it is treated as a logically separable part.

A diacritic mark can be treated in different ways when defining a character repertoire. You could define a character like é (letter "e" with acute accent) as a separate character, or you could define the base character "e" and the diacritic ´ as two distinct characters. In the latter approach, you would need to define the diacritic as combining (nonspacing), or otherwise indicate that it be rendered as attached to the character, not as a separate character after it.

For example, the ISO-8859-1 character code contains a collection of letters with diacritic marks, such as é, but no combining marks. It contains the acute accent ´, but as a normal (spacing) character, which is not combined with any other character in any way.

The Unicode standard uses *nonspacing mark* as a term that covers diacritic marks but can be seen as somewhat more general in nature. The term "diacritic mark" is often used to denote accents and other marks attached to Latin, Greek, Cyrillic, and other letters, whereas "nonspacing mark" also covers Hebrew points, Arabic vowel marks, etc. In this book, "diacritic mark" is used in a broad sense, as a synonym for "nonspacing mark."

Precomposed and decomposed form

In Unicode, a character with a diacritic mark can often be represented in two ways. You can express é as a *precomposed* character or as *decomposed*—i.e., as a character pair consisting of "e" and a combining acute accent. Both representations are possible for a large number of commonly used characters, though not for all characters with diacritics.

This means flexibility, but it also creates a pile of problems. What happens if a database contains é as decomposed but a search string typed by the user contains it as precomposed? This is just the beginning of the problems. For example, a character with several diacritic marks can be represented as several different decompositions.

Unicode contains separate characters called *combining diacritical marks*. The general idea is that you can express a vast set of characters with diacritics by representing them so that a base character is followed by one or more combining (nonspacing) diacritic mark(s). A program that displays such a construct is expected to do rather clever things in formatting —e.g., selecting a particular shape for the diacritic according to the shape of the base character.

In Unicode, a combining diacritic mark always *follows the base character* in data. It may visually appear above, below, or on either side of the base character. The logical order differs from the order in many methods of typing characters with diacritic marks. For example, on many keyboards, you could first press a key labeled ´, and then the "e" key, to produce é. However, if this letter is represented in data as decomposed, it has the combining diacritic mark after the base letter "e."

The order in typing mechanisms reflects the methods used on mechanical typewriters. They may contain a ´ key, which is non-advancing—i.e., the writing position is not moved forward. Therefore, the next character will overprint the symbol, resulting in a coarsely constructed accented letter. In Unicode, combining diacritic marks are supposed to be rendered as combined with the preceding character in a more elaborate way.

Combining marks: powerful, but still poorly supported

Many programs currently in use are totally incapable of doing anything meaningful with combining diacritic marks. However, there is at least some simple support for them in word processors and web browsers, for example. Regarding advanced implementation of the rendering of characters with diacritic marks, consult Unicode Technical Note #2, "A General Method for Rendering Combining Marks," *http://www.unicode.org/notes/tn2/*.

Using combining diacritic marks, we have wide range of possibilities. We can put, say, a dieresis on a gamma, although "Greek small letter gamma with dieresis" does not exist in Unicode as a character with a code position of its own. The combination U+03B3 U+0308 consists of two characters, although its visual presentation looks like a single character in the same sense as ä looks like a single character. A word processor may display it as γ̈, which might be of poor quality (the dieresis is not correctly placed with respect to the base character), but probably legible. Many programs fail to display it at all. For practical reasons, in order to use a character with a diacritic mark, you should primarily try to find it as a precomposed character.

A *precomposed character*, also called a *composite character* or a *decomposable character*, is one that has a code position (and thereby identity) of its own but is in some sense equivalent to a sequence of other characters. There are lots of them in Unicode, and they cover most of the needs of the languages of the world, but not all. Special notations, such as the International Phonetic Alphabet by IPA, may require several different diacritic marks that can be combined with characters, in a manner that makes it quite infeasible to try to define all the combinations as precomposed characters.

For example, the Latin small letter "a" with dieresis ä (U+00E4) is, by Unicode definition, decomposable to the sequence of the two characters: Latin small letter "a" (U+0061) and combining dieresis (U+0308). Almost always, however, the letter ä is entered in its precomposed form, though it might then internally be decomposed. Generally, by decomposing all decomposable characters, you could in many cases simplify the processing of textual data, and the resulting data might be converted back to a format using precomposed characters.

Features that are not diacritic marks

Many letters that do not contain a diacritic mark in the Unicode sense have historically been formed from a base letter by adding some mark to it. For example, the Norwegian and Danish ø is originally an "o" with a slanted line over it. Its name, "Latin small letter o with stroke," reminds of this and could even be read as suggesting that it is a combination of an "o" and a diacritic mark called "stroke." Similarly, the letter Ł, "Latin capital letter L with stroke," used in Polish, would seem to be an "L" with the same diacritic, though with a different visual shape.

Although such letters are often understood as letters with diacritic marks, they are classified as independent letters in Unicode. The characters ø and Ł are not decomposable in any way. They have no defined relationships with "o" and "L" in Unicode, except in the sense that in the default collating order (see the section "Collation and Sorting" later in this chapter), ø is sorted in the same primary position as "o," and Ł is sorted in the primary position as "L."

This approach does not exclude the possibility of treating such characters in some special way in application programming or in language-dependent general rules. Since they are intuitively understood as variants of some base characters, it would be natural to define *input methods* that relate to such intuition. For example, in MS Word, you can produce ø by using the sequence Ctrl-Shift-7 o. This is relatively easy to remember if your keyboard has the solidus / as Shift-7, so that you can think you are using Ctrl-/ o.

Compatibility Mappings and Canonical Mappings

The Unicode character database defines a *decomposition mapping* for each character. This mapping associates another character or a sequence of characters with the given character, and this association is indicated as a *canonical mapping* or as a *compatibility mapping*, also called *decomposition*. Typical cases include the following:

- A character with a diacritic mark has a canonical mapping to a sequence of a base character and a combining diacritic mark. For example, é has a canonical mapping to "e" followed by a combining acute accent.

- A ligature has a compatibility mapping to a sequence consisting of the constituent letters. For example, ligature fi has compatibility mapping to "f" followed by "i."

- A character that is treated as a variant of another character often has a compatibility mapping to it, although sometimes the mapping is defined as being canonical. For example, many characters have so-called fullwidth forms for use in East Asian texts, where normal forms of symbols like $ might look odd, when other characters are "wide" (basically, designed to fit into a square). These forms, such as fullwidth dollar sign $ (U+FF04), have compatibility mappings to the normal characters.

Difference between canonical and compatibility mappings

Canonical and compatibility mappings are rather fundamental in Unicode, and they are commonly confused with each other. One reason for this is that in many cases, the choice of the mapping type was debatable, if not arbitrary. For example, the micro sign µ has *compatibility* mapping to the Greek small letter mu, but the ohm sign Ω has *canonical* mapping to the Greek letter capital omega. Yet both of them are basically Greek letters that have been taken to special usage, perhaps modifying the shape of the glyph a little.

In some notations—e.g., in the Unicode code charts—the character ≡ (identical to, U+2261) is used to indicate canonical mapping—e.g., Ω U+2126 ≡ Ω U+03A9. Handy as this may be, it can be misleading, since the two characters are not identical, though they may be treated as essentially similar by programs. The relation expressed by the ≡ symbol here isn't even symmetric, contrary to its normal use in mathematics. The symbol is best read as "has canonical mapping to."

Similarly, the character ≈ (almost equal to, U+2248) is often used to indicate compatibility mapping—e.g., µ U+00B5 ≈ µ U+03BC. This symbol is best read as "has compatibility mapping to."

The short characterizations are:

- If A has *canonical* mapping to B, then A and B are really two different ways of encoding the *same symbol* in Unicode. As codes or sequences of codes, they are different, but they have the same ultimate meaning and normally the same rendering.

- If A has *compatibility* mapping to B, then A and B denote *fundamentally similar* characters, which may differ in rendering, as well as in scope of usage. In practice, they may differ in meaning, too.

The Unicode Normalization Form C (discussed in the section "Normalization") is often applied to Unicode data. It applies all canonical mappings (e.g., loses the distinction between ohm sign and capital omega), but not compatibility mappings (e.g., it keeps micro sign and small mu as distinct).

Although compatibility mapping is not meant to imply semantic difference, the Unicode standard admits (in UAX #15): "However, some characters with compatibility decompositions are used in mathematical notation to represent distinction of a semantic nature; replacing the use of distinct character codes by formatting may cause problems." A simple example of this is the superscript two ^{2}, which has compatibility mapping to the digit two, 2. Applying this compatibility mapping in, for example, the expression 5^2 yields 52 and therefore distorts the meaning. In some cases, this can be fixed by using markup or formatting instructions, but in plain text, that's not possible.

Canonical and compatibility equivalence

Although canonical and compatibility mappings are one-directional and do not mean equivalence, we can define equivalence relations based on them. Canonical and compatibility equivalence are defined for *sequences of characters* (i.e., strings), naturally regarding a single character as a special case. The exact definitions will be given later in this chapter, but the basic idea is the following. Strings are canonical equivalent, if their canonical decompositions, obtained by applying all canonical mappings, are the same. Thus, in particular, if A has a canonical mapping to B, then A and B are canonical equivalent. Compatibility equivalence is defined in a similar way, except that both compatibility and canonical mappings are applied.

 The term "canonical equivalent" is from the Unicode standard, so we use it in this book, instead of the grammatically more correct expression "canonically equivalent."

The meaning of canonical mapping

We already mentioned that canonical mapping does not mean identity, despite the symbol commonly used to denote it. A relationship like Ω U+2126 ≡ Ω U+03A9 is a relation between two distinct characters. We should expect that programs often make no distinction between them, but a distinction *may* be made.

For example, a program might recognize U+2126 but not U+03A9, or vice versa. It would then behave differently for them, of course. If it recognizes both, it need not treat them the same way, but any program conforming to the Unicode standard *may* do so. Thus, if a program sends another program the character U+2126 and the latter acknowledges having received U+03A9, it is accepted behavior, and the sender should be prepared for this.

Differences in glyphs for equivalent characters

A character may be visually distinct from its compatibility mapping. For example, a font that contains both U+2126 and U+03A9 may have different glyphs for them, although we would expect them to have the same basic shape. The Unicode standard explicitly says that replacing a character with its compatibility mapping may lose formatting information.

In practice, a character may visually differ from its canonical mapping, too, although the general idea is that this shouldn't happen. For example, many fonts have different glyphs for μ U+00B5 and μ U+03BC. In some cases, there is no difference in any font, but the appearances may still differ! For example, if a font contains the Kelvin sign K (U+212A), it looks just the same as the Latin capital letter "K," K, in that font. But if you create, for example, a web page containing the Kelvin sign, it will often look different from the letter "K," since a browser uses its default font for the letter "K" and picks up the Kelvin sign from a different font.

How the mappings are defined

When you need to know about the canonical or compatibility mapping of a particular character, you can consult some of the resources mentioned in Chapter 4, which also described the overall structure of the Unicode database.

The *UnicodeData.txt* file in the Unicode database contains, for each character, a field (the sixth one) that specifies whether the character has a decomposition mapping, as well as the specific decomposition and its nature (canonical or compatibility). Let us consider the following line at *http://www.unicode.org/Public/UNIDATA/UnicodeData.txt*:

```
00B5;MICRO SIGN;Ll;0;L;<compat> 03BC;;;;N;;;039C;;039C
```

Here, the notation <compat> 03BC means that the character has compatibility mapping to U+03BC. Instead of <compat>, the field could also contain a more specific notation, such as <super>, which also indicates the nature of the presentational difference. For example:

```
00B2;SUPERSCRIPT TWO;No;0;EN;<super> 0032;;2;2;N;SUPERSCRIPT DIGIT TWO;;;;
```

Superscript two (^{2}) is an ISO Latin 1 character with its own code position in that standard. In the Unicode way of thinking, it would have been treated as a superscript variant of digit two (2), if there had not been a particular reason to do otherwise. This does not mean that in the Unicode philosophy superscripting (or subscripting, italics, bolding, etc.) would be irrelevant; rather, it is to be handled at another level of data presentation, such as some special markup or styling. Since the superscript two character is contained in an important standard, it was included into Unicode, though only as a compatibility character, with <super> 0032 in the sixth field in its entry in the database. The practical reason is that now one can convert from ISO Latin 1 to Unicode and back and get the original data unchanged.

The sixth field might also contain just the number of a character, or numbers of characters, without any indication of compatibility. For example:

```
212B;ANGSTROM SIGN;Lu;0;L;00C5;;;;N;ANGSTROM UNIT;;;00E5;
```

The field 00C5 means that the angstrom sign U+212B has *canonical* mapping to the Latin capital letter "A" with ring above Å (U+00C5). Since no notation like <compat> or <super> is present in the field, it indicates canonical mapping and not compatibility mapping.

You can also find information on decomposition mappingials in the Unicode code charts, where they appear more legibly, as illustrated in Figure 5-2, though divided into a large

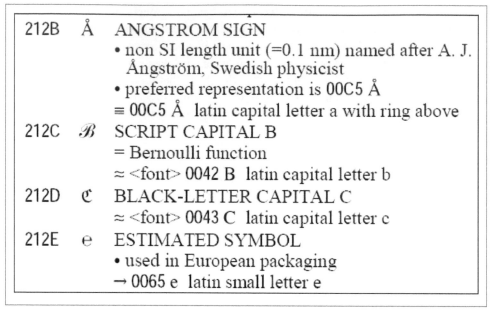

Figure 5-2. Descriptions of four characters in a code chart

number of PDF files. In the charts, characters at the start of an item under a character's name have meanings as follows:

- ≡ indicates canonical mapping.

- ≈ indicates compatibility mapping.

- = indicates a synonym (not any mapping).

- • indicates an informal note (not any mapping).

- → is a cross reference, which can be read as "compare with"; it does not mean any mapping, and it explicitly warns against confusing the character with another one.

The last example in Figure 5-2 illustrates that a character does not always have a decomposition even if it greatly resembles another character. The estimated symbol is surely derived from the letter "e," but it is treated as an independent character in Unicode.

The *compatibility formatting tag* `<super>` looks like an HTML or XML tag, but it is just a notation used in the Unicode database to indicate the value of the property dt = Decomposition Type. The "tags" do not appear in actual data, of course. On the other hand, characters with such mappings can often be replaced by markup elements that contain the non-compatibility character. For example, modifier letter small "h" (U+02B0) with compatibility mapping "<super> 0068," might be replaced by the markup `<sup>h</sup>` in HTML, though this is often debatable (see Chapter 9).

The meanings of compatibility formatting tags used in the compatibility mappings are given in Table 5-2. The words "narrow" and "wide" refer specifically to presentation forms used in East Asian writing systems.

Table 5-2. Compatibility formatting tags

Tag	Meaning
<circle>	An encircled form
<compat>	Otherwise unspecified compatibility character
<final>	A final presentation form (Arabic)
<font>	A font variant (e.g., a blackletter or italics form)
<fraction>	A vulgar fraction form, such as ½
<initial>	An initial presentation form (Arabic)
<isolated>	An isolated presentation form (Arabic)
<medial>	A medial presentation form (Arabic)
<narrow>	A narrow (hankaku) compatibility character
<noBreak>	A no-break version of a space, hyphen, or other punctuation
<small>	A small variant form (CNS compatibility)
<square>	A CJK squared font variant
<sub>	A subscript form
<super>	A superscript form
<vertical>	A vertical layout presentation form
<wide>	A wide (zenkaku) compatibility character

Canonical Decomposition and Compatibility Decomposition

Canonical and compatibility decomposition are based on the canonical and compatibility mappings discussed earlier, but decompositions may consist of *successive application* of the mappings. For example, the angstrom sign Å (U+212B) has canonical mapping to Latin capital letter "A" with ring Å (U+00C5), which in turn has canonical mapping to letter "A" followed by a combining diacritic. Successive application of mappings is often called "recursive," but it's really not recursion, rather it's iteration.

Decomposition replaces a character by a sequence of characters that are in some sense more basic. From the perspective of the Unicode standard, decomposition is something that you may or may not perform, just as you find suitable for your purposes. Other standards and rules may make decomposition compulsory in some contexts.

There are two kinds of decomposition defined in the Unicode standard: canonical and compatibility. They relate to the two kinds of mappings, although in a somewhat more complex way than you might expect.

Canonical decomposition

Canonical decomposition of a character means the following: if the character has a canonical mapping, you replace it with the character or string in the mapping. Then you check whether any character in the result has a canonical mapping, and you proceed until no further mapping exists. The mappings have of course been defined so that the process ends after a finite number of steps, without going to a loop.

For example, the canonical decomposition of the angstrom sign Å (U+212B) is the two-character sequence U+0041 U+030A (letter "A" and combining ring above). As explained previously, two mapping steps are taken in this case.

In fact, canonical decomposition involves two additional algorithms. By definition, canonical decomposition consists of the following:

1. Successively apply all the canonical mappings defined in the *UnicodeData.txt* file and by the Conjoining Jamo Behavior, until no such mapping can be applied. The Conjoining Jamo Behavior, defined in section 3.12 of the Unicode standard, deals with Hangul (Korean) characters and describes an algorithm for decomposing a Hangul syllable character.

2. Then reorder nonspacing marks according to Canonical Ordering Behavior. This deals with situations where two or more nonspacing marks appear in succession.

Canonical Ordering Behavior

Canonical Ordering Behavior is based on the ccc = Canonical Combining Class property, which assigns an integer to each character. For nonspacing marks, this value describes the position of the mark with respect to the base character, and it is also used for ordering the marks. For characters other than nonspacing marks, this value is zero.

The Canonical Ordering Behavior, described in detail in section 3.11 of the Unicode standard, reorders consecutive nonspacing marks in increasing order by their Canonical Combining Class property. This removes some variation. For example, the letter "e" with a circumflex above and a dot below can be represented in five ways in Unicode:

- As a fully composed character: Latin small letter "e" with circumflex and dot below ệ (U+1EC7)

- As fully decomposed in two ways, using two different orders for the combining marks

- As partly composed in two ways: ê followed by combining dot below, or ẹ followed by combining circumflex accent

In canonical decomposition, canonical mappings remove part of the variation: the result is fully decomposed. However, the combining marks may appear in two different orders, depending on the initial data. Canonical Ordering Behavior removes this variation, if the combining marks belong to different combining classes. In our example, combining circumflex accent (U+0302) has combining class 230, whereas combining dot below (U+0323) has combining class 220. The one with lower class comes first, so canonical

---

decomposition changes the five ways in the above list to a single representation: U+0065 U+0323 U+0302 (letter "e," combining dot below, combining circumflex accent).

Canonical decomposition does not remove all variation in the order of combining marks. If two marks belong to the same combining class, their mutual order is not changed. The reason is that the order can be significant, since being in the same class, the marks may interact typographically, and this interaction may depend on the mutual order. For example, U+0065 U+0306 U+0302 and U+0065 U+0302 U+0306 (letter "e" followed by combining breve and combining circumflex accent in either order) remain as different after decomposition. The combining breve and the combining circumflex accent both have combining class 230, because they are in essentially the same position with respect to the base character. Thus, an adequate rendering process will produce different visual results: "e" with a breve above it and with a circumflex above the breve, or "e" with a circumflex above it and a breve above it. (A poor implementation produces an "e" with a breve and circumflex overprinting each other.)

Canonical equivalence

The Unicode character defines canonical equivalence of strings, and it is an equivalence relation in the mathematical sense. It is reflexive (i.e., any string is equivalent to itself); it is symmetric (i.e., if A is equivalent to B, then B is equivalent to A); and it is transitive (i.e., if A is equivalent to B and B is equivalent to C, then A is equivalent to C).

Strings are by definition canonical equivalent, if their canonical decompositions are identical. For example, the five ways of representing "e" with dot below and circumflex discussed in the previous section are all canonical equivalent.

Compatibility decomposition and equivalence

Compatibility decomposition is defined the same way as canonical decomposition, except that *compatibility decomposition includes canonical decomposition*. Canonical decomposition of a string consists of the following:

1. Successively apply all the compatibility mappings and canonical mappings defined in the *UnicodeData.txt* file and by the Conjoining Jamo Behavior, until no such mapping can be applied.
2. Then reorder nonspacing marks according to Canonical Ordering Behavior.

For example, the compatibility decomposition of the (rather artificial) string "½ µé," where µ is the micro sign, is the string "1/2 µe´," where µ is the Greek letter mu and ´ denotes the combining acute accent.

Compatibility equivalence of strings is defined in the obvious way: strings are compatibility equivalent, if their compatibility decompositions are identical. It follows from the definitions that canonical equivalent strings are compatibility equivalent, too.

Canonical and compatibility decomposable characters

The Unicode standard uses a large number of rather redundant terms. We need to mention them, since you may encounter them when reading about Unicode: A character that is canonical equivalent to something other than itself is said to be *canonical decomposable*. Similarly, if a character is compatibility equivalent to something other than itself, it is *compatibility decomposable*. Often such decomposability really means that a character can be decomposed into constituents—e.g., ä can be decomposed into "a" and a combining dieresis. However, many of the "decompositions" just map one character to another character, as in the case of Ω U+2126 ≈ Ω U+03A9, mentioned earlier in the chapter.

Compatibility Characters

Unicode contains a large number of characters described as "compatibility characters." Many of them are variants of other characters. The overall tone of the standard is that compatibility characters should be avoided, except in legacy data. However, it does not explicitly deprecate them; on the contrary, it says: "The status of a character as a compatibility character does not mean that the character is deprecated in the standard." There is a separate concept of deprecation, for characters that really should not be used at all but have been preserved in Unicode according to its design principles.

Compatibility characters were included into Unicode for compatibility with other character codes—i.e., just because the characters exist in one or more character code. One reason for this is that data presented using some other code can be converted to Unicode and back, or from one character code to another using Unicode as an intermediate code, without losing information. The Unicode standard says:

> Compatibility characters are those that would not have been encoded except for compatibility and round-trip convertibility with other standards. They are variants of characters that already have encodings as *normal* (that is, non-compatibility) characters in the Unicode Standard.

Many, but not all, compatibility characters have *compatibility decompositions*, which specify the character's relationship to other characters. There has been some confusion around this, since not all compatibility characters have such decompositions. The Unicode standard itself mentions that the phrase "compatibility character" is also used in a narrower sense, which refers to *compatibility decomposable* characters—i.e., those characters that have compatibility decompositions. The phrase "compatibility composite (character)" is also mentioned as a synonym, but that sounds quite redundant and confusing.

For example, the micro sign µ (U+00B5) is a compatibility decomposable character. It has compatibility mapping to the Greek small letter mu µ (U+03BC).

The Unicode character database rigorously defines for each character whether it is a compatibility decomposable character, as well as the eventual decomposition. The same information is presented in a more readable form in the code charts, where the ≈ character indicates canonical decomposition, as illustrated in Figure 5-3. The question exclamation mark (U+2048) is defined as a separate character, but with compatibility mapping to the character pair U+003F U+0021—i.e., ? followed by !.

The more general concept of compatibility character is defined in prose only, and it includes, for example, deprecated alternate format characters, which have no

---

Figure 5-3. Sample definition of a compatibility decomposable character

decomposition, as well as CJK compatibility ideographs, which have *canonical* decompositions, not compatibility decompositions. This wider concept of compatibility character is basically just descriptive; rules and algorithms operate on the decompositions.

The concept "compatibility decomposable character" has been defined formally, whereas the concept "compatibility character" is informal but sometimes important. If a character is a compatibility decomposable character, it is a compatibility character; the reverse is not true.

For example, as discussed previously, the angstrom sign Å (U+212B) is defined so that it has a *canonical* decomposition, not a compatibility decomposition. Yet, it is a compatibility character—because it has been declared as such in the prose of the Unicode standard. Generally, when a character is defined to have canonical mapping to a single character, the explanation is that it has been included into Unicode for compatibility only and it is regarded as so similar to the other character that their renderings are expected to be the same.

Thus, canonical mapping means different things in different cases, depending on whether a character has canonical mapping to one character or to a sequence of characters. For example, Latin capital letter "A" with ring above Å (U+00C5) has canonical mapping to U+0041 U+030A (letter "A" followed by combining ring above), but it is not a compatibility character. It is simply a "normal" character that is decomposable into two "normal" characters.

Compatibility Decomposable Characters

Replacing a compatibility decomposable character by the corresponding normal character or sequence of characters does not, by Unicode definition, change the meaning of text, but it may change formatting and layout. For example, the micro sign and the small mu are expected to look similar, but not necessarily identical.

This definition is subject to some criticism, though. It can be argued that the micro sign is quite different in meaning from the small mu. The micro sign unambiguously denotes a multiplier of a unit. The small mu is a letter of the Greek alphabet, and it is normally used when writing Greek words, although it could also appear in a variety of special meanings. The Unicode standard does not recommend that such distinctions should be made, or that they should not be made. Rather, the micro sign is included for compatibility with old character codes and it in fact implies that the distinction *can* be made, if desired.

Many compatibility characters are in the Compatibility Area but others are scattered around the Unicode coding space. They belong to different types, such as the following:

- Variants of letters used in specialized meanings, such as the micro sign
- Variants such as superscripts (e.g., ^{2} as variant of "2")
- Ligatures, such as fi
- Contextual forms of Arabic letters
- Fullwidth forms of ASCII characters, for use in East Asian writing systems
- Special-purpose combinations of characters, such as care of % (which has compatibility mapping to c/o)
- Fixed-width space characters like thin space, used for typographic purposes

Avoiding Compatibility Characters

The general idea in the Unicode standard is that compatibility characters should be avoided in new data, but it expresses this somewhat indirectly. However, in subsection 3.7, "Decomposition," the standard is rather explicit about compatibility decomposable characters:

> Compatibility decomposable characters … support transmission and processing of legacy data. Their use is discouraged other than for legacy data or other special circumstances.

In practice, it is not always feasible to avoid compatibility characters in plain text. If plain text contains the string 3^2, the normal interpretation is that it means 3 to the power 2. Replacing the superscript two with the corresponding non-compatibility character would turn the data into 32, which means something completely different.

In formats other than plain text, it is often possible and suitable to avoid compatibility characters by using markup or other tools. There is a document titled "Unicode in XML and other Markup Languages," at *http://www.w3.org/TR/unicode-xml/*, produced jointly by the World Wide Web Consortium (W3C) and the Unicode Consortium. It discusses characters with compatibility mappings: should they be used, or should the corresponding non-compatibility characters be used, perhaps with some markup and/or stylesheet that corresponds to the difference between them? The answers depend on the nature of the characters and the available markup and styling techniques. For example, for superscripts, the use of `sup` markup (as in HTML) is recommended—i.e., `<sup>2</sup>` is preferred over the superscript two character ^{2} (and its representation as an entity, ²). This is a debatable issue, partly because superscripting has two essentially different uses: semantic, as in mathematics, or stylistic, as in abbreviations like 1st for "first" or French Mlle for "mademoiselle." This will be discussed in more detail in Chapter 9.

In practice, compatibility characters are widely used in new Unicode data, too. Many of them work more reliably than the corresponding "normal" characters. For example, the micro sign belongs to ISO Latin 1 and therefore appears in almost any font used in the Western world, whereas the letter mu has less support. Existing software for processing measurement data may well recognize "μm" as denoting micrometer but fail to recognize "µm" (where the letter mu is used).

In using characters, it's often best to do what everyone else does. Suppose, for example, that you decide to use the letter mu instead of the micro sign as a unit prefix. If people open your document in a program and use the program's search function, the odds are that they type "μm" using the micro sign. (After all, it's often easier to write than the letter mu.) They would not find anything, unless the search function uses advanced techniques that handle compatibility mappings somehow.

Compatibility Characters for Ligatures

Some compatibility characters have compatibility decompositions consisting of two or more characters so that it can be said that they represent a ligature of those characters. For example, Latin small ligature "fi" fi (U+FB01) has the obvious decomposition consisting of letters "f" and "i." It is a distinct character in Unicode, but in the spirit of Unicode, we should not use it except for storing and transmitting existing data that contains the character. One practical reason for this is that most programs do not treat a ligature as matching the corresponding sequence of characters in comparisons, searches, etc.

As mentioned in Chapter 4, Unicode has two control characters for affecting ligature behavior, zero-width joiner ZWJ U+200D and zero-width non-joiner ZWNJ U+200C. This is intended to prevent the use of a ligature or cursive connection. Formally, ligature characters such as U+FB01 are *not* defined in a manner that involves a zero-width joiner. Instead, U+FB01 has compatibility mapping to U+0066 U+0069 (i.e., "f" followed by "i"), although it might conceivably have been declared as having mapping to U+0066 U+200D U+0069.

Normalization

In data processing, *normalization* generally means conversion of data to a form that has been defined as *normal form*, among different possibilities. This does not mean that other forms would be incorrect or nonstandard. On the contrary, the normal form is usually just one of the correct forms. In some contexts, there is a difference between "normal form" and "normalized form," but we will treat them as synonyms here.

Consider the Latin small letter "e" with acute accent é. This character can be represented in Unicode as a separate character with a code point of its own, U+00E9. Equivalently, in the sense of canonical equivalence, it can be represented as a two-character sequence: Latin small letter "e" (U+0065) followed by combining acute accent (U+0301). The rendering should be exactly the same, and we might say that well-designed software should handle them both—and identically. Due to its design goals, Unicode contains a lot of ways to represent things in canonically equivalent ways.

However, processing of data becomes easier if the variation is reduced. For some purpose and context, we might decide that one of the forms is the normal form. We might then use preprocessing software that converts the data to the normal form. This would make the coding of the actual processing easier. For example, text searching is easier if we can assume that all data has been normalized, so that when a search for é is performed, we know exactly what to look for.

Normalization operates at the level of code points, not encodings. Different encodings, such as UTF-8 and UTF-16, will be discussed in Chapter 6. Encoding issues are independent of normalization.

Normalization Versus Folding

In the Unicode context, the term "normalization" is used only to denote normalization forms that deal with canonical and compatibility decompositions and compositions. For example, the representation of é as U+00F9 or as U+0065 U+0301 is a normalization issue in this narrow sense. Mapping, for example, É to é for case-insensitive comparisons or ignoring diacritic marks (mapping é, è, etc., all to "e") is not called normalization but *folding*, although the goals are often the same as for normalization.

Folding issues are discussed in the Draft Unicode Technical Report (UTR) #30, "Character Foldings," *http://www.unicode.org/reports/tr30/*. Typically, the foldings described there are mappings that perform some of the canonical or compatibility mappings, such as removal of canonical duplicates or subscript folding, which turns subscript characters to corresponding normal characters. However, they also include quite different mappings, such as accent removal.

According to UTR #30, all folding operations involve canonical decomposition, and they may involve composition as the last step. The general idea is to apply folding rules, then canonical decomposition, and then to repeat these steps until the data is stable—i.e., does not change anymore in these steps. Thus, folding resembles normalization but contains additional operations.

Overview of Normalization Forms

Unicode defines several normalization forms, which can be used for different purposes. They are summarized in Table 5-3. The principles are simple: first decomposable characters are decomposed, using either canonical or compatibility decomposition. This may be followed by canonical composition, as described later in the detailed descriptions of Normalization Forms C and KC.

Table 5-3. Unicode normalization forms

Code	Name	Meaning
NFD	Normalization Form D	Canonical decomposition
NFC	Normalization Form C	Canonical decomposition, canonical composition
NFKD	Normalization Form KD	Compatibility decomposition
NFKC	Normalization Form KC	Compatibility decomposition, canonical composition

In the codes, "D" stands for decomposition, "C" for composition, and "K" for compatibility. Composition implies prior decomposition.

For example, consider the word "fiancé" written so that it starts with the ligature fi (U+FB01) and ends with the composite character "e" with acute accent (U+00E9). These characters have compatibility and canonical mappings, respectively. The normalization forms of the word are presented in Table 5-4, denoting a combining acute accent U+0301 by the acute accent ´ for clarity.

Table 5-4. Normalization forms of the sample word "fiancé"

Form	"fiancé" normalized	Explanation
NFD	fi a n c e ´	é has been decomposed (canonical)
NFC	fi a n c é	é was decomposed but then composed back
NFKD	f i a n c e ´	Both fi and é have been decomposed
NFKC	f i a n c é	Only fi has been decomposed (compatibility)

In the example, the NFC form is the same as the original string. This is typical, since NFC deals with canonical mappings only, and it first decomposes, and then composes. The NFKD form is fully decomposed, whereas in the NFKC form, the character é was first decomposed, then composed back (canonical composition).

Unicode data may contain characters such as é in both precomposed and decomposed form. Normalization to NFD (or NKFD) ensures that they will all be in (completely) decomposed form. Normalization to NFC (or NKFC) ensures that they will all be in precomposed form if possible. The "if possible" part comes from the fact that not all characters with diacritic marks have precomposed forms in Unicode.

No normalization form performs any "compatibility composition." For example, normalization never composes the letters "f" and "i" into the ligature fi.

For quick checks on the normalization forms of individual characters, you can use the Normalization Charts at *http://www.unicode.org/charts/normalization/*. They show the four normalization forms for each character, except for those that are invariant under all normalizations. The charts are illustrated in Figure 5-4. Note that the glyphs are usually the same although the normalization forms (code number sequences) differ, so the most relevant information is in the code numbers below the glyphs. Generally, normalization to the C or D form should not change the rendering of a character, whereas normalization to KC or KD form may change it, since they involve compatibility mappings.

There is also an offline tool for checking the normalization forms of a string, Charlint. It can be downloaded from *http://www.w3.org/International/charlint*. It corresponds to Unicode Version 3.2, so newer characters cannot be checked.

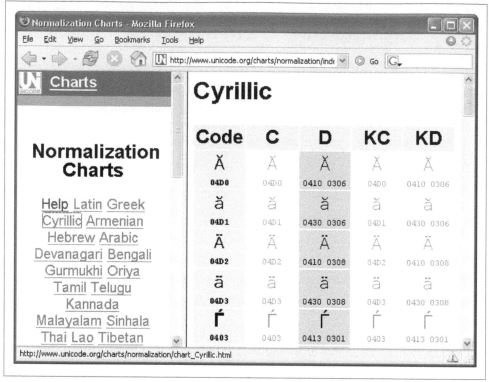

Figure 5-4. The Normalization Chart for some Cyrillic characters that have canonical decompositions

Use of normalization forms

In practice, the different normalization forms have rather different usage:

- Normalization Form C (NFC) is favored as the basic form, for example, by the World Wide Web Consortium (W3C) in the Character Model for the Web, for use in XML and related formats; see *http://www.w3.org/TR/charmod/*. Some general purpose subroutine libraries and utilities require that their input be in NFC.

- Normalization Form D (NFD) can be useful in situations where you prefer to process all characters with diacritics as decomposed—e.g., because you wish to simply ignore all diacritics.

- Normalization Forms KD and KC (NFKD, NFKC) should be used with caution, after a careful analysis of the possible effects, since these normalizations may lose essential information (e.g., by normalizing 4^2 to 42). They can be useful in applications where you intentionally want to simplify character data.

Invariance of Basic Latin characters

The Basic Latin block in Unicode, corresponding to ASCII, has been designed so that strings consisting of Basic Latin characters only are not changed in any normalization. That is, they have no decomposition mappings, and there are no compositions that operate on sequences of Basic Latin characters. Therefore, the basic syntactic constructs in programming and markup languages remain invariant in normalization, as long as they use Basic Latin characters only. This goal explains why, for example, the grave accent ` does not have canonical mapping to space followed by the combining grave accent, although for example, there is a canonical mapping for the acute accent ´ (which is outside Basic Latin, in the Latin-1 Supplement).

Normalization Form C

As mentioned, NFC means canonical decomposition followed by canonical composition. This may sound odd: why decompose something that will be composed back again? The explanation is that decomposition ensures, among other things, that multiple diacritic marks will be handled in a uniform manner.

The exact definition of canonical composition requires some auxiliary concepts:

Starter
> A character is called a starter, if its combining class is 0—i.e., the value of the property ccc = Canonical Combining Class for the character is zero. This includes all characters that are not combining characters as well as some combining characters.

Blocked
> In a string that begins with a starter, a character C is said to be blocked from the starter S, if there is a character B between them such that either B is a starter or it has a combining class value as at least as high as C's.

Primary composite
> A character is said to be a primary composite, if it has a canonical mapping and it has not been explicitly excluded from composition by assigning the value yes (True) to the property CE = Composition Exclusion for the character. See subsection "Composition Exclusions" later in this chapter.

We can now define that the construction of the NFC for a string consists of the following:

1. Construct the canonical decomposition of the string. (Note that this includes reordering of consecutive nonspacing marks.)

2. Process the result by successively composing each character with the nearest preceding starter, if it is not blocked from it. Composing character C with a starter S means that if there is a primary composite Z that is canonically equivalent to the string consisting of S followed by C, then S is replaced by Z, and C is removed.

This is a bit complicated, so let us consider a simple example. Assume that the initial string is U+00EA U+0323—i.e., ê followed by combining dot below. The process of converting it to NFC is presented stepwise in Table 5-5. For clarity, the combining diacritic marks are visualized as ^ (denoting circumflex above) and . (denoting dot below). The operations in the composition phase are based on the canonical mappings defined for U+1EB9 and U+1EC7.

Table 5-5. Normalization Form C step by step

Phase	Representation of e with circumflex above and dot below	Comments
Original data	U+00EA ê U+0323 .	Partly composed
Decomposition	U+0065 "e" U+0302 ^ U+0323 .	Canonical decompose ê
Decomposition	U+0065 "e" U+0323 . U+0302 ^	Reorder nonspacing marks
Composition	U+1EB9 ẹ U+0302 ^	Compose mark with starter "e"
Composition	U+1EC7 ệ	Compose second mark

Normalization Form KC

NFKC is defined in a manner very similar to the definition of NFC. The only difference is in step 1, which involved compatibility decomposition instead of canonical decomposition. The construction of NFKC for a string consists of the following:

1. Construct the compatibility decomposition of the string. (Note that this includes applying both canonical and compatibility mappings and then reordering of consecutive nonspacing marks.)

2. Process the result by successively composing each character with the nearest preceding starter, if it is not blocked from it. Composing character *C* with a starter *S* means that if there is a primary composite *Z* that is canonically equivalent to the string consisting of *S* followed by *C*, then *S* is replaced by *Z*, and *C* is removed.

Composition Exclusions

As defined in the previous section, characters with a "yes" value for the CE = Composition Exclusion property are excluded from composition in normalization, because they are by definition not primary composites. These characters are listed, with comments, in the Unicode database file *CompositionExclusions.txt*. They are divided into the following groups:

- *Script-specific* precomposed characters that are generally not the preferred form for particular scripts and therefore declared as to be excluded from composition. Currently these include some Devanagari, Bengali, Gurmukhi, Oriya, Tibetan, and Hebrew characters.

- *Post Composition Version* precomposed characters, which means precomposed characters added after Unicode Version 3.0. By Unicode policy, such characters are always excluded from composition. There are just a few symbols in this group.

- *Singleton Decompositions*—i.e., characters whose canonical decomposition consists of a single character; e.g., the ohm sign (with capital omega as its decomposition).

- *Non-Starter Decompositions*—i.e., characters whose canonical decomposition starts with a character with a nonzero combining class. There are just a few of such characters—e.g., combining Greek dialytika tonos U+0344, which represents two combining diacritic marks (dialytika and tonos).

Definition of Compatibility Decomposable Character

We can now formally define what it means to be *compatibility decomposable*: it means that a character's compatibility decomposition differs from its canonical decomposition —i.e., its normalization form D is different from its normalization form KD. That is, character *c* is compatibility decomposable, if $\mathrm{NFKD}(c) \neq \mathrm{NFD}(c)$.

For example, the micro sign is compatibility decomposable, since it has compatibility mapping to the Greek letter small mu, which is thus its NFKD, whereas its NFD is the micro sign itself (since it has no canonical mapping to anything). On the other hand, the ohm sign is not compatibility decomposable, since it has canonical mapping to the Greek letter capital omega, thus having that character as its NFKD and as its NFD.

 Not all compatibility characters are compatibility decomposable. Many of them have decompositions that are canonical.

W3C Normalization

The World Wide Web Consortium (W3C) favors Normalization Form C on the Web, and it additionally suggests stronger normalization rules in HTML and XML documents. The stronger rules are external to Unicode, since they relate to markup, not plain text. They are briefly described here due to their practical impact. The rules are described in more detail in the document "Character Model for the World Wide Web 1.0: Normalization," *http://www.w3.org/TR/charmod-norm/*. However, it needs to be noted that document is officially a Working Draft (work in progress) only.

The W3C normalization rules require that text be in NFC and additionally forbid the occurrence of character references and entity references that would make the text non-normalized, if replaced by the characters that they denote. For example, by Unicode rules, NFC does not allow the appearance of "e" followed by a combining acute accent, since this combination must be replaced by the precomposed character é. The W3C normalization rules also forbid the indirect appearance of the combination, for example, as in é (where ́ is a character reference that denotes the combining acute accent U+0301).

On the Web, expressions like é are rarely used in practice, since the corresponding precomposed character (either written as such or as a character reference like é or é or as an entity reference like &#eacute;) works much better. However, suppose that you have a database that contains characters in decomposed form. Unless you are careful, software that presents data extracted from it in HTML or XML format might treat data like U+0065 U+0301 so that U+0065 is represented directly as "e" (which should cause no problems), whereas U+0301 is converted to ́ for safety. This would result in data that is not W3C normalized, and this involves unnecessary risks. A simple way to avoid this is to normalize (to NFC) the character data extracted from the database before making any decisions on using character references to represent some characters.

Case Properties

Some writing systems, such as Latin, Greek, and Cyrillic, make a distinction between cases of letters. Historically, *uppercase* letters, also known as *capital* letters or as *majuscules*, reflect the original shapes of letters. In the middle ages, *lowercase* letters, also known as *small* letters or as *minuscules* were invented to make writing by hand faster. Uppercase letters were preserved for special use—e.g., for emphasis, for abbreviations, and for use as initials in proper names and in the first word of a sentence.

Usually an uppercase letter is larger than the corresponding lowercase letter. In some cases, this is the only essential difference; e.g., compare "O" with "o." Usually there is also a shape difference, which can be considerable; e.g., between "E" and "e." If you see letters of a script unknown to you, you might have difficulties in recognizing their case. For example, which of Þ and þ is uppercase? (Hint: uppercase letters usually do not extend below the baseline of text, in most fonts.)

Not all writing systems make a case distinction, even if they use letters. For example, there is no such distinction, even though the shape of a letter may vary considerably for other reasons (by position within a word).

The use of uppercase letters varies by language. For example, German writes all nouns with initial capitals, and most European languages write names of months in all lowercase, unlike English. There is also considerable stylistic variation; in some styles, headings and even entire paragraphs are written in all uppercase. The Unicode standard does not try to describe such variation. Instead, it describes properties that can be used to deal with the variation—e.g., to recognize or convert the case of a letter.

Recognizing Uppercase, Lowercase, and Titlecase

The Unicode names of letters generally contain the word "capital" for uppercase letters and the word "small" for lowercase letters. However, there are exceptions to this, and there is no reason to rely on the names. Instead, you can use several defined properties of characters, such as the General Category property values, listed in Table 5-1. The value of the property is Lu for uppercase letters, Ll for lowercase letters, Lt for the few letters that are of a special titlecase form, and Lm or Lo for letters that make no case distinction.

"Titlecase" refers to a character used at the start of a word written with a capital initial, as common for most words in titles of books, articles, etc., in English. Note that the capitalization conventions of English do not apply to some words like prepositions; thus, not all words in a title begin with a titlecase letter. For most characters, titlecase is the same as uppercase. However, for some letters that are originally ligatures, only the first component is in uppercase version in the titlecase form. For example, if you have the letter dž (U+01C6), converting it to uppercase gives DŽ (U+01C4), but conversion to titlecase gives Dž (U+01C5).

If you find it more convenient, you can also use the derived Boolean (yes/no) properties Uppercase and Lowercase. There is no derived property for detecting titlecase, though.

Case Mappings

Suppose that you have a file or database containing character data and you wish to create a program for searching data from it using simple searches by keywords. If your data contains the word "Newton," you would probably like to make a search find it even if the user enters the word as "newton" or "NEWTON." In effect, you wish to perform a case-insensitive match in the search. That is what people intuitively expect from a search.

You could use *case folding*, converting all your data to uppercase, or to lowercase, and doing the same for any user input. This would usually be awkward, since you normally want to display the data normally, in mixed case. Therefore, you might wish to perform delayed case folding: keep both the data and the user input in mixed case but convert them to a single case just before performing a comparison (matching) in the search. You might also avoid any case folding and just use a routine that performs a case-insensitive search (although it might internally perform case folding for the purpose).

Mapping (converting) characters from lowercase to uppercase or vice versa is more complex than you might expect. The Unicode database contains, in the basic file *Unicodedata.txt* (described in Chapter 4), values for the properties Simple Uppercase Mapping, Simple Lowercase Mapping, and Simple Titlecase Mapping. The word "Simple" is there for a reason. The properties are intentionally limited to character-to-character mappings. For example, the Latin small letter sharp "s" ß (U+00DF) has no Simple Uppercase Mapping defined—i.e., it remains invariant in such a mapping. However, such behavior violates the rules of the only language where the character is used (German): the rules say that the uppercase equivalent is the character pair "SS" (e.g., "Fuß" becomes "FUSS").

 Simple case mappings are meant to be used only when it is not possible to perform the correct case mappings—e.g., because the length of a string cannot be changed in the mapping. In practice, however, existing software often performs simple case mappings only.

There are additional mapping rules in the *SpecialCasing.txt* file. They are meant to be used in order to override and augment the simple mapping rules. For example, the Latin small ligature "fi" fi (U+FB01) has no simple uppercase or titlecase mapping, since it is not possible to present them as single characters. The *SpecialCasing.txt* file however contains:

```
FB01; FB01; 0046 0069; 0046 0049; # LATIN SMALL LIGATURE FI
```

This line specifies that for U+FB01, the lowercase form is the character itself, the titlecase form is U+0046 U+0069 (i.e., "F" followed by "i"), and the uppercase form is U+0046 U+0049 (i.e., "F" followed by "I").

In addition to letters like ß and ligature characters with no single-character uppercase mappings, the additional mapping rules cover letters with diacritic marks, in situations where the uppercase form does not exist as a precomposed character. There are also conditional mappings, such as mapping Greek capital letter sigma Σ to lowercase by a special rule for its use at the end of a word: there lowercase sigma is ς as opposed to the normal σ. Some mappings are language-dependent (for Lithuanian, Turkish, and Azerbaijani). Of course, they can be applied only in situations where the language of text is known.

In different languages, styles, and applications there are other deviations from the general principles, and they need to be handled separately. It is rather common (though perhaps disapproved by language authorities) to omit diacritic marks from uppercase letters, especially when writing words in all uppercase. This means that you would post-process the result of conversion to uppercase by removing the marks.

Case Folding in Unicode

In Unicode, case folding mostly maps everything to *lowercase*, but there are some complications. The case folding mapping is separately defined in the Unicode database file *CaseFolding.txt* by explicitly giving the case folded form for each character that changes in case folding. This mapping is defined formally as independent of other mappings, but in practice, there is logic behind it, connecting the mappings.

We can conceptually think of the case folding mapping as mapping everything to uppercase, and then to lowercase. The reason for this apparently absurd complexity is that otherwise the case folded form would not do its job in removing case distinctions. For example, the sharp "s" ß has "SS" as its uppercase equivalent in full case mapping. Therefore, it is mapped to "ss" in full case folding. Otherwise, full case folding would not map "Fuß" and "FUSS" (which differ in case only) to the same string.

The *CaseFolding.txt* file contains rules for both simple and full mappings, as opposed to the use of two distinct files as for uppercase, lowercase, and titlecase mappings. The file contains lines like the following:

```
00DE; C; 00FE; # LATIN CAPITAL LETTER THORN
00DF; F; 0073 0073; # LATIN SMALL LETTER SHARP S
```

Here, as usual in the Unicode database, the first item on a line is the code number of the character to which the mapping applies, and anything from # onward is a comment. The lines say that U+00DE is case folded to U+00FE (which is Latin small letter thorn) and U+00DF is case folded to U+0073 U+0073 (which is "ss"). The letter in the second field, here "C" or "F," specifies the applicability of the rule as follows:

- "C" means "Common"—i.e., the rule is always applied in case folding.
- "F" means "Full"—i.e., the rule is applied in full case folding only.
- "S" means "Simple"—i.e., the rule is applied in simple case folding only.

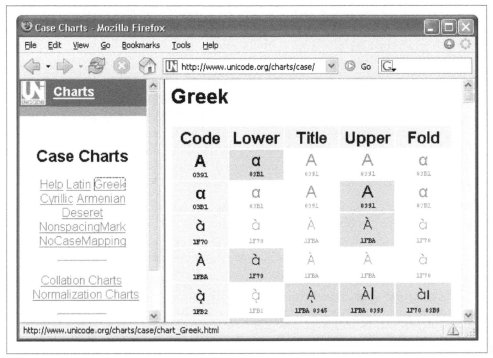

Figure 5-5. Viewing Case Charts for some Greek letters

- "T" means "Turkic," which means that the rule is optionally selectable for use in case folding by the principles on handling dotted and undotted "i" ("İ" versus "ı") in Turkish and Azerbaijani.

Viewing the Mappings

If you just want to view the mappings for different characters, the Unicode Case Charts at *http://www.unicode.org/charts/case/* are very handy, as illustrated in Figure 5-5. They show the uppercase, lowercase, titlecase, and case folded form for each character that has any difference between the forms. As usual in such matters, the rendering of glyphs can be problematic due to font problems, especially on Internet Explorer.

Character Case Mappings Versus Visual Mappings

The mappings discussed in the previous section need to be distinguished from purely visual mappings. You could store and process character data as such in mixed case and perform mapping to uppercase, lowercase, or titlecase in visual rendering only. Usually you would map to uppercase in order to highlight a piece of text as a heading or just for emphasis.

The difference between character-level mappings and visual mappings is illustrated by two functions in MS Word:

- If you select a piece of text, and then use the command Format → Change case, you can have the text case mapped to uppercase, lowercase, titlecase, or "sentence case," which means that the first word is in titlecase, other words are in lowercase. Such operations are irreversible—i.e., there is no general way to get the original form back, except naturally in the sense that you might do the Undo operation next.

- If you select a piece of text, and then use the command Format → Font and check (on the Font pane) the checkbox "All caps" (under "Effects"), then the text will be displayed in all uppercase. The character data is preserved as such, however, so if you later select the text again and uncheck the checkbox, the original form becomes visible. You can also use this approach when defining a style in MS Word, since the style settings have font formatting options, too.

Both of these mappings might perform simple mapping only, so they should be used with caution; e.g., for texts in German and Turkish. Also note that mapping to titlecase does not produce grammatically correct results for English, since it capitalizes every word, but by English rules, words like "a" and "to" should be left lowercase.

In HTML or XML authoring, you might use a Cascading Style Sheet (CSS) declaration like `text-transform: uppercase`. Applied to a string, it performs a conversion to uppercase when selecting glyphs for rendering the characters. The other values of the property are `lowercase`, `capitalize` (= titlecase), and `none`.

Such operations can be a better choice than conversions at the character level, since keeping the data itself in mixed case helps in editing, spellchecking, etc. Moreover, character-level case mappings are irreversible: there is no way to deduce the original form from the case-mapped string.

Such an approach also lets you use different stylesheets for the same data, using conversion to uppercase only when it is judged to be the best way—e.g., for headings (typically, due to lack of better typographic possibilities). However, beware that such transformations might not work by Unicode rules for all characters and that they might apply simple mappings. CSS specifications do not specify how the mappings are performed. In practice, if you write `<h1>Fuß</h1>` in HTML and have the rule `h1 { text-transform: uppercase }` in CSS, you probably get "FUß" or even "FUS" (incorrect) depending on the browser, instead of the full case folded result "FUSS."

Collation and Sorting

Sorting is a well-known concept: we put data into a specific order, such as alphabetical order. *Collating order* is a more technical concept, but closely related: the collating order of characters and strings is the order by which sorting of character data takes place. The collating order says, for example, that "a" < "b" or that "&" < ".", using the less than sign to mean "precedes (in the ordering)." Sorting is often called "alphabetizing," although it generally operates on strings in general, not just alphabetic characters.

Sorting is relevant when we present a large amount of text data to users and the data has some key component, such as a person's name in a telephone catalog or a term in a glossary. People are used to scanning through lists and tables, expecting them to be in an alphabetic order (or, more generally, collating order) they have learned at school. In the global context, it is important that different people have learned different orders.

The relative importance of sorting has diminished due to the advance of automatic searching tools. When you use a CD-ROM encyclopedia, you can type a word and expect a program to show you the corresponding entry; alphabetic order is irrelevant here. However, you might be uncertain of the spelling and would like to browse through consecutive entries.

Sorting still has many other uses as well. For example, when you need to present countries in some order, difficult political problems may arise unless you can apply some reasonably neutral or traditional order, such as alphabetic order by the name of the country in French. Moreover, even for small amounts of entries—e.g., in a list of links—alphabetic order is often the best, when there is no other natural order. It is then easy to a user who is looking for a particular entry to check whether it is the list. Sorting is also relevant to operations that extract a range of values from some data.

Sorting Characters Versus Sorting Strings

For sorting, we need an order for characters, but this may not be sufficient. A trivial method for ordering strings, once a character order has been established, is to compare the first characters of the strings, then the second characters, until a difference is found. The first difference found will determine string order. Thus, "AAB" < "AAC", since "B" < "C". This simple method is often called *lexicographic* order or *dictionary order*.

However, when you look at a real dictionary, you may notice that entries are often ordered in a more complex manner. As an alternative to "letter by letter" ordering, a "word by word" ordering can be applied. Technically, such matters are reflected in the treatment of spaces, hyphens, and other punctuation marks. It is often better to ignore them, in order to produce an order that corresponds to readers' expectations. For example, it might be better to treat "cat eyed," "cat-eyed," and "cateyed" as basically the same in sorting.

For such reasons, the Unicode definitions related to collation are somewhat complex. They specify methods for applying special rules in addition to the simple lexicographic order, in a manner that allows different sets of rules to be used.

Collation and Unicode

The Unicode standard does not define a collating order. Thus, Unicode characters have no inherent order, but they can be sorted according to different orders.

The Unicode Consortium has issued a separate standard on collation: "Unicode Collation Algorithm," Unicode Technical Standard #10, *http://www.unicode.org/reports/tr30/*. It is an independent standard: conformance to it is not required for conformance to the Unicode standard.

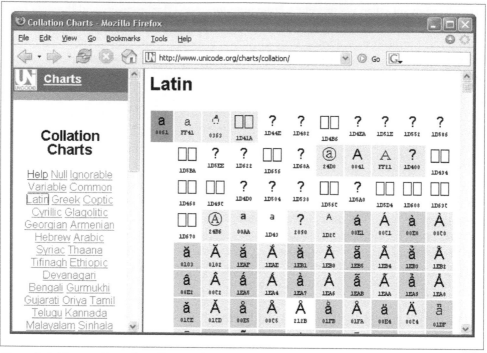

Figure 5-6. Viewing Unicode Collation Charts

The Consortium has also prepared *collation charts*, which present the collating order visually. The charts are at *http://www.unicode.org/charts/collation/*, and they can be used as a handy checking tool, as is illustrated in Figure 5-6. There you can see some of the characters that are historically based on the letter "A," in collating order. Much of this order is a matter of arbitrary decisions that just had to be made. (Due to font limitations, not all characters are displayed correctly when viewing the charts; this is why there are question marks and boxes.)

Layered Model of Collation

Collation order is language-dependent, and it may vary even within a language. For example, in German, the letter ö is placed after "o," and the difference between them is made only for words that are otherwise the same. In Swedish, ö is the last letter in the alphabet, after "z," å, and ä. Thus, when looking for a word like "Öhman" in an alphabetic list, different people start at different places. Moreover, in some countries, different sorting principles are applied in different contexts—e.g., in dictionaries versus telephone catalogs.

Technically, we can say that collating order depends on a *locale*, which can be defined as a cultural environment, or as a collection of cultural conventions. For example, the combination "ch" was traditionally regarded as a single letter in Spanish, so that all words beginning with "ch" were placed after the set of all other words beginning with "c." People might still prefer the old style—i.e., to use a Spanish locale with the old sorting rules. Part of the Common Locale Data Repository (CLDR) activity (described in Chapter 11) is the collection of data on such variation, for use in implementing tools that automatically perform collation in a locale-dependent manner.

Ultimately, a locale is a matter of user preferences, based on a user's cultural and personal background, habits, views, and decisions. For example, should "foo" appear before or after "Foo" in collation? There might be standards on such matters, but in practice, they depend on what you are accustomed to or you find most natural.

 Collating order should meet user expectations, rather than the standards of the information producer. Ideally, it would be customizable by users.

The variation between locales is described as exceptions to a default collating order, which should thus be understood as a useful tool for defining language-specific orders, rather than an attempt at a universal order to be used everywhere. On the other hand, definitions of collating orders often deal with many special characters that are usually not very relevant in sorting. For example, indexes in books are usually alphabetic but may contain entries with special characters, such as "% operator" in a book on programming. They need to put somewhere, and different authors, publishers, and standardizers have handled them differently. We can expect that the situation will become more uniform: language-specific orders will mostly cover only characters commonly used in a language, and all the rest is easiest to order according to default collating order.

More generally, the modern approach to collation is based on a layered model, where each layer may modify or replace the rules set on lower layers. For example, the layers could consist of the following, in descending order of priority:

1. Application-specific rules, such as "treat v and w as identical" (for some particular reason)

2. Company-specific rules; e.g., reflecting the traditions and decisions of a publishing house in their glossaries

3. Locale-specific rules; e.g., describing the collation rules of Swiss German, to the extent that they deviate from pan-European rules

4. Rules common to many locales by tradition or convention, such as pan-European rules

5. Universal default rules, such as Unicode default collating order

Thus, Unicode collating order is not meant to unify sorting rules across languages and cultures. On the contrary, it constitutes an essential part of a model designed to support cultural variation, providing the lowest layer of rules. It simplifies the definition of locale-specific sorting, since only deviations from default rules need to be specified. It also ensures that the collating order is defined for all characters, no matter how rare and little known they are.

Code Point Order Versus Collating Order

Code points are numbers (integers), and therefore they have an order defined by the normal ordering of numbers (0, 1, 2,…). However, this order is not meant to be used as collating order, except for special purposes.

Code point order is unnatural

It would be impossible to allocate code points so that their order, as numbers, would match the collating order of characters. Different languages have different collating orders. For example, the character ö is treated as a separate letter at the end of the alphabet in some languages but as a variant of "o" in many other languages. Moreover, the structure of the Unicode coding space imposes serious limitations, since the grouping of characters into blocks largely reflects old practices and other character standards.

Some small *subsets* of Unicode have code points that correspond to the *mutual* order of the characters. For example, the Latin letters A through Z are in consecutive code points in the "right" order in Unicode, as well as in ASCII and most other character codes. However, even for the basic Latin letters, the code point order is not suitable as a collating order, since all lowercase letters appear after all uppercase letters. In code point order, A < B < … < Z < a < b … < z, but the normal collating order has A < a < B < b < … < Z < z (so that "A" and "a" are equivalent at the primary level, etc.). As we proceed to Latin letters with diacritics, it becomes even more obvious that code point order differs from collating order.

Using code point order as a fallback in definitions

Some definitions of collating order have defined things so that they specify meaningful order only for characters that are expected to appear in normal data. They use Unicode code point order for the rest, just to have it sorted out *somehow*, in some known order.

Although you can define your collating order as you like, it is usually not necessary to use anything as arbitrary as code point order. You can use Unicode default collating order instead. Both of these orders are more or less arbitrary, but the default collating order tries to pay attention to sorting principles in human languages.

Code point order sorting for technical reasons

Sometimes you might decide to use code point order as the collating order simply because you need some known order. For example, some algorithms require that data be placed in some order, but it does not matter which. Code point order is easy to implement, and it can be described easily. The simplicity of description is essential, if data sorted by a program will be processed by another program that expects sorted data.

Although code point order is technically very simple, it poses some problems when the data is in encoded form, as opposed to just a sequence of code points. Some Unicode encodings, described in Chapter 6, are very easy in this respect, since they use fixed-size storage units for all characters. The encodings used in practice tend to be more complicated. Methods for performing code point order sorting on UTF-8 and other Unicode encodings are described in the Unicode standard in section 5.17 "Binary Order." It discusses the even more technical orders based on numeric ordering of code units (such as octets that constitute UTF-8 encoded data) rather than code numbers.

Problems of legacy software

In simple programming tasks, comparisons of character and string data are sometimes based on comparisons of code points. This applies basically to basic Latin letters in contexts where it can be assumed (or it just is assumed) that we need not deal with any other letters and that the case of letters is fixed (e.g., due to previous case folding). This explains code like if((ch >= 'A') & (ch <= 'Z')) for testing whether the value of ch is an (uppercase) letter. Such code can be efficient, but nowadays it is usually better to use library subroutines (e.g., if(isletter(ch))), making the code more readable and more portable without sacrificing efficiency. We will discuss such methods in Chapter 11.

As a user of programs, you may encounter sorted data and sorting routines that apply to simple code point order. For example, if you use a tool for automatic generation of an index for a publication, you might notice that the index will be sorted that way. If the entries are dominantly English words, the result may look mostly OK, but the handling of spaces, punctuation marks, special characters, and case of letters may differ from the applicable rules of sorting. Therefore, you may need to fix the order separately, "by hand." Make sure you first know the rules; there are differences that depend on language, style, and publisher.

Unicode Collation Algorithm

The Unicode Collation Algorithm (UCA) uses *multilevel comparison* in order to deal with the complexities of sorting. Instead of simply putting all characters in a single order and defining the collating order of strings according to their first difference (simple lexicographic ordering), UCA defines different levels of ordering between characters. For example, you can define the difference between "o" and ö as primary (as in Swedish) or as secondary (as in German). By default, UCA works with three levels:

1. Alphabetic ordering (e.g., "a" < "b")
2. Diacritic ordering (e.g., "a" < "á" < "à")
3. Case ordering (e.g., "a" < "A")

Surprisingly, UCA uses by default a case ordering where lowercase precedes uppercase, resulting in, for example, mime < Mime < MIME. The usual dictionary is opposite to this.

Canonical equivalents are essentially different ways of representing the same character (e.g., ö as a precomposed character or as an "o" followed by a combining dieresis). It is therefore natural to expect them to behave identically in collation. However, when desired, a distinction between them can be made, when everything else is the same ("tie-break situation").

A collation algorithm needs to be able to work on text elements larger than individual characters, in order to be suitable for general use. For example, in some languages, the letter æ might be treated as a separate letter, different from other letters at the primary level, but in other languages or contexts, it might be treated as equivalent to the letter pair "ae." In English, æ is often understood as just a ligature of "a" and "e," even though Unicode defines it differently. Thus, in sorting material in English, you might wish to make "Cæsar" appear where "Caesar" would appear, not after "cat."

Formally, UCA is described as an algorithm that takes as input a string and a *Collation Element Table*, which contains mapping data for characters. The output is a *sort key*, which is a sequence of 16-bit integers. These integers are not code numbers (though they may coincide with the character's code number) but weights that describe the position of the input string in the collation order, in a manner that lets us sort strings by their sort keys. Comparison of sort keys means simple comparison by numeric values. By convention, the 16-bit integers are written in hexadecimal, using four digits.

The algorithm can be used for different collating orders by using different Collation Element Tables. The UCA definition contains the *Default Unicode Collation Element Table (DUCET)*, which you may choose to use as such or as a basis for defining your own table. In particular, you may define collating order for characters that are important in your application and leave all rest as in DUCET. This ensures that the collating order is defined for all Unicode characters.

A Collation Element Table maps characters (code points) to *collation elements*. A collation element is a sequence of three or more weights (16-bit integers), and the order of the weights corresponds to their levels. Thus, the first integer indicates the primary weight, which typically corresponds to the basic alphabetic order. The principles of interpreting collation elements are the following:

- The order of elements is the order of their primary (first level) weights, if these weights are different. If the weights are equal, the order of the secondary (second level) weights is used, etc.

- However, a weight of 0000 means that the collation element is ignorable at the level of that weight.

The DUCET table is available at *http://www.unicode.org/Public/UCA/latest/allkeys.txt*. It does not contain mappings for all characters, since UCA defines weight derivation— i.e., calculation rules for weights that are not explicitly listed in a table.

A simple example of an entry in DUCET:

```
0041  ; [.0F6C.0020.0008.0041] # LATIN CAPITAL LETTER A
```

The example defines the mapping for "A" U+0041. The weights are given in square brackets, separated with periods. The primary weight is 0F6C, etc. The text starting with # is a comment, as in the Unicode database in general.

The first character inside brackets has a special meaning. If it is a period . as above, the collation element is a normal one. If it is an asterisk ∗, the collation element is *variable*. Variable elements include spaces, punctuation marks, and most symbols. They have defined weights, but an implementation of UCA may support alternate weightings. This means that a program switch called a *variable weighting tag* can change the status of variable elements so that they are ignored, except in the absence of other differences between strings.

For example, consider the following entry in DUCET:

```
002D  ; [*0221.0020.0002.002D] # HYPHEN-MINUS
```

This means that the hyphen-minus character "-" has primary weight 0221, putting it among many other punctuation marks and symbols, before any letters. This makes, for example, "X-men" sort before any string that begins with an "X" and a letter, such as "Xanadu." When alternate weighting is used, the hyphen-minus is more or less ignored, making "X-men" sort basically the same way as "Xmen." The setting of the variable weighting tag affects this behavior as follows:

Blanked (ignorable)

This setting sets the weights of variable collation elements to zero at the first three levels. This makes collation work as if variable collation elements were not present at all. However, as the last resort, Unicode code number order of character will be used for tie-breaking. Therefore, this would result, for example, in the order "X men" < "X-men" < "Xmen" < "X–men" (with en dash) while all of these would be treated as "Xmen" with respect to other strings.

Non-ignorable

Variable collation elements have their weights unchanged. Thus, for this value, an implementation supporting alternate weightings behaves the same way as an implementation that does not.

Shifted

The first three weights are set to zero, as for Blanked, but the original primary weight is made the fourth-level weight. In this case, all non-variable collation elements get the maximal fourth-level weight of FFFF. Therefore, we would get an order like "X men" < "X-men" < "X–men" < "Xmen," since now the mutual order is not by code number order but by the original first-level weight (which is 0209 for space, 0221 for hyphen-minus, and 0227 for en dash).

Shift-trimmed

This is the same as Shifted except that all trailing FFFF weights are trimmed from the sort key. This feature is intended to simulate POSIX behavior. The effect is similar to that of Shifted, but with the strings containing variable collation elements placed *after* an otherwise identical string without them. For example, "Xmen" < "X men" < "X-men" < "X–men."

Control and formatting characters, except line breaks and horizontal tabs (which count as whitespace), are completely ignored in the default order.

We have discussed some general principles of UCA only, and you need to consult UTS #10 for the detailed algorithm and notations. In practice, you will probably not work with Collation Element Tables directly. Rather, you will use higher-level constructs, such as the `Collator` and `RuleBasedCollator` classes in Java programming. These classes let you specify your modifications of the default collating order using simple, readable notations like "c < ch < d," which says that "ch" is to be treated as if it were a character between "c" and "d."

Text Boundaries

In text processing, we often need to work with text elements larger than individual characters. For example, we might need operations like "delete next word" or "move one sentence forward in the text." Therefore, we need to recognize boundaries between elements of text, collectively called text boundaries.

Text boundary principles are defined in a separate document, Unicode Standard Annex (UAX) #29, "Text Boundaries." It specifies boundaries for three types of text elements:

- Grapheme cluster, which is characterized informally as "user character"
- Word, which partly corresponds to the word concept in natural languages
- Sentence, which is recognized from punctuation by some coarse rules

The concept "grapheme cluster" is the most obscure of the three. It is meant to correspond to the idea of a character as a user sees it, on the basis of her cultural background. For example, it could be a digraph (two-character combination) like "ch" if understood as a single letter in some language, or a combination of a base character and one or more diacritic marks, or a sequence of Unicode characters that represent one syllable and are displayed as a unit. Therefore, "grapheme cluster" depends on the writing system and on conventions, but UAX #29 still tries to specify how to recognize it in general. Expressions like "grapheme" and "logical character" have been used too, but all names seem to be prone to misunderstanding. In particular, this is not a matter of graphemes in the linguistic sense.

The default, or language-independent, boundary rules are specified in UAX #29 at the general level, referring to certain special properties of characters. The values of these properties are defined in the Unicode database files *GraphemeBreakProperty.txt*, *WordBreakProperty.txt*, and *SentenceBreakProperty.txt*. The general approach in the definitions is the same as for line breaks, as described in section "Line-Breaking Properties" later in this chapter.

To illustrate the nature of boundary rules, which are not yet widely implemented along these lines in existing software, we will consider the word boundaries. Described informally and somewhat loosely, the principles are:

- Treat consecutive alphabetic characters as belonging to the same word. This applies to characters for which the Alphabetic property has the value "yes" (True), except characters belonging to Thai, Lao, or Hiragana writing system, as well as to the no-break space character (somewhat surprisingly?).

- Treat digits and other numeric characters as comparable to alphabetic characters (e.g., treat "3A" as one word).

- Do not break a numeric string at a character that has a LineBreak property value of IN = Infix, numeric (except for ":"). For example, treat "1.000,00" as one word.

- Treat connector punctuation such as "_" (with General Category value of Cp = Connector, punctuation) as comparable to alphabetic characters (e.g., treat "foo_bar" as one word).

- Treat a grapheme cluster as if it were one character.

- Regard the following as part of word when they appear between alphabetic characters: apostrophe ' (U+0027), right single quotation mark ' (U+2019), middle dot · (U+00B7), hyphenation point ‧ (U+2027), colon : (U+003A), and Hebrew punctuation gershayim ״ (U+05F4).

For example, the principle mentioned last in the list works well for some strings that need to be treated as words, such as "cat's" and "c:a" (an abbreviation of a word in Swedish). On the other hand, the principle also brings things together although they should be treated as separate words, as in the Italian expression "dell'arte" (where "dell'" is a contraction of a preposition).

The default boundary rules in UAX #29 are not meant to work as a basis of advanced processing of natural languages, such as syntactic analysis. Rather, they are meant to help in implementing useful operations in editing. For example, you can typically double-click in a word processor to select a "word," and perhaps triple-click to select a "sentence." The text boundary rules are meant to define what is selected that way.

Directionality

You might never encounter problems with directionality, if all texts you work with are written exclusively left to right. But when you need to work with other texts, you may have considerable conceptual problems. Therefore, in order to be prepared to meet such problems, it is useful to gain some basic understanding of directionality. Moreover, the topic is culturally interesting in itself. People may think that left-to-right writing is the only possibility, or the only natural way, and consequently think that right-to-left writing is unnatural or wrong.

Directionality as discussed here deals with *horizontal* writing direction. Vertical writing —i.e., writing a text line from top to bottom (or from bottom to top)—is a different issue and handled outside Unicode, although it has some implications for Unicode, as we'll see in Chapter 7.

Writing Direction of Text

Right-to-left writing is older than left-to-right writing. Hieroglyphs and oldest Greek were mostly written right to left, though alternating direction was used, too. Arabic and Hebrew scripts have preserved the original direction. The Greek script changed the direction, and

Figure 5-7. Progress or regress?

the Latin writing system was derived from a version of Greek writing system that already had established left-to-right writing direction.

The writing system that we learn in our childhood and use throughout our life makes us think that things *progress* in a particular way in the horizontal direction. If we write left to right, we think that movement rightward means progression in time: given "AB," we think that "A" is before "B" in a natural order of things.

Even if we consider purely graphic presentation, our built-in way of reading left to right or right to left will affect our understanding. If you think left to right, you probably see Figure 5-7 as indicating growth of some kind. If you are accustomed to reading right to left, you might see a decrease there. Naturally, the interpretation depends on the context, such as the presence of left-to-right or right-to-left text. Presented in isolation, graphic presentation can be thoroughly misunderstood: your attempt to describe "before" and "after" situations might be read the other way around.

When you read about writing direction, you probably read about it in English, or in another language written left to right. Therefore, the mental model of "natural" writing order is in front of your eyes even in texts that try to give you a broader view. When I say that, in Hebrew, the letters alef (aleph) א and bet (beth) ב in that order are written as אב, the explanation is confusing. The letters have already appeared in the English sentence in a particular order horizontally, so now it looks like the order was reversed.

I wrote אב in MS Word by using the Insert → Characters command, first selecting א from the Character Map, and then selecting ב. Word displays the combination as אב, since it knows that these characters must be written right to left. Things would have gone all wrong if I had thought that *I* need to reverse the order. Directionality is about visual order, so it is best handled by software that is responsible for formatting text on screen or paper.

 Using Unicode, you type characters in the logical order—i.e., in the order in which they would be mentioned if words were spelled out. In simple cases, properties of characters and the software you use take care of writing direction. When punctuation and special characters intervene, you may need to add control characters to make writing directions correct.

Bidirectionality

Using exclusively left-to-right writing, or exclusively right-to-left writing, is relatively simple to handle. When you have a document that contains, say, both English and Arabic, it becomes challenging to deal with changes in writing direction. Problems arise, among other things, from punctuation characters that are used in different writing systems and therefore need to have their directionality set by the context. The Unicode way of handling such things is described in Unicode Standard Annex #9, "The Bidirectional Algorithm," *http://www.unicode.org/reports/tr9/*.

Directionality and Character Codes

There are several ways to deal with directionality in an environment where both writing directions may appear:

- Specify that the content of a file or string is to be always written left to right, and arrange things so that characters appear in an order suitable for that. This is sometimes applied to Hebrew texts: a file contains the character in a completely reversed order, but when written left to right, the order becomes correct (for reading right to left). Confusingly, data is then said to be coded in "visual order," implying eye movement from left to right!

- Indicate the direction explicitly with invisible control characters. At the simplest, one control character says that subsequent characters are to be written left to right, and another control character switches the direction to the opposite.

- Assign inherent directionality to characters.

Although the first approach may look most natural and the third one most complicated, Unicode uses inherent directionality, enhanced with the possibility of using control characters for exceptions.

Directionality of Characters

The Unicode approach to writing direction is based on the inherent directionality defined for each character. For example, Latin and Greek letters have inherent left-to-right directionality; Hebrew and Arabic letters have inherent right-to-left directionality. Programs that display text need not know the language, at least not for directionality purposes. They use the much more technical information that is contained in the Unicode database: a table that assigns directionality to each character.

It would even be incorrect to deduce directionality from language information. The HTML specification explicitly says that browsers must not deduce the directionality of text from its declared language (the `lang` or `xml:lang` attribute, if present). This is natural if you think about transliterated Arabic, for example. When an Arabic word is written in Latin letters according to some transliteration scheme, it is still an Arabic word, but it is to be written left to right (except in some scientific contexts).

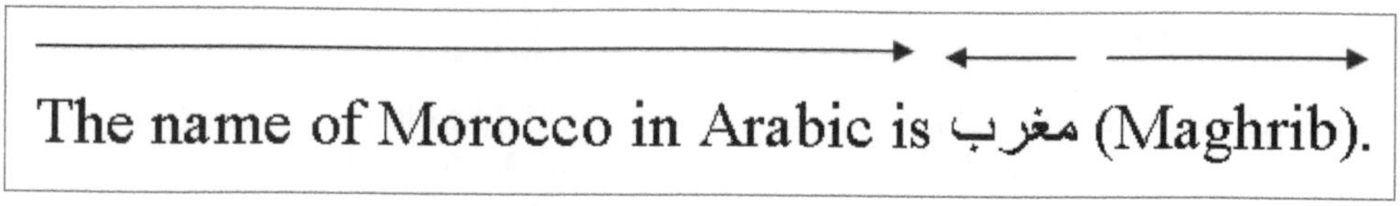

The name of Morocco in Arabic is مغرب (Maghrib).

Figure 5-8. English text with an Arabic word in it, with reading directions marked with arrows

The directionality issue is complicated by the use of directionally neutral characters. Some punctuation and other characters are used both in left-to-right and in right-to-left writing. Further complication is caused by merging texts written in different directions. For example, an English document may quote some Arabic in Arabic writing, or Arabic text may contain English words in Latin letters. The reader is assumed to be able to change the reading direction: when she sees some Arabic writing like مغرب, she jumps to the right end of that part of the text, reads leftward, and then jumps back to the right over the Arabic writing she had read. This is illustrated in Figure 5-8.

To deal with the complications, the directionality property of a character has several possible values, not just two. These values classify characters so that bidirectional algorithm can handle most situations well. Officially, the directionality property is called BiDi Class, referring to bidirectionality.

The values are named in Table 5-6, where the second column indicates whether the value indicates strong (S), weak (W), or neutral (N) directionality.

Table 5-6. BiDi Class values (directionality property values)

Code		Name	Characters that have this value
AL	S	Arabic Letter	Arabic, Syriac, and Thaana letters, etc.
AN	W	Arabic Number	Arabic-Indic digits, etc.
B	N	Paragraph Separator	Line feed, carriage return, etc.
BN	W	Boundary Neutral	Most formatting and control characters
CS	W	Common Number Separator	Comma, full stop, colon, NBSP, etc.
EN	W	European Number	European and some other digits
ES	W	European Number Separator	Plus sign, minus sign, hyphen-minus, etc.
ET	W	European Number Terminator	Degree sign, currency symbols, etc.
L	S	Left-to-Right	Most letters, ideographs, etc., and LRM
LRE	S	Left-to-Right Embedding	LRE
LRO	S	Left-to-Right Override	LRO
NSM	W	Non-Spacing Mark	Characters in General Category Mn or Me
ON	N	Other Neutrals	Characters not belonging to other classes
PDF	W	Pop Directional Format	PDF
R	S	Right-to-Left	Hebrew letters etc., and RLM
RLE	S	Right-to-Left Embedding	RLE

Code		Name	Characters that have this value
RLO	S	Right-to-Left Override	RLO
S	N	Segment Separator	Horizontal tab
WS	N	Whitespace	Spaces, form feed, etc.

Control Characters for Directionality

There is small collection of control characters that affect directionality. They are not needed in pieces of text that contain only left-to-right characters (e.g., Latin letters) or only right-to-left characters (e.g., Arabic letters). These characters have been placed into the General Punctuation block, somewhat illogically, since they are not visible punctuation marks but invisible controls. Due to their meaning, these characters should be ignored in any processing except visual rendering.

The characters are presented in Table 5-7, along with their HTML and CSS equivalents, to be discussed shortly.

Table 5-7. Control characters for directionality

Code	Name	Abbr.	Entity	HTML	CSS
U+200E	Left-to-right mark	LRM	‎		`direction: ltr;`
U+200F	Right-to-left mark	RLM	‏		`direction: rtl;`
U+202A	Left-to-right embedding	LRE		`dir="ltr"`	`unicode-bidi: embed; direction: ltr;`
U+202B	Right-to-left embedding	RLE		`dir="rtl"`	`unicode-bidi: embed; direction: ltr;`
U+202D	Left-to-right override	LRO		`<bdo dir="ltr">`	`unicode-bidi: bidi-override; direction: ltr;`
U+202E	Right-to-left override	RLO		`<bdo dir="rtl">`	`unicode-bidi: bidi-override; direction: rtl;`
U+202C	Pop directional formatting	PDF		Suitable end tag	

The left-to-right mark and the right-to-left mark set the directionality for preceding and following characters with *weak or neutral directionality*. Thus, you cannot change the writing direction of a string like "ABC" with these marks. Technically, these marks are zero-width (i.e., invisible) characters with strong directionality.

The *override* characters, left-to-right override (LRO) and right-to-left override (RLO), have a stronger effect. They affect the directionality of *all* characters, up to the next override or embedding or pop directional formatting (PDF) character. Thus overriding any natural directionality, they can be used even to make normal English text run right to left. The LRO character or the corresponding markup is needed for "visual Hebrew"—i.e., Hebrew written backward—so that modern programs still show it the intended way.

The *embedding* characters, left-to-right embedding (LRE) and right-to-left embedding (RLE), start and end a new level in directionality, in the following sense: Text between an LRE and a PDF, or between an RLE and a PDF, is treated as embedded (as a whole) inside the surrounding text. Embedding can be nested: you can, for example, have English text with an embedded Arabic quotation, which contains an embedded English word.

The *pop directional formatting* (PDF) character acts as a closing symbol that terminates the effect of preceding and matching LRO, RLO, LRE, or RLE.

Bidi Mirroring

Many characters can appear both in left-to-right and in right-to-left writing but with different glyphs depending on the writing direction. For example, the greater than sign > points to the smaller of its operands, when seen as an arrowhead. To preserve this relationship in right-to-left writing, the character must be displayed as mirrored. A glyph for the less than character < can be used for this.

For example, consider an expression like "a > b" when written in Hebrew text and using Hebrew letters instead of "a" and "b." If you type the Hebrew letter alef א, the greater-than sign >, and the Hebrew letter bet ב, you should get the visual appearance ב<א assuming that the program supports the Unicode bidirectional algorithm or the writing direction has been explicitly set to right to left. The character that looks like a less-than sign there is still the greater-than sign; it just has a mirrored glyph.

In many cases, mirroring can be described superficially as a character-level correspondence. We can say that > and < correspond to each other in mirroring, and so do "(" and ")." However, it is really a glyph-level correspondence: the rendering engine just uses a normal (i.e., normal in left-to-right writing) glyph for a character to render another character.

Not all mirrored characters can rendered by "borrowing" a glyph from another character. For some characters, such as angle ∠ (U+2220), a separate mirrored glyph needs to be used. This means that an implementation that supports the character and supports both writing directions must have two different glyphs for it. However, this is not common in practice, since it requires both adequate programming and a suitable font using advanced font technology.

The Bidi Mirrored property is a normative binary (yes/no) property that simply tells whether a character is mirrored or not. The Bidi Mirroring Glyph property is an informative property that suggests, for many mirrored characters, a character whose glyph might be used to render the mirrored character in right-to-left writing. For example, the following lines in the file *BidiMirroring.txt* suggest that a glyph for) can be used to render (as mirrored, and vice versa:

```
0028; 0029 # LEFT PARENTHESIS
0029; 0028 # RIGHT PARENTHESIS
```

Directionality in HTML and CSS

We will briefly discuss directionality in HTML, since the topic is often neglected, or presented incorrectly, in HTML material. In HTML authoring, you have three ways to affect directionality:

- Insert Unicode control characters; this is discouraged in UTR #20 (see Chapter 9) except for the left-to-right mark and the right-to-left mark (which you can write in different ways, including the entity references ‎ and ‏).

- Insert HTML markup to indicate directionality (dir attribute for setting directionality inside an element, and bdo element for bidirectional override).

- Use Cascading Style Sheets (CSS) rules (direction and bidi-override properties) on a suitable markup element, introducing extra markup for that if needed.

For example, to make the string "ABC" written right to left, you could use any one of the following constructs in HTML (where the last one uses essentially CSS):

```
&#x202e;ABC&#x202c;
<bdo dir="rtl">ABC</bdo>
<span style="unicode-bidi: bidi-override; direction: rtl;">ABC</span>
```

Setting the dir attribute in HTML for any element but bdo corresponds to using left-to-right mark and therefore does not affect characters with strong directionality. Thus, ABC would appear as ABC. Similarly, the direction property in CSS does not override natural strong directionality, unless the bidi-override property is set as well.

HTML specifications explicitly warn that the declaration of the language used in a document, via lang or xml:lang attribute, shall *not* set directionality. The overall default in HTML is left-to-right directionality. Thus, a document in Arabic should normally have <html dir="rtl"> as its first tag. Using the attribute lang="ar" there as well can be useful for other purposes, but it does not set directionality.

Web browsers, especially Internet Explorer, have flaws in directionality features. For example, text that contains only right-to-left characters and neutral characters should be displayed correctly without any extra markup, but this does not always happen. Using logically redundant markup with dir attributes may help.

 HTML authors who create right-to-left or mixed-direction content should use dir attributes even in contexts where they are not required by the specifications.

For additional explanations, examples, and advice, please consult Andreas Prilop's "Bidirectional text" at *http://www.unics.uni-hannover.de/nhtcapri/bidirectional-text.html*.

Directionality of Formatting

The dir attribute in HTML and the direction property in CSS should be used with caution, since they do not affect the directionality of characters only. They also affect the direction of document formatting. This is natural in many ways. If you have, say, a bulleted list, then the bullet should apparently be placed near the start of each item. If the character directionality in the items is right to left, this means that the bullets should appear on the right and the text should be right-aligned. Setting directionality in HTML or CSS affects the following:

- Writing direction of text as just described
- The layout direction of blocks that appear side by side
- The layout direction of columns in tables
- The direction of horizontal overflow, when content does not fit into its block
- The default value of horizontal alignment of text lines (the align attribute in HTML, the text-align property in CSS)
- The alignment of the last line of a block of text that is justified on both sides

Line-Breaking Properties

The need for line breaking arises from the simple fact that horizontal space is usually limited by factors such as paper or screen width. In addition, for readability, line length should be kept within reasonable limits. Typographic recommendations usually suggest a maximum of 80 or 90 characters and an optimum of 55 to 60 characters. On small devices —e.g., when displaying text messages in a mobile phone—the line length can be very small, for example, 13 characters.

Plain text is often preformatted so that it is divided into lines with explicit line breaks, typically making lines shorter than 80 characters. Such text may need to be reformatted, though, due to changing requirements on line length. Moreover, it is nowadays very common to avoid preformatting. In word processors, web authoring, and even in plain text, explicit line breaks are often omitted, marking just paragraph boundaries. Therefore, paragraphs need to be dynamically formatted into lines.

In old manual typography, line breaks were decided by professional typesetters with years of experience. In the modern world, line breaking of prose text is mostly automated, though sometimes people inspect and check the results. This may mean preventing undesirable line breaks, suggesting line-breaking opportunities, or adding forced line breaks. It might also be possible to do such things even in the writing phase, and this is the only feasible way if the author cannot see the formatted results (e.g., in normal web authoring).

Preformatted text is still used in many contexts, such as poetry. Typically, forced line breaks of some kind are used to create lines, when using lines so short they need not be broken in any normal circumstances.

Conformance Criteria

Line breaking is a very complex issue, and the Unicode standard deals with it at a rather technical and low level only. Unicode has, in addition to explicit line break characters, some special control characters for suggesting or prohibiting line breaks at specific points and some general line-breaking rules. The rules mostly operate very locally only, for a single character or a pair of consecutive characters. Therefore, these rules constitute just a coarse technical basis, which often needs to be augmented and overridden by higher-level rules, such as language-specific hyphenation. Moreover, they are just an optional basis. Some features in line breaking are normative (i.e., must be obeyed if line breaking is performed at all), but the algorithm as a whole is not.

 Conformance to the Unicode standard does not require conformance to the Line Breaking Algorithm. The algorithm specifies default rules that software designers may wish to use as a basis.

A program can separately claim conformance to the Unicode Line Breaking Algorithm. Even then, the algorithm may partly be overridden by higher-level rules, or as "tailored," provided that the existence of such rules is mentioned. Detailed documentation is not required; a statement like the following is acceptable: "This program uses the Unicode Line Breaking Algorithm as specified in Version 4.1.0 of the Unicode Standard, as tailored to the Vogon language."

Characters for Special Control over Line Breaking

Let us first look at some Unicode characters that are meant for controlling line breaks in text, either by preventing an undesired break or by suggesting a break. The general idea is that programs divide text into lines according to some general principles, such as the default Unicode rules for line-breaking or application-specific rules. Characters that can be used to override general rules are presented in Table 5-8. Some of the characters are control characters; some are graphic characters with special line-breaking properties. Note that here we do not discuss forced line breaks, generated with line break characters such as Carriage Return; they will be discussed in Chapter 8.

Table 5-8. Characters for special control over line breaking

Code	Unicode name	Description
U+00A0	No-break space	Like space U+0020, but prevents line break
U+2011	Non-breaking hyphen	Like hyphen U+2010, but prevents line break
U+00AD	Soft hyphen	Invisible; indicates allowed hyphenation point
U+200B	Zero-width space	Invisible; indicates allowed line break
U+2060	Word joiner	Invisible; prevents line break

Preventing line breaks

The word joiner (WJ) character exists for the sole purpose of preventing a line break. It can be used when general line-breaking rules would allow a line break but a break is considered inappropriate. Do not confuse it with the ZWJ U+200D and the ZWNJ U+200C, which relate to ligature behavior. Unfortunately, there is such confusion in several versions of MS Word. When you select Insert → Symbol and select the Special characters pane, there are options like "No-Width Optional Break" and "No-Width Non Break." Selecting them means actually ZWJ and ZWNJ, respectively. MS Word treats them the way it describes, but if the text is transferred to a program that conforms to the Unicode standard in this issue, their effect changes essentially.

Previously, the zero-width no-break space (ZWNBSP) U+FEFF has been defined as an invisible character that prevents line break. However, such usage is not recommended anymore; instead, the word joiner should be used. The zero-width no-break space retains its use in an unrelated purpose, as a byte order mark.

Only a few characters, such as the space, have "non-breaking clones." Technically, the "clones" are characters with a compatibility decomposition containing the <noBreak> tag, indicating that a line break is prohibited after the character. In practice, there can be other differences, too, between a character and its "non-breaking clone" (see notes on no-break space in Chapter 8).

For other characters, different techniques must be used. To disallow a line break after a solidus /, for example, you cannot use a non-breaking version of that character. Instead, you can use the normal character and add a word joiner character after it.

Suggesting line break opportunities

The zero-width space (ZWSP) allows a simple line break, without adding any hyphen. It is typically used in strings that are not words, although in the Thai script, it can be used to separate words. It may be useful, for example, when a long URL is mentioned in text. You can add ZWSP in places where a line break is acceptable.

The soft hyphen is supported by some programs, ignored by some, and treated as a visible hyphen by some other software. When supported according to the Unicode standard, it suggests (allows) hyphenation—i.e., division of a word so that a hyphen is placed at the end of the first line.

For example, if you insert a soft hyphen U+00AD between "c" and "d" in "abcdef," you allow the string to be divided so that "abc-" appears at the end of a line. If you insert a zero-width space U+200B instead, you allow the string to be divided so that "abc" without a hyphen appears at the end of line. In the latter case, the reader cannot really know (except from an explicit explanation or by guessing right) that the text contains "abcdef" and not "abc def."

Limited support

Software like Microsoft Word may not interpret all line-breaking control characters as defined in the Unicode standard. Program-specific tools, which operate at levels other than character level, can be more effective in practice. Some techniques are mentioned later in this chapter, and Chapter 9 presents some ways to prevent line breaks in markup languages like HTML.

 Characters in Table 5-8 are inconsistently supported in popular software such as word processors. Check the software documentation, or run some tests, before taking them into use, and stay tuned to problems in data transfer between programs. The no-break space is well supported, though.

Principles of Line Breaking

In very simple processing of English texts, line breaking consists of breaking between words. Technically, this means the principle that a line break is allowed after a space but not elsewhere. Conceptually, this means that there is a space at the end of a line but it is ignored (not even counted as lengthening the line). Many text editors, browsers, and other programs still apply such a simple model. They may treat a hyphen (or hyphen-minus) as an allowed break point, too.

In the Unicode context, the problem is more complex, since not all writing systems use spaces between words. Moreover, technical or otherwise special texts can contain long strings of symbols with no spaces. There are six basic modes of line breaking (although the Unicode standard lists only the first, the fourth, and the fifth as "principal styles"):

Western—i.e., word-oriented (without hyphenation)
A line break may be introduced after a space, and possibly after a hyphen as well. This can be applied to Latin, Greek, Cyrillic, and many other scripts that have a concept of written word that consists of letters, with words separated by spaces.

Western with hyphenation
Additional line breaks may be introduced on the basis of hyphenation of words so that a word is broken to two lines and a hyphen is added at the end of a line to indicate this. Hyphenation may be based on language-specific algorithms, on hyphenation dictionaries, or on invisible hyphenation hints.

Symbolic
Line breaks should generally be avoided, but when necessary, line breaks can be introduced between major components of a construct, such as a mathematical expression, a chemical formula, a pathname of a file, or a URL. Quite often, simpler methods are needed, and they are often based on allowing breaks after certain characters.

East Asian
Line breaks are allowed everywhere except after or before certain characters. This is used for East Asian languages written using an ideographic or syllabic system. Korean, however, uses spaces between words.

South East Asian
> Line breaks are allowed at syllable boundaries, to be detected in a morphological analysis. This is used for languages like Thai, written without spaces between words and allowing a line break between syllables in general.

Emergency breaks
> A line break is made as required by an imposed maximum line length when the limit is reached, irrespectively of any line-breaking rules. Emergency breaks are normally applied as the last resort only, when there is a long string that cannot be broken at all by the line-breaking rules being applied.

If you use a program that applies Western-style line breaking, it is clear that East Asian or South East Asian texts won't work well, even if you could type them in that program. In such a case, short fragments of symbolic text work reasonably, but long expressions can be difficult to handle, especially if you cannot use spaces in them.

In all modes, special characters for explicit line break control can be used as an additional device, if supported as defined in the Unicode standard. Sometimes they might be entered automatically—e.g., by processing URLs by programs that insert invisible line break control characters.

Unicode line-breaking rules are mostly oriented toward handling Western, Symbolic, and East Asian modes. Thus, the rules address just a relatively small part of the problem. On the other hand, being defined in a uniform manner, they let you work with documents containing a mixture of scripts and languages. This has partly been achieved by somewhat artificial decisions. It is easy to start defining line-breaking rules so that Latin letters and other characters used in Western scripts have properties suitable for the Western mode, etc., but there are many borderline cases, especially since many characters are used in several scripts, or for several essentially different purposes within a script.

Emergency Breaks

The oldest forms of alphabetic writing can be described as using emergency breaks as the normal mode. Words were written with no space between them, and the entire available writing width was used, with no regard to word boundaries. This saved writing material, which was very expensive (e.g., parchment). We can see such things (although with spaces between words) happen again, for example, on small devices where the line length is small. Applying emergency break mode throughout makes things unambiguous, if readers know about it and if a space is written even when a line break occurs between words. Applying emergency breaks as the last resort may introduce ambiguity. In particular, it means breaking a word without displaying a hyphen, even when the normal mode is (or the user may think it is) Western with hyphenation.

When a program applies some line-breaking rules and observes that a line would exceed the allowed width, since there is no line-breaking opportunity within a long string, there are several ways to handle the situation, such as the following:

Emergency break
> Break the line so that the maximum width is used and continue at the start of the next line, with no indication that a break has occurred.

Visible overflow
> Let the line exceed past the allowed width (to a page margin, on paper).

Horizontal scrolling (on screen)
> Only the part of the line that fits is visible, but a scrollbar can be used to see the entire line.

Invisible overflow
> Make the part of text that exceeds the width invisible, perhaps thereby making the last visible character appear in part only.

Truncation
> Similar to invisible overflow, but indicated with some symbol like "…" at the end of a line.

Negative kerning
> Reduce the spacing between characters or words or both, making the text fit within the width at the cost of reduced legibility.

All these approaches have considerable drawbacks, so a choice between them is usually about the lesser of evils. The problem is particularly difficult when the data comes from an unpredictable source. For example, discussion forums on the Web can be sabotaged by entering a message with very long strings that are unbreakable by the rules that web browsers apply. On the other hand, a message could meaningfully contain such a string —e.g., a URL. Therefore, displaying the message in an area that has horizontal scrollbar when needed is probably the best option, as a rule. (You would use overflow: scroll in CSS for this.)

When processing data to be presented on paper, it is best to perform at least some pre-processing to decide whether there will be long unbreakable strings. For example, if you know that the rendering engine does not perform any hyphenation and does not observe Unicode line-breaking rules (as a whole), you can estimate that any string that has no spaces in it and is longer than, say, 30 characters will probably cause serious problems. You could then modify the string by adding an explicit line-breaking opportunity—i.e., zero-width space U+200B—after some special characters that you expect to be common in such strings. Of course, you would first need to make sure that the rendering engine understands U+200B. (Otherwise, you might insert something that has a similar effect in a particular situation, perhaps the nonstandard tag <wbr> in HTML authoring.) The special characters should be chosen so that a break after them is not too disturbing and could be understood by the users. If you expect the long strings to be usually URLs, you could insert a break opportunity after any /, ?, and &, for example.

Unicode Line-Breaking Rules

The Unicode standard specifies "line-breaking behavior" of characters in an apparently complex way, but the rules really operate at the level of individual characters and character pairs. The rules answer questions like "is it permissible to break between these two characters" with no regard to what appears before or after them.

Previously, there were different descriptions of "line-breaking behavior" in different parts of the Unicode standard. The assignments of line-breaking property values to characters, too, have changed between Unicode versions. This is one reason why you should not expect to find complete implementation of the rules even in layout software. However, for new software, a designer might decide to use a subroutine library that implements the rules (such as Unicode::Wrap in the CPAN archive for the Perl language). In that case, care should be taken to check which version of line-breaking rules it implements.

 Unicode line-breaking rules have not been widely implemented yet. Programs typically implement at most a part of them, possibly according to some older version of the rules.

The definitions have now been collected into Unicode Standard Annex (UAX) #14, "Line Breaking Properties." Despite being issued as a separate document, it is an integral part of the standard. It discusses the line-breaking rules in different ways. It is not obvious which parts are the ultimate definitions. The longish Chapter 5, "Line Breaking Properties," is explanatory, or "narrative" as it calls itself, and Chapter 7, "Pair-table Based Implementation," with a tabular presentation of some of the rules, is descriptive, too: it explains a possible implementation.

The authoritative specification of line-breaking properties (both normative and informative) consists of the first part (before Table 1) of Chapter 2, "Definitions," and the formalized rules in Chapter 6, "line-breaking Algorithm," of UAX #14 and the *LineBreak.txt* file. The former describes the rules in terms of LineBreak properties; the latter assigns a LineBreak property to each character. All the rest is attempted explanations or illustrations, and might be just confusing.

Values of the LineBreak property

Although the values of the LineBreak property are meant to be somewhat mnemonic (e.g., PR stands for "Prefix (Numeric)"), they are not meant to constitute a classification in a general meaning (like the General Category property). For example, the dollar sign $ has the LineBreak value of PR, but this just reflects its treatment as a prefix character in line-breaking, due to common use in front of a number in English usage. The mnemonic interpretations names should be read with the implied text "treated as … in the context of line-breaking" around them.

The values are briefly described in Table 5-9. The descriptions are meant to be illustrative, not part of the formal definitions. What really constitutes the defined meaning of the values is the set of rules that use these values to describe line-breaking opportunities. The descriptive names in the second column, though taken from the standard, are not even defined synonyms of the values, just concise characterizations.

Table 5-9. LineBreak property values

Value	Descriptive name	Example(s) of characters
AI	Ambiguous (Alphabetic or Ideographic)	½, ×, ¡
AL	Ordinary Alphabetic and Symbol	A, >
B2	Break Opportunity Before and After	— (em dash)
BA	Break Opportunity After	Thin space, soft hyphen
BB	Break Opportunity Before	´ (U+00B4), ˌ (U+02CC)
BK *	Mandatory Break	LS (U+2028), PS (U+2029)
CB *	Contingent Break Opportunity	U+FFFC
CL	Closing Punctuation	),]
CM *	Attached Characters and Combining Marks	Combining grave accent (U+0300)
CR *	Carriage Return	CR (U+000D)
EX	Exclamation/Interrogation	!, ?
GL *	Non-breaking ("Glue")	No-break space (U+00A0)
H2	Hangul LV Syllable	가 (U+AC00)
H3	Hangul LVT Syllable	각 (U+AC01)
HY	Hyphen	- (hyphen-minus)
ID	Ideographic	Chinese ideographs
IN	Inseparable	horizontal ellipsis: …
IS	Infix Separator	, (comma), . (full stop)
JL	Hangul L Jamo	ㄱ (U+1100)
JT	Hangul T Jamo	ㄲ (U+11A9)
JV	Hangul V Jamo	ㅏ (U+1161)
LF *	Line Feed	LF (U+000A)
NL *	Next Line	NL (U+0085)
NS	Non Starter	Small kana letters (in Japanese)
NU	Numeric	0, 1
OP	Opening Punctuation	(, [
PO	Postfix (Numeric)	"%", "¢"
PR	Prefix (Numeric)	$, +
QU	Ambiguous Quotation	" and other quotation marks
SA	Complex Context (South East Asian)	ก (Thai character ko kai)
SG *	Surrogates	(should not appear)

Value	Descriptive name	Example(s) of characters
SP *	Space	" " (space)
SY	Symbols Allowing Breaks	/
WJ *	Word Joiner	WJ (U+2060)
XX	Unknown	Private use code points
ZW *	Zero Width Space	ZWSP (U+200B)

Some of the descriptive names are slightly misleading. In particular, "Inseparable" does not mean that the character cannot be separated from other characters by a line break. It only means inseparability from some types of characters.

The property is normative for the following values: BK, CB, CM, CR, GL, H2, H3, JL, JT, JV, LF, NL, SG, SP, WJ, ZW, denoted by an asterisk * in Table 5-9. The property is informative for other values. Basically, normative values must be applied as defined by conforming implementations, if they do line breaking at all, whereas informative properties are just suggested defaults. However, even the normative values can be overridden at levels other than plain text—e.g., by explicit formatting instructions.

Characters with same LineBreak property value are said to constitute a *line-breaking class*. Some classes are very small (e.g., the class corresponding to the value SP contains the space character only), because some characters need to have very specific line-breaking behavior.

The format of LineBreak.txt

The *LineBreak.txt* file is of rather simple format, explained on comment lines (starting with #) at the start of the file itself. Each entry consists of one line, containing three fields: Unicode value (code number, four hexadecimal digits); value of the LineBreak property, two characters; and Unicode name, which is purely a comment here, since the code number identifies the character uniquely. Consider the following line:

```
00B0;PO # DEGREE SIGN
```

It says that for the Unicode character U+00B0 (which has the name degree sign), the value of the LineBreak property is PO—i.e., the character belongs to line breaking class PO (which is by the way abbreviated from the word "postfix"—not very mnemonic, is it?).

Character ranges are denoted as in the Unicode database in general. Example:

```
4E00..9FBB;ID # <CJK Ideograph, First>..<CJK Ideograph, Last>
```

This means that all characters between U+4E00 and U+9FBB, inclusively, have the value ID (ideographic) for the LineBreak property.

All code points, assigned and unassigned, that are not listed explicitly are given the value XX.

The following is an extract of *LineBreak.txt*, covering the printable characters in the ISO Latin 1 range (U+0020 to U+007E and U+00A0 to U+00FF) and excluding letters with

AL as the value of the LineBreak property (e.g., basic Latin letters). Note that not all letters have that value and not all characters with that value are letters in a normal sense:

```
0020;SP # SPACE
0021;EX # EXCLAMATION MARK
0022;QU # QUOTATION MARK
0023;AL # NUMBER SIGN
0024;PR # DOLLAR SIGN
0025;PO # PERCENT SIGN
0026;AL # AMPERSAND
0027;QU # APOSTROPHE
0028;OP # LEFT PARENTHESIS
0029;CL # RIGHT PARENTHESIS
002A;AL # ASTERISK
002B;PR # PLUS SIGN
002C;IS # COMMA
002D;HY # HYPHEN-MINUS
002E;IS # FULL STOP
002F;SY # SOLIDUS
0030;NU # DIGIT ZERO
  …
0039;NU # DIGIT NINE
003A;IS # COLON
003B;IS # SEMICOLON
003C;AL # LESS-THAN SIGN
003D;AL # EQUALS SIGN
003E;AL # GREATER-THAN SIGN
003F;EX # QUESTION MARK
0040;AL # COMMERCIAL AT
005B;OP # LEFT SQUARE BRACKET
005C;PR # REVERSE SOLIDUS
005D;CL # RIGHT SQUARE BRACKET
005E;AL # CIRCUMFLEX ACCENT
005F;AL # LOW LINE
0060;AL # GRAVE ACCENT
007B;OP # LEFT CURLY BRACKET
007C;BA # VERTICAL LINE
007D;CL # RIGHT CURLY BRACKET
007E;AL # TILDE
00A0;GL # NO-BREAK SPACE
00A1;AI # INVERTED EXCLAMATION MARK
00A2;PO # CENT SIGN
00A3;PR # POUND SIGN
00A4;PR # CURRENCY SIGN
00A5;PR # YEN SIGN
00A6;AL # BROKEN BAR
00A7;AI # SECTION SIGN
00A8;AI # DIAERESIS
00A9;AL # COPYRIGHT SIGN
00AA;AI # FEMININE ORDINAL INDICATOR
00AB;QU # LEFT-POINTING DOUBLE ANGLE QUOTATION MARK
00AC;AL # NOT SIGN
00AD;BA # SOFT HYPHEN
00AE;AL # REGISTERED SIGN
00AF;AL # MACRON
```

```
00B0;PO # DEGREE SIGN
00B1;PR # PLUS-MINUS SIGN
00B2;AI # SUPERSCRIPT TWO
00B3;AI # SUPERSCRIPT THREE
00B4;BB # ACUTE ACCENT
00B5;AL # MICRO SIGN
00B6;AI # PILCROW SIGN
00B7;AI # MIDDLE DOT
00B8;AI # CEDILLA
00B9;AI # SUPERSCRIPT ONE
00BA;AI # MASCULINE ORDINAL INDICATOR
00BB;QU # RIGHT-POINTING DOUBLE ANGLE QUOTATION MARK
00BC;AI # VULGAR FRACTION ONE QUARTER
00BD;AI # VULGAR FRACTION ONE HALF
00BE;AI # VULGAR FRACTION THREE QUARTERS
00BF;AI # INVERTED QUESTION MARK
00D7;AI # MULTIPLICATION SIGN
00F7;AI # DIVISION SIGN
```

The formal rules

The line-breaking rules themselves in the standard (in UAX #14) consist of formal rules accompanied by verbal notes. The notes try to explain the content of the rules as well as their motivation, though much of the motivation is explained in the descriptions of the values. The formal rules use values of the LineBreak property to indicate any character with that value and the symbols specified in Table 5-10. There is no particular reason for using these specific symbols, but you may think of ! as commanding (a break), × as joining characters together, and ÷ as permitting division (into lines).

Table 5-10. Operators used in line-breaking rules

Symbol	Meaning	Example
! (exclamation mark)	Mandatory break	LF ! means: always break after linefeed
× (multiplication sign)	No break allowed	× QU means: never break before quote
÷ (division sign)	Break allowed	ZW ÷ means: allow break after ZW

The rules are numbered LB1, LB2, etc., but there are holes in the numbering. When rules are removed in an update to the Unicode standard, the numbering of other rules is kept the same. The rules are in *order of priority*. The general idea is to specify a set of rules that forbid some line breaks, and then allow everything else (using the special symbol ALL to refer to all characters). This may sound strange, but the rules explicitly forbid line breaks between alphabetic characters, for example. Thus, when checking whether a line break is allowed at a particular point, the final rule that says "break everything else" will be applied rather rarely (for English text, for example).

The rules are presented in Table 5-11. The first column contains the rule number, the second column contains the rule itself, and the third column explains the rule in loose prose, perhaps using just example characters. The symbol "sot" means start of text, and "eot" means end of text. For brevity, the verb "break" alone indicates that a line break is allowed, whereas "always break" means an obligatory line break. A notation of the form

(A | B) is used to denote "A or B." An asterisk * after a value indicates that a character in the corresponding class may appear zero or more times.

Table 5-11. Line-breaking rules

Nr.	Formal rule	Informal description
1	Resolve AI, CB, SA, SG, and XX into other line-breaking classes	Use external info to decide what to do with ambiguous classes.
2 a	× sot	No break at the start of text.
2 b	! eot	Always break at the end of text.
3a	BK !	Always break after LS or PS.
3b	CR × LF	No break between CR and LF.
	(CR | LF | NL)!	Always break after CR, LF, and NL.
3c	× (BK | CR | LF | NL) !	No break before hard line break.
4	× (SP | ZW)	No break before space or ZWSP.
5	ZW ÷	Break after zero-width space.
7b	Treat X CM* as if it were X, for any class X except BK, CR, LF, NL, SP, or ZW	Bind combining marks with the preceding character.
7c	Treat any remaining CM as if it were AL	Treat an isolated combining mark as alphabetic.
8	× (CL | EX | IS | SY)	No break before), !, ;, /.
9	OP SP* ×	No break after (, even when it is followed by spaces.
10	QU SP* × OP	No break between a quote and (, even if spaces intervene.
11	CL SP* × NS	No break between (and small kana, even if spaces intervene.
11a	B2 SP* × B2	No break between em dashes, even if spaces intervene.
11b	× WJ	No break before word joiner.
	WJ ×	No break after word joiner.
12	SP ÷	Break after a space.
13	× GL	No break before a Glue.
	GL ×	No break after a Glue.
14	× QU	No break before a quote.
	QU ×	No break after a quote.
14a	÷ CB	Break before Contingent Break Opp.
	CB ÷	Break after Contingent Break Opp.
15	× (BA | HY)	No break before a hyphen.
	× NS	No break before small kana.

Nr.	Formal rule	Informal description
	BB ×	No break after an acute accent.
16	(AL | ID | IN | NU) × IN	No break between alphabetic etc. and an ellipsis.
17	ID × PO	No break between ideograph and %.
	AL × NU	No break between letter and number.
	NU × AL	No break between number and letter.
18	CL × PO	No break in)%.
	(HY | IS | NU) × NU	No break in -9 or .9 or 89.
	NU × PO	No break in 9%.
	PR × (AL | HY | ID | NU | OP)	No break in +a or +-, etc.
	SY × NU	No break in /9.
18b	JL × (JL | JV | H2 | H3)	No break inside a Korean syllable.
	(JV | H2) × (JV | JT)	
	(JT | H3) × JT	
18c	(JL | JV | JT | H2 | H3) × (IN | PO)	No break between Korean syllable block and "…" or %.
	PR × (JL | JV | JT | H2 | H3)	No break between + and a Korean syllable block.
19	AL × AL	No break between letters.
19b	IS × AL	No break in :a.
20	ALL ÷	Break after anything else.
	÷ ALL	Break before anything else.

Note that rules that appear before LB12 and prohibit a line break before a character (e.g., × CL) imply that a break is not allowed even if the character is preceded by a space. This means that if normal text contains a special notation starting with a special character like a period (e.g., "use the .htaccess file"), the rules forbid breaking the text so that the special character appears at the start of a line. The reason is such rules beat out rule LB12, which allows a line break after a space.

As an example of the motivation behind the rules, explained to some extent in UAX #14, consider the following statements there in the description of the class IS:

> Characters that usually occur inside a numerical expression may not be separated from the numeric characters that follow, unless a space character intervenes. For example, there is no break in "100.00" or "10,000", nor in "12:59".

> Infix separators are sentence ending punctuation when not used in a numeric context. Therefore they always prevent breaks before.

The first statement explains the rule IS × NU, which is part of LB 18. It also explains the name IS, which is short for Infix Separator. The use of IS characters in a quite different meaning, in normal sentence punctuation, is the reason for the rule × IS, which is part of

LB 8. There is also a comment saying that rule IS × AL (LB 19b) prevents abbreviations like "e.g." being broken. This may sound complicated, and it really is, because the rules deal with characters with multiple usage, with no way to differentiate between them except coarsely on the basis of adjacent characters.

Applying the rules

In principle, it is relatively straightforward to apply the Unicode line-breaking rules. Consider for example the question of whether line breaks are allowed within the string "/%7ej" (without the quotation marks). The LineBreak properties of the characters in the example string can be found in the *LineBreak.txt* file:

```
002F;SY;SOLIDUS
0025;PO;PERCENT SIGN
0037;NU;DIGIT SEVEN
0065;AL;LATIN SMALL LETTER E
006A;AL;LATIN SMALL LETTER J
```

Then, taking the characters in order and applying the rules in Line Breaking Algorithm in order (as they have been specified to apply), we find:

- Between / and %, a line break is permitted, since no rule forbids it and the last rule LB 20 says "break everywhere else."
- Between % and 7, a line break is permitted on the same grounds.
- Between 7 and "e," no line break is allowed, according to rule LB 17: NU × AL.
- Between "e" and "j," no line break is allowed, according to rule LB 19: AL × AL.

This explains, in part, why you might see printed matter containing a URL like *http:// www.cs.tut.fi/%7ejkorpela/* divided into lines in an odd way, *http://www.cs.tut.fi/%* and *7ejkorpela/*.

Somewhat surprisingly, a line break is not allowed before / even after a space (rule LB 8). Thus, if you have text like "it's in directory /usr/spool" and you would like to allow a line break after the word "directory," you would need to insert a zero-width space U+200B before the first /. This works because the rule permitting a line break after a zero-width space appears before the other rules discussed here, hence has a higher priority. On the practical side, although you may observe the problem on some web browsers for example, the cures may not work; instead of a zero-width space, you could use the nonstandard HTML tag <wbr> to suggest a permitted line break.

At each step in considering whether a line break is permitted before two consecutive characters *A* and *B*, we need to consider the LineBreak properties of both characters. If there is no rule (formulated in terms of the LineBreak property values) that forbids a line break between *A* and *B*, or after *A* in general, or before *B* in general, then a line break is permitted between them.

Pair table implementation

For efficiency reasons, the line-breaking algorithm is usually implemented using table lookup techniques. UAX #14 describes how most of the rules can be implemented using a pair table that tells, for any pair of line-breaking classes, whether a break between two characters is allowed. The table does not deal with character pairs only but also situations where characters have one or more spaces between them. The pair table cannot express all aspects of line-breaking behavior, though.

A pair table, shown as Table 5-12, can also be used for *quick checks*.

Table 5-12. Pair table for line-breaking behavior

To check whether a line break is permitted between two characters, you first look up their line-breaking classes and then use them as row and column index to the table. The symbols in the table have the following meanings (note that the notations here differ somewhat from those used in UAX #14):

" " *(space, empty cell in the table)*
> Indirect break opportunity only; this means that no line break is allowed if the characters appear in succession, but a break is allowed if one or more spaces intervene.

÷
> A direct break opportunity—i.e., a line break is allowed (even when no space intervenes).

^
> A prohibited break, in the sense that no break is allowed even if spaces intervene; formally, $A^\wedge B$ means A SP* × B, where SP is the space character.

Line-breaking behavior for pairs involving the following line-breaking classes must be resolved outside the pair table: AI, BK, CB, CR, LF, NL, SA, SG, SP, and XX.

For example, suppose you need to check whether a line break is permitted between an exclamation mark ! (U+0021) and a horizontal ellipsis … (U+2026). You would first find their line-breaking classes, EX and IN, from the Unicode database file or some other source. Then you would find the row EX and the cell in column IN on that row, and find ÷, which means that a line break is permitted.

Tailoring

Unicode line-breaking rules can cause highly undesirable line breaks or prevent quite adequate line breaks. The rules have been written mainly with "normal" text in mind. For specialties like technical notations and mathematical expressions, the rules may result even in ridiculous results. Even relatively normal expressions often cause problems, if they are short and contain nonalphabetic characters. For example, "c/o" can be broken into "c/" and "o" by the algorithm, since a break after / is generally permitted.

UAX #14 allows tailoring, as long as the normative values of LineBreak are implemented as defined. Examples of tailoring include changing the line-breaking class of some characters, adding rules, and modifying rules. It is also possible to try to recognize some special constructs, like URLs or mathematical formulas, and process them by quite different rules.

In a program designed for displaying text written in a script that uses spaces between words, probably the most useful simple tailoring would consist of a rule that prevents breaking a very short "word" or by separating just one or two characters from a "word." Here "word" means just a string of characters not containing any space or other whitespace. Most people probably would not like to see "w/o" divided at all, or "Formula/ X" divided after the "/" even if they might agree on treating "/" as a break opportunity in general. The implementation of such restrictions requires an approach that does not work just at the level of character pairs, of course.

Some background and criticism

Years ago, the Internet Explorer 4 browser was observed to use very strange line breaks —e.g., breaking a string like "a-b" to "a-" at the end of a line and "b" at the start of the next line, or even breaking "-b" to "-" and "b." Newer versions of the browser have exhibited the problems in varying forms, with no documentation. This has caused a lot of frustration. Attempts to use characters for explicit line break control, such as word joiner, were generally unsuccessful, due to lack of support for such characters. Other browsers have had similar problems to some extent. For details on the problems, please refer to the web page *http://www.cs.tut.fi/~jkorpela/html/nobr.html*.

The problem is that web browsers may apply Unicode line-breaking rules blindly, indiscriminately. Although breaking after a hyphen-minus "-" is very often suitable, perhaps even desirable, it is absurd to apply the rule permitting it to a very short string like "a-b." Unfortunately, the Unicode standard does not mention such considerations.

The Unicode line-breaking rules are largely based on estimates (or maybe just guesses) on the suitability of line breaks before or after a character or between two characters. It may well be that in most cases, a line break after the / character is acceptable whereas a line break before it is not. But rules formulated that forbid quite a many perfectly reasonable line breaks, like before the solidus in "it's in directory /usr/spool," and allow some really absurd breaks, like after either solidus in our example or in "c/o."

It is very confusing to see a string broken into lines just because some mechanical rules have allowed it. A string that is mixture of Latin letters, digits, and various symbols is most probably part of some special notation, such as a URL, or a variable in a programming language, or some code. It is unacceptable to have a string like foo%bar broken, especially when it occurs with no indication of what has happened. It can even distort information or corrupt data. For example, if you write about a programming language that uses the character % at the start of variable names, you will not be pleased by line-breaking rules that break "%foo" into "%" and "foo" on separate lines.

"Customization" or "tailoring" can be used to solve such problems, when you design or modify software. This does not help against more or less general purpose software that implements just the Unicode line-breaking algorithm and cannot realistically be modified to suit the needs of different types of text.

It would probably be best to remove all prohibitions against line breaks after spaces. After all, the no-break space can be used instead of a normal space in such cases, or language-specific higher-level protocols can be applied (e.g., to prevent line breaks in French text between a space and a question mark).

Rules for breaking things like URLs (when they appear as text) to two lines to prevent too long lines belong to higher protocol levels. It is probably best to override Unicode line-breaking rules in such situations, using a few carefully selected principles, such as breaking primarily after /, ?, or &, and never after - (to avoid ambiguity on whether the hyphen-minus is part of the URL).

Any breaking of a URL to several lines should be accompanied with the use of suitable delimiters, as recommended in Appendix E of RFC 3986. It recommends surrounding a URL with whitespace (spaces or line breaks) or, when used in text, enclosing a URL in quotation marks or between the characters < and >. Many publishers use yet another method: they print a URL in a font that differs from the normal font. Similar considerations can be applied to strings other than URLs: avoid breaking a string without indicating somehow that the parts belong together.

Unicode Conformance Requirements

As mentioned in Chapter 4, full presentation of the conformance requirements relies on concepts related to character properties, and it was therefore postponed to be given here.

Conformance to the Unicode standard is voluntary. The motivation for making software conformant is that it can then be honestly marketed as Unicode conformant and it can be expected to cooperate with other Unicode conformant software in a predictable manner.

Note that wording like "this program supports Unicode" does not really make a claim on conformance. In practice, this often means just that the software internally operates on Unicode representations of characters. Conformance to the Unicode standard means more: several rules on the interpretation and processing of characters must be satisfied.

On the other hand, conformance does not require the ability to deal with all Unicode characters. You could write a program that conforms to the Unicode standard but processes and displays just a small repertoire of characters—say, ASCII characters or Thai letters. If such a program interfaces with other software, participating in a chain of programs where it receives input from a previous program in the chain and sends output to the next one, it must correctly pass forward all Unicode characters it receives—unless, of course, its defined task includes acting as a filter.

There is currently no mechanism for officially certifying a claim on conformance. The conformance requirements are rather exact, though, so in most cases, it can be determined objectively whether some software conforms or not.

An Informal Summary

Before presenting the conformance requirements, let's list their essentials in an informal manner. The Unicode FAQ contains a brief summary of the requirements at *http://www.unicode.org/faq/basic_q.html*; the following list is a somewhat different formulation. Here "you" refers to software that is meant to be conforming, although intuitively you can read it as referring to people who create or modify such software:

- You don't need to support all Unicode characters.
- You may be ignorant of a character, but not plain wrong about it.
- You can modify characters if that's part of your job, but not arbitrarily.
- Don't just garble what you don't understand.

- Treat unassigned code points as taboo: don't generate, don't change.

- Surrogates are unassigned as code points, but you must recognize surrogates as code units in UTF-16.

- Noncharacters, including U+FFFE and U+FFFF, are not characters. If you get one, pass it forward, or drop it.

- Canonical equivalents should normally be treated as the same character, but they may be treated as technically different.

- Interpret and generate UTF-8 & Co. according to specifications.

- Treat ill-formed input (violating UTF-8 & Co. rules) as errors.

- Recognize the byte order mark (BOM) on input, and imply big-endian, if there is no BOM.

- If you include Arabic or Hebrew, you need to implement the bidirectional algorithm.

- If you include normalization, apply it by the standard.

- If you do things with the case of letters, follow Unicode rules.

Notations and Terms Used in the Requirements

The conformance requirements will be presented here as annotated quotations from the Unicode standard. The quotations contain somewhat difficult language, but due to their authoritative role, they have been preserved verbatim. The annotations (explanations) use simpler and more common terms. The numbering (C4, C5,…) is the same as in the standard, which preserves the numbering of previous versions of the standard. Therefore, some numbers are missing, since some old requirements have been superseded. This is why the first requirement is currently C4. Some numbers have letters attached to them, since requirements have been inserted without changing the numbering of old requirements—e.g., C12a was added between C12 and C13.

The requirements use the term *abstract character* in an attempt to be exact, but actually this causes some vagueness. In Chapter 1, we discussed the various meanings of this term. An abstract character need not have a code number of its own in Unicode; it may consist of a character followed by one or more diacritic marks, for example.

The word *process* is used a lot in the conformance requirements, but it is not defined in the Unicode standard. It can mostly be understood as meaning software in a broad sense that covers applications, databases, etc.

Unassigned Code Points

> C4 A process shall not interpret a high-surrogate code point or a low-surrogate code point as an abstract character.

Although Unicode contains two large blocks for so-called surrogates, the code points in those blocks are not meant to be used at all in character data. Instead, the corresponding *code units* may be used in the UTF-16 encoding. This sounds confusing, but the gist is that the idea of representing some Unicode characters as "surrogate pairs" consisting of two values operates at the encoding level only. If surrogate code points are detected at the character level—e.g., after an encoding has been interpreted as a sequence of code points (and thereby characters)—an error of some kind has occurred.

The conformance requirements do not specify any particular error processing in such a situation, but they disallow the treatment of surrogate code points as characters:

> C5 A process shall not interpret a noncharacter code point as an abstract character.

Noncharacter code points (e.g., U+FFFF) are code points in the Unicode coding space that are permanently defined as not denoting any characters ever. They are thus logically impossible in character data. In practice they may appear in data as indicators (e.g., as indicating, upon return from an input routine, that no input was obtained), sentinel values, or structural delimiters between strings:

> C6 A process shall not interpret an unassigned code point as an abstract character.

This is similar to the previous requirement but applies to code points in the Unicode coding space that have not (yet) been assigned in any way. They are free locations that may later be filled with something, in an update to the standard, and this is the reason for disallowing their use at present, and for now.

A conforming program may use code points in "private" meanings—e.g., to represent characters that have not yet been included in Unicode. But it must not use unassigned code points for that; instead, private use characters should be used.

Interpretation

> C7 A process shall interpret a coded character representation according to the character semantics established by this standard, if that process does interpret that coded character representation.

"Coded character representation" means a sequence of code points, say U+0041 U+0301. A program is not required to interpret it, but if it does, it must do so in accordance with the normative properties of U+0041 and U+0301:

> C8 A process shall not assume that it is required to interpret any particular coded character representation.

This effectively means that software *need* not assume that it has to understand all Unicode characters. Thus, this is not really a requirement, but permission to implement software that supports just a subset of Unicode characters. It need not even document that subset, although it's often wise to do so, to help users as well as future developers:

> C9 A process shall not assume that the interpretations of two canonical-equivalent character sequences are distinct.

This requirement does not mean that software has to treat canonical equivalent sequences (such as ä and its decomposition, "a" followed by combining dieresis) as the same. It is allowed to treat them differently. The general idea in the Unicode standard is that canonical equivalent sequences should be treated identically and as denoting the same abstract character. The standard mentions, however, in this context, that "there are practical circumstances under which implementations may reasonably distinguish them."

For example, it is permissible, though usually not wise, to treat a character differently from its canonical decomposition on display. A program might render ä using a glyph for the character in the current font but the canonical equivalent decomposition by displaying "a" and putting a dieresis over it, using some algorithm for the placement. You may actually see such things happen; it's a bit simpler to implement things that way.

It is allowable, for a program that conforms to the Unicode standard, to fail to interpret combining diacritic marks—i.e., to treat them as unknown characters. Such a program would probably render ä well when represented in precomposed form but as "a" followed by some indication of unknown character when in decomposed form.

Conforming software must not *rely* on having the distinction made in other conforming software. A program that prepares data to be sent to another program for further processing shall not assume that the other program treats, for example, ä and its decomposition as different.

Modification

> C10 When a process purports not to modify the interpretation of a valid coded character representation, it shall make no change to that coded character representation other than the possible replacement of character sequences by their canonical-equivalent sequences or the deletion of noncharacter code points.

A conforming program may interpret character data in many ways, of course. It might even be a decipherment program! The requirement, however, discusses a situation in which a program makes a claim that it does not modify the interpretation of character data. In that case, the data itself must not be modified except perhaps by:

- Replacing a string with a canonical equivalent string (e.g., by replacing a precomposed character like ä with its decomposition, or vice versa)
- Removing code points that are defined as not denoting any characters, such as U+FFFF

This means that (under the given condition) a program must *not* remove any characters, such as characters that it does not recognize. For example, if a program "collapses" consecutive space characters into a single space (as web browsers do), this constitutes a modification of the interpretation of character data.

On the other hand, transcoding is allowed. That is, the representation of data may be changed from one encoding to another, perhaps changing the byte order.

Character Encoding Forms

> C11 When a process interprets a code unit sequence which purports to be in a Unicode character encoding form, it shall interpret that code unit sequence according to the corresponding code point sequence.

Code units are storage units used for the low-level representation of character data, and their size varies by encoding. The size is 8, 16, or 32 bits for UTF-8, UTF-16, and UTF-32, respectively. The requirement says that conforming software must be able to deal with Unicode encodings and must do so according to the specification of each encoding.

> C12 When a process generates a code unit sequence which purports to be in a Unicode character encoding form, it shall not emit ill-formed code unit sequences.

Here "ill-formed" means a sequence that is prohibited by the encoding used, as defined in the specification of the encoding. This is, of course, part of generating data as correctly encoded.

> C12a When a process interprets a code unit sequence which purports to be in a Unicode character encoding form, it shall treat ill-formed code unit sequences as an error condition, and shall not interpret such sequences as characters.

This corresponds to the previous requirement but relates to input. Note that although ill-formed data is to be treated as an error, there are no requirements on error processing, except that such data must not be treated as characters. A program is not required to issue an error message. It may just ignore the data. The standard explicitly permits representing an ill-formed code unit with a marker such as U+FFFD, though this seems unnatural, since that special character is defined to indicate an unrepresentable character rather than ill-formed data.

Conformance clauses C12 and C12a do not mean that programs should never process ill-formed code units. The phrase "purports to be" is interpreted freely in the standard. A conforming program may read data "as such"—i.e., as a sequence of octets or other storage units, without paying any attention to its internal structure. For example, copying Unicode data as such, preserving its internal representation, can most efficiently be performed as raw copying. This could mean copying octets in a loop, or a block copy instruction, depending on computer or communication architecture. The point is that the copying software need not check the data, if it does not try to interpret it according to some encoding.

Character Encoding Schemes

> C12b When a process interprets a byte sequence which purports to be in a Unicode character encoding scheme, it shall interpret that byte sequence according to the byte order and specifications for the use of the byte order mark established by this standard for that character encoding scheme.

The requirement is a verbose way of saying that byte order rules be observed. This means that a program, when reading UTF-16 encoded data, must recognize the byte order as defined in the specification of UTF-16, and apply it, instead of implying some particular fixed byte order.

Byte order specifies whether the most significant byte (octet) or the least significant byte comes first in a 2-byte quantity. If the most significant byte comes first ("big end first"), the order is called "big-endian"; otherwise, it is "little-endian." A conforming program must be able to handle both, no matter which byte order is used in the "native" data format of the system where the program runs.

Bidirectional Text

C13 A process that displays text containing supported right-to-left characters or embedding codes shall display all visible representations of characters (excluding format characters) in the same order as if the bidirectional algorithm had been applied to the text, in the absence of higher-level protocols.

This requirement relates to the display of characters that belong to writing systems that are written right to left (e.g., Arabic), as well as to the use of explicit codes (control characters) for setting the writing direction. Conforming programs that perform such operations are effectively required to implement the Unicode bidirectional algorithm, which is defined in Unicode Standard Annex #9. Technically, the formulation of the requirement is more abstract: it is sufficient that the program behaves as if it used that algorithm.

Normalization Forms

C14 A process that produces Unicode text that purports to be in a Normalization Form shall do so in accordance with the specifications in Unicode Standard Annex #15, "Unicode Normalization Forms."

C15 A process that tests Unicode text to determine whether it is in a Normalization Form shall do so in accordance with the specifications in Unicode Standard Annex #15, "Unicode Normalization Forms."

C16 A process that purports to transform text into a Normalization Form must be able to produce the results of the conformance test specified in Unicode Standard Annex #15, "Unicode Normalization Forms."

This is a way of requiring conformance to the specification of Unicode normalization forms. The formulation is somewhat complex, since a conforming program need not understand normalization at all. The requirement says that if it plays with normalization (in the sense of producing normalized data, testing for data being normalized, and transforming to normalized form), it must play by the rules in the annex.

Normative References

C17 Normative references to the Standard itself, to property aliases, to property value aliases, or to Unicode algorithms shall follow the formats specified in Section 3.1, Versions of the Unicode Standard.

Informally, for example, when saying "I ♡ Unicode," you can use whatever style you prefer to refer to Unicode. The same applies even to official documents, as long as you are not making a normative reference. A normative reference claims or requires conformance. For example, in a contract on building some software, you might wish to specify that the product will conform to the Unicode standard, and then you should be exact. This means that you refer to a specific version, and do that unambiguously. For safety, you may wish to use the exact citation format specified in the standard, such as the following:

The Unicode Consortium. The Unicode Standard, Version 4.1.0, defined by: *The Unicode Standard, Version 4.0* (Boston, MA, Addison-Wesley, 2003. ISBN 0-321-18578-1), as amended by *Unicode 4.0.1* (*http://www.unicode.org/versions/Unicode4.0.1/*) and *Unicode 4.1.0* (*http://www.unicode.org/versions/Unicode4.1.0/*).

Note that a conformance claim does not imply support to all characters defined in a particular version of Unicode. There is not even a formal requirement to specify the repertoire supported. In order to know what a software vendor really promises when it claims conformance to Unicode, you need check what it says about the repertoire.

References to *properties* should use long names (aliases), not abbreviations, and should cite the standard version as well. The example given is the following, followed by an exact reference to the standard version:

The property value Uppercase_Letter from the General_Category property, as defined in Unicode 3.2.0

This makes the references rather verbose, of course. What is important in practice is to use long names, not abbreviations like "Lu" and "gc," which can be rather cryptic. Specifying the Unicode version is important to definiteness, since properties and their values may change, though they usually don't.

References to *Unicode algorithms* (see below for a definition) should specify the name of the algorithm or its abbreviation and cite the version of the standard, as in this example:

The Unicode Bidirectional Algorithm, as specified in Version 4.1.0 of the Unicode Standard.

See Unicode Standard Annex #9, "The Bidirectional Algorithm," (*http://www.unicode.org/reports/tr9/*).

Where algorithms allow tailoring, the reference must state whether any such tailorings were applied or are applicable:

C18 Higher-level protocols shall not make normative references to provisional properties.

A property may be designated as provisional in the standard. This means that it has been included as potentially useful but immature. Officially, it is a "property whose values are unapproved and tentative, and which may be incomplete or otherwise not in a usable state."

The phrase "higher-level protocol" means any agreement on the interpretation of Unicode characters that extends beyond the scope of the Unicode standard.

For *data*, there is no defined format for claiming or requiring conformance. When you say, for example, that an application accepts Unicode data as input, the meaning of this statement depends on what Unicode version is implied or expressed.

Unicode Algorithms

C19 If a process purports to implement a Unicode algorithm, it shall conform to the specification of that algorithm in the standard, unless tailored by a higher-level protocol.

The term *Unicode algorithm* is defined as "the logical description of a process used to achieve a specified result involving Unicode characters." Despite the broad definition, it is meant to refer only to algorithms defined in the Unicode standard.

Although the word "algorithm" is used, the essential meaning is the result, not the execution of specific steps in a specific manner. This means that an implementation may use some other approach, as long as the results are always the same.

The term *tailoring* refers to a different kind of allowed variation. Even the logical description—i.e., the relationship between input and output data—may differ from the one specified in the algorithm, if the algorithm is defined to be tailorable. For example, the algorithms for normalization and canonical ordering are not tailorable, whereas the bidirectional algorithm allows some tailoring.

Default Casing Operations

C20 An implementation that purports to support the default casing operations of case conversion, case detection, and caseless mapping shall do so in accordance with the definitions and specifications in Section 3.13, Default Case Operations.

The basics of casing were described in the section "Case Properties" earlier in this chapter. The casing may be simple or full, and it must be based on the Unicode case mappings. Conformance to the standard does not exclude language-specific tailoring of the rules. Testing the case of a string must be logically based on normalizing the string to NFD and then case mapping it. However, an implementation may perform the test more efficiently, if the results are the same. Similarly, caseless (case insensitive) comparison of strings must logically involve mapping both strings to lowercase.

Unicode Standard Annexes

Conformance to the Unicode standard requires conformance to the specifications contained in the following annexes of the standard. The annexes contain both descriptive (informative) and normative material; only the normative parts are relevant to conformance.

- UAX #9: "The Bidirectional Algorithm"
- UAX #11: "East Asian Width"
- UAX #14: "Line Breaking Properties"
- UAX #15: "Unicode Normalization Forms"
- UAX #24: "Script Names"
- UAX #29: "Text Boundaries"

The annexes are available via *http://www.unicode.org/reports/*. The page contains links to other Unicode Technical Reports (UTR), too. However, only a UTR designated as UAX is part of the Unicode standard. There are also Unicode Technical Standards (UTS), which are normative documents issued by the Unicode Consortium, but separate from the Unicode standard. Conformance to them is not required for conformance to the Unicode standard. Moreover, there are UTR documents labeled as UTR! Such documents are informative (descriptive), not normative. Thus, we can loosely describe the relationships between these types of documents by the formula UTR = UAX + UTS + UTR, naturally reflecting the two meanings, broader and narrower, of "UTR."

There are also Unicode Technical Notes (UTN), at *http://www.unicode.org/notes/*, but they have no normative or otherwise official status whatsoever. In contrast with a UTR, which is produced by the Unicode Technical Committee even if the UTR is not normative, a UTN can be one person's product, which is just made available through the Unicode web site. In practice, the author of a UTN is an expert, and a UTN can be a helpful tutorial, an interesting proposal, an in-depth treatise of a special topic, or otherwise useful.

Effects on Choosing Characters

In Chapter 1, we discussed some reasons to be strict (or picky) in choosing the right character, as opposed to using a character that only looks right. At this point, we can return to such issues with a better technical background: what is the impact of the formally defined *properties* of characters?

We discussed the simple example of using the letter sharp "s" ß (U+00DF) as a replacement for the Greek small letter beta β (U+03B2). The idea might be tempting, and it has been applied, in situations where you can safely use the ISO Latin 1 repertoire of characters (as you can very often) but not the Greek letters, and you have just a casual need for a beta. Yet, even ignoring all the other arguments, if you compare the formally defined properties of the characters, you can see that they are fundamentally different. They are both letters, but from different scripts, and they have quite different uppercase mappings. Of course, in many contexts, you might get away with this, if no program processes the text in any manner where the differences in properties matter.

Even if you try to avoid any tricks based on visual similarity, trying to use the right character, you may find yourself puzzled. Unicode has about 100,000 characters, and even though very large portions thereof can be classified as belonging to particular scripts, there is still quite a lot to choose from. This applies in particular to characters that can be classified as "symbols" in the sense that they do not belong to any particular script, though perhaps to a very specialized area of application like some branch of science or technology.

Example: Some Mathematical Operators

As a simple example, consider scalar and vector products in mathematics (and physics). They are operations on entities called vectors and conventionally denoted by bold face letters. Normally the scalar (or dot) product of vectors **a** and **b** is denoted as **a** · **b**, and their vector (or cross) product is denoted as **a** × **b**. Mathematical handbooks and standards do not usually identify these operators as characters in some code—e.g., by their Unicode code number. (The world is changing in this respect, but slowly.) This leaves us rather uncertain about the correct way to represent these characters.

There are two obvious candidates for the symbols: the middle dot · (U+00B7) and the multiplication sign × (U+00D7). This is a convenient choice, since the characters belong to the ISO Latin 1 repertoire. In fact, it is very often the best choice, given the existing limitations. It would be theoretically more adequate to use the dot operator · (U+22C5) and the vector or cross product × (U+2A2F), respectively, since they have more specific meanings. In practice, these characters (especially the latter) are available far less often, due to font limitations and other problems. We might regard the more common, mixed-usage characters as just as good. However, if we look at the properties of characters, we see many differences, as illustrated in Table 5-13. Generally, the property values of the dot operator correspond to its specific meaning as mathematical operator, whereas the middle dot, with multiple semantics (described in Chapter 8 to some extent), has less informative, more neutral property values.

Table 5-13. Comparison of properties of two "dot-like" characters

Property	Value for middle dot	Value for dot operator
General Category (gc)	Po (Punctuation, other)	Sm (Symbol, math)
Line Break (lb)	AI (= alphabetic/ideographic)	AL (= alphabetic/symbol)
Math (= mathematical)	No	Yes
Word Break (WB)	MidLetter	Other
East Asian Width (ea)	A (= ambiguous)	N (= narrow)

Most people probably don't even consider using the dot operator, since they've never heard of the character. After careful analysis, you might decide to do the same, since the practical benefits of using the middle dot are more important than the considerations of semantics and properties. The line-breaking property values, for example, are not essentially different: default line-breaking rules will not break before or after a middle dot or a dot operator, unless a space intervenes.

Consequently, people often use characters that are not "quite right" and do not have the properties that the theoretically most adequate characters would have. When processing texts, you need to be prepared to deal with input where "wrong" characters are used. For example, if you edit a mathematical journal, you should expect that authors use different characters as symbols for scalar and vector product. Authors might use almost anything that looks close enough to them, using, for example, a bullet operator • (U+2022) or even the normal period (full stop) "." as a symbol of dot product. It would be your responsibility to unify the notations (or to make a conscious decision not to do that), and this might mean that you need to use a program that lets you check the codes of the characters in the text easily.

Similarly, any attempt to process mathematical texts should not assume much about the use of characters, unless it has been carefully verified. You cannot expect, for example, that characters used to denote mathematical operators have the appropriate formal properties. Their general category might be something quite different from "Sm" (Symbol, math), for example "Po" (Punctuation, other).

Any processing by the formal properties of characters should be made with care. It might be suitable as a fallback, after you have dealt with all "expected" characters, including characters commonly used as replacements for newer, semantically exact characters.

CHAPTER 6

Unicode Encodings

This chapter describes UTF-8 and other encodings for Unicode in detail, including the algorithmic descriptions and the practical considerations on choosing an encoding. It concentrates on the UTF-8, UTF-16, and UTF-32 encodings, which are the current official Unicode encodings. However, some older encodings are described as well, even though not all of them are formally character encodings in a strict sense.

If you are not interested in the technicalities of encodings, you might read just the last section of this chapter ("Choosing an Encoding"). It summarizes the practical criteria, but they can really be understood well only if you know the technical foundations.

Unicode Encodings in General

As described in Chapter 3, an *encoding* is a mapping from code numbers (which represent characters) to sequences of code units. A code unit is in practice an octet (8-bit byte), a double octet (16-bit quantity), or a quadruple octet (32-bit quantity). The reason for using such units is that modern computers have been designed to work on such data objects efficiently.

Thus, the simplest encoding for Unicode is to map each code number to a quadruple octet representing the number as a single integer in binary notation. Such an encoding, UTF-32, is however too inefficient for most practical purposes.

Within a code unit of 16 or 32 bits, the order in which the octets are interpreted depends on "endian-ness," which belongs to the level of *encoding scheme* in the Unicode terminology. Often the encoding scheme is coupled with the encoding even in the name, so that we use, for example, the name "UTF-16LE" to refer to the UTF-16 encoding represented with a little-endian (LE) encoding scheme.

The names of the encodings contain abbreviations "UCS" for "Universal Character Set" and "UTF" for "Unicode Transformation Format." These expansions should not be taken too seriously; treat the names as historical oddities.

For illustration, Figure 6-1 shows the string "pâté" in some encodings. The string is represented used precomposed characters, so that there are just four characters in it. As a

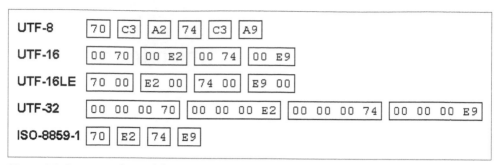

Figure 6-1. Some encodings of the string "pâté"

Encodings	
HTML Entity (decimal)	&#119813;
HTML Entity (hex)	&#x1d405;
How to type in Microsoft Windows	Alt +01D405
UTF-8 (hex)	0xF0 0x9D 0x90 0x85 (f09d9085)
UTF-8 (binary)	11110000:10011101:10010000:10000101
UTF-16 (hex)	0xD835 0xDC05 (d835dc05)
UTF-16 (decimal)	55,349 56,325
UTF-32 (hex)	0x0001D405 (01d405)
UTF-32 (decimal)	119,813
C/C++/Java source code	"\uD835\uDC05"
	More...

Figure 6-2. Encodings of a character (U+1D405) as displayed by FileFormat.info

sequence of code points, the string is U+0070 U+00E2 U+0074 U+00E9. Each box indicates a code unit, with its content expressed in hexadecimal digits, paired so that each pair corresponds to one octet.

To check the representation of a character in one or more Unicode encodings, you can use the service *http://www.fileformat.info/info/unicode/char/search.htm*. It lets you type in the code number and get information that contains the encodings, among other data, as illustrated in Figure 6-2.

Technically, Unicode encodings are defined as representations of *Unicode scalar values* as sequences of code units. This somewhat odd (and practically rare) term refers to all Unicode code numbers except those corresponding to surrogates. This means in practice the ranges U+0000 to U+D7FF and U+E000 to U+10FFFF. The in-between range from U+D8000 to U+DFFF is the surrogates area, and those code points need not be represented, since they are not meant to appear in Unicode data.

On the other hand, the Unicode encodings are defined for noncharacters and for unassigned code points, too. If some data contains, for example, the code point U+FFFF, which is defined to be a noncharacter, the data is incorrect as Unicode character data. However, it is processed in a well-defined way when encoding the data in UTF-8, UTF-16, or UTF-32. This guarantees that conversions between Unicode encodings do not remove such errors but allow them to be detected.

The encodings UTF-8, UTF-16, and UTF-32 are all *self-synchronizing*. This feature, also known as *auto-synchronization*, means that if malformed data (i.e., data that is not possible according to the definition of the encoding) is encountered, only one code point needs to be rejected. The start of the representation of the next code point can be recognized easily. This helps guard against errors caused by data corruption in transfer or storage: the effects of errors are local. If you have data like "Foobar" and the character "b" is corrupted in storage or transfer, the data appears as "Foo?ar" (where ? indicates corrupted data). In some other encodings, all data following a corrupted character might appear as corrupted.

Sample program code, in the C language, for conversions between the Unicode encoding forms is available at *http://www.unicode.org/Public/PROGRAMS/CVTUTF/*.

UTF-32 and UCS-4

UTF-32 uses a 32-bit code unit to represent a code number (and hence a character). That is, a code unit is simply a sequence of 32 bits (four octets) that represents the code number as an integer in binary notation. Since Unicode code numbers are guaranteed to fit into 21 bits, this wastes space; the most significant 11 bits in a code unit are always zero.

On the other hand, addressing of 32-bit units is efficient in modern computers. UTF-32 is otherwise suited for data processing, too, since it allows fast data access. To address the nth character of a string, a program would just add $4 \times (n - 1)$ to the base (start) address of the string.

UTF-32 is robust in the sense that if a code unit is corrupted, all the rest of the data remains intact. Each code unit represents a code number, independently of other code units.

Since the Unicode coding space is limited to 21 bits, and since UTF-32 does not use surrogate code units (only UTF-16 does), UTF-32 encoded data contains code units from the following ranges only (expressed in hexadecimal): 0000 to D7FF and E000 to 10FFFF. This can be used as a basis for a rough check: if you take a reasonably large file that contains other than UTF-32 data and interpret it as 32-bit units, the odds are that there are many values outside those mentioned earlier in this chapter.

UCS-4 is effectively the ISO 10646 equivalent of UTF-32. The registered MIME name of UCS-4 is ISO-10646-UCS-4. Previously, UCS-4 and UTF-32 were different in principle, since UCS-4 operated on a 31-bit coding space, UTF-32 on a 21-bit coding space. The decision to stick to 21-bit coding space removed the distinction. The difference is now nominal, and it is more natural to use the name UTF-32.

UTF-16 and UCS-2

The UCS-2 and UTF-16 encodings use 16-bit code units. In these encodings, all characters in the Basic Multilingual Plane (BMP), and hence most characters that people use these days, are represented directly: a character is represented as one code unit. It represents the code number of the character as one unsigned 16-bit integer. Thus, the encodings are structurally simpler than UTF-8.

UCS-2 Is BMP Only

UCS-2 is by definition limited to BMP. It is therefore not a full Unicode encoding: you cannot represent all Unicode data in UCS-2. On the other hand, UTF-16 is basically UCS-2 enhanced with a mechanism (surrogate pairs) for representing Unicode characters outside BMP. If you don't use such characters, UTF-16 effectively behaves as UCS-2.

Thus, UCS-2 can be regarded as mainly historical. It is however still part of the ISO 10646 standard—but not part of the Unicode standard. The registered MIME name of UCS-2 is ISO-10646-UCS-2.

Surrogate Pairs in UTF-16

UTF-16 uses *surrogate pairs* to overcome the 16 bit limitation. This means that some 16-bit values have been reserved for use as a *high* (leading) or *low* (trailing) value in a pair of code units. Together these values denote a Unicode character outside BMP. The word "surrogate" is not very descriptive, and it has caused much confusion; in reality, the "surrogates" are simply an extension mechanism.

More exactly, a high surrogate is a code unit in the range D800 to DBFF, and a low surrogate is in the range DC00 to DFFF. We use hexadecimal numbers here without the "U+" prefix to emphasize that the surrogates are code units, not code points. Two consecutive surrogate code units together denote one code point, which is outside BMP—i.e., in the range U+10000 to U+10FFFF.

Surrogate code units have a defined meaning only when they appear in a pair of a high surrogate and a low surrogate. Otherwise, they have no defined meaning, and they are data errors.

A surrogate code unit pair is constructed by the following algorithm:

1. Given a Unicode code point outside BMP—i.e., with value > FFFF—represent it as a 21-bit integer, with leading zeros as necessary.

2. Divide this sequence of 21 bits to parts with 5, 6, and 10 bits; denote the parts with u_1, u_2, and u_3, respectively.

3. Subtract 1 from u_1, and consider the result as a 4-bit sequence. Note that this loses no information, since the original u_1 is at most 10000 (because the Unicode range ends at 10FFFF hexadecimal, 100001111111111111111111 binary).

4. Construct the high surrogate code unit as $110110u_1u_2$ (by simple catenation of bit sequences).

5. Construct the low surrogate code unit as $110111u_3$.

For example, consider the code point U+1D405. (It denotes mathematical bold capital "F," but its meaning is irrelevant here.) Writing it as a 21-bit binary integer, we get 000011101010000000101. When split, this gives $u_1 = 00001$, $u_2 = 110101$, and $u_3 = 0000000101$. After subtraction, $u_1 = 0000$. Now we can construct the surrogate code units: 1101100000110101 and 1101110000000101. In hexadecimal, they are D835 and DC05.

The example calculation was performed only to illustrate the algorithm. In practice, we don't do such calculations by hand or even write program code for them, except perhaps as an assignment when learning programming. We use existing software such as conversion programs and routines.

The algorithm implies the following arithmetic relationship between a code number U and the corresponding surrogate pair consisting of H (high surrogate) and L (low surrogate):

$$U = (H - D800) \times 400 + (L - DC00) \times 10000$$

Here all numbers are expressed in hexadecimal. Although the formula contains multiplications, they contain multipliers that are constant and powers of two. Such multiplications can be implemented efficiently as shifts that move bits to the left, which is essentially faster than normal multiplications on a computer.

Some Properties of UTF-16

Using UTF-16, you cannot access the nth character of a string directly. You need to scan the string and count the characters, since some characters (those in BMP) occupy one code unit, others take two code units. UTF-16 is robust, though, in the same sense as UTF-32: if a code unit is corrupted, then only one character is corrupted. If a normal code point is corrupted so that it becomes a high surrogate, for example, the next code unit will still be interpreted correctly. Since it is not a low surrogate, we can know that the previous code point is erroneous data.

If you access a code unit in a UTF-16 string, you can immediately recognize it as a BMP character or as a component of a surrogate pair, simply by checking whether it falls within the ranges for surrogates. If it is a high surrogate, you need to read the next code unit to determine a character. If it is a low surrogate, you need to read the preceding code unit.

Since conformance to the Unicode standard does not require support for all Unicode characters, it is quite permissible for an implementation to be ignorant of all characters outside the BMP. It could be incapable of rendering any of them or processing them in any useful way. However, for conformance, an implementation must be able to recognize that there is a surrogate code unit pair UTF-16 encoded data. It must not treat the code units in it as two characters but as a representation of one character, although perhaps a completely unknown character.

UTF-8

UTF-8 uses 8-bit code units, and it represents characters in the Basic Latin (ASCII) range U+0000 to U+007F efficiently, one code unit per character. On the other hand, this implies that all other characters use at least two code units, which all have the most significant bit set—i.e., they are in the range 80 to FF (hexadecimal). More exactly, they are in the range 80 to 9F. This means that when there is a code unit in the range 00 to 7F in UTF-8 data, we can know that it represents a Basic Latin character and cannot be part of the representation of some other character.

These structural decisions imply that UTF-8 is relatively inefficient, since it leaves many simple combinations unused. There is yet another principle that has a similar effect. In a representation of any character other than Basic Latin characters, the first (leading) code unit is from a specific range, and all the subsequent (trailing) code units are from a different range.

UTF-8 Encoding Algorithm

For a character outside the Basic Latin block, UTF-8 uses two, three, or four octets. You might encounter specifications that describe UTF-8 as using up to six octets per character, but they reflect definitions that did not restrict the Unicode coding space the way it has now been restricted.

The UTF-8 algorithm is described in Table 6-1. The first column specifies a bit pattern, in 16 or 21 bits, grouped for readability. The other columns indicate how the pattern is mapped to code units (octets), represented here as bit patterns.

Table 6-1. UTF-8 encoding algorithm

Code number in binary	Octet 1	Octet 2	Octet 3	Octet 4
00000000 0xxxxxxx	0xxxxxxx			
00000yyy yyxxxxxx	110yyyyy	10xxxxxx		
zzzzyyyy yyxxxxxx	1110zzzz	10yyyyyy	10xxxxxx	
uuuww zzzzyyyy yyxxxxxx	11110uuu	10wwzzzz	10yyyyyy	10xxxxxx

Thus, the UTF-8 encoding uses bit combinations of very specific types in the octets. If you pick up an octet from UTF-8 encoded data, you can immediately see its role. If the first bit is 0, the octet is a single-octet representation of a (Basic Latin) character. Otherwise, you look at the second bit as well. If it is 0, you know that you have a second, third, or fourth octet of a multioctet representation of a character. Otherwise, you have the first octet of such a representation, and the initial bits 110, 1110, or 1111 reveal whether the representation is two, three, or four octets long.

Thus, interpreting (decoding) UTF-8 is straightforward, too. You take an octet, match it with the patterns in column "Octet 1" in Table 6-1, and read zero to three additional octets accordingly. Then you construct the binary representation of the code number from the bit sequences you extract from the octets. Naturally, nobody wants to do this by hand, but the point is that this can be implemented efficiently, as operations on bit fields. A correct implementation of Unicode has to signal an error, if there is data that does match any of the defined patterns.

A quick way to find out the UTF-8 encoding of a string is to visit *http://www.google.com* on any modern browser, type the string into the keyword box, and hit Search. Then just look at the address field of the browser. For example, if you type **pâté**, the address field will contain *http://www.google.com/search?hl=en&lr=&q=p%C3%A2t%C3%A9*, so you can see that â is encoded as the octets C3 A2 and é as octets C3 A9. (In some situations, this does not work since Google does not use UTF-8. In that case, use the URL *http://www.google.com/webhp?ie=UTF-8* to force the input encoding to UTF-8.)

UTF-8 Versus ISO-8859-1

UTF-8 is not compatible with ISO-8859-1, and still less with windows-1252 (which is often, but incorrectly, called "ANSI"). The Basic Latin (ASCII) range is treated the same way, but the Latin 1 Supplement (the upper half of ISO-8859-1) is represented as one octet per character in ISO-8859-1, and two octets per character in UTF-8. The octets that denote Latin 1 Supplement characters in ISO-8859-1 have their first bit set to 1, and such octets are used as components of multioctet representations of characters in UTF-8.

If UTF-8 encoded data is by mistake interpreted as ISO-8859-1 encoded, a Latin 1 Supplement character will appear as Â or Ã followed by another character. The reason is that the first octet of the encoded form is 11000010 or 11000011 in binary, C2 or C3 in hexadecimal, which means Â or Ã in ISO-8859-1. The second octet has "10" as the first 2 bits, so it would be interpreted as some Latin 1 Supplement character or as a C1 Control. For example, if you type the text "Here is my résumé." and send it with a program that UTF-8 encodes it but does not adequately specify the encoding, the recipient may well imply ISO-8859-1 or windows-1252 encoding and display your text as "Here is my rÃ©sumÃ©." The text looks strange, but with some guesswork and experience, it is legible.

Some Properties of UTF-8

Due to the algorithm, the octets appearing in UTF-8 are limited to certain ranges, as shown in Table 6-2. In particular, octets C0 and C1 and F5 through FF do not appear in UTF-8. Other octets may appear in specific contexts only. This means that if you have a large file that is not, in fact, character data in UTF-8 and you try to read it as UTF-8, it is most probable that errors will be signaled.

Table 6-2. Octet ranges in UTF-8

Code range	Octet 1	Octet 2	Octet 3	Octet 4
U+0000..U+007F	00..7F			
U+0080..U+07FF	C2..DF	80..BF		
U+0800..U+0FFF	E0	A0..BF	80..BF	
U+1000..U+CFFF	E1..EC	80..BF	80..BF	
U+D000..U+D7FF	ED	80..9F	80..BF	
U+E000..U+FFFF	EE..EF	80..BF	80..BF	
U+10000..U+3FFFF	F0	90..BF	80..BF	80..BF
U+40000..U+FFFFF	F1..F3	80..BF	80..BF	80..BF
U+100000..U+10FFFF	F4	80..8F	80..BF	80..BF

Similarly to UTF-16, UTF-8 makes it impossible to access the *n*th character of a string directly. UTF-8 is robust, though: if a code unit is corrupted, other characters will be processed correctly. The reason is that UTF-8 has been designed so that a code unit starting the representation of a character can be recognized as such, even if the preceding code unit is in error.

Although the authoritative definition of UTF-8 is in the Unicode standard, with content as described here, there is also a description of UTF-8 as an Internet standard, STD 63. It is currently RFC 3629, "UTF-8, a transformation format of ISO 10646," and available at *http://www.ietf.org/rfc/rfc3629.txt*. It contains additional recommendations (by the IETF) regarding the use of UTF-8 on the Internet, especially with regards to protocol design.

Byte Order

A unit that consists of two or four octets, such as the code units in UTF-16 and UTF-32, has a logical order of octets. For example, if you interpret a two-octet unit as a single unsigned integer (in the range 0..FFFF in hexadecimal, 0..65,535 in decimal), one of the octets is treated as more significant than the other.

Strange as it may sound, the physical order of octets within a unit may differ from their logical order. This might be compared to storing a string like "42" so that "2" appears first in storage, then "4." Specifically, the physical order of octets in a two-octet unit might be less significant octet first. For a four-octet unit, you might in theory define several possible orders. In practice, unless the natural order from the most significant to the least significant is used, it's the exactly opposite order.

The term *byte order* refers to the mutual order of octets (bytes) within a unit of two or four octets. Computers that use a reverse order (least significant to most significant) of octets within a storage unit are called *little-endian*. Those with the logical order are called *big-endian*.

Within a single computer, endian-ness seldom causes trouble. In programming, if you access individual octets, you may need to know the endian-ness. However, for most practical purposes, the software—including library routines—that you use can be expected to handle the endian-ness, so that you can work with the logical order only.

In data transfer, on the other hand, endian-ness becomes a problem. Suppose that you create a file in UTF-16 encoding, for example, on a big-endian computer and send the file to a little-endian computer. How does the recipient know that it needs to reverse the order of octets within a code unit? There are three possible approaches:

- The recipient might try to interpret the data according to either byte order, and if the data does not m ake sense that way, switch to the other order. This is of course very unreliable. How can you make a program analyze whether some arbitrary string of characters makes sense?
- You might indicate the byte order explicitly when sending the data—e.g., in email message headers or HTTP headers—much the same way as you indicate the encoding. In fact, there are encoding names that have byte order information embedded into them—e.g., "UTF-16LE," where "LE" means "little-endian."
- The byte order could be indicated in the data itself. This may sound impossible, since you need to know the byte order before you can interpret the data in the first place. In reality, since there are just two possible orders, a rather simple method will do: we use a byte order mark at the start of data.

The second approach can be applied in the context of Unicode encodings by using the encoding names UTF-16LE and UTF-16BE. They denote UTF-16 in little-endian and big-endian byte order, respectively. In these encodings, no byte order mark is allowed. Using just UTF-16 means an unspecified byte order, but so that big-endian is implied, if the data itself does not indicate the byte order. Similarly, for UTF-32, you can use the specific names UTF-32LE and UTF-32BE.

Although the second approach looks logical, it is not universal. One problem with this is that not everything is sent with Internet message headers. Even if you can declare the byte order outside the data, things might get separated and your data might need to be processed without any outside declaration.

For example, data received as an email attachment or via HTTP may have headers that specify the byte order, but when it is saved locally, this information may get lost. Filesystems often lack tools for saving information about encoding and byte order. Indicating the byte order in the data itself, using a byte order mark, helps quite a lot.

 When you use UTF-16, it is safest to use a byte order mark at the start of data.

The way to indicate the byte order in the data itself is to start the data with a *byte order mark (BOM)*. This means a Unicode code point reserved for this specific purpose, namely U+FEFF. Note that you use the same code point, irrespective of byte order. When your data is represented in UTF-16 encoding in a specific byte order, the first two octets will be either FE FF or FF FE. From this, the recipient can infer big-endian or little-endian byte order, respectively.

In practice, the byte order mark also works as a strong indication of the fact that the data is UTF-16 in the first place. This is useful in situations where the software has no direct information about the encoding. If a program opens a disk file, it might guess from the filename extension (such as *.txt*) that it is a text file, but how can it guess the encoding?

If the first two octets are FE and FF, in either order, it is very unlikely that the data is any other encoding but UTF-16. It cannot be ASCII encoded, since the octets are not in the ASCII range. If it were ISO-8859-1 or windows-1252 encoded, the file would start with the character pair "þÿ" or "ÿþ." These characters are rather rare, and their combination is impossible in any natural text. (The thorn, þ, is used in a few languages like Icelandic, and "y" with dieresis, ÿ, is used only in French—after a vowel.) The data cannot be UTF-8 encoded either, since UTF-8 does not use either FE or FF (see Table 6-2).

Note that although the octet sequence FF FE may thus appear in UTF-16 encoded data, the code point U+FFFE is not allowed; it is defined to be a noncharacter. If you receive data claimed to be in big-endian UTF-16 and the first two octets are FF FE, you know that something is wrong—probably the claim about byte order is wrong.

Similarly, when data is known or expected to be in UTF-32 encoding, but in unspecified byte order, it should start with the octets 00 00 FE FF or 00 00 FF FE, from which you can deduce the byte order (big-endian or little-ending, respectively). If it does not start in either way, it should be assumed to be big-endian without BOM.

The Unicode standard does not require the use of BOM. Other standards or specifications may require or recommend its use. In general, there's no reason not to use BOM in UTF-16 and UTF-32. It is a cheap way to help in correct interpretation of data.

In UTF-8, there is no byte order issue, since the code unit size is one octet. Therefore, using BOM serves no purpose. It is nevertheless allowed, though discouraged. The most common situation for its presence is that data has been converted from UTF-16 or UTF-32 without removing BOM. (In UTF-8, BOM is the octet sequence EF BB BF.)

The BOM is to be treated as indicating the byte order only, not as part of the data. Previously, code point U+FEFF was defined to have the meaning of a zero width no-break space (ZWNBSP), too, and it could appear in the middle of text, too. This usually did not cause problems, but such usage has now been deprecated. In theory, when you detect U+FEFF at the start of UTF-8 data, you cannot know for sure whether it is meant to be a byte order mark or just a no-break space as part of the data proper. In practice, this seldom makes a difference, since an initial no-break space doesn't really matter. However, if you concatenate files, for example, it might matter.

If U+FEFF is encountered within text, it should be treated as ZWNBSP, which acts as invisible "glue" that prevents a line break between characters. However, you should not use it that way in new data; the recommended "glue" character is word joiner U+2060. Unicode implementations are allowed to convert U+FEFF (inside data) to U+2060.

There is no way in Unicode to change the byte order within a file. If U+FEFF appears anywhere else except at the start of character data, it must be interpreted according to the no-break space semantics (or not be interpreted at all).

Due to the stability principles of Unicode, code point U+FEFF preserves "zero width no-break space" as its Unicode name.

Conversions Between Unicode Encodings

When you need to convert data between UTF-8, UTF-16, and UTF-32 encodings, you normally use tools like programs or routines that can read and write text data in the different encodings, as described in Chapter 3. For an overview of these encodings and their use, we will however discuss the nature of the conversions here. A conversion from UTF-32 to UTF-16 means the following:

- Characters in the BMP are represented by omitting the two most significant octets (which are zero in UTF-32 for BMP characters).

- Other characters are replaced by surrogate code unit pairs. This means replacing one 32-bit code unit by two 16-bit code units.

A conversion in the opposite direction naturally means extension with two zero octets for BMP characters and decoding a surrogate code unit pair into a code number, to be represented as a 32-bit quantity.

A conversion from UTF-32 to UTF-8 simply means that the UTF-8 encoding algorithm, as presented in Table 6-1, is applied. The reverse conversion is straightforward, too, since it can operate octet by octet, using the first few bits of an octet to determine its role.

Conversions between UTF-8 and UTF-16 are best performed via an intermediate representation that corresponds to UTF-32. This does not require the creation of an actual UTF-32 coded representation of the file or data stream. Instead, you can operate on just the code points: read code units from UTF-8 (or UTF-16) encoded data as much as needed to determine the Unicode code number that they represent, and then encode this number in UTF-16 (or, respectively, in UTF-8).

Other Encodings

In addition to the encodings defined in the Unicode and ISO 10646 standards, there are several encodings that have been used or at least proposed for Unicode data. We will discuss some of them, summarized in Table 6-3 in alphabetic order by name. For completeness, the table contains also the previously discussed UTF and UCS encodings.

Table 6-3. Encodings used for Unicode data

Name of encoding	Nature and usage of the encoding
Base64	General purpose encoding, used as "transfer encoding"
BOCU-1	A compression scheme for Unicode; not used much
CESU-8	A mixture of UTF-8 and UTF-16 for special usage
GB18030	"Chinese Unicode," technically a separate character code
Modified UTF-8	Used in Java programming; CESU-8 with an additional change
Punycode	An encoding for Internationalized Domain Names (IDN)
Quoted Printable	Transfer encoding especially for email
SCSU	A standardized compression scheme for Unicode; little used
UCS-2	A two-octet encoding, restricted to Basic Multilingual Plane
UCS-4	ISO 10646 equivalent of UTF-32
URL Encoding	Special encoding for URLs and form data on the Web
UTF-1	Obsolete, historic only
UTF-7	Obsolete encoding; little used; not part of the Unicode standard
UTF-8	A standard Unicode encoding, very widely used
UTF-16	A standard Unicode encoding, widely used
UTF-16BE	As UTF-16, but with Big Endian byte order fixed
UTF-16LE	As UTF-8, but with Little Endian byte order fixed
UTF-32	A standard Unicode encoding; wastes space, easy to process
UTF-32BE	As UTF-32, but with Big Endian byte order fixed
UTF-32LE	As UTF-32, but with Little Endian byte order fixed
UTF-EBCDIC	Designed to be compatible with IBM computers using EBCDIC
Uuencode	General purpose encoding of data; sometimes used for text

SCSU Compression

SCSU is defined in Unicode Technical Standard (UTS #6), "A Standard Compression Scheme for Unicode," *http://www.unicode.org/reports/tr6/*. SCSU was designed to achieve compactness comparable to language-specific 8-bit encodings. It has not been widely adopted, but some organizations use it internally.

SCSU works best when the text contains mostly alphabetic characters from one or a few scripts. It can be described as switching between blocks of characters and using efficient one-octet references to characters within a block. SCSU internally switches to UTF-16 to handle non-alphabetic languages.

Although SCSU is registered as a character encoding in the MIME sense, it is not suitable for subtypes of the MIME type text. For example, SCSU cannot be used directly in email and similar protocols. Moreover, for good performance, SCSU requires an implementation with a lookahead in the character stream.

This encoding, like the next one, has been designed as a compression method rather than encoding. However, their usefulness is limited by the fact that widely used general purpose compression mechanisms, such as zip and bzip2, can produce better results, rather independently of encoding issues. SCSU is useful for short strings of text, where general compression mechanisms would require many octets of overhead.

BOCU-1 Compression

BOCU-1 is also a compression scheme for Unicode, and it has been registered as an encoding in the MIME sense. It is defined and described in the Unicode Technical Note (UTN) #6, "BOCU-1: MIME-Compatible Unicode Compression," available at *http://www.unicode.org/notes/tn6/*. Thus, its official status is lower than that of SCSU.

The name "BOCU" comes from "Binary Ordered Compression for Unicode." The encoding preserves code point order.

CESU-8

CESU-8 mixes UTF-8 and UTF-16 so that it uses UTF-8 for all characters in the Basic Multilingual Plane (BMP) but switches to UTF-16 for other characters. CESU-8 is oriented toward systems that internally process characters as 16-bit entities. It is defined in Unicode Technical Report #26, "Compatibility Encoding Scheme for UTF-16: 8-Bit (CESU-8)," *http://www.unicode.org/reports/tr26/*. The report says about CESU-8:

> *It is not intended nor recommended as an encoding used for open information exchange.* The Unicode Consortium does not encourage the use of CESU-8, but does recognize the existence of data in this encoding and supplies this technical report to clearly define the format and to distinguish it from UTF-8. This encoding does not replace or amend the definition of UTF-8.

Instead of encoding a character outside the BMP as a sequence of four octets according to the UTF-8 algorithm, CESU-8 first represents it as a pair of surrogate code points as in UTF-16), and then encodes these individually, each with three octets. This implies that CESU-8 uses six octets for any non-BMP character. More exactly, CESU-8 encoding consists of the following:

1. Replace any character outside the BMP with the surrogate pair that represents it according to UTF-16.

2. Encode the data according to the UTF-8 algorithm as presented in Table 6-1. Note that only mappings that result in one, two, or three octets will be used, since there are only 16-bit values to be encoded.

For example, consider the three-character string U+004D U+0061 U+10000. In UTF-8, its encoding is 4D 61 F0 90 80 80, since the two characters in the Basic Latin block are represented each as one octet, and the non-BMP character U+10000 is mapped to a sequence of four octets by the algorithm. In CESU-8, the first two characters are treated the same way, but U+10000 is first replaced by the surrogate pair U+D800 U+DC00. (Here we speak of surrogates as if they were code points and denote them that way, and this reflects the thinking behind CESU-8, but in principle, they are just code units in an intermediate representation.) The components of the pair are then each encoded by the UTF-8 algorithm: U+D800 gives ED A0 80 and U+DC00 gives ED B0 80. Thus, the final CESU-8 encoded string is 4D 61 ED A0 80 ED B0 80.

CESU-8 has the same *binary collation* as UTF-16. That is, if you compare strings by comparing their encoded representations as raw data, as bit sequences, you get the same order in CESU-8 as in UTF-16. CESU-8 is designed and recommended only for systems where such collation equivalence is important.

Modified UTF-8

Although UTF-8 could be modified in different ways, the phrase "Modified UTF-8" is a term that denotes a specific modification. It differs from UTF-8 in two ways: it mixes UTF-16 into UTF-8 the same way as CESU-8, and it has special treatment for U+0000.

Modified UTF-8 is used in the Java programming language. Java uses UTF-16 internally, but it supports a nonstandard modification of UTF-8 for writing and reading text data as "serialized" to an octet stream.

Modified UTF-8 represents the null character (NUL) U+0000 in a special way, as two octets C0 80—i.e., 11000000 10000000 in binary. This combination does not appear in UTF-8, but as you can see from Table 6-1, it is what you would get if you encoded U+0000 according to the branch of the UTF-8 algorithm that applies to the range U+0080..U+07FF. In UTF-8, the null character is encoded as one octet with value 0.

Such a representation of the null character means that there are no octets with value 0 ("null bytes") in the encoded data. This guarantees that the encoded string can be processed by routines that treat an octet with value 0 as a string terminator, according to the old convention in the C language and its many derivatives.

The second difference is that Modified UTF-8 represents characters outside the BMP the same way as CESU-8. The reason behind this is the difference between modern Unicode and the Java character model. In Java, a character is 16 bits long, reflecting the design of Unicode before the merge with ISO 10646 and expansion of the coding space. Thus, in Java, you process "Java characters," which are identical with Unicode characters for the BMP but cannot directly correspond to anything outside the BMP. In effect, Java treats surrogate code points as "Java characters." When a Java program reads a string in Modified UTF-8, the decoding process produces a string of "Java characters." Additional program logic is then needed to deal with them by Unicode rules, since a program needs to recognize any surrogate pair and treat it as indicating one Unicode character.

The Java routines that write or read in Modified UTF-8 format also produce or recognize a byte count before the start of the data itself (see Chapter 11).

Base64 Encoding of Data

Base64 is not really a character encoding. It is a general encoding mechanism, which can be used to represent any data (any sequence of octets) as a string of characters from a subset of ASCII. Since those characters in turn are represented as octets, by the ASCII encoding, Base64 logically defines a mapping from sequences of octets to sequences of octets. As you may guess, the length of the sequence increases, by the ratio 4:3.

The role of Base64 in the representation of characters is that it can be used as an encoding applied to data that is already in an encoding, such as UTF-8, UTF-16, ISO-8859-1, or ASCII. Base64 lets you represent data in a format that can safely be transmitted and processed in situations where, for example, some octets used in UTF-8 might cause trouble. Base64 is used especially in email. Technically, it is not regarded (or registered) as a character encoding but as a "content transfer encoding."

The name "Base64" reflects the idea of using a positional number system with base 64. To convert data to Base64, you take three octets—i.e., 24 bits of data—and represent the 24-bit integer in a base 64 number system. As digits, you use basic Latin letters (uppercase and lowercase), digits, and two other characters.

To express the idea in another way, without reference to number systems, and somewhat more exactly, we can say that data is encoded into Base64 as follows:

1. Pick up the next 24 bits (three octets) from the input. If there is not enough data left to encode, fill the missing bit positions with zeros.
2. Divide the bits to four groups of 6 bits.
3. Interpret each of the groups, in succession, as a 6-bit unsigned integer (in the range 0 to 63) and map it to a character by using it as an index to the (64-character) string "ABCDEFGHIJKLMNOPQRSTUVWXYZabcdefghijklmnopqrstuvwxyz0123456789+/".
4. If there were only one or two octets (instead of three) available at the last step of processing input data, replace, respectively, the last two or one characters generated in step 3 with the = character.
5. Represent the characters according to the ASCII code.

For example, if you take the string "Here's my résumé." and encode it in UTF-8, then apply Base64 encoding and interpret the result as ASCII, you get the following:

```
SGVyZeKAmXMgbXkgcsOpc3Vtw6kuDQoNCg==
```

When interpreted as ASCII data, a Base64-encoded string looks like a random alphanumeric string, perhaps interspersed with the occasional + or / and possibly terminated one or two = characters. Therefore, Base64 encoding is sometimes used as a poor man's encryption method. It is of course trivial to experts to break the "encryption." Moreover, email programs are typically capable of decoding Base64 automatically.

The choice of the number 64 is based on the fact that 64 is a power of two, and this makes the algorithm fast, since it essentially works with shift operations. The next higher power of two is 128, which is too large, since there are not that many printable ASCII characters. The characters used in Base64 are very "safe": they belong to the invariant subset of ASCII. Naturally, the method relies on the distinction between uppercase and lowercase letters.

Many programs can do Base64 encoding and decoding, but there are also online tools for the purpose. You can find them by entering the search string **"base64 converter"**.

There are several variations of the Base64 encoding, including the following:

- In MIME email, a line break is inserted after every 76 characters of Base64 encoded data, to keep the line length acceptable to all email software.

- The padding = characters at the end may be omitted, when the length of the data is known to the recipient from other information.

- The characters + and /, which might be unsafe in some contexts where Base64 is used (e.g., in filenames), are replaced by other characters in some variations.

- In particular, "URL and filename safe" Base64 alphabet uses the hyphen-minus "-" instead of + and the underline _ instead of /.

- When Base64 is used to produce encoded strings that will be used as XML name tokens, the underline _ and the colon : might be used instead of + and / in order to meet the requirements of XML name syntax. However, the colon has a special meaning in XML names.

The Base64 encoding and some similar encodings are described in the informational RFC 3548, "The Base16, Base32, and Base64 Data Encoding."

Quoted Printable Encoding

Quoted Printable (QP), too, is a content transfer encoding, not a primary encoding of characters. It is widely used especially for delivery of non-ASCII data by email. QP is defined in the MIME specifications, namely in RFC 2045, "Multipurpose Internet Mail Extensions (MIME) Part One: Format of Internet Message Bodies."

Like Base64, QP encodes any data, any octet stream. When used for character data, this means that the data is already in some encoding, and QP applies another encoding on top of it. In particular, you can have UTF-8 encoded data but encode it with QP to make it safer for sending it through software that might munge octets with the first bit set.

Logically, QP maps an octet string to an octet string, but we usually describe the result string in terms of ASCII characters. If the original data is ASCII encoded, QP leaves most printable characters intact. Similarly, if the data is UTF-8 encoded, most printable characters in the ASCII range remain unchanged.

QP uses an escape notation of the form = *xx*, where *xx* are two hexadecimal digits, for representing non-ASCII characters as well as some ASCII characters. The digits *xx* indicate the numeric value of the octet. The escape notation must be applied even to many ASCII characters (all code values are expressed here in hexadecimal):

- Most control characters must be escaped. For example, the ASCII form feed, code value C, must appear as =0C.

- If the data contains a line break, it shall be represented as CR LF (carriage return, line feed), as such (octets in ASCII encoding, not encoded).

- The horizontal tab character (code 9), need not be escaped (as =09), unless it appears at the end of a line.

- The space character (code 20) may be represented as such, except at the end of a line, where it must be escaped (as =20).

- The equals sign = (code 3D) must be escaped (as =3D), to avoid confusing it as data character with its use in escape notations.

The maximum line length in QP coded data is 76 characters (counted by characters, or octets, in the encoded form). Therefore, QP has a special "soft line break" convention: a line can be ended with an equals sign = alone, and neither that character nor the line break after it will be treated as part of the data itself.

For example, suppose you configure your email program to send messages as UTF-8 encoded, using QP as the transfer encoding. You could write a message body that contains just "Here's my résumé." (with a typographically correct apostrophe ' U+2019 instead of the ASCII apostrophe ' U+0027). A recipient who looks at the raw data of your message interpreted as all ASCII characters would see the body as follows:

```
Here=E2=80=99s my r=C3=A9sum=C3=A9.
```

Looking at the message headers, the recipient would see, among other things:

```
Content-Type: text/plain;charset="utf-8"
Content-Transfer-Encoding: quoted-printable
```

This contains information for adequate interpretation of the message. Of course, most people would never directly apply such information. We normally use email programs that do such things for us, recognizing the headers, decoding the data, and displaying just the characters for us. Mostly we would know nothing about the encoding issues, unless something goes wrong. (However, too often something really goes wrong.)

In the example, the letter é (U+00E9) appears as =C3=A9, which is the QP encoded form of the two octets C3 and A9 that constitute the UTF-8 encoded form of U+00E9. As you probably remember, UTF-8 uses at least two octets for any character outside the ASCII range, even for Latin 1 Supplement characters. (If you had sent email as ISO-8859-1 encoded, with QP encoding, the letter é would appear as =E9.) The character ' (U+2019) appears as =E2=80=99, which is the QP encoded form of the three octets that constitute the UTF-8 encoded form of U+2019.

QP has often been criticized for being "quoted unreadable" and unnecessarily messing things up. There is a good point here. Quite often, QP is used in wrong contexts, like Usenet messages, where 8-bit characters work better. However, much of the criticism is unjust. When viewed on a program that does not support QP, you may still get a fairly good picture of the content. The data looks messy, because there is so much readable in the text. Base64, for example, is completely unreadable, if not interpreted properly.

Uuencode

QP and Base64 are just examples of content transfer encodings, but they were selected due to their relatively common use for character data, especially in MIME email. Other transfer encodings, such as Uuencode, Binhex, and yEnc, are typically best known for their use in embedding binary data such as images or executable programs into text. However, they can also be used for text data. You could, for example, first encode text as UTF-8, and then apply Uuencode to the octets, to get a representation that can safely be transmitted over connections, gateways, and software that might mess up UTF-8 as such.

Here we will only consider Uuencode, which has lost importance but can still be found as one option for data transmission—e.g., in email programs. The u's in the name "Uuen-code" do not refer to Unicode but to Unix: it's originally "Unix to Unix encode." Uuencode was designed to make it possible to send any data from one Unix computer to another with tools like old email systems, which process only ASCII data (octets in the range 0 to 7F hexadecimal) reliably. On virtually any Unix system, you can find a command uuencode for performing the encoding and uudecode for decoding it.

Uuencoded data appears as a block of the following form:

```
begin mode filename
data lines
end
```

Here *mode* is the "file mode" in the Unix sense, specifying the file's read, write, and execute permissions as three octal digits, and *filename* is the name to be used when saving the decoded data into a file. Although there is no indication of the media type or primary encoding of the data, some guesses can be based on the filename extension that was chosen when generating the encoded data.

The encoded data itself is first constructed as follows (cf. to Base64 encoding):

1. Pick up the next 24 bits (three octets) from the input. If there is not enough data left to encode, fill the missing bit positions with zeros.

2. Divide the bits to four groups of 6 bits and interpret the groups as integers in the range 0 to 63 (decimal).

3. Add 32 (decimal) to each of the integers. After this, the range is thus 32 to 95 in decimal, 20 to 5F in hexadecimal.

4. Represent the characters according to the ASCII code.

ASCII characters greater than 95 may also be used; however, only the six right-most bits are relevant. This means that number 64 decimal, 40 hexadecimal may be added to the ASCII code. For example, instead of a space (20 hexadecimal), a grave accent (60 hex-adecimal) may be used.

When all the data has been processed that way, the algorithm continues as follows:

1. Write each group of 60 output characters (corresponding to 45 input octets) as a separate line preceded by an encoded character that gives the number of octets in

the original data that are represented on that line. For all lines except the last, this will be the letter "M" (ASCII code 77 = 32+45).

2. Finally, a line containing just a single space (or grave accent `) is output, to be followed by one line containing the string end that terminates the encoded data.

Sometimes each data line has extra dummy characters (often the grave accent) added to avoid problems with software that strips trailing spaces. These characters are ignored when decoding the data.

For example, if you have a file that contains the string "Hello world!" and you Uuencode it, specifying *hello.txt* as the filename to be used, you get the following:

```
begin 644 hello.txt
,2&5L;&\@=V]R;&0A

end
```

Thus, Uuencode produces an encoded form that is completely unintelligible without decoding. On the other hand, the initial and final line indicate the presence of encoded data in a recognizable way, and some email programs can recognize Uuencoded data embedded into the body of a message.

UTF-7

UTF-7 is an obsolete encoding, which is not part of the Unicode standard. However, it is a registered encoding, and you might still encounter it somewhere.

Analogously with UTF-8, UTF-16, and UTF-32, we can regard UTF-7 as an encoding that uses 7-bit code units. In practice, the code units are stored and transmitted as 8-bit bytes (octets), usually with the first bit set to zero. In principle, the first bit could be used for other purposes—e.g., as a parity bit for checking. In any case, it is considered external to the encoding.

The idea was to define an encoding that can be safely transmitted over 7-bit connections, notably data transfer systems that cannot be trusted to pass 8-bit bytes correctly. Such connections existed, in particular, for transmitting ASCII data. You could even send UTF-7 data over an old email connection that had been designed to work with ASCII only. Of course, UTF-7 is not ASCII, but since UTF-7 uses octets in the ASCII range only, the transfer works fine. It is then up to the recipient to know how to interpret it.

UTF-7 uses up to eight octets per character. Characters in the ASCII range remain unchanged, except for the plus sign +, which is escaped as +- due to its special role in the encoding. Other characters are represented using modified Base64 encoding and surrounded by octets corresponding to characters + and -.

For example, the string "£500" is "+AKM-500" in UTF-7 (when we represent the octets of UTF-7 representation as ASCII characters). The characters "500" are unchanged, but the pound sign £ (U+00A3) becomes "+AKM-" as follows: The code point 00A3 is first represented by octets 00 A3, which means 00000000 10100011 in binary. The bits are grouped and the 6-bit groups are mapped to ASCII characters according to the Base64 algorithm, giving 000000 (decimal 0) → A, 001010 (decimal 10) → K, and 001100 (decimal 12) → M. The last zeros in 001100 are fill bits.

The UTF-7 encoding is defined in the informational RFC 2152, "UTF-7: A Mail-Safe Transformation Format of Unicode."

UTF-1

UTF-1 was the first transfer encoding for the Universal Character Set (hence the number "1"). It was defined in the ISO 10646 standard, and it was formally registered as an encoding in the MIME sense, under the name ISO-10646-UTF-1. It never gained much use; it was removed from ISO 10646, and it has been obsolete for years.

UTF-1 used one to five octets per character. One of the reasons for its failure was inefficiency: the algorithm required integer divisions, which are much slower than operations on bit fields. It also lacked the "self-synchronizing" feature.

UTF-EBCDIC

The EBCDIC code, briefly described in Chapter 3, has been widely used on large IBM computers. To facilitate the use of Unicode on such computers, using EBCDIC as their "native" character code, UTF-EBCDIC, was designed. It is defined in the Unicode Technical Report #16, "UTF-EBCDIC," *http://www.unicode.org/reports/tr16/*.

UTF-EBCDIC is "EBCDIC-friendly Unicode." It is similar to UTF-8 but uses EBCDIC codes for some characters and handles code points U+0080 to U+009F in a special way, in order to make the control characters used in EBCDIC have the same representations as in EBCDIC. More exactly, the algorithm is:

1. Starting from a sequence of Unicode code points, construct first an intermediate format, called "UTF-8-Mod" or "I8," using a special mapping that resembles the UTF-8 algorithm. The mapping represents U+0000 to U+009F each as one octet and other code points as two to five octets.

2. Map the octets 00 to 9F to the octets that represent the characters U+0000 to U+009F in the EBCDIC code (with some modifications on line break conventions), and map other octets to remaining octets according to a specifically designed table. As a whole, this step is a simple table-driven operation.

This allows some old EBCDIC applications to handle Unicode data to some extent. To them, UTF-EBCDIC looks like EBCDIC, and although the meanings of some octets are different, the printable characters in the ASCII repertoire as well as the EBCDIC control characters are the same. Problems may still arise due to differences between variants of EBCDIC.

UTF-EBCDIC is intended for use in homogeneous systems and networks that use EBCDIC. It is not meant for use in public networks. In reality, UTF-EBCDIC is not used much. EBCDIC-based IBM mainframes generally use UTF-16 for Unicode support.

GB 18030, "Chinese Unicode"

GB 18030 has been characterized as the Chinese equivalent of UTF-8, with a capability of representing all Unicode code points and maintaining compatibility with GB 2312/GBK, and older character code for Chinese. However, GB18030 also defines a character code (code points) in a manner that differs from Unicode. In practice, due to the well-defined mappings, we can informally describe GB 18030 as "Chinese Unicode."

GB 18030 is formally called "Chinese National Standard GB 18030-2000: Information Technology -- Chinese ideograms coded character set for information interchange -- Extension for the basic set." The letters GB are short for "Guojia Biaozhun," which is a transcription of the Chinese words for "National Standard." Support for GB 18030 is mandatory for all computer operating systems sold in the People's Republic of China.

The MIME name of the encoding has no space: "GB18030."

There is a more detailed description of GB 18030 and its background available at *http://examples.oreilly.com/cjkvinfo/pdf/GB18030_Summary.pdf.*

Punycode, Encoding for Domain Names

Punycode is an encoding, or an escape scheme (depending on how you look at it), for a specific purpose: implementing Internationalized Domain Names (IDN). The idea is that people can use Unicode characters in Internet domain names through special conventions that map strings to ASCII strings. Software that supports IDN is expected to recognize certain types of constructs in domain names as indicating that they should not be interpreted as such but by the special conventions.

Suppose, for example, that we would like to register the Internet domain name "härmä.fi," reflecting the Finnish name "Härmä." Previously, such issues were resolved simply by dropping the diacritic marks (e.g., "harma.fi") or by using some replacement notation (e.g., writing "muenchen" instead of "München"). This is rather unsatisfactory, if the diacritics really make a difference in a language. For languages that use a non-Latin script, the situation was even more problematic.

Since it would not have been realistic to change the entire domain name system to use Unicode as such, a tricky method was developed. Special notations that start with "xn--" (letters "x" and "n" and two hyphen-minus characters) are used to signal that the method, Punycode is used. You would register, for example, the domain name "xn--hrm-qlac.fi," which contains ASCII characters only and therefore does not create technical problems. Web browsers are expected to behave so that if the user types "härmä.fi," the browser internally applies Punycode to it, producing "xn--hrm-qlac.fi." Then the browser uses this name to ask a domain name server to tell the numeric IP address to be used. The browser is expected to show "härmä.fi" in the address field, so that from the user point of view, the non-ASCII characters seem to work smoothly in the domain name.

There is no reason to use two consecutive hyphen-minus characters in a normal domain name. Therefore, the Punycode convention will hardly clash with meaningful non-Punycode domain names.

Technically, Punycode converts a sequence of Unicode characters to a form that contains only characters that are allowed in components of domain names: ASCII letters, digits, and hyphen-minus. For example, in the Punycode form "xn--hrm-qlac.fi," the string "xn--" and the hyphen "-" are delimiters, and between them, you have the ASCII characters of the field "härmä." The "qlac" part is the Punycode way of representing the two occurrences of the non-ASCII character ä and their positions within the string. As you may guess, this involves some relatively sophisticated computation.

Punycode is defined in RFC 3492, which carries a long name: "Punycode: A Bootstring encoding of Unicode for Internationalized Domain Names in Applications (IDNA)."

Old browsers may need an update in order to support Punycode. Partly for such reasons, organizations that acquire an internationalized domain name also keep or acquire a simplified, pure ASCII domain name (such as "harma.fi").

There is an online service for Punycode conversions at *http://mct.verisign-grs.com/*.

Punycode has raised some serious security issues, as any method of using Unicode in domain names would. There have long been attempts to mislead users by reserving Internet domain names that resemble others. For example, someone might try to register the domain name "orei11y.com" and send bulk email containing a link to a web site in that domain. Users might think they are visiting oreilly.com, especially if they see the domain name in a font that does not make a clear distinction between "1" (digit one) and "l" (lowercase letter "l"). When the character repertoire is extended, there are much more possibilities for such tricks. For example, if you wrote "oreilly.com" so that the first "o" is the Cyrillic small letter "o," it would look exactly the same as "oreilly.com" in all Latin letters, since no usual font distinguishes between Latin "o" and Cyrillic "o." Yet, the characters are distinct, and so are the domain names. In Chapter 10, we will discuss attempts at preventing abuse of IDN without restricting ease of use too much.

URL Encoding

URL Encoding relates to Uniform Resource Locators (URL), often loosely called "web addresses," but it is not limited to them. It has an important role in encoding form data, when the user has filled out a form on a web page and submits it to processing. The encoded form data may in fact constitute a URL, but it need not.

Introduction: URL Encoding for form data

Suppose that you use Google search and enter the word **Dürst** into the text box. (You can do this even if your keyboard has no ü key; see Chapter 2 for some methods.) Looking at the result page that Google produces, you might see its address (URL) as:

```
http://www.google.com/search?hl=en&q=D%C3%BCrst&btnG=Google+Search
```

You might be somewhat disappointed at the results, since by default Google treats "Dürst" and "Durst" as basically the same (when the user language is set to English; the matching principles of Google vary by language). To make Google look for "Dürst" only and not for "Durst," you would prefix the string by a plus sign, which means "exact match" to Google: +Dürst. But this was a digression, although perhaps a useful one.

The point in mentioning the URL is that the letter ü appears as %C3%BC in it. To be honest, this depends on your browser and its settings, but what we discuss here is the most common case in modern browsers. The browser has actually encoded your string according to UTF-8 (namely as octets C3 and BC), and then applied another encoding to the result.

The original URL Encoding

Originally, URL Encoding was defined for data that is restricted to ASCII, and the reason for the encoding was that not even all ASCII characters are "safe" in all contexts. In addition to national use variation (described in Chapter 3), some characters were deemed "unsafe" because some software was known to use them for special purposes. The encoding mechanism is simple: for an "unsafe" ASCII character, use the notation %*xx*, where *xx* is the ASCII code number of the character in two hexadecimal digits. Naturally, this implies that the percent sign % itself needs to be escaped (as %25). In a %*xx* notation, uppercase and lowercase letters are equivalent; e.g., %5B is equivalent to %5b.

URL Encoding is meant to be applied to all use of URLs, both in plain text and elsewhere —e.g., in HTML and in HTTP. For example, if a URL contains a space, the space must always appear as URL Encoded, as %20. When a browser follows a link containing such a URL, the browser should not decode %20 in any way but keep it in the request it sends to the server. Only the server is allowed to interpret %20 as a space—e.g., when mapping a URL to a filename.

URL Encoding was also used as a basis for defining the format in which form data is sent by default. A browser is supposed to collect all the relevant fields of a form and their values and construct a data set from them, and then URL Encode the data set. However, there is one modification: before applying URL Encoding, the browser is required to replace any occurrence of a space by a plus sign, +.

To encode or not to encode?

During the history of URL specifications, which have been issued as RFCs, the definitions have become more permissive. Fewer characters are declared as "unsafe" than in the original specification. Moreover, what is "safe" depends on the context—i.e., the part of a URL where a character appears. The situation has stabilized, since now the general syntax of URLs, including the URL Encoding mechanism, is defined in an Internet Standard, STD 66, "Uniform Resource Identifiers (URI): Generic Syntax." Currently STD 66 is RFC 3986. "URI" is a theoretical concept that is a generalization of URL.

According to STD 66, the characters that are always "safe" in URLs are letters "A" to "Z" and "a" to "z," digits 0 to 9, hyphen-minus -, period ., underline _, and tilde ~. These characters need not, and should not, be encoded using a %*xx* notation. For historical and practical reasons, the tilde is still often encoded (as %7E). Characters outside the "safe" set may need to be encoded, depending on context.

URL Encoding is special in the sense that the need for encoding characters depends on the context, and the same character might even appear as such or as encoded, with a difference in meaning. When a character is defined as constituting part of URL syntax, as a punctuation character in it, it need not and it must not be encoded. For example, a URL may contain a query part that begins with ? and consists of parts of the form *name=value*, separated from each other by ampersand & (as in our previous Google example). In such constructs, the characters ?, =, and & must not be encoded, since they appear in special meanings. If, however, a *value* in such a construct needs to contain one of those characters (e.g., because the user input in a Google search contained such a character), it needs to be encoded—otherwise, it could be mistakenly regarded as part of the syntax and not part of the value.

Generalized URL Encoding

There is an obvious way to generalize URL Encoding to strings in an 8-bit encoding such as ISO-8859-1 or windows-1252. You would just use %*xx* for values of *xx* up to FF, instead of the upper limit of 7E (as defined by the range of printable ASCII characters). This means that you would encode, for example, ü (U+00FC) as %FC, using its code number in ISO-8859-1. Although such a technique works in many situations, the problem is that the character encoding of a URL is unspecified, and we don't want to give ISO-8859-1 a special status. Besides, ISO-8859-1 is insufficient for true internationalization.

Modern, UTF-8-based URL Encoding

The modern approach to allowing a wide repertoire of characters in URLs uses UTF-8 together with URL Encoding of octets. The proposed convention, generally supported by modern browsers, is the following:

1. Encode the characters in a URL using UTF-8. This of course leaves ASCII characters intact, but for example, ü becomes the octet pair C3 BC.

2. Encode octets from 80 to FF (as well as "unsafe" ASCII characters) using the %*xx* mechanism. For example, octets C3 BC become encoded as %C3%BC.

You may wonder how it is possible that both this modern way and the old way, implying ISO-8859-1 or some other encoding, can work in browsers. How can the browser know how to interpret the data? The HTML specification recommends that upon processing a link with a URL with a %*xx* notation outside the ASCII range, browsers should first try to interpret it the modern, UTF-8-based way. If the result does not resolve to a working address, the browser could try to interpret the notation according to the character encoding of the document in which the link appears.

Auto-Detecting the Encoding

The encoding of data should be explicitly told to any potential recipient. In particular, on the Internet, special headers have been designed for informing the encoding of a web page or a message, as described in Chapter 10.

However, quite often we are faced with data that is known or suspected to be in a Unicode encoding, but we don't know which. Moreover, we might not wish to trust the indication of the encoding without performing some simple checks. Table 6-4 presents basic methods for guessing the encoding from the first few octets of data. Beware that the result is at best a good guess. The second column shows how the first few octets, shown in column one in hexadecimal, look when interpreted according to the ISO-8859-1 encoding (which is what many simple editors and software for dumping data in text format use by default). If the data starts in some other way, it could still be in a Unicode encoding, but without a byte order mark.

Table 6-4. Heuristics for detecting Unicode encoding

First octets of data	ISO-8859-1 view	Probable encoding
FE FF	þÿ	UTF-16
FF FE	ÿþ	UTF-16LE
00 00 FE FF	(nul)(nul)þÿ	UTF-32
00 00 FF FE	(nul)(nul)ÿþ	UTF-32LE
EF BB BF	ï»¿	UTF-8
0E FE FF	(Ctrl-N)þÿ	SCSU
DD 73 73 73	Ýsss	UTF-EBCDIC

Choosing an Encoding

The Unicode standard explicitly says that the Unicode Consortium "fully endorses the use of any of the three Unicode encoding forms [UTF-8, UTF-16, and UTF-32] as a conformant way of implementing the Unicode Standard." As far as the Unicode standard is concerned, it expresses no preference and leaves the choice is up to you.

The forms are not equally suitable in practice, though. For use on the Internet, the Internet Engineering Task Force (IETF) has expressed a strong preference for UTF-8. In programming, you may find UTF-16 (or sometimes UTF-32) most suitable due to its simplicity. There are also efficiency differences.

> UTF-8, UTF-16, and UTF-32 all support exactly the same repertoire of characters, the full Unicode repertoire. Thus, they can all be used for all languages. However, the language of the text matters when you consider which encoding is most efficient.

Storage Requirements

The storage requirements for the encodings in octets are summarized in Table 6-5. If almost all characters in the text are Basic Latin characters, as in English, UTF-8 is clearly the most compact. The second class of characters, range U+0080 to U+07FF, currently contains the following blocks: Latin-1 Supplement, Latin Extended-A, Latin Extended-B, IPA Extensions, Spacing Modifier Letters, Combining Diacritical Marks, Greek and Coptic, Cyrillic, Cyrillic Supplement, Armenian, Hebrew, Arabic, Syriac, Arabic Supplement, and Thaana. Thus, for this collection of alphabetic scripts, UTF-8 and UTF-16 use the same number (2) of octets per character.

Table 6-5. Size of characters in UTF encodings, in octets

Class of characters	Range of characters	UTF-8	UTF-16	UTF-32
Basic Latin (ASCII)	U+0000 to U+007F	1	2	4
Latin 1 Suppl., ..., Thaana	U+0080 to U+07FF	2	2	4
Rest of BMP	U+0800 to U+FFFF	3	2	4
Outside BMP	U+10000 to U+10FFFF	4	4	4

Storage requirements naturally affect data transfer time as well. For example, for a document distributed on the Internet, the use of disk space (on a server, and on users' workstations) is relatively unimportant, unless the document is very large. However, the time required for transmission over the network is almost proportional to file size, at least unless some compression is applied. The transfer time is important especially on slow connections and for files that are requested very often. On the other hand, the size of text files is often a relatively small factor in material that contains images, videos, and other nontext files.

Efficiency of Processing

What you lose in use of storage might be gained in processing simplicity and speed. In UTF-32, you have one character per code unit, and a 32-bit code unit typically corresponds to the integer type in modern computer architectures. If you process BMP characters only, as you probably do, UTF-16 sounds tempting, especially since UTF-16 is the representation form of characters in many programming languages, such as Java. However, when dealing with arbitrary data, you cannot really be sure of never getting any characters beyond BMP.

UTF-16 is internally used in all modern versions of Windows. This makes it efficient for system-oriented programming, or generally for programming that uses the built-in functions of Windows. Subroutine libraries have often been written to assume UTF-16 (or perhaps just UCS-2) representation of character data.

In processing, UTF-32 has the benefit of using exactly one code unit per Unicode character. UTF-16 shares this property for BMP characters, which constitute the vast majority of all characters that you process. However, the simple correspondence between code units and characters is somewhat illusionary. Even using UTF-32 and UTF-16, something that constitutes a character in the user's thinking need not correspond to a single code unit. For example, the character é might be represented in decomposed form, as two code points (for letter "e" and a combining mark), hence as two code units. Thus, even a simple operation like "move one character forward" might need to be more complicated than just proceeding to the next code unit.

UTF-8 is also suitable for work with old programming languages like C, where the character data type is identified with an octet (byte) concept. When you use a string in such a language, you can store UTF-8 encoded data as such, but you need to handle the interpretation (decoding) of octet sequences as characters yourself.

Specific Limitations

In any of UTF-8, UTF-16, and UTF-32, octets with the most significant bit set may appear. Thus, they cannot be safely transmitted over connections or software that are not "eight-bit-clean" but may mask out the most significant bit, interpret it as a sign bit or parity bit, or otherwise process it incorrectly. In such situations, you could use UTF-7, but it is usually better to use some of the standard UTF encodings and an additional transfer encoding, usually Base64 or Quoted Printable.

The software you use may impose restrictions on the use of encodings. However, if a program can handle any of UTF-8, UTF-16, and UTF-32, it can probably handle the others as well. Some old software, reflecting the original 16-bit design of Unicode, might effectively support UCS-2 only, which means that you can use UTF-16 but you need to limit the character repertoire to the BMP.

Favoring UTF-8 on the Internet

UTF-8 is typically the preferred encoding form for Unicode data on the Internet, including web pages in HTML format. UTF-8 is explicitly recommended by the Internet Engineering Task Force (IETF). The document "IETF Policy on Character Sets and Languages," published in 1998 as RFC 2277 and also labeled as Best Current Practice (BCP) 18, is written basically as a policy on Internet protocols:

> Protocols MUST be able to use the UTF-8 charset, which consists of the ISO 10646 coded character set combined with the UTF-8 character encoding scheme...for all text.

> Protocols MAY specify, in addition, how to use other charsets or other character encoding schemes for ISO 10646, such as UTF-16, but lack of an ability to use UTF-8 is a violation of this policy....

In practice, web browsers generally accept both UTF-8 and UTF-16, if they handle Unicode at all (as the great majority of browsers do). However, important software like the Google search engine has been reported to fail to recognize UTF-16 properly.

UTF-32 is not suitable for use on the Internet. For example, Internet Explorer 6 does not recognize it at all. Moreover, UTF-32 wastes storage and transfer time.

However, there is nothing wrong with using UTF-16 or even UTF-32 internally in databases, for example. If desired, you can store the data in such a format and operate on it but accept user input and present results to the user in UTF-8, or in any encoding that suits the user.

PART III

Advanced Unicode Topics

Each of the chapters in this part covers a specialized topic, and the chapters can be read in any order. The chapters discuss language issues with characters, the use of some practically important classes of characters, the character level versus other protocol levels, characters in Internet protocols (including encoding issues on the Web), and characters in programming.

CHAPTER 7

Characters and Languages

The chapter describes some IT-related requirements of different languages and writing systems, such as how to deal with right-to-left writing (a common source of confusion). This includes transliteration, transcription, and simplifications. The interaction between encoding, language, and font settings is described. Moreover, language codes, language metadata, and language markup are described, illustrated with XML examples.

Information about the language of text is more important when using Unicode than with older character codes. The reason is that the unification principle of Unicode (described in Chapter 4) removes many distinctions between language-dependent variants of characters. For example, Unicode often uses the same code position for a Chinese character and a historically and semantically related but different Japanese character. To express the difference, you would include information about language—e.g., by using markup.

Writing Systems and IT

In information technology, we often deal with text just as any data, with no regard to its internal structure or meaning. When sending a plain text file, for example, we consider at most issues like efficiency, encoding, and checking that the data arrives unchanged. However, operations like page layout, searching, indexing, and word processing need to be sensitive at least to some features and variation of writing systems.

Internationalization (i18n) and Related Issues

Character code problems are part of a topic called *internationalization*, jocularly abbreviated as *i18n*, where 18 stands for the 18 letters between "i" and "n" in this difficult word. It is really not a matter of being international; rather, a matter of letting people use their national languages and notations. Typically, international communication on the Internet is carried out in English, but "internationalization" is meant to create realistic possibilities for communication in any language.

Internationalization mainly revolves around the problems of using various languages and writing systems (scripts). It includes questions like text directionality, which was discussed in Chapter 5. This book discusses mostly just the character-level aspects of internationalization.

Internationalization is related to *localization*, sometimes abbreviated as *l10n*. Localization means that data and systems are adapted to specific linguistic, cultural, and local habits and rules, collectively called a *locale*. In the modern approach, localization is usually based on internationalization. It is often much better to start from a neutral basis and develop mappings to different locales than to map from a specific locale to another.

The word *globalization* is used to denote the general idea of making things work globally as well as different practical methods and aspects. Quite often, this means internationalization followed by localization. However, it can also mean things like supporting different repertoires of characters, for any use whatsoever. The terms are often used interchangeably, or vaguely, but perhaps a useful division is the following:

- Internationalization turns the internal representation of data into a neutral, easily processable and well-defined format. For example, for processing monetary data, we aim at using an internal format that always identifies the currency but does not fix the way in which such data is displayed.

- Localization implements the presentation of data to users in a manner that adapts to their expectations and preferences. A sum of money stored in an internationalized format as the number 42.5 and the currency code USD (U.S. dollar) might be presented as "$42.50" to a U.S. user and as "42:50 $" to a Swedish user.

- Globalization is an umbrella term that covers internationalization, localization, and other ways of making data presentation and processing truly global, so that different languages, notations, and conventions can be used.

Note that most people and most documents probably use the word "internationalization" in a broad sense that roughly corresponds to our definition of "globalization." Sometimes "globalization" is used as a very specific term to refer to software that has been internationalized and that supports localization at runtime—i.e., switching between locales without restarting the program.

Aspects of Writing and Their IT Impact

In information technology, we usually do not need to know about the *sound values* of letters and other symbols. Obvious exceptions to this include language processing such as automatic speech synthesis or loose comparison of strings by their phonetic similarity (e.g., in search systems). Similarly, the *meanings* of words formed from characters are irrelevant to most data processing applications. There are, however, somewhat more technical aspects of writing that can be significant.

Writing direction

In normal text processing, some basic features of the *writing system* used in the text are significant. The problem of left-to-right versus right-to-left writing was discussed in the section "Directionality" in Chapter 5. The writing direction affects text rendering in many ways, though many people do not realize this, since they have always used left-to-right writing only.

Vertical writing means writing text in lines that run vertically from top to bottom, or sometimes from bottom to top. Whether such vertical lines—i.e., columns—run right to left or left to right is a different issue. East Asian writing has traditionally been vertical, but horizontal writing is now used, too, partly because many computer systems have been unable to produce vertical layout. Another reason is that it makes it easier to insert text (such as names and formulas) in Latin letters into a document.

Vertical writing as such is handled outside Unicode and above the character level in general, using layout tools that produce it. However, the possibility of writing vertically has some impact. The shape of some Japanese punctuation marks is different in vertical writing; for example, the colon, :, is rotated 90 degrees. This should be handled by the rendering software as a glyph selection issue. However, there are some variants of such characters for vertical text, *vertical forms*, in the CJK Compatibility Forms block. Moreover, there are *half-width* and *fullwidth* variants of ASCII characters, for use in vertical writing, which in practice requires characters to be of fixed width. This width is either the width of a display cell (square) or half of it.

What does a language setting really set?

The language of text is crucial for many data processing tasks, though much of processing is completely independent of language. The effect of languages has been greatly obscured by software and documents that mix quite separate concepts with each other: writing system, language, character repertoire, character encoding, keyboard layout, etc. These are interrelated but fundamentally different things. In particular, it is crucial to distinguish between the following language settings:

- The language of a program's user interface, affecting menus, error messages, etc.
- Keyboard settings, which have usually been designed for some particular language and named according to it (e.g., "French keyboard")
- The language of a document being written, viewed, or otherwise processed, perhaps with variation inside a document (since it may contain texts in several languages)
- The user's preferred language for accessing some content, in situations where a document is available in several languages

These are all logically independent of each other, and of character encoding as well as of fonts.

The user interface language is often fixed by the program designer, according to the estimated user community. Many programs are available as different language versions, and, in some cases, you might even be able to buy a multilingual version, where the language can be changed on the fly, or at least between sessions with the program.

In Chapter 2, we discussed how the different needs of different languages could be taken into account in keyboard design, especially when using virtual keyboards. The current keyboard setting is often displayed at the bottom of the screen, using language codes like "EN" for English, etc. However, such settings really relate to the keyboard only. I am writing this with the keyboard set to "FI" (Finnish), even though I am writing in English and have the language set to English in the word processor. The reason is that I want my keyboard keys work the way that the keycaps suggest. The user interface language of the word processor (e.g., the language of commands like "File," "Edit," etc.) is yet another thing. Finally, if I visit a web page, I might have set my browser to ask primarily for a German version of a page, if available, if my native language were German.

We will next discuss the two other meanings of "language settings" by simple examples.

Setting the Language in Word Processing

Advanced word processors typically support more than one language, and they need to know or to guess the language of the text. The support might include:

- Automatic operations on punctuation to match the rules of the language
- Hyphenation and language-sensitive line breaking in general
- Spellchecking (while typing, or upon specific request)
- Grammar checks
- Hints on synonyms for a word upon request
- Translation tools of varying kind—e.g., showing translations for a word upon request

When you acquire a word processor or other text-related software, it is important to consider not only the user interface language but also the language support you will need. However, you might be able to buy extra modules later, extending the program with support to new languages.

Automatic operations on punctuation

As an example, if you type the data **"foo"** in MS Word, with suitable language packs installed if needed, you will see and your document will actually contain:

- "foo" if the document language is set to English
- « foo » if the document language is set to French
- „foo" if the document language is set to German
- "foo" if the document language is set to Danish

This means that you can use an ordinary keyboard with just one key for a quotation mark, since the program converts it to language-specific characters. There will be some other examples on fixing punctuation by language-specific rules later in this chapter.

This is just fine when it works right. However, several things can go wrong. If the word processor has a wrong idea of the language of the text, it will not perform the conversion at all, or it will perform a wrong conversion, which is even worse. When editors combine texts from different authors and sources, they might fail to check such things. As a result, a publication might contain a mixture of styles (like "foo" and "foo" and "foo"). Unfortunately, there is often no simple way to fix such things, since the conversions take place when typing; changing the language for already typed text does not change its punctuation.

On the other hand, sometimes a conversion, although correct for the language used in the text in general, is not correct in some specific occasion. Your English text might contain a block quotation in French, and inside it, French punctuation should be used. (Whether quoted text should preserve its original punctuation is a matter of style and rules. The point here is that situations exist where people wish to preserve it.)

Sometimes a conversion of quotation marks is not desirable at all. You may need to use ASCII quotation marks, since you are writing about a computer language. In that case, you can use Ctrl-Z immediately after typing a quotation mark that was converted by MS Word. The reason is that such operations undo the automatic replacement. Thus, to produce "foo" with straight quotes, you would type "^Zfoo"^Z where ^Z denotes pressing Ctrl-Z. Alternatively, you could change the MS Word settings to disable any automatic replacement of quotation marks.

Spelling and grammar checks

Word processors and other text-oriented software often contain automatic tools for spellchecking, perhaps even for grammar and style checks. A spellchecker typically detects misspelled words and may suggest corrections. A grammar or style check operates on constructs larger than a word, and it is based on some linguistic analysis of sentences. A grammar check could detect, for example, the lack of a predicate verb in a sentence.

Opinions on the usefulness of such checks vary greatly, and so does the quality of checkers. When writing specialized text with many special terms and rare words, a spellchecker typically flags a large number of words as potentially misspelled. It may also suggest alternatives to such words, often letting the user fix his error easily, but sometimes presenting something absurd.

When writing for a wide audience, spellchecking is a very good idea. If a spellchecker does not recognize some special word that you use, odds are that many readers won't either.

When you set the text of language in a word processor, the effect depends on the extent of support for that language in the program. Perhaps the program simply records the information about language without using it in any way. It might still pass the information forward when the text is transferred to another program. Moreover, other versions of the program might use the information in a useful way. Support to a language might consist of some simple operations on punctuation marks, as described earlier. It might also include a spellchecker, grammar checker, style checker, readability checker, synonym dictionary, etc.

If you set the language and see something useful happening (e.g., quotation marks turning to chevrons when the language has been set to French), the program might still fail to do any spellchecks, even if you have enabled checking in general. The software might lack a spelling dictionary and other spelling support for a language. An easy way to check this is to write something nonsensical, like qffqgfq, and see whether the program flags it as an error.

Determining the language of text

A word processor could deduce the language of a document or a fragment of a document in different ways. In particular, MS Word uses the following techniques:

Heuristic recognition

> MS Word analyzes the text and deduces the language by statistical analysis. This feature can be disabled, though. When it is enabled, you can start typing text, and after a few words, MS Word probably guesses the appropriate language and switches to it. You may observe that words indicated first as misspelled or suspicious with a red wavy underline turn into normal words.

Explicit information from user

> As a user, you can click on the language indicator text at the bottom of MS Word window (e.g., the word "English" there). This opens a small window as in Figure 7-1, and there, you can select a language. This will apply to text you will type, until the language setting is changed. If you have first selected some text—e.g., by double-clicking or painting—only that fragment of text will be affected. Thus, if you have typed some text in English, and then noted that MS Word flags a name like Rhône as potentially misspelled, you can select the word by double-clicking on it and set the language to French—for that word only. (You can also right-click after the selection, to get a pop-up menu with language settings as one of the available functions.)

Embedded information

> If you open an existing MS Word document, it contains language information corresponding to what was deduced or expressed when writing it. MS Word will read and use that information. Similar things may happen with some other document formats as well—e.g., when opening an HTML document in MS Word.

Exercise

This exercise requires MS Word or some other word processor with some support for different languages. You also need to know some basic functions in it, or to consult a manual on learning about them. With these premises, this exercise may illustrate the benefits of indicating the language:

1. Open some small document in a word processor.
2. Select all text in the document (e.g., with Ctrl-A in MS Word) and perform a spellcheck on it.
3. Set the word processor to check spelling when typing.
4. Then add some long word in another language supported by the program. Insert the word in several places. You should now see the word indicated as misspelled.

Figure 7-1. Setting the language of text in MS Word (the style and content of this window depends on the version of MS Word and previous use of languages in a document)

5. Set the program to use justification on both sides and word division as needed. You should now see the long word incorrectly divided, or left undivided. (If this does not happen, add it to suitable places.)

6. Click on one of the occurrences of the long foreign word and set its language to the correct one. You should now see the misspelling indication vanish and the word split correctly, provided of course that its language is sufficiently well supported by the word processor.

This paragraph illustrates the topic of the exercise. It contains the longish word Haupteigenschaft. If a word processor does not treat it as a German word, it probably leaves the word undivided, often causing poor formatting (too much or too little spacing between words), or divides it improperly. The proper division points are as in Haupt-ei-gen-schaft. When the word processor knows the language, the writer need not know the hyphenation rules of that language, except perhaps to fix the hyphenation of some special words.

Setting Language Preferences in Browsers

We will briefly discuss the language settings in web browsers. Although they are usually not very important (they relate to "language negotiation" described in Chapter 10), they have caused some confusion that needs to be cleared up. In particular, they have been confused with other, more important language settings.

A dialog for setting language preferences in Mozilla Firefox can be invoked with the command Tools → Options → General → Languages, and the dialog window is shown in Figure 7-2. In IE 6, you would enter a similar dialog by selecting Tools → Internet Options → General → Languages → Language Preferences. As we mentioned in Chapter 1, these

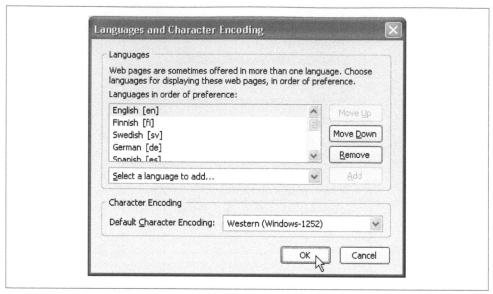

Figure 7-2. Setting language preferences in Firefox

preferences are typically coupled with the setting of the default encoding (to be implied for pages that do not specify their encoding), which is something quite different.

The settings may include one or more languages, in order of preference. In the dialog, the user can typically add (or remove) languages and move them up and down in the order. Ideally, the user should list all languages she understands to some extent at least. Such settings are sent by the browser when it sends a request to a web server. The server may then use the information to select a particular language version of the requested page. Examples of this include *http://www.debian.org/* and *http://www.altavista.com*. However, this is rare, and most bilingual or multilingual sites do not use such technology but typically just explicit language versions.

> The language preferences in browsers have no effect except when a web page is available in several languages, using a particular protocol.

For completeness, we need to mention, though, that Netscape and Mozilla software may include information about the user's language preferences (into message headers), when such software is used to post an article to Usenet. This is in principle a threat to privacy.

Script = Writing System

The word "script" is often used instead of "writing system," and we follow suit in this book, even though some confusion is possible. To many people, "script" means a (small) program or a command file, which is very different from a writing system for human languages. Here "script" means basically a collection of letters and other characters, meant for writing human languages in a systematic way.

A script, as a writing system, is not an exact concept but matter of judgment and convention. We say that languages such as English, German, Icelandic, and Vietnamese use the Latin script, although they have different repertoires of characters. German has, in addition to the basic Latin letters "a" to "z," letters like ä. Icelandic has accented letters like á and the extra letters ð and þ, which are regarded as Latin letters by convention. Vietnamese uses multiple diacritics, although they are often dropped due to technical limitations or ignorance.

Thus, "Latin script" is a broad concept. It contains much more characters than most people imagine. What is common is the historical basis, the letters used in writing classical Latin. Different diacritic marks and even completely new characters have been added, to deal with sounds that cannot be conveniently expressed using the basic Latin letters. The reason why the Icelandic ð and þ are counted as Latin letters is not in their shape but their use in a language that uses letters "a" to "z" as the basis of the alphabet. The Latin script also contains, by convention, a large set of phonetic (IPA) characters, although some of them have been rather directly derived from Greek letters, such as Latin small letter gamma ɣ (U+0263).

Other scripts include Greek, Cyrillic, Arabic, Hebrew, Hangul (Korean), and Han (Chinese) script. Although many scripts have common ancestors—in fact, the scripts used by mankind can be traced back to just a few different original scripts—they may have diverged considerably. The Greek and Cyrillic scripts, for example, resemble the Latin script quite a lot, but there are so many changes in the alphabet as a whole that they are classified as separate scripts. For information on the nature and use of different scripts, consult the web site *http://www.omniglot.com/writing/*.

Many languages use and have always used a particular script. For some languages, the script has been changed to another in course of time. Turkish was once written in the Arabic script, now in the Latin script. Some languages have changed script several times, often for political reasons. Since changes often take time, a language might have two scripts in use at the same time, and such a situation might become even relatively permanent.

Categories of Scripts

In the section "Variation of Writing Systems" in Chapter 1, we described some basic categories of scripts: alphabetic, consonant, syllabic, and ideographic. The differences between these categories are more difficult to handle in automatic processing than the variation of character repertoires. For example, Greek text is displayed basically the same way as English: you put one character after another, left to right, with lines running bottom up, and breaking lines between words, unless you have some hyphenation routine. Displaying Arabic, on the other hand, requires writing right to left and selecting the shape of a character according to its position in a word. Much data-processing software and systems has been designed with the implicit assumption that everything is written pretty much the same way as English, although perhaps with some other letters.

Need for script information

In some contexts, it is useful to be able to specify the script used in a document or part of a document in a manner suitable for automatic processing. Moreover, most characters can be classified as belonging to one script only. For example, suppose that a document has been specified to be in the Latin script, or has been inferred to be in the Latin script by an analysis of its content. If the document contains an isolated Cyrillic letter, this could be an error (e.g., a user has entered a Cyrillic "A" by mistake), and in any case, it is something special that may need human attention.

Script information can also be used in pattern matching. For example, you might wish to use a pattern that corresponds to any sequence of characters in the Cyrillic script. In practice, patterns should normally also include the script name "Common," which refers to characters that appear in several scripts. Script information can be specified at different levels:

Document
> The script of a document can be expressed informally, in prose (e.g., "this document contains old Turkish, written in the Arabic script"), or it can be guessed from the context, language, or even encoding. In the future, the script can also be specified formally as part of the language code specified for the document.

Fragment of a document
> This could be a section, a paragraph, a sentence, or even an individual word, or other part of a document. For example, a scholarly work could be written in English but with Greek quotations in Greek letters. You might be able to use markup or out-of-the-band information to indicate the script of a fragment—e.g., as part of language code.

Character
> This level is covered well in the Unicode standard. As we can see, the standard assigns each character a script.

Although many blocks in Unicode contain characters from one script, and might have been named according to a script, there is no one-to-one correspondence between blocks and scripts. Some blocks contain characters from different scripts, and some scripts have been divided into several blocks (e.g., Basic Latin, Latin-1 Supplement, Latin Extended-A, etc.). Therefore, the Unicode standard defines a separate property that specifies the script of a character, Script (sc).

Scripts and spoofing

Script information has become more important due to use of mixing characters from different scripts in order to misguide people by "spoofing." The idea in the kind of spoofing discussed here is to present text to the user in a format that looks correct but internally means something different. Spoofing is possible even within one script. The familiar example is the use of "l" (lowercase letter "l") instead of "1" (digit one), or vice versa, making use of the fact that in many fonts, they are hard to distinguish. Another old example is the confusion between "O" (capital letter "o") and "0" (digit zero), although they are rather different in most modern fonts, when you see both of them.

Spoofing is a relatively modern phenomenon, since it revolves around the difference between visible shapes of characters and their internal digital representation. In the old times, it did not matter much if you typed "O" for "0" in a number, since the character you entered existed only on paper and was judged only on its appearance. In fact, some old typewriters forced people to type that way, since they lacked digits "0" and "1" altogether. In the modern world, it matters a lot whether an address, a password, or a variable name contains the letter "l" or the digit "1," since they have completely separate internal representations.

Spoofing might be accidental: people make mistakes in typing and confuse characters with each other. Spoofing might also be used with good aims: some instructions on choosing good passwords suggest that you spoof—e.g., use "l" in place of "1"—to make it more difficult to steal your password from a casual glimpse of it or to crack it with dictionary attacks.

For the most part, spoofing is used in attempts to break into systems or otherwise compromise their security. Perhaps the best known form of spoofing is to use Internet domain names that misleadingly resemble another. If there is a widely known web server at *www.paypal.example*, an attacker might set up *www.paypal.example* and send, say, a million copies of an email example asking people to login at the following site: *http://www.paypal.example*. They are then asked to change their password, to protect their account against some threat. The attacker would have set up a server that looks and acts like the real service being imitated but actually steals the user ID and password given on login. Such operations have often succeeded even when they rely on something as simple as the similarity of "l" and "1" in many fonts.

The particular form of spoofing that is used to mislead people into logging in somewhere and giving their confidential information is called "phishing." Users could resist such attacks by refusing to click on addresses shown in email messages, but many people are careless and lazy. It's so much easier to click (or cut and paste) than to type.

Unicode, with its large repertoire of characters, has opened new possibilities for spoofing. This is relevant in cases where national characters are used in Internet domain names. (Their use in web addresses otherwise might be relevant, too, but usually it's the domain name part, the server name, that is crucial in spoofing.) If you were able to distinguish "paypal" from "paypal," perhaps because you were using a font that makes the difference obvious, how about "paypal"? This string actually contains two occurrences of the Cyrillic small letter "a" (U+0430). It is highly unlikely that you would be able to distinguish them from the Latin small letter "a" by their appearance only, since in practically all fonts, they look exactly the same.

Proposed solutions include the display of URLs or strings in general in a manner that highlights any abnormal changes of script—e.g., by bolding any Cyrillic letter that appears between Latin letters (**paypal**), or showing it in red. Alternatively, such mixtures might be banned completely, forbidden in some contexts like domain names. For a discussion of the problems and solutions, see the Unicode Technical Report #36, "Security Considerations for the Implementation of Unicode and Related Technology." In any case, such methods require easy access to machine-readable information about the script of each character.

Codes and names for scripts

A script can be identified in several ways, described in some detail below:

- A four-letter code, such as "Grek" (for use in many contexts—e.g., in language codes)
- A longer and more natural code name, such as "Greek"
- A three-digit numeric code, such as "200" (not used much)
- A name in some natural language; the name in English often coincides with the longer code name, but for other languages, it could be completely different (e.g., "Griechisch" or "Греческая")

There are two systems of codes for scripts, and they differ in some details: the international standard ISO 15924, "Code for the Representation of Names of Scripts," and the Unicode Standard Annex (UAX) #24, "Script Names," which is available from *http://www.unicode.org/reports/tr24/*. The Unicode Consortium is the Registration Authority for ISO 15924; see *http://www.unicode.org/iso15924/*.

UAX #24 defines both four-letter codes (such as "Latn" and "Cyrl") and more legible longer, more name-like codes (like "Latin" and "Cyrillic") for scripts. The four-letter codes match those used in ISO 15924, and they are used as components of language codes. Both types of codes are listed in the Unicode database in *http://www.unicode.org/Public/UNIDATA/PropertyValueAliases.txt*.

The ISO 15924 standard defines codes for some scripts that can be regarded as variants of a basic script, such as "Latf" and "Latg" for old Fraktur and Gaelic variants of the Latin script. The reason for this is existing bibliographic classification, where different versions of a book printed in normal Latin (Roman), Fraktur, or Gaelic letters are recorded separately. In the UAX #24 approach, such variation is not considered as a script difference but as something to be handled at the font and glyph level. Therefore, UAX #24 defines just "Latn" as the generic identifier for the Latin script.

Somewhat similarly, UAX #24 has just the generic "Hani" script for CJK (Han) characters, whereas ISO 15924 lets you differentiate between "Hant" (traditional Chinese) and "Hans" (simplified Chinese).

On the other hand, UAX #24 basically defines the codes for scripts as used when identifying the script of a character as a member of the Unicode set of characters. In other contexts, more specific codes (referring to typographic variants) may be used.

The registry of ISO 15924 contains a table of script codes together with their "names" in English and French, at *http://www.unicode.org/iso15924/iso15924-codes.html*. Some of the "names" are actually short descriptions, and they may differ from the longer codes. For example, there is a script with the short code "Ital," the long code "Old_Italic," and the English name "Old Italic (Etruscan, Oscan, etc.)" and the French name "ancien italique (étrusque, osque, etc.)." The standard also defines three-digit numeric codes, which are not used much, but they might be used internally, if you need integer-valued identifications for scripts.

When information about the script of a character, fragment, or document is presented to a user, it should preferably be presented in the user's own language. The Common Locale Data Repository (CLDR), described in Chapter 11, contains names of scripts in different languages. A large comparison chart of such localized names is available at *http://www.unicode.org/cldr/data/diff/by_type/localeDisplayNames_scripts.html*. There are two special script codes:

Common (Zyyy)
> This value is assigned to characters that are used in several scripts, such as punctuation characters and special symbols. Most letterlike symbols, such as the copyright sign ©, are classified as Common, not by the script of the letter from which they have been derived. Such symbols are typically used across scripts. Unassigned code points, too, have this value.

Inherited (Qaai)
> This indicates that the character is to be assumed to be in the same script as the (logically) preceding character. This value is assigned to nonspacing marks. For example, the script of the combining acute accent (U+0301) is Inherited, so that when it follows a Latin letter, it is treated as belonging to the Latin script, and when it follows a Greek letter, it is treated as belonging to the Greek script.

In technical and scientific contexts, Greek letters may appear in the midst of text otherwise written in the Latin script—e.g., in names like "β-carotene" and "γ rays." Although the Greek letters usually appear in specialized meanings as symbols, Unicode treats them as Greek letters, belonging to the Greek script. However, there are exceptions for symbols encoded as separate characters. For example, the micro sign μ (U+00B5), although compatibility equivalent to Greek small letter mu, is defined as belonging to the Common script. Thus, replacing a character with its compatibility equivalent may change the script.

The short (four-letter) and long codes for scripts are summarized in Table 7-1. The table also acts as an overview of writing systems, although it does not include all the historic scripts that have been used. The short code in the first column is the ISO 15924 code, and the second column contains the longer code as defined in UAX #24, using an underline character instead of a space.

Table 7-1. Short and long codes for scripts

Code	Property value alias	Explanations
Arab	Arabic	Used for Arabic, Persian, and other languages
Armn	Armenian	Used for the Armenian language
Bali		Used for Balinese in Indonesia
Batk		Used for Batak languages in Indonesia
Beng	Bengali	Used for Bengali, Assamese, etc.
Blis		Bliss symbols; easy-to-learn pictorial symbols
Bopo	Bopomofo	An alphabetic writing system for Chinese
Brah		Brahmi, an ancient script used in India
Brai	Braille	Braille; symbols touchable by fingertips
Bugi		Buginese, used in Sulawesi, Indonesia
Buhd	Buhid	Used for Buhid in the Philippines (island of Mindoro)
Cans	Canadian_Aboriginal	Unified Canadian Aboriginal Syllabics
Cham		Cham, used in Cambodia and Vietnamese
Cher	Cherokee	A syllabic script for the Cherokee language
Cirt		Cirth, a Runic-like script invented by J.R.R. Tolkien
Copt		Coptic; was used for ancient Egyptian, now liturgic
Cprt	Cypriot	An ancient script used in Cyprus
Cyrl	Cyrillic	Cyrillic; used for many Slavic and non-Slavic languages
Cyrs		Cyrillic, Old Church Slavonic variant
Deva	Devanagari	Used for several languages in India, including Hindi
Dsrt	Deseret	Invented in the 1850s (for English), still used by Mormons
Egyd		Egyptian demotic
Egyh		Egyptian hieratic
Egyp		Egyptian hieroglyphs
Ethi	Ethiopic	Used for several languages in Ethiopia
Geok		Khutsuri, a script previously used for Georgian
Geor	Georgian	Used for Georgian (Mkhedruli), spoken in the Caucasus
Glag		Glagolitic (Glagolitsa), an old script for Slavic languages
Goth	Gothic	Was used for a now-extinct Germanic language
Grek	Greek	Greek (both ancient and modern)
Gujr	Gujarati	Used for the Gujarati language in western India
Guru	Gurmukhi	Used for the Panjabi language in northern India
Hang	Hangul	The currently most common script for Korean

Code	Property value alias	Explanations
Hani	Han	Chinese-Japanese-Korean, known as Hanzi, Kanji, Hanja
Hano	Hanunoo	Used for Hanunóo in the Philippines (island of Mindoro)
Hans		Chinese, Simplified writing system
Hant		Chinese, Traditional writing system
Hebr	Hebrew	Used for Hebrew, Yiddish, Ladino, etc.
Hira	Hiragana	A cursive syllabic script for writing Japanese
Hmng		Pahawh Hmong, used for Hmong in East Asia
Hrkt	Katakana_Or_Hiragana	Alias for Hiragana + Katakana
Hung		Old Hungarian, a Runic system used before AD 1000
Inds		Indus (Harappan); ancient script
Ital	Old_Italic	Ancient Italic (Etruscan, Oscan, etc.)
Java		Javanese, used for the Javanese language in Indonesia
Kali		Kayah Li, used in Burma (Myanmar)
Kana	Katakana	A non-cursive syllabic script for writing Japanese
Khar		Kharoshthi, an ancient script that was used in Asia
Khmr	Khmer	Used for the Cambodian language
Knda	Kannada	Used for Kannada (Kanarese) in southern India
Laoo	Lao	Used for Lao, the main language of Laos
Latf		Latin, Fraktur (Gothic) variant
Latg		Latin, Gaelic variant
Latn	Latin	Used for a wide range of European and other languages
Lepc		Lepcha (Róng), used to write a Tibeto-Burman language
Limb	Limbu	Used for Limbu, a Tibeto-Burman language
Lina		Linear A, an ancient script used on Crete
Linb	Linear_B	Linear B, an ancient script used to write a form of Greek
Mand		Mandaean, used for Mandaic, a Semitic language
Maya		Mayan hieroglyphs
Mero		Meroïtic, used for a now-extinct language in Egypt
Mlym	Malayalam	Used for Malayalam in southern India
Mong	Mongolian	Used for Mongolian; a cursive script, complex shaping
Mymr	Myanmar	Used for Burmese in Burma (Myanmar)
Nkoo		N'Ko, used for Mandekan languages in western Africa
Ogam	Ogham	Was used in the fifth and sixth centuries for early Irish

Code	Property value alias	Explanations
Orkh		Orkhon, used to write Uyghur, a Turkic language in China
Orya	Oriya	Used for the Oriya language in eastern India
Osma	Osmanya	Used for the Somali language in Africa
Perm		Old Permic (Abur), previously used for the Komi language
Phag		'Phags-pa, was used for Mongolian and other languages
Phnx		Phoenician, an ancient consonantal alphabet
Plrd		Pollard Phonetic, used to write the Miao language in China
Qaaa		Reserved for private use (start)
Qabx		Reserved for private use (end)
Roro		Rongorongo, was used on the Easter Island
Runr	Runic	A historic European script
Sara		Sarati, a "Middle Earth" script invented by J.R.R. Tolkien
Shaw	Shavian	Shavian (Shaw), invented for phonetic writing of English
Sinh	Sinhala	Used for Sinhala (Sinhalese) in Sri Lanka
Sylo		Syloti Nagri, used for Sylheti in Bangladesh and Indica
Syrc	Syriac	Used for the Syriac language, but also for Arabic
Syre		Syriac (Estrangelo variant)
Syrj		Syriac (Western variant)
Syrn		Syriac (Eastern variant)
Tagb	Tagbanwa	Used for Tagbanwa in the Philippines (island of Palawan)
Tale	Tai_Le	Tai Le (Dehong Dai), used in southwest China
Talu		New Tai Lue, used to write Lue in East Asia
Taml	Tamil	Used for the Tamil language in India, Sri Lanka, etc.
Telu	Telugu	Used for the Telugu language in southern India
Teng		Tengwar, a script invented by J.R.R. Tolkien
Tfng		Tifinagh, used to write Berber languages like Tamasheq
Tglg	Tagalog	Was used to write Tagalog and other Filipino languages
Thaa	Thaana	Thaana, for the Dhivehi languages (in the Maldives)
Thai	Thai	Used for Thai, the main language of Thailand (Siam)
Tibt	Tibetan	Used for Tibetan, spoken in Tibet and Bhutan
Ugar	Ugaritic	An ancient cuneiform script used to write Ugaritic
Vaii		Vai, a syllabary used to write the Vai language in Liberia

Code	Property value alias	Explanations
Visp		Visible Speech, a phonetic and "organic" script
Xpeo		Old Persian Cuneiform
Xsux		Cuneiform, Sumero-Akkadian
Yiii	Yi	A large syllabary used to write Yi (Lolo) in China
Zxxx		Code for unwritten languages
Zyyy	Common	Code for undetermined script
Zzzz		Code for uncoded script

The Script property: the script of a character

The data file that specifies values of the Script (sc) property, i.e. the script of each Unicode character, is *http://www.unicode.org/Public/UNIDATA/Scripts.txt*. It uses the longer names for the scripts. Its entries look like the following:

```
0993..09A8    ; Bengali # Lo  [22] BENGALI LETTER O..BENGALI LETTER NA
```

This sample line says that characters U+0933 through U+09A8 belong to the script "Bengali." Such information is sufficient for automatic classification of characters by script. The rest is a comment, mentioning the general category (Lo), the number of characters in the range (22), and the range expressed by names of characters.

For readability, the data in the file has been grouped by script. This lets you see quickly which characters are contained in a given script, but it makes it more difficult to find the script of a given character.

Character Requirements of Languages

Although Unicode contains almost all characters used in currently used languages, it is still and will always be relevant to consider the character requirements that different languages impose. Here we will first list some of the reasons for this, and then analyze the concept of "character requirements," and finally study some specific languages.

The Impact of Character Repertoire

As mentioned in the section "Definitions of Character Repertoires" in Chapter 1, there are good reasons to try to estimate the repertoire of characters that will appear in a document or in an application. In more detail, the reasons include the following:

- A font typically supports a limited character repertoire only. Full Unicode fonts are rare, and usually not suitable for copy text.

- In particular, artistic or otherwise special fonts, such as those used for headings and buttons, often have a very limited character repertoire.

- A program that will be used for processing your document in some way might be prepared to handle a limited repertoire only.

- Special characters in normal text often result from mistyping or other errors. When checking input data, it is often useful to detect any "unusual" characters and issue warnings about them.

- In particular, character recognition (in scanning text or in processing handwritten characters) works best if the assumed repertoire is small. It can be very difficult to distinguish between similar-looking characters like ă and ǎ ("a" with breve and "a" with caron). Things are much easier if you can expect only one of them to occur.

At the technical level, there is also the consideration that if you restrict yourself to a small repertoire of characters, you have more options when choosing the encoding. For example, if you use just the characters normally used in English, you can use almost any encoding, including ASCII, ISO 8859 encodings, etc. If you decide that the copyright symbol © is needed, too, then you exclude both ASCII and several of the ISO 8859 encodings (unless you can use "escape notations" like © in HTML).

Such technical limitations are slowly losing their importance, but other limitations persist. For example, when designing methods for user input, we should focus on characters that will be used frequently, support some less common characters in a reasonably easy way, and leave the rest up to some generic way, which is not very convenient. In a sense, it is good to make the entry of rarely used characters difficult; thereby they will not appear by mistake so often.

Languages and Characters

Languages have very varying requirements on the repertoire of characters. English can be written using less than a hundred different characters, whereas Chinese needs thousands of characters, or tens of thousands, if you count the rare characters too. Moreover, the needs are difficult to analyze. Is é needed in English, because it appears in words like "fiancé"? Normal English text, even in a newspaper, may contain special characters like μ on science pages, ♣ in a bridge column, and ® in an advertisement.

What constitutes a character?

Language affects the way people look at characters and what they identify as a single character. This primarily applies to a person's native language. If English is your native language, you may well classify the œ in the French word "œuvre" as just a way of writing "o" and "e" together. After all, in English, expressions like "hors d'oeuvre" are commonly written with separate "o" and "e." If French is your native language, you might treat œ as a single letter and "oe" just as a replacement that is used out of necessity. Perhaps an even better example is æ, which is certainly a separate letter to people who speak Danish and Norwegian but just a typographic variant of "ae" to many English-speaking people, who either never noticed æ or saw it only in contexts where it is apparently just a way of writing "ae" (e.g., in "Cæsar" for "Caesar").

The way we identify characters affects how we count characters. How many letters are there in the string "Cæsar"? This makes instructions, limitations, and operations on character count relative. If you are prompted for some information, to be written in less than 42 characters, how do you know how some program counts characters? When exactness is important, as it might be in contracts, it might be suitable to define explicitly that characters are counted by the number of Unicode characters when the text is in Unicode Normalization Form C. Unfortunately, few people understand what that means, but the same applies to many other exact definitions.

Does Unicode support all languages?

Short descriptions of Unicode often present it as more universal than it really is. They might, in particular, claim that Unicode supports all languages, or at least all living languages, or that it contains all characters used by humanity.

The question "Does Unicode support all languages?" is vague on several counts. To begin with, does "Unicode" refer to the collection of Unicode characters, or to the Unicode standard, or to the Unicode Consortium? What does "support" mean? And what do you mean by "language," and specifically by "all languages"?

Thus, any reasonable answer needs to clarify the question. Here is an attempt at a short answer: Almost all living languages, and many dead languages, can be written in their normal writing system(s) using Unicode characters. However, this might not quite mean what you intuitively expect it to mean. Note, in particular, the following points:

- Some languages use characters that cannot be represented as single Unicode characters but need to be written as combinations (sequences of Unicode characters). For example, some accented characters cannot be written as a single character but as base characters followed by some combining diacritic mark(s). In this sense, the claim that Unicode "provides a unique number for every character" (as the Consortium's page "What is Unicode?" says) is somewhat misleading.

- Some orthographic and typographic differences that could be expressed in plain text cannot be expressed in Unicode. This results from the unification policy, which often treats, for example, the differences between Chinese and Japanese characters as typographic.

- Some of the properties of characters as defined by the Unicode standard do not correspond to their behavior in different languages. For example, Unicode line-breaking rules previously permitted a line break after a colon :, but some languages use it inside words, and a line break after a colon can seriously violate the rules of the language.

- Unicode is meant to describe plain text only, so it generally lacks any support that might be needed for display and processing of text by language-specific rules.

These points reflect the design of Unicode, not failures or incompleteness in achieving its goals. On the other hand, there are also some characters used in living languages that have not yet been included in Unicode. Those languages are used by very small communities, and your odds of ever seeing them written are rather small, unless you are an ethnologist or linguist. For example, Unicode 4.1 lacks some Cyrillic characters that are used by some ethnic groups (Enets, Chukchi, etc.) in Russia.

The first point means that when writing some languages, we cannot use a single Unicode character (code point) to denote what people intuitively understand as one character in that language. For example, a language may have the letter "i" with macron and grave accent, but in Unicode, it can only be written using two or three characters. In Chapter 4, we described some concepts and techniques meant to help with this. Yet, people may think that Unicode puts such languages to a different position than others.

As a thought experiment, let us suppose that the letter "w" had not been included into ASCII or other character codes but written as "vv," and that Unicode had not changed this. When people would then ask for the letter "w" to be included into Unicode, the answer would be that it is just a typographic variant of "vv" written as a ligature (as it historically is, in fact). Maybe after much debate, we would then be told to use the combination of three Unicode characters, "v," word joiner, and "v." Maybe we could officially register this as a character sequence. Yet, could we then really say that Unicode supports the English alphabet, for example?

The discussion above deals with "living languages," a subject that is itself a somewhat vague concept. There are extinct languages that are not used as anyone's native language, or otherwise in normal speech or writing, but might still be used quite a lot in scholarly documents, or perhaps used by hobbyists who wish to revive a language. Constructed (artificial) languages have usually been created for use as people's second (or maybe even first) language, but the great majority of them have no actual use, or no use outside a very small circle. Esperanto is the best-known exception; it is well covered by Unicode. Finally, there are languages that might be classified as fictional, such as the Klingon language (from the Star Trek TV series) and the languages of Middle Earth (from the books of J.R.R. Tolkien). Such languages may lack full description, actual usage by human beings, and an established writing system. If fictional languages cannot be written in Unicode, the reason may well be that they are not written at all, but it is also possible that they can be classified as written languages, perhaps with some characters that wait for inclusion into Unicode.

Attempts at technical definitions of character requirements

In 1995, an Internet draft titled "Characters and character sets for various languages" was composed by Harald Alvestrand. Although it expired soon and was in many ways incomplete, it was long used for checking character requirements. After all, if you were asked to design software that can handle characters in some languages that you don't know, you have to start somewhere. The draft is still available at the address *http://www.eki.ee/ itstandard/docs/draft-alvestrand-lang-char-03.txt*. For some languages, it listed "important characters" in addition to "required characters."

There was an attempt at creating a "cultural registry" that describes character requirements along with some other information about languages. The structure was described in the ISO 15897 standard (approved in 1999). The registry was not populated with much data, except for some Nordic languages, and the information in it was not used much. The registry technically still exists, at *http://anubis.dkuug.dk/cultreg/*, but it has not been updated for years. Probably the main reason for the failure was lack of interest and participation by major software vendors—i.e., the organizations on which the wide use of such information mainly depends.

The Common Locale Data Repository (CLDR), described in Chapter 11, contains two data fields for describing a language's character requirements with regards to letters:

Basic characters (exemplarCharacters)
> Letters needed for normal writing of the language. For English, this consists of the letters a to z only. (Uppercase forms are implicitly included.)

Auxiliary characters (exemplarCharacters with type="auxiliary")
> Additional letters that may appear in texts in the language, typically in (relatively) common foreign words. For English, this currently consists of the following set: áà éè íì óò úù âêîôû æœ äëïöüÿ āēīōū ăĕĭŏŭ åø çñß. As you can see, it is a rather mixed collection and contains several characters outside the Windows Latin 1 repertoire.

The description of the CLDR database makes it clear that the basic exemplarCharacters set should be rather narrow:

> In general, the test to see whether or not a letter belongs in the set is based on whether it is acceptable in that language to always use spellings that avoid that character. For example, the exemplar character set for en (English) is the set [a-z]. This set does not contain the accented letters that are sometimes seen in words like "résumé" or "naïve", because it is acceptable in common practice to spell those words without the accents.

The content of the exemplarCharacters fields in the CLDR is available, formatted as a table, at *http://www.unicode.org/cldr/data/diff/by_type/characters.html*.

The structure of the CLDR is being developed, and the descriptions of character requirements will probably evolve quite a lot. On the other hand, even at the present stage, the CLDR constitutes the best available overall description of such matters. It should however be used with caution due to the following problems:

- The description, with just two levels of requirements, is too coarse (see below).
- The description only covers letters, not, for example, punctuation.
- Not all data has been checked sufficiently carefully by authorities and experts on a language.
- The data is insufficient—e.g., with regards to the description of auxiliary characters, which have been specified for a few languages only.

Which characters does a language need?

Questions like "Which characters does language *X* need?" are both very important and very difficult. It isn't even a well-defined question before you spend quite some time on it. Yet, it affects, or should affect, keyboard design and settings, font choices, input checks, text scanning, etc. Even though Unicode lets you use any characters, roughly speaking, it is still relevant to know which characters will actually be used, or needed.

People may disagree on what really belongs to a language, even at the character level. Orthographic rules on punctuation have often been defined so that it is debatable what Unicode characters are meant. For example, the rules may discuss "dash" without telling whether it is an em dash or an en dash or whether either of them could be used. There can also be dispute on whether a character difference should be made between some letters that look very similar to each other.

Instead of trying to find a one-dimensional answer, we can specify classes of characters needed in a language in a layered manner. Some characters are essential, some are auxiliary, and some are rare visitors. In a closer analysis, we might consider the following classes:

Core characters
> This class includes the characters that are regarded as absolutely necessary for normal writing of the language. It roughly corresponds to the "exemplarCharacters" definition in CLDR. For English, this class contains small and capital letters "a" to "z," digits 0 to 9, some punctuation marks, and a few special characters like $ and &. The exact repertoire of punctuation marks is debatable, since we are accustomed to using, for example, the ASCII quotation mark " instead of proper quotation marks. We can often include ASCII special characters like *, due to their wide availability, even though they are not common in ordinary texts.

Commonly used other characters
> These are less common characters that can be regarded as belonging to the language in the broad sense, such as é due to its occurrence in words of French origin, @ due to its appearance in the Internet context as well as in unit price indications, and the ellipsis, "…". Most of these characters can be replaced by the use of core characters, with some loss in typography and style. (For example, "e" could be used for é, and three period characters "..." could be used instead of the ellipsis "…".)

Additional characters in foreign words and names from "neighboring" languages
> These are characters that belong to other languages but appear relatively often due to cultural connections. In English, it is not uncommon to use loanwords and names taken directly from French, Spanish, and German, for example. Therefore, characters like è, ñ, and ü are often needed in English texts. Their relevance depends on the nature of the text as well as cultural context. Typically, these characters are letters with diacritic marks, and the marks can usually be omitted without making the text incomprehensible, but it is regarded as good style to preserve them.

Other characters of the same script
> This class differs from the preceding one on cultural and historical grounds, often with technological connections. In English, it is common to omit diacritic marks from, e.g., Polish or Czech names (writing, e.g., Łódź as Lodz), partly because such

characters might not belong to ISO Latin 1, partly because they are regarded as culturally more remote than, for example, French letters.

Additional symbols

In different types of text, many additional characters other than letters are needed. The need greatly depends on the topic area. It is difficult to specify which characters might be needed in "normal" text as opposite to specialized scientific or technical usage. Their repertoire also varies by time, and in the modern world, previously unknown or rare characters like \ or ≈ have become known to many people from technical contexts. We can probably include, e.g., Greek letters α and π into this class due to their use as symbols (rather than letters) in several special contexts.

Characters from other scripts

This class is the most marginal: it includes characters that are almost never used in the language, since they belong to completely different writing systems. For English and other languages written in Latin letters, this includes Cyrillic, Thai, and Chinese characters, for example. The reason is that Russian, Thai, or Chinese words are normally written as transliterated or transcribed when used in English texts. Rare exceptions appear in some linguistic and other scientific use and textbooks of foreign languages. However, the situation is somewhat asymmetric: letters of the Latin script are relatively often used in other scripts, for writing names and other notations.

Language Coverage of ISO Latin Alphabets

The ISO Latin alphabets are defined by ISO 8859 standards as listed in Table 7-2. There are other ISO 8859 standards, but they define character sets that contain the ASCII characters and some collections of non-Latin letters (see Chapter 3). Note that ISO Latin 5, 6, 7, 8, 9, and 10 correspond to ISO 8859-9, -10, -13, -14, -15, and -16, respectively.

The ISO Latin alphabets were primarily designed to meet the needs of some languages used as official or regional languages in Europe and written in Latin letters. Table 7-2 summarizes the suitability of ISO Latin alphabets for them. The information is mainly derived from the ISO 8859 standards. For example, the table says that Croatian can be written in ISO Latin 2 or in ISO Latin 10 (i.e., ISO-8859-16).

As a side effect, all or some of ISO Latin alphabets cover other languages as well, such as Afrikaans, Indonesian/Malay, Swahili, and Tagalog. This issue will not be explored here.

Support to a language in some repertoire of characters is often subject to interpretation and even debate. In particular, the descriptions in the ISO 8859 standards deal with the availability of letters, not punctuation marks. Moreover, the considerations are limited to modern forms of the languages and to use "for general purpose applications in typical office environments," as ISO 8859 standards put it. To point out some other problems, some entries are marked with an asterisk *, with explanations after the table.

Table 7-2. *Coverage of European languages by ISO Latin alphabets*

Language	ISO Latin										Notes
	1	2	3	4	5	6	7	8	9	10	
Albanian	1	2			5			8	9	10	
Basque	1		3		5			8	9		
Breton	1				5			8	9		
Catalan	1		3		5			8	9		
Cornish	1				5			8			
Croatian		2								10	
Czech		2									
Danish	1			4	5	6	7	8	9		
Dutch	1				5				9		ij ligature?
English	1	2	3	4	5	6	7	8	9	10	
Esperanto			3								
Estonian				4		6	7		9		
Faroese	1					6			9		
Finnish	1*	2	3	4	5*	6	7	8*	9	10	š, ž?
French	1*		3*		5*			8*	9	10	œ, Ÿ?
Frisian	1				5				9		
Galician	1		3		5			8	9		
German	1	2	3	4	5	6	7	8	9	10	
Greenlandic	1			4	5	6		8	9		
Hungarian		2								10	
Icelandic	1					6			9		
Irish	1				5*	6*		8	9*	10*	New orthography
Italian	1		3		5			8	9	10	
Latin	1	2	3	4	5	6	7	8	9	10	
Latvian				4			7				
Lithuanian				4		6	7				
Luxemburgish	1				5			8	9		
Maltese			3								
Manx Gaelic								8			
Norwegian	1			4	5	6	7	8	9		
Polish		2					7			10	
Portuguese	1				5			8	9		
Rhaeto-Romanic	1				5			8	9		
Romanian		2*								10	Diacritics on s, t?

Language	1	2	3	4	5	6	7	8	9	10	Notes
Sámi				4*		6*					Not Skolt Sámi
Scottish Gaelic	1				5				9		
Slovak		2									
Slovenian		2		4		6	7			10	
Sorbian		2									
Spanish	1		3		5			8	9		
Swedish	1			4	5	6	7	8	9		
Turkish			3*		5						3 deprecated
Welsh								8			

Explanations to Table 7-2:

- Dutch has (arguably) an ij ligature, which does not belong to any ISO Latin alphabet.
- Finnish official orthography contains š and ž, which are not covered by ISO Latin 1, 5, and 8.
- French has the letter œ and capital Ÿ, which are not covered by ISO Latin 1, 3, 5, and 8.
- Irish can be written with the indicated alphabets when the new orthography is used. ISO Latin 5, 6, 9, and 10 are not suitable when the old orthography is used.
- Romanian uses letters "s" and "t" with a diacritic mark below them. According to the Romanian Standards Institute, this diacritic mark is not a cedilla but a comma below. According to this interpretation, no ISO Latin alphabet except the ISO Latin 10 is suitable for Romanian. However, according to ISO 8859-2, Latin alphabet No. 2 can be used "subject to the agreement of originator and receiver in information exchange." Effectively, "s" and "t" with cedilla (ş, ţ) can be used as substitutes.
- Sámi is a collection of languages that have partly different spelling systems. ISO Latin 4 and 6 cover the requirements of most Sámi orthographies, but for Skolt Sámi, no ISO Latin alphabet is sufficient.
- Turkish can be written in ISO Latin 3 and ISO Latin 5, but the use of ISO Latin 3 for Turkish is deprecated.

We will next consider in more detail the character requirements of two languages, French and Spanish. They are rather similar in their writing systems and use of characters, as compared with the variation of world's languages. Yet, problems emerge in the details.

Example: Spanish

The basic character requirements of Spanish include (in addition to ASCII characters):

- Accented characters á, é, í, ó, and ú (and their uppercase forms)
- The letter ü (and Ü)

- The letter ñ (and Ñ)
- Inverted exclamation mark ¡, used at the start of an exclamation
- Inverted question mark ¿, used at the start of a question
- Characters ª and º, used when an ordinal number has been written with digits (e.g., 2ª = segunda "second (feminine)" and 2º = segundo "second (masculine)"
- Em dash "—"
- Quotation marks: double angle quotation marks («bien»), double quotation marks as in English ("bien"), and single quotation marks as in English ('bien'), with some differences in usage

Except for the dash and the curly quotation marks, Spanish is covered by the ISO Latin 1 character repertoire, and the Windows Latin 1 repertoire adds the missing characters, as well as the euro sign, €. For the purposes of writing Spanish, ISO Latin 9 (ISO 8859-15) is the same as ISO Latin 1 with the addition of the euro sign, but ISO Latin 9 is little used. Some other ISO Latin alphabets could be used for Spanish, too, but most of them lack the inverted exclamation mark and the inverted question mark.

Spanish also uses ellipsis points, "puntos suspensivos," but they are usually unspaced, unlike in recommended English practice. Therefore, they can be represented as sequences of three periods (U+002E U+002E U+002E) rather than as the horizontal ellipsis character (U+2026).

MS Word helps in writing Spanish, if it has recognized the language from the text or you tell it via Word commands. In Spanish mode, MS Word does not convert three periods to English-style ellipsis as it would otherwise do. It also changes an ! or ? at the start of a sentence to an inverted exclamation or question mark, and it changes, for example, "2a" to "2ª." Somewhat strangely, MS Word produces English-style quotation marks ("bien") in Spanish mode, even though Spanish literary usage favors guillemets («bien»).

In Spanish, the acute accent indicates the vowel as stressed, and this may imply a difference in meanings of words. However, in names, the accent rarely has a distinctive meaning. Accented letters are not counted as separate letters in the alphabet, and the accent is taken into account in alphabetic ordering at the secondary level only (i.e., for words that are otherwise the same). By the official rules, accents are used in uppercase letters, too, although it is not rare to deviate from this.

Traditionally, the combinations (digraphs) "ch" and "ll" (which denote specific phonemes in Spanish) have been regarded as separate letters, as components of the alphabet position between "c" and "d," and "l" and "m," respectively. However, in 1994, the association of academies for the Spanish decided to accept the treatment of these combinations as pairs of letters, in alphabetic ordering. Previously Spanish had, for example, "correo" < "chico," since "c" < "ch," but now the official sorting rules follow the international pattern.

The details of official Spanish orthography can be found in the document "Ortografía de la lengua española," available online via *http://www.rae.es/*.

Example: French

The basic character requirements of French include (in addition to ASCII characters):

- Several vowels with diacritic marks: à, â, é, è, ê, ë, î, ï, ô, ù, û, ü, ÿ (and their uppercase forms)
- The letter ç (and Ç)
- The letter œ (and Œ)
- Debatably, the letter æ (and Æ), in words of Latin or Greek origin (e.g., "ægosome")
- Em dash "—"
- Quotation marks: double angle quotation marks (« bien »), double quotation marks as in English ("bien"), and single quotation marks as in English ('bien'), with some differences in usage

Except for the character œ, the dash, and the curly quotation marks, French is covered by the ISO Latin 1 character repertoire, and the Windows Latin 1 repertoire adds the missing characters, as well as the euro sign, €.

However, there is an essential feature in French orthography that cannot be properly addressed in plain text even using Unicode. The orthography rules require thin space (espace fine) after or before some punctuation marks—e.g., before an exclamation mark. Naturally, such a space should be nonbreaking. This problem is discussed in the section "General Punctuation" in Chapter 8.

The letter œ, "oe" ligature, has often been written as the character pair "oe" due to character code limitations. The letter œ was one of the reasons for defining the ISO-8859-15 code (ISO Latin 9), which has not gained much popularity, since you can use œ in windows-1252, and naturally in any Unicode encoding. A normal French keyboard still has no key for œ, so some special technique is needed to type it.

There is no simple way to type æ either on a French keyboard. In practice, "ae" is very often used instead, although the dictionary of the French Academy uses æ spellings.

MS Word helps in writing French, for example, by turning, in French mode, the ASCII quotation mark to French-style quotation marks (e.g., turning the input "bien" into « bien »). Like Spanish, French uses unspaced periods for ellipsis.

Diacritic marks are essential in French, and should be used on uppercase letters, too, according to the recommendation of the French Academy. However, there are differences of opinion and expectations in this area. Therefore, programs often contain a user-settable option for allowing or disallowing accents on capital letters in French text. When they are disallowed, conversion of "égalité" to uppercase would produce "EGALITE." In MS Word, the setting is Tools → Options → Edit → Allow accented uppercase in French. The default setting for this may depend on the version of French (e.g., so that it is normally off for the French of France, but on for Canadian French).

On a typical French keyboard ("azerty keyboard"), the methods for typing letters with a diacritic mark are different for different characters. In particular, there is no obvious way to enter the capital letters É and Ç, so the user needs to know and to use some special technique (such as Alt-0201 and Alt-0199, or Ctrl-' E in Word). The letter œ (or Œ) cannot be typed in any obvious way either.

Since French uses several diacritic marks, it's easier to get them wrong than in Spanish. For example, "e" with grave, è, and "e" with acute, é, are often confused with each other by foreigners, even though their main purpose is to indicate a difference in pronunciation. When spellchecking is enabled and French is supported in it, such confusion will almost always be detected.

There was a large reform of the use of diacritic marks in French in the 1990s. Generally, their use was reduced. Old texts and even old programs (e.g., spellcheckers) might still reflect the old rules. The new rules are described in the document "Rectification de l'orthographe," *http://www.academiefrancaise.fr/langue/orthographe/plan.html*.

Transliteration and Transcription

A conversion between essentially different writing systems, such as writing Greek names in Latin letters, operates at a higher level than the character level. It presupposes the existence of characters and some methods of rendering them. For example, you could take some piece of Unicode-encoded Greek text and replace the Greek letters with Latin letters according to some simple scheme. This would produce a file that is Unicode-encoded, too, so that the scheme could be described as a mapping from the set of Unicode characters into the same set. If the encoding is changed in this context, it would be something logically quite distinct from the replacement operation. Thus, the operation would be similar to modifying text with some editing commands, and generally outside the scope of character set standards.

Conversions between writing systems produce, however, some specific problems in the use of characters. The conversion schemes, especially those used in science, often use diacritic marks and special characters. Writing Greek or Japanese in Latin letters may mean that you use letters like "o" with macron, ō, which is more problematic than basic Latin letters. Writing Arabic in Latin letters according to a scientific scheme requires apostrophe-like characters, which need to be distinguished from similar-looking characters. Moreover, when considering how to automate conversions, it is essential to distinguish between simple character-to-character conversions and more complicated schemes.

The conversions discussed here need to be distinguished from *adaptation* of names and other words from one language into another. For example, name of the capital of Russia, Москва, can be written in Latin letters as "Moskva," but many languages have their own form for the name, such as "Moscow," quite independently of any conversion schemes. However, such adapted forms (sometimes called exonyms) are mostly used for very common names only. The general trend among cartographic and other authorities is to use original names of places, in latinized form when needed, instead of adapting them in different ways to different languages.

Solutions to Readers, Problems to Implementers

Transliteration and transcription convert text from one writing system to another. For example, the Modern Greek name Ηράκλειο (for the capital of Crete) might be transliterated as Herakleio, Hērákleio, or Īrákleio, or transcribed as Iraklio. The transliterations correspond to the written form, although in different ways, whereas the transcription tries to tell the pronunciation.

When the target writing system is a Latin script, transliteration or transcription is often called *romanization* or *latinization*. There are often technical reasons for using romanization: Latin letters, especially the basic letters A to Z, are widely available on computer keyboards and character encodings. You might even find Greek people communicating with each other in Greek using some romanization, since their computers do not allow them to type and read Greek letters.

Transliteration and transcription make foreign names much easier to read to people who do not know the original writing system. They also make texts typographically more uniform. Even in English texts written for people who know Greek well, it is customary to transliterate or transcribe Greek names and other words, except perhaps in linguistic texts that discuss the Greek language itself.

In addition to convenience to readers, transliteration and transcription may help writers. It is easier to work with English text when you need not consider the problems of using Greek letters. However, this issue has lost some of significance.

In processing character data, transliteration and transcription are often problematic, since several mutually incompatible schemes are used. Moreover, most schemes are not reversible—i.e., you cannot always reconstruct the original form from a transliterated form, still less from a transcribed form. This means that if you receive, say, data containing Greek words from different sources, you have a big problem in unifying their spelling into any well-defined single system.

Since different transliterations and transcriptions are used, it is often a good idea to include the original spelling of a word in parentheses—e.g., "Then take the road to Iraklio (Ηράκλειον)." If you write a travel guide, your readers may appreciate such spellings even if they do not know the foreign script. In science, such notes are often needed for exactness. This means that a document otherwise in English and in Latin letters only might need to contain foreign letters, and perhaps to use a Unicode encoding.

If you need to transliterate texts programmatically, the main problem is the choice of a transliteration scheme. Can you use a simple, systematic scheme, or do you need to use a less systematic but more widely understood scheme? Once a scheme has been decided on, the rest is usually simple. Pure transliteration is just a simple one-to-one mapping that can be efficiently implemented using a table. Other transliteration schemes may require some contextual considerations, such as omitting a character at the end of a word but mapping it to a character elsewhere.

Transliteration Converts Letters

Although the terminology varies, we use the word *transliteration* to denote a transformation that replaces letters in an alphabet with letters of another alphabet and *transcription* to denote any other transformation between writing systems. Often "transliteration" is used as a term that covers both kinds of transformations.

There is no strict border between transliteration and transcription. For example, a pure transliteration of Arabic would produce an almost unreadable result, since short vowels are normally not written in Arabic. For practical reasons, most transliteration systems for Arabic express the implied short vowels; therefore, their application requires good understanding of the text.

Sometimes the word "transliteration" is used to denote code conversion (transcoding), but such usage is very confusing. Transliteration is often coupled with code conversions. For example, when transliterating from Cyrillic to Latin script, it might be practical to change the data representation from one 8-bit encoding to another. Yet transliteration is independent of character encoding: transliteration is a mapping between abstract characters.

Transliteration does not always mean a simple one-to-one mapping from one alphabet to another. In fact, most transliteration systems use digraphs or trigraphs (combinations of two or three letters) for a single character in the source alphabet—e.g., "sh" for the Cyrillic letter sha, ш. They may also map two or more distinct letters of the source alphabet to a single letter in the target alphabet, thereby losing information of course. In transliterating Greek, for example, both omicron (o) and omega (ω) might be mapped to "o."

Most of the international transliteration schemes defined by ISO, the International Organization for Standardization, are different: they strive for an ideal, one-to-one mapping. Consequently, they typically require additional letters, often making heavy use of diacritic marks. This is one reason why ISO schemes have not been used much—mostly just in some scholarly texts and to some extent in cartography. On the other hand, such schemes are easy to implement in software, they require no understanding of the text, they lose no information in the transliteration, and they are fully reversible—i.e., the original spelling can be unambiguously constructed from the transliterated text.

For example, Table 7-3 shows the transliteration of a Ukrainian name, Ющенко, in a few systems. The ISO 9 scheme is very logical: each Cyrillic letter is mapped to one Latin letter, and the result has six letters, just as the original. However, the result is unrecognizable to anyone who has not separately learned this system. The other systems produce forms that are known to people in some cultural environments and reflect the orthographies of different languages. English-speaking people are used to understanding "sh" as a particular sound, the French recognize "ch" similarly, the German "sch," and so on. If the transliteration systems get mixed, confusion arises.

Table 7-3. Sample transliterations of a Ukrainian name

Transliteration	System (scheme)
Ûšenko	ISO 9 (current, 1995 version)
Juščenko	Previous version of ISO 9
Yushchenko	Common system in English texts
Juschtschenko	Common system in German texts
Iouchtchenko	Common system in French texts
Jusjtjenko	Common system in Swedish texts
Juštšenko	Finnish standard

There are many transliteration tables as well as transliteration software available. There is a collection of transliteration and transcription tables at *http://transliteration.eki.ee/*. They are in PDF format and often contain a comparison of different transliteration systems.

The reliability and usefulness of transliteration tables varies greatly. In particular, the tables, even in standards, often describe the mappings on paper only, identifying characters just by showing some glyphs. Therefore, it can be difficult to identify them as Unicode characters. Although letters, including diacritics, can usually be interpreted unambiguously, the same is not true for special characters. This applies especially to apostrophe-like characters that have several interpretations.

Transliteration is widely used in libraries, which mostly apply schemes developed for bibliographic use. These include the ALA-LC romanization tables of the U.S. Library of Congress, *http://www.loc.gov/catdir/cpso/roman.html*. These tables cover several scripts, and they are applied outside libraries, too. They use USMARC codes to identify characters, and these codes have defined mappings to Unicode numbers. The mappings can be found via *http://www.loc.gov/marc/specifications/*.

Descriptions in the Unicode standard and elsewhere suggest the following interpretations of transliteration standards and tables, at least in scientific transliteration:

- In transliteration of Cyrillic texts, the soft sign ь (U+044C) is transliterated as the modifier letter prime ′ (U+02B9).

- Similarly, the hard sign ъ (U+044A) is mapped to the modifier letter double prime ″ (U+02BA).

- In transliteration of Arabic texts, the hamza ء (U+0621) (or, in some systems, the alef ا, U+0627) is transliterated as the modifier letter right half ring ʾ (U+02BE).

- Similarly, the ain ('ayn) ع (U+0639) is mapped to the modifier letter left half ring ʿ (U+02BF).

In simplified transliterations, these characters are often replaced by the ASCII apostrophe, the ASCII quotation mark, the right single quotation mark, or the left single quotation mark, respectively. In even more simplified transliterations, these characters are omitted, or the single quotation marks are replaced by the ASCII apostrophe.

Transcription Converts Sounds

In practice, transcription is usually based on some method of expressing sounds in some writing system. This usually means converting text from one system to another, but it can also mean recording spoken language as text, even for a language that is normally not written at all.

For example, in Russian, foreign names are usually transcribed. Instead of trying to replace Latin letters with Cyrillic letters according to some scheme, the pronunciation is taken as the basis, and then the word is written as you would write any Russian word. This means that the sounds are mapped to their closest Russian equivalents. However, some double letters may be preserved to reflect the Latin spelling; e.g., the name Scott would become Скотт, even though doubling the consonant has no effect in Russian. In transcription, some sounds of English or other languages can be interpreted in different ways. For example, Russian has no "w" sound, and Russian has a system of vowels that is rather different from English. Thus, the name Walter may become Вальтер or Уолтер. This example also illustrates what may happen if such a transcribed word is transliterated to Latin script instead of recognizing it as an English name, for example; it would become Val'ter, Valter, or Uolter.

Romanization of Chinese needs to be transcription, since the Chinese writing system is not alphabetic at all—i.e., there are no letters to start from. Different transcription systems have been developed. The Wade-Giles system used to be common, but now there is a strong tendency to use the pinyin system everywhere. The two systems are rather different, and neither of them corresponds well to the English writing system. Instead, the letters and letter combinations denote sounds by special conventions. For example, the Chinese name of the capital of China is "Pei-ching" in Wade-Giles, "Beijing" in pinyin, but you really cannot guess the Chinese pronunciation from either of these.

In the Western world, pinyin is usually applied in a simplified form, omitting *tone marks*. Chinese is, however, a strongly tonal language where the tone—i.e., the melody of a syllable—plays a very important role. The tone can be expressed in pinyin by using a diacritical mark on a vowel or, less satisfactorily, with a superscript digit after the vowel. For example, the word "pinyin" itself should be written as "pīnyīn" (or "pin[1]yin[1]"), where the macron on the vowels (or superscript 1 after the syllables) indicates high level tone. Other tones are indicated with acute accent (high rising tone), caron (low dipping tone), and grave accent (high falling), so that the shape of the diacritic suggests the nature of the tone. When storing Chinese names in a romanized form in a database, it is probably best to store them in full pīnyīn with diacritics, and drop the diacritics on output if needed. There's a service at *http://www.pin1yin1.com* for checking the romanization, if you know how to input a name in Chinese characters.

Transcription may require a thorough understanding of the language being processed and its pronunciation. It is generally not possible to implement phonetic transcription without lexical information—i.e., detailed data about the words of a language and their pronunciation. Outside elaborated linguistic applications, it is often best to record the original form and the transcribed form of a name separately, without assuming that one can be constructed from the other. Similarly, recognizing transcribed names requires good understanding of the text.

Phonetic Transcription in IPA

The IPA is the most widely used system of phonetic writing. It is used for describing the pronunciation of languages that have some writing system but also to express individual and contextual variation of speech. Moreover, the IPA is used to write languages that have no ordinary writing system—i.e., those that exist only in spoken form.

The abbreviation "IPA" stands both for "International Phonetic Association" and for "International Phonetic Alphabet," which is the most important product of the association. In the latter meaning, the IPA actually contains many writing principles such as the use of diacritic marks, not just a collection of letters. Yet, as mentioned earlier, the IPA is not regarded as a script of its own. All the IPA letters are classified as belonging to the Latin script. They are effectively caseless, and their shapes resemble lowercase letters, and their names may carry the words "small letter."

The IPA is widely used in scientific contexts. Worldwide, it is also used in teaching foreign languages, in dictionaries and grammars, and in pronunciation instructions in encyclopedias. Some IPA characters have even been taken into use as letters in normal writing, when designing an orthography for a previously unwritten language. In such situations, the letters usually have separate lowercase and uppercase forms. For example, the Latin small letter schwa ə (U+0259) is originally just an IPA character, denoting a neutral vowel, but due to its use in some orthographies, it has an uppercase form as well: Latin capital letter schwa Ə (U+018F).

In the English-speaking world, the public does not know the IPA very well, since dictionaries and reference books generally use varying notations for pronunciation information. Often the notations are based on the rules of English, with many additional conventions and added marks, so they might not be more intuitive than the IPA. However, British publishers often use the IPA.

The IPA uses many basic Latin letters in meanings that correspond to their phonetic values in English and in many other languages. However, to express sounds exactly and systematically, the IPA uses many additional symbols as well. For example, the common British pronunciation of the word "international" in English is [ɪntəˈnæʃənəl] when written in the IPA. The vowels are denoted by unambiguous symbols, and the stress is indicated with a special symbol before a stressed syllable. The French word "amber" is [ɑ̃bʀ] in the IPA. Here the tilde indicates nasalization. Diacritic marks can be used to indicate detailed variants of pronunciation, but in nonscientific works, rather coarse transcriptions are used.

The main problem with using the IPA on computers has been the lack of suitable fonts. Although fonts that cover a practically useful part of the IPA are widely available, the commonly installed fonts might be insufficient. Moreover, linguists have often used software that lacks Unicode support, or they have for other reasons used tricky implementations of the IPA, typically with some ad hoc 8-bit encoding. In many forms of communication, such as email and Internet discussion groups, it is common to use some "IPA ASCII" system—i.e., some convention on representing the IPA characters using ASCII characters only (e.g., letting @ stand for ə). One common "IPA ASCII" system is described at *http://www.kirshenbaum.net/IPA/*.

On modern computers, the IPA can usually be used, with some caution. In addition to general caveats on the recipients' ability to deal with rich character repertoires and Unicode encodings, there are some technical details:

- The stress mark mentioned earlier, modifier letter vertical line ' (U+02C8), does not belong to some fonts that have otherwise relatively good IPA support. It is therefore common to use the ASCII apostrophe ' (U+0027) instead.

- The length mark, modifier letter triangular colon : (U+02D0) is even more problematic. It is often replaced by the ASCII colon : (U+003A). Although the symbols are rather different, no ambiguity arises, since the colon is not used in the IPA.

- All diacritic marks work more or less unreliably, although in most cases, a single diacritic on a letter works sufficiently well.

The web site of the association, *http://www.arts.gla.ac.uk/ipa/ipa.html*, contains detailed information about the IPA. In particular, the page "The International Phonetic Alphabet in Unicode," *http://www.phon.ucl.ac.uk/home/wells/ipa-unicode.htm*, is very useful if you need to write or interpret IPA notations. The reason is that the original definition documents do not identify the IPA symbols in Unicode terms.

Transcription Inside a Script?

Usually no transliteration or transcription is applied to a foreign word when both the original spelling and the surrounding text use the Latin script. Thus, "Churchill" is "Churchill" even in languages that use "ch" to denote a different sound (e.g., the "k" sound as in Italian) or do not use it all. Although letters may have quite different phonetic values, it would just cause too much confusion to change the spelling. However, there are some exceptions:

- Diacritic marks are often omitted, though usually due to ignorance or technical difficulties rather than conscious decisions. Thus, "Žīgure" may become "Zigure."

- Diacritic marks might even be replaced by other diacritic marks, which are more widely known to the audience (or the writer) or easier to produce. For example, ī (i with macron) might be written as î, which is often far easier to type. Such practices easily cause confusion, at least if not explained in the document.

- Letters with diacritic marks are sometimes replaced with letter combinations. The most common cases are probably "ae" for ä or æ, "oe" for ö or ø, "ue" for ü, and "aa" for å. These replacements are more or less accepted for German, Danish, and Norwegian words.

- Additional letters that do not belong to the basic alphabet are often replaced by other notations. For example, in Icelandic names, the letters ð (eth) and þ (thorn) are often replaced with "d" and "th." Such letters are officially regarded as (additional) Latin letters, but they look odd to many. However, the real reason is often the writer's unwillingness to spend time to check how to type the strange letters. This is also reflected by the common use of "ae" for æ and "oe" for œ.

- In some languages, foreign names are often transcribed so that they are written according to the language's own system, even if both writing systems are Latin-based. For example, Turkish uses the Latin script with some additions, but sometimes changes the spelling of foreign names—e.g., "Churchill" into "Çörçil." Similarly, the name is often written as "Čerčil" in some Slavic languages that use the Latin script.

- Some widely known names have different forms in different languages. This mostly applies to geographic names but also to names of kings and popes as well as first names of other famous people. Thus, the city that Italians call "Venezia" is "Venice" in English, "Venedig" in German, etc. This is really a different issue, since we are talking about the change of a word, not just spelling. But there are borderline cases: sometimes just dropping a diacritic is all that happens when a name is adapted to a language. Usually the difference is clear: "München" is a German name, "Munich" is the English name for the city, and "Munchen" is just a misspelling.

- Loanwords are usually, but not always, adapted to the language's own orthography. Sometimes unadapted and adapted (and intermediate) forms coexist, such as "rôle" and "role" in English, but orthography and style guides usually favor one of the alternatives. This, too, is about adapting words, not just spelling, though it looks like transliteration, if only the spelling is affected in particular cases.

The first two points imply that although we should try to be careful in using the right diacritic marks, we need to be prepared to process data that does not contain them. Moreover, people inevitable make mistakes in using diacritic marks: trying to be correct, they put such marks even where they do not belong. Thus, in particular, *string matching* should often be made without regard to diacritic marks. This is what most search engines do, for example, though they may have optional tools for more specific searches, too.

When using the Cyrillic script, all foreign words are usually transcribed, even if the original spelling uses the Cyrillic script. Thus, text in Bulgarian that mentions the name Yushchenko does not use the original Ukrainian spelling Ющенко but writes it according to Bulgarian orthography: Юшченко.

Language Metadata

Metadata is data about data. For example, the string "elf" is text data, and we can associate with it the metadata that the text is in English. This does not change the identity of characters in the data, but it may affect the interpretation and processing of the data. If accompanied with metadata that says that the string "elf" is in German, the correct interpretation would be that it is a numeral that means "11" (the word is a cognate of English "eleven").

Normally metadata is invisible, when represented using a digital data format that has provisions for metadata. In plain text, you cannot make a distinction between data and metadata. You can write "This document is in English" if you like, but structurally that would be just part of the text. In markup languages and in data formats used by word processors, metadata can be stored and processed separately.

It is difficult to specify what constitutes a language, but in this context, "language" means definitely "human language" as opposite to computer languages such programming, command, and data description languages. Text in a computer language may be characterized as belonging to some human language, to some extent. For example, for the purposes of speech synthesis, comments and variable names in computer source programs need to be interpreted as belonging to some human language.

Need for Language Information

In data processing, there are several situations where information about the language of text is necessary or useful. Typical examples include spelling and grammar checks, speech synthesis, and limiting searches to documents in a particular language. For example, if you are looking for information about elves and therefore search for documents containing the word "elf," you will not be very happy to see hits where the string "elf" appears as a German word that means "eleven."

Information about the language of text (either a document as a whole, or a larger or smaller part thereof) could in principle be used for the following purposes, but beware that most of the uses are, in most situations, just possibilities rather than reality:

- Choice of fonts and glyphs (to suit language-specific typographic conventions, including appropriate use of ligatures)
- Spellchecks
- Grammar and style checks
- Restricting searches for texts in particular languages
- Speech synthesis
- Presentation of text on Braille devices (as dot patterns, to be read with fingertips), since the methods of such presentation are language-dependent

- Automatic operations on text—e.g., fixing punctuation to match the rules of a language, showing synonyms or dictionary definitions of a word to the user, or automatically translating words or fragments of text
- Informing the user about the language (e.g., responding to a user action that corresponds to the question "What's the language of this strange word?")
- Hyphenation and language-sensitive line breaking in general

Language-dependent exceptions to *collating* (sorting) rules should not depend on the language of the text being sorted. Instead, they should depend on the locale setting (see Chapter 11). For example, the index of a book should be alphabetized according to the rules of the language of the book, not by the rules of the languages of the words in the index.

In the Unicode context, the importance of language information is increased by the unification principle (discussed in Chapter 4). Since Unicode, when encoding text, often loses the distinction between variants of a character as used in different languages, it becomes important to be able to indicate the language. This is particularly relevant to East Asian languages. The same string of Unicode characters should be rendered differently depending on whether it is Chinese or Japanese, and this cannot generally be deduced from the characters themselves.

In practice, the user can make the choice of language-dependent presentation "manually" by using a program command or switch. However, this won't work for multilingual documents containing a mixture of Chinese and Japanese, for example. Although such documents are mostly scholarly, they might appear, for example, in user interfaces for language selection as well. This calls for a method for detecting language changes within a document, from markup or otherwise. It needs to be said, though, that often the typographic context dominates. For example, Chinese quotations in Japanese dictionaries usually use Japanese-style characters.

Methods of Determining Language

The language of a document or a part of a document can be determined from:

- Human user's view of the textual content
- Automatic analysis of the content—i.e., recognition of language
- Internet message headers for the document
- Language markup, such as the lang attribute in HTML or xml:lang attribute in XML
- Language tag characters, which are defined in Unicode, but not used much

For example, a speech synthesizer might start reading a document, but then the user realizes that it's all wrong, and he changes the program's mode so that it starts reading by French rules. Some speech synthesizers are able to read different languages, but they usually need to be told which language the text is in.

Automatic analysis is widely applied by search engines like Google and AltaVista. They can search for documents in a particular language, and for this, they need to recognize the language of each document. The methods they use have not been disclosed to the public, but they are probably simple statistical methods. Word processors, too, are often able to recognize the language and select their operating mode such as hyphenation algorithm or spellcheck vocabularies and methods accordingly. There are even "language guesser" demos and services on the Web. Typically, one line of text is sufficient for guessing the language rather well.

Unfortunately, search engines seem to be immune to explicit metadata about language. If Google misanalyzes your Norwegian page as Danish (thereby preventing people from finding it when they restrict the search to pages in Norwegian), there is no simple way to tell Google to reclassify it. It may help to check the spelling of your text and to make sure that there are not too many foreign words (e.g., foreign names) near the start of the document.

Internet message headers are not used much for determining language. The Content-Language header has been defined for indicating the language of the intended audience, and some authoring software generates it. However, "consumers" like browsers do not use it, except in rare cases and inconsistently.

Language Markup

Language markup has been discussed much in different specifications and guides, but it is not widely used in practice yet. It has the obvious drawback that it can only be used in markup systems, not in plain text, and only in markup systems that have been designed with language markup in mind. Moreover, software for processing marked-up text usually makes little or no use of language markup. For example, if Google misanalyzes your Danish web page as being in Norwegian, you cannot fix this by explicitly declaring its language in markup. Yet some programs, such as word processors and web browsers, make some use of language markup.

Attributes for language in HTML and XML

In HTML markup, the attribute for indicating language is lang, whereas in XML, it is xml:lang. In XHTML, you can use both. The attributes can be used for practically any markup element for which it could possibly make sense to declare its language. There are also methods for language markup in other data formats, such as XSL, SVG, SMIL, RTF, and DocBook, but here we will concentrate on the common case of HTML and XML.

The value of the attribute is a language code, according to a system that will be explained shortly. Mostly the language code is just a two-letter code, such as "en" for English, "fr" for French, and "de" for German (derived from Deutsch, the name of the language in the language itself).

For example, if you have the tag `<html lang="en">` near the start of your HTML document, you are saying that the textual content of your document is in English, except perhaps for inner elements that have their own lang attribute. If the document contains a block of quoted text in French, you can use the markup `<blockquote lang="fr">…</blockquote>` for it.

There is also a defined way of specifying the language of a document in Dublin Core (DC) metadata, see *http://www.dublincore.org*. The DC metadata can also be embedded into HTML—e.g., `<meta name="DC.Language" content="en">`. However, DC metadata is not used much, and it only applies to a document as a whole.

Language markup is by essence logical (descriptive), not prescriptive markup. It simply says, for example, "this is in French," instead of giving any specific processing instructions. Programs may use the information the way they like, or ignore it. A good implementation will use language markup in any operations where language might matter. For example, if a program performs word division or generates speech, it is natural to expect that it uses the information about language given in markup, if available. Yet, it is possible that the program you use can perform language-specific word division or language-sensitive speech generation, yet lack support for French there. You might expect that at least a warning is given, but usually your expectations would not be met.

The working draft "Authoring Techniques for XHTML & HTML Internationalization: Specifying the language of content" at *http://www.w3.org/TR/i18n-html-tech-lang/* discusses several problems of language markup and its implications.

The impact of language markup

Despite all the potential uses for information expressed in language markup, web browsers mostly ignore it or use it for font selection only. Actual usage includes the following:

- Several browsers recognize the language of text for the purposes of choosing the font to be used when a document does not specify the font or the text contains a character that is not present in the specified font.

- Some speech-based browsers recognize some language codes and are able to select the correct reading mode automatically.

- Some browsers show the language in an element in a pop-up window, if the user requests information about an element (typically, by right clicking on it and selecting a suitable action).

- Some browsers support language selectors in CSS stylesheets, allowing easier creation of styles that display different languages differently.

- Some online translator programs, when asked to translate an HTML document, make some use of language markup (especially in the root element, `<html lang="…">`) to recognize the source language.

The font selection features imply that it is generally not useful to use language markup for transliterated or transcribed text. Logically, the name Достоевский remains a Russian word if transliterated as Dostoyevsky (or in some other way). Yet, if you use language markup like `lang="ru"` for it, browsers may display it in a font different from the normal font of the text, since they use a font assigned to Russian text. This could make the name stand out in a distracting way.

Granularity of markup

Language markup is very easy in simple cases. You just add an attribute to the tag for the root element of a document (in HTML, the `<html>` tag). If you have quotations in another language, you add language markup for them. The same applies to names of books and other longish fragments of text. However, as you get down to the level of individual words, what should you do with words like "status quo" (that's Latin, isn't it?) or "fiancé" (French, even if used in English text?) or with proper names of people and things? For example, the Web Accessibility Initiative (WAI) recommendations say that you should indicate all changes of language in a document, and this is a Priority 1 requirement. Yet, the WAI documents themselves don't do that for proper names.

Thus, language markup is easy for large portions of text and doesn't take much time, but in such cases, programs could well deduce the language by heuristic methods. Using language markup for very small fragments of text, like words and even parts of a word, would take much time and markup. Yet, it would be essential for detecting changes in language, since a program can hardly deduce from a lone word that it is in a language different from that of the surrounding text. If a document in English mentions that the French word for "garlic" is "ail," it is unrealistic to expect that programs will recognize this (without any markup) and treat that "ail" as a French word and not an English word.

Somewhat similarly, it might be impossible to deduce from a medium-size piece of text whether it is supposed to be U.S. English or British English. The text might contain spellings like "colour" and "favor," but how could a spellchecker know which one is right and which one is misspelled. The language would need to be expressed in markup using a more specific code than "en" (which indicates English in general), namely "en-US" for U.S. English or "en-GB" for British English. Although this would be easy if the author of a document knows it, you would need to add extra markup if your document in U.S. English quotes British authors, or vice versa—and most writers hardly think that they need to indicate the language of quoted text if they quote text in English in a document in English.

The paradox of language markup: it's easy when it's not needed.

Taken to the extremes, or applied logically, language markup would apply even to parts of words in many cases. After all, if you take, say, an English word and use it in a language that uses suffixes for inflexion, the suffix and the base word logically belong to different languages. For example, "Smithin," the genitive form of "Smith" when used in Finnish, would be marked up as `<span lang="en">Smith</span>`in inside a document in Finnish. This would be awkward to do even with good authoring tools, and it could in practice make things worse. A speech synthesizer, for example, might pause between the base word and the suffix, when it switches mode.

There are many other problems in using detailed language markup. Thus, it is best to limit it to major parts of a document only, such as expressions longer than a few words.

Language Codes

In order to express the language of some text in a machine-processable way, we need a system of language codes. Preferably, the codes should be easy to recognize in a program, but most importantly, they need to be systematic. We cannot really work with information about language expressed in everyone's own style and language, like "English," "anglais," or "engl."

The confusion of codes

Just as there is a confusion of languages in the world, there is a confusion of language codes. Several incompatible systems are used to encode information about language in a short identifier, typically a two- or three-letter alphabetic code or a number. To some extent, the codes can be mapped to each other. However, there is no universally accepted list of languages, or anything close to that. Language code systems in use include:

- The ISO 639 standard (see below), with two- and three-letter alphabetic codes as well numeric codes
- The Ethnologue system, also known as SIL code, with three-letter codes; see *http://www.ethnologue.com*
- MARC Code, used in libraries; see *http://www.loc.gov/marc/languages/*
- Systems used in various computing environments; see the draft list "Language Codes: ISO 639, Microsoft and Macintosh," available at *http://www.unicode.org/unicode/onlinedat/languages.html*, and the "List of Windows XP's Three Letter Acronyms for Languages," found at *http://www.microsoft.com/globaldev/reference/winxp/langtla.mspx*

The definitions of language code systems typically identify a language by its name in English (and perhaps in French, too). However, the same name might be used about different languages in different code systems. One code's language might be another code's dialect, or another code's group of languages. There isn't even a universally approved operative definition of what constitutes a language in principle. The oft-quoted statement "a language is a dialect with an army and a navy"—which exists in different variants; e.g., requiring an air force as well—might describe some of the social and political aspects involved, but it isn't really a serious definition.

ISO 639

Frustrating as the confusion might be, there is luckily some uniformity in those language codes that are relevant at the character level. Such codes are generally based on the ISO 639 family of standards, often augmented by additional definitions and principles given in RFC documents about the use of language codes on the Internet.

ISO 639, titled "Codes for the representation of languages," currently has two parts. ISO 639-1 defines two-letter codes for a relatively small set of languages, and ISO 639-2 defines three-letter codes for the same languages and many additional languages. There is however work in progress to extend the standard with new parts, which is shown in

Table 7-4. In particular, ISO 693-3 is meant to cover all languages of the world, which means thousands of languages as opposed to hundreds of languages as in ISO 693-2. This is expected to be largely based on Ethnologue codes, for languages that have not yet been covered by existing ISO 693 codes.

Table 7-4. Parts of ISO 639, current and planned

Part	Content	Notes
ISO 639-1	Alpha-2 code	Example: "en"
ISO 639-2	Alpha-3 code	Example: "eng"
ISO 639-3	Alpha-3 code for comprehensive coverage of languages	Planned, 2006?
ISO 693-4	Implementation guidelines and general principles	Planned, 2007?
ISO 693-5	Alpha-3 code for language families and groups	Planned, 2006?

For 22 languages, ISO 639-2 defines two three-letter codes, bibliographic (ISO 639-2/B) and terminological (ISO 639-2/T), such as "fre" and "fra" for French. In practice, this does not matter much, since these languages also have two-letter codes (such as "fr") defined in ISO 639-1. Policies on language codes on the Internet favor ISO 639-1 codes.

By ISO 639-2, Alpha-3 codes from "qaa" to "qtx" have been reserved for local use. Thus, they will not be assigned to languages in a standard, and they can be used for special purposes by agreements between interested parties.

The registration authority for ISO 639-2 is the U.S. Library of Congress, and the up-to-date list of codes is at *http://www.loc.gov/standards/iso639-2/*. The list contains the ISO 639-1 codes as well. Some widely used ISO 639-1 codes are listed in Table 7-5.

Table 7-5. ISO 639-1 codes for some languages

Language	Code	Comments
Afrikaans	af	Spoken in South Africa
Arabic	ar	Exists in several forms that differ substantially by country
Chinese	zh	Much variation by dialect and writing—e.g., zh-Hant and zh-Hans
Dutch	nl	Spoken in the Netherlands, in Belgium, etc.
English	en	Difference between en-US and en-GB relevant in spelling
Esperanto	eo	The most widely used constructed (artificial) human language
French	fr	Some variation exists—e.g., between fr-FR and fr-CA (Canadian)
German	de	Orthographic differences exist between language forms
Greek	el	Modern Greek (Ancient Greek has three-letter code "grc")
Hebrew	he	Written in Hebrew script
Hindi	hi	Spoken in India
Italian	it	Spoken in Italy
Japanese	ja	Written using different scripts

Language	Code	Comments
Korean	ko	Currently mostly written in specific Korean script, Hangul
Latin	la	Used for ancient, medieval, and modern Latin
Polish	pl	Spoken in Poland; a Slavic language written in the Latin script
Portuguese	pt	Orthographic differences between pt-PT and pt-BR (Brazilian)
Russian	ru	Written in the Cyrillic script
Spanish	es	Spoken in Spain, Latin America, and elsewhere
Vietnamese	vi	Currently mostly written in Latin letters, with many diacritics

Language codes on the Internet

In 1995, RFC 1766 was issued under the title "Tags for the Identification of Languages." Here "tag" really means "code." The idea was to specify that an ISO 639 conformant language code is used as the primary code, optionally followed by a hyphen and a subcode, which is usually a two-letter country code as defined in ISO 3166.

ISO 3166 defines code systems for countries and some other territories. Among the systems, the two-letter alphabetic code (e.g., "FR" for France) is most widely used. Usually, but not always, this code coincides with the code used in the two-letter code of the Internet domain of the country (e.g., ".fr").

Both language codes and country codes are case-insensitive. However, the recommendation is to write language codes in lowercase, country codes in uppercase. For example, the language code for Italian is usually written as "it," whereas the country code for Italy is written "IT." As in this example, a language code is often the same as the country code for a country where the language is common. There are many exceptions, though. For example, Chinese is "zh" but China is "CN."

Thus, for example, "en-US" means English as spoken in the U.S., and "en-GB" means British English, or English as spoken in the United Kingdom of Great Britain and Northern Ireland, commonly known as the U.K. Note that the ISO 3166 country code is "GB," while the Internet domain for the U.K. is ".uk."

 Although some primary language codes are the same as country codes, the two code systems are separate. In general, there is no one-to-one mapping between languages and countries.

Several Internet protocols refer to RFC 1766, but the references should probably be interpreted as referring to the newest definition of language codes. In 2001, RFC 1766 was superseded by RFC 3066. There is work in progress to create the successor of RFC 3066, see *http://www.w3.org/International/core/langtags/rfc3066bis.html*.

The general structure of language codes according to RFC 3066 is the following: a language code consists of a primary code ("primary subtag") and optionally one or more additional codes ("subtags"), each preceded by a hyphen-minus character "-". In practice, an underline is often used as a separator instead of a hyphen-minus—e.g., "en_US"—

since in many contexts, the syntax of codes does not allow a minus-hyphen. The principles on primary language codes according to RFC 3066 are the following:

- Any two-letter primary code shall be as defined in ISO 639-1.
- Any three-letter primary code shall be as defined in ISO 639-2. Such codes must not be used for languages that have a two-letter code (e.g., "eng" is not allowed, since English has the ISO 693-1 code "en").
- The primary code "i" is reserved for language codes registered at the Internet Assigned Numbers Authority (IANA). Such registrations have not been made much. Codes so registered should not be used, if an ISO based code is available.
- The primary code "x" can be used by agreements between interested parties.
- No other primary code shall be used.

The rules for the secondary code ("second subtag") in a language code are:

- No one-letter code shall be used.
- Any two-letter code shall be a country or other territory code as defined in ISO 3166.
- A code of length three to eight may be registered at IANA. It may indicate a dialect or other variant. The registry is at *http://www.iana.org/assignments/language-tags*.
- Codes longer than eight characters should not be used.

In practice, only a few combinations of a primary code and a secondary code have practical significance at present. Although the structure of language codes permits more complicated codes, such as de-AT-1996 (Austrian variant of German, orthography as reformed in 1996), they have even less use. However, any software that processes language codes should be prepared to parse a structured code, instead of just performing simple string matching against primary codes like "en," "fr," etc.

This work on the development of language codes as used on the Internet will probably result in some additional specific rules on the use of additional codes. In particular, several additional codes could be used according to the following principles:

- The additional codes, if present, would appear in the order *language-script-region-variant-extension-privateuse*.
- Additional codes may be omitted, and mostly the lengths of codes resolve any ambiguities. For example, "en-US" has language and region only, with the script omitted (implied).
- The script can be indicated by using a four-letter code. However, it should be omitted (implied) for languages that are normally written in one script only. There will be a registry of such cases. For example, "en" implies the Latin script, "Latn," and the code "en-Latn" should not be used. On the other hand, it would be adequate to use "ru-Latn" for transliterated Russian text, though this would still be vague, since you would not be able to express the transliteration scheme used.
- The region code can be a two-letter country or territory code (as by ISO 3166) or a three-digit code, to be interpreted according to an IANA registry that contains a

subset of numeric codes for areas (such as continents) according to a system developed by the United Nations.

- Variant codes can be used for well-recognized variants of a language, such as dialects. They are at least five characters long if they start with a letter and at least four characters long if they start with a digit. For example, in "de-1996" the code "1996" identifies the orthographic variant of German defined by the reform in 1996. Specifying this variant, or the "1901" variant (referring to the older orthography), for German can be essential to having spellchecks performed as intended. (At present, you use settings—applicable to the entire document—of a word processor to select between such orthographic variants, if it supports them at all.)

- Extension codes are application-oriented and start with a code consisting of a single letter. A registry is to be set up for extension codes.

- Private use codes indicate distinctions in language important in a given context by private agreement and they start with a code consisting of the letter "x." Thus, in the code "en-GB-a-some-stuff-x-foobar," "a-some-stuff" is an extension part, and "x-foobar" is a private use part.

Language codes and user interfaces

Language codes are based on names of languages, although often on the English name rather than the name in the language itself. When presented to users, language codes should preferably be mapped to localized language names—i.e., names in the language that the user prefers. For such purposes, the CLDR database (discussed in Chapter 11) contains localized names for languages.

In practice, user interfaces like language selection menus often identify the languages either by English names or by two-letter ISO 639 codes, or both (as in Figure 7-2 or on the main page of the European Union web site *http://www.eu.int/*). Short codes are used especially in contexts where several languages need to be expressed compactly. Sometimes flags of countries are used, raising many objections. For example, on the page *http://www.google.com/language_tools*, flags are used adequately to indicate countries, whereas the choice of language is by language name.

The most logical method for selection between versions of documentation in different languages—for example, in a document that acts as an entry page only—would be to use the name of each language in the language itself. Of course, this often requires a rich repertoire of characters. It also raises the problem that people get confused with the mixture of languages, especially if they see "strange characters" and cannot easily figure out what the information is about. Ordering the languages is difficult too; often they are ordered by the ISO 639 code.

Language Tags in Unicode

There are special characters for language tagging in Unicode, but their use is *strongly discouraged*, in general. Language tag characters are control characters that contain metadata about text. They are invisible, although they may indirectly affect the rendering of normal characters. They are meant for use in plain text (as opposed to HTML or XML, for example) and in special circumstances only.

The block Tags, U+E0000..U+E007F, is used for the purpose. It contains clones of ASCII characters, defined as invisible tag characters and used to indicate language using language codes such as "en" or "en-US." For example, to indicate that subsequent text is in English, you would use the two characters U+E0065 U+E006E (clones of "e" and "n"). Any software that does not recognize language tag characters probably behaves oddly upon encountering them—e.g., trying to render them visibly, instead of just ignoring them.

There is a free utility LTag for constructing language tags, to be used with plain text editors in Windows. It is available from *http://users.adelphia.net/~dewell/ltag.html*.

Languages and Fonts

Although languages using the same script may have different typographic conventions and practices, setting the language of text (in markup or with a word processor command) will usually not affect the visible rendering of text. When desired, such typographic issues need to be handled at the font level. This typically means that you select the font so that its typographic features are suitable for the main language of your text. However, most widely used fonts are intentionally rather "neutral." In OpenType technology, it is possible to have language-dependent variants of a character as different glyphs within the same font. Software that makes use of such possibilities is still rare.

Example: Shape of the Acute Accent

In Polish typography, the acute accent is more vertical than the acute accent used, for example, in French. It is also positioned differently: more to the right. Commonly used fonts typically make compromises but are closer to the French typography. Compare, for example, the French-style é of Times with the mixed-style é of Georgia and the rather Polish style é of Arial. In practice, selecting a font on such grounds is seldom possible, since there are so many other issues to consider. However, it is one criterion to be considered.

The situation is so frustrating to some people that they claim that the Polish diacritic is not an acute accent at all but a separate diacritic, "kreska." See, for example, the illustrated description at *http://www.twardoch.com/download/polishhowto/kreska.html*. However, it is unlikely that Unicode will be amended by the kreska. This means that the difference cannot be made at the character level.

In some distant future, we might be able to use fonts that have acute accents of different shapes—e.g., Western, Polish, and Greek—simply by setting the language of the text. At present, don't expect anything like that to happen. There are, however, issues in East Asian languages that can sometimes be handled by making language-dependent font choices, to some extent.

Chinese Characters and Language Information

Due to the nature of the Chinese writing system and its unification in Unicode, it is in principle useful to indicate the language of text containing Chinese-Japanese-Korean (CJK) ideographs. This allows the selection of appropriate glyphs as intended, either by the choice of a font or by the choice of glyphs within a font that supports variation by language.

For Chinese, there are two major writing systems, called "Traditional" and "Simplified." The latter is much more common especially in mainland China. In addition to simplifying the shapes of many characters, it removes some distinctions made in the Traditional script by mapping two or more characters into one. For an illustrated explanation, see *http://people.w3.org/rishida/scripts/chinese/*.

The CJK ideographs share a common origin but may differ between the languages. The unification process recognized some differences as so essential that different code points were assigned for characters that originate from one old Chinese character. In such cases, it is of course an author's responsibility to use the correct code points; font settings will not help. However, most differences were deemed typographic only. In such cases, a reader is expected to recognize a character in any of the variants (most important, Japanese, Chinese Traditional, and Chinese Simplified). Despite this, it is natural to try to make the text appearance correspond to the user's expectations.

In practice, authors mostly decide on the representation of CJK ideographs by selecting a specific font. In particular, when setting the style of some element in a word processor, you might see separate settings for "Asian" or "East-Asian" and other text. There you can select a font that is suitable for the language you are using. In web authoring, you could similarly set a specific font, or a list of alternative fonts, in a stylesheet.

Although explicit font settings are still often the most effective way, there are some problems with them. The author's font choice might be ignored or overridden—e.g., because the document has been sent to a computer that lacks the chosen font. The user may dislike a font and may wish to override author-supplied font settings. Moreover, setting a specific font normally means setting it by the name, and many fonts exist in different versions (with different character coverage) under the same name.

In web authoring, you can set the language of text in markup, instead of or in addition to suggesting specific fonts. The idea is that browsers may then map different languages to different fonts.

For Japanese and Korean, there is no fundamental problem: you would use language codes "ja" and "ko," respectively. For Chinese (code "zh"), things are different, since it is relevant to indicate the difference between the writing systems, "Traditional" and "Simplified." Usually a font that contains CJK characters has them as according to one of these systems, or as in Japanese, or as in Korean.

The language codes "zh-CN," "zh-TW," and "zh-HK" have often been used to specify the version of Chinese used. The real purpose has usually been to specify Simplified

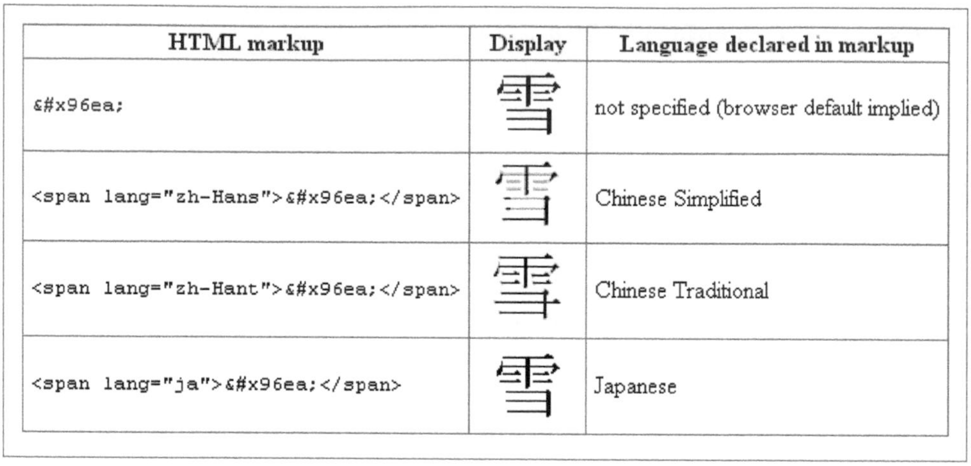

HTML markup	Display	Language declared in markup
`&#x96ea;`	雪	not specified (browser default implied)
`<span lang="zh-Hans">&#x96ea;</span>`	雪	Chinese Simplified
`<span lang="zh-Hant">&#x96ea;</span>`	雪	Chinese Traditional
`<span lang="ja">&#x96ea;</span>`	雪	Japanese

Figure 7-3. Effect of language markup on CJK characters on Firefox

Chinese when using "zh-CN" and Traditional Chinese in the other cases. The reason in that in mainland China (code CN), the Simplified system is normally used, whereas in Taiwan (code TW) and Hong Kong (code HK), the Traditional system is more common.

It is in principle more adequate to use script codes, since the issue is really about scripts, not territories. The codes "zh-Hans" and "zh-Hant" denote Simplified and Traditional Chinese, respectively. Modern software often recognizes them, though some programs might recognize only the previously mentioned notations with territory codes. As you can guess, "s" stands for Simplified, "t" stands for Traditional; "Han" is one of the names of the Chinese writing system.

The potential effect of language markup is illustrated in Figure 7-3, which shows how language markup alone (with no font settings on a web page) may affect the display of CJK ideographs. You may need to take a close look at the ideograph glyphs to see how they differ. In this case, the browser, Mozilla Firefox, uses Japanese glyphs by default. The actual fonts used depend on the settings of the browser.

The effect of language markup on the rendering of CJK ideographs depends on several things, including the browser, its font settings, and its internal logic in selecting glyphs. See some data on this at *http://www.w3.org/International/tests/results/langandcjkfont*.

At the end of Chapter 1, we mentioned how browsers may let the user select different fonts for different scripts. The script concept used there is not the same as the script concept described in this chapter. Rather, it involves the script proper, the encoding of the page, and other factors. One of the factors might be the script as declared in HTML markup, using, for example, the attribute lang="zh-Hans". Such markup may enable the automatic selection of different fonts for different parts of a document. It is however questionable whether this is useful. For example, a Japanese user might prefer seeing even Chinese text written using Japanese glyphs.

CHAPTER 8

Character Usage

This chapter describes different character blocks and collections that are practically important, especially in the Western world. The first section is of a more generic nature and discusses the relationship of character standards, orthography, and typography. All the Unicode blocks are briefly characterized to give an overview, but the emphasis is on ASCII, different Latin supplements, General Punctuation, and mathematical and technical symbols.

 For information on ideographic characters and processing of East Asian languages, see Ken Lunde's *CJKV Information Processing* (O'Reilly).

Basics of Character Usage

The use of characters has many aspects, but here we are mainly interested in selecting the most suitable character, when there is a choice between similar-looking characters. The choice may affect the appearance of text, but also the processing of text.

Orthography Sets Rules for Writing

Orthography, or "correct writing," sets rules for using characters. This is largely a matter of writing words correctly, according to rules that some authority has set, or according to established habits and conventions. You might use dictionary and spellcheckers for this. But there are also rules that relate to grammar rather than dictionaries. For example, English orthography has rules for quotations, and different forms of English have somewhat different rules. In U.S. English, you usually "quote," but in British English, you normally 'quote' with single quotation marks.

Although the orthography rules themselves are beyond the scope of this book, there are issues that relate to the identity and coding of characters. For example, the rules of a language might say that a dash is used in some contexts, such as a range notation "0–40." The rules might not identify what "dash" means, and they might even explicitly leave the length of a dash unspecified, to be regarded as a typographic issue. For the purposes of writing text on a computer, you simply have to decide on the identity of a dash. In coded character sets, there is no dash as such. You need to use the em dash, the en dash, or some other specific dash character. Modern orthographic guidelines resolve such issues.

Typography Is About Appearance

Typography is about typesetting and other tuning of text appearance. Typography deals with fonts, spacing, and line length, for example. Typographic rules suggest, for example, that an expression like "0–40" should have some small spacing on both sides of the dash, so that it does not touch the surrounding digits. Usually this does not mean the insertion of any characters. Instead, you might use program-specific tools, such as those mentioned in Chapter 2.

In many writing systems, typography is an essential part of writing, not just optional fine-tuning. In English, we may worry about fonts, word division, etc., or we might just unconsciously accept the default settings of a program. Arabic writing, on the other hand, requires the use of appropriate forms for each character according to its immediate context. In typesetting mathematical texts, typography is often essential for readability and un-derstandability. You may need to combine characters from different fonts, and you need to make sure that the intended meaning is clear in spite of this.

Liberal in What You Accept

An old principle in Internet protocol design is "be conservative in what you send, liberal in what you receive." This was formulated in 1981 as follows by Jon Postel in RFC 791:

> The implementation of a protocol must be robust. Each implementation must expect to interoperate with others created by different individuals. While the goal of this specification is to be explicit about the protocol there is the possibility of differing interpretations. In general, an implementation must be conservative in its sending behavior, and liberal in its receiving behavior. That is, it must be careful to send well-formed datagrams, but must accept any datagram that it can interpret (e.g., not object to technical errors where the meaning is still clear).

The principle applies to characters and strings as well as datagrams (certain types of mes-sages), and between programs as well as in Internet communication. The idea is that you should play strictly by the rules but not assume that others always do so.

For example, consider the expression of a temperature in centigrade (degrees Celsius). By international standards, the orthographically correct way is to use a space between and the number and the degree sign and to use the character degree sign U+00B0 followed by the letter C, as in "42 °C." Moreover, you should prevent line breaks between the number and the unit, by using a no-break space or by other tools.

However, when reading or otherwise processing data, you should expect to see different temperature notations, such as "42°C" or "42 C." The variation that you can and should deal with depends on the circumstances. For example, if you detect that "42 °C" actually contains a masculine ordinal indicator ° and not the degree sign °, it is practically certain that you still know *what was meant*. If you design a program that detects such a situation, it should probably process the data under the assumption that the degree sign was meant, without even issuing a message about this—although sometimes it might be suitable to issue a mild warning. On the other hand, "42 C" is a more difficult case, since it could conceivably be the correct notation for 42 coulombs, for example.

Similarly, if a program reads a Unicode text file and interprets its content as numeric data, it should recognize, for example, "-42" (with hyphen-minus), "–42" (with en dash), and "−42" (with minus sign) all as indicating a negative number. That is, you should not be picky about the use of the minus sign but accept characters that are widely used in the role of a minus sign. Note that common library routines for reading numeric data, like scanf in C, generally treat only the hyphen-minus character as a minus sign—i.e., they reflect the old and widespread usage and do not accept the "real" minus sign even as an alternative.

Conservative in What You Send

The note in the previous section illustrates the difficulty of being conservative with characters. If you prepare data for an application that is fully equipped to process Unicode data, the conservative way is to use the Unicode minus sign to denote a negative number. It is the most adequate character for the purpose in that context. On the other hand, if you prepare data for an unknown application or a multitude of applications, it is probably much better to use a hyphen-minus character "-" as a replacement for the minus sign.

Even if the immediate target application is Unicode-capable, your data might be transferred from it to something much more limited. For example, a multilingual database could (and normally should) internally use Unicode, but it might be accessed using connections, software, and devices that seriously limit the output and input possibilities. Ideally, the database should contain all text data in the most appropriate Unicode format, and various restrictions on character repertoire should be taken into account when data is sent from it or received by it. As practical principles in being conservative in this sense, we can recommend:

- In email messages, use ASCII (Basic Latin) only, by default, unless working with a community that can be expected to be able to deal with other encodings.

- In communication within a language community that generally uses a particular character repertoire, use it. For example, in French, German, or Spanish, use Latin 1 Supplement in addition to ASCII (i.e, use ISO Latin 1).

- When a wider character repertoire is indispensable, try to limit the use of characters to a subset of Unicode that is known to work widely. For example, in European multilingual contexts and in simple mathematical and technical texts that need special symbols, try to restrict the repertoire to the Minimum European Subset 2 (MES-2). As a more practical criterion, use characters in the Windows Glyph List 4 (WGL 4), which is what the most common fonts cover, more or less.

- For text-processing and publishing purposes, try to identify and document in advance the set of characters you will need, and test how the relevant software can handle it. This will help you in identifying the fonts that can be used.

ASCII (Basic Latin)

In Chapter 3, we briefly described the ASCII characters and their encoding. Here we go into the details of the meanings of these characters. For technical reasons, ASCII characters are widely used even when more appropriate characters exist in Unicode. This is partly caused by the history, partly by the fact that ASCII characters are well-known and easy to type and process, and they work reliably across platforms. But this implies that many of the characters have *multiple uses* or, to put it in other words, multiple semantics.

In the Unicode framework, ASCII characters constitute the very first block of Unicode, called Basic Latin and ranging from U+0000 to U+007E.

Names of ASCII Characters

The names of ASCII characters have a long history, and they can be rather misleading. For example, " (U+0022) is called "quotation mark," although it is not a correct quotation mark in English or human languages in general. The name "grave accent" for ` (U+0060) reflects one of the original intended uses, rather than actual practice. Many of the special characters in ASCII have a large variety of names in common usage, and the name used in Unicode usually corresponds to the choice made in ASCII.

Generally, the Unicode name of an ASCII character might be suitable in some official contexts, but not necessarily in more normal usage. As an example of the differences, Table 8-1 presents some ASCII characters for which the Unicode name and the name normally used in O'Reilly books are different.

Table 8-1. Some variation in names of ASCII characters

Chararcter	Code	Unicode name	Name(s) used in O'Reilly books
#	U+0023	Number sign	Hash sign, sharp sign
.	U+002E	Full stop	Period, dot
/	U+002F	Solidus	Slash
@	U+0040	Commercial at	At sign
\	U+005C	Reverse solidus	Backslash
^	U+005E	Circumflex accent	Caret, circumflex
`	U+0060	Grave accent	Backquote, backtick

Alphanumeric Characters

The ASCII set contains the uppercase characters A–Z and the lowercase characters a–z as well as the common digits 0–9. The letters are often called basic Latin letters, though

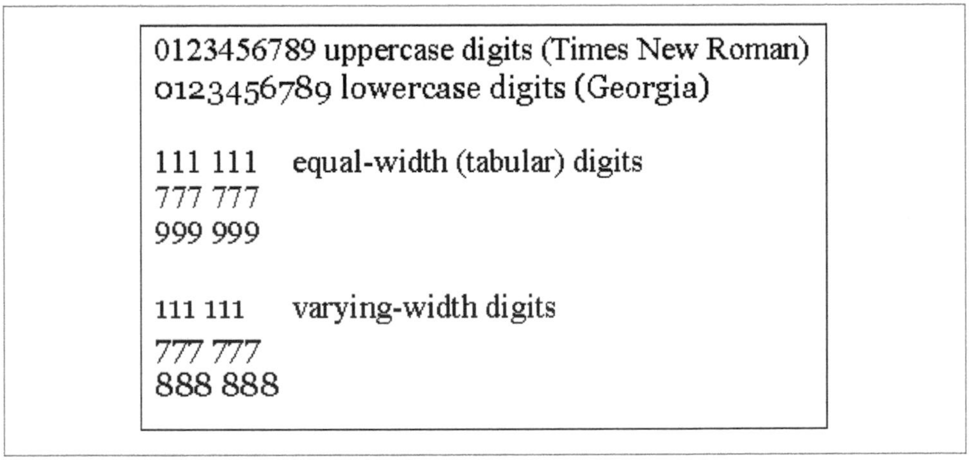

```
0123456789 uppercase digits (Times New Roman)
0123456789 lowercase digits (Georgia)

111 111     equal-width (tabular) digits
777 777
999 999

111 111     varying-width digits
777 777
888 888
```

Figure 8-1. Different renderings of common digits

Latin has no "w" letter. It is more adequate to refer to the ASCII letters as letters of the English alphabet. The digits 0–9 are often called Arabic digits, but they differ from the original Arabic digits (٠,١,٢,٣, etc., also called Arabic-Indic digits), which are still in wide use in the Arabic world.

In many computer languages, the ASCII alphanumeric characters are what you can use in names (identifiers), usually with the added requirement that the first character must be a letter. However, quite often a computer language allows more latitude, such as the use of the underline character "_" and possibly other characters as well in identifiers. Typographically, there are different presentations of digits, illustrated in Figure 8-1:

Uppercase versus lowercase digits
> Uppercase digits all have the same height, usually the same as the height of uppercase letters. They are also called *modern style* or *lining* digits (or figures or numbers). Lowercase digits vary in height and have ascenders and descenders. They have been traditionally used in print typography in running texts. They are also known as *old style* or *non-lining* digits. According to typographic rules, lowercase digits should not be used in an expression formed from digits and uppercase letters, like "ABC-123."

Equal-width (tabular) versus varying-width digits
> In tabulated data, digits normally need to be of equal width to produce good appearance where numbers line up. Inside text, the widths of digits may vary. Often only the digit "1" has a width different from other digits.

Unicode, or character standards in general, does not make either of these distinctions. Thus, in plain text you cannot have both lowercase and uppercase digits. The distinction can be made at font level, when suitable fonts are available. Expert fonts may contain two sets of digits, lowercase and uppercase. Some techniques use Private Use characters for this—i.e., allocate, for example, lowercase digits to code positions that have been reserved for use by private agreements only. This is risky because the data becomes cryptic if information about the particular agreement is lost in data transfer and processing.

Most fonts commonly used in computers have equal-width uppercase digits. However, the Georgia font has lowercase varying-width digits. If you use such a font in the text of your document, you should use a different font for tabulated numbers.

Parentheses

ASCII contains three sets of paired parentheses:

Common parentheses, (and)
> Called *left parenthesis* and *right parenthesis* in Unicode. They are widely used both in natural languages and in computer languages. In natural languages, they usually enclose a parenthetic (less important) remark. In computer languages, they have different uses that might not have anything to do with importance. For example, arguments of a function are usually written in parentheses, as in mathematics—e.g., f(42, x+y).

Square brackets, [and]
> Called *left bracket* and *right bracket* in Unicode. They are sometimes used in natural languages in special contexts (such as in a parenthetic remark inside a parenthetic remark [like here], or to indicate an addition or change in quoted text). In phonetics, brackets are used to denote that pronunciation is specified. In mathematics, square brackets are sometimes used as outer parentheses when parentheses are nested, as in 2×[(a + b)/c]. In computer languages, brackets have a wide range of uses, often including the use in subscripted variables or array component selectors like a[i].

Braces, { and }
> Called *left curly bracket* and *right curly bracket* in Unicode. They are rare in natural languages but relatively common in computer languages. In mathematics, they are sometimes used when parentheses are nested several levels. More commonly, they are used to denote sets; e.g., {5, 42, 83} is a set of three numbers.

The Unicode names of these characters have the attributes "left" and "right," although they are logically treated as opening and closing parentheses (and called that way in some standards). This is relevant because the physical appearance adapts to the writing direction of the text (see Chapter 7). Thus, if you have Arabic or Hebrew text containing a parenthetic expression, then the "left parenthesis" is located to the right of the enclosed expression and the "right parenthesis" is on the left side, since the text generally runs right to left. On the other hand, the parentheses are displayed as mirror images, so that the opening "left" parenthesis looks like a right parenthesis.

The characters < and > are often used in a parenthesis-like manner and referred to as left and right angle bracket. Such usage, as well as "real" angle brackets, is discussed in the section "General Punctuation" later in this chapter.

Other Graphic Characters

The other graphic characters in ASCII will be described here in alphabetic order by their Unicode name, which deviates from the common name in some cases.

Ampersand & (U+0026)

In natural languages, this character normally means just "and." In some programming and command languages, it has a comparable meaning, as logical AND operator, as bitwise AND operator, string concatenation operator, or as a sequential operator. But the ampersand also appears in many technical uses that have nothing to do with the meaning "and." For example, in the C programming language, &x denotes the address of x.

The visual appearance of this character varies a lot. In some designs, the character's origin as a ligature of "ET"—the Latin word for "and"—can readily be seen.

Apostrophe ' (U+0027)

This character has mixed usage, usually as a punctuation character. In normal text, it is used either as an apostrophe as in the English word *don't* or as a single quotation mark. (In Unicode Version 1.0, this character was named "apostrophe-quote" to reflect this.) In both types of usage, the apostrophe is just a replacement used to overcome character repertoire limitations. It should not be confused with the typographically correct apostrophe, and it can be called "ASCII apostrophe" to emphasize this.

With regards to use as a single quote, compare to notes below on the use of the quotation mark. Analogously with the quotation mark, the apostrophe is defined (in Unicode) as having a "neutral (vertical)" glyph. This reflects its use as both an opening single quote and a closing single quote. However, in practice it may get displayed as slanted or even curved. As with the quotation mark, it is sometimes difficult to find out what really happens, since word processors may convert an apostrophe to a different character, often to a language-specific quotation mark.

Unicode defines modifier letter prime ' (U+02B9) and prime ' (U+2032) as distinct characters. The former is used mainly in linguistics to denote primary stress or palatalization (e.g., when transliterating Cyrillic soft sign). The latter is used to denote minutes or feet, and in mathematics, to denote a derivative (differentiation). When only ASCII (or only ISO Latin 1) is available, the apostrophe can be used as a surrogate for those characters. It might look natural to use the acute accent ´ (which is slanted) for some of such purposes, but since the whole idea is to use a replacement due to character repertoire restrictions, it is best to use a replacement that works most widely (due to being an ASCII character).

In ASCII, the apostrophe was intended to have secondary usage as acute accent, to be overprinted on a letter. This explains, in part, why the glyph is often slanted.

Asterisk * (U+002A)

The asterisk has a wide range of uses, including the following:

- In natural languages, an asterisk or a sequence of asterisks is sometimes used as a reference to a footnote or a margin note*. Several other symbols, such as daggers and (superscript-style) digits and letters, are used for such purposes too. Due to glyph problems discussed below, it is probably best to avoid the use of asterisks for such purposes and use some other notations. *The footnote or margin note itself begins with the asterisk or sequence of asterisks.

- The asterisk is sometimes used when indicating the year or date of birth—e.g., * 1952.

- Especially in command languages, the asterisk is often used as a wildcard character that matches any string of characters. For example, `*.txt` as a command argument might refer to all filenames ending with *.txt*.

- In regular expressions, the asterisk often denotes possible repetition. For example, depending on the particular regexp syntax, xy* might denote the set of strings consisting of an x followed by any number (including zero) of y's—i.e., x, xy, xyy, xyyy, etc.

- In mathematics, the asterisk has several uses as an operator symbol of some kind. Generally, such uses are surrogate notations for various star-like symbols with more specific semantics. A double asterisk ** sometimes indicates exponentiation.

- In linguistics, a leading asterisk before a word can be used to indicate a reconstructed form (e.g., "the word *king* probably derives from old Germanic *kuningaz*"); it may also indicate an ungrammatical expression.

- In Usenet postings and some other plain text contexts, the asterisk may also be used for *emphasis* (though using _underlines_ is more common).

- One of the early uses was to make a series of asterisks a "check protector," to flank the amount of a check so one could not kite or change the value. That method was applied in punch cards and printers too, and it's still often used, for example, in password input, to help the user count characters but protect the password from prying eyes.

- The asterisk is sometimes used to indicate a "masked out" character, as in "G*d."

- In several programming languages, asterisk is the multiplication symbol, but it may also have other uses. For example, `int *p;` declares p as a pointer to `int` in C.

When writing or quoting expressions in computer languages that have the asterisk as part of language syntax, the asterisk shall be preserved of course. On the other hand, such usage should not be extended to other contexts, unless the limitations of the character repertoire prevent the use of better symbols. Specifically, in ISO Latin 1 there is a separate multiplication sign. In some contexts the middle dot (·) is, somewhat arguably, an adequate multiplication symbol.

The glyphs for the asterisk vary, but generally it appears in a more or less superscript style, perhaps in a rather small size. It is difficult to say what an asterisk *should* look like, given its mixed usage. When used as an operator of some kind, it should be vertically positioned the same way as, for example, the plus sign. When used as a reference sign, and perhaps in some other uses too, it should appear in superscript style. It seems that most font designs reflect the latter style, making expressions like a*b look somewhat odd. If you cannot use a symbol with less ambiguous meaning, you might try to help things by using a font where the asterisk looks more operator-like, such as the Courier font, though even the Courier * is somewhat raised. Quite often it might be better to use a monospace font for all expressions (like a*b) quoted from programming and command languages, etc.

The Unicode standard mentions that asterisk is called "star" on phone keypads. It also mentions that the asterisk is distinct from Arabic five-pointed star * (U+066D), asterisk operator * (U+2217), and heavy asterisk ✳ (U+2731). Note that this list of Unicode characters resembling the asterisk in appearance is far from complete; there are many more, especially in the Dingbats block.

Circumflex accent ^ (U+005E)

This character, often called just "circumflex" or "arrow," is used for a variety of technical purposes—e.g., in programming and command languages. It might, for example, be used as an exponentiation operator in linear notation ($a^b = a^b$). In regular expression syntax (see Chapter 11), the circumflex matches the start of a string.

This character was introduced into ASCII for several purposes, including the use as a diacritic mark, with overprinting techniques. This never became common, and the usual shape of the character reflects much more the technical use: it is operator-like, relatively large, and rather different from a circumflex accent as used in a character like â. The name of the character is thus rather misleading.

In ASCII, this character has the primary name "upward arrow head," and "circumflex accent" appears there as a secondary name only.

Colon : (U+003A)

This character is used as a punctuation symbol in natural and other languages. The rules for using it vary from one language to another, and even from one authority to another.

The colon is also used when presenting ratios (proportions) as in "2:3," but in Unicode, you can use a more specific character, ratio U+2236.

Comma , (U+002C)

Primarily this character is a punctuation symbol in natural languages. The rules for using it vary from one language to another and even from one authority to another.

In numbers, some languages (mainly English) use comma as thousands separator (e.g., "1,234" means one thousand two hundred thirty-four) whereas in many other languages it is used as a decimal point (e.g., "1,234" means the same as "1.234" in English). The Unicode standard mentions "decimal separator" as another name for the comma.

In ASCII, the comma was intended to have secondary usage as cedilla.

The comma should not be confused with the Unicode character single low-9 quotation mark "," (U+201A), which is used in quotations in some usages.

Dollar sign $ (U+0024)

This character is a famous currency symbol, but its exact meaning is not quite clear. The Unicode standard explicitly says that this character is unambiguously dollar sign, not a generic currency symbol. On the other hand, this is not meant to limit the use to only those currencies that are named "dollar," still less the U.S. dollar only. The Unicode standard mentions "milreis" and "escudo" as alternative names for dollar sign, so obviously the symbol can be used to denote those currencies, too.

According to the Unicode standard, a glyph for the dollar sign may have one or two vertical bars. That is, the number of bars is a glyph difference, not character difference.

In computing, the dollar sign has secondary uses that may have nothing to do with any currency. For example, it can be a character that is allowed in identifiers, perhaps used to signal a reserved or otherwise special identifier.

Commercial at @ (U+0040)

This character was originally used in English in conjunction with unit prices in the meaning "each." Its name still reflects such usage, which is relatively rare, and often unknown in other languages.

This character has become most widely known as a separator in Internet email addresses, where it can be read as "at" rather naturally, as in *jkorpela@cs.tut.fi*. It has many other special uses, too, for example, in Perl to indicate that a symbol denotes an array.

There are many names in use in different languages for this character. Many of the names use words that try to describe the visual appearance or connotations, such as a monkey or a sitting cat and a long tail.

Equals sign = (U+003D)

This character is used to denote equality both in mathematics (as in $2 + 2 = 4$) and in other areas. It is distinct from the Unicode character $\equiv$ (identical to U+2261).

In programming languages, the equals sign very often means assignment—e.g., a = b + c means that the sum b + c is computed and the result is assigned to the variable a. This means that usually some other operator (such as ==, eq, or .EQ.) is used in a logical expression to test for equality.

Exclamation mark ! (U+0021)

This character is basically used as a punctuation character at the end of an exclamation. It is also used in mathematics to denote a factorial (as in "5!," which denotes $1 \times 2 \times 3 \times 4 \times 5$). Many other special usages exist; e.g., in the C programming language, the exclamation mark denotes a "not" operator (negation)! The Unicode standard mentions the alternate names "factorial" and "bang."

This character is also used as a substitute for a similar-looking character, Latin letter retroflex click (U+01C3) used in the orthography of some African languages, to denote a click sound—e.g., in the name "!Kung" (denoting a people in southern Africa). In principle, the two characters are distinct, despite similarity in glyph appearance.

Full stop "." (U+002E)

In U.S. English, this character is known as "period" (which was the name used for it in Unicode Version 1.0). It is commonly used as a punctuation character but also for other purposes. The Unicode standard mentions the alternative names "dot" and "decimal point."

The Unicode standard uses this character to illustrate the principle that "a character may have a broader range of use than the most literal interpretation of its name might indicate" and admits that the name of a character can be misleading. It says: "U+002E full stop can represent a sentence period, an abbreviation period, a decimal number separator in English, a thousands number separator in German, and so on." Note that the use of the full stop as a thousands separator is discouraged in several standards, which recommend the use of some space character instead.

In addition to such usages, programming languages and other notations often use the full stop for purposes that do not correspond to natural-language punctuation (or the name "full stop"!) at all. In particular, it is often used as a separator between components of a hierarchic name, so that foo.bar could denote the bar component of a structure named foo (which might be read as "foo's bar").

The Unicode standard mentions that this character "may be rendered as a raised decimal point in old style numbers." This is to be taken as a warning against interpreting such a character as a middle dot (·).

Grave accent ` (U+0060)

This character, often called just "grave," is used for a variety of technical purposes—e.g., in programming and command languages. For example, in many Unix shells, the grave accent is a quoting character with a special meaning, "command substitution" (sometimes even called "grave command"!). In such a case, the value of the expression `foo` is the output from executing the command foo.

This character was introduced into ASCII for several purposes, including the use as a diacritic mark, to produce characters like è with overprinting techniques. This never became common. The technical uses of the character also remained relatively limited because the character is not very visible and because it is easily confused with some other characters.

Sometimes the grave accent is used in normal text as a single quote, especially to create the appearance of "smart" (asymmetric) quotes. In such style, people use the grave accent instead of an opening single quote and either the apostrophe or (less often) the acute accent ´ instead of a closing single quote, as in `this' or `this´. In some fonts, this looks relatively correct because the glyphs for the grave accent and the acute accent are (rather questionably) curly, quote-like. In processing natural language texts, it is usually reasonable to assume that a grave accent is meant to act as a quotation mark of some kind, since there is not much other usage for it in normal text. However, sometimes, for example, e` might be used to mean è.

When the American National Standards Institute adopted ASCII as national standard, it added a provision for overloading the code positions 60 and 27 (hexadecimal) with the typographic characters left and right single quotation mark. This practice become widely used in some communities in the United States and is now found in numerous and still even some contemporary English-language ASCII files. Naturally, unless output routines specifically handle the issue, this means that text meant to display as 'foo' will appear as `foo'. The design of the grave accent and the ASCII apostrophe in fonts may reflect attempts to make things less distracting by making them resemble single quotes.

Greater-than sign > (U+003E)

This character primarily denotes a mathematical relation. It is widely used for some secondary purposes as well, such as in the role of a closing angle bracket, as described earlier.

Some programming languages avoid using > as an operator, or use it for some data types. A language might even have, say, > and "gt" as different "greater than" operators.

The character pair >= has often been used to mean "greater than or equal to." In Unicode, you can use the character greater-than or equal to ≥ (U+2265) instead.

Hyphen-minus "-" (U+002D)

This is a dual-purpose character: it can be used as a hyphen (punctuation character) or as a minus sign (mathematical symbol). It is usually called "hyphen" or "minus" depending on the context and meaning. The term "hyphen-minus" is used mostly in character standard contexts only. The Unicode standard mentions "hyphen or minus sign" as a synonym, but it is best avoided, since it often makes statements ambiguous.

Unicode contains two characters that can be used instead of the hyphen-minus character to resolve the ambiguity at character level: hyphen (U+2010) and minus sign (U+2212). This may help to produce a better visual appearance, too. Usually the hyphen is relatively short and the minus sign is rather long, comparable to an en dash. One of the problems with hyphen-minus is that its glyph is usually so short that it does not look good and prominent enough in expressions like "-1" (for "minus one").

It is common to use a hyphen or two hyphens "--" as a replacement for an en dash "–" or em dash "—", when the dashes cannot be used. There are other hyphen-like characters in Unicode as well, to be discussed later in the Punctuation section.

Less-than sign < (U+003C)

This character primarily denotes a mathematical relation. It is widely used for some secondary purposes as well, such as in the role of an angle bracket, as described earlier.

Some programming languages avoid using < as an operator, or use it for some data types. A language might even have, say, < and "lt" as different "less than" operators.

The character pair <= has often been used to mean "less than or equal to." In Unicode, you can use the character less-than or equal to ≤ (U+2264) instead.

Low line _ (U+005F)

This character is usually known as "underline" or "underscore."

Probably the most typical use of this character is to make long identifiers more readable in programming languages. Due to their general syntax, such languages generally do not allow spaces in identifiers; but several programming languages allow underscores in identifiers. For example, one could write number_of_events in such languages.

In plain text—e.g., in Usenet discussions—it is customary to use a low line before and after a word or phrase to indicate underlining of enclosed text, usually to denote emphasis (e.g., "this is _very_ important") due to lack of better methods. Some software automatically recognizes the notation and renders the expression in a more advanced way (e.g., "this is very important" or "this is *very* important").

One of the original ideas was to use the low line for underlining text using overprinting. This is irrelevant these days, but the character might be used to create a horizontal line in plain text. It depends on the font whether successive underline characters are joined (____) or not (_ _ _ _).

Number sign # (U+0023)

The name of this character reflects its use to mean "number," as in "item #42" (meaning "item number 42, the 42nd item"). Such usage is mostly limited to U.S. English. More often, the word "number" is abbreviated as nr., no., n., or N°. In U.S. English, the character is sometimes used to denote pound as a unit of weight (mass)—e.g., in the paper industry "70#" means "70 lb."

In computer languages, this character has many different uses, and it is usually called a *hash*. In some of these uses, it relates to ordinal numbers. For example in HTML and XML, &#n; denotes the character that occupies code position *n* in Unicode. Mostly the # character is just a separator (e.g., indicating the rest of the line as comment) or has some special meaning assigned to it more or less arbitrarily, with no connection with numbering. It is used in web addresses (URL references), and the URL syntax specification calls it "crosshatch" character. Many other names are used as well, such as "octothorpe."

The number sign character unambiguously occupies code position 23 hexadecimal in ISO Latin 1 and in Unicode. The Unicode standard mentions "pound sign" as an alternative name, but here "pound" means the unit of weight, not currency. Further confusion has been caused by the varying definitions of ASCII and ISO 636, since some definitions allow the position 23 to be used either for # or for £ (the pound sterling sign), as "agreed between interested parties." Some programs and devices might still reflect this in their behavior (displaying £ when the data contains #).

In Unicode (and ISO Latin 1), the pound sign £ (as a currency symbol) is a completely independent symbol in its own code position, U+00A3.

The number sign has also been used as a surrogate for music sharp sign U+266F, due to some similarity in appearance.

Percent sign % (U+0025)

This character is used after numbers, in the meaning "in the hundred" or "of each hundred." It is commonly used immediately after a number (e.g., 50%), but quite often, the official spelling requires a space (e.g., 50 %), although this depends on authority. In computer language notations, a space is often disallowed. For example, in a CSS stylesheet, `width: 50%` is correct, whereas `width: 50 %` would be incorrect. On the other hand, in natural languages, as well as in notations related to the International System of Units (SI), the official recommendations often require a space. If a space is used, it should be a no-break space, for obvious reasons.

In some situations, expressions like "o/o" are used instead of the percent sign. This might be a practical choice in a context where the per mille sign ‰ (U+2030) would be needed too but cannot be used due to technical restrictions. You might then use "o/oo" as a replacement, and therefore "o/o" too, for uniformity. However, contrary to popular belief, the percent sign has not evolved from "o/o" or "0/0" but from an abbreviation of the Latin words "pro cento," which mean "for a hundred."

In computer languages, the percent sign has very different uses, which might have nothing to do with percentages. For example, % is a modulus operator in C, and it indicates an identifier as a hash in Perl.

Plus sign + (U+002B)

This is the well-known plus sign, primarily used to denote addition and as a unary plus. It has many technical uses that have little or nothing to do with addition. It may indicate string concatenation, for example.

Question mark ? (U+003F)

This character is basically used as a punctuation character at the end of a direct question. The detailed rules for using it vary from one language to another and even from one authority to another. In some languages, some space is left before the question mark. In formal notations such as regular expressions, the question mark has special meanings. It could, for example, be a wildcard character that represents any single character.

Quotation mark " (U+0022)

This punctuation character is a "symmetric" quotation mark as opposite to "smart" or "asymmetric" quotation marks. That is, when this character is used to mark quotations, the opening quote is identical with the closing quote. Its glyph should be "neutral" (vertical) to reflect this. The Unicode standard explicitly says about it: "neutral (vertical), used as opening or closing quotation mark." However, in practice, the appearance varies, and some fonts have a slightly slanted glyph for the quotation mark.

It is sometimes difficult to find out what really happens, since text-processing programs (word processors) like MS Word typically convert a quotation mark to a different character, as described in Chapter 2. Pressing the " key often inserts a language-specific quotation mark, perhaps to a "smart" (curved) quotation mark in English text, a chevron (« or ») in French text, etc. Note that this means a replacement at the character level: the different quotation marks are different characters, not just different glyphs.

The name "quotation mark" is a historical relic: this character was the only double quotation mark used in computers when ASCII was developed. It was natural to call it just "quotation mark," and this name was kept even in Unicode. This creates problems, since often we need to talk about quotation marks in general (as we will do later in the section "General Punctuation"), but there is no official name for U+0022 that would let us identify it in such contexts. Thus, we may need to identify it by its code, or use an unofficial name like "ASCII quotation mark" or "machine quotation mark." Typographers may call the character an inch symbol, but this is actually incorrect: although the ASCII quotation mark is often used as a substitute for an inch symbol, the appropriate Unicode character for inch is the double prime U+2033.

When typewriters were designed, several simplifications were made to the use of characters. For physical and economic reasons, the character repertoire was kept small. Early typewriters often lacked even the digits 0 and 1, on the grounds that you could use letters "O" and "l" instead! Similarly, only one double quotation mark was included. The key cap might actually have a curved glyph like ", to confuse us more. This approach was copied to early computer keyboards, and that's what we still mostly live with.

At the character level, this means that there is a huge amount of text data (both plain text and other formats) that uses the ASCII quotation mark for normal quotations. The use of ASCII quotation marks has become so common that you often find it even in printed matter and in other contexts where the author had no compelling technical reason to do so.

Why would you use the ASCII quotation mark in text processing? Well, if your text discusses C or JavaScript code or Unix commands, then the ASCII quotation mark is the correct character—e.g., in an assignment like `str = "foo"`. Using a "smart" (curved) quotation mark would not be smart at all in such cases.

The Unicode standard explicitly says that "APL quote" is identical with the quotation mark. In addition to that, the quotation mark is used in many other programming and command languages, typically to delimit string constants. In some of such languages, a string can be delimited using either quotation marks or apostrophes with no change in meaning, whereas in some others there is a definite difference. For example, in the C language, quotation marks delimit string constants whereas apostrophes delimit character constants; in Perl, quotation marks allow variable substitution within the string, whereas apostrophes indicate a pure literal.

The quotation mark is often used instead of different symbols such as the inch sign, due to similarity in appearance. Table 8-2 shows some of them.

Table 8-2. Symbols that are often replaced by a quotation mark

Name	Code	Character	Proper use
Double prime	U+2033	″	Inches or (in angles and times) seconds
Ditto mark	U+3003	〃	Repetition of information, "the same"
Modifier letter double prime	U+20BA	″	E.g., transliteration of Cyrillic "hard sign"

In ASCII, the quotation mark was intended to have secondary usage as dieresis (see section "Diacritic Marks" later in this chapter). That is, you were supposed to overprint, say, the letter "a" with a quotation mark to produce something that looks like ä. This was an odd idea, but it may have affected the design of some fonts.

Reverse solidus \ (U+005C)

This character is best known under the name "backslash." It has a wide range of uses in technical contexts—e.g., as a separator in hierarchical filenames in Windows and in several "escape notations," such as '\n', which denotes line break character in many programming languages (see Chapter 11 for more examples). The reverse solidus was taken into character repertoires for special usage, such as to allow the construction of symbols ∨ and ∧ for logical *and* and logical *or* from the reverse solidus and the solidus. This never became common, but quite different other uses were invented.

The reverse solidus is especially suitable for use in "escape notations" just because it is, in a sense, an artificial creation. Since it is not used in normal text, it will less likely be confused with normal data characters than other characters that might be used for "escaping." However, confusion may still arise when different notational systems that use the reverse solidus (for different purposes) are combined.

In Unicode, the reverse solidus is regarded as distinct from set minus U+2216, which is used in mathematics as an operator on sets (meaning set difference), but conceivably, \ can be used as a surrogate for that character.

Rather often, the reverse solidus is confused with the solidus (slash) character, /. They are similar in shape, just slanted differently. But they are quite distinct characters and have different uses. They are rarely interchangeable. However, Internet Explorer treats the reverse solidus in a URL (where it is not permitted by the URL syntax) as the solidus.

Semicolon ; (U+003B)

This character is used as a punctuation symbol in natural and other languages. It is often used as a separator in lists of numbers with commas as the decimal separator (for example, "1,2; 1,3; 1,5," corresponding to "1.2, 1.3, 1.5" in common English notation). In many programming languages, semicolon is the statement separator or terminator.

Solidus / (U+002F)

The name "solidus" was taken from British English. This character is much more widely known as "slash" (which was its name in Unicode Version 1.0). It is sometimes called "virgule" or even "shilling" (which are alternative names mentioned in the Unicode standard) or "diagonal." Do not confuse it with the reverse solidus (backslash, \). Sometimes the solidus is called "forward slash" to distinguish it from the backslash.

The solidus is used for many different purposes, typically as a separator of some kind. Ambiguities easily arise. For example, a date notation like 3/4 might mean the 3rd of April, or the 4th of March. In the ISO 8601 notation for dates, the solidus is used when expressing a time interval (e.g., 1998-03-04/04-03 unambiguously means "from 4th of March to 3rd of April in 1998").

Sometimes the solidus separates alternatives—e.g., on a form, with the suggestion to strike out the inapplicable alternative(s). In natural languages, the solidus is often used in a very confusing way, so that "foo/bar" might mean "foo or bar" or "foo alias bar" or "foo and bar," or something else. The ambiguity created that way might be intentional.

In HTML (and in other SGML- or XML-based markup languages), start and end tags are distinguished from each other by the presence of a solidus in the end tag, so that, for example, `</cite>` means "end of cite element."

In web addresses and other URLs, the solidus is a separator between hierarchic components. This usage is historically based on similar usage in pathnames in hierarchic filesystems.

Unicode defines fraction slash U+2044 and division slash U+2215 as characters distinct from solidus and from each other. The fraction slash is meant for use in fractional numbers, whereas the division sign is a division operator. In Unicode encoded data, you do not *need* to use these characters with more specific semantics; Unicode just *allows* you to make a distinction. The fraction slash may have a special visual effect, creating a vulgar fraction, as discussed in the section "The Number Forms Block" later in this chapter.

Space " " (U+0020)

This is the well-known space character, also known as "blank." The abbreviation SP is often used for the name of the character. Sometimes the character symbol for space ␠ (U+2420) is used in instructions and descriptions referring to the use of a space. The ISO 8859-1 standard defines the space character formally as follows:

> This character may be interpreted as a graphic character, a control character or as both. As a graphic character it has the visual representation consisting of the absence of a graphic symbol.

Usually a font contains a glyph for a space, but the glyph is empty (blank): it just takes some space. The width of a space varies considerably. Programs might also interpret a space as a control character—e.g., so that instead of using a particular glyph, the program just leaves some empty space. The width of this spacing may vary by circumstances. In particular, the inter-word gaps can be of different widths in visual presentation especially when text is justified on both sides. Thus, spaces might be "stretchable" as well as "shrinkable." This will be discussed in "General Punctuation" later in the chapter.

The term *whitespace character* is often used in programming and markup contexts. It is a generalization of the space character and denotes a set of characters, typically including at least the space, some line break characters, and horizontal tab. The vertical tab is often included, too. For example, in the C programming language, the standard function `isspace()` tests for its argument being a whitespace character, not just a space.

Tilde ~ (U+007E)

This character has mixed usage. The word "tilde" is of Spanish origin and refers to a wavy diacritic mark, as in Spanish ñ (although in Spanish, the word "tilde" often denotes the acute accent, too!). The name of this character thus reflects one of the originally intended uses. Currently such use has little to do with tilde as an ASCII and Unicode character. In jargon, names like "squiggle" and "twiddle" are used.

In practice, tilde is used for a variety of technical purposes according to specific rules— e.g., in programming and command languages. For example, in many Unix shells, ~ denotes the user's home directory. Reflecting this tradition, on many web servers, people's web pages are named in a manner that involves the tilde character. In Windows systems, the mapping of Windows filenames to DOS-compatible filenames ("8+3 characters") uses tilde; e.g., *LONGFILENAME.TXT* may get mapped to *LONGFI~1.TXT*. In the C language, the tilde denotes a bitwise operator that complements each bit. In Perl, the tilde is used in matching operators.

The glyph for tilde has varying shapes. Sometimes it looks like a diacritic tilde, but much more often it looks like an operator, placed vertically at the same level as a hyphen "-" or a little higher. The different uses of the tilde make it impossible to design a glyph that would be suitable for all, or even most, of the uses.

The overall tone in the Unicode standard is that the tilde character could and should often be replaced by characters with more specific semantics and more appropriate visual appearance. Care must be taken, however, since many computer languages explicitly define the tilde as the character to be used. Thus, the following recommendations apply basically to other contexts, such as prose texts, and only with caution:

- For a symbol for *negation* in formal logic, use the not sign ¬ (U+00AC).
- As a symbol for *approximate value*, use the almost equal to sign ≈ (U+2248).
- In other *mathematical* meanings like "varies with," "is proportional to," "is similar to," etc., use the tilde operator ∼ (U+223C).
- As punctuation to denote *alternation* as well as in dictionary usage to indicate *repetition* of the defined term in examples, the visually wider character swung dash U+2053 is preferred in principle. However, almost all fonts lack this character, which was added to Unicode in Version 4.
- As a spacing clone of a *diacritic tilde* (i.e., spacing counterpart of combining tilde U+0303), use the small tilde ˜ (U+02CD).

In ASCII, the tilde character has the primary name "overline" and a corresponding appearance; "tilde" was a secondary name only.

Vertical line | (U+007C)

This character is commonly known as "vertical bar" or just "bar." It is most typically used in formal languages (such as Backus–Naur Form, BNF) between alternatives, corresponding to the word "or." In mathematics, vertical lines are used around an expression to denote its absolute value—e.g., |−42| = 42. In some dictionaries, a vertical line is used to indicate a possible hyphenation point; there is also a quite different dictionary usage: to separate the invariable part of a word from the rest in a paragraph that describes several words that begin the same way (e.g., imitat|e ... -ion ... -ive). Several other usages exist, too, especially in technical contexts. In Unix shells, for example, this character is used to denote "piping," and the character itself is then often known as "pipe." For example, in Unix shells, ls | more means "execute the ls program directing its output to the more program as input."

When discussing characters in general, the name "vertical line" is preferable to "vertical bar," since in Unicode, there are several other characters named as vertical bar symbols. Among them, even light vertical bar U+2658 is intended to be thicker than vertical line!

In some old fonts and keyboards, this character appears as a broken vertical line. However, in Unicode (and Latin 1), the broken bar (¦) is a completely distinct character, though very little used.

ASCII Control Characters (C0 Controls)

Character codes often contain code positions that are not assigned to any visible character but might be used for control purposes. For example, in communication betwee n a terminal and a computer using the ASCII code, the computer could regard octet 3 as a request for terminating the currently running process. Some older character code standards contain explicit descriptions of such conventions. Newer standards just reserve some positions for such usage, to be defined in separate standards or agreements such as "C0 controls" (discussed below) and "C1 controls," or specifically ISO 6429, which is equivalent to ECMA-48, available from *http://www.ecma-international.com*.

ASCII, Unicode, and other standards reserve some code positions for eventual use for control purposes. Usually only a few of them, mainly those for line breaks, are defined in the standard itself. Somewhat confusingly, a standard may assign a *name* to such a code position. Such names (as in Table 8-3) may relate to actual or proposed usage, but they must not be taken as defining the meaning, or even as describing the most common usage.

Unicode does not assign official names to control codes, but in practice, various names and abbreviations taken from other standards are used. For example, U+000A is commonly called "line feed" (or "linefeed") or briefly "LF."

Control characters or control codes?

It is a matter of rather arbitrary definition whether you regard "control characters" as characters or just codes (code positions reserved for control purposes). In character code standards, they are usually called characters. It is however important to realize that a "control character" has no visual appearance as such (not even emptiness). Instead, their control effects may include visual formatting.

When people read or write about characters, their idea of character may or may not include control characters. Usually the context and content will help in resolving this. For example, if someone says that a font has the same width for all characters, he is clearly excluding control characters, since they normally have no width.

Types of control characters

Control codes can be used for *device control* such as cursor movement, page eject, or changing colors. Quite often, they are used in combination with codes for graphic characters, so that a device driver is expected to interpret the combination as a specific command and not display the graphic character(s) contained in it. For example, in the classical VT100 controls, ESC followed by the code corresponding to the letter "A" or something more complicated (depending on mode settings) moves the cursor up. To take a different example, the Emacs editor treats `ESC a` as a request to move to the beginning of a sentence. Note that the ESC control code is logically distinct from the ESC key in a keyboard, and many other things than pressing ESC might cause the ESC control code to be sent. Also note that phrases like "escape sequence" are often used to refer to things that do not involve ESC at all and operate at a quite different level, such as writing \" to include the character " as data, instead of having it interpreted as a delimiter.

One possible form of device control is changing the way a device interprets the data (octets) that it receives. For example, a control code followed by some data in a specific format might be interpreted so that any subsequent octets to be interpreted according to a table are identified in some specific way. This is often called "code page switching," and it means that control codes could be used to change the character encoding. It is then more logical to consider the control codes and associated data at the level of fundamental interpretation of data rather than direct device control. The international standard ISO 2022 defines powerful facilities for using different 8-bit character codes in a document. However, such approaches did not gain popularity, and nowadays, Unicode has made them rather unimportant.

Widely used *formatting* control codes include carriage return (CR), linefeed (LF), and horizontal tab (HT), which in ASCII occupy code positions 13, 10, and 9. The names (or abbreviations) suggest generic meanings, but the actual meanings are defined partly in each character code definition, partly—and more important—by various other conventions above the character level. The formatting codes were previously often seen as a special case of device control, but nowadays, they are rather treated as indicating the line structure of text; see the section "Line Structure Control" later in this chapter.

The *horizontal tabulation* HT (TAB) character, or tab for short, was previously used for real "tabbing" to some predefined writing position (tab stop), as on typewriters. The tab character is nowadays not used much for such purposes, partly because tab stop settings may vary, partly because more advanced tools (such as tables) exist. However the tab is often used to indicate data boundaries, without implying any particular presentational effect. In particular, the "tab separated values" (TSV) data format is used to transfer data between spreadsheet applications, using line breaks to separate records (rows) and tabs to separate fields (cells) within records.

Visible symbols for control characters

Although a control character cannot have a graphic presentation (a glyph) in the same way as normal characters have, we sometimes use visual symbols to indicate the presence of control characters in a data stream. In Unicode, there is a separate block, Control Pictures, for such purposes. These characters have different shapes in different fonts—e.g., $^{E}_{SC}$ or $^{E}_{SC}$. They are of course quite distinct from the control codes they symbolize. The symbol for escape $^{E}_{SC}$ (U+241B) is not the same as the escape U+001B.

In manuals and instructions where you need to explicitly indicate the use of spaces, you might use the blank symbol ␢ (U+2422) or the open box ␣ (U+2423). The latter is probably more common and more easily recognizable. There is no specific character for indicating the Enter or Return key; a small image probably works best. Sometimes the symbol for newline ␤ (U+2424) is used. Beware that glyphs for it vary considerably, though they generally contain the letters "NL" in some style.

If you display a text file containing octets in the C0 Controls on MS-DOS or in the DOS-like mode in Windows, you may get graphic characters like ☺. This is because in some Windows code pages (such as CP 437), octets in that range are treated as graphic characters. For a list, see *http://czyborra.com/charsets/codepages.html*.

On the other hand, a control code might occasionally be displayed, by some programs, in a visible form, perhaps describing the control action rather than the code. For example, upon receiving octet 3 in the example situation just described, a program might echo back (onto the terminal) *** or INTERRUPT or ^C. All such notations are program-specific conventions. Some control codes are sometimes named in a manner that seems to bind them to characters. In particular, control codes 1, 2, 3,... are often called control-A, control-B, control-C, etc. (or CTRL-A or Ctrl-A or C-A). This is associated with the fact that on many keyboards, control codes can be sent to a computer by using a special key labeled "Control" or "Ctrl" or something like that together with letter keys "A," "B," "C," etc. This in turn is related to the fact that the code numbers of characters and control codes have been assigned so that the code of "Control-X" is obtained from the code of the uppercase letter "X" by a simple operation (subtracting 64 decimal). However, such things imply no real relationships between letters and control codes. The control code 3, or "Control-C," is not a variant of letter C at all, and its meaning is not associated with the meaning of C.

Summary of C0 Controls

Although the meanings of control characters depend on specific agreements and often vary greatly, many of them have typical uses, which are reflected in their commonly used names. The following table contains additional notes on the usage, especially in text data. If you design an application or data format that uses C0 Controls, it is up to you to assign meanings to them. It is however advisable to use assignments that correspond to common usage, partly because this helps to avoid clashes with assignments in software that might interact with your system.

The C0 Controls consist of the first 32 code positions (U+0000..U+001F) in Unicode and ASCII as well as the last position in ASCII, U+007F. Table 8-3 lists their ASCII names. The primary Unicode names are somewhat different: U+0009 is character tabulation, U+000C is line tabulation, and U+001C..U+001F are information separator four, three, two, and one.

Table 8-3. C0 Controls

Code	Abbr.	Name	Ctrl-x	Typical usage
0000	NUL	Null	Ctrl-@	Data or time fill, or terminator
0001	SOH	Start of heading	Ctrl-A	Starts a message header
0002	STX	Start of text	Ctrl-B	Starts a message body
0003	ETX	End of text	Ctrl-C	End of text entity
0004	EOT	End of transmission	Ctrl-D	End of sending one or more texts
0005	ENQ	Enquiry	Ctrl-E	Asks for identification
0006	ACK	Acknowledge	Ctrl-F	Affirmative response
0007	BEL	Bell	Ctrl-G	Alarm, often audible (beep)
0008	BS	Backspace	Ctrl-H	One character position backward
0009	HT	Horizontal tabulation	Ctrl-I	Move to next tab stop; separator
000A	LF	Line feed	Ctrl-J	One line downward; line break
000B	VT	Vertical tabulation	Ctrl-K	Move downward
000C	FF	Form feed	Ctrl-L	Page eject; page separator
000D	CR	Carriage return	Ctrl-M	Move to start of line; line break
000E	SO	Shift out	Ctrl-N	Shift out from alternate code page
000F	SI	Shift in	Ctrl-O	Switch to alternate code page
0010	DLE	Data link escape	Ctrl-P	Data transmission control
0011	DC1	Device control one	Ctrl-Q	Resume data transmission
0012	DC2	Device control two	Ctrl-R	Special mode of device operation
0013	DC3	Device control three	Ctrl-S	Pause data transmission
0014	DC4	Device control four	Ctrl-T	Deactivate ancillary device
0015	NAK	Negative acknowledge	Ctrl-U	Negative response to sender
0016	SYN	Synchronous idle	Ctrl-V	Synchronization of transmission
0017	ETB	End of transmission block	Ctrl-W	Transmission of data in blocks
0018	CAN	Cancel	Ctrl-X	Ignore preceding data
0019	EM	End of medium	Ctrl-Y	End of medium or recorded data
001A	SUB	Substitute	Ctrl-Z	Indicates invalid/erroneous data

Code	Abbr.	Name	Ctrl-x	Typical usage
001B	ESC	Escape	Ctrl-[	Starts a control command
001C	FS	File separator	Ctrl-\	Delimits a set of data (file)
001D	GS	Group separator	Ctrl-]	Delimits a data group
001E	RS	Record separator	Ctrl-^	Delimits a line or other record
001F	US	Unit separator	Ctrl-_	Delimits a unit (field) of data
007F	DEL	Delete		Data or time fill

The DEL character was originally used on punched tapes to delete a character by making all seven bits to one. This explains its code position. Later it has been used as a fill in a data stream. Do not confuse it with the effect of a Delete (or Del or Rubout) key, which often sends the code for backspace (BS, Ctrl-H).

Normal plain text data seldom contains C0 Controls except CR and LF to indicate line breaks, sometimes HT to indicate tabbing, and rarely VT or FF for vertical spacing. When reading text data in a program, occurrences of other C0 Controls can typically be treated as symptoms of data errors, unless there is a special agreement to use them.

C1 Controls include, loosely speaking, the corresponding set of control characters in the upper half of 8-bit character codes, Unicode range U+0080..U+009F. However, there are different assignments for those positions, see *http://www.itscj.ipsj.or.jp/ISO-IR/2-6.htm*. Note that in Windows and Macintosh character sets, many of these positions have been assigned to graphic characters.

Latin-1 Supplement (ISO 8859-1)

The Latin-1 Supplement block in Unicode is the same as the upper half of ISO 8859-1. In ISO 8859-1, these characters are those that have the most significant bit set—i.e., characters in code positions from 128 to 255 in decimal. This means the range U+0020 to U+00FF in Unicode.

Like the ASCII repertoire, the Latin-1 Supplement contains a mixture of characters for historical reasons, sometimes for no good reason. This means that many of the characters in it would belong to other blocks, if blocks were formed purely according to the meanings of characters. For example, the multiplication sign × would really belong to the Mathematical Operators block. However, Unicode was designed to preserve all the code point assignments in ISO 8859-1.

While all printable ASCII characters have got some widespread use at least in specialized notations, many of the Latin-1 Supplement characters have very little use. There was less need for assigning arbitrary meanings to characters. You will hardly find any use for a character like broken bar ¦, for example.

The Latin-1 Supplement was designed to cover the needs of most languages spoken in Western or Northern Europe. These languages use the Latin alphabet as the basis but also contain various diacritical marks, a few extra letters. In its repertoire of punctuation characters, the Latin-1 Supplement is illogical: it contains, for example, the chevrons (« and ») but not the "smart quotes" used in English. However, it can be argued that the ASCII quotation mark can be reasonably used as a substitute for smart quotes but not chevrons.

Diacritic Marks and Letters with Them

The Latin-1 Supplement contains Latin letters with diacritic marks as used in languages of Western and Northern Europe. It covers only a small fraction of all such characters. As we can see from Table 8-4, the characters do not constitute a systematic grid. Even more unsystematically, the uppercase form of ÿ (Ÿ, U+0178) does not belong to the Latin-1 Supplement.

Table 8-4. The unsystematic grid of diacritic marks in the Latin-1 Supplement

Lowercase letters					
à	á	â	ã	ä	å
è	é	ê		ë	
ì	í	î		ï	
ò	ó	ô	õ	ö	
ù	ú	û		ü	
	ý			ÿ	
			ñ		
					ç

The use of diacritic marks is strongly *language-dependent*. It will be discussed later in the section "Diacritic Marks" (where we mention some additional marks, too).

The following characters are spacing clones of diacritic marks, and they have very little use as characters (see notes in the section "Diacritic Marks" later in this chapter):

- Acute accent ´ (U+00B4), which is a clone of the combining acute accent U+0301.
- Cedilla ¸ (U+00B8), which is a clone of the combining cedilla U+0327.
- Dieresis ¨ (U+00A8), which is a clone of the combining dieresis U+0308.
- Macron ¯ (U+00AF), which is a clone of the combining macron U+0304.

The acute accent is often used as an apostrophe (e.g., "John´s"), since it resembles a typographically correct apostrophe more than the ASCII apostrophe does. Such usage may confuse both human readers and computer programs.

The macron occasionally has some special uses. The Unicode standard mentions "overline" and "APL overbar" as synonyms for this character. Consecutive macrons connect in many fonts, so the character can be used to create a long line (‾‾‾‾).

Other Letters

The feminine ordinal indicator ª (U+00AA) and the masculine ordinal indicator º (U+00BA) can be regarded as letters, too. These characters are defined as compatibility characters that are equivalent to letters "a" and "o" in superscript style, but they are meant to be used in specific contexts only. They are used in Spanish after numbers to indicate an ordinal number of feminine or masculine gender, respectively. For example, 1^a = primera, 1° = primero, both meaning "first." The masculine ordinal indicator is very often confused with the degree sign (see "Mathematical, Logical, and Physical Symbols" later in this chapter).

Characters in Table 8-5 are regarded as independent letters, although some of them are historically combinations of two letters or a letter and a diacritic. Only the short names are given here; full names are "Latin capital letter AE," "Latin small letter ae," etc.

Table 8-5. Special letters in Latin-1 Supplement

Glyphs	Codes	Name	Usage notes (not exhaustive)
Ææ	U+00C6, U+00E6	Letter ae	Scandinavian languages, English, IPA
Ðð	U+00D0, U+00F0	Eth	Icelandic (as voiced "th" in English)
Þþ	U+00DE, U+00FE	Thorn	Icelandic (as unvoiced "th" in English)
Øø	U+00D8, U+00F8	O with stroke	Danish, Norwegian, Faroese, IPA
ß	U+00DF	Sharp s	German, denotes unvoiced "s" sound

In modern German orthography, the sharp "s," ß, is used after a long vowel only. It has no uppercase equivalent. When converting data to uppercase, ß is replaced by "SS."

The following characters are not regarded as letters, despite being historically formed from stylized letters: ¢, £, ¥, ©, ®, and µ (micro sign).

Superscript Digits (¹ ² ³) and Vulgar Fractions (¼ ½ ¾)

In Unicode, there are versions of digits used as superscripts or subscripts coded as separate characters. Only the superscripts corresponding to 1, 2, and 3 belong to Latin-1 Supplement. The first one is not used much, but the others have common usage—e.g., in denoting square meter (m^2) and cubic meter (m^3). The others are in the block Superscripts and Subscripts, discussed later. The Latin-1 Supplement contains two characters that may *look* like superscript 0: the degree sign (°) and the masculine ordinal indicator (°).

The so-called vulgar fractions are characters denoting fractional numbers as single characters. In Latin-1 Supplement, there are such characters for the fractions 1/4, 1/2, and 3/4 (namely ¼, ½, and ¾). This reflects the character repertoire on many typewriters. Depending on the font, the bar (which corresponds to fraction slash) can be horizontal or slanted.

For usage notes, see the section "Mathematical and Technical Symbols" later in this chapter.

Punctuation

Latin-1 Supplement has just a few punctuation characters:

- Left-pointing angle quotation mark « (U+00AB) and right-pointing angle quotation mark » (U+00BB), often called *guillemets* or *chevrons* and used as normal quotation marks—e.g., in French, as in the following: Il a dit : « L'État, c'est moi. »

- Inverted exclamation mark ¡ (U+00A1). It is used in Spanish and some other languages at the beginning of an exclamation. The exclamation is terminated by a normal exclamation mark—for example: ¡Buenos días, señor!

- Inverted question mark ¿ (U+00BF). It is used in Spanish and some other languages at the beginning of a question. The question is terminated by a normal question mark —for example: ¿Cómo está usted?

- Soft hyphen (U+00AD), which is either rendered as normal hyphen-minus "-" or not rendered at all (and treated as invisible hyphenation hint). It will be discussed later in conjunction with other hyphen-like characters in the section "General Punctuation" later in this chapter.

Currency Symbols

Cent sign ¢ (U+00A2) is used in many countries. It is most widely known as the symbol for "cent" as one hundredth of the U.S. dollar. In the English language, this character is written immediately after a number—e.g., 75¢. It is never used when writing a sum of money that begins with dollar sign ($); in such cases, cents are indicated as fractions of dollar—e.g., $0.75, $49.95.

The currency unit euro is divided into 100 cents, also known as eurocents. There is no recommendation on using the cent sign as a symbol for cent in that meaning. Different abbreviations like "c" and "ct" are used for the eurocent.

Currency sign ¤ (U+00A4) has no definite semantics. It is hardly ever used in normal text. Most naturally, it is used as a *generic* currency symbol: a placeholder for actual currency symbols. Localization settings in software may use the currency sign in patterns used to specify the formatting of monetary quantities. For example, in such settings, the string "1,1 ¤" might be the way to tell the system to put the currency symbol (to be specified in another setting) after the number and separated from it with a space.

When data in ISO 8859-15 encoding is displayed by a program that does not support that encoding or does not properly recognize information about the encoding, the program typically defaults to displaying the data as if it were ISO 8859-1 encoded. Thus, an octet intended to represent the euro sign € would be displayed as the currency sign, ¤.

Pound sign £ (U+00A3) is best known as denoting the pound as the currency unit of the United Kingdom. It may be used for other currencies as well. The Unicode standard distinguishes the pound sign from the lira sign ₤ (U+20A4), which has two crossbars, as opposed to one crossbar in the pound sign. On the other hand, the standard says that the lira sign is not used much and that the preferred sign for lira is £ (U+00A3).

Yen sign ¥ (U+00A5) has an alternative name "yuan," reflecting its dual use for the currencies of Japan and China. A glyph for the character may have one or two crossbars, with no difference in meaning.

The euro sign, €, does not belong to the Latin-1 Supplement block but to the Currency Symbols block, discussed in the section "Other Blocks" later in this chapter.

Mathematical, Logical, and Physical Symbols

There is a limited and rather haphazard set of mathematically oriented symbols in Latin-1 Supplement. Together with the characters in Basic Latin, such as +, -, and /, they let us write very simple arithmetic expressions.

Degree sign ° (U+00B0) denotes temperature in degrees (e.g., 100 °F, 38 °C) or degrees when expressing angles (e.g., 90° angle). Notice that when a temperature is expressed in kelvins, the degree sign is not used; the symbol of kelvin is simply K (e.g., 311 K).

According to the rules of the SI system of units, a space should be used between a numeric value and a unit symbol, with the exception of angle notations like 30°22′8″. When the degree sign is used for temperatures, the normal rule applies (e.g., 42 °C). A no-break space can be used instead of a normal space to prevent undesired line breaks.

In practice, you may find the degree sign used for different other purposes, too. The Unicode standard even mentions (in 14.2: Letterlike Symbols): "Legacy data encoded in ISO/IEC 8859-1 (Latin-1) or other 8-bit character sets may also have represented the numero sign by a sequence of 'N' followed by the degree sign (U+00B0 DEGREE SIGN). Implementations interworking with legacy data should be aware of such alternative representations for the numero sign when converting data." This statement describes legacy data rather than adequate use of the degree sign.

The degree sign is not the same as masculine ordinal indicator (º), although the glyphs for the two characters may look similar. In Chapter 1, we discussed some of the reasons for being strict in such issues. The degree sign is not to be confused with superscript zero U+2070 (digit "0" in superscript style) either.

Division sign ÷ (U+00F7) is a mathematical symbol that mostly denotes division. Its intended scope of use is unclear. It has been used in school mathematics, as in "100 ÷ 5 makes 20." In some numeric keypads of computer keyboards, there is a key with the ÷ symbol, which means division in calculator usage but may generate the solidus / when used for character input.

It is probably best to avoid using the division sign, except in special cases where its meaning can be made clear. It has no tangible benefits over using the solidus /. Moreover, the symbol ÷ is also used to denote *subtraction* in Denmark and elsewhere in Europe.

Micro sign μ (U+00B5) corresponds to the prefix "micro-" and denotes division by one million when used as prefix of a unit. For example, "μm" is micrometer—i.e., one millionth of a meter (previously called "micron" and denoted by "μ" alone).

This character is historically based on the Greek letter mu. In Unicode, these characters are however distinct. On the other hand, Unicode defines micro sign as a compatibility character which has Greek small letter mu U+03BC as its compatibility decomposition.

In Unicode Version 4, the sample glyphs for the micro sign and the letter mu look very similar, if not identical. In many fonts, however, there are differences, which vary from hardly noticeable to substantial. In Times New Roman, for example, the glyphs are µ (micro) and μ (mu).

Multiplication sign × (U+00D7) is a mathematical symbol denoting multiplication. Examples: "2×2 makes 4," where × can be read as "times"; "a 5×10 metres area," where × can be read as "by." In biology, this character is used when naming hybrids—e.g., *Salix ×capreola* indicates that the species results from hybridization, and *Agrostis stolonifera × Polypogon monspeliensis* is a "hybrid formula" that indicates the hybrid of two named species. The Unicode standard mentions an alternative name "z notation Cartesian product," reflecting the usage for Cartesian (direct) product of sets. Cf. to the middle dot (·), discussed in "Specialized Characters" later in the chapter.

Not sign ¬ (U+00AC) denotes logical negation, though mostly in formal logic texts only, not in programming languages. Even logic texts often use the Basic Latin character ~ (tilde) instead. The Unicode standard also mentions that in typography, this character is called an "angled dash."

MS Word displays an "optional hyphen" (i.e., an invisible hyphenation hint) as ¬ when in "show formatting" (Show ¶) mode. It was probably chosen partly because the not sign looks like a hyphen with a special mark on it, and partly just because it is a conveniently available character that rarely appears in running text.

Plus-minus sign ± (U+00B1) means "plus or minus." It has different uses:

- It is sometimes used to refer to two quantities at the same time, as in "the solutions of the equation $x^2 - 4 = 0$ are ±2," meaning that the solutions are +2 and −2.

- It is also used to indicate an interval of uncertainty in measurements and estimates, as in "according to the measurements, the weight is 42.4 kg ± 0.5 kg." This means that the weight is expected to be between $42.4 - 0.5$ and $42.4 + 0.5$ kilograms. Typically, this does not specify absolute limits; the quantity after the ± sign is often some statistical measure like standard deviation. According to rules for using the SI, notations like $42.4 ± 0.5$ kg should not be used; you should either repeat the unit as above or use parentheses: $(42.4 ± 0.5)$ kg to make it "completely clear to which unit symbols the numerical values of the quantities belong."

- Yet another (informal) usage seems to be to let ± denote "about, circa" (e.g., "he is ±50 years old"), which can be quite confusing.

When the character repertoire is limited to Basic Latin, the string "+/-" is commonly used instead of ±.

Specialized Characters

Broken bar ¦ (U+00A6) has no specific meaning. In some old fonts (and keyboards), the vertical line | character appears as a broken line. For no apparent reason, this variant has been coded as a separate character in Latin-1. The Unicode standard mentions that an alternative name for the character in typography is "parted rule."

Copyright sign © (U+00A9) consists of letter C in a circle, and it is used in copyright statements, such as "© 2006 Jukka K. Korpela." The character can be used instead of or in addition to the word "copyright," partly because the character is, in principle, language-neutral and universal.

Middle dot · (U+00B7) is a multi-purpose character, which was originally included into Latin 1 due to its use as punctuation in the Catalan language. It is more often used as a special character, usually as multiplication sign of a kind. Uses include the following:

- In the SI system of units, a middle dot, called "half-high dot" or "raised dot" in that context, can be used when denoting the product of two or more units—e.g., "N·m" (newton multiplied by meter). An alternative is to use a space (e.g., "N m"). See notes on multiplication symbols in "Mathematical and Technical Symbols" later in this chapter.

- In *mathematics*, a middle dot is often used as a multiplication symbol. If such a symbol is needed—note that in algebra it is often implied: *ab* means *a* multiplied by *b*—then it is usually better to use the multiplication sign (×).

- In *chemistry*, a middle dot is used in some cases to separate major parts of a complex formula such as components of a double salt. Example: $K_2SO_4 \cdot Al_2(SO_4)_3$.

- In *Catalan*, the middle dot is used to distinguish between "ll" and "l·l," which are pronounced differently. In Unicode, there are separate characters Latin capital letter "l" with middle dot (U+013F) and Latin small letter "l" with middle dot (U+0140), but they are compatibility equivalent to letter "L" or "l" followed by the middle dot. However, typographers have differing views on Catalan middle dots.

- In *dictionaries*, the middle dot is used as a surrogate for hyphenation point U+2027 —i.e., to indicate correct word breaking as in dic·tion·ar·ies.

- In *Greek*, the middle dot is often used for a punctuation character "ano teleia," which should actually appear higher than the middle dot. Unicode has Greek ano teleia (U+0387) as a separate character, but it has the middle dot as its canonical mapping. However, in several fonts, Greek ano teleia is an upper dot, not a middle dot, so it is a better punctuation character for Greek texts when it is available.

Note that a raised decimal point should not be interpreted as a middle dot but as a full stop "." character in particular usage and style.

The middle dot is distinct from the following characters: bullet (U+2022), one dot leader (U+2024), bullet operator (U+2219), dot operator (U+22C5), and hyphenation point (U+2027). However, it is often used as a surrogate for them—e.g., as a small list bullet, although it is not visually suitable for such use, since the glyph for middle dot is typically rather small.

No-break space " " (U+00A0) is used in place of a normal space character as a "binding space," to prevent a line break between words or other expressions. It will be discussed in detail in "General Punctuation" later in this chapter.

Pilcrow sign ¶ (U+00B6) is a "section sign in some European usage," as the Unicode standard puts it. In old manuscripts, there was a tendency to present a new paragraph by writing a pilcrow sign and continuing in-line, due to the considerable cost of the recording media in those days. However, such usage is now largely outdated, and the character is used as a marker for special notes.

The pilcrow sign appears as paragraph sign (and is typically called that way) in some U.S. usage, in much the same way as the paragraph sign (§) is often used in Europe. For example, clause 6 of an agreement or verdict is referred to by "¶ 6" and clauses from 20 to 28 are referred to by "¶¶ 20–28."

Many word processors display paragraph breaks as ¶ when requested to "show formatting." This does not mean that the data itself (e.g., as saved onto disk) would contain such characters; it is usually just a visual indication on the screen.

Registered sign ® (U+00AE) consists of letter R in a circle. It is written after a name or other expression to indicate it as a registered trademark (at least in some country). There is considerable variation in glyphs for this character. The letter R inside the circle may have different shapes, but in addition to that, the size and position may vary. For example, in the Lucida Sans Unicode font, ® is a small superscript, whereas in Verdana, ® extends below baseline (making the R in the symbol line up with the baseline), and the symbol is relatively large.

Section sign § (U+00A7) is used as a section sign especially in the U.S., and as a paragraph sign in some European usage, especially when referring to paragraphs in laws, contracts, rules, etc. For that reason, § is often used to symbolize law in general. Reflecting the variation, the character is called *paragraph sign* in many standards.

Other Latin Letters

The Latin-1 Supplement covers most languages spoken in Western and Northern Europe. There are many other languages that use a script based on Latin letters. The ISO 8859 set of standards contains various sets of 8-bit codes with different upper halves that cover some of those languages. In Unicode, however, the structure is different. It has:

- Latin Extended-A block (U+0100..U+017F), which contains a large set of Latin letters with diacritic marks as well as some additional letters. They appear in a more or less alphabetic order and include letters used in East European languages written in Latin letters (Polish, Lithuanian, Czech, etc.): Ā ā Ă ă Ą ą Ć ć … Ż ż Ž ž ſ

- Latin Extended-B block (U+0180..U+024F, which contains a set of additional letters, which are less widely known and often modified variants of Latin letters: Ƀ Ƃ Ƅ Ƅ ƅ ƅ Ɔ Ƈ ....
- Latin Extended Additional block (U+1E00..U+1EFF), which is yet another supplement: Ḁ ḁ Ḃ ḃ ... Ỹ ỹ.

When looking for a Latin letter with a diacritic, or a supposedly "Latin letter" in the broad sense, you should normally look for the Latin 1 Supplement first (especially if the text is in a Western European language), then the Latin Extended-A block. Sometimes you need to check the other two blocks as well. This is somewhat inconvenient of course and demonstrates how Unicode has been built up in a piecewise manner, rather than systematically designed from scratch.

Other European Alphabetic Scripts

There are some writing systems in Europe that have the same structural principle (i.e., that are alphabetic) as the Latin script but different letters. The letters look partly similar to or even identical to Latin letters, largely due to common origin. Beware of the differences, though. For example, the Greek capital letter rho, Ρ, and the Cyrillic capital letter er, Р, look very similar to the Latin capital letter "P," but they denote an "r" sound and historically relate to R rather than P.

Greek Script

The letters α, β, γ,... used in modern Greek have been included into the Greek and Coptic block (U+0370..U+03FF), which is similar to an 8-bit character code, ISO 8859-7. This code, in turn, deviates from windows-1253 in a few code points, in addition to the difference that windows-1253 contains some extra characters in the range 80..9F. Although there is variation in *encodings*, the *characters* themselves are well supported.

For ancient Greek as written in modern times, however, other characters are needed. They include vowels with different diacritic marks, indicating three kinds of intonation of stressed vowels. The term *polytonic Greek* is used to denote such a form of written Greek. The marks were preserved (until the 20th century) long after the intonation had been lost. Modern Greek has only one type of stress mark (called *tonos*), and it is called *monotonic Greek*.

The additional characters needed for polytonic Greek, as well as some other characters, have been included into the Greek Extended block, U+1F00..U+1FFF. Basically, you need Unicode to write polytonic Greek properly. On the other hand, various font-based techniques have been used for polytonic Greek—i.e., encodings implicitly defined by the design of an 8-bit font.

Cyrillic Script

The Cyrillic script is historically derived from a version of the Greek script, with many modifications, including addition of some characters taken from the Hebrew script. Although you may know the Cyrillic script primarily as used for Russian, it is used (in many variants) for many other Slavic and non-Slavic languages as well. Throughout history, the writing system of some languages has been changed from Latin to Cyrillic or vice versa for political reasons.

The Cyrillic letters as used in Russian are covered by several 8-bit encodings. Among them, the most common are KOI-8R and windows-1251. KOI8-R is specifically for Russian and does not cover most other languages that use the Cyrillic script. The ISO-8859-5 and windows-1251 encodings cover the Cyrillic letters used for Slavic languages, though not many of the letters in other languages using the Cyrillic script.

Even when Unicode is used, problems may arise. Russian is normally written without accent marks, despite the fact that the stress is varying and can be distinctive. However, an acute accent is often used in dictionaries and textbooks, and occasionally in normal text as well—e.g., to distinguish бо́льшой "bigger" from большо́й "big" (with stress on the second syllable). This creates a problem, since Unicode does not contain Cyrillic vowel letters with acute accent as precomposed characters. Consequently, you need to use the combining acute accent U+0301 after a vowel letter and try to use software that can handle this. Unfortunately, the result is often typographically poor, though there is more and more software that implements combining diacritic marks well.

When Cyrillic text is transliterated into a Latin script, confusion is often caused by varying transliteration systems. Without knowing the transliteration method, it is impossible to know the original Cyrillic spelling (and hence pronunciation).

Armenian and Georgian Scripts

Characters needed for writing the Armenian and Georgian languages, spoken in the Caucasus, have been included into separate blocks named according to the languages. The languages have relatively small sets of letters, so they can each also be written using an 8-bit encoding.

Modern Georgian makes no case distinction for letters. (Old Georgian had separate upper- and lowercase, though.) In fact, such a situation is common in the writing systems of the world, though most European scripts are an exception. It is also older; the case distinction was invented in medieval Europe.

Diacritic Marks

Diacritic marks are small signs added to letters or other characters, such an acute accent added to letter "e" to produce é or a tilde added to "a" to produce ã. Usually the mark is placed above the letter, but it could also appear below the letter, as in ç, or in another position. If your native language does not use diacritic marks, you might regard them as decorations only. However, they may fundamentally affect the meanings of words.

Why Diacritic Marks?

Diacritic marks are used to create variants of letters, often because a language that uses Latin letters has more sounds that can be expressed using the basic letters.

Diacritic marks often originate from letters that were written above another letter. For example, the tilde was originally a small "n," so that, for example, "an" was first written with a small "n" above the "a," and then the "n" was simplified, producing ã. When, for example, the sound combination "an" had changed to a nasalized "a" (i.e., the vowel "a" pronounced through the nose, with no consonant "n"), it was natural to denote this sound with a single letter, ã.

People who have designed writing systems for previously unwritten languages often find the basic Latin alphabet insufficient. If there are more essentially different sounds (phonemes) in the language than there are basic letters, you could invent new letters or take them from other alphabets. However, the most common solution is to add diacritic marks on letters, often imitating the orthographies of other languages.

The meanings of diacritic marks vary greatly by language. For example, in French, the acute on é affects the quality of the vowel in pronunciation; in Hungarian, the acute indicates that the vowel is long; in Spanish, that the vowel has stress. It is not a matter of small nuances only; the differences can be crucial to making distinctions in meaning. The French verbs "pêcher" (to fish) and "pècher" (to sin) are quite different.

Sometimes diacritic marks are used just to make a distinction between words that are pronounced the same way and otherwise written the same way, but have different meanings. The Italian words "e" (and) and è (is) are pronounced similarly, but the diacritic marks help readers to see the difference in meaning from the word itself, without context analysis.

In many languages, diacritic marks have an essential role. Speakers of such languages often regard characters created with diacritic marks as completely independent letters. For example, in Swedish, ö is a separate letter, placed at the end of the alphabet. From the Unicode perspective, however, it can also be regarded as letter "o" with a diacritic, the dieresis.

Diacritic marks can also be combined. Letters with two diacritic marks are rare in European languages but common in Vietnamese, for example.

In special notations, such as phonetic writing (e.g., IPA notation) and mathematical formalisms, diacritic marks are often deployed extensively. Their use could not be covered with a reasonable number of combinations of a base letter and a diacritic mark. For example, the Uralic Phonetic Alphabet (UPA) rather routinely uses three or four diacritic marks on a letter to describe various nuances of pronunciation.

Diacritic marks are often omitted, though, especially by people who are not familiar with the rules of a language that uses diacritic marks. People might not know how to write the diacritic marks in a particular program, or they might fear—not without reason—that diacritic marks cause problems in data transfer.

Publishers' policies differ on the use of diacritic marks. The most logical and polite approach is to preserve all diacritic marks in foreign words, excluding those that have been specifically adapted to another language. Thus, in English you should reserve the diacritic in "Rhône" (name of a river in France) but may drop it in a loanword like "rôle," for which the spelling "role" is more common in English. Some names have been adapted in a form without diacritics—e.g., "Aland" (Swedish "Åland"). Similarly, the unit name "angstrom" is often written without diacritics, but the scientist's name must have them: "Ångström."

Early Approaches

In the early days of character data processing on computers, diacritic marks were not used. Later, attempts were made to produce them in a coarse manner similar to those used on typewriters. To produce ô, for example, you typed "o" followed by a control character that moves the writing position backward (to the left), then the character ^ (i.e., the circumflex as a separate character). The control character used was normally the ASCII backspace, BS.

The results were of course esthetically poor, since the same diacritic was used for all letters, lowercase and uppercase. Moreover, for economic reasons (like saving keyboard keys and coding space), the characters used as diacritic marks were often not designed for the purpose. Instead, existing characters were overloaded with new meanings and uses. For example, ASCII does not contain an acute accent, but the ASCII apostrophe was meant to be used as an accent too. Since the ASCII apostrophe had to serve so many different purposes, its appearance had to be neutral, hence not really suitable for any of the uses.

Once some characters had been introduced for use as overprinting diacritic marks, new uses were invented for them. After all, there was a very limited character repertoire available. Thus, for example, since the circumflex ^ looks like an upward-pointing arrow head, it was taken into special usage such as exponentiation: x^y is often used to denote x to the power y. This in turn implied that the glyph for the character had to be clearly visible, even in low-quality rendering that was common at that time. That way, the circumflex became rather big in shape. It then became rather unsuitable as a diacritic mark, but it mostly wasn't used for that purpose anyway.

Coded Combinations

In Latin-1 and other 8-bit character sets, some character positions were assigned to letters with diacritic marks as needed for writing particular languages. For example, Latin-1 contains characters such as é and ü for the needs of Western European languages. Due to the limitations of the coding space and the practical nature of the character sets, the assignments do not follow very regular patterns. For example, Latin-1 contains the letter ÿ,

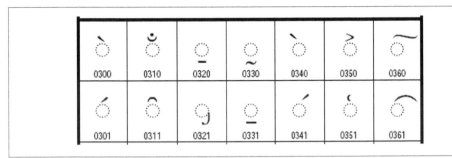

Figure 8-2. Sample glyphs for combining diacritic marks

but not the corresponding uppercase letter—the letter is rare in itself and its uppercase variant is very rare.

Although Unicode contains "precomposed" characters as well, it turned out to be unsatisfactory to define all the possible combinations as separate characters. The concept of "combining diacritic marks" was introduced to allow, in principle, free combinations. You can use almost any character as a base character and attach any diacritic marks to it. Some of the combinations result in characters that already exist in Unicode as precomposed, and this raises the problem of dual presentations that are addressed in the so-called normalization.

The general idea is that new precomposed characters, consisting of a Unicode character and a Unicode diacritic, will normally not be added to Unicode anymore. This has caused some controversy for obvious reasons, since precomposed characters, with their own code positions, are often regarded as "more real" than the combinations. Partly for such reasons, the concept Unicode Sequence Identifier (USI) was introduced, which is described in Chapter 4.

Combining Diacritic Marks

A combining diacritic mark is a character that is meant to be presented in conjunction with a base character, not as such. For example, when the combining acute accent U+0301 appears after the letter "a," this character pair is to be rendered as á. Should you wish to render the combining acute accent itself, you could put it after the space (or no-break space) character—i.e., combine it with a graphically empty character. This would normally create the same rendering as the acute accent ´ (U+00B4), which is treated as the "spacing clone" of the combining acute accent. In code charts, combining diacritic marks are often shown using a dotted circle to symbolize a generic base character, as in Figure 8-2.

You might think of a combining diacritic mark as corresponding to backspace followed by the corresponding spacing (noncombining) character. That is, you might regard U+0301 as resembling backspace U+0008 followed by acute accent U+00B4. Although such thinking paints a picture that is useful up to a point, it easily becomes misleading after that.

Programs that support combining diacritic marks in rendering are really supposed to do much more elaborated operations than backspacing and overprinting. A program is supposed to analyze the base character and the combining diacritic and pick up a suitable glyph (designed, as an element of a font, by a typographer), such as á, if possible. As a second option, a program should construct a visual rendering that places the diacritic on the base character intelligently. For example, to produce á and Á that way, the program should at least pay attention to the different heights of "a" and "A."

Existing software is often deficient in supporting combining diacritic marks. It might get simple cases right, but it might also use simplistic methods that correspond to overprinting. This might result in a rendering where the diacritic is barely visible, or not visible at all. It is currently much safer to use precombined characters when possible. The Unicode Normalization Form C (see Chapter 5) is suitable for such purposes.

There is a particular danger when a program has been instructed to use one font as the primary font and another font, or other fonts, as fallback for characters that do not have glyphs in the primary font. The data might contain combining diacritic marks that do not appear in the primary font. Consider what would happen if a program, when presenting the data U+0061 U+0301 (small letter a, combining acute accent), used the Times font for the first character and Arial Unicode MS for the latter. Since the proportions of glyphs are different, the diacritic will not be placed well on the letter. This would result in á, which is typographically inferior; compare it with the precomposed character in the two fonts: á and á. A program can avoid this particular case by using the precomposed character, but in the general case, such a character may not exist, or the basic font used might lack it.

 If you use combining diacritic marks, be aware that not many fonts contain them. Select a suitable font, and make sure it is used for the base characters, too.

The combining marks used for Latin letters, as well as many other marks, are in the block "Combining Diacritical Marks" ranging from U+0300 to U+036F. The grouping of these characters is shown in Table 8-6. The attribute "combining" has been omitted from the character names here for brevity. The "Ordinary diacritics" group is by far the most common. Note that there are combining marks outside this block, too.

Table 8-6. Classification of combining diacritic marks

Range	Name of group	Sample diacritic name
U+0300..U+0333	Ordinary diacritics	Grave accent
U+0334..U+0338	Overstruck diacritics	Tilde overlay
U+0339..U+033F	Additions	Right half below
U+0340..U+0341	Vietnamese tone marks (deprecated)	Grave tone mark
U+0342..U+0345	Additions for Greek	Greek perispomeni

Range	Name of group	Sample diacritic name
U+0346..U+034A	Additions for IPA	Bridge above
U+034B..U+34E	IPA diacritics for disordered speech	Homothetic above
U+034F	Grapheme joiner	Grapheme joiner
U+0350..U+0357	Additions for UPA	Right arrowhead above
U+035D..U+0362	Double diacritics	Double breve
U+0363..U+036F	Medieval superscript letter diacritics	Latin small letter a

The "ordinary" diacritic marks in the block are listed in Table 8-7, in alphabetic order by name, omitting the attribute "combining." The first column shows the character as combined with the letter "a."

Table 8-7. Ordinary combining diacritic marks

Character	Code	Diacritic mark
á	U+0301	Acute accent
ạ	U+0317	Acute accent below
ă	U+0306	Breve
ạ	U+032E	Breve below
ạ	U+032A	Bridge below
å	U+0310	Candrabindu
ă	U+030C	Caron
ạ	U+032C	Caron below
ạ	U+0327	Cedilla
â	U+0302	Circumflex accent
ạ	U+032D	Circumflex accent below
ȧ	U+0313	Comma above
a'	U+0315	Comma above right
ạ	U+0326	Comma below
ä	U+0308	Dieresis
ạ	U+0324	Dieresis below
ȧ	U+0307	Dot above
ạ	U+0323	Dot below
ă	U+030B	Double acute accent
ȁ	U+030F	Double grave accent
a̳	U+0333	Double low line
̋a	U+030E	Double vertical line above
ạ	U+031E	Down tack below

Character	Code	Diacritic mark
à	U+0300	Grave accent
ą	U+0316	Grave accent below
ả	U+0309	Hook above
a'	U+031B	Horn
â	U+0311	Inverted breve
ą	U+032F	Inverted breve below
ą	U+032B	Inverted double arch below
à	U+031A	Left angle above
ą	U+031C	Left half ring below
ą	U+0318	Left tack below
a	U+0332	Low line
ā	U+0304	Macron
a	U+0331	Macron below
ą	U+0320	Minus sign below
ą	U+0328	Ogonek
ā	U+0305	Overline
ą	U+0321	Palatalized hook below
ą	U+031F	Plus sign below
ą	U+0322	Retroflex hook below
à	U+0314	Reversed comma above
ą	U+0319	Right tack below
å	U+030A	Ring above
ą	U+0325	Ring below
ã	U+0303	Tilde
ą	U+0330	Tilde below
à	U+0312	Turned comma above
ą	U+031D	Up tack below
à	U+030D	Vertical line above
ą	U+0329	Vertical line below

Some diacritic marks are often confused with each other. In particular, the caron (hacek) is often confused with the breve, which typically indicates that a vowel is short. The marks may look rather similar, but the caron is angular, v-like in shape, often characterized as inverted circumflex, whereas the breve is at least mildly curved, a little bit u-like. Although the visual differences can be very small, there is a fundamental difference in the coded representations of the characters. Nobody knows where the name "caron" (used mostly in character standards only) comes from, and the common name for this diacritic is "hacek" (from the Czech word "háček").

Combining macron below (U+0331) and combining low line (U+0332) both indicate underlining of a kind, but the latter is supposed to join on both sides. That is, for two consecutive characters with combining low line, you would expect the underlining to be continuous. These combining marks should only be used when underlining is part of a writing system—e.g., when the orthography of a language uses an underlined letter to indicate something different from the base letter. For underlining used, for example, for emphasis or decoration, it is much better to use markup, word processor commands, or other tools.

The double diacritics U+035D to U+0362 are special in the sense that such a diacritic applies to the two characters *around* it. This is an exception from the rule that in Unicode, a combining diacritic appears after its base character. For example, to write an underlined "ts" so that there is just one long underline that applies to both characters, you would use U+0074 U+035F U+0073 ("t," combining double macron below, "s"). The character U+035F is poorly supported, but you might have better success, for example, with combining double inverted breve U+0361: U+0074 U+0361 U+0073 might produce t͡s.

The double diacritics are meant to be used in special cases where they belong to a script or notation (such as IPA). Note that the word "double" occurs in names of diacritics somewhat confusingly. For example, combining double low line U+0333 is not a double diacritic as discussed here, just a doubled low line under one character (a̳).

There are additional diacritic marks in the block "Combining Diacritical Marks for Symbols," U+20D0..U+20FF. As the name suggests, they are mainly meant for use with mathematical and other symbols. They have rather limited support in software and fonts. For example, to write letter "x" with a rightward arrow above it, you could in theory use "x" followed by combining right arrow above U+20D7. However, few fonts contain it, and it might even be incorrectly marked as a normal graphic character →, not a combining diacritic mark. Thus, for formulas and texts containing such symbols, it is probably better to use special software like formula editors, instead of trying to represent them as plain text.

Variation in Appearance

The visual appearance of a diacritic mark may vary greatly by font. In handwriting, there is even more variation; for example, a handwritten ä may look like ã or ā.

The Latin small letter "a" with breve, ă is often written using a tilde as the diacritic ã. Such appearances can often be regarded as substitutions of one character for another, and they may have technical reasons. For example, ã (being an ISO Latin 1 character) might be available where ă is not. Whether the variation causes problems depends on the character repertoire of the language and the context. Although people can use ã instead of ă in Romanian, since this has become common and will probably not cause confusion, it would be risky to use ā, since the reader could not immediately see whether it stands for ă or for â, which are both used in Romanian.

Some of the variation is language-dependent. For example, the acute accent in French typically looks different from the acute in Polish. This can be reflected in the dislike of fonts and even in labeling some fonts as "foreign."

Unicode has even unified the modern Greek stress mark, tonos, with the acute accent, although the name "tonos" appears in the names of characters. For example, the Greek letter small alpha with tonos ά (U+03AC) is defined as compatibility equivalent to normal alpha followed by combining acute accent, U+0301. Despite this, the shape of the diacritic in such characters differs from the acute in, for example, é. The difference is more striking in, for example, the Greek letter capital alpha with tonos U+03AB, since in Greek typography, the tonos is positioned to left of the base character in such a case: Ά.

Some diacritic marks have a regular appearance that deviates from what you might expect from their name. The Latin capital letter "T" with caron, used in Czech and Slovak, looks as you'd expect: Ť. However, its lowercase counterpart, Latin small letter "t" with caron U+0165, has a comma-like diacritic in most fonts: ť. This means that the diacritic mark looks like a comma or an apostrophe but it is called caron and treated as caron in Unicode (e.g., in the canonical decomposition). Although this sounds unnatural, it would also be unnatural to have "T" with caron mapped to, say, "t" with comma above right in an uppercase-to-lowercase mapping.

Spacing Diacritic Marks

When a combining diacritic mark is applied to a space character, we get the diacritic itself as a visible character. Alternatively, we might use a character that itself represents a spacing diacritic mark, often called "spacing clones" of diacritic marks. Such characters appear, for historical reasons, in different blocks, such as Latin-1 Supplement and Spacing Modifier Letters.

Starting from of Unicode 4.1, the recommendation is to apply a combining diacritic mark to a no-break space U+00A0 rather than space U+0020. The reason is "potential conflicts with the handling of sequences of U+0020 space characters in contexts like XML." However, the formal definitions still to define decompositions using the space. For example, the acute accent ´ (U+00B4) is by definition compatibility equivalent to a two-character sequence consisting of a space U+0020 and a combining acute accent U+0301.

Spacing diacritic marks do not have much use. Sometimes we might wish to mention a diacritic in text, such as "the acute ´ has varying shapes." More often, the spacing diacritic marks are used mistakenly (or questionably) as replacements for more appropriate characters (e.g., the acute as an apostrophe).

Some Basic Latin (ASCII) characters are historically derived from diacritic marks but are now treated as characters on their own. For example, the tilde ~ (U+007E) is not treated as a spacing clone of the combining tilde U+0303—that would in fact be odd, since the tilde has a rather different appearance. Instead, there is a separate character, small tilde ˜ (U+02DC), which is by definition compatibility equivalent to U+0020 U+0303.

Letterlike Symbols

This block contains a large number of characters that are historically based on letters or letter combinations but might be shaped differently and, most important, are used in specialized meanings. For example, a symbol formed from the letter "R" by doubling its vertical line or all lines (ℝ) is conventionally used to denote the set of all real numbers in mathematics. Frequently used characters of this type include:

- Estimated symbol e (U+212E), originally letter "e" in a particular shape but defined by the European Union as a specific symbol used in packaging to denote that a certain accuracy is guaranteed in designating volume, mass, or other quantity,

- Numero sign № (U+2116), used in some languages (with some glyph variation by language) to mean "number" (e.g., "№ 1" means much the same as "#1"). Compatibility equivalent to the letter pair "No".

- Trademark sign ™ (U+2122), used much the same way as the registered sign ® but about unregistered trademarks. Compatibility equivalent to the letter pair "TM" in superscript style, but glyphs vary a lot.

This block does not contain all Unicode characters that have originally been formed as stylized variants of letters. Some such characters belong to other blocks due to the history of character codes.

Some characters in this block are redundant duplicates of normal letters but included into Unicode for compatibility. For example, although there is a character named "kelvin sign" in this block, it is not meant to be used instead of the normal letter "K" when expressing thermodynamic temperatures. The "kelvin sign" has been taken into Unicode only to allow existing data to be converted to Unicode so that a distinction between normal "K" and a kelvin sign is preserved, if it exists in the original data.

Thus, contrary to what many people think after finding this block, many characters in it are not more appropriate than the corresponding normal letters. It is true that using "kelvin sign" for example would contain more semantic information, since the letter "K" as such has a large number of different uses and interpretations. However, it would not be feasible to disambiguate characters by using different codes for something that is essentially identifiable as a single character. We will return to this issue in the discussion of using letters in SI notations.

General Punctuation

The General Punctuation block (U+2000..U+206F) is very important, since many characters in it are used frequently. It is however a mixed set, and only under a very liberal interpretation can we regard all characters there as punctuation. For example, the per mille sign ‰ (U+2030) is comparable to a unit symbol rather than the comma or the colon.

On the other hand, there are important punctuation characters elsewhere. The Basic Latin and Latin 1 Supplement blocks contain many very common punctuation characters like the comma. Moreover, characters that are used in only one script have usually been placed in the same block as the letters or other characters of the script.

Space Characters

In ASCII, there is only one space character, space. The Latin 1 supplement adds the no-break space, which is meant to be used instead of a space between words and expressions when line breaking should be disallowed there. There are several other space characters in Unicode, but they are of rather limited usefulness and use.

Space

The space character U+0020 normally creates horizontal empty space. Depending on the rendering software, the spacing could be of fixed width (for any particular font), or it could vary, especially in typesetting when the text is justified on both sides. The spacing might also be affected by commands of the typesetting program or other means, such as a stylesheet (e.g., using the `word-spacing` property in CSS) when authoring in HTML.

Often texts can be reformatted so that spaces are replaced by line breaks or vice versa. In technical terms, Unicode describes this so that a line break is normally permitted after a space character. The space that is left at the end of a line is then ignored in formatting.

It is common to omit spaces in situations where orthography rules would require a space but both the width adjustments and the breakability would cause undesired effects. For example, the rules of the SI, the International System of Units, require a space between a number and a unit, as in "5 m" (five meters), but people often write "5m." Of course we don't want a line break between "5" and "m" or even a wide gap as in "5   m," when text justification requires increased spacing between words. Usually, however, we can prevent such effects and still comply with orthography rules, by using a no-break space.

No-break space: use it!

The no-break space character U+00A0 is similar to a normal space but does not allow a line break after it. That is, if you have "foo bar" with a no-break space between the words, then the words are kept on the same line when the text is rendered or reformatted. Note that you use a no-break space instead of a normal space, not in addition to it. The no-break space is also called a "hard space" or "required space," though these unofficial names may also allude to other meanings, which are often coupled with the non-breaking behavior.

In addition to its basic meaning, the no-break space usually has the property of being of *fixed width*, for any given font. That is, it is neither expanded nor shrunk in text justification. This behavior is not defined in the Unicode standard, but it is very common. It is probably often caused by the way programs deal with the no-break space: they treat it as a printable character, just with an empty glyph (of a particular width), not as a character that controls spacing. It's like an alphabetic character, just empty.

Some programs, such as web browsers, by default collapse consecutive spaces. That is, any sequence of space characters might be treated as equivalent to a single space. The programs usually treat no-break space characters as *non-collapsing*. This is natural, since no-break space is usually treated as a fixed width character, as just explained.

The no-break space has some special uses. In the HTML source code if web pages, you might find table cells that contain nothing but a no-break space, usually written as an HTML entity, . The reason is that web browsers commonly treat empty cells differently from nonempty cells (e.g., empty cells may lack borders), and they typically treat a cell with a normal space as empty, a cell with a no-break space as nonempty.

The no-break space belongs to all ISO-8859 encodings, so it is widely available. However, it is not used very widely yet, partly because people do not know about it or how to type it simply. When using MS Word, for example, you can type a no-break space almost as easily as a normal space: just keep the Ctrl and Shift keys pressed down when you hit the spacebar. You can make no-break spaces visible in MS Word by selecting the Show ¶ mode (often by clicking on the ¶ button); Word then shows a no-break space as a degree sign, °. In other programs, things can be different, but often you can define a keyboard shortcut you can use.

The difficult part is to adopt the *habit* of using no-break spaces. The following list suggests some common cases where you might routinely use a no-break space:

- Between a number and a unit, as in "5 m"
- Between a word and a closely associated number or symbol, as in "section 1" or "letter x"
- Within a number or a code that contains spaces, as in "1 000 000" in languages that use a space as thousands separator, or in phone numbers like "+358 9 888 2675"
- In short expressions like "U = V" or "a < 0"
- Before the last word of a paragraph, if that word is very short

If you find this too difficult, you might decide to use no-break space only when you notice a particularly bad line break in your text. However, texts are very often edited and reformatted so that you cannot predict line breaks well.

On the other hand, when the formatting is important (e.g., in headings and headlines), you might use no-break spaces even more extensively. For example, you might wish to prevent a short word that starts or ends a sentence from being separated from the rest of the sentence. Remember, however, that preventing line breaks increases the odds for bad formatting in other parts of a paragraph.

Fixed-width spaces: rarely used

Unicode contains a set of space characters, shown in Table 8-8, that are similar to the common space but have a fixed width. This means that they are normally not adjusted by typesetting programs. On the other hand, such programs may contain commands for inserting something such as a thin space, which might not be the Unicode thin space character but an internal code that affects spacing. In that case, the spacing effect is often controllable via the program's commands in a detailed manner.

Table 8-8. Fixed-width space characters in Unicode

Code	Name	Width
U+200B	Zero width space (ZWSP)	Nominally no width, but may expand
U+200A	Hair space	Defined as "narrower than thin space"
U+2006	Six-per-em space	1/6 em (0.166... em)
U+2009	Thin space	1/5 em (0.2 em) or sometimes 1/6 em
U+205F	Medium mathematical space	4/18 em (0.222... em)
U+2005	Four-per-em space	1/4 em (0.25 em)
U+2004	Three-per-em space	1/3 em (0.333... em)
U+2002	En space	1 en (0.5 em)
U+2000	En quad	1 en (0.5 em)
U+2003	Em space	1 em (the size of the font in use)
U+2001	Em quad	1 em
U+2008	Punctuation space	The width of a period (full stop) "."
U+2007	Figure space	The width of a digit (tabular width)
U+3000	Ideographic space	The width of ideographic (CJK) characters

The fixed-width characters have been included into Unicode mostly for compatibility reasons. They are rarely used in practice. They may have some special uses, however. For example, *figure space* could be used for alignment purposes in numerical tables. If you have, say, a column with values like 1.2, 1.151, and 1.41, you could right-pad the values with figure spaces so that they have the same number of characters to the right of the decimal point. Then aligning the column to the right would make the values aligned to the decimal point. This is useful in contexts where you have no direct method for such alignment—e.g., in HTML authoring. The Unicode line breaking rules in UAX #14 (see Chapter 5) specify that the figure space is non-breaking and even recommend it: "This is the preferred space to use in numbers. It has the same width as a digit and keeps the number together for the purpose of line breaking." In practice, it is seldom a good choice, due to lack of support.

In particular, *zero-width space* (ZWSP) can be used to suggest line breaking possibilities inside a string that could otherwise cause problems in typesetting. The ZWSP character is basically invisible, yet allows a line break after it. Do not confuse this with discretionary hyphens; when a string is broken after a ZWSP, no hyphen is added at the end of a line. For example, a long URL like *http://www.cs.tut.fi/~jkorpela/unicode/spaces.html* (when used in text) might be modified to contain ZWSP after some slash (/) characters. The ZWSP does not prevent increased spacing between the characters around it, if such spacing is applied—e.g., in order to justify text.

Beware that implementations may fail to implement fixed-width spaces according to the Unicode descriptions. Programs may lack any particular support to fixed-width space characters in the sense that they would adjust spacing. Instead, programs might just insert a glyph for the fixed-width character if available—and most fonts lack them, so the result is often a symbol for unrepresentable character. To make things worse, the glyphs are often incorrect. For example, the thin space can be narrower or much wider than it should, and most fonts that contain a punctuation space have a far too wide a glyph for it.

Among commonly used fonts, only a few, such as Arial Unicode MS, Lucida Sans Unicode, and Code2000, contain glyphs for all or most fixed-width spaces.

 Fixed-width spaces should be used only after checking the appearance in the particular font used and only when you can be reasonably sure that the text will always be rendered using that font.

The fixed-width spaces just listed (all except the figure space) have the basic semantics of a space in the sense that a line break is permitted. This is often a problem. For example, French orthography rules require "fine spaces" around some punctuation characters, as in « Voilà ! ». Although thin spaces would give roughly the correct spacing, they would also permit highly undesirable line breaks. Thus, no-break spaces are safer, though this would mean that the amount of spacing should be controlled elsewhere, above the character level.

Adjusting spacing in other ways

As mentioned earlier, fixed-width characters are not used very much. In fact, even if a typesetting program may have a command for inserting "thin space" for example, this need not mean that the Unicode thin space character is actually used. Instead, the program might internally adjust spacing between characters, using tools above the character level. This explains why such programs often let you modify the width of the "thin space" you insert.

In MS Word, you can use the Format → Font command to enter a dialog where you can adjust character spacing. If you select a string with the mouse and then set character spacing for it that way, you actually add the specified spacing *after* each character. In particular, if you do that for a single character, the spacing before it is not affected. You can also use negative spacing to bring characters closer to each other, and even overprint each other. This is normally not a good idea if any other tools are available.

For example, to produce letter "a" with a line (macron) above it, you could try writing "a" and a macron ¯ (U+00AF), then adjusting the spacing for the "a" suitably so that the macron appears above it. Such tuning would however depend on the font. Usually better tools exist. You could use the small letter "a" with macron (ā), or you could use "a" followed by a combining macron, or you could use a formula editor.

Additional no-break space characters

The character U+202F, narrow no-break space, would appear to address some common problems in spacing, since it is both narrow and nonbreaking. However, support to it in programs and fonts is still rather limited. It was included in Unicode (in Version 3.0) for special purposes: for use in the Mongolian script. It has been defined just as being narrower than a no-break space, without specifying the width, so it cannot give any precise control even in principle.

Finally, there is U+FEFF, zero-width no-break space (ZWNBSP). As its name suggests, it is really an invisible connector. It would prevent a line break inside a string even if a break would otherwise be permitted. The recommended character for such usage is now U+2060, word joiner (WJ). The reason is that ZWNBSP also has a different usage: it is used as a byte order mark (see Chapter 6). However, in practice, ZWNBSP is more widely supported in software at present.

In theory, you could use a "nonbreakable thin space" (e.g., between numbers) by using a thin space followed by a word joiner, U+2009 U+2060. In addition to being clumsy, this would be unreliable, since it uses two characters that are not widely supported. Far too often, U+2060 displays as a box or as a question mark. You would get better results with U+FEFF instead of U+2060, but even then the method would work with some fonts only.

A practical approach to thin spaces

In contexts like French punctuation or the use of a space as a thousands separator (as in 500 000), we would like to use a thin space character that is non-breaking. Since this is almost impossible at present at the character level, we have two options, illustrated here with implementations in HTML and CSS:

- Use no-break space characters and adjust the amount of spacing—e.g., in a stylesheet; for example:

  ```
  <span style="word-spacing: -0.08em">500 000</span>
  ```

  or:

  ```
  <span style="margin-right: -0.08em">500</span> 000
  ```

- Use thin space characters and prevent line breaking using a stylesheet or markup; for example:

  ```
  <span style="white-space: nowrap">500 000</span>
  ```

  or:

  ```
  <nobr>500 000</nobr>
  ```

The first method, where non-breakability is expressed at the character level and spacing adjustment is handled otherwise, is usually more practical. The no-break space character is far more widely supported than the thin space. As a variation of this method, you could use HTML markup rather than CSS for affecting the amount of spacing—for example, using 500<small> </small>000.

Disallowing and allowing line breaks

The Unicode standard recommends the use of WJ when you wish to prevent line breaks and ZWSP when you wish to allow line breaks, overriding normal line break rules. However, at present such line break control at the character level does not work very widely and should not be expected to be portable across text-processing applications. It is often better to use other methods, such as markup, stylesheets, or typesetting commands. For example, in HTML authoring, people even use nonstandard but widely supported markup such as <nobr>...</nobr> (prevents line breaks inside) and <wbr> (allows a line break; corresponds to ZWSP).

Quotation Marks

In Unicode, there are several pairs of asymmetric quotation marks, but of them, only the double angle quotation marks « and » belong to ISO Latin 1. Notice in particular that the normal quotation marks in U.S. English, namely left and right double quotation marks (U+201C, U+201D), do not belong to ISO Latin 1 (although they belong to Windows Latin 1). In Unicode, most quotation marks belong to the General Punctuation block.

The quotation marks vary greatly from one language to another and even within a language. When ISO Latin 1 has to be used, there are not many choices: you have to live with ", ', «, and ». It is better to use these typographically inferior characters for quotations than to try to ``construct'' smart quotes from characters that are not quotes.

Language-specific quotation marks

In Chapter 2, we described how word processors can automatically generate language-dependent quotation marks. Beware, however, that the applicable rules are somewhat debatable, especially regarding nested punctuation. This means that the automatically generated marks do not always comply with official rules. Even versions of the Unicode standard have contained erroneous examples of the use of quotes. See "Using Common Locale Data Repository" in Chapter 11 for information about language-specific rules.

The most common quotation marks are listed in Table 8-9. The names are partly misleading, since a "left" quote does not always appear to the left of the quoted text.

Table 8-9. Quotation marks

Code	Character	Name
U+00AB	«	Left-pointing double angle quotation mark
U+00BB	»	Right-pointing double angle quotation mark
U+2018	'	Left single quotation mark
U+2019	'	Right single quotation mark
U+201A	,	Single low-9 quotation mark
U+201B	'	Single high-reversed-9 quotation mark
U+201C	"	Left double quotation mark
U+201D	"	Right double quotation mark
U+201E	„	Double low-9 quotation mark
U+201F	"	Double high-reversed-9 quotation mark

Code	Character	Name
U+2039	‹	Single left-pointing angle quotation mark
U+203A	›	Single right-pointing angle quotation mark

The apostrophe versus the single quotation mark

People often ask how to distinguish the apostrophe, as in "can't," from the right single quotation mark, as the closing quote in 'hello' (using British-style quotation marks). The short answer is that in Unicode, you don't. The answer often makes people uneasy, but we cannot really change this anymore.

Version 2.0 of the Unicode standard said that the preferred character for apostrophe is the modifier letter apostrophe U+02BC, but this was changed in Version 2.1. The modifier letter apostrophe is preferred where the character is to represent a modifier letter (for example, in transliterations to indicate a glottal stop). But as a punctuation apostrophe, as in "We've been here before," the right single quotation mark (U+2019) is preferred.

This means that in processing text data, you cannot tell a punctuation apostrophe (used as part of a word) from a right single quote without considering the context. This is practically not very serious, since there is in any case some variation in the ways that a punctuation apostrophe might be represented in data. The person who typed the data in the first place may have used the ASCII apostrophe, or the acute accent.

Hyphens and Dashes

It has become common to use the hyphen-minus character for a wide range of purposes, simply because it is the only hyphen-like character in ASCII. This is detrimental to typography, since different hyphen-like characters need different appearance. Sometimes two consecutive hyphens "--" are used to emulate an em dash, but this results in poor appearance, since the hyphens do not connect.

In Unicode, there is a rather large collection of hyphen-like or dash-like characters. Specifically, there is an official list (in Chapter 6 of the Unicode standard, Table 6-3), which is presented in Table 8-10 as amended with additional reference information. This table also contains the soft hyphen, which belonged to the corresponding table in Unicode 3 but is just mentioned after the table in the current version of the standard.

Table 8-10. Hyphens and dashes in Unicode

Glyph	Code	Name	Notes on meaning and usage
-	U+002D	Hyphen-minus	The well-known ASCII hyphen, with multiple usage, or "ambiguous semantic value"; the width should be "average"
~	U+007E	Tilde	The ASCII tilde, with multiple usage; "swung dash"
-	U+00AD	Soft hyphen	"Discretionary hyphen"
-	U+058A	Armenian hyphen	As soft hyphen, but different in shape

Glyph	Code	Name	Notes on meaning and usage
‐	U+1806	Mongolian todo hyphen	As soft hyphen, but displayed at the beginning of the second line
‐	U+2010	Hyphen	Unambiguously a hyphen character, as in "left-to-right"; narrow width
‑	U+2011	Non-breaking hyphen	As hyphen (U+2011), but not an allowed line break point
–	U+2012	Figure dash	As hyphen-minus, but has the same width as digits
–	U+2013	En dash	Used, for example, to indicate a range of values
—	U+2014	Em dash	Used, for example, to make a break in the flow of a sentence
–	U+2015	Horizontal bar	Used to introduce quoted text in some typographic styles; "quotation dash"; often (e.g., in the representative glyph in the Unicode standard) longer than em dash
~	U+2053	Swung dash	Like a large tilde; often missing in fonts
⁻	U+207B	Superscript minus	A compatibility character, equivalent to minus sign U+2212 in superscript style
₋	U+208B	Subscript minus	A compatibility character, equivalent to minus sign U+2212 in subscript style
−	U+2212	Minus sign	An arithmetic operator; the glyph may look the same as the glyph for a hyphen-minus, or may be longer
〜	U+301C	Wave dash	A Chinese/Japanese/Korean character
〰	U+3030	Wavy dash	A Chinese/Japanese/Korean character

The hyphen bullet U+2043 is not listed among the hyphen dash characters, despite its name. There is no cross-reference in the description of the hyphen bullet in the code chart. Apparently, the hyphen bullet is really meant to be a bullet character that looks like a hyphen (of a kind), rather than comparable to hyphens and dashes. Note that in ASCII text, the hyphen-minus is often used in the role of a bullet in a bulleted list. Some typographic conventions favor the use of a hyphen-like bullet even when a rich character repertoire is available, though the bullet • and dashes like the en dash "–" are more common in such usage. Typically, list bullets are generated by word processors or other programs, rather than written explicitly into documents.

Use of hyphens and dashes

When a sufficient character repertoire is available, the following usage rules are suitable, since they comply with old typographic and orthographic principles and the defined Unicode meanings of characters:

- The hyphen-minus character should be used only in computer languages and other contexts where this ASCII character belongs to the language syntax. Thus, for example, the C language statement a = b - c; must be written using the hyphen-minus character, despite the fact that it there denotes mathematical subtraction; the reason is that C language has been defined to use hyphen-minus as such an operator. Similar considerations apply to most programming, scripting, command, and markup languages, since they generally use ASCII characters only at least in the core language.

- The hyphen character should be used as a normal hyphen in natural languages.
- The non-breaking hyphen should be used instead of a normal hyphen when a line break is undesirable, as in the string "Latin-1."
- The minus sign should be used as mathematical minus sign, both as a binary operator and as a unary operator (or simply as the sign of a number).
- The en dash is used to indicate a range of values, such as 2000–2500. However, there are often other possible notations, like "2000 to 2500" or "2000…2500."
- The em dash can be used to make a break—like this—in the flow of a sentence, or to make a parenthetic remark.

The en dash and em dash especially have language-dependent uses. The uses mentioned in this list (as taken from the Unicode standard) should primarily be taken as typical uses in American English. For example, in Europe, it is much more common to use an en dash with spaces around it – like this – for parenthetic remarks. Historically, the spaces compensate for the shortness of the en dash.

The soft hyphen

The soft hyphen is defined as "discretionary hyphen" in Unicode. This means that it is normally not displayed at all but indicates a permissible hyphenation point. For texts in a Latin script, hyphenation means that a word may be broken so that the first part appears at the end of a line, with a hyphen after it.

Hyphenation hints useful for words that would not be properly hyphenated by a program's normal algorithms—e.g., for foreign words or for words like "record" that have different hyphenations depending on meaning (verb "re-cord," noun "rec-ord"). In many programs, the occurrence of a soft hyphen prevents automatic hyphenation in the word—i.e., the word can *only* be hyphenated at a soft hyphen. Thus, for long words, it might be advisable to indicate all hyphenation points.

The reason why Unicode 4 does not list the soft hyphen as a hyphen is that the standard tries to clarify its meaning: "it marks a position for hyphenation, rather than being itself a hyphen character."

Though supported by some software, the soft hyphen does not work reliably across programs. In addition to the MS Word specialty discussed below, the soft hyphen is treated as a normal hyphen by various programs, including some web browsers.

MS Word specialties

Microsoft Word has an Insert → Symbol function, which was described in Chapter 2. It contains a quick menu for some commonly used characters: "Special Characters." Some entries there are rather misleading:

- "Nonbreaking Hyphen" (often with shortcut Ctrl-Shift--) does not insert the Unicode character non-breaking hyphen U+2011 but instead the control character U+001E. Word displays it as a hyphen and does not break a line after it. If the document is saved as plain text, Word turns the control character to a hyphen-minus. If you cut and paste text, the character turns into a question mark, ?.
- "Optional Hyphen" (often with shortcut Ctrl--) does not insert the Unicode character soft hyphen U+00AD. Instead, it inserts the control character U+001F, which is interpreted by Word as indicating a possible hyphenation point. This information is usually lost when saving in other formats or when cutting and pasting.

However, when saving data in HTML format, Word 2002 generates ‑ (character reference that means U+2011) from its internal "Nonbreaking Hyphen" and the U+00AD soft hyphen character from its internal "Optional Hyphen."

It is possible to insert U+2011 or U+00AD—e.g., using the "Symbols" pane or, in sufficiently new systems, by typing `2011 Alt-x` or `ad Alt-x`, respectively. The non-breaking hyphen U+2011 then works properly, assuming the font in use contains a glyph for it. The soft hyphen U+00AD however is displayed as a visible hyphen. Thus, MS Word does not support the soft hyphen as defined in Unicode. Internet Explorer, on the other hand, supports the soft hyphen, but some other web browsers do not.

Ellipsis

In English, three spaced dots are often used to indicate omission. The notation can be identified with the horizontal ellipsis "…" (U+2026), which belongs to windows-1252, too. This character is compatibility equivalent to a sequence of three period (full stop) characters ("...") with a presentation that has more spacing between the periods. MS Word automatically converts three periods to horizontal ellipsis (by default).

In some other languages, recommendations or practices may favor the use of unspaced periods. There is no Unicode character for such a combination, so it is naturally written as three periods. MS Word obeys such conventions: if it has recognized the language, for example, as French or Spanish (by inference or from an explicit setting of language), it leaves "..." intact.

In mathematics, other ellipsis characters are used, too. The most common of them is mid-line horizontal ellipsis "⋯" U+22EF. It is used, for example, in sums like $a_1 + a_2 + \cdots + a_n$.

Angular brackets

There is great confusion about various characters called angle brackets. Here we will refer to them collectively with the name "angular brackets," since the words "angle bracket" appear in the names of specific Unicode characters. Quite often, when someone says "angle bracket," he does not mean any of those characters but the less-than sign < and the greater-than sign >.

In mathematics and some other special notations, angular brackets are used for special purposes. Sometimes they are used as an additional type of brackets when you have run out of other types—i.e., normal parentheses ( ), square brackets [ ], and curly braces { }. More often, angular brackets are used to denote other things, such as the following:

- Pairs, triplets, or n-tuples, instead of the more common use of normal parentheses. For example, ⟨x,y,z⟩ might mean an ordered triplet of coordinates, more commonly denoted as (x,y,z). This is potentially misleading, due to the other uses.

- An inner product of two functions or vectors, often denoted as ⟨f | g⟩.

- Specifically the L^2-inner product, also called bracket product.

- An expectation value: ⟨X⟩ is the expectation value of a variable X.

In any case, the identity of angular brackets in terms of Unicode characters usually remains unspecified. In many references, the less-than sign and the greater-than sign are described as being angle brackets or as identical in shape to them. Yet, there is considerable difference between those signs and the usual shapes of angular brackets in good mathematical typography. Usually angular brackets have a rather obtuse angle.

Further confusion is caused by the fact that the less-than sign and the greater-than sign, being ASCII characters, have been taken into many computer language for use as delimiters. We can say that they are *used as* (i.e., in the role of) angular brackets, but it would be incorrect to say that they *are* angular brackets. This includes the well-known use in HTML and XML tags like <body>. Of course, in such notations you must use the less-than sign and the greater-than sign, since they are part of the defined syntax. Partly imitating such usage, they are also used as delimiters in Unicode notations like <small> in compatibility mappings, in writing URLs in text (e.g., as *<http://www.w3.org>*), in handwritten typesetting instructions like <sc> for small caps, and in pseudo-markup like <joke> on Internet discussion forums.

 There is some established use of less-than sign and greater-than sign as delimiters. There are also rare cases where you need typographically correct angular brackets—e.g., in mathematics. Apart from such usage, angular brackets are best avoided.

The main reason for avoiding angular brackets is that the widely available less-than sign and the greater-than sign are typographically unsuitable for such use, and they are also heavily loaded with other meanings and uses. Other characters that might be considered for use as angular brackets are less widely available; some of them exist in a few fonts only. Moreover, they are easily confused with each other both by writers and by readers.

Table 8-11 lists several Unicode characters that might be understood as angular brackets in some sense. For simplicity, only "left-pointing" (or "opening") characters are considered. The corresponding "right-pointing" character usually appears in the next code position or otherwise close. The glyphs (in the second column) for the characters are shown in the Arial Unicode MS font; as you can see, some of the characters are missing even in this relatively large font.

Table 8-11. Unicode angular brackets

Code	Glyph	Name	Block
U+003C	<	Less-than sign	Basic Latin
U+2039	‹	Left-pointing angle quotation mark	General Punctuation
U+2329	〈	Left-pointing angle bracket	Miscellaneous Technical
U+276C		Medium left-pointing angle bracket ornament	Dingbats
U+27E8		Mathematical left angle bracket	Misc. Math. Symbols-A
U+29FC		Left-pointing curved angle bracket	Misc. Math. Symbols-B
U+3008	〈	Left angle bracket	CJK Symbols and Punct.

Although angle quotation marks (guillemets, chevrons) have occasionally been used as angular brackets, as in ‹foo›, such usage is very problematic. Their size and shape differs from typographic angular brackets, and they might be incorrectly taken as quotation marks —not only by human readers but also by software, since they *are* quotation marks by Unicode definitions. Thus, they may confuse, for example, the automatic processing of quotations.

In the Dingbats block, there are also some other ornamental brackets in addition to U+276C. Generally, Dingbats characters are unsuitable for normal text and should be considered as decorations only, unless used by some special convention.

The characters in the blocks Miscellaneous Mathematical Symbols-A and Symbols-B are relatively new additions to Unicode (added in Version 3.2), and therefore poorly supported. Although U+27E8 (also known as "bra," matching "ket," which is a synonym for mathematical right angle bracket U+27E9) would theoretically be most adequate for use as an angular bracket, U+2329 is usually a much more practical choice.

Yet, the Unicode standard says about U+2329 and the right-pointing angle bracket U+232A that they are "discouraged for mathematical use because of their canonical equivalence to CJK punctuation." They have indeed been defined as canonical equivalent to U+3008 and U+3009, though displayed as visually different. The Unicode names of these characters, "left angle bracket" and "right angle bracket" are misleading, since they give no hint of their nature. They are meant for use in East Asian writing along with Chinese-Japanese-Korean ideographs. Consequently, they have some surprising properties.

A glyph for the left angle bracket 〈 (U+3008) has to suit its use with ideographs designed to fit into a square, such as 懌. Therefore, the left-pointing angle bracket 〈 (U+2329) is much more suitable, for example, for mathematical texts in English. However, the canonical equivalence means that software conforming to the Unicode standard may effectively treat them as identical, and mapping to any Unicode normalization form will replace U+2329 with U+3008.

Thus, if you really need angular brackets (in mathematics, for example):

1. Use the mathematical brackets U+27E8 and U+27E9, if you can be reasonably sure that these rarely available characters will be displayed and printed correctly.

2. Otherwise, use the left-pointing and right-pointing angle brackets U+2329 and U+232A (which are available in a few fonts), if you can guarantee that no problems will arise from normalization or other operations based on canonical equivalence.

3. Both of the above failing, use the less-than sign and the greater-than sign, and give appropriate explanations so that readers will understand them as delimiters.

Line Structure Control

For practical reasons, text usually needs to be divided into lines when presented visually. This is caused by the properties of media like papyrus scroll, sheet of paper, or computer screen. If we used continuous tapes for writing, things would be different.

Different Approaches to Line Structuring

When text is presented in digital coded form, it seems natural to leave out the line division. It can be handled by the rendering software, which selects the line length according to the rendering situation and styling instructions. This is typically the approach in modern text processing: a paragraph does not contain any line structure information. The same applies to data formats such as HTML and TeX: although the source format may contain line breaks, they are normally ignored (treating them as equivalent to spaces). You would use explicit markup, such as br in HTML, to force a line break.

However, in the early days of computing things were different, and this is still reflected in important ways. Text data files were line-oriented, since the files were treated more or less as images of a deck of punched cards (with 80 characters in each card), line printer output (typically consisting of 132 character wide lines), or computer screens (usually 80 characters wide). This means that the digital files were internally divided into lines as well, using some of the coding methods we will discuss shortly.

Line structure became semantically important, too. In the absence of more advanced methods, text was formatted using blank lines between paragraphs and other blocks of text. Indentation was created by using spaces at the start of a line. Spaces were also used to create table-like display of data or pictures formed from characters ("ASCII graphics"), and naturally this implied that line structure is essential.

Line structure is also used for presenting tabular data in formats such as Tab Separated Values (TSV) or Comma Separated Values (CSV). They are commonly used for transferring data as text between spreadsheet programs and other software. A row of a table is presented as one line of text, with a horizontal tab or comma or other character as separator between cells.

Many computer languages have been designed to be line-structured. Although in most *programming languages* (excluding original FORTRAN, Python, and few others), line structuring is just visual formatting for the human eye, most *command languages* use a line as a fundamental concept. Typically, a command consists of one line.

In particular, *Internet protocols* typically use command (or control) languages that are line structured. For example, an email message header is a logical line, beginning with a key word and a colon—e.g., From: or Subject:—and extending to the end of line. In such headers, the continuation line convention is that a line beginning with at least one space is treated as a continuation of the preceding physical line.

Lines and Records

Lines are often called "records," or "physical records" to distinguish them from a logical record concept. A logical record may correspond to one physical record or a sequence of physical records (e.g., a postal address record consists of several lines, or physical records), or the correspondence can be more complicated. In any case, logical and physical records are at different conceptual levels, and logical record structure is either not explicit at all or it is expressed using tools above the character level.

The situation is somewhat more complex, though. Although a physical record (in text data) normally corresponds to a line, it may actually span several lines. To express this somewhat confusing situation, we can distinguish between physical line and logical line.

In line-structured languages and data, it may happen that a line needs to be longer than conveniently fits into one physical line. In such cases, some *continuation line* convention is applied so that one logical line can consist of several physical lines. Even in programming languages that are not line structured, continuation line conventions are useful for constructs that do not permit a line break inside them, most important, string constant literals. The conventions vary. A common one is that a reverse solidus \ (backslash) at the end of line indicates that the logical line continues at the start (character position 1) of the next physical line and the \ itself is not treated as data. In such a convention, \ before a line break effectively nullifies the line break (and the \ character itself).

Continuation lines are not a Unicode issue, since the continuation line conventions operate at a higher level. In Unicode, the distinction between physical line and logical line as just described does not exist.

Methods of Coding Line Structure

Several methods have been deployed for expressing a line structure at the character level:

- Precede each line by data that expresses the length of the line in octets. Writing characters must be line-buffered: they are written to an internal buffer that is flushed out when the line is complete and its length can be written out before the line itself.
- Make all lines of the same, fixed and known length, such as 80 characters, using spaces or other neutral characters for padding. Essentially, a text file is then structurally equivalent to a deck of punched cards with no separator between the cards. This is wasteful but simple, and it was widely used in the early days of computing.

You can still find legacy data and even legacy systems that use such an approach. Care must be taken when dealing with trailing spaces, since some of them might be significant and not just padding.

- Use control characters for start of line and end of line. Although this may seem unnecessarily explicit, as compared with indicating just line breaks, it is the line structure model used in SGML, for example. By default, SGML uses line feed as start of line (record start, RS) and carriage return as end of line (record end, RE). In implementations, it is common to use line break control as described next, and programs are expected to infer the missing start of line (and end of line) characters.

- Use control characters between lines. The expression "line break" is often used to refer to one or more control characters used for the purpose. This is the most common approach nowadays, but the problem is that there are several line break conventions. Even the last line is usually terminated by a line break, although it is then ambiguous whether the data ends with an empty line or not. The control characters used in different environments are listed in the next table.

The line break characters are summarized in Table 8-12. Note that CR and LF, the most common control characters for line breaks, are seriously ambiguous.

Table 8-12. Line break characters in Unicode

Abbr.	Code	Unicode name	Comments
LF	U+000A	Line feed	Line break or paragraph break; "control-J"
VT	U+000B	Vertical tabulation	Line break in MS Word; "control-K"
FF	U+000C	Form feed	Page break, implying line break; "control-L"
CR	U+000D	Carriage return	Line break or paragraph break; "control-M"
NEL	U+0085	Next line	Line break in some systems
LS	U+2028	Line separator	Unambiguous, but used very little
PS	U+2029	Paragraph separator	Unambiguous, but used very little

Commonly used conventions on line breaks include the following:

- Some systems (e.g., Macintosh) use CR between lines.

- Some systems (e.g., Unix) use LF between lines; XML follows this practice in the sense that XML processors canonicalize line breaks to LF.

- Many systems use a CR LF pair (carriage return immediately followed by line feed) to indicate a single line break, and this is a basic convention in most Internet contexts, for example.

On Windows systems, CR LF is normally used as a line break. However, in text-processing software such as MS Word, CR LF separates *paragraphs*. In such usage, there is normally no line structure inside a paragraph, so a paragraph is like a long line, as far as line break controls are considered.

Editors, Word Processors, and Data Transfer

The differences described in the previous section are a common source of problems in data transfer between programs, even inside a single computer. The programs commonly used for processing text can be roughly divided into two categories. An *editor* processes plain text and is often line oriented, and lines are typically separated by LF (or CR or CR LF). At the simplest, an editor uses one font only, and it stores no font information in a file it creates. Widely used editors include Notepad and Emacs. A *word processor* such as MS Word can handle different fonts, underlining, tabular formatting, and many other kinds of visual enhancements. This means that it saves data in a particular internal format that contains formatting data in addition to the text itself.

Normally a text processor can read or write plain text files, too. Thus, data can be transferred between a text processor and an editor in plain text at least. There are pitfalls, however. Differences in line break conventions often cause trouble. If you use MS Word and tell the program to save a document as plain text, there is a considerable difference between "plain text" and "plain text with line breaks" in the format menu of the "Save As" function. In "plain text," a paragraph is saved as one long line, and this may cause trouble if you try to open the file in an editor. "Plain text with line breaks" splits a paragraph into lines, separated with CR LF, according to the current visual rendering (which depends on the window width). This is usually much more digestible to an editor. It may imply that information about paragraph breaks is lost, though.

Mathematical and Technical Symbols

There is a large and growing amount of characters that are used as special symbols in mathematical and technical texts, often in highly specialized meaning and context. The use of mathematical notations is increasingly common even in social sciences and humanities. Rules for usage are generally well established, though with some typographic and other variation. See, for example, the extensive international standard ISO 31-11, "Quantities and Units. Part 11: Mathematical signs and symbols for use in the physical sciences and technology." The MathWorld web site *http://mathworld.wolfram.com* illustrates and explains the conventional mathematical notations.

In Unicode, digits and other numeric symbols appear in different script-specific blocks, including Basic Latin, of course. There are also some very commonly used mathematical operators and other symbols in blocks like Basic Latin, Latin-1 Supplement, and General Punctuation. In addition to these, there are several blocks for mathematical and technical symbols, allocated in a rather confusing way for historical reasons. An overview of this situation is given in Table 8-13. For more information, consult the Unicode Technical Report 25, "Unicode Support for Mathematics," *http://www.unicode.org/reports/tr25/*.

Table 8-13. Blocks containing mathematical and technical symbols

Code range	Name of block	Notes
0000..007F	Basic Latin	E.g., 0, 1, +, %, =, <
FF00..FFEF	Halfwidth and Fullwidth Forms	Clones of symbols, for CJK
0080..00FF	Latin-1 Supplement	E.g., ¬, ±, ², ×, ½
0300..03FF	Greek and Coptic	Used as symbols, e.g., π
2000..206F	General Punctuation	E.g., fraction slash,/
2150..218F	Number Forms	Fractions, Roman numerals
2070..209F	Superscripts and Subscripts	Digits, parentheses, etc.
2100..214F	Letterlike Symbols	E.g., ℰ, ℕ, ℵ
1D400..1D7FF	Mathematical Alphanumeric Symbols	Bold, italic, etc., variants
2190..21FF	Arrows	E.g., →, ↔
2200..22FF	Mathematical Operators	E.g., ∂, Δ, ∏, ∞, ≈
2A00..2AFF	Supplemental Mathematical Operators	Variants of operators, etc.
27C0..27EF	Miscellaneous Mathematical Symbols-A	Modal logic, etc.
2980..29FF	Miscellaneous Mathematical Symbols-B	Brackets, fences, angles, etc.
27F0..27FF	Supplemental Arrows-A	Long arrows, etc.
2900..297F	Supplemental Arrows-B	Arrows with strokes, etc.
2B00..2BFF	Miscellaneous Symbols and Arrows	White and black arrows, etc.
25A0..25FF	Geometric Shapes	E.g., □, ▲, ◇, ◙
2500..257F	Box Drawing	E.g., ┌, ─, ┐, ╠, =, ╝
2580..259F	Block Elements	E.g., ▜, ▄, ▓
2400..243F	Control Pictures	Names of controls, e.g., ␕
2300..23FF	Miscellaneous Technical	E.g., ⌀, ⌂, ⎰, ⌊, ⌋, ⌘, ⌽

Superscripts and Subscripts

Superscripts are used partly as stylistic variation, as in writing "first" as "1st" and not "1st." On the other hand, superscripting is used to indicate exponentiation and other semantic relations; for example, "2^3" is certainly not just a stylistic variant of "23." Subscripting is mostly a matter of established notational convention, as in "H2O."

Both superscripting and subscripting are mostly something applied to character data, rather than part of the data itself. However, largely reflecting the practices of older character codes, Unicode contains some characters that are superscript or subscript variants of other characters, usually defined as compatibility equivalents. Many of them are letters, such as masculine ordinal indicator º (U+00BA), which is a superscript letter "o," and modifier letter small "h" ʰ (U+02B0), which is a phonetic symbol.

Superscript variants that can be used for mathematical purposes exist in Unicode for digits 0–9, letters "i" and "n," plus and minus sign, equals sign, and normal parentheses. For historical reasons, superscript variants of 1, 2, and 3 are not in the Superscripts and Subscripts block but in the Latin-1 Supplement. Subscript variants exist for digits 0–9, plus and minus sign, equals sign, and normal parentheses.

Thus, you could write relatively complicated superscripts or subscripts. However, this is not very common and it would not take you very far. You would inevitably meet restrictions in writing superscript or subscript expressions. Normally other methods are used, such as markup languages or special formatting, as discussed in Chapter 9.

The Number Forms Block

The Number Forms block covers the range from U+2150 to U+218F and contains some relatively uninteresting characters, which are *special presentations of some numerals*. Almost all of them are compatibility characters. Currently the block contains only characters for Roman numerals and for some vulgar (common) fractions.

Roman numerals

The characters for Roman numerals are not meant to be used in normal text. Instead of U+2162 Roman numeral three, Ⅲ, you normally use a sequence of capital letters, "III." The special characters for Roman numerals have been included in Unicode for compatibility with other character codes.

It has been argued, though, that the special characters for Roman numerals might be preferable due to their more specific semantics. The character U+2160 Roman numeral one unambiguously denotes a number, while the Latin capital letter "I" has multiple uses. A speech generator, for example, would in principle be in a much better position to decide how to pronounce the notation. But this will probably remain just theory.

Fractions

Fractional numbers such as 1/4 (one fourth) are commonly written in linearized notation, using normal digits and a normal solidus (slash) character. However, in typesetting traditions, fractions are often presented in a different style, perhaps using special glyphs, like ¼. There are two basic variants of the style: "shilling" fractions, where the numerator and denominator are separated by a slanted slash, and "vertical" fractions, where the numerator is right above the denominator and there is a horizontal line between them.

Some frequently used fractions have been included into Unicode as separate characters. For example, there is the character U+00BC, vulgar fraction one fourth (¼), which is compatibility equivalent to the three-character sequence 1/4. In most fonts, the appearance is "shilling" fraction.

The only such fractions in ISO Latin 1 are ½, ¼, and ¾. They appeared in some typewriter keyboards and may still appear in some computer keyboards. Moreover, when you type, say, the characters 1/4 in succession, your word processor might convert the sequence to ¼, as described in Chapter 2. This can be undesirable especially if your document contains other fractions, like 1/3, which would appear in a quite different style.

In Unicode, the Number Forms block contains a few more fraction characters, namely for 1/3, 2/3, 1/5, 2/5, 3/5, 4/5, 1/6, 5/6, 1/8, 3/8, 5/8, 7/8, as well as for numerator one (1/). However, only a few fonts contain glyphs for them.

As a different approach, you could use the U+2044 fraction slash character. This character, absent in many fonts, has an appearance similar to that of the common solidus, though it is often more slanted, even in an 45° angle, as in ⁄. More important, it has special semantics, as suggested by its name. It unambiguously separates the numerator and the denominator of a fraction and never has any other meaning. Moreover, a program that is capable of rendering fractions in a classic typographic style should do that automatically. However, such behavior is not common in programs. In MS Word, you probably get just something like the following: 1⁄4 (i.e., normally rendered 1 and 4 separated with the fraction slash).

Thus, if you wish to produce typographically formatted fractions, you mostly need tools above the character level, such as typesetting commands. The web page "How to create fractions in Word," *http://word.mvps.org/FAQs/Formatting/CreateFraction.htm*, illustrates some techniques in producing both "vertical" fractions and "shilling" fractions.

Characters in SI Notations

This subsection discusses the character-level issues of presenting values of physical quantities according to the SI, the International System of Units (Système international). For general information on the SI, please refer to the Metric System FAQ *http://www.cl.cam.ac.uk/~mgk25/metric-system-faq.txt*. Note especially its item 1.12, "What is the correct way of writing metric units?," which also mentions some practical typing methods not discussed here.

The organization responsible for the definition of SI units is the General Conference on Weights and Measures (CGPM), *http://www.bipm.org/en/convention/cgpm/*. Official information is also available from the Bureau International des Poids et Mesures (BIPM), see *http://www.bipm.org/en/si/*, and the National Institute of Standards and Technology (NIST), see *http://physics.nist.gov/cuu/Units/*. There are also international ISO standards and national standards on the use of the SI.

Conceptual levels of SI notations

The use of the SI can be considered at different levels, which are defined by different standards, conventions, and other norms:

- Physical definitions of units, established by international conventions; the definitions are often complicated in order to be exact; and they need to name the units somehow, but the different language-dependent names are not defined in this context; example: "The meter is the length of the path travelled by light in vacuum during a time interval of 1/299 792 458 of a second."
- Names of units, such as "metre" (British English), "meter" (U.S. English), "Meter" (German), "metri" (Finnish), etc.; these are defined by various language authorities, or just by common usage in a language community.

- Symbols of units, such as "m" for the meter; these symbols are defined by international conventions and are intended for international use as such; however, in some cultures, otherwise applying the SI, language-dependent abbreviations are used as symbols, such as кг for kilogram in Russian.

- Use of prefixes for multiples and submultiples of units, such as "km," written as "kilometre" in British English, for 1 000 m; these are defined by international conventions, but other norms, such as national standards, have added further recommendations, such as the recommendation to avoid the prefix "h" ("hecto-" in English), except perhaps for special use; similarly to units, the prefixes are supposed to have an internationally standardized, language-independent symbol and language-dependent names (generally sharing a common origin).

- Expression of quantities using a numeric value and a unit, perhaps with a prefix, such as "1,5 km" or "1.5 km," depending on language, or maybe, for example, "1.5×10^3 m"; this is defined by international conventions, with additional recommendations from other sources, including national standards and publishers' rules.

- The exact identification of characters used to write the expressions. Since the conventions generally do not identify characters except by showing them, this is a somewhat gray area; but it is the level that we are mostly interested in here.

- Typography, such as the width of a space used to separate a number from a unit, or the use of a particular font to render a character like "m," such as Times New Roman "m" or Arial "m"; this is generally not standardized but left to typographers, except that there is a strong recommendation to use "upright" letters and not an italics font.

Here we mostly consider the last but one level, characters, or abstract characters to be more exact.

Notes on individual characters

Most characters used in SI notations can easily be identified as abstract characters, or more specifically, as Unicode characters. For example, the symbol of the meter, "m," is apparently the character named Latin small letter "m" in Unicode, with the code position 6D in hexadecimal, therefore it's often denoted by U+006D in Unicode contexts. But the following characters need to be considered:

- The multiplication symbols, which are used in numeric expressions like the alternative notations "$1,5 \cdot 10^3$" and "1.5×10^3." They can apparently be identified with the Unicode characters middle dot (U+00B7) and multiplication sign (U+00D7). The former is also used in symbols for compound units such as "N·m" (newton meter; often written less suitably as "N m" or questionably as "Nm"). However, it can be argued that middle dot is a punctuation character and that the dot used for multiplication (called "half-high dot" in the ISO 31-0 standard) should be identified with U+22C5 dot operator, which is classified as a mathematical operator. A practical argument in favor of this is that the representative glyph for dot operator in the Unicode code chart is a larger dot than that of the middle dot, hence more noticeable and more suitable for use as an operator. And in the Arial Unicode MS font—one of the few fonts that has a fairly good repertoire of mathematical symbols—the situation is the same and dot operator is at a somewhat higher position. It is positioned in a way that corresponds better to the notion of a multiplication operator. You can see this from the following samples that contain (in Arial Unicode MS) the expression for pascal second first using the middle dot, then using the dot operator: Pa·s Pa·s

- The division symbol used for constructing derived units like "m/s" (meters per second) is most logically identified with the division slash U+2215. However, this character is not present in most fonts, so it is normal to use the ASCII solidus U+002F, also known as slash, character as surrogate. In theory, division slash would be preferable, since it has a more exact meaning.

- The minus sign used before a number (in an exponent, too), is logically to be identified with the minus sign, U+2212. However, instead of this character, the en dash, U+2013, or (far more often) the ASCII hyphen-minus U+002D is used. A problem with these is that Unicode line breaking rules permit a line break after these characters. This creates the risk of having the sign appear at the end of a line and the number at the start of the next line. (This should not happen for the real minus sign.) There are various ways to try to avoid this problem—e.g., by using the nonstandard nobr markup in HTML authoring.

- The space between a numeric value and a unit (or between unit symbols when multiplication of units is indicated in this less satisfactory way). It is difficult to say how the space is to be interpreted in Unicode, considering the multitude of space characters in Unicode. Presumably, any space character, excluding those with zero width, is acceptable. Using the no-break space U+00A0 character would help in preventing undesired line breaks between the number and the unit. Using the thin space U+2009 character would help in making the space narrower than a normal space between words. The problem is that these two cannot be combined in a single Unicode character, in the present repertoire of Unicode. There are different possible approaches:

- The exponents used in some numeric values (such as "1.5×10^3") as well as in many compound unit symbols (such as "m^2" or "s^{-1}"). The numbers 2 and 3 as exponents can easily be represented using the characters for them, superscript two U+00B2 and superscript three U+00B3. Unicode contains also other digits and the minus sign as exponent, but these characters have very limited support in programs and fonts. Hence, it is better to use the tools of text-processing systems or other methods (such as sup markup in HTML) for superscripting for them. For typographic reasons, it is best to represent all superscript that way if you need anything other that just 2 or 3. Otherwise, the visual difference in superscripting of, for example, 2 and -1 is too disturbing.

- The symbol of micro prefix, corresponding to multiplication by 10^{-6}. An apparent candidate is the micro sign (U+00B5), μ, which is widely available in fonts. However, Unicode defines micro sign as a compatibility character that has Greek small letter mu U+03BC as its compatibility decomposition. This means that the two are distinct characters but the micro sign has been included for legacy reasons only, and the two are equivalent except perhaps for formatting information. In practice, the characters are very often similar in appearance. Since the micro sign is more widely available, it is probably to be preferred. It might also be argued that it has unambiguous semantics, whereas Greek small letter mu is primarily a letter and has varying other uses as well.

- The symbol for ohm can be identified with the ohm sign Ω (U+2126, in the Symbols Area). It has a specific meaning, but it is defined as canonical equivalent to Greek capital letter omega Ω (U+03A9), and the Unicode standard recommends using the latter. The ohm sign has somewhat wider support in fonts. If a font contains both, they may look somewhat different.

- The degree symbol is naturally the degree sign ° (U+00B0). As explained in the description of the Latin-1 Supplement, it is important to distinguish this symbol from the masculine ordinal indicator, U+00BA.

- The symbols for minutes and seconds in expressions for angles should be identified with the prime (U+2032) and the double prime (U+2033). However, these characters are rarely available, so it is common to use the ASCII apostrophe (U+0027) and the ASCII quotation mark (U+0022) as surrogates. In visual appearance, prime and double prime are clearly slanted, whereas apostrophe and quotation mark should have straight (vertical) glyphs according to Unicode, and they often have.

- Several letterlike symbols in Unicode denote characters used in the SI context, in a sense. However, this is mostly an illusion, and a misleading one. For example, the script small "l" (U+2113), is often used as a symbol for liter. However, the NIST Guide to SI units explicitly says: "The script letter ℓ is not an approved symbol for the liter." Such confusions will be separately discussed in the next section.

Letterlike symbols and the SI

People interested in unit symbols and Unicode have become surprised when they have found that, for example, the unit "degree Celsius" has a symbol of its own, U+2103, presenting °C as a single character. Similarly, for degree Fahrenheit (a completely non-SI unit of course), there is U+2109; for siemens, U+2127; and for Kelvin, U+212A, for example, in the Letterlike Symbols block. Educated people may well think that it is better to use such specific characters, with limited semantics, especially if dealing with documents that might be read by a text-to-speech converter later on, or otherwise processed by software that might use semantic information about characters. They might also be seen as typographically suitable, since they allow detailed formatting that corresponds to the specific meanings.

But in addition to being poorly supported in most fonts, such characters are inadequate in principle, by Unicode rules. For example, degree Celsius U+2103 is compatibility equivalent to U+00B0 U+0043 (i.e., degree sign followed by letter C). It has little to do with typographic correctness. Rather, it is a matter of compatibility, so that data containing that character in some non-Unicode encoding can be encoded in Unicode without losing the distinction between that character and the U+00B0 U+0043 pair, should someone wish to retain that distinction. This means that the data can also be converted back to the original encoding and get the original data exactly. It is not recommended for use in new, originally Unicode data. The Unicode standard says, in the discussion of unit symbols:

> **Unit Symbols**. Several letterlike symbols are used to indicate units. In most cases, however, such as for SI units (Système International), the use of regular letters or other symbols is preferred. U+2113 SCRIPT SMALL L is commonly used as a non-SI symbol for the liter. Official SI usage prefers the regular lowercase letter l.

> Three letterlike symbols have been given canonical equivalence to regular letters: U+2126 OHM SIGN, U+211A KELVIN SIGN, and U+211B ANGSTROM SIGN. In all three instances the regular letter should be used. In normal use, it is better to represent degrees Celsius "°C" with a sequence of U+00B0 DEGREE SIGN + U+0043 LATIN CAPITAL LETTER C, rather than U+2103 DEGREE CELSIUS. For searching, treat these two sequences as identical.

Unfortunately, the Unicode standard has wrong information about the symbol for the liter. The official position in the SI system is that both "l" and "L" are allowed, with no expressed preference (although in the U.S., "L" is preferred by national authorities).

The special letterlike characters discussed here were taken into Unicode due to their presence in some character codes used in East Asia, such as the Japanese JIS X 0212. These characters do their job in allowing conversions between character codes without losing information. Problems arise when people use utilities like the Character Map (described in Chapter 2) without knowing the background and looking just at the characters and their names.

To conclude, it is acceptable and recommendable to use normal Latin letters as SI unit symbols, such as "K" for kelvin.

Other Blocks

Some Unicode blocks of general interest are described here. For information on blocks that relate to a particular writing system or a specialized application area, please refer to the appropriate section in the Unicode standard. The overall effect of writing systems on character usage was discussed in Chapter 7.

Spacing Modifier Letters

Some characters in this block are "spacing clones" of diacritic marks. That is, they are defined as being compatibility equivalent to space U+0020 followed by a combining diacritic mark. However, this block includes quite a few other characters as well. They are mostly written after a letter, though some of them are actually used as independent letters —e.g., the different apostrophe-like characters that are used to transliterate the Arabic character hamza.

For example, the first of the characters in this block, modifier letter small "h" (U+02B0), is used to indicate aspiration of the preceding consonant in phonetic notations (e.g., in pronunciation instructions in encyclopedias). This character is a compatibility character, which is defined to be compatibility equivalent to letter "h" in superscript style. The results of using U+02B0 (from a font where it exists) and using "h" formatted in superscript style may differ, of course, especially since programs often implement superscripting simply by decreasing the size of a glyph and putting it in a higher position. Good font design tries to make the appearance better, perhaps modifying the shape to suit the needs of small-size rendering. Compare the following ways of denoting an aspirated pronunciation of "k," using first U+02B0, and then "h" as a superscript: kʰ kʰ.

Currency Symbols

Currencies can be denoted in several ways: words, currency symbol characters, or various abbreviations or codes. The optimal choice depends on the context and intentions. When uniqueness, definiteness, and internationality (as neutrality with respect to national languages) are essential, the three-letter codes as defined in ISO 4217 should be used—e.g., "GBP 42." In localized notations, the formats vary—e.g., "£42" versus "42 £"—and so do currency names, of course. The Common Locale Data Repository, described in Chapter 11, contains extensive information on such localized formats. Currency symbol characters (general category Sc) appear in different blocks in Unicode:

- The dollar sign $ is in the Basic Latin block.
- The cent sign ¢, the pound sign £, the currency sign ¤, and the yen sign ¥ are in the Latin-1 Supplement block.
- There are several currency symbols in script-specific blocks, such as the Thai currency symbol baht ฿ (U+0E3F) in the Thai block.
- Other currency symbols are in the Currency Symbols block, U+20A0..U+20CF. It includes important symbols such as the euro sign € (U+20AC) but also some characters that are historical only, such as the French franc sign ₣ (U+20A3). The euro-currency sign ₠ (U+20A0) is not even historical but only a symbol that was once planned and allocated, and it has not been removed, due to Unicode principles.

Phonetic Characters

Phonetic characters are used in writing systems that indicate the pronunciation. The most widely known and used phonetic alphabet is the *International Phonetic Alphabet (IPA)*. Originally designed for use in linguistics, IPA is also used in language teaching and in pronunciation instructions in dictionaries and encyclopedias, though in English material, other pronunciation notations are more common. In developing writing systems for languages that previously existed in spoken form only, some IPA characters are often used along with normal Latin letters.

IPA is a fairly old alphabet and was originally defined by indicating the visible shapes of characters only. For computer applications, the characters had to be defined more exactly. Some characters were identified with normal Latin (lowercase) letters, such as "b." Some were identified with other characters that are used in normal writing too, such as æ (which belongs to the Latin-1 Supplement). But most IPA characters were separately coded in the IPA Extensions block.

No writing system can accurately describe all details of spoken language. Even IPA notations are just approximations. Moreover, they are approximations of different degrees. Simple IPA writing can be used, for example, in dictionaries, whereas transcription of speech in linguistics uses more exact descriptions, using diacritic marks to indicate nuances.

The needs of IPA transcription differ from conventions of general purpose typesetting. This is not surprising, since IPA attempts a precision of phonetic representation that is well beyond that of the normal alphabet of any Latin script language. For this purpose, IPA uses diacritic marks, but it also assigns a distinctive meaning to forms that in general purpose typography are considered purely stylistic variants of the same letter. The most obvious case is that IPA includes both the common (ASCII) letter "a" and a variant of the letter "a" that denotes a vowel of different quality. The latter letter is oddly named: Latin small letter alpha ɑ (U+0251).

For such reasons, IPA characters do not follow typical typographic conventions in the distinction between roman and italic styles. In simple terms, an italic IPA font needs to be something akin to an oblique version of roman, rather than a distinct style of lettering. Thus, IPA involves a specialized technical kind of typesetting, not very different from, for example, mathematical typesetting in the way that it assigns distinct meaning to stylistic variants of letterforms.

Many characters in the IPA Extensions blocks are turned or otherwise modified versions of Latin letters. For example, the Latin small letter schwa ə (U+0259) is originally a rotated image of "e." It denotes the neutral and often reduced vowel that is so common in English, and it is present in some fonts that do not otherwise contain IPA Extensions.

For example, the standard British pronunciation of the English word "international" can be written in IPA as ɪntəˈnæʃənəl. The character "n" there, for example, is the common Latin letter, whereas the character æ is the same Latin small letter "ae" (U+00E6) as used, for example, in Danish and old English. Some other characters, such as the schwa, are from the IPA extensions block. The IPA stress mark, modifier letter vertical line ˈ (U+02C8), is not common in fonts, and often other characters such as the (ASCII) apostrophe ' (U+0027) are used instead.

The official description of IPA is available at the site *http://www.arts.gla.ac.uk/ipa/ ipachart.html*. Since characters used in IPA appear in different blocks in Unicode, you may find the following document useful: "The International Phonetic Alphabet in Unicode," *http://www.phon.ucl.ac.uk/home/wells/ipa-unicode.htm*.

Due to the heavy use of diacritic marks, IPA transcription often requires implementations that support combining diacritic marks, since most of the combinations needed do not appear as precomposed characters in Unicode. However, for simple usage of IPA, relatively simple implementations of such marks are tolerable.

For simple IPA, the Arial Unicode MS font is sufficient and suitable. For more advanced purposes, you may wish to use the Doulos SIL font, available from *http://scripts.sil.org*.

In addition to IPA, there are other phonetic writing systems. One of them, the Uralic Phonetic Alphabet (UPA), has been included into Unicode. The added characters are in the Phonetic Extensions block.

Specials

The Specials block contains just a few code positions, U+FFF0 through U+FFFF, and they are indeed special:

- U+FFF0 through U+FFF8 are unassigned (reserved for eventual future use).
- U+FFF9 through U+FFFB are interlinear annotation characters, explained below.
- U+FFFC is an *object replacement character*, which is an invisible placeholder for a nontextual object, such as an image, to be inserted (by some external tools). In code charts, 〔OBJ〕 appears in place of this character.
- U+FFFD is a *replacement character*, for use in data converted from a code other than Unicode, to indicate a character that has no Unicode counterpart. This is somewhat similar to U+001A (substitute, Control-Z) in the ASCII range. However, U+FFFD has a visible shape ◆ (although it appears in a few fonts only). In the Java programming language, U+FFFD is traditionally used to indicate Not a Number (NaN)—i.e., undefined result of a mathematical operation; this does not comply with the meaning of U+FFFD in Unicode.
- U+FFFE and U+FFFF are noncharacters—i.e., code positions that do not and will not ever represent any characters. They can be used as sentinels or for checking purposes. Any occurrence of these code points in character data (i.e., in data being interpreted as characters) indicates an error of some kind.

Interlinear annotation characters are invisible indicators (control characters, in a sense) that separate interlinear annotations from normal text. "Interlinear" means "between the lines" and refers to information presented between normal lines in small font. Interlinear annotations, called *ruby* or *furigana*, are typically used in Japanese books for children or for foreigners studying Japanese, and they usually show the pronunciation of words. The name "ruby" is originally the name of a font size.

Although interlinear annotations primarily relate to East Asian languages, they might conceivably be used for other purposes as well. They could be used to indicate the pronunciation of foreign words in English text, or to add editor's or translator's short notes, or even to create documents with lyrics with guitar chords so that the chords will be displayed above the respective text. However, software that supports interlinear annotations may do so in a manner designed for annotations of East Asian texts—e.g., using a very small font by default.

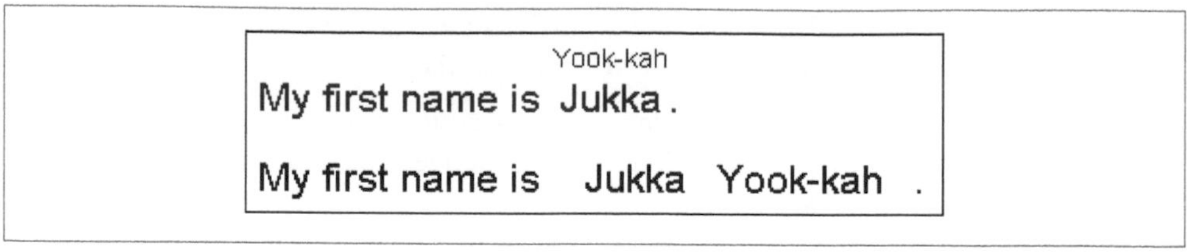

Figure 8-3. Display of interlinear annotations on IE 6; the first alternative uses Ruby markup, the second tries to use interlinear annotation characters in Unicode

Interlinear annotations are best described at higher protocol levels, such as the markup elements in the Ruby module of XHTML. The Ruby module belongs to XHTML 1.1 and has some limited support in Internet Explorer (IE) since Version 6.

The interlinear annotation characters in Unicode are of rather limited usefulness. Very few programs support them. When they are not supported, something odd may appear in their place, and the annotations would appear in normal text. However, the characters might conceivably be used if you need to represent the annotations in plain text format and you have (or you can create) software that supports them. The characters are:

- U+FFF9 interlinear annotation anchor indicates the start of normal text that has an annotation attached to it; corresponds to markup `<rb>` in Ruby in XHTML.

- U+FFFA interlinear annotation separator indicates the end of the text being annotated and the start of the annotation; corresponds to `</rb><rt>` in Ruby.

- U+FFFB interlinear annotation terminator ends the annotation, so that subsequent characters will be taken as normal text; corresponds to `</rt>` in Ruby.

The following piece of XHTML markup uses first Ruby markup, then interlinear annotation characters (via character references) to add information about the pronunciation of a name. The markup method is the one that has the best chance of working. This is illustrated in Figure 8-3:

```
<p>My first name is <ruby><rb>Jukka</rb><rt>Yook-kah</rt></ruby>.</p>
<p>My first name is &#xfff9;Jukka&#xfffa;Yook-kah&#xfffb;.</p>
```

Dingbats

Dingbats are essentially graphics coded as characters. One might say that the meaning of a dingbat is its graphic appearance. This makes dingbats rather special. On the other hand, in practice, some of the dingbats have a fairly well-defined logical meaning, and putting them into this block has been a rather arbitrary decision.

Dingbats are used by switching to a special font. This means that data is typically in an 8-bit encoding but by font change, characters are visually turned into something quite different. Thus, you could type the letter "a," and then change the font to a special one, and get checkmark ✓ (U+2713). However, this is not the Unicode way.

This block of Unicode in general does not contain all the graphics that have been implemented in different specialized fonts. For example, corporate logos are excluded. Many of the symbols in the Windings fonts commonly available in computers have not been coded as characters in Unicode at all.

Summary of Blocks

Table 8-14 lists all blocks as defined in Unicode Version 4.1 and planned for Version 5.0. The up-to-date summary information on blocks is in the file *Blocks.txt* in the Unicode character database, available online at *http://www.unicode.org*. Many blocks correspond more or less directly to some specific scripts (writing systems) discussed in Chapter 7.

Table 8-14. Unicode 4.1 blocks

Code range	Name of block	Notes
0000..007F	Basic Latin	ASCII
0080..00FF	Latin-1 Supplement	Upper half of Latin 1
0100..017F	Latin Extended-A	
0180..024F	Latin Extended-B	
0250..02AF	IPA Extensions	Phonetic symbols
02B0..02FF	Spacing Modifier Letters	
0300..036F	Combining Diacritical Marks	
0370..03FF	Greek and Coptic	
0400..04FF	Cyrillic	
0500..052F	Cyrillic Supplement	
0530..058F	Armenian	
0590..05FF	Hebrew	
0600..06FF	Arabic	
0700..074F	Syriac	
0750..077F	Arabic Supplement	
0780..07BF	Thaana	
07C0..07FF	NKo	Proposed (Unicode 5.0)
0900..097F	Devanagari	For Indic languages
0980..09FF	Bengali	
0A00..0A7F	Gurmukhi	
0A80..0AFF	Gujarati	
0B00..0B7F	Oriya	
0B80..0BFF	Tamil	
0C00..0C7F	Telugu	
0C80..0CFF	Kannada	
0D00..0D7F	Malayalam	

Code range	Name of block	Notes
0D80..0DFF	Sinhala	
0E00..0E7F	Thai	
0E80..0EFF	Lao	
0F00..0FFF	Tibetan	
1000..109F	Myanmar	
10A0..10FF	Georgian	
1100..11FF	Hangul Jamo	
1200..137F	Ethiopic	
1380..139F	Ethiopic Supplement	
13A0..13FF	Cherokee	
1400..167F	Unified Canadian Aboriginal Syllabics	
1680..169F	Ogham	
16A0..16FF	Runic	
1700..171F	Tagalog	
1720..173F	Hanunoo	
1740..175F	Buhid	
1760..177F	Tagbanwa	
1780..17FF	Khmer	
1800..18AF	Mongolian	
1900..194F	Limbu	
1950..197F	Tai Le	
1980..19DF	New Tai Lue	
19E0..19FF	Khmer Symbols	
1A00..1A1F	Buginese	
1B00..1B7F	Balinese	Proposed (Unicode 5.0)
1D00..1D7F	Phonetic Extensions	Mostly for UPA
1D80..1DBF	Phonetic Extensions Supplement	
1DC0..1DFF	Combining Diacritical Marks Supplement	
1E00..1EFF	Latin Extended Additional	
1F00..1FFF	Greek Extended	
2000..206F	General Punctuation	
2070..209F	Superscripts and Subscripts	
20A0..20CF	Currency Symbols	
20D0..20FF	Combining Diacritical Marks for Symbols	
2100..214F	Letterlike Symbols	

Code range	Name of block	Notes
2150..218F	Number Forms	
2190..21FF	Arrows	
2200..22FF	Mathematical Operators	
2300..23FF	Miscellaneous Technical	
2400..243F	Control Pictures	
2440..245F	Optical Character Recognition	
2460..24FF	Enclosed Alphanumerics	
2500..257F	Box Drawing	
2580..259F	Block Elements	
25A0..25FF	Geometric Shapes	
2600..26FF	Miscellaneous Symbols	
2700..27BF	Dingbats	
27C0..27EF	Miscellaneous Mathematical Symbols-A	
27F0..27FF	Supplemental Arrows-A	
2800..28FF	Braille Patterns	
2900..297F	Supplemental Arrows-B	
2980..29FF	Miscellaneous Mathematical Symbols-B	
2A00..2AFF	Supplemental Mathematical Operators	
2B00..2BFF	Miscellaneous Symbols and Arrows	
2C00..2C5F	Glagolitic	
2C60..2C7F	Latin Extended-C	Proposed (Unicode 5.0)
2C80..2CFF	Coptic	
2D00..2D2F	Georgian Supplement	
2D30..2D7F	Tifinagh	
2D80..2DDF	Ethiopic Extended	
2E00..2E7F	Supplemental Punctuation	
2E80..2EFF	CJK Radicals Supplement	
2F00..2FDF	Kangxi Radicals	
2FF0..2FFF	Ideographic Description Characters	
3000..303F	CJK Symbols and Punctuation	
3040..309F	Hiragana	
30A0..30FF	Katakana	
3100..312F	Bopomofo	
3130..318F	Hangul Compatibility Jamo	
3190..319F	Kanbun	

Code range	Name of block	Notes
31A0..31BF	Bopomofo Extended	
31C0..31EF	CJK Strokes	
31F0..31FF	Katakana Phonetic Extensions	
3200..32FF	Enclosed CJK Letters and Months	
3300..33FF	CJK Compatibility	
3400..4DBF	CJK Unified Ideographs Extension A	
4DC0..4DFF	Yijing Hexagram Symbols	
4E00..9FFF	CJK Unified Ideographs	Main block of CJK
A000..A48F	Yi Syllables	
A490..A4CF	Yi Radicals	
A700..A71F	Modifier Tone Letters	
A720..A7FF	Latin Extended-D	Proposed (Unicode 5.0)
A800..A82F	Syloti Nagri	
A840..A87F	Phags-pa	Proposed (Unicode 5.0)
AC00..D7AF	Hangul Syllables	
D800..DB7F	High Surrogates	
DB80..DBFF	High Private Use Surrogates	
DC00..DFFF	Low Surrogates	
E000..F8FF	Private Use Area	
F900..FAFF	CJK Compatibility Ideographs	
FB00..FB4F	Alphabetic Presentation Forms	
FB50..FDFF	Arabic Presentation Forms-A	
FE00..FE0F	Variation Selectors	
FE10..FE1F	Vertical Forms	
FE20..FE2F	Combining Half Marks	
FE30..FE4F	CJK Compatibility Forms	
FE50..FE6F	Small Form Variants	
FE70..FEFF	Arabic Presentation Forms-B	
FF00..FFEF	Halfwidth and Fullwidth Forms	
FFF0..FFFF	Specials	
10000..1007F	Linear B Syllabary	
10080..100FF	Linear B Ideograms	
10100..1013F	Aegean Numbers	
10140..1018F	Ancient Greek Numbers	
10300..1032F	Old Italic	

Code range	Name of block	Notes
10330..1034F	Gothic	
10380..1039F	Ugaritic	
103A0..103DF	Old Persian	
10400..1044F	Deseret	
10450..1047F	Shavian	
10480..104AF	Osmanya	
10800..1083F	Cypriot Syllabary	
10900..1091F	Phoenician	Proposed (Unicode 5.0)
10A00..10A5F	Kharoshthi	
12000..123FF	Cuneiform	Proposed (Unicode 5.0)
12400..1247F	Cuneiform Numbers and Punctuation	Proposed (Unicode 5.0)
1D000..1D0FF	Byzantine Musical Symbols	
1D100..1D1FF	Musical Symbols	
1D200..1D24F	Ancient Greek Musical Notation	
1D300..1D35F	Tai Xuan Jing Symbols	
1D360..1D37F	Chinese Counting Rod Numerals	Proposed (Unicode 5.0)
1D400..1D7FF	Mathematical Alphanumeric Symbols	
20000..2A6DF	CJK Unified Ideographs Extension B	
2F800..2FA1F	CJK Compatibility Ideographs Supplement	
E0000..E007F	Tags	Language tagging
E0100..E01EF	Variation Selectors Supplement	
F0000..FFFFF	Supplementary Private Use Area-A	
100000..10FFFF	Supplementary Private Use Area-B	

CHAPTER 9

The Character Level and Above

In representation of texts, characters form but one protocol level, above which there are higher levels such as markup level, record structure level, and application level. Guidelines will be given about the coding of information at different levels when there is choice, such as using markup versus character difference (largely still an open problem despite the efforts of the World Wide Web Consortium and the Unicode Consortium). This is particularly important to processing of legacy data and to avoiding too fine distinctions at character level. The chapter ends with a section on media types for text and the difference between plain text, other subtypes of text, and application types such as text processing formats.

Levels of Text Representation and Processing

The Unicode standard defines the term *higher-level protocol* as denoting "any agreement on the interpretation of Unicode characters that extends beyond the scope of this standard." It adds a note: "Such an agreement need not be formally announced in data; it may be implicit in the context."

For example, an agreement such as the XML specification says that a sequence of characters like π will be understood as a character reference (denoting the Greek small letter pi π, U+03C0, in this case). This is an example of a very explicit agreement. The scope of this agreement consists of XML documents, though it can, by separate conventions, be extended to apply elsewhere as well.

The same information can often be expressed at different protocol levels—e.g., at the character level or in a program-specific data format. There is no simple answer to the question of which level should be used. Factors to be considered include the following:

- What can be expressed at each protocol level? For example, at the character level, you can specify underlining of a character but not its font size.
- Are there recommendations on using the different methods in applicable standards and specifications? In particular, the Unicode standard defines distinctions that can be made at the character level but more or less deprecates their use.

- How well are the different methods supported by existing software? For example, although you can express the language of text using special Unicode characters, this is very poorly supported (in addition to being deprecated).

- How will the data be processed and transferred, and is it important that information is saved when converting the data to plain text or other data formats?

- How easy are the methods to people who produce texts? For example, they may know well the formatting tools of a word processor but not the ways to enter arbitrary Unicode characters.

Plain Text, Rich Text, and Markup

Roughly speaking, we can characterize some basic formats of text as follows, using widely known software as examples for concreteness:

- Plain text is what you write with a simple editor like Notepad, and it's "text as such."
- Rich text is what a word processor like MS Word generates when you ask it to save in the RTF format.
- Markup is HTML, XML, or something similar, and you could generate it with web publishing software like FrontPage or Nvu.

The normal data formats used by word processors are not text at all in the sense discussed here. This may sound surprising, since when people use such software to create a document with a filename suffix like *.doc*, they usually think they work with text. After all, that's the normal way of typing text to many people. The explanation to this paradox is that such formats (as well as, for example, PDF documents and text databases) *contain* text, but their overall data format is not textual. There is more about this in the last section of this chapter ("Media Types for Text").

When you send a document, or request for a document, by email or otherwise, it is important to specify the format in an understandable way. Do not assume that most people know the distinctions described here. It is often best to specify the format exactly (e.g., "RTF format") rather than generally (e.g., "rich text"), since the specific formats are more widely known. When requesting documents, it is nice to offer a list of allowed formats. Beware, however, that *conversions* between plain text, rich text formats, and markup formats may lose information and may require human intervention (interaction)—i.e., cannot be reliably automated in general.

Data (whether text or not) can be accompanied by information (metadata) that tells how it should be interpreted—i.e., what its data format is. Such information is often included in Internet message headers, as explained in Chapter 10. It should not be confused with markup, which is part of the data itself and typically applies to parts of a document, not the document as a whole. The information about data format should be available before any markup in the document is interpreted, for example, since the format specifies whether anything in the data is to be treated as markup in the first place.

Plain text

A plain text file, such as a file written with Notepad, is just a sequence of characters. It is true that it has a line structure, but that structure is expressed using control characters. When displayed, the text appears in some font, but this is just a choice that can be made for the text as a whole. A plain text file does not contain any font information.

When we move from plain text to word processing—e.g., in MS Word—the most obvious change is that we can use different font faces and sizes for different parts of text. Font changes are not encoded into the characters but expressed using internal data, which is not shown to the user as such but is used to modify the rendering of characters. If you select File → Save As and pick up the plain text format (*.txt), all the formatting information disappears; only the character data is saved.

In a typical word processor, there is much more data that is not shown as part of the document, such as authorship information, date stamps, language information, styling information, and perhaps even a revision history. Styling includes margins, text justification, character and word spacing, etc.

Rich text formats

Data that consists of text and associated formatting or structural information is often called *rich text*. This general concept should not be confused with particular formats such as Rich Text Format (RTF), which is a specific format used for interchange of text between word processors so that formatting information is retained. Rich text is also called *styled text*.

For example, in the RTF format, underlined text like foo is written as {\ul foo}.

There is no clear line between rich text and markup. Usually, however, we use the name "rich text" for formats with presentational information that is typically generated by a word processor, email program, or other software, to encode the effect of the formatting commands that the user has given. Markup might also be generated in a similar way, but often markup is oriented toward describing document structures, with some separation of structure from presentation. Markup usually contains elements for the overall structure and layout of a document, and markup could be generated programmatically, or even written "by hand" (i.e., using a text editor).

Text with markup

If formatting or structural information is written using normal characters, it is usually referred to as markup. The most widely know markup is the HTML markup used on web pages. For example, the string <h2>Summary</h2> can be interpreted as containing the textual content "Summary" surrounded by the two tags, <h2> and </h2>. If a program interprets the data according to HTML rules, it would treat the textual content as a second-level heading. If it applies some other interpretation—for example, in an XML context—the tags might mean something completely different. Anyway, such interpretations mean that the data is not taken as plain text but as marked-up text. The interpretation could lead to a particular rendering of the textual content, or it might affect automatic processing such as the construction of a table of contents. Alternatively, a program could interpret `<h2>Summary</h2>` just as a string and display it as such, for example.

One of the practical differences between markup like HTML and the internal formats used by word processors is that markup can be viewed and edited as text. You can work with HTML using just a plain text editor and writing all the tags yourself. This is however impractical in many cases. Markup is often so verbose and complicated that an HTML or XML document is very hard to read as such, as "source." Instead, people use various specialized tools, like WYSIWYG (What You See Is What You Get) editors, which handle most of the markup invisibly. In practice, this means that the distinction between markup and word processors' data formats has been obscured—even more so when word processors use an XML-based format, as they often do these days.

Quasi-markup

As an intermediary between plain text and marked-up text, people often use notations created with special characters, such as slash (solidus) characters around a word to simulate writing it in italics. Some software such as email programs might interpret the special characters in a markup-like manner, displaying /foo/ as *foo* in italics (perhaps retaining the slashes: */foo/*). This may cause problems when a message contains the string /foo/ and this should be interpreted and displayed literally. Most of the time, however, such markup-like conventions in plain text work reasonably well, even if some readers see them literally and need to understand the underlying convention. Common conventions of this kind include using asterisks for strong emphasis or bolding (*foo* means **foo** in bold face) and underscores (low lines) for underlining or emphasis (_foo_ means foo underlined or emphasized in a manner that corresponds to using italics: *foo*).

Thus, we cannot really say that some text is plain text or marked-up text as such. Rather, it can be *interpreted* or *processed* as plain text, or according to some markup rules.

The border between plain text and rich text or marked-up text is not absolute. In a sense, punctuation characters could be regarded as markup. A good example is the Spanish use of paired question marks: the text ¿Cómo? is structurally similar to XML markup like `<question>Cómo</question>`. The main reason for not regarding punctuation marks as markup is that they became a traditional part of writing systems long before the age of computers.

Conversion to plain text

You may need to convert rich text or marked-up text to plain text for various reasons— e.g., when filling out a form that accepts plain text only or when inserting text into an email message body that needs to be plain text. Quite often, you could just cut and paste the text, but you could also open a text file in a word processor and use the "Save As" command to create a plain text version.

Irrespective of the method, the conversion may lose information, as described later in this chapter. If you convert 10^6 (with "6" in superscript style, not as the character superscript six) to plain text, you get 106, which is all wrong. There is no simple way to check whether such things happen, but superscripts are a common reason to stay alert.

Moreover, even if the data is reasonably convertible to plain text, there are practical reasons to consider character encoding issues as well. Often, the reasons for converting to plain text imply the necessity of restricting the character repertoire as well. In email message bodies, for example, you often need to stick to ASCII, or at least to ISO-8859-1.

For example, if you use MS Word to save a Word document's content in plain text, you first select File → Save As. Then, in the menu for file type selection, select "Encoded text" or "Plain text" or something similar (depending on the version of Word). When you click on "Save" in the dialog, you will be prompted for the encoding. If you select ASCII, for example, Word performs some conversions like replacing "smart" quotes with "straight" quotes and dashes with hyphens. The replacements are rather coarse and mechanic, and for any tailored conversion, you need to use a separate converter or use the Find and Replace function of a word processor or a text editor.

Example: Nonbreaking Hyphen

As mentioned in section "General Punctuation" in Chapter 8, the common way of inserting a "nonbreaking hyphen" in MS Word does not insert the Unicode character with that name. Instead, when you press Ctrl-Shift-hyphen in Word, you insert the control character U+001F. MS Word displays it as a normal ASCII hyphen.

For an illustration, open MS Word, type an ASCII hyphen, and then Ctrl-Shift-hyphen, and finally insert a nonbreaking hyphen (U+2011)—e.g., by typing Alt-8209. You get something like "---," where the last hyphen is usually different from the other two. This is because since the nonbreaking hyphen character is not present in many fonts, Word often needs to take it from another font. When the nonbreaking hyphen is from another font, a trained eye may notice a disturbing typographic difference between various hyphens.

Thus, the MS Word approach of using a control character is in some ways safer than using a special character. It works with any font. On the other hand, it is program-specific. If you save a document as plain text or cut and paste text containing the control character, you may get nothing, or a space, or an error, depending on program.

If you use *markup* such the HTML markup `<td nowrap>foo-bar</td>`, where the `nowrap` attribute forbids line breaks inside the `td` (table cell) element, you achieve the same effect as using a nonbreaking hyphen (`<td>foo&#8209;bar</td>`). That way, you avoid the risks involved in this relatively poorly supported character. On the other hand, if the content is saved as plain text from a browser or copied and pasted, the information in the markup is lost.

Example: Formatting in Word Processing

Suppose that you need to write the notation K_a when composing a document in a word processor. The practical method is to write the letters "Ka," then select the letter "a" with the mouse and use the word processor's tools for making text appear as subscript. For example, in MS Word you would use the command Format → Font, and then check the box for "Subscript." The character data, as Unicode characters, does not change, but formatting information is added to it, in the internal format that the word processor uses.

You can exchange data between different word processors without losing such formatting information. Word processors can often read files in formats written by other word processors. Moreover, you can save the document in the RTF format (Rich Text Format), which preserves the formatting, including subscripting.

In theory, you could alternatively use the Unicode character Latin subscript small letter "a" (U+2090). This would let you use subscripts even in plain text. The character U+2090 is, however, hardly available in fonts that people use. It was added to Unicode in Version 4.1. In some applications, the approach could be feasible, though. You could, for example, store data using such characters into a database and make sure that all software that extracts and renders data from it contains code that deals with the subscript characters. For example, it could be converted into a data format like the one used by MS Word or, much simpler, into HTML format (`<sub>a</sub>`), for display with a web browser.

Similar considerations apply to almost all subscripts, superscripts, underlining, italics, and other formatting, even when it indicates basic differences between symbols and not just emphasis or styling. Some exceptions to this were mentioned in Chapter 8.

Example: HTML Markup and CSS

Consider the following fragment of markup from a web page. It is rather obvious intuitively what it means, if you know or guess that nobr means "no break." This is not meant to be an example of good, modern HTML markup:

```
<nobr>Hello <font color="red" size="+1">world</font></nobr>
```

When rendered by a web browser, this displays as "Hello world" with the second word in larger font and in red. Moreover, a line break will never appear between the words. The markup is deprecated and even nonstandard, but it illustrates the simple idea of inserting markup into a stream of characters. The font markup affects features that are beyond the scope of character standards, such as text color and font size. The nobr markup, on the other hand, affects things that could be affected at the character level too, using a no-break space character instead of a normal space.

In a more modern approach, features of character presentation are not expressed in HTML but in CSS (Cascading Style Sheets), although CSS constructs could be embedded into HTML, for example, as follows:

```
<div style="white-space: nowrap">Hello <span style=
"color:red; font-size: larger">world</span></div>
```

We could adopt a more structured approach by moving the CSS code away from the document itself, making the HTML code, e.g.:

```
<div class="greeting">Hello <span class="emphatic">world</span></div>
```

$$m = \frac{m_0}{\sqrt{1 - \left(\dfrac{v}{c}\right)^2}}$$

Figure 9-1. A mathematical equation written with a simple formula editor

In that case, a separate CSS file (which would be referred to in the HTML document) would contain the formatting instructions, as "out of band" information:

```
div.greering { white-space: nowrap; }
span.emphatic { color:red; font-size: larger; }
```

In such an approach, as in the pure HTML approach, the formatting instructions would be completely independent of the character data. This means that the formatting is not preserved when data is transferred as plain text. The formatting information might be converted as part of conversion to another data format, such as RTF or PDF, but this requires specific conversion software.

Linear Text Versus Mathematical Notations

Although several character repertoires, most notably Unicode, contain mathematical and other symbols, the presentation of mathematical formulas is much more than just a character level issue. At the character level, symbols such as integral and n-ary summation can be defined, and their code positions and encodings defined, and representative glyphs shown, and perhaps some usage notes given. However, the construction of real formulas —e.g., for a definite integral of a function—is a different thing, no matter whether one considers formulas abstractly (how the structure of the formula is given) or presentation-ally (how the formula is displayed on paper or on screen).

To mention just a few approaches to such issues, the TeX system is widely used by mathematicians to produce high-quality presentations of formulas, and MathML is an ambitious effort for creating a markup language for mathematics so that both structure and presentation can be handled. In practice, people often use simpler tools such as formula editors, some of which are included in word processors.

To illustrate how the problems of mathematical notations exceed the character-level, consider the relatively simple formula shown in Figure 9-1. The formula was created using the built-in formula editor of MS Word, invoked via the Insert → Object command. In plain text, even using full Unicode, you cannot come closer to approximating the appearance of the formula than "m = m_0 / $\sqrt{(1 - (v/c)^2)}$." Moreover, this plain text representation uses characters that are not widely available in fonts, especially the subscript zero.

If you use a formula editor to produce expressions that will appear as separate blocks, you have the problem that symbols that you use in text may look rather different from the same symbols in the blocks. For example, your formula editor might let you express subscript zero or a square root nicely, but in text paragraphs, you would need to resort to other

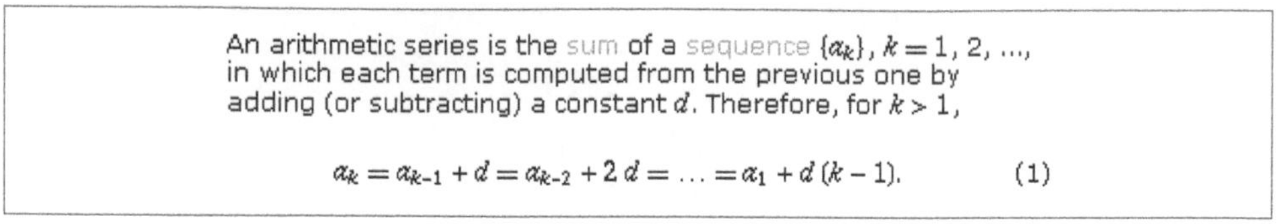

An arithmetic series is the sum of a sequence $\{a_k\}$, $k = 1, 2, ...,$ in which each term is computed from the previous one by adding (or subtracting) a constant d. Therefore, for $k > 1$,

$$a_k = a_{k-1} + d = a_{k-2} + 2d = \ldots = a_1 + d\,(k-1). \qquad (1)$$

Figure 9-2. A sample from MathWorld, containing text as images

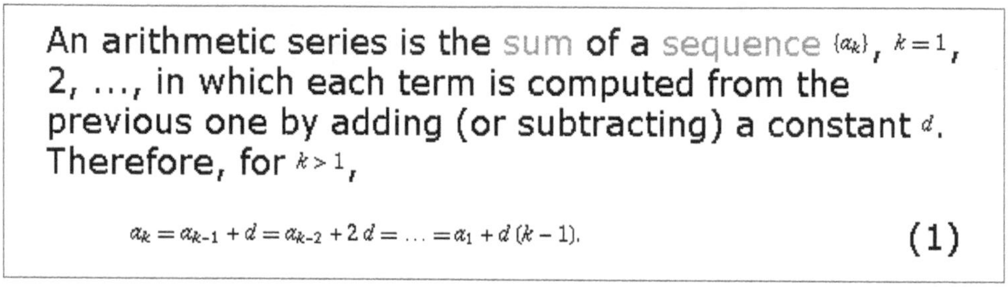

An arithmetic series is the sum of a sequence $\{a_k\}$, $k = 1, 2, ...,$ in which each term is computed from the previous one by adding (or subtracting) a constant d. Therefore, for $k > 1$,

$$a_k = a_{k-1} + d = a_{k-2} + 2d = \ldots = a_1 + d\,(k-1). \qquad \mathbf{(1)}$$

Figure 9-3. MathWorld sample with increased font size

methods, like the square root character, $\sqrt{\ }$. At worst, your readers might not recognize the symbols in the text as the same as those in separate formula blocks.

Similar considerations apply to the use of images. Especially in web publishing, it is common to present any complicated formulas as images, created using, for example, a formula editor or the TeX software. For example, MathWorld (available at *http://mathworld.wolfram.com*) contains an impressive amount of mathematical expressions, but almost exclusively as images. Probably partly to prevent mismatch between symbols in text and in block formulas, the site uses images even inside text, "inline images." The pages have been designed so that you might not notice this but think that those images are normal text characters, as illustrated in Figure 9-2.

However, if you change the font size (this may require a special override of document-specified font sizes)—e.g., because you cannot read small text—you notice a difference. The images are not scaled, as illustrated in Figure 9-3. Note that apart from one use of a subscript, all symbols used in the text could well be written in characters.

You will often be forced to use images for text, especially in formulas. As the example shows, it might be the lesser of evils to use special characters and not images inside linear text, within reasonable limits, even though this might make a symbol in text look different than a symbol in a formula block. For high-quality typesetting, you would need to use software that avoids both problems.

Unicode and Mathematics

Unicode can't do math, of course. You can't compute even $1 + 1$ in Unicode. You can only write mathematical expressions in Unicode. As explained in the previous section, even this has serious limitations, since much of the conventional mathematical notations are not linear text—i.e., text that can be written simply as lines.

In addition, there is very large (and increasing) number of mathematical symbols that are typographic variants of letters, with specialized meanings, such as the mathematical sans-serif italic small "a" U+1D4B6 (which more or less looks like *a*). Although many mathematical symbols have been included in Unicode, they are not widely supported in fonts or in programs.

The crucial question is whether it is necessary and possible to make the distinction between a normal letter and a mathematical symbol in plain text. Quite often, other data formats are more suitable, such as HTML, TeX, or MathML. In HTML, for example, maybe you should not use U+1D4B6 (or the equivalent reference 𝒶) but markup like `<i style="font-family: sans-serif">a</i>`. The latter surely works more widely in current browsers, but is the meaning the same? We will discuss such problems, in a more general framework, in the section "Selecting the Appropriate Level of Expression" later in this chapter.

There are other issues, too, in presenting mathematical notations. They are discussed in the Unicode Technical Report UTR #25, "Unicode Support for Mathematics," *http://www.unicode.org/reports/tr25/*. Much of the material there is largely theoretical at present, due to lack of support in software, and it competes with other approaches, such as MathML, the mathematical markup language.

To take a simple example, you probably know that even in elementary algebra, we often write a product without using any multiplication symbol. We can write the product of *a* and *b* as *a×b* or as *a·b*, but also as *ab*, when there is no ambiguity. This is problematic in processing, since how could a computer program know that *ab* here denotes a product, instead of just being a variable or something else? In a markup language, you could indicate it as a product using, for example, the following (made-up) markup:

```
<product><factor>a</factor><factor>b</factor></product>
```

Using markup, you could express the structure, to be potentially used in any program that recognizes the markup, without necessarily affecting rendering in the least. Software that recognizes markup in general but not this particular markup could simply ignore the tags and use just the textual content. In order to allow such information to be expressed in plain text as well—i.e., even when no markup is available—Unicode contains the character invisible times (U+2062). As the name suggests, it is invisible (has no width), and it is basically defined as having a logical meaning only. In essence, it corresponds to logical markup. Similar characters exist for a few other logical constructs as well, such as the function application (U+2061), which you could use before the left parenthesis in an expression like *f*(*a*+*b*) to indicate the presence of a function invocation rather than, for example, a product or other use of parentheses.

You may ask, what's the point of using invisible markup-like characters? And that's a good question. Their usefulness will probably be limited to applications where you need to work with plain text (e.g., in a database or in the internal strings in a program) but need to include structural information expressible with those characters. On output or on transfer of data to other applications, you would probably need to remove those characters, possibly inserting equivalent markup.

Characters Outside the Repertoire

The available repertoire of characters is limited by several factors:

- The character code used
- The input mechanisms you can use to enter characters
- The font(s) used
- Data processing and transfer software, which may fail to accept, or even pass forward, characters that you might otherwise use

Methods for exceeding different limitations are discussed in various parts of this book. Here we ask what to do if no such method helps.

The ultimate limitation is the character code. Naturally, you can often override such a limitation by switching to another character code, such as from ASCII to an ISO 8859 code or to Unicode. It is, however, possible that such solutions cannot be applied, perhaps because the character you need is not even in Unicode. You might need a very rare character—e.g., because it appears in an old manuscript that you need to convert to a digital form, or because you want, or someone else wants, to introduce a new symbol for use in mathematical, technical, or otherwise special text. You probably cannot wait several years until the character can be added to Unicode and implemented in fonts.

Different workarounds

Independently of the nature of the limitation that you need to overcome, there are three basic ways to use a character outside the available repertoire:

- Design a font that contains a glyph for the character, and encode the character using a Private Use code point in Unicode.
- Create an image that represents the character, and embed the image into text.
- Represent the entire paragraph or block of text as an image, and insert it between normal text blocks.

The first approach can work only in an environment where you can control font usage. The approach as such does not violate Unicode principles, if you use the Private Use area instead of code points allocated to characters in the Unicode standard. Naturally, the approach would depend on "private agreement," and texts using it would not be portable across systems and applications.

The second approach has mostly been used in situations where the character repertoire is limited by practical constraints that do not allow the use of full Unicode. You can still find web pages that represent special characters as images, since authors do not know about Unicode, or since they estimate that the characters are not widely enough available on users' systems. Thus, a character like black spade suit ♠ (U+2660) might be represented using a tag for image embedding, `<img src="spade.gif" alt="spades">`, rather than the character as such or the character reference `&#x2660;`. The image would need to represent the character in a size that matches the font size. Using a stylesheet (CSS), you could specify that the size be scaled so that it depends on the font size, but the scaling performed by browsers can be rather coarse. Moreover, it is difficult to make the embedded image appear smoothly as if it were a character; its shape and exact size might not match the font design, and the spacing around it may differ from normal character spacing.

Some of the typographical problems are avoided in the third approach, which represents an entire paragraph or other block, such as a long mathematical equation, as a single image. The idea is to use a tool such as a formula editor or a typesetting program to produce nicely formatted text, containing special characters, as an image that can be embedded into a document where the character set is more limited. This approach is often used when presenting mathematical expressions on web pages.

Using a character versus using a small image

Quite often, people insert characters as small images, typically in GIF format. This looks like a simple solution to the problem of presenting special characters, and it has several benefits:

- You can use it to present any character.
- You can select the specific shape of the character, using an image of your choice.
- You can use a multicolor image.
- The method works in any data format where images can be embedded.

On the other hand, the method has several drawbacks:

- The image normally has a fixed size in pixels, so it does not scale automatically when the font size of the text is changed.
- The image may cause uneven line spacing; note that the image normally needs to have a height smaller than the font size to prevent this (since the image is normally placed on the baseline of text but the font size includes descenders, too).
- The method fails when the data is converted to plain text (though some data formats let you specify alternate text—e.g., in HTML using the `alt` attribute in an `<img>` tag).
- When the data is transferred to another program, the image may cause problems, because the conversion routine cannot handle it properly.
- A publisher's rules or a publishing program may prevent you from using images embedded into text.
- You often need to design and implement the image yourself, and this is more difficult than it may sound.
- It is particularly difficult to select or design an image that matches the design of the font of the text.

Button-like symbols

A typical case of using an image in place of a character is in an instruction manual where you need to refer to a particular symbol in a button or other user interface. You may need to write, for example, "then press the ⌫ key" or "look for places marked with the ⌘ symbol." The symbols used in the examples actually exist in Unicode as characters (erase to the left U+232B and place of interest sign U+2318), but you might need to use symbols that have not been encoded in Unicode. You might also wish to use images for symbols that exist in Unicode but are not well supported in fonts or have shapes too different from what suit your needs.

Consider the case of an instruction manual where you need to tell the user to press a particular button, labeled with a symbol that is not in Unicode. It is normally vain to hope that the symbol will be added to Unicode. Generally, Unicode contains characters used in text, not graphic symbols in general. Although some symbols that you might wish to use may conceivably appear in many texts like instruction manuals, the same applies to virtually all small graphic symbols. There would be no end to adding characters that might casually appear in text as depicting graphic symbols.

There are some Unicode characters that seem to contradict the above, such as the watch ⌚ (U+232A), but they have mostly been included due to their presence in other character codes or for some special reasons. Computer keyboard symbols and common symbols seen on a computer screen seem to have made their way to Unicode relatively easily, perhaps due to their assumed need to be included in written instructions.

A graphic symbol that is essentially *iconic*—i.e., an image that imitates another image (such as something engraved into a button)—is best regarded as a symbol that is not a character. The imitated image may have a symbolic meaning (e.g., it could stand for "pause" in a key that makes something pause), but this does not make it a character. If it is used in texts only to stand for the imitated image, it is still essentially an image. If people started using it as a general shorthand notation for the concept or word "pause," effectively turning it into an ideograph, it would become a character. For example, people nowadays often use a heart symbol ♡ in text to mean love (e.g., "I ♡ Unicode"), and this would justify encoding it, if it did not exist in Unicode already (white heart suit, U+2661).

Suppose, for example, that you are writing an instruction manual for a device that has a control panel with physical buttons, with some symbols on them. For example, it might have a double vertical rectangle on a pause button—a common convention, though the specific shape varies. There is one possible form of such a button in Figure 9-4. Such a symbol does not exist in Unicode. It might be added some day to Unicode, but that's questionable. What benefits would it produce? You could use it in texts, assuming you have a font that contains it, so you could write some things in some instructions using plain text, instead of embedding an image. However, this would mean that the shape of the character varies. When writing a manual for a particular device, it would be better to use the specific shapes (and perhaps colors) that appear on its buttons. On such grounds, it is better to use embedded images instead of, for example, a Private Use character or a simulation of the shape using Unicode characters with similar appearance, such as the box

Figure 9-4. A pause button symbol, not available as a character

drawings double vertical ‖ (U+2551) or two copies of the medium vertical bar ❙ (U+2759). When limited to plain text, you could just explain the image verbally, perhaps using a very coarse approximation of the shape as an auxiliary hint—e.g., "Looks somewhat like ‖" (where ‖ is just two copies of a common ASCII character, the vertical line U+007C).

Computer keyboard symbols are a somewhat different issue, since people may wish to use generic symbols when writing, for example, a manual for software that may be used with different keyboards. The same applies to symbols in some other equipment, such as telephones, and to symbols that may appear on screen with variation in shape but with a recognizable identity. It can be useful to be able to write "press the option key ⌥" using a character (option key, U+2325) rather than a small image, since you wish to refer to generically to a key assumed to exist in the user's keyboard as marked with a symbol, but in varying shapes. This is one reason why there are several such symbols in Unicode, especially in the Miscellaneous Technical block.

Sometimes the name of a Unicode character suggests a more "iconic" use than it is meant for. The eject symbol (U+23CF) consists of a solid triangle above a horizontal bar, and it might be understood as a symbol of a button. However, it is described under the heading "Keyboard and UI symbols" and with the note "UI symbol to eject media." Thus, it relates to user interface (UI) symbols used in computer software. There are also some keyboard symbols from the ISO 9995-7 standard, for example. Generally, button-like symbols are available as Unicode characters only when they are computer-oriented. Even in such cases, the use of images is often a better choice, since the characters are relatively new and do not belong to most fonts.

Using an image for esthetic reasons

For example, in many widely used fonts such as Times New Roman, the male and female sign, ♀ and ♂, look somewhat disproportionate. Their appearance in Arial (♀♂) is even worse. Therefore, it might be esthetically better to use small well-designed images when visual quality is important, unless you can ensure that some font with a better design for these characters will be used.

Many of the aspects discussed here also apply to the use of images to present texts like a heading, a product name, or button text. For example, in order to make letters multicolored (as in the Google logo), you need to use an image.

Selecting the Appropriate Level of Expression

We often have a choice between expressing some information at the character level and expressing it in text formatting, markup, or other methods. Some specific questions of this type have been discussed previously in this chapter, and there will be some further discussion in the section "Characters and Markup" later in the chapter. Here we will consider some general criteria and the impact of different choices.

As an example, consider the expression m^2. It normally means "square meter," though in mathematics or physics, it might have other meanings, too. There are several ways to express the superscript in a document:

1. Use the character superscript two ² (U+00B2).

2. Use the character superscript two but write it using some notation like the character reference ² in HTML or XML or the entity reference ² in HTML.

3. Use the character digit two "2" (U+0032) (writing "m2"), but use a word processor's formatting or styling tools for making it a superscript.

4. Use the character digit two, but surround it with markup that indicates it as superscript. For example, in HTML, you could write m².

5. Use the character digit two, with the explicit or implicit instruction to readers to understand "m2" as m^2.

Similarly, assuming you wish or need to conform to the convention that a number and a unit be separated by a space, you could write an expression like "5 m" (for "five meters") in several different ways. The ways depend on whether you wish to express that the space should be non-breakable (i.e., a line break between "5" and "m" is not permitted) and whether you wish to affect the exact amount of spacing. The ways also depend on whether you try to express these things at the character level or elsewhere. Some ways were discussed in the section "General Punctuation" in Chapter 8.

There is no universal answer to the question about the choice between character level and other protocol levels. It depends on many aspects, some of which are summarized in Table 9-1. You could well use different strategies in the same document. For example, you could write "5 m^2" using the superscript two character but using a normal space, expressing the non-breakability and the width of spacing in a stylesheet. Checking the criteria in the table, it is relatively easy to see the benefits of using the superscript two character, whereas the no-break space could be more problematic. (For example, it can cause surprises in text justification, since it is typically of fixed width.)

Issue	Character level	Higher protocol levels
Does it work in practice?	Greatly depends on the rarity and novelty of the character used.	Depends on the software used to process the data.
Requirements on encoding	You often need to use a Unicode encoding.	You can often use 8-bit encodings.
Maintainability of data	You need to know the Unicode characters used in order to work with data (e.g., edit it).	It is sufficient to know the formatting tools or markup used.
Preserving the information	Usually well preserved in processing, except perhaps in normalization.	Often lost when converting to other data formats (e.g., between word processors).
Ease of coding	Often clumsy, if the character is needed repeatedly, though defined keyboard shortcuts may help.	Often easily manageable in a centralized manner—e.g., in a style definition.
Side effects	May result from ambiguous semantics of characters and their Unicode properties.	Usually rare; e.g., usually "bolding" means just bolding.
Tuning the rendering	Rather limited possibilities, mostly just font choice.	Often good possibilities; e.g., via a stylesheet.

When information is expressed at the *character level*, by the choice of specific Unicode code points, the information persists through all processes that correctly preserve the identity of plain text characters. For example, cut and paste operations may or may not preserve formatting information (such as fonts), but they can be expected to preserve character identity. If the target of pasting is in a program that does not support Unicode, characters may be lost. However, an implementation of Unicode is required to preserve characters, instead of, for example, dropping out characters that it does not recognize. It may well fail to display them, but they should be available in the data by other means.

For example, for the expression m², the first two methods just discussed imply that in cut and paste, the result preserves the information: m². (For method 2, we assume that you cut from the formatted document, not from XML or HTML source.) For methods 3 and 4, cut and paste normally converts the text to "m2," unless the operation takes place inside a program or between programs that recognize the method used. Thus, if you copy and paste the string "m²" where "2" is formatted as a superscript, the formatting is preserved when working inside a word processor, but not when copying from it into a plain text editor like Notepad. When method 5 is used, the data copied is of course "m2."

Similarly, when data is read *by a program*, information expressed at the character level is always available to the program, though it may not make use of it. Information expressed in markup is normally available, too, since programs normally read the markup source, but they would need to recognize the markup—at least to the extent that it can skip it, instead of treating markup as data! Reading data in a word processor's internal format is possible, too, but requires complicated software. Mostly, if you wish to process, say, Word or PDF documents programmatically (e.g., to compute word concordances or to compute statistics on the text), you would first convert the document to plain text or some other easily processable format.

Availability of information at the character level is not always an asset. It may imply that a program for processing the data must deal with a larger variation of characters. For example, if the expression "5 m²" is written using the no-break space and the superscript two, what will happen if the expression is used as input to a program that is prepared to handle ASCII data only? If you wish to write a program that can handle *all* the ways in which the expression could be written in Unicode, in principle, you have lots of cases to consider. For example, someone might write the letter "m" using the fullwidth Latin small letter "m" (U+FF4D), for some good reason. Even if you have no use for the information involved in this choice, you would need to deal with this possibility. You might convert the data to a suitable normalization form (prior to other processing) to reduce the variation considerably.

The following list suggests guidelines on choosing the level where information is given, with an emphasis on what should or should not be done at the character level:

Color
> The color of text cannot be expressed at the character level, except in the sense that in a few cases, there are "white" and "black" versions of a symbol in Unicode, such as white chess knight ♘ and black chess knight ♞ (where the distinction is essential: it indicates which player's piece is referred to). "Black" and "white" in characters really mean "foreground color" and "background color," which can usually both be set using word processor tools or markup.

Size
> The size of characters isn't expressible at the character level either. The size of a character depends on the font size but also on the font face, since the relative sizes of characters vary greatly by font design. (For example, "m" in Times is considerably smaller than m in Verdana, using the same font size.) Exceptionally, some symbols have been coded in Unicode as separate characters with size difference, such as the tilde ~ (U+007E) and the small tilde ˜ (U+02DC), but usually this involves differences other than just size. For many characters, there are narrow and wide forms, but this relates to East Asian typography that needs to adapt foreign characters to the principles of ideograph usage. Note that reduction of font size inside text has varying meanings, and this affects the kind of markup you would use for it; in English, reduced font size usually means less important text, while in some other writing systems, it means more important. Size variation may have other semantics, too.

Spacing
> Horizontal spacing between characters can be affected to some extent at the character level, especially using fixed-width spaces. However, they often work inconsistently or do not work at all. Modern typography uses formatting tools at higher protocol levels. For other spacing, such as line height and margins, higher levels are usually

the only feasible option. (Sometimes spaces and extra line breaks are used for such spacing, but such methods are very coarse.)

Underlining and overlining

In almost all cases, use higher-level protocols. The possibilities of using combining marks to achieve underlining or overlining are mostly theoretic.

Italics, bolding, and other font variation

Generally, use higher-level protocols, except perhaps for some special symbols (e.g., in mathematics). If you try to make, for example, words in normal text italicized by the use of Unicode characters of italics shape, you will end up with something very unreliable and clumsy.

Subscripts and Superscripts

The need for subscripts or superscripts is one of the most common cases where plain text appears to be insufficient. Most subscripts and superscripts that are needed in practice could be written as Unicode characters, but such an approach is often not feasible. As described in Chapter 8, the repertoire of such characters is relatively large, but only superscripts 1, 2, and 3 are widely supported.

The use of subscripts and superscripts can be classified as follows:

Purely stylistic

Superscripting is used in many languages as a conventional device in writing some expressions, like ordinal numbers in English (1st, 2nd, etc.) and abbreviations like Mlle in French. Somewhat more debatably, the subscripting in common chemistry formulas like H_2O could be regarded as stylistic only, since there is no change in meaning and no ambiguity if a normal number is used instead (H2O). In notations like ^{14}C (for carbon-14, an isotope), ambiguities could arise if superscripting were removed.

Structural

The use of superscripts as exponents is clearly structural, and in general, removing the superscripting may completely change the meaning (e.g., turning 2^3 to 23). In many cases, though, no real ambiguity arises (e.g., when writing m^2 as m2 in ordinary text). In phonetics, superscripting of letters is structural, too: a superscripted letter has a phonetic value that is different from that of the normal letter.

In-between usage

Much of the use of subscripts and superscripts falls between purely stylistic and purely structural. In mathematics, if you name variables a_1, a_2, etc., subscripting might be treated as stylistic, so that your variables are really just a1, a2,…. But if you then refer to a_i, using a generic index i, we need to regard subscripting as more or less structural. A mathematical notation like "A^*" (with * as an operator placed after its operand) might be understood as using superscripting for stylistic reasons only, but in "A^+" superscripting is more essential, to avoid confusion with other uses of a + sign.

Purely stylistic superscripting or subscripting is best handled above the character level, in styling of some kind. Structural superscripting or subscripting should be handled at markup level when possible, and expressing it at the character level is better than making it purely stylistic, though often impractical. The in-between cases are more difficult, and we can only give some general guidelines about them. Many notations are mostly unambiguous even if subscripting or superscripting is removed, but they may create a risk of confusion in special cases. For example, notations for isotopes in chemistry, such as ^{14}C, conventionally use a superscripted number, but omitting the superscripting does not usually cause any ambiguity. In rare cases, however, the text might also contain notations like 14C in a completely different meaning (e.g., as codes of some kind or perhaps as hexadecimal numbers). It is probably best to treat in-between usage as *structural*, unless there are good reasons to treat it as presentational. Note that in chemistry, notations like C-14 are recommended when superscripting is impossible.

Visual appearance of subscripts and superscripts

When considering the use of subscript or superscript characters in Unicode, note that the appearance will in general be different from what you get by using other tools. The characters have a fixed appearance in each font. You have no tools for affecting, for example, the vertical position of the superscript with respect to the base letter, except coarsely by trying different fonts. Superscripts are typically more legible in sans-serif fonts than in serif fonts; compare, for example, a^2 in Times with a^2 in Arial.

If you use font formatting commands in a word processor to create subscripts and superscripts, the appearance is different from subscript and superscript characters. Moreover, the appearance can be modified with the tools of the program more flexibly. Compare, for example, the expressions m^2 and m2. The appearance of the latter, containing the digit two in superscript style, can be modified with styling commands. For example, in MS Word, you could select the "2" and choose Format → Font to set the font size smaller or to make the character appear in a lower or higher position. This may look clumsy, but general purpose style settings can make this easier. When the superscript two character is used, its glyph shows the digit in smaller size and in a raised position, and the details of such features depend on the font and are difficult to modify.

Similar notes apply to using sub or sup markup in HTML or similar markup in other markup languages. Their appearance and effect can be tuned in CSS by using the properties font-size, vertical-align, and line-height. If you create your own markup system that has elements for subscripts or superscripts, these three properties should be set suitably in your CSS stylesheet.

When different methods for expressing subscripts or superscripts are mixed, the result is usually typographically poor due to style variation. Therefore, do not express superscript and subscript numbers using the Unicode characters unless you can be reasonably sure that you can consistently use that method for all superscripts and subscripts in the document.

Replacement notations for superscripts and subscripts

Since superscripting is often structural, especially in mathematics, different methods have been used to describe superscripting in plain text. To express x to the power y, x^y, programming languages typically use x^y or x**y or a functional notation like pow(x,y).

Such notations are often used even in normal text, but you should not expect people to know them in general without explanations, or find them natural. Notations like x↑y or power(x,y) might be somewhat more understandable, though the upward arrow ↑ (U+2191) is often not available when you are limited to plain text. Note that the circumflex accent ^ is essentially computer programming jargon and has multiple uses as such.

Subscripting can often be removed without affecting the basic meaning, but if you need some replacement, an underscore might be best, writing a_i as a_i when needed.

Suggested policy on subscripting and superscripting

There is really no simple general answer to the question of whether you should use subscript and superscript characters or other methods, such as word processor commands or markup. Some guidelines can be given, though:

- If you only need digits 1, 2, and 3 as superscripts (e.g., you just need m^2 and m^3), use the characters for them. Being Latin 1 characters, they work widely.

- Otherwise, use markup when available, or other techniques. Be consistent: represent even superscript 1, 2, and 3 using the same method as you use for other superscripts.

- When restricted to plain text, omit superscripting and subscripting when they are presentational only or they can be inferred from the context (e.g., 1st, H2O, m2), and use special notations instead of them when they are structural (e.g., 2^n could be written as 2↑n, 2^n, 2**n, or super(2,n)).

- If you need or wish to affect the specific visual appearance of subscripts and superscripts, such as their size and vertical position with respect to the baseline of text, it is probably better to use higher-level protocols rather than subscript and superscript characters. For example, in a word processor, you can probably use its styling tools to specify a common style for all text that you designate as subscripts or superscripts.

- On the other hand, when you use subscript and superscript characters, you need not worry about line spacing, since their glyphs have been designed for rendering within the height of the font. Using any other technique for subscripting or superscripting, there is a definite risk of uneven line spacing. There are usually some tools against that, but they typically mean setting the overall line spacing larger than normal.

- In special cases—such as when your data needs to be stored as plain text (e.g., in a database)—analyze whether Unicode contains all the characters you'll need as subscripts and superscripts, and use them. Beware that special processing may be needed on output.

- In particular, non-numeric subscripts and superscripts are very poorly supported in fonts. Since they largely exist for special purposes like phonetic notations, their appearance may not suit your needs. (Here, "non-numeric" means anything but digits 0 through 9, plus sign, minus sign, parentheses, and equals sign.)

- Note that Unicode characters allow no nested subscripts or superscripts. You can represent the subscript in "x_i" as a character (Latin subscript small letter "i," U+1D62), but not the subscript in "x_{i_j}."

Characters and Accessibility

Accessibility means making content and services available to anyone irrespective of physical or mental disability. In a broader sense, accessibility means availability to anyone irrespective of variation between people and between the situations where they act. There are worldwide recommendations and national guidelines and even legal rules on accessibility, especially in the digital and networked environment. There are W3C recommendations on accessibility at *http://www.w3.org/WAI/*. In the U.S., the so-called Section 508 legislation makes accessibility considerations mandatory in some contexts that involve federal funding, see *http://www.section508.gov/*.

Characters in non-visual presentation

The most commonly presented example of accessibility is how to make web pages and other digital content available to the blind. Tools used for this usually involve speech synthesis: textual content is used as input to an automatic speech synthesizer, which reads the text audibly. The synthesizer may use metainformation presented in markup, for example, in order to read headings emphatically and to leave pauses between paragraphs. Alternatively, text could be presented via a Braille "display," which is a device that renders a character using a combination of dots (a Braille pattern) that can be sensed by the user's fingertips.

These examples deal with a very narrow part of accessibility, but they illustrate well how accessibility deals with the character level, too. Unicode is oriented toward characters that are displayed visibly. The very character concept deals with elements of written text, even though it does not mandate a particular presentation. Strings of Unicode characters can, however, be presented in other ways, too.

Speech synthesis needs much more than just characters. It must be strongly language-dependent to be correct or even to get close. Braille display works more directly at the character level, but different schemes exist for converting text to sequences of Braille patterns. Those patterns have been encoded into Unicode in a block of their own, but they are defined just as dot patterns, without assigning any specific character or other meaning to them. Therefore, Braille rendering is language-dependent, too.

Both speech synthesis and Braille rendering were originally designed to handle a small repertoire of characters, such as a subset of ASCII characters. Therefore, you often have problems in such modes of rendering even for characters that work well in most visible presentations, like accented letters. In visible rendering, the user mostly has the option of changing the font in order to see whether some other font would work better. Perhaps he could even download additional fonts. In non-visual rendering, problematic characters might not be rendered at all, or they might be indicated by their names or numbers.

Understandability of characters

In all modes of presentation, failures are possible since the user might not understand the character used, even if it is presented in a technically flawless way. If you write "5 µm," it is quite possible that the µ character gets messed up in the presentation, but even if it does not, the reader might simply not recognize and understand it. Similarly, the phonetic symbol ə, though widely used by linguists, is unknown to most people, so an essential part of a pronunciation instruction using it might not be understood at all.

There is no simple cure for the problem. We need to be cautious, and we need to explain the special characters, as well as special notations, that we use. Unicode lets you use a huge number of characters, but most people understand just a small subset.

Although the understandability of characters and the technical possibilities of rendering them are quite different aspects, they are interconnected in practice. If you use technically "safe" characters such as ASCII characters only, for example, the odds are that people understand the characters and that specialized software, like Braille devices, can handle them well. People and programs understand the "safe" characters because they are widely used in computers. Even if they don't know exactly what you mean by an asterisk, *, the character probably looks familiar to them. If you use a more fancy star-shaped Unicode character, like the black star ★ (U+2605), in your text, it will not work technically in all circumstances, and it may make people wonder whether it is a typo or something. Therefore, make sure you have a good reason to take these risks.

Explaining characters

When you use characters that are not widely known to your audience, you should try to explain them. Usually the explanations should be presented in normal textual content, perhaps in the copy text, perhaps in footnotes or some other way; the choice depends on how important the explanation is. Identifying characters by Unicode numbers or names or both can be useful in specialized technical contexts, but it can be alienating when writing for the general public. A mixed explanation like the following might be useful in a legend, though, if readers may need to use the character themselves and therefore need its Unicode identification:

> The character ə is a phonetic symbol that denotes a neutral vowel, as the one at the start of the English word "about." The character is called "schwa," or formally "Latin small letter schwa" (U+0259) in Unicode.

In hypertext, you could make the "U+0259" a link to a more detailed technical description of the character, such as *http://www.fileformat.info/info/unicode/char/0259/*.

Characters and Markup

XML (and SGML) markup has often been characterized as "semantic" or "logical," instead of presentational or physical. However, markup can be used for many purposes, including formatting and typography. If you need to store text data in a way that contains formatting information, nothing prevents you from using XML markup for that. To mention examples from HTML, `<i>` markup is used to indicate italics, and markup like `<font face="Arial">`, though deprecated, is still used to specify the font family.

On the other hand, many Unicode characters are typographic variants of other characters, coded as separate characters for different reasons. Many of them are compatibility characters and have been included only due to their existence in other character codes. However, there are other cases as well. The difference between normal (upright) and italics style may indicate a semantic distinction in mathematics or other special notations

Most things that are expressed in markup have no character-level counterpart. For example, designating some text as a heading, in the logical structure, cannot be done at the character level. What comes closest to that is writing the heading text in all uppercase with line breaks before and after, as we often do in plain text. If you consider markup for indicating the structure of a price list that is never meant to be displayed as such, only through special formatting processes and rules, it should be obvious that you cannot do anything at the character level to indicate some text as "product name" and some other text as "unit price" for the product.

Thus, the question of whether information should be expressed at the character level or in markup primarily deals with *presentational* distinctions, or distinctions that might at least arguably be regarded as presentational. It is an important special case of the problem of selecting an appropriate level of expression in such cases. There are specific guidelines on it suggested in a joint report by the Unicode Consortium and the World Wide Web Consortium (W3C). Note that text processors increasingly use XML markup in their data formats, so the principles apply to using their tools, too, at least indirectly.

Markup and Styling

In this context, "markup" really means "markup and styling," in most cases. Modern markup tends to be logical rather than presentational, and therefore markup alone does not usually imply any particular rendering style. In particular, if you use generic XML, inventing tags as you need and with the intention of specifying rendering in a stylesheet, then no markup has any rendering style as such, only through the stylesheet.

Although the `i` markup in HTML, for example, specifically means "italics," we cannot say the same about the (rarely used) `var` markup, which means "variable, placeholder." Yet, in contexts where it is suitable to replace a compatibility character with a normal character and `i` markup, it can be just as suitable, if not more so, to replace it by the normal character and `var` markup, provided that two conditions are met. First, the intended meaning should correspond to the defined meaning of the markup. Second, we should have reasonable expectations on having it rendered in italics. The expectations might be based on information about typical browser defaults, or on the use of a stylesheet that explicitly suggests such rendering (`var { font-style: italic; }`).

Document-wide Versus Local Decisions

The question "character level or markup?" has two levels:

- Should you use plain text or marked-up text as the format of some information? Choosing plain text excludes all markup. Choosing marked-up text does not exclude the possibility of expressing information at the character level rather than in markup.

- Inside marked-up text, should you express some information (say, the use of italics for a character) in markup, or at the character level, or perhaps both ways?

The alternative "both ways" can usually be excluded. Although it may sound ideal to get the best of both possible worlds, you easily end up with getting the worst of them. Besides, you might get nasty cumulative effects. Consider the simple example of writing the expression x^4 (x to the power of 4). You could use the superscript four (U+2074), or you could use a higher-level protocol, such as markup (e.g., sup element in HTML) or superscript style in a word processor. Trying to use both—e.g., using x^{⁴} in HTML—will probably combine the drawbacks of both alternatives: in rendering, it fails whenever U+2074 does not belong to the fonts in use, and it tends to mess up line spacing the way sup markup often does. Besides, it's illogical. It means double superscripting, and this will probably make the superscript appear as very small if at all, since a browser uses superscript 4 and reduces its size.

Moreover, as noted earlier in this chapter, if you express some superscripts as superscript characters and other superscripts using markup, they easily look disturbingly different. Any automated processing of the data, such as conversion to another format, would need to deal with two representations of superscripts instead of one.

You can mix markup with formatting information expressed at the character level, but you should normally not use both ways for the same information in a document.

There are a few exceptions, though. Sometimes there are two ways to present the same formatting information so that no harm arises from the duplication. For example, in HTML authoring, you could write a table cell as <td nowrap>42 m</td> so that the space between "42" and "m" is a no-break space U+00A0 (which you could write as   in HTML). That would mean expressing both at the character level and in markup, with the nowrap attribute, that the cell content must remain on one line. Both ways are "safe" in practice. Although there is no particular benefit from using both, no harm is caused either, so such duplication need not be avoided, for example, when generating table markup automatically.

Unicode Versus Markup

The document "Unicode in XML and other Markup Languages" has been published as Unicode Technical Report UTR #21 at *http://www.unicode.org/reports/tr20/* as well as a W3C Note at *http://www.w3.org/TR/unicode-xml/*. It is not part of the Unicode standard.

It has been approved just as a Technical Report, though other documents may make normative references to it. In the W3C terminology, a Note is a document that has been endorsed by a working group but not reviewed or endorsed by the W3C as a whole (or by "W3C Members").

Nevertheless, UTR #21 is the best available general guideline on whether information should be expressed at the character level or in markup. We need to use it with discretion, partly because the report considers markup in general and not the specific features of various markup languages and systems. For example, in cases where the report recommends markup, the markup language we use might lack elements that could be used for the purpose, or their implementation in software might be wanting.

In practice, the report revolves around XML, which covers both generic XML (where you can invent tags as you go) and specific XML-based markup languages such as XHTML (the XML-ized version of HTML), MathML, MusicML, or SVG (Scaleable Vector Graphics, a language for two-dimensional graphics in XML, with a possibility of including text as character data). However, the markup concept is more general and covers SGML too, including classic HTML, which is nominally SGML-based. Even notations such as RTF and other rich text systems can be regarded as markup, even though their general syntax is different.

Differences between markup and plain text

Plain text is linear: a character follows another in a sequence. Although the visual rendering can be more complicated—e.g., due to combining diacritic marks and to alterations in writing direction—plain text is still processed linearly. Markup, on the other hand, expresses tree-like structures, even if it is written linearly. As any good book on markup will tell you, a notation like <x><y>foo</y><z>bar</z></x> describes a tree structure, with elements y and z as "children" (subtrees) of x. The marked-up text needs to be processed (parsed) in order to construct the tree structure, which in turn can be linearized into text. A markup element can be very large. In XML, the entire document is treated as one element, with subelements, which contain subelements, etc.

Information expressed at character level works on different grounds. Either the difference between characters as such carries some information (e.g., using ² instead of 2 expresses that we have a superscript), or a character affects the interpretation or processing of the preceding or sometimes the following character. Some characters may set some internal state in interpretation or processing, such as writing direction. They might be compared to start tags in markup. Even then, such characters usually affect a state in a simple way, setting it to a specific value. There is normally no *nesting* involved as in markup.

Thus, character level is normally useful for rather *local* information only. On the other hand, it is generally simple and compact to use when it applies. Compare the simplicity of using a character (code point) for ² as opposed to markup like ², where you need start and end tags even though you are saying something about a single character only.

Obviously, information at the character level is suitable for linear processing where you read a stream of characters and process them in succession. Similarly, marked-up text, once parsed, is suitable for structured processing where you start from a tree and process it by the structure.

Characters that should not be used in marked-up text

UTR #20 declares some characters, listed in Table 9-2, as "unsuitable for use with markup." Some of them might have use in plain text or other formats, but not in XML, for example. Most of these characters would rarely come into your mind anyway when using markup. Note, however, that U+FEFF has been used to some extent in marked-up text as an invisible joiner (to prevent undesired line breaks), and in practice, it still does the job more reliably than the suggested replacement, U+2060.

Table 9-2. Characters not suitable for use with markup

Character(s)	Description	Reason for avoiding
U+2028..U+2029	Line and paragraph separator	Use markup (like p and br in HTML)
U+202A..U+202E	Bidi embedding controls	Use only markup to avoid conflicts; however, see notes after the table
U+206A..U+206B	Activate or Inhibit Symmetric swapping	Deprecated in Unicode
U+206C..U+206D	Activate or Inhibit Arabic form shaping	Deprecated in Unicode
U+206E..U+206F	Activate or Inhibit National digit shapes	Deprecated in Unicode
U+FFF9..U+FFFB	Interlinear annotation characters	Use Ruby markup (see Chapter 8)
U+FEFF	Zero width no-break space (ZWNBSP)	Use only as byte order mark (see, however, the note at the beginning of this section)
U+FFFC	Object replacement character	Use markup for embedding—e.g., img or object in HTML
U+1D173..U+1D173A	Scoping for Musical Notation	Use an appropriate markup language, as it becomes available
U+E0000..U+E007F	Language tag characters	Use language markup—e.g., lang or xml:lang attribute (see Chapter 7)

As described in Chapter 5, the Line Separator (LS) U+2028 and the Paragraph Separator (PS) U+2029 were introduced to provide unambiguous means to denote line breaks and paragraph delimiters in plain text. This was meant to avoid the ambiguity caused by different uses of ASCII control characters like Line Feed. In practice, LS and PS have not been used much. If they appear in plain text being converted to marked-up text, they should be replaced by appropriate markup. In HTML, you use
 (or <br /> in XHTML) for a forced line break, and you surround each paragraph with the tags <p> and </p>. UTR #20 recommends that an occurrence of LS or PS in marked-up text be treated as whitespace —i.e., as equivalent to a space.

According to UTR #20, the Bidi embedding controls U+202A..U+202E (see Chapter 5) are "strongly discouraged" in the HTML 4 specification, which however actually just warns about possible conflicts between those controls and equivalent markup. It recommends that preferably one or the other should be used exclusively, and adds:

> The markup method offers a better guarantee of document structural integrity and alleviates some problems when editing bidirectional HTML text with a simple text editor, but some software may be more apt at using the UNICODE characters. If both methods are used, great care should be exercised to insure proper nesting of markup and directional embedding or override, otherwise, rendering results are undefined.

UTR #20 suggests that markup be used instead of the controls on the following grounds:

> The embedding controls introduce a state into the plain text, which must be maintained when editing or displaying the text. Processes that are modifying the text without being aware of this state may inadvertently affect the rendering of large portions of the text, for example by removing a PDF [= Pop Directional Formatting].

Although this recommendation is usually adequate, there are situations where markup cannot be used for Bidi embedding. Attributes of elements cannot contain markup, only text, and some elements may contain only text. Thus, if Bidi control is needed—e.g., a `<title>` element or an `alt` attribute of an `<img>` element—the control characters are the only possibility.

Formatting characters that may be used in marked-up text

According to UTR #20, the characters listed in Table 9-3 may be used in XML documents or other marked-up text, even though they are invisible formatting characters or characters with formatting information. This does not mean that they should be used, or that it would always be appropriate and best to use them. Rather, they are regarded in principle as compatible with the ideas and practices of markup. This means that the potential risks of mixing character-level information and markup are not relevant, or they can be controllable enough. On the practical side, many of the characters listed are poorly supported or could be replaced by markup. The no-break space U+00A0 is often used and useful, whereas most of the other characters have little use in texts written in Latin letters, except for the soft hyphen U+00AD in some word processors.

Table 9-3. Formatting characters acceptable for use with markup

Character(s)	Name(s)	Notes
U+00A0	No-break space	Latin-1 character
U+00AD	Soft hyphen	Hyphenation hint
U+034F	Combining grapheme joiner	See explanation below
U+0600	Arabic number sign	Subtending mark

Character(s)	Name(s)	Notes
U+0601	Arabic sign sanah	Subtending mark
U+0602	Arabic footnote marker	Subtending mark
U+0603	Arabic sign safha	Subtending mark
U+06DD	Arabic end of ayah	Enclosing mark
U+070C	Syriac Abbreviation Mark (SAM)	Supertending mark
U+0F0C	Tibetan mark delimiter tsheg bstar	<noBreak> U+0F0B
U+180B..U+180E	Mongolian variation selectors and vowel separator	Required for Mongolian
U+200C..U+200D	Zero-width joiner and non-joiner (ZWJ and ZWNJ)	For ligature behavior; see Chapter 5
U+200E..U+200F	Directional marks (LRM and RLM)	See Chapter 5
U+2011	Non-breaking hyphen	<noBreak> U+2010
U+202F	Narrow No-Break Space	Narrow form of U+00A0
U+2044	Fraction slash	Or use markup (MathML)
U+2060	Word Joiner	Prevents line break
U+2061	Function application	Mathematical use
U+2062	Invisible times	Mathematical use
U+2063	Invisible comma	Mathematical use
U+2FF0..U+2FFB	Ideographic character description	Graphic characters
U+303E	Ideographic variation indicator	Graphic character
U+FE00..U+FE0F	Variation selectors	Glyph selection indicators
U+E0100..U+E01DF	Variation selectors	Glyph selection indicators

The combining grapheme joiner (U+034F) is a combining mark rather than a formatting character. It does not affect cursive joining or ligation (as ZWJ and ZWNJ do). Neither does it combine or join graphemes, so its Unicode name is misleading. It has two uses, related to collation (sorting) of strings and to canonical reordering of combining marks. See the Unicode FAQ, *http://www.unicode.org/faq/char_combmark.html*.

Subtending marks are used in the Arabic and Syriac scripts to indicate that a mark be placed below a string of characters—e.g., below a sequence of digits, to indicate a year. The Syriac abbreviation mark is used similarly but placed above a string, as a supertending mark, and the Arabic end of ayah is a similar but enclosing mark. In character data, a subtending mark precedes the affected characters; the end of the affected range is defined implicitly, usually by the first non-alphanumeric character. There is currently no markup that can replace these subtending, supertending, or enclosing marks.

Variation selectors were discussed in the section "Unicode and Fonts" in Chapter 4. They are used to select a glyph variant of the preceding character. Although they could in principle be replaced by markup and styling (glyph selection), this cannot be done in practice now. UTR #20 comments on them as "Not graphic characters," which is technically correct: they are not visible characters but meant to affect the rendering of another character.

Characters with compatibility mappings

The characters listed in Table 9-2 and Table 9-3 usually do not cause much of a problem when deciding what characters to use in marked-up text. Most of them would not be used anyway, and the rules for them are rather straightforward, though the practical considerations (would this formatting character work?) might require some study.

The third and last group of characters discussed in UTR #20, those with compatibility mappings, is more problematic, and more important—e.g., in texts in English. As we noted in Chapter 5, compatibility mappings exist for different reasons and have varying meanings. The difference between a character and its compatibility mapping can vary from practically ignorable to substantial difference in meaning or appearance or both. The expression "characters with compatibility mappings" is admittedly clumsy, but the equivalent term "compatibility decomposable character" is also clumsy, and the simpler term "compatibility character" does not mean quite the same thing. (There are compatibility characters that have no compatibility mapping.)

The recommendations on using characters with compatibility mappings in marked-up text may appear to conflict with general Unicode principles on avoiding such characters in new data (see Chapter 5). The main reason is that these recommendations mainly deal with *marking up existing character data* rather than creation of completely new data. For example, the use of characters for ligatures (such as "fl" as one character) in new data should normally be avoided. However, if such data exists in plain text, it should not be indiscriminately replaced by its decomposition (such as letters "f" and "l"), especially if we have no idea of how the ligature behavior could be expressed in markup or otherwise.

The recommendations of UTR #20 are summarized in Table 9-4 and commented (and criticized) after the table. The report presents them primarily as applicable when XML markup is *first added* to text that has no markup. It does not necessarily mean that existing marked-up text should be modified. The first column in the table specifies a "compatibility tag" as defined in the Unicode database. As explained in Chapter 5, such tags are metasymbols used to indicate the nature of the compatibility mapping, and they should not be confused with markup tags. For two tags, the recommended treatment is different for different characters, and this is indicated by specifying the applicability by code range in column 2. (For compactness, the "U+" prefix is omitted here.)

Table 9-4. What to do with characters with compatibility mappings

Tag	Code range	What to do	Description of characters and/or notes
\<circled>		Retain, or use list markup	Circled letters and digits
\<compat>	2002..200A	Retain	Fixed-width spaces; see comments
	2100..2101	Retain	℀ and ℁; used as symbols

Tag	Code range	What to do	Description of characters and/or notes
	2105..2106	Retain	% and ‰; used as symbols
	2121, 213B	Retain	ᵀᴱᴸ and facsimile sign
	2160..217F	Retain, or use list markup	Roman numerals, usually used as list item markers
	2474..249B	Retain, or use list markup	Parenthesized or dotted number, usually used as list item marker
	249C..24B5	Retain, or use list markup	Parenthesized letters, usually used as list item markers
	3131..318E	Retain	Compatibility Hangul Jamo
	3200..3229	Retain, or use list markup	Parenthesized Korean characters and ideographic numbers
	322A..3243	Retain, or use list markup	Parenthesized ideographs
	32C0..32CB	Retain	Ideographic telegraph symbols for months
	all other	Retain	Maintain, semantic distinctions apply
<final>		Normalize	Arabic presentation forms
<font>		Retain	Variant letter forms used as symbols
<fraction>		Normalize	"As long as fraction slash is supported!"
<initial>		Normalize	Arabic presentation forms
<isolated>		Normalize	Arabic presentation forms
<medial>		Normalize	Arabic presentation forms
<narrow>		Retain	Half-width characters
<noBreak>		Retain	Non-breaking variants; see notes below
<small>		Retain	Small forms of characters; see notes
<square>	3300..3357	Retain	Single display cell cluster containing multiple lines of kana for vertical layout
	3358..337D	Retain	Ideographic symbols
	33E0..33FE	Retain	Ideographic telegraph symbols for days
	all other	Retain	Symbols used in vertical layout
<sub>		Use markup, or retain	Subscript characters
<super>		Use markup, or retain	Superscript characters
<vertical>		Normalize	East Asian Presentation forms
<wide>		Retain	Fullwidth characters

In this context, "normalize" means conversion to *Normalization Form KC*. As described in Chapter 5, this means compatibility ("K") decomposition followed by canonical composition ("C"). Only a few types of characters are normalized, according to UTR #20. Most compatibility characters are retained.

The treatment of characters with compatibility mappings needs to be more complicated than expressed in the summary table. In fact, there are internal inconsistencies in UTR #20 between the summary table and the prose explanations. Here it is interpreted according to the prose, which is more detailed, and some apparent errors have been corrected.

Most important, we need to consider the intended meaning of using a character with a compatibility mapping. If the purpose is just visual formatting, it should be replaced by the use of normal characters and markup (and a stylesheet). If there is a semantic difference involved, the character should be retained. The report illustrates this with a simple example of *italicized* characters:

- It would be inappropriate to use compatibility characters like h (U+210E), e (U+212F), etc., to write the word *hello* in italics. This should be rather obvious on several accounts: the names of the characters, the variation in their glyphs (which are not based on any uniform "italics design"), and the rather practical fact that these characters are poorly supported.

- On the other hand, the character h (U+210E) is adequate for denoting the Planck constant, used in physics. In fact, "Planck constant" is its name and suggests its meaning. The report says that we should not use just an italicized "h," or specifically the HTML markup `<i>h</i>`, to denote the Planck constant. In practice, we often don't have a choice, due to character repertoire limitations. But the principle is clear: in cases like this, the compatibility character is to be preferred. The principle can be criticized, though: why would the Planck constant be an exception, when we use, for example, just an italicized c to denote the speed of light?

In the following, we present additional rules, explanations, and comments related to Table 9-4, organized in the same order as the table.

Characters with <circled> mapping

These are circled letters and digits such as ① (U+2460). They are most often used as list item markers, as footnote markers, or in text when referring to items in a numbered list. Although the report suggests in its summary that such characters be retained, the detailed rules rather suggest that when used as list markers, they should be replaced by *list markup*. On the other hand, this might be impractical if you wish to preserve the circled appearance of the markers. As the report warns, such formatting can be difficult or impossible. (In MS Word, for example, you can set up a numbered list, and then change its appearance to use circled numbers, up to the value of 20. In HTML or CSS, on the other hand, you cannot format a numbered list that way in practice.) In any case, if the characters are used both as list markers and in text as referencing list items, any replacements of the characters should preserve reasonable visual similarity between the markers and the references.

Characters with <compat> mapping in general

The report vaguely describes that "the <compat> label was given to a set of compatibility characters whose further classification was not settled at the time the standard was created." This seems to ignore the possibility of simply replacing the character with its compatibility mapping—e.g., writing ℅ as "c/o." Perhaps the idea is to say that if the formatting or the special meaning is to be preserved, there is usually no other way than to retain the character. In some situations, such as vertical layout, it is necessary to keep the symbol as single character, and vertical layout is one of the reasons why the characters have been used in the first place. Besides, due to relatively poor support in fonts, most characters in this category are rarely used for purely typographic reasons. Therefore, it might be safest to assume, at least in automatic conversions, that if these characters appear, there is a particular reason for that, so they should be retained as such. On the other hand, if you know that, say, the character Roman numeral seven Ⅶ (U+2166) has been used just for typography or by mistake, it's hard to see why you could not replace it with the three-character string "VII," optionally with some styling.

Fixed-width spaces

The report recommends that these characters be retained. However, as described in Chapter 8, most fixed-width spaces work unreliably and could often be replaced by the use of normal spaces and formatting commands or stylesheets.

Roman numerals

These characters each represent a Roman numeral, such as "VII," as a single character. Similarly to characters with <circled> mapping, they are often used as list item marks in a numbered list, and they could be similarly replaced by list markup. List styling tools (e.g., in HTML and CSS) usually support well the formatting of numbers as Roman numerals. In other usage, these characters should be retained; see earlier notes on <compat> mapping in general.

Parenthesized numbers

These characters, U+2474 to U+2487, have <compat> mappings like "(1)" and consist of a character in parentheses, such as ⑴ (U+2474). They are used much the same way as circled characters, and the report recommends, in its prose, the same approach for them. The feasibility of replacing these numbers with list markup and styling varies; for example, in CSS, it is currently not possible to make list markers appear as parenthesized numbers.

Dotted numbers

These characters, U+2488 to U+249B, are similar to parenthesized numbers but have <compat> mappings like "1." (i.e., a number followed by a full stop). Similar considerations apply. Note that many default renderings of numbered lists have a dot after the number; it can actually be difficult to get rid of it!

Parenthesized letters

These characters are similar to parenthesized numbers. The summary in the report says "use list item marker style or normalize," but this is probably an oversight. Instead, if it is infeasible to use list markup and marker styling, it is best to treat them the same was as other characters with <compat> mappings: retain them as such, unless you know that they can safely be replaced by their mappings (i.e., normalized).

Other parenthesized symbols

> Characters U+3200..U+3229 and U+322A..U+3243 are parenthesized symbols, often used as list markers. Due to their scope of use, they are usually best retained.

Ideographic telegraph symbols for months

> These characters have <compat> mappings consisting of a number (of month) followed by an ideograph. Due to their use in vertical layout, they are retained.

Arabic presentation forms

> Characters with <final>, <initial>, <isolated>, or <medial> mapping are compatibility characters that represent specific contextual forms of Arabic writing. The report recommends that these be normalized—i.e., replaced with the corresponding generic characters. Note that text using contextual forms is difficult to edit, since the forms would need to be changed, and search operations are difficult, too. However, some rendering software might be able display the contextual forms but unable to select appropriate glyphs when normalized text is used. If you decide to retain contextual forms for such reasons, beware that there are many pitfalls. For example, you may need to specify directionality explicitly even for purely Arabic text.

Characters with <font> mapping

> The report recommends that these be retained. This is cautious policy, based on the fact that the use of these characters *may* involve semantic distinctions. For example, the Planck constant "*h*" (U+210E) belongs to this category. If it has been used properly, it should be retained, in principle, though you may have good reasons to deviate from this. If, on the other hand, we can know that this character has been mistakenly used just to produce the letter "h" in italics style, with no specific semantics, the letter "h" and suitable markup and styling should be used instead.

Fractions

> Characters with <fraction> mapping are "vulgar fractions." The report somewhat oddly recommends that they be normalized "as long as fraction slash is supported!" In reality, the fraction formatting as requested by the use of the fraction slash is poorly supported. When converting to mathematical markup, fractions should apparently be replaced by the use of constructs like the general mfrac element in MathML. However, the real choice is usually between retaining these characters and replacing them with linearized fractions (e.g., mapping ½ to "1/2" so that / is the normal slash, or solidus) or maybe using a different notation instead of a fraction (e.g., "0.5"). See suggestions on writing fractions in Chapter 8.

Half-width (narrow) characters

> Characters with <narrow> mapping are half-width forms of characters, for use in East Asian writing that normally uses glyphs designed to fit into a full square. There is no equivalent markup in general.

Non-breaking characters

> Characters with <noBreak> mapping are non-breaking variants of characters. Currently this means no-break space (U+00A0), Tibetan mark delimiter tsheg bstar (U+0F0C), figure space (U+2007), non-breaking hyphen (U+2011), and narrow

no-break space (U+202F). (In fact, all of these except the figure space already appear in Table 9-3.) Otherwise, prevention of line breaking needs to be handled using invisible characters or at a higher protocol level, as explained in Chapter 5. The report says enigmatically: "The compatibility mapping is merely a way to indicate the equivalent character that is not non-breaking. The distinction must be preserved." In reality, there are several alternate ways to express non-breakability, in markup or in a stylesheet. But non-breakability information should surely not just be dropped.

Small forms

Characters with <small> mapping are versions of some ASCII characters and a few other characters, for use in East Asian writing. The report says: "Precise usage unknown. Maintain, but do not generate."

Square forms

Characters with <square> mapping are presentational forms of characters and strings, for use in vertical layout. Although this category contains different types of characters, the report recommends that they all be retained. Typically, the characters are symbols composed of Latin or Japanese kana letters, digits, and slash, designed to fit into a square that can be used as a single cell. For many simple implementations, this is the only way to present, for example, metric units (say, "km") and common abbreviations in a manner suitable for vertical text.

Subscript and superscript characters

Characters with <sub> or <super> mapping are subscript or superscript variants of characters, such as ². The summary in the report recommends replacing them by the use of sub and sup markup, respectively, apparently referring to HTML markup or similar markup. (Of course, there is no guarantee that an arbitrary XML-based markup language contains such elements, or that they have these names; in MathML, the names are msub and msup.) As discussed previously, the situation is rather complicated, and the text of the report acknowledges many of the problems. In the absence of information about the intended meaning, it is generally best to *retain* these characters. The report explicitly says that when subscripts and superscripts are to reflect semantic distinctions, "it is easier to work with these meanings encoded in text rather than markup, for example, in phonetic or phonemic transcription" and that especially for letters, the distinction can be essential (in phonetic notations, the meaning of "kʰ" is different from the meaning of "kh").

Vertical forms

Characters with <vertical> mapping are presentational forms of characters, for use in East Asian writing when it runs vertically and not horizontally. The report recommends that they be normalized (replaced by the mapping). This is feasible if the rendering software can be assumed to select vertical forms automatically as needed.

Fullwidth (wide) characters

Characters with <wide> mapping are fullwidth forms of characters, for use in East Asian writing that normally uses glyphs designed to fit into a full square. There is no equivalent markup in general.

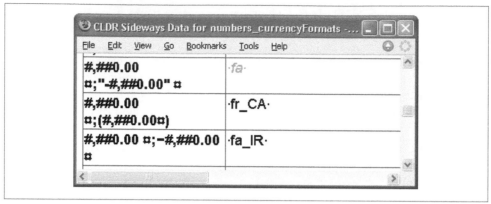

Figure 9-5. An extract of a table with highly undesirable line breaks

Preventing Line Breaks

We return to the issue of preventing line breaks, discussed in this chapter as well as in Chapter 5 and Chapter 8. The reason is that it is so common to have poorly formatted data, especially tables, just because no method for preventing undesired line breaks has been used. Here we summarize the different methods and present some examples.

To illustrate the problem, consider the extract of tabular data presented in Figure 9-5. It is localization data from the CLDR (discussed in Chapter 11) and somewhat complicated in itself, but undesirable line breaks make things much worse. The first row shown in the figure is meant to specify that for the Farsi (Persian) language (language code fa), a positive monetary amount is expressed in the format #,##90.00 ¤ and a negative monetary amount in the format "-#,##0.00" ¤. Here you can see the currency symbol ¤ in actual use: it is a placeholder for a code, name, or symbol for a currency. The problem here, apart from the difficulty of understanding the notations of the formats, is that a web browser has broken the string #,##90.00 ¤;"-#,##0.00" ¤ (where the semicolon is just a separator between the formats) in a disturbing manner. Breaking at the space obfuscates the data. Similar things happen on the two other rows.

Especially in tables, horizontal space is often a scarce resource. When rendering software tries to fit a multicolumn table within some limited space, it may squeeze some columns so that even cell content like "5 m" is broken into two lines. Breaking it to "5" and "m" can be confusing, and it surely makes the appearance bad. In HTML authoring, specifically, there are many ways of preventing such breaks. They are presented in Table 9-5. Note that some of the ways are just theoretical, though they may illustrate techniques that are useful in other contexts.

Table 9-5. Methods of preventing line breaks in an HTML table cell

Description	Sample markup	Notes
No-Break Space	`<td>5 m</td>`	Could use U+00A0 itself, too
Word Joiner	`<td>5 &#x2060;m</td>`	Theoretical alternative
Markup attribute	`<td nowrap>5 m</td>`	Deprecated markup in HTML
Markup element	`<td><nobr>5 m</nobr></td>`	Nonstandard, widely supported
Style sheet (CSS)	`<td style="white-space: nowrap">5 m</td>`	Better done with external CSS

When using a stylesheet, it is usually better to put CSS code into a separate file, rather than embed it into HTML markup using the `style` attribute, as in the example. Normally you would use just a `<td>` tag without attributes, or such a tag with a `class` attribute, and the styling would be done outside the HTML document.

Although all the methods mentioned in Table 9-5 might be expected to have the same effect, the Word Joiner (WJ) method—which might be regarded as theoretically the most adequate—fails on almost any browser. The other methods mostly have the same effect, but if there is an explicit width set for the table cell, both the markup attribute method and the stylesheet method fail to prevent the line break. This is just one example of the practically important oddities that you may encounter. Using the character-level method, no-break space, is usually the simplest and most effective method here. Note that the use of the entity reference ` ` is equivalent to using the no-break space character itself as data, and we use it here just for clarity.

Things change if you need to consider potential line breaking points other than spaces. In that case, you usually don't have a character like the no-break space that you could use. In particular, to prevent a line break after a hyphen, as in `<td>555-123</td>`, the character level methods (using the nonbreaking hyphen or the Word Joiner) hardly work in practice. You would thus use one of the last three methods mentioned—i.e., the `nowrap` attribute, the `nobr` element, or a stylesheet (or maybe a combination of these).

Finally, as a practical observation that often makes things easier, note that it is often sufficient to prevent line breaks in one cell in a column. Typically, you would work on the cell with largest width requirement when written on one line. If you prevent a line break in a cell containing "1 000 000 $," then surely a cell with "42 $" in the same column won't be broken either.

Breaking the Flow of Text

Markup can be used even for parts of words. Should it affect the way in which the textual content is processed, such as recognition of words? Consider the (old-fashioned) HTML markup `<b>F</b>oo`, intended to make the word Foo appear so that first letter is bold. Could search engines, for example, treat it as two words, "F" and "oo"?

Search engines generally parse HTML in a manner that effectively ignores most tags. It is however possible that some programs do otherwise, either because they have poorly written parsers or because they have intentionally been programmed to honor markup, in a way. The latter would be quite natural for markup like `<p>xxx</p><p>yyy</p>`, where the two elements should be treated as paragraphs and the strings xxx and yyy as separate, not as xxxyyy.

In practice, search engines differ. Google treats `<b>F</b>oo` as "Foo," whereas AltaVista treats it as two words, "F oo." Moreover, search engine behavior may vary by situation and version. It is thus best to avoid using markup that breaks words, unless you have real need for it.

For a markup language like HTML, it would be natural to think that inline (text-level) markup (like b for bold face font) does not separate characters in any way, whereas block-level markup (like p for paragraph) acts as a separator. However, neither HTML specifications nor the Unicode standard discuss this issue, and search engines can hardly be expected to make such distinctions.

In a more general setting, such as XML, things become even more complicated. There is no division into inline and block-level elements in XML itself, though in XML-based languages, such a division might be made.

Thus, we should be prepared for both alternatives. In some situations, inline markup could separate strings. It might also fail to do that even when we would expect that, so markup like `<p>xxx</p><p>yyy</p>` is not safe; it is better to insert a space or a line break between the elements.

Similarly, if we write `<font color="red">f</font>i`, it may happen that the string "fi" is not presented as a ligature even if a browser would use a ligature when the font markup is not there. If we use ē in HTML (or XML), we may expect to see ē (letter "e" and a combining macron, U+0304), and this may well happen. But if we write e`<font color="red">`̄`</font>`, the situation may change, depending on the browser. The font tag might act as an invisible barrier between a character and a combining diacritic mark. Different browsers could render this as ē in normal color, as ē with a red macron, or as e̅ with a red macron, or even (incorrectly) as just "e." The example may sound contrived, but people really want to use such markup at times—e.g., in linguistic contexts when drawing attention to a diacritic mark.

In any case, markup used inside words, even for individual characters, tends to make the markup hard to read. This is one of the reasons why UTR #20 allows several formatting characters that could in principle be replaced by markup. Compare, for example, the string foo-bar-1 (where the second hyphen is the nonbreaking hyphen, U+2011) or even foo-bar‑1 (using a character reference for U+2011) with the markup foo-`<span style="white-space:nowrap">bar-1</span>`.

Why Not Markup in Unicode?

Unicode contains a large number of characters that are, more or less, typographic variants of more basic characters. This, and reasons for it, were discussed in Chapter 4. To some extent, such characters can be explained by the universality principle: they have been taken into Unicode, since they exist in other character code standards. However, this does not explain the addition of more and more characters of this kind, especially for the needs of mathematics (e.g., mathematical bold capital "A," mathematical bold italic capital "A," mathematical sans-serif capital "A," and many, many others).

Since most of such characters can be described in terms of basic characters and a number of features such as "bold," "italic," and "sans-serif," it is natural to ask whether a more systematic approach could have been used. In fact, they could have been implemented more efficiently by adding a limited number of formatting characters into the Basic Multilingual Plane (BMP). That way, you would use such a formatting character before or after a normal letter to create a special variant. This would give much more flexibility, and it would be in accordance with the principles applied to characters with diacritic marks. The Unicode FAQ answers:

> It would have provided too much flexibility, and would have tempted people to use such characters to create "poor man's markup" schemes rather than using proper markup such as SGML/HTML/XML. The mathematical letters and digits are meant to be used only in mathematics, where the distinction between a plain and a bold letter is fundamentally semantic rather than stylistic.

This means that there are two distinct points:

- The Unicode standard intentionally excludes anything resembling general font markup. The expressed reason is that people should use "proper markup" instead.
- The Unicode characters that can be classified as font variants are usually not just typographic variants but have specific meaning. However, Unicode defines the meaning rather abstractly by designating characters as "mathematical," for example.

In practice, if you decided to use, say, mathematical bold capital "A" (U+1D400) just to produce a bold **A**, you would not break any formal rule of Unicode. But in addition to breaking the spirit, it would almost always be unwise. The character U+1D400 has very limited support in fonts and in automatic processing in programs. Besides, programs that recognize it may treat it in a way that corresponds to its role as a mathematical symbol, rather than just a variant of the common letter "A."

Media Types for Text

When data is stored in a file or transferred between systems and applications, it is essential to keep track of the format of data. This is especially important on the Internet, where the recipient of data may be prepared to handle different formats of data but needs to know the format. For example, if some data is included in an email message as an attachment, the message should internally carry information about the format of the data, such as plain text (which can be rendered directly very simply) or rich text (which needs to be processed in a rather complicated way in order to display it properly).

Internet media types (MIME types), described in Chapter 10, are used to specify the general nature of a data set (file), such as image versus text, as well as its more specific format. Here we will consider the major type text and its subtypes.

The Type text

The MIME specification (RFC 2046) defines the type text as follows:

> The "text" media type is intended for sending material which is principally textual in form. A "charset" parameter may be used to indicate the character set of the body text for "text" subtypes, notably including the subtype "text/plain," which is a generic subtype for plain text. Plain text does not provide for or allow formatting commands, font attribute specifications, processing instructions, interpretation directives, or content markup. Plain text is seen simply as a linear sequence of characters, possibly interrupted by line breaks or page breaks. Plain text may allow the stacking of several characters in the same position in the text. Plain text in scripts like Arabic and Hebrew may also include facilities that allow the arbitrary mixing of text segments with opposite writing directions.
>
> Beyond plain text, there are many formats for representing what might be known as "rich text." An interesting characteristic of many such representations is that they are to some extent readable even without the software that interprets them. It is useful, then, to distinguish them, at the highest level, from such unreadable data as images, audio, or text represented in an unreadable form. In the absence of appropriate interpretation software, it is reasonable to show subtypes of "text" to the user, while it is not reasonable to do so with most nontextual data. Such formatted textual data should be represented using subtypes of "text."

In most cases, data of type text is completely textual, not just principally textual. However, rich text formats may contain facilities for embedding images directly into the file format.

This definition might be read so that "rich text" is a catchall name for anything that is text but not plain text. However, "rich text" normally refers to formats that contain text and formatting instructions (for italics, bolding, font selection, spacing, etc.). HTML or XML documents are hardly "rich text," since they mostly do not contain direct formatting instructions.

Data formats such as TSV (Tab Separated Values) aren't really "rich text" either. Rather, they specify a very simple structure for tabular data: each line of text (separated by line breaks) corresponds to one row of a table, and some designated character (typically, tab, semicolon, or comma) is treated as a separator between cells. Naturally, that designated character must not appear in the data itself.

The Character Encoding

The text type has an optional charset parameter that can be used to specify the character encoding of the text. For example, text/plain;charset=utf-8 means plain text that shall be interpreted as UTF-8 encoding.

What happens if the encoding is not specified that way? Since the content is text—i.e., characters—there is really no meaningful way to process it in any way without knowing, guessing, or implying some encoding. In Chapter 10, we will take a detailed look at this practically important problem for HTML documents on the Web. The problem is of a more general nature, though. For example, if you open a plain text file locally in a system, there is usually no encoding information for the file. Most filesystems contain no direct data about media types in the MIME sense or about the encoding.

At the general level, there are different ways to deal with a situation where a subtype of text does not specify the encoding with charset:

Imply an encoding

> This has been very common in the past, usually implying ASCII, or (especially on the Web) ISO-8859-1. According to MIME specifications, the default must be ASCII for all subtypes of text, but other Internet protocols (e.g., HTTP) impose other rules. Thus, it is unsafe to assume any specific default. If you open a plain text file on the local disk, the program you use might imply a system-dependent default.

Specify a default encoding for a subtype

> It might be natural to specify a default encoding for a subtype on practical grounds. In particular, the effective default encoding for text/html is usually windows-1252 or ISO-8859-1. In principle, this is not the case, and the MIME specification apparently disallows subtype-specific defaults.

Deduce the encoding from the data itself

> Various techniques can be used to try to guess the encoding from the data content. In particular, some data formats contain mechanisms for specifying the encoding inside the data (e.g., a meta element in HTML and the XML prologue in XML). Although logically odd, these mechanisms often work reasonably well.

Let the user decide

> Rather naturally, a program could prompt for a user action to choose between encodings, when adequate information about encoding is not available. If the dialog contains a method for previewing the content in different encodings, this may work well, when the user is experienced.

As an implication, if you have Unicode data in UTF-8 encoding, it is very probable that characters in the ASCII range get interpreted correctly. All the rest is more or less unsafe. This is one reason why the basic structural elements of computer languages, such as markup tags, are usually still limited to ASCII.

According to MIME specifications, if a program does not recognize a subtype of text, it should treat it as text/plain, provided that it knows how to handle the character encoding (charset). If the character encoding unrecognized, too, the subtype should be should be treated as application/octet-stream, which effectively means "lump of binary data." Upon receiving such data from a network, well-behaved software normally prompts the user for an action, asking her to specify whether the data should be stored on the local disk or processed in some other user-specified way. In reality, programs might just imply the ASCII encoding (or some other) instead.

The text Type Versus the application Type

In the type classification, many formats that can intuitively be understood as text formats are defined as being of major type application. For example, the data formats that word processors normally use are classified as application types. As a rough rule of thumb, if a format is designed for processing with a specific program or family of programs, it is classified as an application type. Formats of text type are meant to be processed with many different programs, and they have been defined by specifying their structural properties and semantics, rather than technical implementation.

For example, the format used by WordPerfect is application/vnd.wordperfect. Names of subtypes defined for vendor-specific software start with vnd. in most cases, but there are some exceptions for historical reasons, such as application/msword.

The PDF format, defined by Adobe, is registered as application/pdf. It is comparable to word processor formats, in the sense that the content is typically mostly text, but the overall structure is not textual. PDF is widely used for the interchange and distribution of documents, especially when it is desirable to deliver them in easily printable format. Officially, "PDF" is short for "Portable Document Format." PDF is often used for documents that contain special characters, since you can, upon creating a PDF file, specify that font information be embedded into the data. This means that recipients can usually view and print the document, even if the fonts on their computers do not contain all the characters used.

In some cases, the same data format can be classified using different media types. For example, an XML document may be classified as text/xml or application/xml, and possibly using other media types as well, depending on the specific markup used.

Subtypes of text

Just as for the application type, the subtype name usually begins with vnd. for vendor-specific subtypes of text. This does not mean that the subtype is private use only. On the contrary, it has been registered so that it can be used generally—e.g., on the Internet.

Table 9-6 presents all subtypes of text except those with names beginning with vnd. (see the full registry at *http://www.iana.org/assignments/media-types/text/*). The last column identifies the registration documents, which usually do not describe the format itself; instead, it lists some basic properties and refers to some documents or organizations for the actual specifications. "I-Draft" means an Internet-Draft, available from the repository *https://datatracker.ietf.org/public/idindex.cgi*. "Registry" means that the definition is in a file in the registry, not published as an RFC or as an Internet-Draft.

Table 9-6. Registered subtypes of text

Subtype	Meaning	Definition
calendar	iCalendarformat, for calendaring and scheduling	RFC 2445
css	Stylesheet, in Cascading Style Sheets (CSS)	RFC 2318
csv	Comma Separated Values, for tabular data	I-Draft
directory	Directoryinformation (e.g., telephone directory)	RFC 2425
dns	DomainName System data	RFC 4027

Subtype	Meaning	Definition
ecmascript	Obsoletesubtype for Ecmascript code	I-Draft
enriched	A simplerich text type—i.e., text with formatting info	RFC 1896
html	HTML (Hypertext MarkupLanguage) document	RFC 2854
javascript	Obsolete subtype for JavaScript code	I-Draft
parityfec	For Real-time Transport Protocol (RTP)	RFC 3009
plain	Plain text: text as such, with no special agreements	RFC 2046
prs.fallenstein.rst	For reStructuredText, a simple markup system	Registry
prs.lines.tags	Consists of lines with simple name: value syntax	Registry
red	For transport of redundant text data via RTP	RFC 4102
rfc822-headers	Internet message headers, when sent as data	RFC 1892
richtext	An obsolete rich text type, see text/enriched	RFC 1341
rtf	Rich Text Format (RTF), a common rich text type	Registry
sgml	Standard Generalized Markup Language (SGML)	RFC 1874
t140	For transmission of data via RTP using ITU T.140	RFC 4103
tab-separated -values	TSV format, for tabular data, similar to text/csv	Registry
troff	Marked-up text, for the troff typesetting programs	I-Draft
uri-list	A list of URIs (URLs) for URI resolution services	RFC 2483
xml	XML (Extensible Markup Language) document	RFC 2023
xml-external-parsed-entity	External parsed entity, as defined in the XML specification; typically, a file of common definitions	RFC 2023

Usually, subtypes of application are used for XML documents. However, RFC 2023 recommends that text/xml (or, in some cases, text/xml-external-parsed-entity) be used, if "an XML document—that is, the unprocessed, source XML document—is readable by casual users." As a practical consideration, software that does not support XML in any particular way will probably treat text/xml as comparable to text/plain and display it as such. Thus, the question is whether a person who does not know the specific markup used will be able to understand (some of) the data intuitively. This may well be the case, if element and attribute names are mnemonic and descriptive, like product and price. Note, however, that displaying an XML document as unprocessed means that character references such as ሴ are displayed literally, probably confusing casual users.

CHAPTER 10

Characters in Internet Protocols

This chapter describes how character encoding information is transmitted in Internet protocols, including MIME and HTTP, and how content negotiation works on the Web, mainly for the purposes of negotiating on character encoding and language. This constitutes a basis for a presentation of some fundamentals of multilingual web authoring at the technical level. Moreover, the use of characters in the protocols themselves, such as in Internet message headers and URLs, is described, with focus on the partial shift from pure ASCII to Unicode. In particular, the technical basis of Internationalized Domain Names and Internationalized URLs is described.

A common situation in which people first encounter problems with character encoding is when they start authoring web pages in new languages. If you have a web site in English, you might never think about encodings, since you can work with default settings. Then, if you want to add a page in Japanese or Arabic, you meet several problems at a time:

- What authoring tools (software) should I use?
- What fonts do I use?
- Which encoding should I use?
- How do I give information about the encoding?
- What tags should I put in my documents to tell the language I'm using?

Many of the difficulties in such situations arise from the common confusion of fonts, encodings, and languages. Other chapters of this book have explained such issues; in this chapter, we mostly concentrate on the encodings. A suitable approach is:

1. Determine the *character repertoire* that you will need (see Chapter 7). Consider both the needs of the language(s) you use and the special symbols that might appear.

2. Select a suitable *encoding* that covers that repertoire and is suitable for use on the Web. Chapters 3 and 6 have described the encodings, but in this chapter, we consider the special conditions of web publishing. In particular, it is possible to use an encoding that does not support all the characters needed, since you can use special notations like character references to overcome the limitations of an encoding.

3. Select *software* that lets you work conveniently with the encoding and with the characters you need. In practice, you may need to consider what software is available before you decide on the encoding. Such topics were discussed in Chapter 2.

4. Make sure that the web server sends *information about the encoding* in one way or another, and possibly in different ways. This is explained in this chapter.

5. Use *language markup* if you know how to use it properly, but do not rely on it. It mostly has no effect except possibly on typography (font selection) on some browsers. See Chapter 7.

6. Worry about *fonts* if you wish or need to, but do not think that font settings solve any of the fundamental problems listed here. Rather, setting fonts is like painting a house, once you have otherwise built it up. Font issues mostly do not belong to the scope of this book. You would normally use Cascading Style Sheets (CSS) to affect fonts in web authoring, but you might also create a PDF version of a document, with fonts embedded into it.

Information About Encoding

When data is sent over the Internet, it needs to be encoded into digital format, ultimately as octets and bits. If the recipient program does not know the *overall format*—i.e., how the data has been encoded, it needs to make guesses, or it might simply fail to do anything sensible with it. A sequence of octets could be intended to present data other than character data, too. It could be an image in a bitmap format, or a computer program in binary form, or numeric data in the internal format used in computers.

Moreover, if the data is text, the recipient needs to know the *character encoding*—i.e., how the octets will be mapped to characters. If you only look at an octet sequence, you cannot even know whether each octet presents one character or just part of a two-octet presentation of a character, or something more complicated. Sometimes the recipient can guess the encoding, but data processing and transfer shouldn't be guesswork.

Information about the overall format and the character encoding should normally be included into *Internet message headers*. The headers contain other information, too. The *MIME* specification defines how the format, the encoding, and other information pertaining to character representation are expressed in Internet message headers. In particular, when non-ASCII data is sent by email, there should be a header that says the MIME is used in the first place (as opposed to old email formats, where ASCII was implied) and a header that indicates the data transmission method. For example:

```
MIME-Version: 1.0
Content-Type: text/plain; charset=ISO-8859-15
Content-Transfer-Encoding: 8bit
```

The header `Content-Transfer-Encoding: 8bit` indicates that the octets representing the data (in this case, in the ISO 8859-15 encoding) are transmitted as such as 8-bit quantities. The original design of Internet email postulated the use of 7-bit quantities only. Most email software can handle 8-bit quantities nowadays, but the octets can be encoded using 7-bit quantities when needed.

What Happens Without Information About Encoding

Because of *default settings*, you might work with computers and the Internet for quite a while without ever worrying about formats and encodings. Suppose that you use just English, or some other language of Western European origin, like Spanish. When you send email, your email program probably sends your message as plain text encoded in ASCII, ISO-8859-1, or windows-1252 (Windows Latin 1). The program may also automatically include a header that tells the format and the encoding. A recipient's email program will often find that header and act accordingly, without bothering its user with any technicalities. In the absence of the header, the program will probably interpret the data as plain text in windows-1252 encoding, and get it right. (ASCII and ISO-8859-1 encoded data gets interpreted correctly when interpreted as windows-1252; see Chapter 3.)

Problems arise when *defaults clash* with each other. Suppose that you send email to Russia. Even if your message is in English, you might use some non-ASCII characters, such as curved quotation marks, dashes, or symbols like µ or €. Your email program might therefore decide to send the message as ISO-8859-1 or windows-1252 encoded. If it does not inform about the encoding, or if the recipient's program does not use the information, the odds are that the recipient sees the non-ASCII characters wrong. Some Cyrillic letters or some special characters (but not the right ones) would appear, when your message is interpreted according to some of the 8-bit encodings commonly used in Russia. This all works in the opposite direction, too. Someone writing in English in Russia might use the character № to mean "number" (incorrectly but understandably thinking the symbol is used in English, too), but when his email program sends it, for example, in windows-1251 (Windows Cyrillic) encoding and your email program interprets it as windows-1252, you will see the symbol as ¹.

It is easy to guess wrong and never realize the truth, if the wrong guess affects a few characters only. This may happen when non-ASCII characters appear only rarely. It also happens when some commonly used encodings are rather similar to each other but not the same. For example, ISO-8859-1 and ISO-8859-15 differ in a few positions only. If you get a lump of data and notice that it looks ISO-8859-1 encoded, you might be quite happy even if the encoding is in fact ISO-8859-15. However, the data that you pass forward or print or otherwise process might contain some wrong characters. For example, octet A8 (hexadecimal) means the dieresis ¨ in ISO-8859-1, and since the dieresis has so little use as a separate character, the texts you look at probably don't contain it. One day, however, the data you get might contain that octet and you would see it as the dieresis, wondering what it means. If the encoding is in fact ISO-8859-15, the octet should be taken as meaning the letter š.

When very different encodings are implied by a sending program and a receiving program, the user will immediately see that there is something wrong. If you send Spanish text (using all accents correctly) to Russia and the recipient's program interprets it according to some encoding commonly used in Russia, all non-ASCII letters will appear replaced by Cyrillic letters. If someone sends you a message in Japanese, using some of the encodings commonly used in Japan for Japanese text, and your program interprets it according to windows-1252, the result will be completely illegible even you read Japanese fluently.

When there is no information about encoding or the information is wrong, the user often has to try to set her program to show the data according to different encodings to find the right one. We discussed this in Chapter 1, but most users do not know such features or they have problems using them. It is difficult to find information about these features in documentation of most programs.

Approaches to Specifying the Encoding

For reliable data transmission, a platform-independent method of specifying the general format and the encoding and other relevant information is needed. Such methods exist, although they are not always used widely enough. People still send each other data without specifying the encoding, and this may cause a lot of harm.

Attaching a human-readable note, such as a few words of explanation in an email message body, is better than nothing. You could write, for example: "The enclosed attachment contains the report you asked for, as plain text, in ISO-8859-1 encoding."

Before the Web, FTP (File Transfer Protocol) servers were used to make documents available on the Internet, and they still have some usage. In FTP, there is no way to indicate the format of documents at the protocol level, except by distinguishing between text ("ASCII") files and all other files, collectively called binary files. It is therefore common and recommendable to include a text file in a directory on an FTP server so that this file, often named conventionally as *README.TXT*, contains a list of all files in the directory. That's a suitable place for explaining not only the content and purpose of each file, but also the file formats and character encodings.

However, since data is processed by programs that cannot understand such notes, the encoding should be specified in a standardized computer-readable form whenever possible. Ideally, computers would do this automatically when sending data, so that people would not need to know anything about it, unless they are computer specialists who work on technologies that make such things possible. In the real world, many people need to know something about the internals of sending information about encoding.

Thus, in most Internet contexts, the normal and recommendable approach is to specify the encoding of data in a *formalized* manner, in a format that can easily be processed by programs. Usually, Internet message headers are used for the purpose.

Practical Recommendations

Most important, make sure that any Internet-related software that you use to send data (such as an email program) specifies the encoding correctly in suitable headers. There are two things involved:

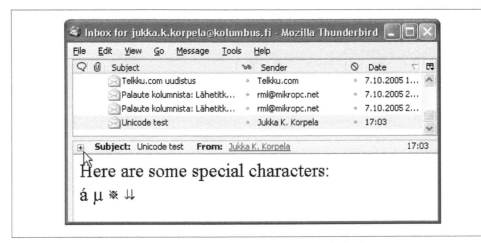

Figure 10-1. Normal view of an incoming email message in Thunderbird

- The header must be present and it must reflect the actual encoding used.
- The encoding used must be one that is widely understood by the (potential) recipients' software.

You often need to make compromises with regards to the latter aim: you may need to use an encoding that is not yet universally supported to get your message through at all. In practice, this mainly means that you may need to use UTF-8, even though not all email programs can handle it in incoming mail. In Chapter 3, we described some of the commonly available encodings and their suitability. ASCII is safe, ISO 8859 encodings are safe in many contexts (in communication between people who belong to the same language community), and UTF-8 is usually the best approach when you need a wide repertoire of characters.

Typically, you should check the headers sent by a program when you first use it, or the first time you intend to send anything but ASCII characters. We discussed this in Chapter 1. However, you should also check that the message has appropriate headers, instead of just looking right by accident.

Looking at the Headers

When you view an incoming message normally, as in Figure 10-1, you see just the content, not the headers. However, some information extracted from the headers may appear; e.g., the "Subject" and "From" information has been taken from them.

Using some program-dependent method, you can change the display of an incoming email message so that all the message headers become visible. In Thunderbird, you would just click on the small box containing + at the start of the line with the Subject of the message, right above the message itself. The headers then appear before the message, as shown in Figure 10-2, and the content of the box changes to the minus sign, – (meaning that if you click on it, the headers are removed from the display).

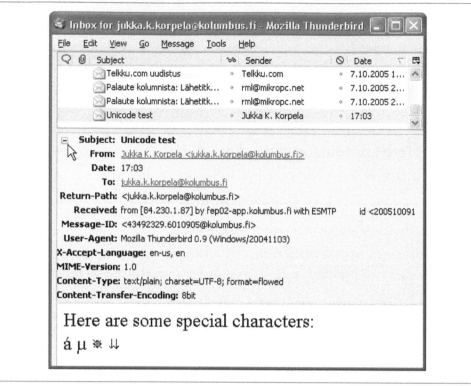

Figure 10-2. View of an incoming email message with headers in Thunderbird

The structure of the email message headers, or MIME headers, will be discussed later in this chapter. Here it suffices to note that the last three headers specify the following:

- The message is in MIME format (specifically, in MIME Version 1.0).
- The content is in plain text format, UTF-8 encoded, and it is subject to a specific convention expressed by format=flowed (which says that the message may be reformatted for display according to certain rules, as opposite to fixed line structure).
- The encoded (UTF-8) content is transferred directly as octets, instead of applying any particular transfer encoding such as Quoted Printable (see Chapter 6).

Alternatively, when viewing a message in Thunderbird, you could select View → Message source, or simply type Ctrl-U, to see the message as "source," or as "raw format." This means that the message is displayed as transmitted on the network and as received by an email program. This format contains first the headers, then a blank line, and then the message itself. Our test message is shown as "source" in Figure 10-3. In this case, the characters in the message are displayed as such, but if some special transfer encoding (such as Quoted Printable) had been used, they would appear as "raw," in the encoded form.

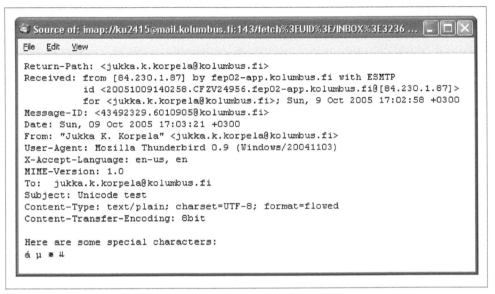

Figure 10-3. View of email message "source" in Thunderbird

Other programs have different methods for making the headers visible or viewing message "source" or "raw format." Typically, the relevant commands are in a "File" menu or in a "View" menu. In Outlook Express, for example, you can normally use File → Properties to access both the source and the raw format.

To test that your email program behaves well, you could send a message with several special characters to a friend who works in a completely different environment—e.g., a Linux or Mac environment, if you use Windows—and ask her to forward the message back to you. Of course, if something goes wrong, you will not immediately see whether the problem is in your system or in hers. However, the headers will help in analyzing the situation.

Characters in MIME

MIME is a protocol that makes it possible to send text data by email using different encodings, not just ASCII, which is the original encoding for Internet email. MIME has other purposes and applications as well, such as sending nontextual data by email.

An email message that uses MIME has special headers as illustrated in the preceding section. The headers are used to specify the general data format of the message as well as its character encoding. It may also specify the transfer encoding (see Chapter 6) used for the data.

Media Types

Internet media types, often called *MIME types*, can be used to specify a major media type ("top level media type," such as text), a subtype (such as html), and an encoding (such as iso-8859-1). They were originally developed to allow the use of email for sending *formats* other than plain ASCII data. They can be (and should be) also used for specifying the *encoding* when character data is sent over a network—e.g., by email or using the HTTP protocol on the World Wide Web.

Originally, "MIME" was short for Multipurpose Internet Mail Extensions. The idea was to extend the capabilities of Internet email from the original content format, which is plain text with ASCII as the implied encoding. Thus, MIME was developed both to let you include characters other than ASCII into the message body and to specify methods for including nontext data, such as images, as attachments. The currently defined major media types are the following:

application
> Application-dependent data format. This includes various binary data formats as well as formats used to represent text in an application-dependent way. The subtype application/octet-stream denotes binary data with unknown or unclassified structure.

audio
> Data representing voice, such as music or speech. For example, audio/basic is a simple audio format.

image
> Data that is meant to be presented in a graphic (visible) form, such as a drawing or a photograph. For example, the subtype image/gif means an image in GIF format.

message
> An Internet message, such as an email message or Usenet posting, along with its message headers. The body is normally plain text, but the headers (though textual) are to be treated in a special way, not as text as such. For example, the subtype message/partial indicates a message that is a part of one logical message divided into parts for delivery.

model
> Modeling data, such as model/vrml, which is data in VRML (Virtual Reality Modeling Language).

multipart
> A format that consists of one or more parts that may be of different formats. For example, multipart/alternative is a general purpose subtype for data that consists of representations of the same data in different formats (e.g., as plain text and as rich text).

text
> Data that consists of characters only, though possibly with some special conventions on the interpretation of some characters (e.g., as tags). The subtype text/plain means text without such conventions.

video
> Video data—i.e., film-like data (moving pictures, possibly with associated sound). For example, video/mpeg.

The media type concept is defined in RFC 2046. The procedure for registering types in specified in RFC 2048. The site *http://www.oac.uci.edu/indiv/ehood/MIME/toc.html* contains a collection of interrelated RFCs (2045–2049) in hypertext format. The official registry of media types is maintained by the Internet Assigned Numbers Authority (IANA) at *http://www.iana.org/assignments/mediatypes/*. Unregistered types are often used, though, especially for data related to new technologies. In principle, an unregistered media type should have a subtype that begins with x- (letter "x" and hyphen-minus)—e.g., text/x-cooltext, but this requirement is often violated.

Character Encoding ("charset") Information

The technical term used to denote a character encoding in the Internet media type context is *charset*, abbreviated from "character set." This has caused a lot of confusion, since "set" can easily be understood as repertoire.

Normally, subtypes of message and text need a parameter that specifies the character encoding used, though this parameter can be omitted (defaulted) in some cases. The parameter is called charset, and it is written like the following example of an email message header:

```
Content-Type: text/plain; charset=iso-8859-1
```

This specifies, in addition to saying that the media type is text and subtype is plain, that the character encoding is ISO-8859-1. Encoding names are case insensitive, and they must not contain spaces. The spaces after : and ; above are optional and used for clarity only.

The official registry of charset (i.e., character encoding) names is kept by IANA at *http://www.iana.org/assignments/character-sets*. This plain text file also contains some references to documents that define encodings. There is also an unofficial tabular presentation of the registry, ordered alphabetically by charset name and augmented with some references: *http://www.cs.tut.fi/~jkorpela/chars/sorted.html*.

Several character encodings have *alternate (alias) names* in the registry. For example, the ASCII encoding can be called ASCII, ANSI_X3.4-1968, or cp367 (plus a few other names). Its preferred name in MIME context is, according to the registry, US-ASCII. Similarly, ISO 8859-1 has several names; its preferred MIME name is ISO-8859-1.

MIME Headers

The Content-Type information in the preceding section is an example of information in a message header, or *header* for short. Headers relate to some data, describing its presentation and other things, but are passed as logically separate from it. MIME headers are a special case of *Internet message headers*, often called RFC 822 headers, although the classical RFC 822 has now been replaced by RFC 2822, "Internet Message Format," available as hypertext at *http://www.rfc-ref.org/RFC-TEXTS/2822/*. In the specifications, "header line" is used instead of "header," but a header may be divided into several physical lines.

Adequate headers should normally be *generated automatically* by the software that sends the data (such as a program for sending email, or a web server) and interpreted automatically by receiving software (such as a program for reading email, or a web browser). In email messages, headers precede the message body. It depends on the email program whether and how it displays the headers. Typically, just a few commonly used headers are displayed by default. The header names themselves, such as Content-Type and Date, are fixed by the email protocol, but the information content of headers might be shown to the user in a localized and customized way. For example, the content type is usually not shown to the user, since it is technical information for interpreting the data, whereas the timestamp in the Date header might be shown with any suitable name in a language understood by the user.

Internet message format and MIME

The Internet message format was originally developed for simple ASCII-based email. It has been extended in content and scope so that, for example, Usenet messages and HTTP messages use the same fundamental format, though partly with different types of headers.

The general approach of MIME and several essential headers are described in the basic MIME specification, RFC 2045, "Multipurpose Internet Mail Extensions (MIME) Part One: Format of Internet Message Bodies." There are additional definitions in RFC 3864, "Registration Procedures for Message Header Fields," and RFC 4021, "Registration of Mail and MIME Header Fields."

Internet message headers have a common general syntax (see the example in Figure 10-3):

- Message headers appear before the message body, separated from it by one completely empty line.
- A header is of the form *name*: *value* normally written on one line. The space after the colon is optional, but is commonly used for legibility.
- A header may be continued to next line by starting the next line with at least one space.
- The message header name starts with a letter and contains name characters: ASCII letters, digits, and hyphen-minus.

- Message header names are case insensitive, but are usually written as capitalized (e.g., From, Subject). Values may or may not be case sensitive, depending on the definition of the header.

- The mutual order of Internet message headers is insignificant. Some orders might be more natural than others, but the meaning is not changed by any reordering. However, for multiple headers with the same name, the order may be significant.

- As in the Internet message format in general, lines are separated from each other by the character pair CR LF (Carriage Return, Line Feed); see Chapter 8.

- The implied character encoding is ASCII (US-ASCII). This means that the headers are written and processed as ASCII data, though specific encoding mechanisms may be used to include other characters even in the headings. The headers may specify that the message body be interpreted in some other encoding.

Within this simple framework, Internet message headers of different kinds can be used for a multitude of purposes, public and private. In theory, you are supposed to use a header name that starts with X- (capital "X" and hyphen-minus), if you use a header that is not defined in a published specification. In practice, people have used "private" or experimental headers without sticking to such conventions. Attempts have been made to describe the actual usage, but it has been very varying. For example, many email programs have used headers of their own in a proprietary manner, so that the same information is often expressed in different headers by different programs.

RFC 3864 establishes a registry, which might clarify the situation: *http://www.iana.org/ assignments/message-headers/message-header-index.html*. It does not directly define the headers but cites the defining documents, many of which just cite other documents for the real definitions.

Headers related to characters

The most important headers that we need for character-related issues have already been mentioned. They are summarized in Table 10-1 along with some other headers. Not all of them relate directly to representation characters. In particular, the Subject header is mentioned here because it should contain the subject of the message in a suitable natural language, and this raises the question how we can represent non-ASCII data there.

Table 10-1. Internet message headers related to handling characters

Header name	Meaning
Accept-Charset	Lists the character encodings accepted (in HTTP).
Accept-Encoding	Lists the transfer encodings accepted (in HTTP).
Accept-Language	Lists the language preference settings of the user.
Content-Encoding	Specifies the transfer encoding of the original data.
Content-Transfer-Encoding	Specifies the transfer encoding applied.
Content-Language	Specifies the language(s) of the content. Rarely used.

Header name	Meaning
Content-Type	Specifies the media type and the character encoding.
MIME-Version	Indicates the use of MIME, and a specific version.
Subject	Specifies the subject (title) of the message.
Transfer-Encoding	Specifies the transfer encoding of the message body.

Headers for transfer encoding

As you can see from Table 10-1, there are several headers that may specify a "content encoding," which means an additional encoding such as compression. Those headers differ in their scope of use. For example, Content-Encoding: gzip might be used by web servers when they send a document as compressed with the gzip algorithm, for efficiency. Web server software might allow the server administration to configure the server to automatically use such compression when sending to browsers that can handle it. This could remove much of the inefficiency involved in some character encodings.

In MIME email, the Content-Transfer-Encoding header is used to specify the encoding (if any) applied to octets (as used in some primary encoding, such as UTF-8 or ISO-8859-1) in order to transmit them in an environment where "raw" 8-bit data might cause problems. The possible values for it are specified in Table 10-2.

Table 10-2. Content-Transfer-Encoding values (for MIME email)

Value	Meaning
7bit	7-bit data sent as such, no transfer encoding
8bit	Textual 8-bit data sent as such, no transfer encoding
base64	Base64encoding (see Chapter 6) has been applied to the octets
binary	Arbitrary 8-bit data sent as such, no transfer encoding
quoted-printable	QPencoding (see Chapter 6) has been applied to the octets

The header Content-Transfer-Encoding: 7bit promises that the message content consists of relatively short (maximum: 998 characters) lines of text, with CR LF between lines. The characters CR and LF appear in such pairs only. All octets are in the range 1 to 7F hexadecimal—i.e., correspond to ASCII characters excluding NUL.

The header Content-Transfer-Encoding: 8bit makes a similar promise, but octets larger than 7F may appear. NUL is excluded here, too. Thus, all octets in the range 1 to FF may appear, though CR and LF appear only in CR LF pairs.

The Quoted-Printable (QP) transfer encoding

The MIME specification defines, among many other things, the general purpose "Quoted-Printable" (QP) encoding, which we described in Chapter 6. Some of the basic points are repeated here, partly to explain them a bit differently, partly to help readers who skipped Chapter 6 because it was too technical.

QP can be used to represent any sequence of octets as a sequence of such octets that correspond to ASCII characters. This implies that the sequence of octets becomes longer, and if it is read as an ASCII string, it can be incomprehensible to human readers. What is gained is robustness in data transfer, since the encoding uses only "safe" ASCII characters, which will most probably get unmodified through any component in the data transfer.

Basically, QP encoding means that most octets up to 7F (hexadecimal) are used as such, whereas octets with higher values and some other octets are presented as follows: octet *n* is presented as a sequence of three octets, corresponding to (ASCII codes for) the equals sign, =, and the two digits of the hexadecimal notation of *n*.

If QP encoding is applied to a sequence of octets presenting character data according to ISO 8859-1 character code, then effectively this means that most ASCII characters (including all ASCII letters) are preserved as such, whereas, for example, the ISO 8859-1 character ä (code position E4 in hexadecimal) is encoded as =E4. For obvious reasons, the equals sign = itself is among the few ASCII characters that are encoded. Being in code position 3D in hexadecimal, it is encoded as =3D.

Encoding, for example, ISO 8859-1 data this way means that the *character code* is the one specified by the ISO 8859-1 standard, whereas the *character encoding* is different from the one specified (or at least suggested) in that standard. Since QP only specifies the mapping of a sequence of octets to another sequence of octets, it is a pure encoding and can be applied to any character data, or to any data for that matter.

Naturally, QP needs to be processed (decoded) by a program that knows it and can convert it to human-readable form. It looks rather confusing when displayed as such. Roughly speaking, one can expect most email programs to be able to handle QP, but the same does not apply to newsreaders (or web browsers). Therefore, you should normally use QP in email only.

How MIME should work

Basically, MIME should let people communicate smoothly without hindrances caused by character code and encoding differences. MIME should handle the necessary conversions automatically and invisibly.

For example, when person A sends email to person B, the following should happen:

1. The email program used by A encodes A's message in some particular manner, probably according to some convention that is normal on the system where the program is used (such as ISO 8859-1 encoding on a typical modern Unix system).
2. A's program automatically includes information about this encoding in an email header, which is usually invisible to both A and B.
3. The message, with the headers, is then delivered, through network connections, to B's system. Its content will normally not be modified in the delivery path. Headers may be modified to reflect the events in the delivery process.

4. The email subsystem where B's mailbox resides (typically, on a server accessed by B from her workstation) may perform some encoding conversions on the message, and should indicate this in the headers.

5. When B uses her email program (which may be very different from A's) to read the message, the program should automatically pick up the information about the encoding as specified in a header and interpret the message body according to it.

Thus, it is by no means necessary that the computers and email programs used by A and B use the same character code. Conversion (transcoding) to B's code, when needed, could be performed automatically in phase 4 or in phase 5. Moreover, A's program might in some situations be able to know what the recipient software wants. In particular, when responding to an email message, your email program might send (at least optionally) your reply in the same encoding in which the original message was received. This is however just extra courtesy; the encoding should still be specified in the headers. Moreover, if there are multiple recipients, you cannot expect all of them to be able to deal with the encoding that the original sender used.

For example, if B is using a Macintosh computer, B's program would automatically convert the message into Mac's internal character encoding, Mac Roman, and only then display it. Thus, if the message was ISO-8859-1 encoded and contained the Ä (uppercase "A" with dieresis) character, encoded as octet C4 (hexadecimal), the email program used on the Mac should use a conversion table to map this to octet 80, which is the encoding for Ä on Mac. If the program fails to do such a conversion, strange things will happen. ASCII characters would be displayed correctly, since they have the same codes in both encodings, but instead of Ä, the character corresponding to octet 196 in Mac encoding would appear, namely, the symbol ƒ. (This example intentionally refers to the old Mac Roman to make a point. New Mac software can usually interpret ISO-8859-1 and Unicode encodings more directly.)

Troubleshooting Examples

Unfortunately, there are deficiencies and errors in software so that users often have to struggle with character code conversion problems, perhaps correcting the actions taken by programs. It takes two to tango, and some more participants to get characters right. This section demonstrates different things that may happen, and do happen, when just one component is faulty—i.e., when MIME is not used or it is inadequately supported by some "partner" (software involved in entering, storing, transferring, and displaying character data).

Typical problems that occur in communication in Western European languages other than English creates situations in which most characters get interpreted and displayed correctly, but some "national letters" don't. For example, the character repertoire needed in German, Swedish, and Finnish is essentially ASCII plus a few letters like ä from the rest of ISO Latin 1. If a text in such a language is processed so that a necessary conversion is not applied, or an incorrect conversion is applied, the result might be that, for example, the word "später" becomes "spter" or "spÌter" or "spdter" or "sp=E4ter." Much of the text will be quite readable, but words containing accented letters look odd.

If the data is in an Internet message, such as an email message, that has appropriate MIME headers, it is straightforward to interpret the data. You may need to use a special program that can decode the encoding used, or you may even need to consult a definition or a mapping table for an encoding or code. Things get worse if there are no headers, or if the headers contain wrong information—i.e., the data does not make sense even technically when interpreted according to it. You might still be able to deduce or guess what has happened, and perhaps to determine which code conversion should be applied, and apply it more or less "by hand."

In the following examples, we assume that you have received (or found) some text data that is expected to be, say, in German, Swedish, or Finnish and that indeed appears to be such text, but with some characters replaced by oddities in a somewhat systematic way. We will consider some situations where you can guess, with reasonable certainty, what has happened. Depending on the case, you may need information about encodings as presented in Chapters 3 and 6 as well as in documents cited there.

You may find it useful to try to solve at least some of the problems below, as an exercise, before reading the explanations.

We will consider the particular letter ä ("a" with umlaut), which is common in all the languages mentioned. We could try to identify some words that should contain the letter ä but have something strange in place of it (as in the examples for "später").

Let us now assume that such identification has been made—i.e., we know (or at least have guessed intelligently) what character or string appears where ä (U+00E4) should appear. In the following, some common cases are analyzed, largely under the assumption that your program interprets the data in ISO-8859-1 or in Windows Latin 1 encoding:

a

The person who wrote the text possibly just used "a" instead of ä, probably because he thought that ä would not get through correctly. Although ä is surely problematic, the cure is often worse than the disease: using "a" instead of ä loses information and may change the meanings of words. This usage, and the next two cases below, is (usually) not directly caused by incorrect implementations but by the human writer; however, it is indirectly caused by them.

ae

Similar to the previous case, this is usually an attempt to avoid writing ä. For some languages (e.g., German), using "ae" as a replacement for ä is a common workaround, but it is much less applicable to Swedish or Finnish—and loses information, since the letter pair "ae" can genuinely occur in many words.

a"

Yet another replacement notation. It resembles an old (and generally outdated) idea of using the quotation mark as a replacement for a diacritic mark, but it is probably expected to be understood by humans instead of being converted to an ä by a program.

d

The original data was actually ISO 8859-1 encoded or something similar (e.g., Windows Latin 1) but during data transfer, the most significant bit of each octet was lost. (Such things may happen in systems for transferring, or "gatewaying," data from one network to another. For example, your terminal device or terminal emulator might have been configured to "mask out" the most significant bit.) This means that the octet representing ä in ISO 8859-1—i.e., E4 in hexadecimal, 11100100 in binary—became 01100100 in binary, 64 in hexadecimal, which is the ISO 8859-1 encoding of letter d.

{

Obviously, the data is in ASCII encoding so that the character { is used in place of ä. It was once common to use various national variants of ASCII, with characters #, $, @, [, \,], ^, _, `, {, |, }, and ~ replaced by national letters or symbols according to the needs of a particular language (see Chapter 3). Thus, they modified the character repertoire of ASCII by dropping out some special characters and introducing national characters into their ASCII code positions. It requires further study to determine the actual encoding used, since, for example, Swedish, German, and Finnish ASCII variants all have ä as a replacement for {, but there are differences in other replacements.

Ã¤

The data is evidently in UTF-8 encoding. Notice that the characters Ã and ¤ stand here for octets C3 and A4, which might be displayed differently depending on the program and device used. Generally, the frequent appearance of uppercase Ã is a strong indication of the problem that UTF-8 encoded data is being interpreted as ISO-8859-1 encoded.

+AOQ-

The data is in UTF-7 encoding.

Ì

The data is most probably in Roman-8 encoding (defined by Hewlett-Packard).

=E4

The data is in Quoted-Printable encoding. The original encoding, upon which the QP encoding was applied, might be ISO-8859-1, or any other encoding that represents character ä in the same way as ISO-8859-1 (i.e., as octet E4 hexadecimal).

ä

The data is in HTML format; the encoding may vary. See Chapter 9.

ä

The data is in HTML or XML format; the encoding may vary.

‰

This character occupies code position E4 in the old Macintosh character code. Thus, what has probably happened is that some program received ISO-8859-1 encoded data and interpreted it as if it were in Mac encoding, and then performed a conversion based on that interpretation. It apparently turned E4 into 89, which is the code position of the per mille sign in the windows-1252 code. The misbehavior might be caused by specifying the encoding as, for example, ISO-8859-15 or windows-1250 or anything else unknown to the receiver, but with ä still in position E4. Some programs refuse to apply the usual ISO-8859-1 to MacRoman transcoding in such a case.

Σ

This character occupies code position E4 in DOS code page 437. As in the previous case, data encoded as ISO-8859-1 (or something similar) has been incorrectly interpreted in another encoding.

(nothing, lack of any character)

Perhaps the data was encoded in DOS encoding (e.g., code page 850), where the code for ä is 84. In ISO-8859-1, octet 84 is in the area reserved for control characters; typically such octets are not displayed at all, or perhaps displayed as blank. If you can access the data in binary form, you could find evidence for this hypothesis by noticing that octets 84 actually appear there. (For instance, the Emacs editor would display such an octet as \204, since 204 is the octal notation for 84 hexadecimal.) If, on the other hand, it is not octet 84 but octet 8A, then the data is most probably in Macintosh encoding.

„ *(double low-9 quotation mark)*

Most likely, the data was encoded in DOS encoding (e.g., code page 850), where the code for ä is 84. Your program is interpreting it according to the Windows Latin 1 code, where this code position is occupied by the double low-9 quotation mark.

Š

Most likely, the data was in the old Macintosh encoding (Mac Roman), where the code for ä is 8A. Your program is interpreting that octet according to the Windows Latin 1 code, where this code position is occupied by Š.

The encodings involved in the examples are largely old encodings that are not used much in modern computers. The reason is that problems with encodings arise mostly when old systems and old software are involved.

Character Encoding on the Web

In Chapter 1, we discussed the character encoding problems of web pages from a user's point of view. Sometimes you need to change your browser settings in order to view a web page correctly, telling the browser to try a different encoding. Here we discuss the authoring side of the matter. This explains the background of the problems that users experience, and this is also important to people who wish to publish something on the Web.

The principles are simple:

- Select an encoding for your HTML documents so that it covers most characters you will need.
- Make sure that the web server where you put your documents sends correct HTTP headers that announce the encoding.
- Additionally, use meta tags in HTML for specifying the encoding.

The use of HTML forms and processing of data posted via forms raises some difficult additional problems, which will not be discussed here but in Chapter 11.

Headers in HTTP

HTTP is the transport protocol of the Web, as well as in intranets and extranets. Contrary to what the name expansion "HyperText Transfer Protocol" suggests, HTTP is not limited to hypertext. It can also transport plain text files, pictures, audio files, executable binaries, etc.

The HTTP technology is based on the client/server model: a client (browser) sends a request to a server, and the server responds to it, typically by sending the requested data and some headers that describe the data. The request normally specifies the requested resource by its URL.

A web server is supposed to specify the media type of the data that it sends to a browser, using a Content-Type header as in email. Normally a browser sends a request without specifying the media type of the requested resource. A browser can actually specify its media type preferences using an Accept header, but that header usually plays no role. Instead, the server sends the requested resource, along with information about its media type. Usually a browser does not show this information, just uses it. (Later in this section, we describe tools for viewing the headers.) For example, when the requested resource is a photograph in JPEG format, the server might send:

```
Content-Type: image/jpeg
```

The general idea is that upon receiving such information, the browser immediately knows what to expect. It can select an appropriate action, possibly affected by user settings that specify how different data formats are to be handled. In particular, if the header specifies plain text as the media type, the browser can simply display it as-is. It could also pass the plain text to another program, such as a simple editor, but browsers normally just show the data in the browser window. The user may then save it locally, if desired.

Sometimes the server response does not contain such a header, and the browser needs to make a guess, or report an error. Some browsers make their guesses even in the presence of a Content-Type header. This mainly applies to Internet Explorer, which uses a relatively complicated scheme to decide how to interpret a server response, possibly using the suffix of the URL (such as *.gif*) or an analysis of the (start of) the content of the resource. Microsoft's own documentation of the mechanism is available at the address *http://msdn.microsoft.com/workshop/networking/moniker/overview/appendix_a.asp*.

Usually this does not cause harm, if the filename suffix matches common conventions and if the file content is of more or less normal kind. However, if you, for example, wish to make a document available on the Web as a plain text resource, you will run into problems if its content looks like HTML markup to IE. Moreover, authors who rely on IE's guessing might fail to check that correct HTTP headers are sent, and this may imply that the file is not correctly processed by other browsers.

Specifying the encoding in HTTP headers

In HTTP, the `Content-Type` header can be used for specifying both the media type and (optionally) the character encoding. For an HTML document in particular, a typical header is:

```
Content-Type: text/html; charset=iso-8859-1
```

Thus, the encoding is specified in a `charset` parameter of the media type. The parameter can also be specified for plain text (`text/plain`) as well as for other subtypes of text. This sounds very simple, and it is, but there are several complications.

For various reasons, servers often do not include a `charset` parameter. We will later in this section discuss what should happen then. What actually happens is that a browser uses some default encoding. If that is not the right encoding and the user realizes this, she may try to tell the browser to use another one, as explained in Chapter 1.

Even when a browser normally honors HTTP headers, you might be able to tell the browser to *override* the `charset` parameter. One reason for this is that servers sometimes send wrong information about encoding, and users might be able to fix this.

On Internet Explorer for example, if you simply select View → Encoding and then pick up some encoding, you will make the browser use that encoding only if the server has not announced the encoding. But if you first uncheck the first item in the encoding menu, "Automatic selection," you make the browser override any encoding that the server has specified. Try it; visit, say, some page in French and change the encoding to some Cyrillic encoding, and you see the accented letters turn to Cyrillic letters. Remember to check "Automatic selection" back again after this test, since otherwise you will need to select it manually on every page.

The choice of encoding does not affect characters that have been represented using entity or character references, since they do not depend on the encoding. For example, if an ISO-8859-1 encoded document contains ï as such (octet EF), then the rendering often changes to another character when the encoding setting is changed. If the character has been written in HTML as ï or ï or ï, it remains as ï.

Which encodings can be used?

In principle, any registered character encoding can be used for documents on the Web. Many encodings are used, and browsers generally support a few dozen different encodings. However, the safest encodings are *ASCII*, *ISO-8859-1*, and *UTF-8*. The *windows-1252* encoding is rather safe in practice, too.

Other encodings commonly supported by browsers include several 8-bit encodings in the ISO 8859 and Windows encoding families. However, especially the newest of such encodings might not be recognized by browsers or by important *search engines* or other software used for automated processing of web pages. ISO-8859-2 is probably supported, but ISO-8859-3 or ISO-8859-13 might be a different matter. Although many search engines can process such encodings, their methods of recognizing the encoding might be faulty.

Although *UTF-8* is fairly safe as far as browsers and search engines are concerned, with few exceptions, there are problems with *authoring software*. You can surely find an authoring tool that lets you create UTF-8 encoded documents, either directly in an authoring program or via some conversion to UTF-8 format. However, if your documents will be maintained or edited by other people, you cannot always assume that they have or they can get and learn to use a UTF-8 capable tool.

There is also a psychological factor involved. If you have a tool that lets you type any Unicode character comfortably, you will be tempted to use the full Unicode repertoire. You would easily use characters that many, if not most, users will not see properly.

Thus, if you expect to need just a few characters outside *ASCII*, you might consider a simple approach that uses ASCII as the encoding and expresses all other characters using entity or character references (see Chapter 2). That way, anyone could edit the documents in any environment, though the references might look somewhat obscure. For understandability, it would be best to use entity references (like é) for all characters that have one and hexadecimal character references (like ♀) rather than decimal character references (like ♀) for other characters. Hexadecimal numbers are somewhat more comfortable than decimal if you need to interpret character references, since Unicode-related information usually uses hexadecimal. (Some old browsers do not understand hexadecimal references or all entity references, but the impact of such considerations is rather small these days.)

Although browsers usually support *UTF-16* as well as UTF-8, some important search engines apparently do not process UTF-16 correctly. Thus, it is not practical to use UTF-16 on the Web. This may change if UTF-16 becomes more common on the Web, but there are little signs of such a development. See also the section "Choosing an Encoding" in Chapter 6.

Opinions differ on the acceptability of *windows-1252* (Windows Latin 1). It is widely supported, since due to its common use, even software on non-Windows platforms has to recognize and interpret it, in order to work well on the Internet. It is also an officially registered encoding. On the other hand, it is not an international standard but a proprietary encoding. In HTML authoring, you do not win much by using windows-1252 instead of ISO-8859-1. The extra characters like dashes and "smart" quotation marks (see Chapter 3 for details) can be relatively well written using entity references like –. However, if your data comes from a document produced using a word processor and containing such punctuation characters, it might be simplest to leave it windows-1252 encoded, if that was the format when you received the data.

HTTP versus HTML

According to the HTTP 1.1 specification (RFC 2626), any subtype of text (such as text/plain and text/html) has ISO-8859-1 as its default encoding. The HTML 4.01 specification, on the other hand, says that no default encoding shall be implied. This effectively means that when the encoding has not been specified, the browser should do its best to guess the encoding from the content, instead of simply assuming ISO-8859-1.

For further confusion, RFC 3023 (XML Media Types), "XML Media Types," specifies the media type text/xml so that for it, the default encoding is US-ASCII. That is, if an XML document is sent with a MIME or HTTP header specifying that media type and without a charset parameter, the recipient must imply that the encoding is US-ASCII.

In practice, the default encoding that a browser uses for a page (when the server or the page itself does not specify the encoding) depends on the browser. The default has often been selected to suit the cultural environment where the browser is used. In any case, if the user has selected the encoding manually, this setting will usually stay in effect as a default.

The moral is, of course, that an author should try to make the web server send a header that specifies the encoding, even if it is ISO-8859-1. If the encoding is UTF-8, there is an even greater reason for specifying it in an HTTP header, of course.

Checking the HTTP headers

In order to check the HTTP headers *sent by a server*, you can use a Telnet program or some similar software. Unfortunately, the Telnet program included in Windows is very simple, but there is, for example, the free PuTTY program, which is distributed as a binary executable via *http://www.putty.nl/*.

Using PuTTY (or Telnet), connect to the server using the applicable port, which is normally 80 for HTTP and can be obtained from the URL if not. (If the server name in the URL is followed by a colon and a number, the number is the port number to be used.) Then you issue a HEAD command and a HOST command and an empty line (i.e., hit Enter twice), and wait for an answer. In the HEAD command, the first argument is the relative URL, starting from the solidus character / that follows the server name in the absolute URL. The second argument specifies the HTTP protocol version. The HOST command is required (in HTTP/1.1) and repeats the server name. Figure 10-4 shows a dialog in which the user, after invoking PuTTY so that it is instructed to connect to *www.cs.tut.fi* at port 80, requests the HTTP headers for the URL *http://www.cs.tut.fi/~jkorpela/chars/*.

Alternatively, you can check the headers using Lynx, the text-based browser available for several environments and often installed on Linux and Unix systems. You would use a command of the form **lynx -head -dump** *address*.

As an author of web pages, you need not check the headers of all of your documents, of course. The headers are normally constructed by the web server by some general rules. Thus, it mostly suffices to check things when you start using a server, or when problems appear that might be related to the character encoding or other things expressed in headers.

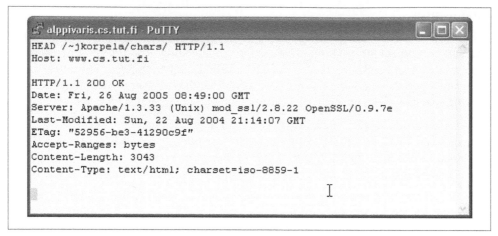

```
HEAD /~jkorpela/chars/ HTTP/1.1
Host: www.cs.tut.fi

HTTP/1.1 200 OK
Date: Fri, 26 Aug 2005 08:49:00 GMT
Server: Apache/1.3.33 (Unix) mod_ssl/2.8.22 OpenSSL/0.9.7e
Last-Modified: Sun, 22 Aug 2004 21:14:07 GMT
ETag: "52956-be3-41290c9f"
Accept-Ranges: bytes
Content-Length: 3043
Content-Type: text/html; charset=iso-8859-1
```

Figure 10-4. Requesting HTTP headers in a simple dialog

This, by the way, is one of the reasons why you should try to specify the URL of your page, rather than just send the contents of a document, when you ask for help with a page. Other people might find problems that you didn't notice—in the headers.

In some situations, you need to check the HTTP headers *sent by a browser* (to a server). In particular, so-called content negotiation may involve such headers for the purpose of agreeing (between a browser and a server) on an encoding to be used. There are services for echoing back the headers—e.g., *http://www.cs.tut.fi/cgibin/~jkorpela/headers.cgi* and *http://www.tipjar.com/cgi-bin/test*. Such services differ in the way they display the headers. Often the header names are preceded by the string HTTP_, which is not part of the headers; it is added by software like CGI. The service at *http://web-sniffer.net* has a particularly detailed and configurable output, and it can show both the headers sent by the browser in the request and the response headers sent by the server.

Server configuration

It depends on the web server software and its configuration whether and how an author can affect the HTTP headers. In typical server software, Apache, the tools for that are simple, though a bit coarse. For example, to specify that files with names ending with *.html* in a directory (folder) be sent with a header that indicates UTF-8, you would create, in that directory, a plain text file with the name *.htaccess* (note the period at the start) and with the following line as its content:

```
AddType text/html;charset=utf-8 html
```

Thus, for example, if you have some HTML documents that are ISO-8859-1 encoded and some that are UTF-8 encoded, you have two simple options:

- Assign different filename extensions, say *.html* and *.htm*, to the two kinds of files, and write two different AddType instructions in your *.htaccess* file. Beware that although the filename extension should not matter to browsers or search engines, it may. The extensions named here are safe, though.

- Put files of one kind in one directory and the rest in another directory—e.g., a subdirectory of your main directory of web pages. Then you just use different *.htaccess* files in the directories, and you can use the same filename extension.

As another example, suppose that you need to put plain text files into one directory on a web server, and some of them are UTF-16 encoded and some are windows-1252 encoded. You could name them so that they have *.u16* and *.wtx* suffixes, respectively. (These are just suffixes invented for this purpose; you can use any suffix that has no conventional meaning.) Then you would add the following lines into the *.htaccess* file:

```
AddType text/plain;charset=utf-16 u16
AddType text/plain;charset=windows-1252 wtx
```

The Apache documentation at *http://httpd.apache.org/docs/* explains additional possibilities. For other server software, different approaches might be needed, though many servers imitate Apache principles. Links to documentation on other server software can be found via *http://www.serverwatch.com/stypes/*.

In practice, many authors have no knowledge about this, and they might even be unwilling to learn about it. It sounds like programming to many, and words like "server configuration" or being asked to do something at the "HTTP level" can be intimidating. In any case, it's quite different from HTML or CSS or the use of a web page editor.

Moreover, a server might have been configured by its maintenance to ignore the settings of individual authors. Server administration might regard per-directory *.htaccess* files as a security threat, and indeed, there are some risky things that authors could do with them to override system-wide settings. An Internet Service Provider might even disable *.htaccess* files on normal accounts in order to charge more for special accounts where they are enabled.

If the server software or administration prevents authors from affecting HTTP headers (e.g., by disabling the use of *.htaccess* on Apache), the server should be configured to send HTML documents with a header that has no charset parameter. Authors should be told how to use meta tags to specify the encoding. Beware that such tags cannot override the charset parameter specified in HTTP headers.

There are also other server technologies that can be used to specify the encoding in HTTP headers. For example, when using PHP, you can write a statement like the following into your document. The PHP processor, running on your server, will recognize it and send actual HTTP headers for the document as specified (and will remove this statement from the document that is sent to the browser):

```
<?php
header("Content-type: text/html; charset=UTF-8");
?>
```

Using a meta tag

It is possible that a server sends HTML files in a fixed manner with a `Content-Type` header that specifies just `text/html` with no `charset` indication. In that case, authors can use the workaround of HTML meta tags, which can be regarded as simulating HTTP headers. For example, the following tag, inside the `head` part of an HTML document, would ask browsers to behave as if the HTML document had been sent with the header `Content-Type: text/html;charset=utf-8`:

```
<meta http-equiv="Content-Type" content="text/html;charset=utf-8">
```

If the HTML used is some version of XHTML, you need to terminate the tag with `/ >` instead of just `>`. Technically, such meta tags are ignored according to XHTML specifications, but they may be used as a method that works on older browsers that process XHTML documents by old HTML rules.

Experts disagree on whether you should use such a meta tag even when the character encoding is specified in a real HTTP header. On one hand, it is a bad idea to hard-wire information about the encoding into the file itself. After all, the encoding could be changed later, without noticing that the tag should be changed too. In principle, the document might be transcoded (i.e., its encoding changed) on the fly as it passes through a network, though is not likely. On the other hand, the `meta` tag is a small insurance against eventual changes in the server. Moreover, if a user saves an HTML document locally on his disk and later accesses it locally, there will be no HTTP headers to tell the encoding. Browsers might (and indeed they should) store the information upon saving the file, in a manner that lets them check it upon any subsequent access. However, browsers do not always behave that way. This is perhaps the most important point here, so in practice, it's usually safest to use the meta tag, even if it is redundant.

When using a `meta` tag to declare the encoding, it is safest to put it before any occurrence of a non-ASCII character. By HTML rules, you can always ensure this by writing the `meta` tag as the first tag inside a document. The tag should apply to the document as a whole, and browsers usually treat it so. However, some browser might start applying it only after encountering the tag in the sequential processing of a document. For example:

```
<meta http-equiv="Content-Type" content="text/html;charset=utf-8">
<title>Liberté, égalité, fraternité</title>
```

You cannot use meta tags in plain text files, of course. Thus, if you wish to make, for example, a UTF-8 encoded plain text file available on the Web, you really need to find a way to make the server send it with `Content-Type: text/plain;charset=utf-8`.

Resolution of conflicts

According to the HTML 4.01 specification, the character encoding of an HTML document can be specified in the following ways, in priority order:

1. In a `charset` parameter in an HTTP header
2. In the document itself, in a `meta` tag corresponding to an HTTP header

3. In a charset attribute in a link that refers to a document

Browsers have ignored the third alternative, but they implement the two other ways correctly, in general. This means that if the server sends a charset parameter in an HTTP header, there is no way to override this in the document itself.

Thus, if you configure a web server and do not want to let authors affect the HTTP headers (e.g., with their *.htaccess* files), you should configure the server to send a Content-Type header without a charset parameter. It would then be appropriate to tell authors to use meta tags to specify the encoding, in all HTML files.

The effect of XHTML

XHTML, the XML-based formulation of HTML, introduces additional ways of specifying the encoding. For XML in general, the rules of the game (explained in more detail in the XML specification *http://www.w3.org/TR/REC-xml/*) are as follows:

- An XML document is treated by default as UTF-8 or UTF-16 encoded. These cases can be automatically distinguished by the presence or absence of a byte order mark (BOM), under the provision that UTF-16 be used with BOM.

- Otherwise, the encoding must be specified in an XML declaration at the start of the XML document, such as <?xml encoding='iso-8859-1'?>.

- However, the encoding can be overridden at the level of a transport protocol such as HTTP or MIME. (This is stated implicitly, but clearly, in the XML specification.)

If your XML document is in ASCII encoding, you need not specify the encoding. The reason is that an ASCII file will be correctly interpreted when it is treated as UTF-8. For ISO-8859-1, however, things are quite different, and the encoding must be specified, either in an XML declaration, or in an HTTP header.

In the special case of XHTML, the same principles are applied. There's actually no room for using a meta tag to specify the encoding. Both an XML declaration and actual HTTP headers are supposed to override any meta tag, and if neither of them is used, then the file is recognized as UTF-8 or UTF-16. This is what seems to happen, too. Yet the XHTML 1.0 specification describes, in Appendix C:

> In order to portably present documents with specific character encodings, the best approach is to ensure that the web server provides the correct headers. If this is not possible, a document that wants to set its character encoding explicitly must include both the XML declaration an encoding declaration and a meta http-equiv statement (e.g., <meta http-equiv="Content-type" content="text/html; charset=EUC-JP" />).

The explanation is that although the meta tag is ignored by XHTML rules, it acts as a backup for browsers—e.g., Internet Explorer (IE) 6—that do not understand XHTML. Such browsers treat the data as HTML, ignoring the XML declaration.

For further confusion, there is strong practical reason to avoid using an XML declaration in XHTML documents on the Web: the XML declaration makes IE 6 go into "quirks mode." This means that IE 6 intentionally simulates previous versions of the browser in the processing of some HTML and CSS constructs, in a manner that violates their specifications. See *http://www.quirksmode.org/* for more explanations.

The bottom line is that if you wish to serve an XHTML document on the Web, it is best to make it UTF-8 encoded (so that you can omit the XML declaration). If that is not possible, you should use actual HTTP headers to specify the encoding.

Heuristics of detecting encoding

When none of the methods just described has been used to specify the character encoding, the browser has to make a guess or give up. Browsers generally try to apply heuristic reasoning rules to deduce the encoding. At *http://www.i18nfaq.com/chardet.html*, you can find a Java version of the heuristic code used in Mozilla.

Remarkably often, browsers make a right guess. It is in principle impossible to determine the encoding of text from the text alone, but in practice, you can often guess right even using automated tools. Different encodings have special properties and known areas of application. More important, a browser knows what to expect.

HTML documents can be expected to start (aside from a possible BOM) with a coded representation of characters from the ASCII repertoire, even if they then go on to present a document body containing a wide range of Unicode. Moreover, there are specific constructs (like a document type declaration and HTML tags) to be expected. There aren't too many different ways of representing the ASCII repertoire, in encodings actually used, so a heuristic has a good chance of recognizing what's going on.

Yet, browsers may guess wrong. The principle that either the server or the document itself should always specify the encoding is not just academic. Browsers have been reported to infer, for a document sent with no indication of encoding, that the encoding is GB2312, a Chinese encoding, when it is in fact ISO-8859-1 encoded and contains almost exclusively ASCII characters. If there are just a few octets with the most significant bit set, the browser might thus think they are part of ideographs and display them all wrong. Heuristics that are oriented toward distinguishing between Asian encodings might thus fail miserably for, for example, English text with a few non-ASCII characters in names.

Which encoding should I use?

Here we are primarily interested in HTML documents, though the principles can be applied to plain text documents as well, with some obvious modifications. In particular, you cannot use character or entity references in plain text. With regards to CSS files, for example, it is usually best to use ASCII only in them. In the rare cases where you need non-ASCII characters in CSS (mainly in generated content), use the CSS escape mechanisms (e.g., \201C for U+201C) mentioned in Chapter 2.

The choice of an encoding for documents on the Web is a matter of compromises between different conflicting needs and limitations. A suggested general policy is presented in Table 10-3. In all cases, the first column describes the characters that are likely to appear frequently in data. Remember that other characters can be expressed using character or

---

entity references, no matter what encoding is used. "Correct punctuation" mainly refers to "smart" quotes, typographers' apostrophes, and dashes like "–" and "—". Potentially suitable 8-bit encodings were discussed in Chapter 3.

Table 10-3. Selecting the encoding for an HTML document

Character repertoire primarily needed	Encoding
English text without correct punctuation	ASCII
English text, with correct punctuation	windows-1252 or UTF-8
Text in other Western European languages without correct punctuation	ISO-8859-1
Text in other Western European languages, with correct punctuation	windows-1252 or UTF-8
Many other languages with small character repertoire (< 200 characters), such as Polish, Russian, modern Greek, Thai, etc.	8-bit encoding (see Chapter 3)
Japanese text	Shift-JIS
Chinese text in Simplified writing	GB2312
Chinese text in Traditional writing	Big5
A combination of languages in classes above (e.g., French and Greek)	UTF-8
Other repertoires, including any text with lots of special symbols	UTF-8

There is a similar but more detailed "decision table" at "Checklist for HTML character encoding," *http://ppewww.ph.gla.ac.uk/~flavell/charset/checklist.html*, by Alan Flavell. The document suggests that if you use ASCII encoding and represent all non-ASCII characters using entity or character references, you declare the encoding as UTF-8. This is technically correct (an ASCII file is trivially UTF-8 encoded, too), and it helps some old browsers render the references correctly.

Avoiding the encoding problem

The method of using entity or character references is in principle unnecessary when UTF-8 is used, except for the few markup-significant characters (<, &, and quotation marks inside attribute values). However, it is still often a practical approach.

Suppose that you have a document that is ASCII or ISO-8859-1 encoded, containing just English for example. If you would like to add a paragraph in Polish, what would you do? Switching to ISO-8859-2 would let you use all the accented Polish letters directly, but you might then have problems with some French letters, if you have used them. Using UTF-8 might require tools and arrangements that aren't available now.

Using character references avoids problems and lets you keep using the encoding you are using now. If you need just a few of them, you could simply look them up from some handy reference. If you have a long paragraph, you would like to use something more automatic. Several conversion programs can do that.

For example, using MS Word, you can proceed as follows:

Figure 10-5. One version of the Unicode Encoded logo

1. Open or create a document containing the text to be added in MS Word.

2. Set the language of the text in MS Word, as described in Chapter 7. This step is not necessary, but it helps to generate markup with correct language information.

3. Select File → Save As.

4. Select the save format as "web page" or, preferably, "web page (filtered)" if available in the menu. This means that the text is saved as HTML. The filtered option means that more compact and more manageable markup will be generated.

5. Open your web page editor, and enter its HTML input mode if needed (i.e., if its normal mode is "what you see is what you get" and does not show HTML tags).

6. Insert the data from the HTML file you just created, using your web page editor's tool for file insertion, or using cut and paste if needed.

For example, suppose that the text is just "This is a Polish name: Wałęsa." Working with it in MS Word, you would click on the name "Wałęsa" and set its language to Polish. Saving this small piece of text as described, you would get the following:

```
<p class=MsoNormal>This is a Polish name:
<span lang=PL>Wa&#322;&#281;sa.</span></p>
```

This can be inserted into an HTML document, irrespectively of its character encoding. (You can remove the attribute `class=MsoNormal`, which is only used by Microsoft Office software internally, but on the other hand, you might as well leave it there.)

The "Unicode Encoded" logo

Some web pages that are Unicode encoded display an image with the text "Unicode Encoded," as in Figure 10-5. The value of such a logo is, however, probably negative on most pages. Visitors are interested in your content, and perhaps your visual design, and the logo is mostly distracting on both accounts. The logo might be useful, though, on pages that specifically sell, demonstrate, or promote Unicode-related products, services, or principles, so that users can be expected to be (or to become) interested in Unicode itself.

Should you wish to use a "Unicode Encoded" logo, note that there are several alternatives available. At *http://www.unicode.org/consortium/uniencoded.html*, you can find specific rules on using them. The basic principles are:

- You are allowed to use a "Unicode Encoded" logo only if your page's encoding is UTF-8 or some other accepted Unicode encoding.

- You are also required to use the W3C HTML Validator to check that the encoding is formally correct. However, markup validity is not required.

- You can select between logos of different design.

- You should copy the selected logo image onto the web server you use, rather than refer to the image on the Unicode site.

- You must make the logo a link to the Unicode Consortium web site (main page).

The markup for the logo as suggested on the Unicode site does not quite conform to good web authoring practices. The following uses more suitable alt and title attributes:

```
<div><a href="http://www.unicode.org/"
title="The Unicode Consortium (main page)">
<img src="unicode-aqua-onwhite.png" width="100" height="16"
alt="This page is Unicode encoded." border="0"></a></div>
```

Content Negotiation and Multilingual Sites

In the web context, content negotiation means *automatic* selection between alternatives, such as different language versions or differently encoded versions of web content. The negotiation takes place between a browser and a server, without direct human interference.

In content negotiation, the browser is supposed to act on behalf of the user, sending the user's preference settings as needed. This is however the weakest practical point especially in language negotiation: users generally haven't checked the settings of the browser. In Chapter 7, we described such features in browsers, but they are not widely known, and the user interfaces are rather inconvenient even to experienced users.

Introduction to Multilingual Web Sites

A web site can be multilingual in many ways. It may contain information about several languages, or information on some topic in different languages, but not the same information. Many sites contain different languages without being multilingual in this sense. It is rather typical that a site contains a short summary page, or a few summary pages, in English—but the content proper is in some other language only. In such situations, you will not encounter the problems (and possibilities) of a multilingual site. However, part of a site might be multilingual—e.g., when some essential information needs to be available in many languages.

Parallel versions in different languages

In this section, multilingualism of a site means that the *same textual content* is available to users in different language versions, for all or at least some of the pages. Even on a multilingual site, each page is usually in one language only, at least for most of it. This is generally recommendable. Sites can be multilingual, but languages should not be mixed within a page, as a rule.

 Using just one language on one page avoids several problems with character encoding, or at least gives more options in solving them.

For example, suppose that you have the same content in French and in Russian. If you use separate pages, the French page can be, for example, ISO-8859-1 encoded and the Russian page, KOI8-R encoded. If you used a single page instead—e.g., with one column in French and another column in Russian—you could not use either of those encodings, or any 8-bit encoding, without special arrangements. (You could, for example, use character references like а to refer to Cyrillic letters in an ISO-8859-1 encoded page, but that would be rather awkward for large amounts of text.) Using UTF-8 would let you mix French and Russian, but UTF-8 is not always a practical choice.

Thus, in most cases, separate pages in separate languages are needed. This creates a terminological problem: the word "page" could refer to some content in general, or its expression in different languages. In the sequel, we will use "page" in the abstract sense, and use expressions like "language versions of a page" when needed.

Pages with a mix of languages

Sometimes multilingualism can be implemented so that one page contains texts in different languages. This is usually practical only if there are just a few languages and the texts are short—e.g., on a page where the main content is an image or a gallery of images, accompanied with short captions in two or a few languages.

Some content is *inherently multilingual*. A dictionary is the most obvious example. In the humanities, it is often appropriate to quote long passages in other languages, since the readers are assumed to know them. In teaching material, critical reviews of translations, etc., it is often necessary to present texts in different languages in parallel. For such content, you should select an encoding that lets you enter text in all the languages directly. Therefore, it is often best to choose UTF-8.

More often, a page contains names or other *short expressions* in different languages. This includes links to versions of the page in other languages, since such links are usually best written using words in the other languages. For short texts, character references are often a feasible way to avoid problems of encoding.

Language negotiation: automatic selection of version

Multilingualism in the sense discussed here normally means that each language version of a page is in a file of its own and can be referred to using a web address (URL) of its own. But since it would be difficult to announce the address of a French version to French-speaking people, the address of a German version to German-speaking people, etc., it would be best if the same address could be used by all.

The general idea is that you would use a single address that resolves to different specific addresses automatically. Everyone would get the page in his own language, or in the language among the available alternatives that is best understood by him. This can be partly achieved using automatic *language negotiation*; on the user side, this only requires that the user specify his language preferences once in the settings of his browser.

The basic principle of language negotiation is simple. When requesting a web page, by specifying the URL, a browser sends a header that specifies the languages that the user understands, with weights that indicate their relative desirability. The web server may then use this information to select one of several versions in different languages, if it such versions exist. The same basic mechanism can also be used to negotiate on the content type (media type)—i.e., to select between plain text, HTML, and Word format when available, as well as on character encoding.

However, for several reasons, the language negotiation mechanism is not sufficient (and it is not indispensable, on the other hand). In any case, the author should write explicit links, through which the user can move—e.g., from a German version to a French version and vice versa. (In some situations, the user would even want to open them simultaneously to compare them or use them in parallel—e.g., if she does not read either language fluently but can make some use of them.)

As an example of a multilingual site—which by the way discusses the creation of such sites—consider the Alis Babel site. Its generic address is *http://babel.alis.com/*. If the browser supports language negotiation, as most browsers in use do, then using this address (e.g., by following that link) will give you a version in English, French, Italian, German, Spanish, Swedish, or Portuguese, according to which of these languages occurs first in the user's language preferences. If, for example, Swedish is the first language there, the user gets the Swedish version, which is also accessible via its specific address *http://babel.alis.com/index.sv.html*. (Note that the browser does not display that but the general address, if the general address was used.)

If the server has no version that matches any of the languages in the user's preferences, then the intent is that the user sees a page that describes the situation and gives a menu of available alternatives. Some browsers however fail to do that; instead they give the user some of the alternatives in a rather random fashion. Even this isn't fatal, if that alternative contains links to the other options.

Language versus country

Quite often, page authors try to perform language selection based on the user's *country*, typically deduced from the Internet address, more exactly, its top-level domain. This is largely just guesswork and guaranteed to fail quite often, partly because many top-level domains (*.com*, *.org*, etc.) are not limited to one country. For example, not everyone in the *.fr* domain (or, more properly, using a computer in the *.fr* domain) speaks French as her native language, or at all. Besides, French-speaking people widely use addresses other than *.fr* addresses, such as *.be* (Belgium) or *.ca* (Canada).

If you still try to make a language selection guess according to the user's domain, re-member that the guess will quite often be wrong. Thus, it is necessary to make available links through which the user can find a page in his preferred language.

Links to Language Versions

Language negotiation can greatly improve the usability of a site. It is however not nec-essary, even if the pages exist in different language versions. Neither should one regard it as sufficient. In any case, linking to different language versions is needed.

There are strong reasons to provide links to different language versions even if the server supports language negotiation and arrangements have been made to use that. The reasons include the following:

- Browser support to language negotiation cannot be trusted. Some browsers have no support, but most important, the general *awareness* about the issue among users is still rather limited. The browser defaults typically reflect the browser's language only. Thus, the information sent by a browser can be in serious conflict with the actual preferences of the user.

- Problems related to *caches* may cause the browser to get the wrong language version.

- Users may wish to *compare* the different language versions or otherwise make use of them. Perhaps someone does not understand a statement in a French version even if French is his native language, but checking the corresponding statement in an English version may help (especially in areas where English is dominant in technical terminology).

- Some users prefer reading the *original* version (among some languages that they know), since they know that something is always lost in translation.

- Users may *encounter language-specific versions* in different ways—by following a link, by using a search engine, or by using an address announced somewhere. This may mean that the entire language negotiation mechanism is bypassed. So the user might run into a page that is all Greek to him but that also exists in a language he knows. Thus, if the page has links to the other versions, it will help.

 It is best to start by linking the versions to each other explicitly. After that, consider whether there is a need and a possibility to use language negotiation, too.

It is difficult to decide whether language-specific or generic links should be used within the site itself and in references to its pages from outside. Normally, generic links are preferable. However, such an approach makes things more difficult, if the user wishes to read pages in a language that is not topmost in his preferences. For example, if I'd like to know what information exists in Italian at the site *http://www.debian.org*, I can select the link to the Italian version on the main page. However, when I follow links there, I will get versions as determined by the language preferences in my browser, since the links are generic. I can switch to the Italian version of each page as I wish, using the explicit link, but I need to repeat this on every page. This however should probably be regarded as an exceptional case, which should be handled by the user—e.g., by temporarily changing the language preferences in the browser. To summarize, links should normally be generic—i.e., point to URLs that are resolved with the language negotiation mechanism.

When you apply the principles suggested here, each page has a language selection menu. You don't need a separate language selection page—i.e., a page that has no real content

Figure 10-6. A set of language links, using codes

but language links or buttons. Such pages tend to frustrate users and cause unnecessary delays.

Writing Link Texts

When referring to different language versions, it is essential how we choose the link text —i.e., the "thing" that acts as a clickable or otherwise selectable part of a page, through which the link can be followed. In principle, that "thing" can be an image, too, but usually textual links work best. Especially in this context, it is not at all a good idea to use an image, since the most natural way to refer to a version of a document in another language is to use words, or maybe something else expressed as text. It is a particularly bad idea to use flags of countries as symbols for languages.

There are several alternatives that may work well for language links:

- The name of the document in the language
- The name of that language, in the language itself (or maybe in English)
- A code for the language, such as a two-letter code (see Chapter 7)
- A combination of the above

One possible exception to using text links is a situation where the link text would be in a language that cannot be presented reliably as text, due to character code problems. Thus, for example, when language names are used as link texts, it might be necessary to use an image to denote Arabic (but naturally one needs to specify a textual replacement for such an image too, using the alt attribute—e.g., alt="Arabic").

The choice depends on the number and nature of the languages involved, as well as on the context. In some situations, when there are many languages, two-letter or three-letters *codes* might be a suitable approach, even though people will have to learn to recognize the codes of the languages that are relevant to them. But it isn't that difficult to learn that en or eng stands for English. Figure 10-6 shows one set of links, using two-letter codes, pointing to versions of a page on the European Union (EU) site *http://www.eu.int*. As you can see, even this compact style requires considerable space. It is not intuitively clear, since the languages do not appear to be ordered by any apparent principle. (The secret order is by the native name of the language: castellano, čeština, dansk,….) However, if the same order is used consistently, people learn to live with it. The approach of using codes has the benefit of requiring basic Latin letters only.

Unavoidably, when we use the names of the linked page in the different languages as link texts, we have to create a page with a mixture of languages, if only in the links. This affects the choice of the character encoding, as described in Table 10-3 (earlier in the chapter). Especially when several scripts (e.g., Latin and Greek) are mixed, UTF-8 may be the best

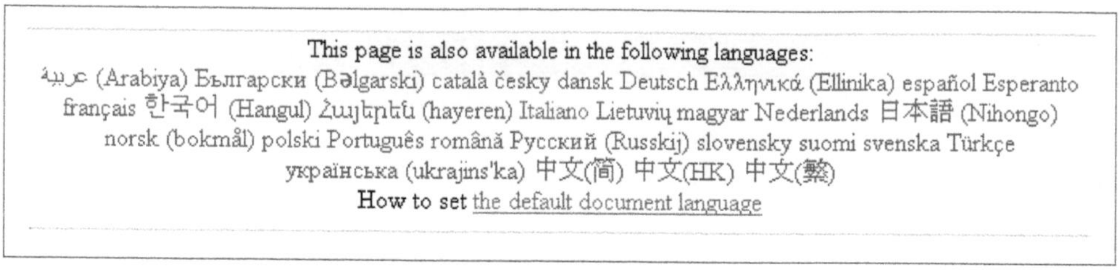

> العربية (Arabiya) Български (Bəlgarski) català česky dansk Deutsch Ελληνικά (Ellinika) español Esperanto français 한국어 (Hangul) Հայերեն (hayeren) Italiano Lietuvių magyar Nederlands 日本語 (Nihongo) norsk (bokmål) polski Português română Русский (Russkij) slovensky suomi svenska Türkçe українська (ukrajins'ka) 中文(简) 中文(HK) 中文(繁)
> How to set the default document language

Figure 10-7. Using names of languages as link texts

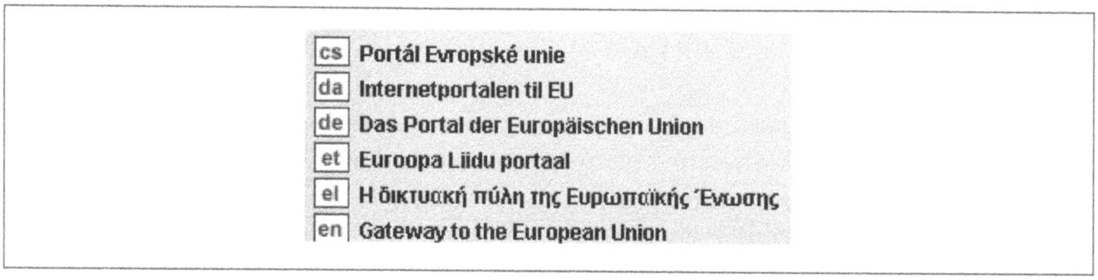

Figure 10-8. Using names of the linked documents as link texts

option. However, since the link texts are typically relatively short, the use of ASCII and character references might be feasible, too.

Rather often, multilingual sites use drop-down menus for a language choice. This may sound suitable when there are many languages and even the two-letter codes would take too much space, in someone's opinion. However, drop-down menus on web pages suffer from usability problems, and their primary benefit (saving space by hiding information, until the menu is opened) is also their basic problem.

A rather verbose approach is illustrated in Figure 10-7, excerpted from a page of the Debian site *http://www.debian.org*. It uses the name of each language, in the language itself, as link text, with a Latin transcription in parentheses for languages that use a non-Latin script. The names are in alphabetic order by the version in Latin letters. (Chinese appears last, with a variant specifier in parentheses.) On the positive side, if you know any of the languages listed there, you can find the right link. The presentation is somewhat messy, because there are no separator characters between the links.

Yet another approach, which might be the best one for the main page of a multilingual site, is to use a list of links with the name of the *page* in each language as the link text. This is illustrated in Figure 10-8, which shows a part of the links on the main page of the EU. Each link is preceded by the two-letter code of the language, to help with identification. (The language codes could also be used as the basis for ordering the links.)

Technically, the language codes on the EU page are actually images, but they could be as well, or better, implemented as styled text. It is probably best to make the code part of the link, since a user might click on the code and not on the text. This means you could use HTML markup like the following, plus some CSS to style the appearance:

```
<a href="index_cs.htm" hreflang="cs"><span class="langcode">cs</span>
<span lang="cs">Portál Evropské unie</span>
```

An advantage is that when someone who knows just one of the languages visits the page, he can both identify the link that is the right one for him and get an idea of what the site is about. As a disadvantage, such links are verbose, and the mixture of languages can be confusing, even alienating. This is one reason why language negotiation may help: when successful, it takes the user directly to the version he understands best.

The *placement* of the language links may vary. Putting them at the start (e.g., in the upper-right corner) makes them easy to note and use but may disturb in situations where the page is used linearly, and it may not fit to the visual design either. When placed at the end, they don't disturb much, but the user might notice them all too late, or not at all.

Language Negotiation in the HTTP Protocol

The language negotiation mechanism is based on the following idea:

- When a browser sends a request to a server, it may specify the user's language preferences in a certain format.
- If the resource that the browser asked for is available in different language versions, the server can be configured to select one of the versions according to the preferences mentioned earlier in this chapter.

At the level of the HTTP protocol, the browser sends an `Accept-Language` header, which lists the acceptable languages and their relative acceptability. More exactly, it lists the languages so that a language indicator (code) can be followed by a *quality value*, which is a number between 0 and 1, specifying the relative acceptability. For example, the header:

```
Accept-Language: fr;q=1, en;q=0.2
```

would say that both French (fr) and English (en) are acceptable, but French is much more acceptable. (This does not necessarily imply that the server always sends a French version, if it is available; a server could also consider the relative "goodness" of the versions.) The notation is a bit strange, since in it, the comma is a stronger separator than the semicolon; additional confusion can be caused by the rather common way of leaving a space after the semicolons.

Language Negotiation: the Server Side

It depends on the server and its settings whether and how an author can make versions of pages in different languages available via the language negotiation mechanism. Here we discuss only the methods that might be used in one widely used server software, Apache, and mainly just one of the two alternative methods there. For details, consult applicable server software documentation such as *http://httpd.apache.org/docs/*.

Apache has two basic methods for content negotiation:

Multiviews

> The alternative versions are in the same directory, and they are named in some uniform way. The author specifies some general rule according to which a generic URL is to be mapped to filenames referring to different versions.

type-map

> For each generic URL, there is a separate file that lists the corresponding language-specific filenames, possibly with some associated properties (e.g., the encoding of the file).

Using Multiviews

If Multiviews is enabled on Apache (as it is by default), you can use language negotiation in the following, though somewhat limited, manner for a directory:

1. Add something like the following into the *.htaccess* file in a directory. Use the two-letter language code as the first argument in these directives, and use whichever suffix you like as the second argument:

   ```
   AddLanguage en .en
   AddLanguage fi .fi
   AddLanguage fr .fr
   ```

2. Name the versions of a document so that the normal filename has the additional suffix as just defined—e.g., using *foo.txt.en* for the English version of *foo.txt* and *foo.txt.fr* for the French version. (You don't need to create a file named *foo.txt*.) Note that language negotiation works well for plain text files, too; the negotiation does not depend on the data format of the file.

3. Now you can use a URL like *http://www.cs.tut.fi/~jkorpela/multi/foo.txt* as a generic URL that works via language negotiation. The specific language versions, like *http://www.cs.tut.fi/~jkorpela/multi/foo.txt.fr*, can be used too whenever desired.

Using type-map

The alternative method for content negotiation can perhaps best be described with a simple example. I have a document in Finnish *http://www.cs.tut.fi/~jkorpela/rfct.html* and a version of it in English *http://www.cs.tut.fi/~jkorpela/rfcs.html*. Into the directory where those files reside, I have written a file named *.htaccess* containing the line:

```
AddHandler type-map var
```

This makes the server handle URLs ending with *.var* in a special way. (This might be a system-default.) I have created, in that directory, a file named *rfc.var* and with the following content:

```
URI: rfcs.html
Content-Type: text/html; charset=iso-8859-1
Content-Language: en

URI: rfct.html
Content-Type: text/html; charset=iso-8859-1
Content-Language: fi
```

This causes the URL *http://www.cs.tut.fi/~jkorpela/rfc.var* to become operational, so that the server will respond by sending a Finnish version or an English version, according to the language preference settings in the user's browser.

When negotiation fails

If a browser sends language preferences such that none of the versions is acceptable by them, Apache sends back the HTTP error code "406 Not Acceptable." By default, the text "Not Acceptable" will be shown to the user, along with a list of links to the alternative versions. The links are not very descriptive. This isn't user-friendly error handling.

There are different ways to improve the error handling—e.g., by creating a specific error page for the error code 406. The best option is, however, probably to append a *generic alternative* to the list: an alternative with no Content-Language specified. Such an alternative will be sent by the server as a response to a request that cannot be satisfied by any other alternative.

The generic alternative should be a page that explains the available alternatives in English, with their names in their own languages. The page could additionally, for the general benefit of the user, give the user some advice on setting his browser's language preferences at least by adding English there, if he understands English.

Language Negotiation: the Browser Side

In Chapter 7, we described the different meanings of "language settings" in software. We mentioned that one of the meanings is to set language preferences in browsers, and illustrated this a bit. It is probably a good idea to check your browser's language preferences now. On Internet Explorer, use Tools → Internet options → Languages. Note that on IE, you can select either a language generically—e.g., English (en)—or a country-specific variant, such as U.S. English (en-US). If you choose a specific variant, it is a good idea to select the language generically, too, as the next option.

The page "Debian web site in different languages," *http://www.debian.org/intro/cn*, contains generally useful instructions (in different languages) on setting language preferences in several browsers.

Most browsers send language preferences to the server according to an ordered list of languages in the browser settings. The browser computes, by some algorithm, quality values to be associated with the language codes, starting from 1 for the first one. For example, if you set the list of languages to Spanish (es), English (en), and Portuguese (pt), your browser might send the following (defaulting the q value to 1 for the first language):

```
es,en;q=0.9,pt;q=0.8
```

Typically the default setting in a browser is that the list consists of one language only, the "own" language of the browser—i.e., the language used in its user interface (menus, buttons, error messages, etc). This naturally implies that if you install, say, an English version of a browser and do not change the language preferences, the settings say that you only know English. This usually isn't fatal, but it usually isn't optimal.

Problems may arise if the same computer and browser is used, at different times—e.g., in a classroom by different people with different language preferences. There does not seem to be any simple solution to that at present. The systems could be configured to reset the settings to something generally reasonable at startup.

Notes on Multilingual Sites

Language negotiation deals with the technical problem of picking up and sending the best possible alternative among versions of a page in different languages. It does not perform any translation. Here we will briefly consider some such aspects. Many of them are discussed in more detail at *http://webtips.dan.info/language.html*.

Producing the translations

When producing different language versions, automatic translation programs might be used to some extent. However, a competent human translator should be responsible for the translation work. Optimally the human translator should know the basics of the HTML language so that he can produce the translation directly as an HTML document. That way, the material to be translated could be delivered in an HTML document, and the translator would replace the texts, leaving (usually) the HTML markup as it is.

As another alternative, the text could be given to the translator either as a plain text file or as displayed by a web browser, for example, as printed on paper. In the latter case, the translator could deduce some relevant information from the appearance of the text. On the other hand, HTML markup could better tell the intended structure of the document, which may have some significance in selecting between alternatives in the translation. In any case, if the translator sends only the translated text, then someone else has to put it into HTML format, in practice, by merging the text with HTML markup. This cannot be done without knowing the language of the translation to some extent.

When working with the HTML format, it is essential to specify the encoding of the documents. The encoding may be different for different languages. This is one reason why MS Word format is often used, since the encoding is normally not a problem there. Conversion from that format to HTML may require quite some work, though.

Translation or different content?

The versions of a page in different languages can be "pure translations" of each other; in practice, that would usually mean that one of the versions is the original one and other versions have been translated from it. A "pure translation" consists of the original document, with the content and form strictly preserved, just expressed in another language. This means, for example, that the translation also contains the same factual errors as the original, the same references to local states of affair, etc.

Quite often, a pure translation is not appropriate for the purposes of the page. On the other hand, it is not adequate to use a language negotiation mechanism to distribute documents with completely different content, just with the same topic. It is sometimes difficult to draw the line.

The specification of the language negotiation mechanism does not require that the versions be exactly equivalent. On the contrary, the mechanism contains the possibility of specifying quality values, which may result in a selection of a version in a language that is lower in the user's preferences than another available language, due to quality difference. For example, if the user knows German a little better than French, he could have specified this in his language preferences; if the server has a version of the requested document in German but also a considerably more up-to-date or more extensive version in French, it might respond by sending the latter. In practice, such situations are probably still rare, partly because popular browsers do not let the users control the quality values associated by languages, only the repertoire and ordering of languages in the user's preferences.

Indicating what is available in each language

When you have a multilingual site, it is crucial to tell people what is really available in different languages. For example, if your site is dominantly in German but has a few pages in English as well, you should make it very clear in the English version that it presents only a small part of the information available in German. Otherwise, a visitor who knows both languages but prefers English might never make real use of the site.

It is mostly sufficient to include such information in the main page in each language. But, for example, if the site contains a news page so that some but not all of the articles are available in German too, then it would be misleading to make the German version contain those articles only. Instead, the news page should minimally say that more news articles are available in English (naturally, the site should include a link with that English page). It could also contain links to English news articles that have not been translated, merged with the news in German. Preferably, the headlines of such news should appear as translated, along with a clear indication of the link pointing to text in English.

Naming the versions

When selecting URLs for versions of documents in different languages, a systematic approach is often desirable, for practical reasons like creating and maintaining the pages. This can be implemented in different ways; the method could, for example, be either of the following:

- The path part of an address contains a separate part that specifies the language—e.g., *http://www.something.example/en/foo.html* (for an English version) and *http://www.something.example/fi/foo.html* (for a Finnish version). In practice, this usually corresponds to having pages in one language in a directory of their own.

- At the end of an address, the part immediately preceding the *.html* (or equivalent) part contains a hyphen (or other punctuation character) and a language code—e.g., *http://www.something.example/foo-en.html* and *http://www.something.example/foo-fi.html*. In practice, this usually corresponds to having pages in different languages in the same directory but with different names, according to a systematic naming scheme.

Both methods have the problem that the "proper name" of the document (in our example, "foo") should be reasonably understandable internationally. This typically means that you use English words there, partly because things are much easier if URLs contain only ASCII characters.

Language preferences and JavaScript

In the JavaScript language, it is under some conditions possible to determine the browser language. This however is almost always useless, and it has nothing to do with the user's language preferences. The browser language is just the language of the browser's user interface.

It is very common to use English versions of browsers just because there are no alternatives or because versions in other languages have confusing translations for terms. The basic use of a browser does not require much understanding of the browser language, since most of the basic functions can be activated using icon buttons or other simple tools so that it suffices to know a very small repertoire of words.

Making use of language preferences in CGI scripts

In CGI scripts, it is possible to use language preferences as sent by browsers. The value of Accept-Language header as defined in the protocol manifests itself to a CGI script as the environment variable HTTP_ACCEPT_LANGUAGE (which needs to be written this way, using uppercase letters).

According to the protocol, the value of this variable contains a comma-separated set of parts, each of which consists of a language code that is optionally followed by the specification of a q value. It is relatively easy to parse this—e.g., in a CGI script written in Perl—using the split function for division into parts. The following code sample performs this and sets the variable $preferred to the language code that corresponds to the language that is primary according to the preferences. Here we set English as the default language, to be implied, if the browser sends no preferences:

```
$accept = $ENV{'HTTP_ACCEPT_LANGUAGE'};
@prefs = split(/,/,$accept);
$preferred = 'en';
$prefq = 0;
foreach $pref(@prefs) {
   if($pref =~ /(.*);q=(.*)/ ) {
      $lang=$1; $qval=$2; }
   else {
      $lang=$pref; $qval= 1; }
   if($qval > $prefq) {
      $preferred = $lang; $prefq = $qval; }}
```

The result can be used, for example, to index a hash containing language-dependent strings. For example, if we would like to have a CGI script in Perl which, when dynamically generating an HTML document, to write texts either in Finnish or in English, we could write the alternate texts into a hash and pick up the right text from it as the following example shows:

```
$gen{'en'} = 'Report generated at ';
$gen{'fi'} = 'Raportin luontihetki: ';
- -
print "<div>$gen{$preferred} $now.</div>";
```

Types of Negotiation

Although we have concentrated on language negotiation, similar mechanisms work for other types of content negotiation, though normally without using user preferences:

Media type negotiation
> You can make the same information available, for example, as plain text, in PDF format, and in HTML format. You could then use the type-map mechanism of Apache for language negotiation, and use different Content-Type headers. The browser is expected to list its media type preferences in an Accept header. This is not very useful in most cases, since browsers often express such preferences in a manner that contains too little information or cannot be trusted in practice.

Encoding negotiation
> Similarly, you can make the same information available in different character encodings. Using the type-map mechanism for example, the Content-Type headers in your definition file would contain charset parameters that indicate the encoding of each version. The browser is expected to list its encoding preferences in an Accept-Charset header. However, many popular browsers do not send such a header at all, which means that they accept any encoding.

Transfer encoding negotiation
> Additional transfer encoding (see Chapter 6) can be agreed upon between the browser and the server. A browser uses Accept-Encoding to specify the transfer encodings it can handle. Figure 10-9 shows how the Opera browser announces that it can handle deflate, gzip, and x-gzip but nothing else. It accepts "identity," which means no transfer encoding, but assigns a quality value of zero to everything else.

Characters in Protocol Headers

The original Internet message syntax restricts the character repertoire to ASCII. For most message headers, this does not cause problems, since the headers names are in ASCII, and most header values are code-like notations designed to be writeable in ASCII.

There are some exceptions, though, such as the Subject header in email and on Usenet. The header should tell what the message is about, and naturally, it should be in the same language as the message content. The sender and recipient headers (such as From and To) contain Internet email addresses, which are normally in ASCII, but they may contain, as comments, real names of people and organizations. If your real name is Matti Meikäläinen, you would like to have it expressed as such, with the ä's, in the From field of your messages. Such practice is often recommended, but it immediately raises the character problems.

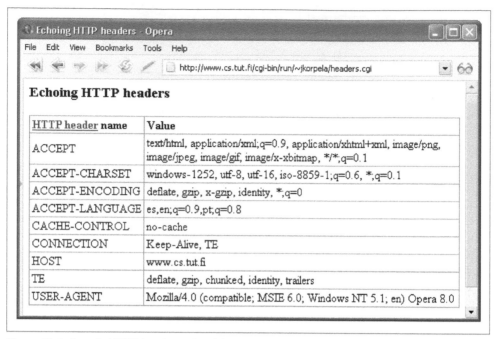

Figure 10-9. Sample HTTP headers echoed (in Opera)

In practice, if you include non-ASCII data in the message headers, things will usually work, if your program sends your messages by the MIME conventions. The headers will specify the encoding for the message body, and most programs that can handle MIME will apply the conventions to the message headers, too. The headers might even contain, for example, Latin 1 Supplement characters as "raw" 8-bit data by the ISO-8859-1 encoding, naturally assuming that there is a Content-Type header that specifies the encoding.

In principle, such methods are not recommended, and they may cause practical problems to some software. Within a country where some 8-bit encoding, such as one of the ISO 8859 family, is widely used, you can probably send email with raw 8-bit data in headings without encountering problems with that. Sending such email to a country where people use dominantly just ASCII may result in unreadable headers, or even make programs crash, because people use software that cannot handle such data.

As a consequence, when sending a message in an *international group discussion*, whether by email or on Usenet, it is safest to use ASCII only in headers, especially in the Subject line. The reason is that when people respond to your message, their messages get the Subject line content from the original message. Although most people's programs can handle MIME properly, sooner or later someone might respond using a program that cannot. It may mess up the Subject line quite a lot.

The Signature Convention May Help

In some cases, you might avoid the problem by using a simplified version of the spelling of your name (e.g., From: Matti Meikalainen <mm@fi.example>) and specify the correct version in a *signature*. A signature, or "sig," is a short piece of text (recommended maximum length is four lines) appended automatically at the end of the email and Usenet messages that you send. It is preceded by a "sig separator," namely two hyphen-minus characters and one space "-- " on a line of its own. For example:

```
--
Matti Meikäläinen
freelance generalist
```

Programs may treat signatures in a special way, distinguishing them from the message body proper. By the protocols, however, a signature is part of the body and may contain non-ASCII characters the same way and under the same conditions as the content.

The Q Encoding

The Q encoding is a general mechanism for overcoming the limitation to ASCII in Internet message headers. Technically, it means that the headers do not crash anything that expects ASCII only, since all octets are in the ASCII range. However, programs are expected to interpret some patterns as indicating a particular character encoding. In that case, part of the heading is to be interpreted according to that encoding. The Q encoding resembles the QP encoding discussed in Chapter 3 but differs from it in a few essential ways:

- Q encoding may be applied in a part of text (header) only.
- A Q encoded part starts with the characters =? and ends with ?=.
- The initial =? is followed by the name of the encoding and the string ?Q?.
- In the data that follows, an octet (to be interpreted in the encoding specified) can be represented as =xx, where xx is its numeric value in hexadecimal. The octet 20 (corresponding to space in ASCII) may also be represented as _ (underline). Octets that correspond to printable ASCII characters, except the space and =, may also be represented as those characters.

Thus, the general format is:

```
=?encoding?Q?data?=
```

For example, if you send email (on a MIME enabled program) and specify the recipient name as Matti Meikäläinen, the program will generate a header like the following:

```
To: =?ISO-8859-1?Q?Matti_Meik=E4l=E4inen?= <mm@fi.example>
```

A recipient who uses an old program that cannot handle MIME will see the name literally that way, but more likely, the recipient's program will interpret the Q encoding and display the name correctly. Here, as usual, things may fail if the recipient's program cannot handle the character encoding used, but ISO-8859-1 will probably work fine.

The B Encoding

The B encoding is similar to the Q encoding but uses Base64 encoding for the data. Since that encoding was described in Chapter 6, we will only give an example here:

```
Subject: =?UTF-8?B?VMOkbcOkIG9uIMK1LXRlc3RpIGphIM6jLXRlc3Rp?=
```

The point is that although modern software recognizes this and decodes the data, it is completely illegible without such decoding. A recipient who is not familiar with encodings might not even realize that there is some sensible data involved.

Summary: Dealing with Non-ASCII Characters in Headers

If it seems that you need to use characters other than ASCII in email or Usenet messages, you can choose between the following options:

Use ASCII only
> This avoids the technical problems but creates problems in human communication. Consider how understandable the data is when mapped to ASCII (e.g., replacing ä with "a," or maybe "ae"; see the section "Escape sequences" in Chapter 2). This is often the only feasible approach in international discussion groups, worldwide email distribution lists, etc.

Use Q encoding
> Modern software often applies Q encoding automatically, if you include non-ASCII characters in headers. This is usually adequate when sending messages in a culturally homogenous environment where the languages normally used need non-ASCII characters, so that most people have MIME capable software.

Use B encoding
> This is hardly useful, since it normally has no significant benefits over Q encoding but serious drawbacks: when presented as such, B encoded data is illegible. Some programs use B encoding by default, at least in some situations.

Use 8-bit characters in headers
> If the program you use has an option for sending 8-bit characters in headers, this means that it uses octets larger than 7F there, too—e.g., passing ISO-8859-1 data as such. This is risky but sometimes works better than Q encoding; for example, some Usenet software ("newsreaders") can deal with 8-bit data but can not decode Q encoding. To use this feature, you would simply select that option, but remember that it will remain in effect until you change it.

Some programs like Outlook Express can be used both for email and for posting to Usenet ("newsgroups"), and they have partly separate settings for these two types of use. You could for example allow 8-bit characters in headers when posting to Usenet but disallow them in email.

It is not possible to give a comprehensive presentation of the ways that email programs should be configured and used with regards to character encoding. The discussion in this section is meant to present the basics for an analysis of the various settings that are available in each program. The bottom line is that anything beyond ASCII in message headers may cause problems, though modern email programs usually understand whatever another modern email program sends.

Characters in Domain Names and URLs

The use of the Web and the Internet in general has become more genuinely global and multilingual than it used to be. This has made it more obvious that we need possibilities for using non-ASCII characters in URLs (web addresses) as well as in Internet domain names. These two are somewhat connected, but not the same thing. You could have a domain name like *école.example* that you wish to use in different contexts, such as email addresses. You could also wish to use a URL like *http://école.example/Noël* where you have a non-ASCII character not only in the server part (the domain name) but also elsewhere.

Internet domain names, especially those of web servers, have become very important in business. Companies typically advertise their web sites by printing the domain name in their brochures and ads, and it is essential that potential users see the name as natural, understandable, and easy to remember. It is therefore understandable that companies and other organizations did not like the limitation to ASCII. If you company's name contains the word Müller, you don't like the idea of having to spell it as Muller or Mueller.

Unfortunately, internationalization of domain names and URLs is still a work in progress, though actually making some progress. Many countries have already allowed the use of non-ASCII characters in the domains that are registered under the country domain. This addresses some of the most critical business issues.

Internationalized Domain Names (IDN)

Internationalization of Internet domain names is based on a special ad hoc method. Instead of extending the character repertoire in any general way, which would mean thorough changes to the infrastructure, we interpret some special combinations of ASCII characters as indicating non-ASCII characters. This is in a sense yet another example of escape notations, which we discussed in Chapter 2.

The IDNA implementation

The Internationalized Domain Name (IDN) idea uses character combinations containing two consecutive hyphen-minus characters (--) for special purposes. Such a combination is hardly meaningful as such; a single hyphen-minus may well appear in a normal domain name, but why would anyone use two of them in succession?

Since 1998, different proposals have been made and debated, but in 2005, "Internationalizing Domain Names in Applications (IDNA)" was chosen as the way to implement IDN. Its basic definition is in RFC 3490, and it works as follows:

1. Start with a domain name that may contain non-ASCII characters. We will here consider the hypothetical example of "www.härmä.fi."

2. Divide the name to components separated by periods, and handle each component separately. In our example, the components "www" and "fi" need no further processing, but "härmä" does.

3. Apply the *Nameprep* algorithm defined in RFC 3491, as a profile of the more general *Stringprep* algorithm. It consists of Unicode normalization to form C (NFKC), case folding (to lowercase), mapping similar-looking characters together, and eliminating certain restricted code points. In our example, "härmä" is unchanged. In more abnormal cases, the component may change essentially.

4. Apply Punycode (see Chapter 6) to the result. In our example, the component "härmä" is changed to "xn--hrm-qlac."

The resulting domain name, *www.xn--hrm-qlac.fi*, is not meant to be written or seen as such. However, technically, it is an Internet domain name, and it can be used as such. In fact, it is *the* domain name in this case. The string "www.härmä.fi" is just a notation that denotes this name, or maps to it, on software that supports IDNA. Thus, on browsers that support IDNA, you can type either of the domain names to access the site, but on other browsers, you need to type the awkward real domain name.

Security threats

As we mentioned in Chapter 6, IDNs raise serious security problems. If the full Unicode repertoire were allowed in IDNs, in any mixture, it would be all too easy to mislead people. For example, someone might register a domain name that has an IDN form like *www.money.example*, where the letter "o" is the Cyrillic small letter "o." Since that letter is indistinguishable from the Latin small letter "o," people would believe they are visiting *www.money.example* (with Latin "o") and type their username and password there. The cheater could then abuse this information to steal money, for example.

Generally, ease of use tends to imply threats to security, and IDNA is meant to make internationalized domain names easy to use. Further problems are caused by people's tendency to follow links in email messages and on web pages, instead of typing in a web address or picking it up from a list of bookmarks (favorites). A large part of the security problem would be avoided if people typed in addresses, or used addresses that they have previously typed in. They would access the real *www.money.example* and not the fake.

However, since people's habits are difficult to change, guidelines have been designed to reduce the risks by restricting the variety of characters and combinations in IDNs. There is a draft Unicode Technical Report #36, "Unicode Security Considerations," which addresses such problems, at *http://www.unicode.org/draft/reports/tr36/tr36.html*. The file *http://unicode.org/draft/reports/tr36/data/draft-restrictions.txt* contains a draft list of characters to be excluded, for one reason or another. The general idea is to allow names of the form that is normally used in a script or language but exclude characters that have no such normal use, such as phonetic symbols and most mathematical symbols. Of course, there are borderline cases.

Characters in URLs

In Chapter 6, we described URL encoding, which was originally introduced as a method for using some ASCII characters that are not allowed as such—e.g., encoding a space character as %20. Later, it was extended to encode octets rather than just ASCII characters. In the modern approach, the implied primary character encoding is UTF-8, and URL encoding then maps the octets used in UTF-8 to *%xx* notations if needed.

Although the mechanisms in principle let you create URLs with non-ASCII characters anywhere, it will take a long time before they work safely. You still need to use addresses that can be written in ASCII without any special conventions, even if they won't be easy to users or natural.

For example, assume that you would really like to use a URL containing the part "skål," such as *http://www.example/skål/*. Maybe you expect your potential visitors to try to type "skål" simply because they are used to that spelling, even they have seen the URL printed with "skaal." Here is a possible strategy:

1. First and foremost, make sure that the address with a simplified spelling ("a" instead of å) works: *http://www.example/skal/*.

2. Consider other ways that people might try to type the name if they just heard it or try to recollect it. If you know that å is often written as "aa" when only ASCII is available, you might set things up (on the server) so that *http://www.example/skaal/* works too, as an alias for the same page.

3. You might also set things up so that *http://www.example/sk%e5l/* works, as an alias, because when people type "skål" into the address box of a browser, the browser may URL encode the string according to ISO-8859-1, mapping å (U+00E5) to "%e5."

4. Then you could make the server recognize *http://www.example/sk%c3%a5l/* as well. This is how *http://www.example/skål/* should be URL encoded by modern principles: take the URL string, encode it as UTF-8, making å the two octets C3 and A5, and then encode these octets as "%c3" and "%a5."

Additional complications arise if you wish to use uppercase characters or to make lowercase and uppercase equivalent. Although servers may have options for making the server treat URLs as case insensitive with regards to basic Latin letters (accepting "foo," "Foo," and "FOO" as equivalent), these options probably do not apply to other letters: Å would still be different than å. Special operations, such as URL rewrite rules, would be needed to make them equivalent.

CHAPTER 11

Characters in Programming

This chapter presents a number of ways to represent character and string data in different programming languages, such as FORTRAN, C, C#, Perl, ECMAScript (JavaScript), and Java, and also other languages such as XML and CSS. It explores both the differences and similarities, illustrated with sample programs to perform simple manipulation of string data. The information is presented to introduce you to using Unicode in programming in different languages. You will need to study language manuals and library documentation in order to do some serious programming.

You need to understand some basics of programming to benefit from this chapter. You should be able to write a program that prints "Hello world," and you should know how to declare variables and assign values to them, write expressions and conditional statements, and use subprograms. Here we will discuss the specifics of processing character and string data. One reason for this is that even people who know programming well may get confused with the fundamental concepts and cannot distinguish, for example, between an empty string, a space character, the NUL character, and the digit zero. Programming language tutorials typically discuss the character concept rather briefly, often assuming that only ASCII data will be used.

The International Components for Unicode (ICU) activity, based on the open source principle, is a large collection of subroutines and modules for Unicode support and localization, for use in C, C++, or Java programs. In addition to saving time, the use of ICU helps to create more robust and more easily localizable software.

The chapter also contains a section on locales and especially the Common Locale Data Repository and its future use in disciplined programming. However, we first discuss some older styles of working with characters, mostly to warn about their problems.

Characters in Computer Languages

What do we really mean when we say that a particular *programming* language has such-and-such a character repertoire? Ranging from the narrowest to the broadest, the interpretations are:

1. The characters you need for writing the *basic constructs* of the language, such as operators and punctuation. This is almost always a subset of ASCII.

2. The characters used in the basic constructs and *identifiers* that the programmer chooses to use as names for variables, arrays, functions, etc. This too is usually a subset of ASCII, but the modern trend is to allow a larger repertoire of letters as identifiers. This lets a programmer name her variables in her native language. The repertoire might even consist of almost all Unicode characters, with special arrangements to make it possible to parse source code unambiguously. After all, we need to know the start and end of an identifier and distinguish identifiers from other symbols.

3. The characters that can be used in the above constructs or in *character and string literals*. Most programming languages do not let you use, for example, an accented letter like é in an identifier, but they may well allow it in literals like 'é' or "égalité".

4. All the characters that are *allowed in source programs*. This includes, in addition to the characters discussed above, characters than can be used in *comments*. Usually you can write anything into comments, but there might be some limitations.

5. All the characters that are *expressible* in source programs. This can be a larger repertoire than the characters that are allowed as such, due to various "escape" mechanisms. Even if a language might not allow you to enter, say, a Cyrillic letter into a source program (even in a literal), it may well let you write a character constant that has a Cyrillic letter as its value, such as '\u042f' (which denotes Я).

6. All the characters that can be *processed* in binary programs created using the language. This may include characters that are not expressible in any way in source programs but can be read as input.

Consider the following line in a Perl program:

```perl
$msg = "§ 1: I \x{2665} Unicode! "; # "Testing" ♥
```

In this example, the dollar symbol, the quotation marks, and the semicolon are basic symbols of Perl (item 1). The string msg contains characters allowed in a name (item 2). Inside a string constant, where the rules can be more permissive (item 3), the non-ASCII character § might be allowed, depending on implementation. Anything following the character # is a comment, so anything goes (item 4), including "smart" quotation marks, which would not be allowed as string delimiters. The string constant contains a notation that refers to U+2665 (black heart suit, ♥), but not that character as such (item 5). Such a reference might work even in circumstances where that character cannot appear as such even in a comment, due to restrictions imposed by the character encoding.

In a *markup* language, the interpretations are similar, except for the last one, which does not exist. You don't process data in markup. The same applies to various descriptive languages, metalanguages, etc.

Thus, whenever you see a statement like "language *X* supports Unicode," you should ask what it means. Usually it means, at most, that Unicode characters are allowed in the sense expressed in items 3 to 6, but sometimes also item 2, though with limitations.

Only a few programming languages have been designed to allow (and require) the use of non-ASCII characters in the basic constructs (item 1). In the early days of computing, some language definitions used special characters like ∧ (logical and, U+2227) as operators. Actual implementations used various replacement notations. Later, even specifications were written to use ASCII only.

The *APL* language is an exception. It is oriented toward processing of arrays and matrices, and it uses a collection of special symbols, all of which have been included in Unicode, some only due to their use in APL. The use of APL has always been relatively small, partly due to the special techniques (a special keyboard or special software) needed for writing it.

Work on a language called *Fortress* has been started, by Sun Microsystems, to create a programming language that allows the use of symbols and notations as in the tradition of mathematics and logic—e.g., $a^2 \in A \cap B$. However, the language defines ways of using symbols constructed from ASCII characters instead of the special characters. Information about Fortress is available at *http://research.sun.com/projects/plrg/*.

By definition, comments are ignored (skipped) by programming language compilers and interpreters or, in the case of a markup language, by parsers and browsers. Thus, it is natural to expect that we can use any characters inside comments, as long as we don't try to use a comment terminator inside a comment.

```
char ch = 'X'; /* A comment: I ♥ C ☺ */
```

However, special characters could cause problems if they are in an encoding that is not recognized by compilers and interpreters. Interpreted wrongly, they might mess up the processing. This should not be a problem if you use an ISO 8859 encoding or UTF-8 and the compiler effectively processes it as ASCII, treating octets outside the ASCII range as unknown characters. It should then simply ignore such octets in comments.

Some old compilers are known to get confused with octets outside the ASCII range even if they occur inside comments only. Try to get a better compiler if this occurs.

Common Escape Notations

Many modern computer languages use "backslash escape" notations for characters inside character and string constants, and possibly in other contexts as well. Escape notations in general were discussed in Chapter 2.

A rather common set of conventions, historically largely based on the C programming language, is presented in Table 11-1. Various languages have deviations from and additions to these notations. Some of the notations, such as \b, are rarely used nowadays but often preserved in the repertoire for historical continuity. The notations are typically allowed in character and string constants that have enclosing quotation marks, but depending on the language definition, they might be allowed, for example, in unquoted values and identifiers, too.

Table 11-1. Widely available escape notations for characters

Notation	Unicode value	Explanation
\a	U+0007	(Audible) alert, BEL
\b	U+0008	Backspace (move one position backwards)
\f	U+000C	Form feed (page eject)
\n	Implementation-dependent	Newline; see "Line structure control," Chapter 9
\r	U+000D	Carriage return (move to start of line)
\t	U+0009	Horizontal tabulation, tab
\v	U+000B	Vertical tab
\\	U+005C	Reverse solidus (backslash) itself
\"	U+0022	ASCII quotation mark
\'	U+0027	ASCII apostrophe

The use of \" and \' is relevant in contexts where the quotation mark or apostrophe could otherwise be taken as terminating a character or string constant. For example, in order to write a string constant that means the three-character string a"b, you may need to write "a\"b".

Usually "backslash escapes" can also be used to specify characters by their *code numbers*. For example, \0 might be used to denote the null character U+0000. However, great care is needed when you change from one language to another, since there are essential differences. Usually the implied numbering is according to Unicode, but the range of permitted numbers varies, and might cover only the ASCII range (0–127) or ASCII and Latin 1 Supplement (0–255).

Moreover, the notations for numbers vary. For example, in C, the number is interpreted as decimal, unless it begins with a zero, in which case it is interpreted as octal (base 8). In Java, the number is interpreted in octal, unless preceded by the letter u, in which case it is interpreted as hexadecimal. Besides, there can be special rules for the amount of digits.

Characters in Markup Languages and CSS

Although markup languages (such as HTML and XML) and CSS, the stylesheet language, are not programming languages, we will discuss them to some extent in this chapter. One reason is that in dealing with characters, they resemble programming languages in many ways. Moreover, they are also used in conjunction with programming languages in a manner that often confuses people. Think about the following attempt at Perl code, meant to generate a piece of HTML code, the tag <p style="em">:

```
print "<p style="em">\n";    # This won't work!
```

This will fail, with an unfriendly error message, because the Perl interpreter treats the second quotation mark as terminating the quoted string. The problem is that we have a quoted string that needs to contain a quoted string in another language. In this particular case, there are many simple solutions, such as using single quotation marks in the HTML code. There are, however, more difficult situations.

Characters in HTML and XML

The methods of using characters, including entity and character references, in HTML and XML were explained in Chapter 2 and Chapter 10. There are some finer points to be discussed here. What exactly is the repertoire of characters that you can use? How do HTML notations interfere with those of programming languages?

HTML and XML derive their escape notations—character references and entity references—from SGML (Standard Generalized Markup Language), which is far less known to most people than its descendants. The escape mechanisms of SGML are rather different from those of programming languages and include characters that cause some clashes. In a character reference like { in SGML, the &# and ; parts are just particular instances (though the default instances) of the general concepts of Character Reference Open (CRO) and Reference Close (REFC). They can be changed to other symbols if desired for the needs of a particular markup system based on SGML. However, both HTML and XML have made such things fixed.

This has some implications especially regarding the ampersand &, which is widely used for special purposes in programming languages and other notations. In particular, the ampersand is used as a separator between fields (*name* = *value* pairs) in the format of data generated from form submission. This means that URLs often contain ampersands. When you include a URL into an HTML document, you must therefore escape the ampersand. For example, to refer to *http://www.google.com/search?hl=en&q=rosebud* in a link in HTML, you should write:

```
<a href="http://www.google.com/search?hl=en&amp;q=rosebud">…
```

Contrary to popular belief, entity references are recognized in attribute values, too. This has often caused confusion, since people have failed to see the difference between a URL (which contains just & here) and the way of writing a URL in an HTML document.

Luckily, the backslash character \ has no special role in HTML or XML. It is just a normal data character.

The HTML and XML specifications define that the *document character set* is ISO 10646. As explained in Chapter 4, this is effectively the same as saying that it is Unicode. However, the document character set relates only to the repertoire of characters that may appear in documents and specifically to the interpretation of character references—i.e., notations of the form &#n; or &#xn;. The document character set is the character code (mapping of integers to characters) according to which the *n* in such notations is to be interpreted.

In particular, HTML and XML specifications do not impose Unicode semantics on characters, for two reasons: they formally refer to ISO 10646, not the Unicode standard, and even if they referred to Unicode, this would not constitute a requirement on conformance to the standard. Of course, software that processes HTML or XML documents may apply Unicode semantics and rules, such as line breaking rules, but this is not a requirement. Only for some features related to directionality do HTML specifications refer to Unicode rules normatively.

The HTML specifications contain some special restrictions on the use of control characters, as listed in Table 11-2. There is usually little reason why control characters other than line breaks and sometimes horizontal tabs would appear in HTML documents. They may, however, appear due to conversions. The rules for them are somewhat different in HTML up to and including HTML 4.01 and in XHTML. (Technically, the SGML declaration for HTML 4.01 disallows U+000C, but the prose discusses it as an allowed character. It would anyway be whitespace and not a page eject character.)

Table 11-2. C0 and C1 Control characters in HTML

Character(s)	Explanation	Use in HTML
U+0000..U+0008	C0 Controls (part)	Forbidden
U+0009	Horizontal Tab	A whitespace character, may tabulate
U+000A	Line Feed	Line break; a whitespace character
U+000B	Vertical Tab	Forbidden
U+000C	Form Feed	Obscure in HTML, forbidden in XHTML
U+000D	Carriage Return	Line break; a whitespace character
U+000E..U+001F	C0 Controls (part)	Forbidden
U+007F	DEL (= Delete)	Disallowed in HTML, discouraged in XHTML
U+0080..U+0084	C1 Controls (part)	Disallowed in HTML, discouraged in XHTML
U+0085	NEL (= Next Line)	Disallowed in HTML, line break in XHTML
U+0086..U+009F	C1 Controls (part)	Disallowed in HTML, discouraged in XHTML

The specific restrictions in XHTML are derived from the XML 1.0 specification, which has a rigorous definition of allowed characters, or rather code points. By the specification, an XML processor must accept any code point (including unassigned code points) except certain control characters, the surrogate blocks, and two noncharacters, as shown in Table 11-3. On the other hand, the XML 1.0 specification declares some characters as *discouraged*. Discouraged characters are allowed and must be accepted by an XML processor, but authors are advised to avoid using them. They are:

- All compatibility characters as defined in the Unicode standard.
- The ranges U+1FFFE..U+1FFFF, U+2FFFE..U+2FFFF, etc.—i.e., the last two code points of all planes except the BMP. They are noncharacters.
- Some other specific ranges of code points; these are indicated in the table as "Discouraged."

Table 11-3. *Characters and other code points in XML 1.0*

Code point(s)	Explanation	Status in XML
U+0000..U+0008	C0 Controls (part)	Forbidden
U+0009	Horizontal Tab	OK
U+000A	Line Feed	OK (line break)
U+000B..U+000C	VT, FF	Forbidden
U+000D	Carriage Return	OK (line break)
U+000E..U+001F	C0 Controls (part)	Forbidden
U+0020..U+007E	Basic Latin (printable)	OK
U+007F..U+0084	Control characters	Discouraged
U+0085	NEL (= Next Line)	OK (line break)
U+0086..U+009F	C1 Controls (part)	Discouraged
U+00A0..U+D7FF	Various BMP characters	OK
U+D800..U+DFFF	Surrogates	Forbidden
U+E000..U+FDCF	Various BMP characters	OK
U+FDD0..U+FDDF	Noncharacters	Discouraged
U+FDE0..U+FFFD	Various BMP characters	OK
U+FFFE..U+FFFF	Noncharacters	Forbidden
U+10000..U+10FFFF	Non-BMP characters	OK with exceptions (see above)

In *XML 1.1*, which has few implementations and less use than XML 1.0, the character concept is somewhat broader: all characters in the range U+0001..U+D7FF—i.e., including most control characters forbidden in XML 1.0—are permitted. The NUL character U+0000 is forbidden even in XML 1.1, to avoid problems with applications that may treat it as a string terminator. On the other hand, XML 1.1 allows C0 and C1 Controls (excluding the line break characters and the horizontal tab) only as character references such as &#1; or &#x1;, not directly as data characters.

Problems in generating markup programmatically

When you write a program that generates markup, you often encounter the problem that the programming language and the markup language have different escape notations. This is, however, mostly a conceptual problem: you need to remember the conventions of both notations and not mix them with each other. Consider the following simple statement in the Perl language:

```
print "<p style=\"em\">\n";
```

Here we have solved the previously mentioned problem with quotation marks by escaping the inner quotation marks. In Perl strings, \" is an escape notation for the quotation mark as a data character. Usually there are many alternative ways of solving such problems.

Here is a perhaps trickier example:

```
print "<p>The price is $100.</p>";    # Will print wrong data
```

The problem is that the dollar sign $, which is just an ordinary data character in HTML, has special meanings in Perl; for example, it starts a scalar variable, and $100 is a special variable. The program is in error, and it probably prints "<p>The price is .</p>" (without any error message or warning, unless you use the -w switch when invoking the Perl interpreter).

 When you mix two languages, check your strings for problems with syntactically special characters and notations in either language.

Problems discussed here can usually be solved by modifying the code in either of the languages, usually with some kind of an escape notation. Moreover, there are typically two or more ways of doing that. In the last example, it would be simplest to solve the problem at the Perl level, either by using single quotation marks (since inside them, the dollar sign loses its special meaning) or by escaping the dollar sign with backslash:

```
print '<p>The price is $100.</p>';    # OK, but implies limitations
print "<p>The price is \$100.</p>";   # A better solution
```

Problems in using scripts inside HTML

There is another way to "nest" HTML and a programming language: putting a program inside an HTML document. You might wish to *show* program source code in an HTML page if you are writing about programming or documenting a program. This would mean that the program source code is normal textual content, so the usual rules for escaping < and & in HTML will apply. Here is an example of HTML markup, for text containing the (somewhat artificial) C language expression &x<y (note that the code markup does not affect the interpretation of <, &, etc.):

```
<p>Consider the statement <code>&amp;x&lt;y</code>.</p>
```

A more difficult question arises if you wish to use program code to be *executed* by the browser—i.e., client-side scripting. You would typically use JavaScript, and you can attach a program (script) to an HMTL document in three ways:

- Write the program into an external file, say *zap.js*, and refer to it in HTML using an element like `<script type="text/javascript" src="zap.js"></script>`. This will avoid all problems discussed here, since in the external file, no HTML rules apply. The file could contain, for example, the JavaScript code `alert("Hello&bye")`.

- Write the program inside a script element—e.g., `<script type="text/javascript">alert('Hello&bye');</script>`. According to HTML specifications up to and including HTML 4.01, the HTML escape rules are not applied inside a script element, so you could and would have to write, for example, the ampersand as such, as in the example. In XHTML, you would need to use the escapes there. This makes things so complicated that it is much easier to write the code in an external script file (i.e., use the first way).

- Write the program inside an event attribute such as `onload` or `onclick`—e.g., `<body onload="alert('Hello&amp;bye')">`. In this case, all HTML escape conventions apply. Moreover, you cannot use the same quotation mark in the JavaScript code as you have used as the attribute value delimiter in HTML. The common style is to use the double quote " in HTML, the single quote ' in JavaScript.

Things can be even more complicated, and that's not even rare. You might have HTML markup that contains JavaScript that generates HTML markup. For example, consider the following HTML element:

```
<script type="text/javascript">
  document.write('<div>Hello world<\/div>');
</script>.
```

In the example, we have written \/, which is a JavaScript escape for the / character. Without such escaping, the browser would see `</div>` as an end tag, causing a syntax error in HTML.

You might now carry out a simple exercise: write a HTML document so that when it is opened, the message "Hello—world" appears in a pop-up window created by the JavaScript function `alert`. The basic code has been presented above, and you just need to find out how to express the em dash character, U+2014. In JavaScript, you can use the escape notation \u2014 for it. But could you also use an HTML character reference, and how would you do that, in the three ways discussed above?

Characters in CSS

A stylesheet written in CSS (Cascading Style Sheets) can use any encoding recognized by a browser on which it will be used. Usually only ASCII characters are used in CSS, so the encoding is not a big issue. However, you might wish to use non-ASCII characters for in some special cases:

- In comments—e.g., `/* © 2006 Jérôme Doe */`
- In identifiers such as element or class names—e.g., `p.Einführung {…}`
- In property values such as font names—e.g., `font-family: Lübeck`
- In strings—e.g., `quotes: "\201d" "\201d";`

CSS code may appear in a separate file or as embedded into an HTML document. In the latter case, it of course shares the encoding of the HTML document. In the former case, the web server (HTTP server) should announce the encoding, as for HTML documents (see Chapter 10). This is problematic, and for casual use of non-ASCII characters, it might be best to use escape notations.

The basic escape mechanism for characters in CSS is simple and similar to the general mechanisms in programming languages. You start an escape with a backslash (reverse solidus) \ and then you write the Unicode code number in hexadecimal. Recognizing the end of the notation is somewhat problematic. The rules were briefly described in Chapter 2, but here we will present them in more detail and also list some alternative notations.

CSS has three kinds of uses for the backslash:

- A backslash immediately followed by a line break is ignored together with the line break. Thus, a \ at the end of a line is used for continuation lines. In practice, it is used inside a string that must not contain a line break, when we wish to keep the physical line length reasonably small.

- Any single character but a hexadecimal number can be escaped by prefixing it with a backslash. This notation is useful when the character itself would not be syntactically permitted or would have a special meaning. Thus, \\ means the backslash itself as data character, \" means the ASCII quotation mark, etc.

- A backslash followed by one to six hexadecimal digits denotes the character with that code number. For example, \2013 means U+2013, the en dash "–". If the notation is followed by a character that is a hexadecimal digit—e.g., you would like to express "1–4"—the end of the notation needs to be indicated. There are two ways to do this: use exactly six digits; e.g., 1\0020134; or put a whitespace character after the last hexadecimal digit; e.g., 1\2013 4. The whitespace character will be ignored by a program that processes the CSS code, and a CR LF pair will be counted as one character in this context. This is a convenient method, and you could use an extra space routinely, even when not needed. However, the convention implies that if the escape notation should be followed by a real space character, the space needs to be doubled or escaped. For example, "1 – 4" would be written as 1 \2013 4 (with two spaces before "4") or as 1 \2013\ 4.

Let us suppose that your HTML document contains `<p class="Einführung">` or, equivalently, uses an entity reference, `<p class="Einf&udier;hrung">`. If you write CSS code in a suitable encoding, you can enter the character ü (U+00FC) directly, but you can alternatively use the escape notation \fc for it, for example:

```
p.Einf\fc hrung { font-size: 120%; }
```

The point is that although HTML and CSS have quite different escape mechanisms, you can escape a character in both languages and have it interpreted the same way. You can also escape a character in one of the languages and use it as such in the other.

If your CSS code is embedded inside an HTML document, it is better to use CSS escapes rather than HTML escapes. One reason for this is that the latter are not always recognized:

- In a style *attribute*, as in `<p style="font-family: Lübeck">`, HTML escapes are recognized. You could write Lübeck or Lübeck there, but the CSS escaped form L\fc beck works, too.

- In a style *element*, as in `<style type="text/css">p { font-family: Lübeck }</style>`, HTML escapes are not recognized according to HTML specifications up to and including HTML 4.01. The CSS escapes work, of course. (In XHTML, the processing of the content of style elements has been defined differently, so that HTML escapes are recognized.)

Identifiers in CSS

The HTML specifications do not prescribe the syntax of class names. It is left to stylesheet languages, and CSS is rather permissive. You don't often see non-ASCII characters in class names, though, because people are afraid of using them, partly for a reason.

In practice, it is safest to use only ASCII letters, digits, and hyphen-minus characters in class names in HTML and CSS. However, a much wider range of characters is permitted in principle. In CSS, class names are identifiers, and CSS identifiers may include:

- Letters "A" to "Z" and "a" to "z"
- Digits "0" to "9"
- ASCII hyphen (hyphen-minus) "-"
- Underscore (low line) "_"
- Any Unicode character from U+00A1 up
- Any Unicode character in an escaped form, such as "\0000A0"

There are limitations on the first character of an identifier in CSS: it must not be a digit, and identifiers starting with the ASCII hyphen are allowed in some contexts only.

The rules for CSS identifiers are important when you use CSS in conjunction with XML, where non-ASCII characters may appear in element and attribute names. Even some ASCII characters may cause problems. For example, using the colon, :, in an attribute name is common in XML (e.g., in the attribute name xml:lang), but the colon is not permitted as such in a CSS identifier. The reason is that it has a special meaning in CSS syntax. It thus needs to be escaped, if the name is used in CSS (e.g., xml\:lang).

Character and String Data

Processing of character data in computers operates on characters represented by code numbers. This is often expressed by saying that characters are treated as small integers, though especially when using Unicode, they need not be that small. A string is usually represented as a sequence of characters in consecutive storage locations. Otherwise, the representation and handling of characters varies greatly by programming language and by software modules.

Constructs and Principles of Processing Characters

For the processing of character data, programming language design needs to solve several problems, and the solutions greatly affect the suitability of the language to string-oriented tasks. You are probably not designing a new programming language, but you may need to select between some existing languages for a project, or to learn or teach a language. In the latter area, the phenomenon that psychologists call *negative transfer* is often problematic: when you have learned one way of doing things in a language (say, the difference between single and double quotes around a literal), you will implicitly assume that another language uses the same way. Even after you have learned the difference, you keep forgetting it. Therefore, it is useful to make some explicit comparisons.

The key features in the processing of character data in a programming language are:

- Repertoire: which characters can appear in data as processed inside a program?
- Typing: is there a particular data type for a character, or a string, and what are its basic properties?
- Characters versus strings: do you treat a character as a special case of a string (a string of length 1), or do you treat a string as a data structure (e.g., array) with characters as its components, or are they two distinct concepts?
- Internal implementation of a character: is it typically (and perhaps by language specification) one octet, two octets, or something different?
- Internal implementation of a string, especially information on its length (e.g., separate character count, or a terminator character, or fixed length).
- Storage allocation for strings: do you need to specify the length, or the maximum length, when declaring a string variable, or do strings automatically expand?
- Literals: how do you write a constant that denotes a single character, or a given string, perhaps an empty one?
- Operators and standard functions, such as extracting the nth character of a string, concatenating two strings, or performing a replacement operation on a string.

Modern programming languages normally have a *character* data type and a *string* data type, or both, but their relationship to each other may vary. In some languages, the character type is one of the basic types and strings are represented as arrays of characters, often with some special features that other arrays do not have. In other languages, which might be called string-oriented, the string type is one of the basic data types (or, at the extreme, the only data type). Variables with values that are individual characters might be treated just as special cases: strings of length 1.

The FORTRAN Model: Hollerith Data

FORTRAN programming was developed in the 1950s for engineering and scientific tasks. Originally, it had just two data types: integer (whole numbers) and real (floating-point numbers). Character data was just string constants added to output as headings to make it more legible. The ways of handling character data in old FORTRAN are mostly a historical curiosity only, but they are briefly described here for comparison.

Originally, FORTRAN allowed you to add explanatory text to output by using Hollerith constants in FORMAT statements, which specified the way in which numeric data was formatted when executing PRINT statements. A Hollerith constant like 5Hhello was taken as indicating a string of five characters following the letter H. That way, it was easy for a compiler to know where the string ends. To a programmer, it was not that convenient: he needed to count the characters, and count them right.

Later, a convenience was added: a quoted string like 'Hello', leaving it to a compiler to recognize the end of the string from the ending quote—actually, the ASCII apostrophe.

However, the programmer still needed to count characters if he wanted to *store* character (string) data to a variable. The reason is that such data was stored to a numeric variable, since there were no other variables. An integer or real variable was able to contain a fixed number of characters, but the number depended on the machine architecture. For example, if an integer value consisted of 36 bits and a 7-bit character code was used, an integer variable was able to contain five characters. Therefore you could write an assignment like MSG = 5Hhello or MSG = 'Hello'. However, the program was not portable to, say, a computer where an integer value is 32 bits and an 8-bit character code is used, allowing an integer variable to hold just four characters. You would, for example, declare MSG as an array and write MSG(1) = 'Hell' and MSG(2) = 'o'.

There wasn't much you could do with character data at that time. It was possible to read, store, copy, and print it, as well as compare for equality. Text processing would have been awkward, since extracting a single character from a string required extra tricks, like shifts and masks. When porting a program from one computer to another, it was often necessary to recode all processing of character data.

Later, a data type called CHARACTER was added to FORTRAN. Despite the name, it is really a string type. When declaring a string variable, you specify the length of the strings it can contain. For example, CHARACTER*20 NAME declares NAME as string of length 20. Its values will effectively be padded with spaces on the right, if you assign a shorter value to it. A substring construct was also added; for example, NAME(2:6) is a substring of NAME from the 2nd character to the 6th.

The C model

C was designed in an environment where an 8-bit byte was the basic unit of storage and any character was assumed to fit into such a byte. More or less implicitly, the character code was assumed to be ASCII, or very similar to it. Later, C has been used to process text in genuinely 8-bit encodings, too. The standard C library locale may be used to find out or to set the specific encoding used, as described in the section "Using Locales" later in this chapter.

Although C++ is very different from C in many ways, it is based on C. In character processing, C++ has copied its constructs from C. However, the I/O system is different.

The character data type

The C language has a data type called char, but in typical implementations, it really corresponds to the concept of an 8-bit byte. It has been used to store a character among other things, but that was just a technicality. C functions often operate on sequences of bytes often with no regard to their content.

In effect, the char type in C is the shortest of integer types. As an aside, it might also be used to store integers that represent characters by their code numbers. There is no type checking involved here. You can declare and assign char ch = 0; and this initializes the variable to NUL—i.e., to the character with code number 0.

However, the definition of C does not fix the range of values of char. It might be 0 to 127, corresponding to ASCII, or 0 to 255. It might even be 0..65,535, corresponding to UTF-16 code units, so that a value of type char occupies two octets. Thus, you might be able to use Unicode simply with the help of the character data type in C, but such software is not portable from one computer system to another.

Strings as arrays

In C, a string is a sequence of values of type char in consecutive storage locations. You can declare a variable that is an array of characters (e.g., char message[20]) and store characters to it using indexed variables (e.g., message[0]), as with other arrays. The index of the first component of an array is zero in C, as in many other languages.

Using the basic operators of C, text processing is awkward, since you basically need to work with individual characters by their indexes. However, there is a standard C library, string, that contains a collection of useful functions for working with arrays of characters. Operations on strings are still somewhat primitive, since you need to keep track of the lengths of strings. An array has a fixed size in C, though you can create the equivalent of an array dynamically so that its length has been computed during execution, rather than fixed when writing the program. The assignment p = malloc(n) would create a memory block sufficient for n characters and assign its address to p, which must be a pointer variable. Then you can use an indexed variable like p[i] just as if you had declared p as an array.

Many descriptions say that in C, strings are "NUL terminated," where NUL means a character with code number zero (U+0000 in Unicode). This is true in the following sense: the functions in the string library, as well as functions for string processing in C programs in general, expect the input strings to be NUL terminated—i.e., to end with NUL, which is not regarded as part of the string. Moreover, when the functions generate strings, they make them NUL terminated. String constants are implemented as NUL terminated strings; thus, the constant "foo" denotes a string of length 3, but its internal representation occupies four octets. As a C programmer, you normally follow suit by treating NUL as a string terminator and by making sure that every string you generate is NUL terminated. However, when you read characters from a file, it is better to accept possible NUL characters and perhaps just skip them on reading. Text files created with other than C programs may contain NUL, and it is possible to output NUL in C, too.

8-bit characters and sign extension

Since ASCII was usually implied, it did not matter whether values of the type were treated as unsigned or signed, since the character values always had zero as the first bit (sign bit). This created problems when C was used with a genuinely 8-bit character code, such as ISO-8859-1. Suppose that you declare and assign char ch = 'ä' and then use the character variable in an assignment with an integer on the left side: int i = ch. Since the value has the first bit set (the code of ä is E4 in hexadecimal, 11100100 in binary), the value is *sign-extended* in the assignment.

Technically, an integer normally occupies two or four octets, and the value is copied to the lowest-order octet, whereas the sign bit is copied to all bit positions in the other octets. In practice, this makes the value a negative number, corresponding to the interpretation of the octet E4 as a signed integer. In the commonly used two's complement method for implementing negative integers, this results in the value −28 (decimal).

Later, a difference was made between unsigned char and the old char type, which may or may not be signed. Declaring a variable unsigned char, you would guarantee that no sign extension is performed when the variable's value is treated as an integer due to type conversions. Compilers have compile-time switches that can be used to make the char type implemented as unsigned, but for portability, it is safer to use the explicit type name unsigned char.

Even if you declare your variables and functions as unsigned char, non-ASCII character *constants* may cause problems. In C, a character constant like 'ä' is in fact of type int (the default integer type), and, for example, a comparison like ch == 'ä' may fail to work properly. The right side could be a negative value when interpreted as an integer and a very large number when interpreted as an unsigned integer. Compile-time switches (like -funsigned-chars in the gcc compiler) might be available for forcing character constants to correct positive values. A more portable alternative is to avoid manifest character constants in statements, using macro definitions. Example:

```
#define AE ((unsigned char) 'ä')
int ch = getchar();
if(ch == AE) { /* 'ä' was received */
```

The example is somewhat confusing, since the variable is declared as int, which means a signed integer type. The reason for this is that the function getchar may return an end of file indicator, which is a negative number. The comparison works, however, since now the right side, being unsigned, is not sign-extended.

The EOF indicator

Since character data was expected to fit into 7 bits, values with the first bit set were used for various purposes such as error indicators. In particular, standard C definitions define the end of file indicator, EOF, as a macro (named constant) that expands to (-1)—i.e., minus one. For example, a function for reading a character normally returns the character but returns EOF, when there is no data left.

Therefore, functions like getchar for reading a single character are declared as being of type int and not char. Normally, the return value of such a function should first be tested against the end of file indicator (ch == EOF), typically exiting from a loop when there was no more data. After that, the value can be assumed to be the code number of a character, in the character code being used. If we work with 8-bit characters only, we could next assign the value to a variable of type unsigned char, for clarity and to protect against undesired type conversions.

The zero byte (NUL byte) convention

One of the specialties of C is that a zero byte—i.e., NUL when interpreted as an ASCII character—is used as a string terminator. Standard C functions that operate on strings effectively operate on arrays (sequences) of characters terminated by NUL. Thus, if you construct a string in C code, you need to write a NUL (conventionally written as '\0' in C, though it really means the same as plain 0) at its end. Using NUL was technically efficient on old byte-oriented computers, since at machine instruction level, testing a byte against zero value was faster than a general test for equality with a given value.

The special rule of NUL in C causes problems, for example, when you have UTF-16 encoded data. If you have, for example, ASCII or ISO-8859 and you encode it in UTF-16, every second octet will be zero. Thus, although C string functions might otherwise be used to process strings with no regard to their internal structure and encoding, this will fail for UTF-16, and for many other encodings.

In any data that might be processed with a C program, a zero octet in data is risky.

The null pointer

Thus, C has no genuine character data type but uses char as a mixed type for characters as well as for small integers and other octets. Moreover, C uses the integer 0, either as such or as explicitly cast to a pointer type, as a null pointer. The null pointer is a special pointer value indicating "not a pointer to anything." Pointer values correspond to addresses of storage units, and they are at least two octets long, often longer. Their implementation depends on the addressing architecture of the computer. In a simple implementation, pointers could be simply numbers of storage locations, with the address 0 unused so that it can be used for the null pointer. However, implementations vary, and the null pointer need not be internally represented the same way as the integer 0.

There is also a predefined name (macro) for denoting the null pointer: NULL, which expands to 0. It is often recommended for use instead of the literal 0, to indicate that a pointer is involved and not an integer. The C compiler is supposed to treat the integer 0 in a pointer context as a null pointer, no matter how the value 0 has been written in the source code and no matter what the internal representation of pointers is.

An implementation of C may also define NULL as (void *) 0. This means the value zero converted to the generic pointer type void *, which is compatible with any pointer type.

Confusion around NUL, NULL, and relatives

The main reason for discussing the null pointer in this book is its name and its predefined symbol, which are often confused with NUL, the character with code number 0 (U+0000 in Unicode). The expression NUL is not part of the C language but just a name for a control character. If desired, you could define NUL as a name in C (using, for example, the directive #define NUL '\0'), but it might easily be misread as NULL.

Such things create many possibilities for confusion, as illustrated in Table 11-4. Similar problems exist in other languages as well, though usually to a lesser degree. In the table, the assumed character code is ASCII or some extension of ASCII. The integer zero is implemented as zero octets, typically as two or four of them. The internal format of a floating-point zero is system-dependent in principle, but in practice, it is usually four zero octets. The internal representation of the null pointer is not shown, since it varies by machine architecture.

Table 11-4. Ways of being "nul" in C

Octet(s) in binary	Notation in C source	Meaning
00000000 …	0	The integer zero
00000000 …	0.	The floating-point number zero
(Null pointer)	(void *) 0	The null pointer
(Null pointer)	NULL	Macro for the null pointer
11111111	EOF	End of file indicator, same as (-1)
00000000	'\0'	The NUL character, U+0000
00100000	' '	The space character, U+0020
00110000	'0'	The digit zero, U+0030
00000000	""	An empty string
00100000 00000000	" "	A string consisting of a space

Further confusion is caused by the fact that both (void *) 0 and '\0' can be written simply as 0. In a pointer context, as in a comparison p==0 or an assignment p = 0, with p declared as a pointer, the integer zero is automatically converted to the null pointer. In a character context, as in comparing a variable against NUL, say ch=='\0', there is a different type conversion. The char type is internally treated as an integer type, and a character constant like '\0' is technically an integer constant written in a special way. The habit of writing ch=='\0' instead of ch==0 is meant to emphasize that we are dealing with character data and with the NUL character, not, for example, the digit zero.

C and Unicode

You might consider using C to process Unicode data in UTF-8 format, where each character consists of one to four octets, or in UTF-16 format, where each BMP character is represented as exactly two octets. We will discuss both approaches in the sequel.

It is however important to note that you should not reinvent the wheel, if you decide to use either of these approaches. There is a lot of existing reusable code, as C function libraries or as C++ class libraries, for operation on UTF-8 or UTF-16 in C. Thus, unless you have a very simple task or a programming assignment on a course, start from looking at existing software, such as the libutf-8 code available from several sites and the ICU code for UTF-16 at *http://icu.sourceforge.net/*.

Unicode with 8-bit Quantities?

Can you process text in Unicode, if the data type for a character is an 8-bit byte, as in classical C? The answer is yes but requires that you distinguish between "string" as a sequence of Unicode characters and "string" as a programming language concept such as a NUL-terminated array of char. You would not store a Unicode character into a variable of type char but as an array or other collection of such variables—e.g., one to four such variables, when using UTF-8.

This means, using the terminology defined in "Unicode and UTF-8" in Chapter 3, that all processing of characters actually takes place at the level of the Character Encoding Scheme. There, the representation of a character is serialized into a sequence of octets. In order to perform even a simple operation—say, scanning through a string to check whether it contains a particular character—you need to interpret the sequence of octets according to the encoding scheme (unserialize it to code numbers).

If you only read Unicode data and copy it as such, preserving the encoding, you can treat the data as if it were binary data, uninterpreted octets. Such situations are rare. However, consider the example of analyzing a logfile that is known to be encoded in some known Unicode encoding. We might be interested in summing things up, without any internal processing of character data.

The approach is used in the following rather naïve program, which expects its input to be UTF-16 encoded, more specifically in low-endian form (UTF-16LE). The program simply reads the code units and checks whether the more significant octet is zero. If not, it prints the code unit in hexadecimal and in decimal. Such processing might be useful if some data is expected to be UTF-16 encoded but mostly contain just Basic Latin and Latin 1 Supplement characters (i.e., characters U+0000..U+00FF), and you wish to list any other code points that appear:

```
#include <stdio.h>
int main() {
  unsigned int first, second;
  unsigned long code;
  while( (first=getchar()) != EOF) {
    if( (second = getchar()) == EOF) {
      fprintf(stderr, "\nError at end of data, first octet: %2X\n",
              first);
      return 1; }
    if(second != 0) {
      code = first * 0x100 + second;
      printf("%4X %6d\n", code, code); } }
  return 0; }
```

Similarly, you could process UTF-8 encoded data using the char type, pointers to char, and arrays of char, as long as you keep track of the situation. Although the string functions of C treat a zero octet (NUL) as a string terminator, this isn't a problem with UTF-8, since UTF-8 uses a zero octet only to encode U+0000. Processing UTF-16 encoded data in a similar way would generally fail, of course.

A value that represents a Unicode code number should be defined as unsigned long (or, more verbosely, unsigned long int) to avoid any surprises. This type is guaranteed to be at least 32 bits. Then you can perform conversions between different encoding forms at input and output only, performing all operations on the characters (code numbers) themselves directly.

You might encounter existing code that uses other integer types, such as the basic integer data type int, for processing Unicode numbers. Implementations of C in most modern computers have int implemented as a 32-bit integer or larger. However, the C standard allows the implementation of int as a 16-bit integer.

Using a specific integer data type such as unsigned int is in principle a clumsy and unnecessarily system-dependent approach. It also makes source code somewhat harder to understand. A more systematic method can be used. You can define a macro like the following:

```
#define UINT32 unsigned long
```

You would then systematically use UINT32 when declaring variables and functions with Unicode character values (e.g., UINT32 ch;).

Wide Characters

In modern versions of C, as well as in C++, you can use "wide characters," which correspond to a character type specified by the current locale. Wideness refers to the storage needed for such a character, not the visual appearance. The storage need not be larger than for normal characters, and it often isn't.

Wide characters need not correspond to Unicode characters. However, they *may* correspond to Unicode characters. Their meaning depends on the underlying system and possibly locale settings. On modern Windows systems, the internal representation is UTF-16, and wide characters are usually implemented as 16-bit quantities. On Unix and Linux systems, the default locale often uses some 8-bit character code, but this can usually be changed to a Unicode encoding. The repertoire of available locales depends on the implementation. Thus, if your program needs to be portable to different computers, you cannot rely on wide characters.

 It is often possible to process Unicode data using wide characters, but not portably.

The type for wide characters is wchar_t, which corresponds to some machine-level "type" (storage unit size) in an implementation-dependent manner. To work on wide character strings, you use standard functions with names beginning with wcs instead of the str prefix in traditional C string functions. For example, you get the length of a traditional string by calling the strlen standard function, and similarly, you use the wcslen function for wide character strings. To create a wide character string constant, you use the normal C string constant syntax but prefix it with the letter "L"; for example, L"Hello". As you may guess, "L" stands for "long," again referring to the storage requirements. It means that the string consists of wide characters.

The standard functions mentioned above, and other features related to wide characters, are included in the wchar and wctype libraries that were added to the C language standard in 1995. Consult suitable textbooks and references for the definitions. The following example illustrates the use of wide characters for a simple problem: reading a UTF-8 encoded file to check for characters beyond the range U+0000..U+00FF. This is similar to the previous example, except that here, UTF-8 encoding is assumed and the techniques are different. In this approach, different encodings can be used simply by changing the attribute of setlocale, if the encoding is supported by the environment:

```
#include <stdio.h>
#include <wchar.h>
#include <locale.h>
int main() {
  wchar_t ch;
  if(!setlocale(LC_CTYPE, "en_US.UTF-8")) {
    fprintf(stderr, "Cannot work in UTF-8 mode!\n");
    return 1; }
  while( (ch=fgetwc(stdin)) != WEOF) {
    if(ch > 0xFF)
      fwprintf(stdout, L"%4x %c\n", ch, ch); }
  return 0; }
```

In order to work with Unicode characters in a reasonably portable way, you could use a type name like UNICHAR and define it with a macro or with a type definition such as the following on a system where wide characters are Unicode characters:

```
typedef wchar_t UNICHAR;
```

You would then consistently use the type name so defined for all character variables and functions. When porting the program to a different system, you would replace wchar_t in this definition with, for example, unsigned int, selecting a type that can contain a Unicode code number. Although this approach, suggested in the Unicode standard, makes software more portable, it has substantial limitations. Many constructs in a program, including the standard functions you use, depend on the specific data type. For portability, you would need to modularize the program so that (ideally) only one module depends on the specific definition of the type used for Unicode characters.

Win32 APIs

An *Application Programming Interface* (API) is a coordinated set of definitions on how computer programs or parts of programs communicate with each other. Usually this involves software at two different levels, such as application programs and system programs. More concretely, an API is a collection of functions and other building blocks that a programmer can use according to their external descriptions, without knowing their internal implementation. The term API is most commonly used to refer to Windows APIs, specifically on relatively modern Windows systems such as Windows NT, Windows 2000, Windows XP, etc., collectively called Win32 APIs. Such APIs are usually described in terms of their manifestation in C or C++.

Win32 APIs support a 16-bit character type, called WCHAR, which ultimately corresponds to a UTF-16 code unit. Internally, Win32 works with such representation of characters and performs code conversions between it and codes used in application programs. As we have seen, UTF-16 code units directly correspond to Unicode characters only on the BMP, but that is sufficient for most practical purposes. Technically, WCHAR is defined as a macro that expands to unsigned short—i.e., the 16-bit unsigned integer type, corresponding to the wchar_t type of standard C.

Using the Win32 API, you can write programs so that they can be compiled to work with some 8-bit encoding (the system's "code page") or with wide characters. In C or C++ programming, you can define the constant (macro) _UNICODE to be 1 (true) or 0 (false) depending on whether you want wide characters or not. You would then declare your character variables for being of type TCHAR, which expands to wchar_t or (8-bit) char, depending on the setting of UNICODE. Similarly, you would declare a pointer to a character (or to a string) as being of type LPTSTR. It expands to wchar_t * or char *, again depending on _UNICODE. You can also use the name LPWSTR, which unambiguously means a pointer to a string of wide characters—i.e., wchar_t *. Win32 APIs that operate on text (strings) exist in two versions:

"A" versions (code page versions)
> These versions operate on 8-bit characters, according to the code page currently in use, such as windows-1252 (Windows Latin 1). The letter "A" reminds us of the misnomer "ANSI."

"W" versions (Unicode versions)
> These versions operate on wide—i.e., 16-bit—characters, or UTF-16 code units, to be exact.

For ease of programming, you can use generic names that will be resolved to "A" or "W" versions during compilation, depending on the setting of _UNICODE. For example, if you call a function with the name SetWindowText, it will be resolved to the name SetWindow-TextW when _UNICODE is set and to SetWindowTextA otherwise.

Multibyte Character Sets (MBCS) Versus Unicode

For comparison, we will briefly describe the use of sequences of octets to represent characters in a manner that differs from Unicode, namely multibyte character sets (MBCS), which are in practice usually double-byte character sets (*DBCS*). You may encounter such techniques in existing software, especially on Windows, where they have been a serious competitor of Unicode techniques. They have been used especially for Chinese and Japanese text.

In DBCS, each character is represented as 1 or 2 bytes (octets). Some bytes, called *lead bytes*, have been reserved for use as the first pair of a double-byte representation and are to be interpreted together with the next byte. Other bytes represent characters as such. The technique implies some underlying character code, often called "code page" in this context. The set of lead bytes depends on the code page, but it could be, for example, the range 81 to 9F (which corresponds to a subset of C1 Controls).

In C programming using a library that supports multibyte characters, function names starting with _mbs are used to handle multibyte character strings, corresponding to standard C string functions with names that begin with str. Thus, for example, _mbslen returns the length of a multibyte character string, as a counterpart to strlen for normal C strings (char strings) and wcslen for wide character strings.

Thus, multibyte characters are not the same as wide characters. Conversions between them are possible, of course, and libraries that support multibyte characters typically contain routines for conversions, such as mbtowc (multibyte to wide character).

It may be desirable in program development to create software that can be set, at compile time, to use 8-bit characters, multibyte characters, or wide character implementation of Unicode. For this purpose, macros that begin with _tcs can be used. They will be resolved at compile time, according to the values of the macros _UNICODE and _MBCS. For example, the name _tcslen resolves to wcslen when _UNICODE is set, to _mbslen when _MBCS is set, and to strlen when neither is set. (Setting both of them makes no sense and causes unpredictable results.)

The Perl Model

The Perl language was primarily designed for processing large amounts of text, though typically text in some fixed format, as one of the expansions of the name suggests: Practical Extraction and Report Language. Yet, Unicode support has been added to Perl only gradually and rather slowly. This book assumes that you are using Perl 5.8 or newer.

We will discuss some basic practical points in using Unicode in Perl. For more information, please refer to the relevant manpages in your Perl environment, in particular, *perluniintro* and *perlunicode*. These manpages are also available on the Web, at *http://perldoc.perl.org/perluniintro.html* and *http://perldoc.perl.org/perlunicode.html*.

Perl uses UTF-8 encoding (or, in some implementations, UTF-EBCDIC) internally. However, if your *Perl source* is UTF-8 encoded, you should use the pragma use utf8 for compatibility reasons. Handling the encoding of input data is a completely different matter and will be discussed in the section "Character Input and Output" later in this chapter.

Strings and characters in Perl

In Perl, a scalar variable may have either a string or a number as its value, and Perl usually converts automatically between the types as needed. There is no separate character type: to handle an individual character, you use a string of length one.

Perl has powerful tools for working with strings. Dealing with individual characters in a string is somewhat clumsier. To extract the fourth character from the value of $foo, you would use the expression substr($foo,3,1). This means using a substring extraction function, where the second argument is the starting position, *counting positions from 0*, and the third argument is the length of the substring.

To get the Unicode code number of a character (i.e., of a single-character string), use the ord function—e.g., ord('é'). The inverse function is chr. For example, chr(9786) or equivalently chr(0x263A), using the Perl notation for integers in hexadecimal notation, means the character U+263A—i.e., ☺.

There is a pitfall for values smaller than 256 decimal. For them, the chr function returns an 8-bit character, in an encoding that might differ from ISO-8859-1. To avoid the potential problems, use the pack function instead of chr for such values: pack("U", *n*) gives the Unicode number with code number *n*. For example, chr(0xE4) usually means ä (U+00E4), but it could mean something different; pack("U",0xE4) certainly yields ä.

The catenation operator "."

Many programming languages use the plus sign, +, both for addition of numbers and catenation of strings. There is a risk of confusion here, since adding up 2 and 5 to get 7 is completely different from catenating the strings to get 25. Languages often deal with this issue by using the *types* of variables and expressions to determine how + should be interpreted. Perl is not a typed language (in a manner that would be useful here), so it uses + for the arithmetic operation and another symbol, the period ".", for string catenation. It is best to leave spaces around the period for readability.

In output statements, you can often use the comma to separate elements, since a function accepts a list of arguments, as in print $foo, $bar;. You could alternatively use the catenation operator: print $foo . $bar;. In that case, there would be only one argument, consisting of an expression. Such an approach is necessary when calling a normal function —e.g., somefun($foo . $bar).

In Perl, double quotes mean evaluation

The use of double quotation marks versus single quotation marks makes a difference, but completely different than in C. In Perl, 'foo' and "foo" mean the same thing, namely, a particular constant string of length 3, so in such simple cases, the difference between the quotes is a matter of style, or coding guidelines. When constructs that could be Perl variables are involved, there is an essential difference:

- '$foo' denotes literally a four-character string that begins with a dollar sign.
- "$foo" denotes a string that consists of the value of the scalar variable $foo at the moment of evaluating this quoted construct.

Thus, single quotes are suitable for normal string constants that need not and should not be processed in any way as expressions. Using double quotes, you can create an expression that will be evaluated by inserting values of variables into it; e.g.:

```
print "The product of $a and $b is $c.\n";
```

The principle that no evaluation takes place between single quotes extends even to "character escapes" like \n (as listed in Table 11-1, earlier in this chapter). They are interpreted inside double quotes, but not inside single quotes. Thus, in the example, \n is interpreted as a line break, but if single quotes were used, even \n would be printed literally.

Notations for Unicode characters

In strings enclosed in double quotation marks, you can use the notation \x{ *number* } to refer to a character by its Unicode number in hexadecimal—e.g., \x{2300}. The braces are needed; without them, the reference has a different meaning. For arguments smaller than 256 decimal, 100 hexadecimal, the results are based on an 8-bit encoding (as in the case of the chr function); thus, use pack instead.

You can also refer to characters by their Unicode names using a notation of the form \n { *name* }, if you first use the pragma use charnames ':full';. Then you can write, for example, \N{DIAMETER SIGN} inside a string constant.

Using properties of characters

Collections of characters can be referred to by Unicode properties. For example, in a regular expression used for matching, p{Lu} denotes any character with General Category value of Lu (Letter, uppercase). You can also use script names in a similar manner. Block names can be used when prefixed by In—e.g., \p{InNumberForms}. The following simple example shows how to replace all Cyrillic characters with question marks: s/\p{Cyrillic}/?/g.

ECMAScript (JavaScript)

The JavaScript language, developed by Netscape for use in client-side scripting on web pages, has been rather widely implemented in web browsers, though with version differences. Different names, such as JScript, are used for trademark reasons.

String oriented

JavaScript is string-oriented, to the extent that it lacks a character type among its basic scalar types. Even numbers are commonly handled as strings. This often causes trouble for beginners, especially since the + operator is overloaded: it means both numeric addition and string catenation, depending on context. If the variable foo contains data obtained, for example, from a form field and the user has typed 42 as the data and you assign foo = foo + 1, you do not get 43 but 421. One way to deal with this is to subtract zero from the value to force it into numeric type: foo = (foo - 0) + 1.

JavaScript has an object concept, and it lets you declare string objects, which have many useful properties. For any advanced string processing, you will find string objects appropriate. The following simple code illustrates some basics. It is a form in an HTML document with one text input field and one button, which invokes a JavaScript function when clicked on. The function takes the input field content, converts it to uppercase, and makes it the new content of the field. Here the field is prefilled with the string "éω" ("e" with acute, small omega), and clicking on the button turns it to "ÉΩ." The function (method) toUpperCase is part of the JavaScript language and defined to work by Unicode rules. It should even perform full case mapping, but in practice, it may perform just simple case mapping.

```
<script type="text/javascript">
function upper(field) {
  var s = new String(field.value);
  field.value = s.toUpperCase(); }
</script>
<form action="...">
<input name="foo" id="fld" value="é&omega;">
<input type="button" value="Upper" onclick=
 "upper(document.getElementById('fld'))">
</form>
```

The ECMAScript standard

The standardized form of JavaScript is called ECMAScript, and it was defined by Ecma (as ECMA 262). The standard is available via *http://www.ecma-international.org/*. Note, however, that the standard mainly specifies the general features of ECMAScript as a programming language, as opposed to specific constructs defined for use on the Web. Those constructs relate to the Document Object Model (DOM) that specifies the mapping between HTML or XML elements and attributes and expressions in scripting languages.

UTF-16 implied

Since Version 1.3, JavaScript uses Unicode for string data. This has been standardized in ECMAScript. More exactly, string data means "Unicode string,"—i.e., a sequence of code units in UTF-16 format. The routines for string processing assume that their input is in Normalization Form C.

Although JavaScript uses UTF-16 (or, in practice, UCS-2), we can safely use UTF-8 on a web page that contains JavaScript code. The web browser is supposed to perform the transcoding internally.

Originally, the basic constructs in JavaScript, including variable names, used ASCII characters only. Other characters were permitted only in strings and comments. Later, the syntax was extended to allow Unicode identifiers, with some added features that allow even more than the default Unicode rules. However, programming practice has largely used ASCII only in identifiers.

The \u escape notation

As many other languages, JavaScript lets you write characters in string constants (in a source program) using a notation that consists of \u immediately followed by a character's Unicode number in hexadecimal. The following trivial program illustrates this. It has been written inside a script element so that it could be immediately embedded into an HTML document.

```
<script type="text/javascript">
var message = "I \u2665 Unicode! \u263A";
alert(message);
document.write(message);
</script>
```

If you view an HTML document containing such a `script` element, you should see the text "I ♥ Unicode! ☺" appear in your HTML document, provided of course that you use a JavaScript-enabled browser. Whether you see the characters properly depends on the font in use. You should also see the same text appear in a small pop-up window, since that's what the `alert` function does. However, the font that a browser uses in such windows is often different from the default font it uses for web pages. This may mean that the special characters are not visible, but small boxes might appear instead. The font used in pop-up windows is under the control of the browser and the operating system and cannot be affected by the document author in any normal way. Thus, avoid special characters in pop-ups.

PHP: Mostly Just 8 Bits

The PHP language, commonly used in web authoring, operates on 8-bit characters only. This applies to PHP 5, too. To get some Unicode support, you need to use the string functions `utf8_encode` and `utf8_decode`, which convert from ISO-8859-1 to UTF-8 and vice versa. See *http://www.php.net/utf8_encode* for their usage. Character and string constants in PHP closely follow the Perl model.

An HTML document created by PHP can, however, contain any Unicode characters, since you can express them as character references like `&#x2665;`.

Java: Rich Support to Unicode

Java has extensive support to Unicode. In addition to basic constructs needed for processing Unicode characters and strings, Java libraries intrinsically work by Unicode models. This means, among other things, that case conversion routines use the definitions in the Unicode character database. Java also allows non-ASCII characters in Java identifiers, though practical considerations still often make programmers avoid them.

Standard Java libraries contain a large number of classes for Unicode support such as input methods for Unicode characters, sorting according to the principles of the Unicode Collation Algorithm, and detection of text boundaries. In modern Java implementations, the output routines support the Unicode bidirectional algorithm as well as contextual shaping of characters as needed for correct rendering of many languages—e.g., Arabic. There are also classes for more technical tasks such as conversions between character encodings, so that you can make a Java program accept data in different encodings. In addition to standard libraries included in Java implementations, there are open source libraries available for Unicode-related operations, such as transliteration.

Characters, strings, objects, and methods

In Java, 'a' is a character constant, whereas "a" denotes an object of type String. The difference is even more fundamental than in C, since in Java, objects can be used in many ways that cannot be applied to simple scalar values. In an object-oriented language like Java, functions are properties of objects and often called *methods* of objects.

A character constant is of type char, which is a simple scalar type, not an object. You can however use the Character class, which wraps a simple character value in an object. You can declare, for example, Character ch = new Character('a') to create a new Character object with a specific initial value.

A function invocation in Java generally consists of the name of a class or object, a dot (period, full stop), the name of the method, and a parenthesized list of arguments. (The class or object may be implied in some situations, in which case the dot is omitted, too.) For example, "Hello world".length() is a function invocation, using a method of a String object. No arguments are passed to the function, since the function operates on the object. As you guessed, this is a standard function that returns the length of a string.

Encodings and escape notations

A Java implementation may read Java source code in different encodings, but internally, it converts it to Unicode. A programmer may create a source file in some Unicode encoding and use characters directly. However, your system might use some other encoding by default. For example, if you work with Java on Unix or Linux, the odds are that the native encoding is ISO-8859-1 and the Java compiler assumes that, too. You can probably specify the encoding of your Java source in a command option when you invoke the Java compiler (note the spelling UTF8 and note that you might not get any error message if you spell it incorrectly!):

```
javac -encoding UTF8 mytest.java
```

Alternatively, you can use some other encoding, such as ASCII, and use the \u notation (\u followed by four hexadecimal digits; e.g., \u00df) to write characters that cannot be typed directly. Unlike ECMAScript, which allows such notations in character and string constants only, Java allows them anywhere in the source. Thus, you could use rôle as a variable name in Java, and you could also write it as r\uF4le. However, it is still common to use only ASCII characters in names, to avoid any potential problems with defective implementations and old software that might be needed in conjunction with Java program.

The following Java program is a little more than a "Hello world" program. First, it includes a special character in its output. Second, it writes the output both in the console and in a message window. The reason is that if you test this program, you may well see the console output without the special character, because the default console font is rather limited:

```
import javax.swing.*;
public class HelloWorld {
    public static void show(String text) {
        JOptionPane.showMessageDialog(null,text);
    }
```

```
    public static void main(String[] args) {
        String msg = "Hello world! \u263A";
        System.out.println(msg);
        show(msg);
        System.exit(0);
    }
}
```

16-bit characters

In Java, the values of type char are 16 bits long. For example, a character constant such as 'x' is automatically implemented that way. Technically, the values are UTF-16 code units, not characters, though these concepts coincide for characters in the Basic Multilingual Plane (BMP). This means that you can directly use any characters in the BMP, but anything outside it needs to be handled differently. Thus, Java is Unicode-oriented, but in an old-fashioned way.

 The character concept in Java corresponds to a BMP character, or a code unit in UTF-16. Other Unicode characters are represented as integers and called "code points" in Java.

Internally, a value of type char is represented by its code number. Logically, characters are distinct from numbers (integers), though. To obtain the Unicode code number of a character variable ch, you can assign it to a numeric variable: int code = ch.

The Java String class (for immutable strings), as well as the StringBuffer class (for strings that may vary in length and content), is based on the char type. Thus, a Java string is really a "Unicode string"—i.e., a sequence of UTF-16 code units, not characters.

If you need characters outside BMP, you can use the integer type int for characters. Java 5.0 has added methods to the Character, String, and related classes for working with text in such representation. As an alternative to this, you could use surrogates—i.e., represent a non-BMP character as a pair of two char values that represent a surrogate pair. You cannot use the \u notation for characters outside the BMP, but you can represent them as integers using a notation like 0x2f81a, (for U+2F81A)—i.e., digit zero and letter "x" followed by the number in hexadecimal.

Java identifiers

Java allows a rich repertoire of characters in identifiers according to the Unicode identifier concept, with the extension that the dollar sign $ and the underscore (low line) _ are allowed anywhere in an identifier. It is however still common to stick to using ASCII in Java identifiers, since programmers do not know about the possibilities or do not dare to use them.

Java identifiers are case-sensitive; isDigit and isdigit are distinct identifiers. It is recommended and common practice to use lowercase and uppercase in identifiers in a particular style. Names of variables and functions (methods) normally start with a low-

---

ercase letter, and uppercase letters correspond to starting a new word in the corresponding natural-language expression (e.g., "is digit" makes isDigit).

Library routines

A modern installation of Java contains a collection of very useful functions and defined symbols for working with characters, in the java.lang.Character class. You need to use the Character. prefix for identifiers defined in the class when you use them in your program. For example, Character.getType(ch) returns the General Category value of the character stored in the variable ch.

For details, consult the documentation at *http://java.sun.com*, such as the description of the class at *http://java.sun.com/j2se/1.5.0/docs/api/java/lang/Character.html*.

The functions (methods) have some naming rules:

is... *methods*
> These are Boolean (yes/no) functions for testing whether a property has the value true for a character, passed as the argument. For example, isDigit. They correspond to yes/no properties formally defined in the Unicode standard, such as the Digit property. (See Chapter 5.)

get... *methods*
> These functions return the value of a property for a character, for a property with something other than a yes/no value. For example, getType gives the value of the General Category property for its argument. The values of this function are defined as symbolic names, formed from the long names of Unicode properties but in all uppercase, with the comma omitted and parts around the comma swapped, and with underscores instead of spaces. Thus, Letter, uppercase is UPPERCASE_LETTER. (There are some deviations from this mapping of names, as indicated in a sample program later.) The getNumericValue function returns the value of the Numeric Value property as an integer, with the convention that it returns -1 if no numeric value exists and -2 if the value is not expressible as an integer.

to... *methods*
> These are various conversion functions. The functions toUpperCase, toLowerCase, and toTitleCase return the uppercase, lowercase, and titlecase form of the argument, respectively. They apply full case mappings, and so do the string functions with the same names. The function toCodePoint takes two Java char values representing a high surrogate and a low surrogate and returns the corresponding Unicode character (codepoint). The toChar function can be used to perform the reverse operation—i.e., to convert a non-BMP character to surrogate form.

Not all Unicode properties have direct Java counterparts, but the available methods cover much of the common needs. The web site *http://www.fileformat.info/info/unicode/char/* contains searchable information about Unicode characters in a format that contains a table of Java method values for a character, but you could easily write a Java program that prints similar information.

To illustrate the use of the functions, here is Java code that traverses through a string and prints all characters that are neither letters nor whitespace characters. Each character is printed on a new line and followed by an indication of the Unicode block it belongs to. The symbol ! denotes negation in Java, && means "and," and the operator + means string catenation when applied to strings:

```java
import javax.swing.*;
public class Hello {
    public static void main(String[] args) {
        String msg = "Hello world! \u263a";
        for(int i = 0; i < msg.length(); i++) {
            char ch = msg.charAt(i);
            if(!Character.isLetter(ch) &&
                !Character.isWhitespace(ch)) {
                System.out.println(ch + " in " +
                    Character.UnicodeBlock.of(ch)); }}
        System.exit(0);
    }
}
```

The program prints the following (except that the smiling face might appear as something different—e.g., ?—due to limitations of a font):

```
! in BASIC_LATIN
☺ in MISCELLANEOUS_SYMBOLS
```

 Unicode property names are case-insensitive, but their Java counterparts are case-sensitive, as are all identifiers in Java. The same applies to values like BASIC_LATIN.

The Java functions corresponding to Unicode properties are listed in Table 11-5 (without the Character. prefix in the function names). The order is by the short name of the Unicode property, as in the description of the properties in Chapter 5. Only a subset of the Unicode properties is directly covered by Java functions.

Table 11-5. Mapping of Unicode properties to Java constructs

Short	Long name of property	Java function
Alpha	Alphabetic	(See note after the table)
bc	Bidi Class	getDirectionality
Bidi M	Bidi Mirrored	isMirrored
blk	Block	UnicodeBlock.of
gc	General Category	getType
IDC	ID Continue	isUnicodeIdentifierPart
IDS	ID Start	isUnicodeIdentifierStart
lc	Lowercase Mapping	toLowerCase
Lower	Lowercase	isLowerCase

Short	Long name of property	Java function
nv	Numeric Value	getNumericValue
tc	Titlecase Mapping	toTitleCase
uc	Uppercase Mapping	toUpperCase
Upper	Uppercase	isUpperCase
WSpace	White Space	isWhitespace

The Java function isLetter doesn't quite correspond to the Alphabetic property, since the latter is true also for characters with General Category value of Nl (Number, letter) and for characters with the OAlpha (Other, Alphabetic) property. For most practical purposes, isLetter is adequate for testing whether a character is alphabetic. In some cases, isUnicodeIdentifierStart is better, since it includes Nl.

In addition to functions like isUnicodeIdentifierStart, there are functions like isJavaIdentifierStart, which are quite similar but allow $ and _, too.

In Java 5.0 and later, most of the functions that correspond to Unicode properties are defined both for character (char) and integer (int) arguments. In the latter case, the argument is treated as a code point, which may refer outside the BMP. Thus, you can relatively conveniently work with non-BMP characters, too.

The return values of functions that correspond to Unicode properties with enumerated values are technically of type byte or int. The values, encoded as integers, have symbolic names, though. For example, the value L (Left-to-Right) of the Bidi Class property corresponds to DIRECTIONALITY_LEFT_TO_RIGHT.

There are some predefined functions in Java that are not directly related to Unicode properties. They are summarized in Table 11-6. The type is indicated in a simple manner, without a static qualifier. In the "Invocation" column, the arguments of functions are specified by the names of their types. The CodePointAt function and relatives (e.g., CodePointBefore) are not listed in the table; they can be used to pick up a code point from a character array or sequence.

Table 11-6. Additional methods in java.lang.Character

Type	Invocation	Meaning
int	charCount(int)	Number of char values (1 or 2) needed to represent the code point
char	charValue()	Value of the Character object as a char
int	compareTo(Character)	Comparison using code numbers
int	digit(char,int)	Numeric value of the character, using the radix specified by the second argument
boolean	equals(Object)	Tests for equality by char value
boolean	isDefined(char)	Tests whether the code point is assigned

Type	Invocation	Meaning
boolean	isDigit(char)	Tests for being a decimal digit—i.e., gc = Nd
boolean	isHighSurrogate(char)	Tests for being a high surrogate code unit
boolean	isISOControl(char)	Tests for being a C0 or C1 Control character
boolean	isLetter(char)	Tests whether gc is Lu, Ll, Lt, Lm, or Lo
boolean	isLetterOrDigit(char)	Either isLetter or isDigit returns true
boolean	isLowSurrogate(char)	Tests for being a high surrogate code unit
boolean	isSpace(char)	Tests for space character: gc is Zs, Zl, or Zp
boolean	isTitleCase(char)	Tests whether gc = Lt

The Preparedness Principle

Well-written program code is prepared for handling any input data, even data that should not occur. Handling may of course consist of simply detecting an error and, for example, skipping erroneous data silently, skipping it with a warning message, or reporting an error and terminating. In writing a subroutine that will not be called from outside our program, we might consider relying on the caller to pass correct data only, to save both programming and execution time. When writing library routines, especially if they perform complex tasks, the programmer should normally check all input data and expect that, for example, a parameter of string type may contain just anything and of any length.

Processing of character data needs to be efficient, too, if the amount of data is large or processing takes place very often. In most applications, the expected character data is from a small repertoire. When processing data that represents people's answers to questions like "How many...?", we should quickly process an answer that consists of common digits. Whether anything else is treated as an error is a different matter. You might decide to accept other digits too, or even some verbal expressions.

Being Prepared for Amount of Data

In particular, in program code to be invoked by other programs or directly by users in an open environment (e.g., CGI scripts on the Web), checking all data is crucial. The software should expect literally anything, such as a gigabyte of junk sent by a confused or malevolent user. Many attempts at breaking into systems or at making them execute code written by a cracker are based on assumed unpreparedness. Typically, a cracker sends special data that is expected to cause buffer overflow—i.e., to make a program store a string larger than the buffer area allocated for it. The overflow may cause the attacker's data to overwrite the program's code so that next it will be executed.

In a form on a web page, even if you use an attribute that is expected to limit the amount of data, it can be overruled. Your form might contain <input name="foo" maxlength="80" size="50">, setting the visible width of a text input field to (about) 50 characters and the maximum amount of data to 80 characters. However, anyone could copy the page, edit the form, and modify or remove the restriction, just to do some experimentation or customization or to break your form handler. This could mean sending data where the field is millions of characters long.

Thus, the classical advice on handling strings in Henry Spencer's *Ten Commandments for C Programmers* is particularly important in the modern world:

> Thou shalt check the array bounds of all strings (indeed, all arrays), for surely where thou typest "foo" someone someday shall type "supercalifragilisticexpialidocious."

Of course, you might not use arrays to implement strings in the programming language you use, but the principle is the same: check the lengths of strings.

Being Prepared for Content of Data

In the modern world, we also need to be prepared for any *content* in strings. Someone someday will type %46\efŵβ⅔ركاﺂﺓ ЯΩ‡♪ or something weirder. There are two basic aspects:

- A string may contain characters that have *special effects* in the program. For example, a program might contain a search operation controlled by a string supplied as data. This may involve security threats by allowing intruders to execute their own code or make the program crash. For examples of what this might mean in the Perl language, and for measures against it, see the Perlmeme.org HOWTO entry "How do I use taint mode," *http://perlmeme.org/howtos/secure_code/taint.html*.

- Some characters may confuse the *data processing* in a program because there is not programmed handling for them. Of course, most programs are meant to handle only a small repertoire of characters in a useful way. A program should however at least skip characters that it does not know.

Methods of handling unexpected characters

When a program encounters a character (or a code point) that it is not prepared to handle normally, it can perform one or several of the following actions. The choice depends, among other things, on the application, its interactivity, and the type of the character.

Pass it through
> The character could be treated as an unknown character, which is just passing by. Even though the program does not "know" the character, it would store it as part of a string and save it or pass it forward to any other program.

Skip (ignore) it
> This means behaving as if the character were not present in the input. The character is removed when storing input data into a program variable or data structure. This can be adequate for characters that are expected to result from conversions, other technical transformations, and software tools used to create a file. For example, data often contains NUL (U+0000) characters for such reasons, and normally NUL has no

meaning in input data. Skipping any Unicode character that a program is not designed to handle is a feasible strategy in some situations.

Warn about it

A program might issue a warning about a character that it cannot handle meaningfully, especially if the character is not expected to appear. The warning might be formulated as an error message, too. The warning should normally identify the character by its Unicode number—e.g., "Unrecognized character (U+1234) detected at line 42 – ignored." The number is probably useless to an end user, but it helps a professional who has been asked to help with the problem. It might be more user-friendly to issue a message that indicates the type of the character (such as "Unrecognized letter (U+1234) ...")—e.g., by its General Category property value, using a suitable library function.

Map it to something else

A program could treat a character as corresponding to another character, which it can handle properly. This is often user-friendly, but it is also risky. For example, a program that does not handle accented letters could treat them as equivalent to the corresponding unaccented letter. If your database stores strings in ASCII format, you could still allow accents in user input, so that searching for "Rhône" would find an entry about "Rhone." When character data is to be stored, you should probably warn the user about the mapping.

Displaying unrecognized or undisplayable code points

A program may need to handle unrecognized characters on display. Any software that renders character data should be somehow prepared for the unexpected. Even if you have some planned processing for any defined Unicode character, the data might contain an unassigned code point, a private use code point, or a noncharacter. Unassigned code points might be assigned later, so handling them means being aware of new versions of Unicode.

When an output routine receives a character that it does not understand, it is usually too late to report an error. Errors should be handled at a higher level in the program logic, and the output routine should expect that this has been done. The Unicode standard mentions, descriptively, the following methods of rendering unassigned code points and private use code points (assuming, of course, that the application does not assign a meaning to such code points):

- Display the code number in four to six hexadecimal digits
- Display a black or white box
- Display a generic, character-like symbol, possibly using different symbols to denote unassigned code points and private use code points
- Display nothing; this is recommended for a collection of code points known as default ignorable code points.

In practice, programs often use the question mark ?, too. This, as well as displaying the code number as such, is problem because it cannot always be distinguished from the display of actual data. If possible, use some special formatting (say, a different color) to indicate that something special has happened. Displaying the code number can be informative to people who know character codes but confusing to others. In any case, it might be a good idea to use some delimiters, such as <E000> or {E000} instead of just E000. If possible, use delimiters that do not normally appear as data characters.

Similar considerations apply to characters that a program recognizes but cannot display, typically due to font restrictions. The standard suggests that the program could display a glyph that reflects the type of the character, as derived from its known properties.

Default ignorable code points

The Unicode standard defines some characters as ignorable in display by default—i.e., to be ignored on output if they are not supported in a constructive manner. These characters have no visible glyph or advance width, but when adequately implemented, they may affect the display, positioning, or adornment of adjacent or surrounding characters. The idea is that if a program does not know how to do so, it should not display anything for the character, not even a symbol for a missing character.

Default ignorable code points are described by the Default Ignorable Code Point (DI) property, defined in the *DerivedCoreProperties.txt* file of the Unicode database. It is a derived property and covers the following:

- Code points with a General Category value of Cf (Other, format), Cs (Other, surrogate, or Cc (Other, control), *except* whitespace characters (e.g., TAB) and interlinear annotation characters U+FFF9..U+FFFB
- Noncharacter code points
- A set of other characters, defined by the Other Default Ignorable Code Point (ODI) property (in the file *PropList.txt*); currently, the set contains the combining grapheme joiner U+034F, some Hangul filler characters, and some reserved code points

Default ignorable code points include the soft hyphen U+00A0, the word joiner U+2060, and the left-to-right mark U+200E and the right-to-left mark U+200F (which all have General Category = Cf). Thus, if a program does not support the functionality expressed with some of these characters, it should completely ignore the character on display.

It is permissible for a program to present default ignorable code points in special circumstances, even when it does not implement them as defined. In particular, word processors and layout design programs often have a display mode where invisible formatting characters are shown in some special way.

Table-Driven Versus Property-Driven Processing

In old-style programs that are meant to read ASCII data only, there are only 128 possible input values. In practice, the program actually reads 8 bits, so it should check that the first bit is zero and do something special if it is not. The processing of any normal data, however, can start with a simple branching that uses, for example, a case or switch statement or something similar (depending on language). It is feasible to handle all the possible 128 cases. Alternatively, you could use a table-driven approach that uses a 128-element table to map an input character to something manageable, such as an indicator of its class, according to an application-dependent classification.

In the simplest cases, a program can just test for an input character being "interesting" in the context of the application and skip all other characters. For example, when reading numeric data, a program could recognize just digits and a few other characters like "." and "-" and ignore the rest. However, it is usually much better to report unexpected characters as errors or at least warnings.

When 8-bit character codes are used, similar simple approaches can still be used. A 256-element decision table (or branching construct) is usually not excessively large. When a program reads Unicode data, the situation changes. Even if we consider only BMP characters, there would be tens of thousands of entries to consider. Although modern computers can store and use large tables, the programming work would be excessive.

The Unicode properties of character are, in part, meant to be used to make program logic simpler and programs smaller. You could, for example, first use the General Category property value for the initial branching. You could even group these values by their initial letter: letter (L), mark (M), number (N), separator (Z), punctuation (P), symbol (S), and other (C).

The following rather simple program illustrates several principles described in this chapter. It is meant to work in an environment in which character display is limited to ASCII. It processes a Unicode string and presents it so that ASCII characters are displayed as such whereas other characters are shown using special notations like "[L:f4]," where "L" indicates the character as a letter and "f4" is its code number in hexadecimal. Such presentation might be useful to a knowledgeable person who needs to inspect the content of a Unicode file that mostly consists of ASCII characters. The program branches according to the General Category (gc) value of the character, as obtained using the getType function; the gc values as defined in the Unicode standard are given in comments:

```java
public class show {
    public static void printc(String symbol, int data) {
        System.out.print("[" + symbol +
                         Integer.toHexString(data) + "]"); }
    public static void main(String[] args) {
        String msg = "Rhône, 42\u00a0§, price £50";
        for(int i = 0; i < msg.length(); i++) {
            char ch = msg.charAt(i);
            int code = ch;
            if(code < 0x7F) {    /* ASCII */
                System.out.print(ch); }
            else switch(Character.getType(ch)) {
            case Character.UPPERCASE_LETTER:        /* Lu */
            case Character.LOWERCASE_LETTER:        /* Ll */
            case Character.TITLECASE_LETTER:        /* Lt */
            case Character.MODIFIER_LETTER:         /* Lm */
            case Character.OTHER_LETTER:            /* Lo */
```

```
    printc("L:", code);
    break;
case Character.DECIMAL_DIGIT_NUMBER:      /* Nd */
case Character.LETTER_NUMBER:             /* Nl */
case Character.OTHER_NUMBER:              /* No */
    printc("N:", code);
    break;
case Character.NON_SPACING_MARK:          /* Mn */
case Character.COMBINING_SPACING_MARK:    /* Mc */
case Character.ENCLOSING_MARK:            /* Me */
    printc("~:", code);
    break;
case Character.SPACE_SEPARATOR:           /* Zs */
    printc(" :", code);
    break;
case Character.LINE_SEPARATOR:            /* Zl */
    System.out.println();
    break;
case Character.PARAGRAPH_SEPARATOR:       /* Zp */
    System.out.println();
    System.out.println();
    break;
case Character.CONTROL:                   /* Cc */
case Character.FORMAT:                     /* Cf */
case Character.SURROGATE:                  /* Cs */
case Character.UNASSIGNED:                 /* Cn */
    if(Character.isWhitespace(ch)) {
        System.out.print(ch); }
    else if(code >= 0xFFF9 && code <= 0xFFFB) {
        printc("A:", code); }
    /* Otherwise: default ignorable, no display */
    break;
case Character.PRIVATE_USE:               /* Co */
    printc("P:", code);
    break;
case Character.CONNECTOR_PUNCTUATION:     /* Pc */
    printc("_:", code);
    break;
case Character.DASH_PUNCTUATION:          /* Pd */
    printc("-:", code);
case Character.START_PUNCTUATION:         /* Ps */
    printc("(:", code);
    break;
case Character.END_PUNCTUATION:           /* Pe */
    printc("):", code);
    break;
case Character.INITIAL_QUOTE_PUNCTUATION: /* Pi */
    System.out.print("[quote]}");
    break;
case Character.FINAL_QUOTE_PUNCTUATION:   /* Pf */
    System.out.print("[unquote]");
    break;
case Character.OTHER_PUNCTUATION:         /* Po */
    printc("!:", code);
    break;
```

```
        case Character.MATH_SYMBOL:                /* Sm */
            printc("+:", code);
            break;
        case Character.CURRENCY_SYMBOL:            /* Sc */
            printc("$:", code);
            break;
        case Character.MODIFIER_SYMBOL:            /* Sk */
            printc("^:", code);
            break;
        case Character.OTHER_SYMBOL:               /* So */
            printc("S:", code);
            break;
        default:
            printc("??:", code);
            break; } }
    System.out.println();
    System.exit(0);
  }
}
```

The program outputs:

```
Rh[L:f4]ne, 42 [S:a7], price [$:a3]50
```

Some old Java implementations classify characters with gc values Pi or Pf as if the values were Ps or Pe, respectively. Therefore, they are unable to recognize the predefined names `INITIAL_QUOTE_PUNCTUATION` and `FINAL_QUOTE_PUNCTUATION`.

Naïve Processing

In old programs, character data is often processed in a naïve manner that assumes a particular character code, typically ASCII. You might even see code like `ch == 32`, which tests for a character being a space, using the ASCII code, instead of the more natural and more portable `ch == ' '`.

Suppose that the variable `ch` contains a single character and we wish to test whether the value is a letter. The following style (exemplified here using the C language notation) is often used in old software:

```
if( ((ch >= 'A') && (ch <= 'Z')) || ((ch >= 'a') && (ch <= 'z')) ) …
```

Here, && means "and" and || means "or," and the expression operates on comparisons that test whether the character's code number is between the code numbers of "A" and "Z" or between the code numbers of "a" and "z." Generally, in programming languages, comparisons of character values operate on the code numbers of characters.

If the data contains only basic Latin letters, the naïve approach works in most cases. The reason is that in most character codes, those letters are in alphabetic order and consecutive —i.e., there is nothing but letters between "A" and "Z" or between "a" and "z" in the code. However, the assumption is not correct for the EBCDIC code, as described in Chapter 3.

A more serious problem is that the approach fails for letters with diacritic marks, or for other than basic Latin letters in general. It would be awkward to write code that compares a character value against all the possible letters that might appear in Unicode data. A modern approach, which has been good style for a long time, is to use subprogram (function) calls that test such things. For example, in C, using the standard function library that you may refer to by using #include <string.h> in your program, you can write as follows:

```
if(isletter(ch)) …
```

This is both simpler and more robust. However, it makes the program depend on the definition of the isletter function, which can be locale-dependent. This can be a problem or an asset (see the section "Using Locales" later in this chapter).

Character Input and Output

In this section, we will discuss some special topics of character I/O. The most general question here is whether we should read and write characters one at a time or by lines. This reflects an old division: in the early days of computing, I/O was line oriented, typically with punched cards (corresponding to lines of exactly 80 characters) as input devices and a line printer (typically with line length of 80 or 132) as an output device. After describing these modes, we consider Java file I/O and some character input problems in web forms.

Character-Oriented and Line-Oriented Processing

In character-oriented input, a program reads a character at a time, typically using a subprogram like getchar() in C. This means that line breaks will appear as characters returned by the subprogram. Normally they are canonicalized, by the programming language's basic I/O routines, to some unified representation. For example, in C, the getchar() function returns the character denoted by the character literal '\n'. The identity of line break varies between C implementations—in practice, it is either CR or LF. In any case, you can test for end of line by using code like if(ch == '\n')....

In line-oriented input, a complete line is read at a time. The data is typically stored to a memory area specified by a parameter of the invocation of the input routine. It is usually the caller's responsibility to allocate sufficient storage for the data. FORTRAN uses primarily line-oriented I/O: one read operation reads at least one line, or (physical) record, to use the FORTRAN terminology.

It is easy to build line-oriented input upon character-oriented input; the opposite is not possible in any direct way. The C language, for example, has line-oriented I/O functions as well, such as gets() for getting an entire line, though it may read just part of a line in some cases. However, many people think that such functions are unsafe, since it is difficult to control the input process and too easy to fail to allocate sufficient storage. Thus, the argument goes, you might just as well write code of your own for reading a line using a function for reading one character.

In Perl, input is essentially line-oriented. It is also implicit in the sense that you do not write a subprogram call but enclose a file handle in the <> operator. The evaluation of a file handle implies the input of a line. Thus, if you write $foo = <STDIN> in Perl, you ask the Perl interpreter to read a line of input from the STDIN file and assign the data (including the trailing end of line character) to the variable $foo. Things can be even more implicit in Perl. If you write while(<STDIN>) { zap(); }, then you have written a loop that reads the entire STDIN file (standard input) one line at a time and executes the subprogram call zap(). Within the subprogram, the current input line can be accessed as the value of the built-in variable $_.

In order to process input character by character in Perl, you would read a line and then use string processing operators to extract individual characters. Moreover, to refer to a single character in a string, you would use substr, the substring operator, and specify a substring of length 1. This may sound clumsy, but Perl programmers are used to it. On the other hand, they try to avoid dealing with characters on such an individual basis and use matching and replacement operators instead.

Perl has the interesting feature that although you read a line at a time, you can make an entire file a single line as far as Perl I/O is considered. The tool to use is the special variable $/, which specifies the character to be recognized as line break. By explicitly setting it to an undefined value, you tell Perl to treat no character as line break. This means that CR or LF will be read and treated as normal data characters. Thus, assuming you have opened a file and assigned the handle DATA to it, the following Perl code would read the entire content of the file into the variable $stuff as one string:

```
$/ = undef;
my $stuff = <DATA>;
```

This is very handy in many situations, where the program can be simplified by treating the input file as one long string stored into a scalar variable. A typical example is a simple replacement operation that should be performed throughout the data. The following program copies a file to another, replacing each occurrence of the euro sign € (U+20AC) with the word "euros":

```
open(IN, "<:utf8", "orig.txt") or die "can't do input";
open(OUT, ">:utf8", "new.txt") or die "can't do output";
$/ = undef;
$all = <IN>;
print $all;
$all =~ s/\x{20AC}/euros/g;
print OUT $all;
```

Perl I/O

Although Perl uses internally UTF-8, it does not interpret input data as UTF-8 encoded by default. Instead, it uses the encoding that is normal in its environment or that has been specified in the locale settings. One reason for this is compatibility: it keeps old programs working. To make programs use UTF-8 on input, you need to specify the encoding.

In Perl, a scalar value is internally accompanied with a utf8 flag, which indicates whether the value is to be interpreted as UTF-8 encoded. String constants, for example, have this flag set. When reading from a file, you normally get data that does not have the flag set. To specify that an input file be read as UTF-8, you can do as follows in order to open a file and to read its first line into a variable:

```
open(IN, "<:utf8", "data.utx") or die "Missing data file";
$dataline = <IN>;
```

In the extra argument "<:utf8", the less-than sign specifies that the file is opened for input only, and the rest specifies the encoding to be used. The filename is given in another argument. As you might guess, you can open an output file for writing in UTF-8 encoding in a similar manner—e.g., open(OUT, ">:utf8", "results.txt").

Alternatively, you can open an input file without the extra argument and convert the data after reading it. For this, you would use the Encode package. The following example shows just the basic approach. It does not contain error processing for the encoding operation, which may fail, since the data might not be valid UTF-8 data:

```
require Encode;
open(IN, "<data.utx") or die "Missing data file";
$dataline = Encode::decode_utf8(<IN>);
```

In the output of Unicode characters in Perl, a common problem is the warning "Wide character in print." Technically, the reason is that you write UTF-8 characters to a stream that has not been opened for such writing. This can be prevented by opening an output stream in UTF-8 mode, as described above. For the standard output stream STDOUT, you use a statement that changes its mode, as in the following example:

```
binmode STDOUT, ":utf8";
print "Hello world \x{263A}!\n";
```

The following demonstration program combines some of the techniques discussed here. It copies a UTF-8 encoded file but replaces Greek letters with inverted question marks, ¿:

```
use charnames ':full';
open(IN, "<:utf8", "data.utx") or die "Missing data file";
open(OUT, ">:utf8", "data2.utx") or die "Cannot open output file";
$line = 0;
while(<IN>) {
    $line++;
    if($count = s/\p{Greek}/\N{INVERTED QUESTION MARK}/g) {
        print "$count replacement(s) on line $line.\n"; }
    print OUT $_; }
```

You can specify other encodings, too, when you open a file. Instead of utf8, you would use a construct of the form encoding(*name*) in the second argument of open. The following program performs a code conversion from windows-1252 to UTF-8:

```
open(IN, "<:encoding(windows-1252)", "dat.txt") or die "No data file";
open(OUT, ">:utf8", "dat2.txt") or die "Cannot write output";
while(<IN>) {
    print OUT; }
```

Java File I/O

In Java, you can perform file output in several ways, such as the following:

- Functions like print and println in the PrintWriter class, for textual output. The format is in the system's native encoding, which may well be a non-Unicode encoding. These functions are polymorphic (generic)—i.e., they accept arguments of different types.

- The write function in the OutputStreamWriter class, which acts as a bridge between streams of characters and streams of octets, encoding character data as needed. The function is polymorphic: the argument can be a character, an array of characters, or a string. The default encoding is the system's native encoding, but the encoding (such as UTF-8) can be specified as a second argument when creating an OutputStreamWriter object.

- The write... functions in the DataOutputStream class. They mean "binary" output, and for character and string data, this means UTF-16 format. You need to select the function name according to the argument type—e.g., writeChars for a string.

- The writeUTF function in the DataOutputStream class. It takes a string argument, so to write anything else, you need to convert it to a string first. The function writes data in the Modified UTF-8 encoding (see Chapter 6). This means that the NUL character and all non-BMP characters are represented differently from UTF-8. Moreover, the function first writes two octets that indicate (when interpreted as a 16-bit integer) the number of octets that constitute the data. Of course, such data is meant to be read by the corresponding input routine, readUTF, or other code that recognizes or at least skips the octets that express the count.

The following program illustrates writing a string into a file in each of the ways described above. The test string is the three-character string written in Java source as Aé\u263a. The first character is an ASCII character, the second one is a Latin 1 character that occupies two octets in UTF-8, and the third one is U+263A, the smiling face:

```java
import java.io.*;
public class output {
    public static void main(String[] args) {

        String msg = "Aé\u263a";
        String filename = "test.txt";
        try {
            OutputStream testf = new FileOutputStream(filename);
            PrintWriter testfile = new PrintWriter(testf);
            testfile.print(msg);
            testfile.close();
            System.out.println("Wrote " + filename);
        } catch(Exception error) {
            System.out.println("Failed to write " + filename); }

        filename = "testu.txt";
        try {
            OutputStream testf = new FileOutputStream(filename);
```

```
        OutputStreamWriter testfile =
            new OutputStreamWriter(testf,"UTF-8");
        testfile.write(msg);
        testfile.close();
        System.out.println("Wrote " + filename);
    } catch(Exception error) {
        System.out.println("Failed to write " + filename); }

    filename = "test16.txt";
    try {
        OutputStream testf = new FileOutputStream(filename);
        DataOutputStream testfile = new DataOutputStream(testf);
        testfile.writeChars(msg);
        testfile.close();
        System.out.println("Wrote " + filename);
    } catch(Exception error) {
        System.out.println("Failed to write " + filename); }

    filename = "test8.txt";
    try {
        OutputStream testf = new FileOutputStream(filename);
        DataOutputStream testfile = new DataOutputStream(testf);
        testfile.writeUTF(msg);
        testfile.close();
        System.out.println("Wrote " + filename);
    } catch(Exception error) {
        System.out.println("Failed to write " + filename); }

    System.exit(0);
}}
```

If the sample program is executed on a system that uses ISO-8859-1 as its native encoding, the first write effectively fails, though no exception is raised and no error message is issued. The character U+263A cannot be represented in ISO-8859-1, so the output routine might write a question mark, ?, instead. (This is questionable, but such things happen.) The other ways work well, though you cannot directly view the file contents on programs that support ISO-8859-1 only. The results are summarized in Table 11-7, which shows the contents of the files by octets (in a big-endian computer).

Table 11-7. File output in Java: encoding of sample text "Aé☺"

Method	Filename	Content (as octets in hex)	Comment
print	test.txt	41 E9 3F	ISO-8859-1, ☺ as ?
write	testu.txt	41 C3 A9 E2 98 BA	UTF-8
writeChars	test16.txt	00 41 00 E9 26 3A	UTF-16, no BOM
writeUTF	test8.txt	00 06 41 C3 A9 E2 98 BA	UTF-8 with octet count (00 06)

The methods for file input are analogous to output methods. We will here give just a rather trivial example: a program that reads a UTF-8 encoded file and prints the (decimal) Unicode code numbers of the characters. The program uses the read function in the InputStreamReader class, which is analogous to the OutputStreamWriter class. Using these

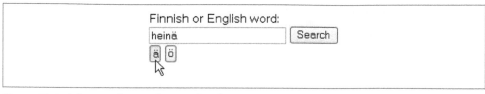

Figure 11-1. A form with extra buttons for character input

classes, you can create a portable program and handle any character encoding supported by the Java implementation. The read function returns the code number of the input character or −1, which indicates the end of file:

```java
import java.io.*;
public class IO {
    public static void main(String[] args) {
        try {
            FileInputStream datafile =
                new FileInputStream(new File("test.txt"));
            InputStreamReader input =
                new InputStreamReader(datafile,"UTF-8");
            int ch;
            while((ch = input.read()) != -1) {
                System.out.println(ch); }
        } catch(Exception error) {
            System.out.println("I/O error"); }
        System.exit(0);
    }
}
```

Buttons for Character Input

In "Virtual Keyboards" in Chapter 2, we discussed the idea of buttons for entering characters in a data entry form. To implement it in an HTML form, you would use an input element of type button and associate an onclick event with it. The event handler would append a character to the content of an input box and focus on that box, so that the user can continue typing with the normal keyboard. The interface is illustrated in Figure 11-1.

The idea can be implemented in JavaScript as follows. For simplicity, the example has just two buttons, for entering ä and ö:

```html
<form action="http://www.tracetech.net:8081/">
<div><label for="word">Finnish or English word:</label></div>
<div>
  <input type="text" id="word" name="word" size="25" maxlength="80">
  <input type="submit" value="Search">
</div>
<div>
  <input type="button" value="ä" onclick="append('ä')">
  <input type="button" value="ö" onclick="append('ö')">
</div>
</form>
<script type="text/javascript">
```

```
var word = document.getElementById('word');
function append(char) {
  word.value += char;
  word.focus(); }
</script>
```

Processing Form Data

The form concept in HTML is rather simple, even simplistic. This has been obscured by the superficial complexity of elements used to construct a form as well as by the variation in technologies for processing form data. The basic idea is the following:

- A form element in HTML defines a data structure for a fill-out form and indicates (in an action attribute) the address of the software that processes the form data when submitted, the *form handler*.

- A form element contains *input fields*, called *controls* in HTML specifications. An input field allows a user to select between alternatives, type in data, insert a file, or submit the form data.

- When a form is submitted, typically by clicking on a submit button (defined by an input field), the web browser takes the contents of all input fields, encodes them in a particular way, and submits this data to the form handler.

- The data may pass through some *interface* (such as Common Gateway Interface) that converts the data to a format that is more easily processed by the form handler.

- The form handler usually *decodes* the form data to a suitable format, often splitting it into different variables corresponding to the fields of the form.

- The rest is up to the form handler. It may, and normally should, send the browser some response, such as search results, a notification or an error message, or the next part of a logical form divided into parts.

Originally, form handling was designed for ASCII data. When the GET method is used (the form element has the attribute method="GET", which is the default), the form data is encoded into a URL using URL encoding as described in Chapter 6. Thereby the character repertoire is restricted to ASCII. Form data processing is undefined in other cases, though in practice, other encodings have been used, relying on extended URL encoding. Using method="POST" is in principle safer, since that way, the form data is passed as a separate block of data, not as part of any URL.

A web author who sets up a form should consider the potential problems caused by non-ASCII input, even if he has no intentions of processing such data. We will here present some basic problems and solutions. More details are available on the page "FORM submission and i18n," *http://ppewww.ph.gla.ac.uk/~flavell/charset/form-i18n.html*.

 You cannot prevent people from writing strange characters in form fields. You can only be prepared to handle them somehow.

Decoding Form Data

The usual tools for decoding form data in programming languages extract the values of form fields and decode the URL encoding. This is typically automatic in advanced programming tools. For example, using Perl and the CGI.pm library for CGI scripting, you would use code like the following to retrieve the value of a field foo to a variable $zap, as URL decoded:

```
use CGI qw(:standard);
$zap = param('foo');
```

Thus, a character that was typed as @ and URL encoded as %40, is again @ after this operation. In PHP, for example, you would do the same thing as follows:

```
$zap = $_GET['foo'];
```

In some cases, you might wish to use functions that specifically URL decode data, such as urldecode in PHP. It is, however, important to avoid URL decoding twice, since decoding already decoded data can result in completely wrong results.

If you wish to use the decoded data on an HTML page, typically in the content of the result page that the form handler sends, you need to escape the markup-significant characters < and & and possibly quotation marks, as usual in HTML. Programming languages often have built-in functions like HTMLescape for the purpose. However, there are problems with this, due to the way browsers may represent special characters, as explained in "Avoid Oddities by Using UTF-8" later in the chapter.

Recognizing the Encoding

Extraction of fields from the form data and URL decoding them is not sufficient. You need to find out the encoding in which the data should be interpreted. The encoding should be the same as on the page where the form appears. Although HTML specifications define an accept-charset attribute for specifying the encoding of form data, it has not been implemented. Instead, browsers use the page's encoding if they can. We cannot always know for sure that a browser has got this right, though.

It is possible that a browser receives a document that is, say, ISO-8859-15 encoded and announced as such, but the browser actually treats it as ISO-8859-1 or windows-1252 encoded. The user would usually observe nothing wrong, especially if all characters used on the page have the same code numbers in all the encodings. However, if she fills out and submits a form, her data might get distorted. If she enters a character that has a different code in ISO-8859-15 than in the code actually used, the form handler interprets it incorrectly.

A simple heuristic check is to include a hidden field in the form and check its value in the form handler. The field should contain some characters that have different codes in encodings that might actually be used by browsers. The euro sign U+20AC, representable in HTML as €, is a useful diagnostic character, since it has different codes in Unicode and windows-1252, and it does not belong to ISO-8859-1 at all. You could also include some other character, one that does not appear in windows-1252. For example:

```
<input type="hidden" name="euro" value="&#8364;">
<input type="hidden" name="Omega" value="&#937;">
```

In the form handler, you can check that the value of this field is what it should be. For example, if your document was sent as ISO-8859-15 encoded, the value should be octet A0 in hexadecimal. If your document was sent as UTF-8, the value should be the UTF-8 encoded form of U+20AC, which is E2 82 AC.

If the test fails, you can know that something went wrong. Normal form processing should be prevented. The form handler could, for example, just send back an error message like the following: "Form data cannot be processed. Unfortunately, your browser is not able to handle the character encoding UTF-8. Therefore, we cannot ensure that your data would be processed correctly."

Avoid Oddities by Using UTF-8

There is a particular reason to use UTF-8 on pages that contain a form. If the user enters a character that cannot be represented in the encoding of the page, there is no rule that says what a browser should do. It would be natural to expect that it issues an error message, or perhaps omits such a character or replaces it with a suitable control character. However, what browsers normally do is convert the character to a character reference (in decimal) and then include this value as URL encoded into the form data.

For example, assume that your page is ISO-8859-1 encoded and contains a form with a text input field. If the user enters, for example, the Greek capital letter omega Ω, browsers will typically convert it to the character reference Ω and then URL encode this to the following: %26%23937%3B. Although this is quite illogical (character references belong to HTML source, not to encoded data) and does not conform to any specification, you need to take it into account. A user may fill out your form using characters he finds natural or necessary, without realizing the limitations of the encoding.

Sometimes you may find it useful to keep special characters as character references. You need to be careful, however. If you use normal tools or algorithms to HTML escape the data retrieved from form fields, you would escape & as & and break the idea. On the other hand, plain & in the data needs to be escaped. In principle, we cannot distinguish the string "Ω" generated by a browser from Ω from the same string typed by the user. Effectively, you need to treat them as equivalent, as a matter of form handler functionality, and you need to use an HTML escape method that leaves character references intact. On the other hand, you could avoid the problem altogether.

By using UTF-8, you avoid the problem, since all Unicode characters are representable in it. On the other hand, you need to handle the encoding, and this would be nontrivial, if your server-side programming language does not support Unicode. However, even when you need to process the data as an octet sequence to be interpreted by your code, you can process ASCII data easily: all octets in the range 0..7F are ASCII characters.

Using UTF-8

The following demonstration code is a Perl script, intended to be used as a CGI script, and it uses the CGI.pm library (see *http://search.cpan.org/dist/CGI.pm/CGI.pm*) for the creation of an HTML form and for processing the form data. The script creates a UTF-8 encoded HTML document containing a form and decodes the form data into UTF-8 format, and then writes the data to a file in UTF-8 encoding, in append mode. (In real life, you would want to include some checks against excessive amounts of data and other abuse.)

```perl
#!/usr/local/gnu/bin/perl
use CGI qw(:standard);
use Encode;

binmode STDOUT, ":utf8";
print header(-charset => 'utf-8');
print start_html(-title => 'Collecting words', -encoding => 'utf-8'),
      h1('Collecting words');

if (param()) {
    if(open(OUT, ">>:utf8", "words.txt")) {
        $word = Encode::decode_utf8(param('word'));
        print OUT "$word\n";
        print p("Thank you for \x{201c}$word\x{201d}!");   }
    else {
        print p("Internal error, sorry!"); exit(0); }}
else {
    print start_form,
          "Some word(s): ",textfield('word'),
          submit(-name => 'Submit'),
          end_form; }

print end_html;
```

Submitting a File

When you use a form with a file input field (`<input type="file">`), the browser creates a special input widget where the user can pick up a file from his system. The contents of the file will be included into the form data as one of the parts of a multipart message. The part has headers of its own, where the encoding could be specified. However, in practice, the browser will just copy the contents of the file octet by octet, and it will insert a header that specifies the media type of the data according to the file system properties. For example, if the filename suffix is *.txt*, the browser includes a header that specifies the media type as `text/plain` without `charset` indication.

The conclusion is that the encoding and even media types of submitted files remain unknown. Human intervention or application-related heuristics is needed to deduce such information. In some cases, you might include a field where the user can specify the encoding of a file, but this would probably be too challenging for most users.

Identifiers, Patterns, and Regular Expressions

In the section "Classification of Characters" in Chapter 5, we preliminarily mentioned the use of defined Unicode properties for the purposes of defining identifiers (names) and patterns of strings. Here we will discuss the issue more technically.

Identifier syntax and pattern syntax had previously been treated as different issues. Unicode combines the two intrinsically to some extent, and the Unicode standard presents them together in Unicode Technical Report #31, "Identifier and Pattern Syntax," *http:// www.unicode.org/reports/tr31/*. One reason for this is that patterns, as used in, for example, search clauses, may need to contain identifiers.

Identifiers

An identifier is a defined name for something. Identifiers are extensively used in many computer languages—e.g., as names of constants, variables, and functions in programming languages or for aggregates and components of data, such as table rows. An identifier is a formal name in the sense that it is formed according to specific rules and it is kept the same, unless explicitly changed. An identifier is often shorter than names used in natural languages. For example, the ISO 3166 standard defines two-letter identifiers for countries, to be used as language-independent immutable code names. (In practice, it does not quite work that way. Sometimes the codes are changed for political reasons.)

Identifiers: internal or external?

In most contexts, identifiers are internal symbols that are not visible to end users of applications. However, usually identifiers are meant to be more or less *mnemonic* and descriptive of their meaning, to make computer code more readable and easier to maintain. Certainly, `totalPopulation` is easier to understand than `x78`. In practice, programmers often use short identifiers such as `n` and `x` especially for variables used very locally. In such style, `c` or `ch` often denotes a character variable and `s` a string variable.

When the native language of a programmer or a group of programmers is not English, it may be desirable to be able to use a wider character repertoire. Especially if the documentation and comments are written in some other language, it would be natural to use that language in identifiers, too. Besides, identifiers might stand for things that have natural names in some language. For example, if you assign identifiers to municipalities of France, it would be natural to use accented letters in them, even if you do not use the French names as such.

Identifiers may become visible to end users, perhaps even as something that they need to type. An example is the naming of Internet domains (such as *www.oreilly.com*), where the components can be regarded as identifiers. (This particular issue was discussed in Chapter 10.) End users often seen identifiers in error messages and user interfaces, even if the programmers may have regarded the identifiers as purely internal and technical. On the Web, pages that use frames need to use identifiers for them. Authors have typically used short and often cryptic names like `frame1` or `left` for them. Problems arise when people use browsers that implement frames in ways that authors did not anticipate—e.g., browsers that read the names of frames aloud, asking the user to choose between them.

Traditional format of identifiers

Each computer language and data format that uses identifiers needs to define its identifier syntax, and there is a lot of variation in it. However, conventionally, the definitions have been relatively simply, allowing just a subset of ASCII. More exactly, the definitions typically allow ASCII letters, digits, and a small collection of special characters.

Usually the first character of an identifier has to be a letter, or in some cases, a character treated as equivalent to a letter, such as _ or $. The reason is that when parsing, for example, a computer source program, you need to be able to distinguish identifiers from other atoms of text, such as numbers and punctuation symbols. For example, when a programming language compiler or interpreter reads "a+b" in program source, it needs to know whether + is allowed in identifiers or not. If + were allowed, special rules would be needed to make it possible to distinguish such use of + from its use as an operator.

For similar reasons, a space is usually not allowed in identifiers. A hyphen is typically not allowed either. Since identifiers are often formed from two or more words of a natural language, this poses a problem. The usual solutions are: just writing words together (e.g., openwindow), using case variation (openWindow), and using the low line (underscore), if the identifier syntax permits that (open_window).

If identifiers occur in a limited context only—i.e., in particular fields of a data structure, there is much less need to use a restricted syntax for them. The typical identifier syntax is designed for use in contexts where identifiers appear in the midst of program code or other data and need to be recognized easily. However, even when identifiers occur in specific contexts only and need not be parsed from text, safety considerations often lead to some restricted syntax.

When using traditional formats of identifiers, a specific syntax for them needs to decide on the following matters:

- Are both lowercase and uppercase letters allowed?
- Which characters are allowed beyond letters and digits? They might include underline (_), dollar sign ($), full stop (.), colon (:), and hyphen-minus (-).
- Is the first character required to be a letter? If it is, are some special characters treated as letters for this purpose?
- Is there a maximum length?

The Unicode names of characters do not conform to this traditional syntax, since the names may contain spaces. When the Unicode names are used as identifiers—e.g., in programming languages—the specific syntax might specify that spaces are replaced by underline characters. However, in some contexts, spaces are permitted.

Case sensitivity

Case sensitivity—i.e., whether lowercase and uppercase letters are equivalent—is an important feature but external to identifier syntax. The syntax only defines the allowed format of identifiers. At the dawn of the computer era, there were no lowercase letters available. Later, they were typically treated as equivalent to uppercase letters, and this is still common in many contexts. A more modern style, such as the one applied in Java and in XML, is to treat lowercase and uppercase as distinct, making a and A two identifiers that are no more connected to each other than a and b are.

The Unicode approach to identifiers

The identifier concept described in the Unicode standard is a generalization of the traditional identifier syntax. It is a basis upon which you can build different syntax definitions for identifiers, rather than a standard identifier syntax per se. As UTR #31 itself puts it, it provides "a recommended default for the definition of identifier syntax." For example, the syntax of programming language identifiers could be defined by saying that it is the Unicode identifier syntax with the addition that the £ character is treated as an Identifier Start character.

The syntax is very similar to the traditional syntax of identifiers, just with a possibility of using much wider repertoires of characters in a convenient way.

Patterns

Patterns are used to describe the format of strings, for the purposes of searching and recognizing components of a string. For example, for reading numeric data, some pattern is needed for recognizing strings that constitute numbers. The specific pattern used determines, among other things, whether ".0" or "0." is a number or whether a digit is needed on either side of the decimal point. Similarly, the pattern specifies whether a period or a comma is used as the decimal separator (or whether either of them is allowed).

The structure of identifiers is a pattern, too. Patterns can be very simple or very complex. For example, a pattern might specify the format of lines in a logfile as just a sequence of characters from a particular set. It could alternatively describe the structure of a line as containing particular fixed strings, intermixed with other strings with some internal structure, such as sequences of digits or letters, perhaps of a particular length.

The word "pattern" as used in the context of string processing has two meanings:

- An abstract pattern, which specifies a general format of strings. Strings that are particular realizations of the pattern are said to *match* it. For example, we could describe a pattern that consists of nonempty sequences of normal digits. Unsigned integers such as 0, 42, and 38389212 match that pattern.

- A pattern as described in some formalized notation. For example, the above-mentioned pattern can be described in Perl as [0-9]+ or equivalently as \d+. Here, the plus sign indicates that the preceding construct may be repeated indefinitely, and [0-9]+ and \d+ are two ways of expressing the concept of normal decimal digit ("0" through "9"). Different notations may use completely different syntax for patterns, though in practice, they tend to be rather similar. Quite often, a pattern is expressed as a construct called a *regular expression*.

We are here interested in patterns in the latter, technical sense. Such a pattern itself is a string of characters. It may contain characters of three kinds:

Syntax characters
> These are characters that have a special meaning by the definition of the formal notation used for patterns. In the pattern [0-9]+, the brackets and the plus sign as well as the hyphen-minus are syntax characters.

Whitespace characters
> A pattern may allow the use of whitespace for readability, with no effect on the meaning of the pattern. For example, the pattern [0-9]+ could be written as [0 - 9] +, if desired.

Literal characters
> All other characters are "literal"—i.e., they denote themselves. Formally, a character that is neither syntactic nor whitespace is a pattern that matches this particular character only.

If a character is defined as a syntax character or as a whitespace character in some formalism, it cannot be directly used as a literal character. The reason is obvious: if you tried to do so, the program that processes the pattern would treat the character by its defined meaning in the syntax or as whitespace. Formalisms typically contain methods for *escaping* characters so that they can be used in the role of a literal character. Several escape mechanisms were mentioned in Chapter 2. A rather common method is to prefix a character with the backslash (reverse solidus) \ (e.g., \\ to escape the backslash itself).

Identifier and Pattern Characters

The Unicode approach distinguishes the following *disjoint* sets of characters for use in identifiers and patterns. The names in parentheses are the long and short name of the property that indicates, for each character, whether it belongs to the set (see Chapter 5):

Identifier Characters (ID Continue, IDC)
> This set is contains Identifier Start (ID Start, IDS) characters, which may appear anywhere in an identifier, and characters that are allowed later in an identifier only. *Identifier Start* characters consist of letters in a broad sense and of ideographs. The latter group, sometimes called *Identifier Continue-Only* characters, contains decimal digits and a mixture of other characters. These sets, described in more detail below, may be extended in future versions of Unicode.

Pattern Syntax Characters (Pattern Syntax, Pat Syn)
> This set contains characters that are used as operators or separators or in other special roles in patterns. This set is fixed—i.e., it will not be extended. There are 2,760 char-

acters in it, as defined in the *PropList.txt* file of the Unicode database. The ASCII characters in the set are: !"#$%&'()*+,-./:;<>?@[\]^`{|}~.

Pattern Whitespace Characters (Pattern White Space, Pat WS)

This set contains characters treated as whitespace in patterns. Whitespace may be needed to separate symbols from each other, but it is otherwise insignificant. This set too is fixed. There are only 11 characters in it: horizontal tab (U+0009), line feed (U+000A), vertical tab (U+000B), form feed (U+000C), carriage return (U+000D), space (U+0032), next line (U+0085), left-to-right mark (U+200E), right-to-left mark (U+200F), line separator (U+2028), and paragraph separator (U+2029).

The policy that Pattern Syntax Characters and Pattern Whitespace Characters are fixed (closed) sets does not mean that actual identifier syntax needs to use exactly those sets. On the contrary, fixing the sets makes it easier to define identifier syntax on a Unicode basis: it can be defined using the Unicode syntax as an immutable base and adding or removing characters as desired. Of course, if a specific identifier syntax definition makes a character such as $ allowed in an identifier, it is removed from the Pattern Syntax Characters set in that syntax; the three sets must be disjoint.

The Identifier Characters and the Identifier Start characters are listed in the *DerivedCoreProperties.txt* file of the Unicode database. As the name of the file suggests, the definitions have been derived from other Unicode properties, in this case, mainly from the gc (General Category) property.

Identifier Start characters include the following:

- Characters with gc value Lu, Lt, Ll, Lm, or Lo (uppercase, titlecase, lowercase, modifier, or other letter); this includes ideographs
- Characters with gc value Nl (Number, letter)
- A small collection of other characters, defined by the Other_ID_Start property; currently this means script capital "p" ℘ (U+2118), estimated symbol e (U+212E), and U+309B and U+309C, which are Japanese (kana) sound marks

Other Identifier characters include:

- Characters with gc value Nd (Number, decimal digit)
- Characters with gc value Mn (Mark, nonspacing) or Mc (Mark, spacing combining)
- Sharacters with gc value Pc (Punctuation, connector)
- A small collection of other characters, defined by the Other_ID_Continue property; currently this means the nine Ethiopic digits U+1369..U+1371

Identifier Syntax

Identifier syntax is defined simply so that an identifier consists of one Identifier Start character followed by zero or more Identifier characters (i.e., Identifier Continue characters). Thus, program code that scans an identifier can be quite simple, if you can use functions that check for a character being an Identifier Start or Identifier Continue character.

The syntax thus generally allows, among other things, words and abbreviations written in languages that use an alphabetic writing system or an ideographic writing system. Examples: años, Ψυχή8, Яблохуz42.

Normalization

The identifier syntax allows nonspacing marks like accents. You can use an identifier like résumé, because é is defined to be a letter, but you could also use an identifier that contains é as decomposed into "e" and a combining acute accent, U+0301. This means that you can also use a combination of a letter and one or more diacritic marks that does not exist in Unicode as a precomposed character.

Nonspacing marks create the question of whether identifiers are regarded as equal if the only difference is that one of them contains a precomposed character like é and the other contains the corresponding decomposed character. The definition of identifier syntax may specify that such identifiers be treated as the same, by specifying that Normalization Form C (as described in Chapter 5) is to be used.

Normalization is an optional feature in identifier syntax. If used, the particular normalization form has to be specified. The definition may list characters that are to be excluded from normalization. There are special rules to be applied if Normalization Form KC is used.

The standard does not define a general method for ignoring diacritic marks in identifiers. If you wish to allow diacritic marks in identifiers, you are more or less supposed to treat them as significant. Outside Unicode identifier syntax you could, however, normalize to Normalization Form D (canonical decomposition only), and then perform a comparison that ignores nonspacing marks.

Case folding

Similarly to normalization, case folding is an optional feature. The definition of identifier syntax may specify either simple or full case folding (as described in Chapter 5). If case folding is specified, identifiers are internally mapped to lowercase. This of course applies to accented letters too, so résumé and RÉSumé would be treated as the same.

Somewhat surprisingly, the standard says: "Generally if the programming language has case-sensitive identifiers, then Normalization Form C is appropriate, while if the programming language has case-insensitive identifiers, then Normalization Form KC is more appropriate." Logically, however, case sensitivity is quite independent of the difference of these normalization forms: Form KC includes compatibility decomposition.

Identifiers (names) in XML

XML1.0 has an identifier syntax that is similar to the general Unicode identifier syntax but is defined in a different way. The definition is fixed: addition of new characters, even letters, to Unicode does not extend the character repertoire in XML identifiers. We will first consider XML 1.0 identifiers, and then the broader XML 1.1 identifier syntax.

XML identifiers are important due to the widespread use of XML for various purposes, often in contexts where identifiers might be shown to or written by end users. Identifiers are used to name elements, attributes, enumerated values of attributes, entities, etc. Of course, XML-based markup systems usually define a finite set of identifiers, and it is still common to use ASCII characters only in them. In designing markup systems and in processing generic XML, it is important to know the exact syntax.

XML identifier syntax, or name syntax as the XML specification calls it, is based on fixed rules derived from "Properties of characters in Unicode version 2.0." These definitions are presented as explicit lists in the XML specification, at *http://www.w3.org/TR/REC-xml/#CharClasses*. It is however much easier to understand the definitions, when you consider the design principles:

- Like the Unicode identifier syntax, the XML name syntax distinguishes between name start characters and name characters in general.

- Name start characters are "XML letters" and the underscore "_" and the colon ":". "XML letters" are: characters with gc value Lu, Lt, Ll, or Lo (uppercase, titlecase, lowercase, or other letters) or Nl (Number, letter), as defined in Unicode 2.0. Moreover, the following characters with gc = Lm are included: U+02BB..U+02C1, U+0559, U+06E5, and U+06E6. Note: the colon ":" has a special meaning in XML, and it should be used only for namespacing purposes.

- Other name characters are: characters with gc value Nd (Number, decimal digit), Mc, Mn, or Me (i.e., spacing combining, noncombining, or enclosing mark), or Lm (Letter, mark), as defined in Unicode 2.0, and some other characters, namely the period ".", the hyphen-minus "-", and the middle dot · (U+00B7) and the Greek ano teleia · (U+0387). However, the enclosing marks U+20DD..U+20E0 are excluded.

- However, characters with compatibility decompositions are excluded. This excludes, for example, Planck constant h (U+210E) and superscript two [2].

- Moreover, all characters in the range U+F900..U+FFDC (compatibility characters such as CJK Compatibility ideographs) are excluded.

Thus, the XML name syntax has been defined rigorously and in a stable manner, but the definition is far from intuitively clear and easy to remember. Table 11-8 summarizes the main points, though it does not express all prohibitions.

Table 11-8. Allowed characters in XML names (identifiers) according to General Category (gc) values as per Unicode 2.0

gc	Description	Sample	Role in XML names
Lu	Letter, uppercase	A	Allowed
Ll	Letter, lowercase	a	Allowed
Lt	Letter, titlecase	Dž	Allowed

gc	Description	Sample	Role in XML names
Lm	Letter, modifier	ʰ (U+02B0)	Allowed; U+02BB..U+02C1, U+0559, U+06E5, U+06E6 not as first character
Lo	Letter, other	א	Allowed
Mn	Mark, nonspacing	` (U+0300)	Allowed, but not as first character
Mc	Mark, spacing combining	ः	Allowed, but not as first character
Me	Mark, enclosing	◌⃝	Allowed, but not as first character, and excluding U+20DD..U+20E0
Nd	Number, decimal digit	1	Allowed, but not as first character
Nl	Number, letter	IV	Allowed
No	Number, other	½	
Zs	Separator, space	(space)	
Zl	Separator, line	(U+2028)	
Zp	Separator, paragraph	(PS)	
Cc	Other, control	(CR)	
Cf	Other, format	(SHY)	
Cs	Other, surrogate	*surrogates*	
Co	Other, private use	(U+E000)	
Cn	Other, not assigned	(U+FFFF)	
Pc	Punctuation, connector	_	Underscore "_" allowed
Pd	Punctuation, dash	-	"-" (U+002D) allowed but not at start
Ps	Punctuation, open	(	
Pe	Punctuation, close	)	
Pi	Punctuation, initial quote	"	
Pf	Punctuation, final quote	"	
Po	Punctuation, other	!	Colon ":" allowed. Period "." and middle dot "·" allowed, but not as first character
Sm	Symbol, math	+	
Sc	Symbol, currency	$	
Sk	Symbol, modifier	^	
So	Symbol, other	©	

In XML 1.1, the approach is different: the identifier syntax is more permissive, based on allowing everything that need not be excluded for specific reasons. However, there are few implementations of XML 1.1. Usually, it is impractical to try to use XML 1.1, unless you need the extended identifier syntax or similar features of XML 1.1 and you can use an XML 1.1 implementation.

The XML 1.1 name (identifier) syntax is simpler than XML 1.0 name syntax. Almost all characters are permitted in names, excluding mostly just characters that need to be treated as punctuation, or generally as delimiters in a context where names are used. Thus, the syntax is best described *negatively*. Table 11-9 lists characters that are disallowed in XML 1.1 names either completely or as the first character. In the "Status" column, "no" means that the character is disallowed, "cont." means that it is allowed as a continuation character only (not at the start), and "special" means that it has special meaning. The XML 1.1 specification contains a non-normative appendix "Suggestions for XML names," which recommends additional restrictions.

Table 11-9. Characters disallowed or with restricted use in XML 1.1 names

Code point(s)	Status	Description
U+0000..U+002C	no	C0 Controls, space, and !"#$%&'()*+,
U+002D..U+002E	cont.	Hyphen-minus "-" and full stop "."
U+002F	no	Solidus /
U+0030..U+0039	cont.	Digits 0 to 9
U+003A	special	Colon :
U+003B..U+0040	no	;<=>?@
U+005B..U+005E	no	[\]^
U+0060	no	Grave accent `
U+007B..U+00B6	no	{|}~, C1 Controls, NBSP, ¡¢£¤¥¦§¨©ª«¬®¯°±²³´µ¶
U+00B7	cont.	Middle dot ·
U+00B8..U+00BF	no	¸¹º»¼½¾¿
U+00D7	no	Multiplication sign ×
U+00F7	no	Division sign ÷
U+0300..U+036F	cont.	Combining marks
U+037E	no	Greek question mark ;
U+2000..U+200B	no	Fixed-width spaces
U+200E..U+203E	no	Various punctuation marks like "—" and ‰
U+203F..U+2040	cont.	Undertie and character tie
U+2041..U+206F	no	Various punctuation marks
U+2190..U+2BFF	no	Arrows
U+2FF0..U+3000	no	Ideographic description characters and ideographic space
U+D800..U+F8FF	no	Surrogates and Private Use
U+FDD0..U+FDEF	no	Noncharacters
U+FFFE..U+FFFF	no	Noncharacters
U+F0000..U+10FFFF	no	Planes F and 10 (Private Use planes)

Although the definition of XML 1.1 names is more concise than the definition of XML 1.0 names and includes large ranges, implying extensibility (new Unicode characters will be automatically allowed), it is still somewhat difficult to use. Some characters (such as

U+037E) have been excluded in a matter that looks random, though there are reasons behind the exclusions (e.g., U+037E is canonical equivalent to semicolon).

Alternative Identifier Syntax

The Unicode standard also specifies an alternate, more permissive syntax for identifiers. It is based on the idea of excluding some characters from use in identifiers and allowing the rest. The characters excluded are those that are reserved for syntactic use, so that identifiers can be distinguished from text.

Syntax analysis based on this approach can be implemented more efficiently, since the exclusion set is fixed and small. Thus, as new characters are added to Unicode, they automatically become available for use in identifiers. In fact, they already are: the approach means that even unassigned code points are allowed in identifiers. If a future version of Unicode assigns a character to a currently unassigned position, nothing happens in the alternative identifier syntax. At another level, though, a document that uses such a code point gains a better status with respect to the Unicode standard.

Thus, a scanner (parser) for identifiers using the alternative identifier syntax need not be changed, if the Unicode standard is changed. On the other hand, the approach has drawbacks, too. The permissive syntax is too permissive for many purposes. It has been described as allowing nonsensical identifiers that lack any human legibility. However, even using the normal syntax, it is easy to write identifiers that have no mnemonic value and intuitive understandability.

The definition of alternative identifier syntax is simple: an identifier is a sequence of characters not containing any Pattern Syntax characters or any Pattern Whitespace characters. This definition can be used as such or as modified in some documented way by adding or removing disallowed characters.

An identifier that is formed according to the alternative syntax is sometimes called an extended identifier or *XID*. The *DerivedCoreProperties.txt* file in the Unicode character database defines the properties XIDS (XID Start), indicating whether a character may start an XID, XIDC (XID Continue), which indicates whether a character may appear in an XID in general. These properties are seldom needed, since the XID approach is based on excluding characters rather than using positive lists.

Pattern Syntax

The pattern syntax recommended in the Unicode standard uses fixed sets of Pattern Syntax characters and Pattern Whitespace characters as described above. Of course, this does not mean that in a particular formalism, every Pattern Syntax character needs to have a defined meaning. Rather, Pattern Syntax characters are what you *may* define for use in the syntax.

The approach allows, and encourages, a design where the formalism requires that Pattern Syntax characters must not be used as literal characters, even if the formalism does not assign a syntactic meaning to them. This means that if such characters would be needed as literals, they must be "escaped" using some suitable mechanism. In such a design, the formalism can later be extended by assigning meanings to Pattern Syntax characters that are now unused.

For example, suppose that you have defined a formalism of regular expressions that does not use the character #. Since it is a Pattern Syntax character, you would still require that it not be used as a literal character but escaped somehow—e.g., as \#. Now suppose that you later extend the formalism by taking the character # into some use. This would mean that the regular expression foo\#bar would still be correct and would have the same meaning (denoting the literal string "foo#bar"). The regular expression foo#bar would become correct, with some meaning. If it were given as input to a program that processes data by the old definition of your formalism, it would generate an error message, due to the attempt to use # as a literal character. This is better than treating it as a literal, since this would not be the intended meaning.

Regular Expressions

A regular expression, or *regexp* (or *regex*) for short, is a string of characters that presents a pattern of strings, for purposes of searching and matching. Strings that correspond to the pattern are said to *match* the regular expression. We can also say that a regular expression defines a set of strings. For example, [a-z][0-9]* is a regular expression that represents the set of strings that start with a lowercase letter "a" to "z" and continue with zero or more common digits 0 to 9.

Different syntaxes are used for regular expressions, but the syntax used in the example is rather common. In simple cases, it is relatively intuitive if you just know one special rule: the asterisk * indicates that characters matching the immediately preceding part of the expression may appear any number of times, including zero. Thus, [0-9]* matches any sequence of digits, including the empty string.

Another common convention is that the period . means "any character." For example, st.p is a regexp that matches "stop" and "step" but also "st8p," "st!p," etc. An alternative convention is that the question mark ? means "any character." This has caused some confusion, since formal descriptions of programming languages typically use a syntax in which the question mark indicates optionality of the preceding construct, so that, for example, c? matches the one-letter string "c" and the empty string.

According to Unicode principles, the characters used in special meanings in regular expression syntax should be selected among Pattern Syntax characters.

Regexp use in programming

Regular expressions are widely used in programming, and many programming languages contain a regexp syntax and matching, searching, or replacement statements where they may be used. They often make it easy to specify the pattern matching to be performed, without needing to write the code that implements the matching.

The following Perl program reads the standard input stream and prints only those lines to the standard output stream that contain the characters "U+" followed by an alphanumeric character (e.g., "U+A" or "U+9"). Note that the character + has been escaped with the backslash \, since otherwise + would have a special meaning. The notation \w denotes an alphabetic character, also called a "word" character:

```
while(<>) {
    if(m/U\+\w/) {
        print; }}
```

Regexp use by end users

Regular expressions have become relevant to end users, too, since search and replace operations in programs often allow their use, at least in some limited form and maybe in a program-specific syntax. In database searches, for example, regexp syntax, if available, is a powerful tool. Unfortunately, the general search engines on the Web do not support regexp syntax, but site-specific search tools may well do so.

Thus, regular expressions can be important to end users of applications, not just to programmers. The concept is not widely known, though. Moreover, finding the tools and the specific syntax in a program may require some experimentation or manuals.

For example, in MS Word, if you start a search (Edit ▯Find or Ctrl-F), click on the "More" button, and check the "Use wildcards" checkbox, you can use regular expressions in the search string. By clicking on the "Special" button, you get a menu of characters and notations that have special meanings in Word regexps. The menu also lets you enter special characters (with no special regexp meaning) that might be difficult or impossible to type normally. The dialog is shown in Figure 11-2. In fact, you can use regular expressions even without checking "Use wildcards," but then you need to precede regexp syntax characters with a circumflex—e.g., ^? instead of just ?.

In Unix and Linux environments, it is common to use programs like *grep* that accept regular expressions as input. The following command would list all lines in file *data.txt* that contain the string "U+" followed by an alphanumeric character (cf. to the preceding example of a Perl program):

```
grep "U\+[A-Za-z0-9]" data.txt
```

Some special characters used in regular expressions are often called *wildcards* (or wildcard characters). The word comes from card games such as poker and canasta where some cards, such as jokers or deuces, may be used in place of any other card.

On the other hand, the word "wildcard" often refers to a more limited syntax that gives some of the capabilities of regexp syntax. For example, in many search operations, you can use a special character, often * or #, to denote an arbitrary string (including the empty string). Thus, a database search interface might let you type synta* or synta# to refer to all words that begin with "synta" (e.g., "syntax," "syntactic," etc.). The exact meaning of such notations depends on the program, but it would typically correspond to what we could express in regexp syntax as synta[a-z]*.

When using regular expressions, we often wish to use constructs that refer to "words" in a meaning that roughly corresponds to words in a natural language. For this, we may need

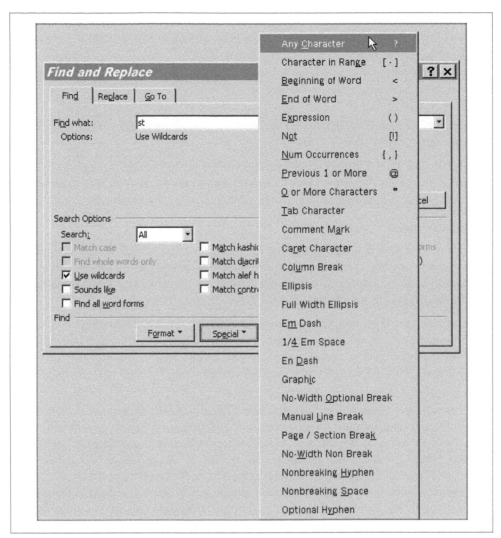

Figure 11-2. Using regular expressions in MS Word

an expression for "letter." An expression like [A-Za-z] that covers only the basic Latin alphabet "A" to "Z" is too limited for most languages written in Latin letters.

Unicode regular expressions

The use of regular expressions in conjunction with Unicode is defined in the Unicode Technical Standard UTS #18, "Unicode Regular Expressions," which is available online at *http://www.unicode.org/reports/tr18/*. It is not part of the Unicode standard but a separate specification issued by the Unicode Consortium.

The specification defines three levels of Unicode support that a program may offer if it recognizes and interprets regular expressions:

Basic Unicode Support

This means that Unicode characters can be used in regular expressions.

Extended Unicode Support

This level additionally includes recognition of grapheme clusters, detection of word boundaries, and canonical equivalence.

Tailored Support

This adds the possibility of tailoring the processing of characters, including language-dependent rules.

The specification UTS #18 does not fix the specific syntax to be used for regular expressions, but it uses a sample syntax, which is based on the syntax used in Perl. The description of the Perl syntax is available via *http://www.perl.com/pub/q/documentation*.

Basic Unicode support

There is no guarantee that a programming language (or an application) that recognizes regular expressions has even basic Unicode support as defined in UTS #18. However, such support is becoming common, and in learning how to use a language, it is useful to know the basic ideas as a background. Basic Unicode support requires:

A general mechanism for specifying a character by its Unicode code number

This could be \u *n* as in many languages or \x{*n*} as in Perl, where *n* is the code number in hexadecimal. Such notations can be combined with other constructs—for example, [\u3040-\u309F] might denote the set of characters from U+3040 to U+309F.

Specifying sets of characters by properties

Some notation is needed for denoting sets of characters by properties. At least the following properties must be supported: General Category, Script, Alphabetic, Uppercase, Lowercase, Whitespace, Noncharacter Code Point, and Default Ignorable Code Point. The specific syntax may vary, but the recommendation is that both abbreviated names and longer, more descriptive names of properties and their values be recognized. Moreover, implementations should apply loose matching of property names, ignoring the case distinctions, whitespace, hyphens, and underlines. Thus, assuming that the specific syntax is of the form \p{name=value} (to denote characters for which a particular property has the specified value), then \p{General_Category=Letter} and \{gc=L} should both be accepted. The properties Script and General Category may have the property name omitted. Thus, simple \p{letter} or p{L} should work, too.

Set subtraction and intersection

A notation is required for specifying the set difference and set intersection of two sets of characters. The operator could be "-" for difference, & for intersection. Thus, [\p{Letter} - Qq] could mean any letter but "Q" or "q," and [\p{Latin} & [\u41 - \u2AF]] could mean Latin letters in the range U+0041 to U+02AF.

Word analysis

An implementation is required to provide at least a simple mechanism for recognizing word boundaries, using a reasonable definition for "word." Minimally, this means that all alphabetic characters as well as zero width non-joiner U+200C and zero width joiner U+200D are treated as word characters. Moreover, a nonspacing mark must be treated as belonging to the same word as their base character. In Perl, the concrete notations that can be used include \w, which matches any word character, and \b, which matches a word boundary.

Case insensitive matching

If an implementation supports case insensitive matching for regular expressions, it must correspond at least to the simple case matching algorithm of Unicode (see Chapter 5). For example, the small sigma σ (U+03C3), the small final sigma ς, and the capital sigma Σ must all match.

Line boundaries

If an implementation provides for line-boundary testing, it shall recognize not only CRLF, LF, and CR, but also NEL (U+0085), PS (U+2029), and LS (U+2028) as terminating a line.

Full code point range

An implementation should handle the full Unicode code point range (U+0000 to U+10FFFF), including planes outside the BMP.

The sample syntax follows the Perl approach even in the rather odd convention that the use of \P instead of \p indicates *negation*. For example, the regular expression \P{Letter} matches all characters that are not letters.

Examples

Utilities like the *grep* program (command) exist in different versions, and modern versions generally support Unicode regular expressions. A Unicode-capable version can be downloaded from *http://www.gnu.org/software/grep/*. The following command illustrates simple use of such a version. The command lists those lines in a file that contain a word that begins with "B" and ends with "n." The special construct [[:alpha:]] matches any alphabetic Unicode character, including accented letters of course (so that the full expression matches, for example, "Bohusvägen" and "Blixén"). However, this functionality may depend on locale settings:

```
grep 'B[[:alpha:]]*n' data.txt
```

The following Perl program reads UTF-8 encoded input and prints all lines that contain a word beginning with é or É. The construct \b matches the start of a word, and the specifier i after the second slash means case-insensitive matching. The letter é is written using the special construct \N{ *name* } to avoid problems that might arise from writing it directly into Perl source:

```
use charnames ':full';
binmode STDIN, ":utf8";
while (<>) {
```

```
if(m/\b\N{LATIN SMALL LETTER E WITH ACUTE}/i) {
    print; }
```

In *Java*, using modern implementations like JDK 1.4, the same operation could be coded as follows. Note that in the string defining the regular expression, "\\b\u00E9", the first occurrence of the backslash needs to be doubled, since the backslash is a special character in Java strings. Thus, in order to include it in the actual string data passed as argument, it must be escaped. A Java compiler interprets the notation \u00E9 as denoting U+00E9— i.e., é—so the backslash must not be escaped. Another specialty is that when using the compile function to define a regular expression, a second argument may be used to specify flags for the matching, and a simple Pattern.CASE_INSENSITIVE would limit case folding to ASCII characters. Using Pattern.UNICODE_CASE, you request Unicode case matching rules. The input routines used here perform input in the system's native encoding:

```java
import java.util.regex.*;
import java.io.*;
public class RegexpExample{
    public static void main(String[] args) throws IOException {
        Pattern regexp = Pattern.compile("\\b\u00E9",
            Pattern.CASE_INSENSITIVE + Pattern.UNICODE_CASE);
        BufferedReader infile =
            new BufferedReader(new FileReader(args[0]));
        String line;
        while ((line = infile.readLine( )) != null) {
            Matcher m = regexp.matcher(line);
            if (m.find()) {
                System.out.println(line);
            }
        }
    }
}
```

International Components for Unicode (ICU)

The International Components for Unicode (ICU) activity is driven by major software companies, but it involves voluntary work too and is based on the open source principle. The ICU software consists of components (subroutines, modules) that are available as source code and portable to different operating systems. ICU is often characterized as a "project," but by its nature, it has to be a continuous activity, to keep up with the development of the Unicode standard and related specifications.

Originally released (in 1999) as "IBM Classes for Unicode" and still substantially supported by IBM and other vendors, ICU has become the first choice for building software that works with Unicode data, when possible. ICU was originally written in Java, and later support to C and C++ has been added. The Java version is called ICU4J, and the C and C++ version is ICU4C.

The official ICU site is hosted at *http://www.ibm.com/software/globalization/icu/*. It contains a handy "Getting started with ICU" section. The other key site is found at *http://icu.sourceforge.net/* and is by SourceForge, the development and download repository of open source code and applications. The sites are linked together in many ways, so you can start in either of them. ICU contains software components for several purposes:

Basic text
  Unicode text handling, character properties, and character code conversions

Text analysis
  Unicode regular expressions and characters, operations on collections (sets) of characters, and detection of word and line boundaries

Sorting and searching
  Language-sensitive collation and searching

Transformations
  Normalization forms, case mappings, transliterations

Locales
  General locale data and resource bundle architecture

Complex text layout
  For example, Arabic, Hebrew, Indic, and Thai

Time and date
  Representation of and operations on dates and times in multiple calendars and time zones

Formatting and parsing
  Reading and writing dates, times, numbers, currencies, messages, and rule-based patterns

Using Locales

Computer technology has mostly been developed in English-speaking environments, and much of the way in which it handles characters and notations reflects the conventions of English. However, the majority of people speak languages other than English as their native language. As computers become a popular commodity, it is increasingly important to let people use them in their own language and according to their cultural conventions. To big software companies, this is essential, since they aim at a worldwide market. It is also important to small companies, due to the competitive advantage.

There are many aspects in making computing technology useable to people with different backgrounds, and part of this is the translation of user interfaces to software. This includes traditional translation work but also new challenges. Increasingly, programs generate texts dynamically, as immediate responses to user queries and responses. Of course, such texts cannot be translated on the fly by human translators.

Suppose that you are designing a program that accepts a search string as input from a user, searches for data in a bibliographic database (i.e., a database containing information about books, serials, etc.), and displays some results to the user. Naturally, the explanations (like "Found 42 hits") should appear in a language of the user's choice, if possible. This is typically straightforward, since it is mostly a matter of translating fixed texts. The book titles may be in any language, and this is a character-level challenge. But the information also contains data such as date of issue and language of the book.

In a well-designed database, data like date and document language is expressed in an unambiguous, easily machine-processable format. For example, the date might be in a format that conforms to the ISO 8601 standard, in year-month-day notation like "1985-11-06," and the language might be expressed using a two- or three-letter code as defined in the ISO 693 family of standards—e.g., with "de" indicating German. When the data is to be presented to a user, however, it should be expressed in a format that the user finds understandable and natural. To some people, this might mean "November 6, 1985" and "German." To some other people, it might mean "6. marraskuuta 1985" and "saksa," or perhaps "6 ноября 1985 г." and "немецкий." The goal is to achieve this without forcing software designers to know about the language-dependent conventions and strings.

The Locale Concept

The data presentation conventions of a language constitute a *locale*. More technically, a locale is an exact, usually formalized specification of some data presentation conventions. Typically, a locale is about a language, so the name "locale" is somewhat misleading, and so is the rather common way of presenting locale settings to a user under a name that primarily refers to country or regional settings. The word "locale" is of course related to the word "local," though there is a difference in meaning as well as in pronunciation. (In "locale," the stress is on the second syllable.)

There is sometimes some locality in a locale, though, since some conventions depend on the country or other area, too. For example, the British English locale differs from the U.S. English locale somewhat—e.g., in the conventions for quotation marks. Even then, language is the primary choice, and the country selection is secondary and optional.

Technically, locales are identified by structured strings with components for language, script (writing system), country or other territory, and variant. The underscore "_" is used as a separator between the components. Only the first component is obligatory, and it is a two- or three-letter language identifier (see Chapter 7). Naming conventions take care of unambiguity when components are omitted. For example, in the identifiers "en_GB" (British English) and "fr_CA" (Canadian French), the second component is a country identifier, since it consists of two letters. A four-letter component is a script identifier; for example, "zh_Hans" means Chinese written in the Traditional script.

In practice, locales are mostly identified by a language code only or by a language code and a country code. This means that they are very similar to language codes with an optional country specifier, though with different punctuation. In principle, the locale "en_US" indicates the notational conventions used by English-speaking people in the United States, whereas "en-US" is a language code for English as spoken in the U.S. In practice, the line between locales and languages is fuzzy.

A locale can be very specific, even relating to the conventions applied by some specific ethnic or cultural group. Ultimately, a locale can even be a personal locale: as a user, you could select a locale according to your native language, then perhaps a specific variant of the language, and add some cultural preferences (e.g., the use of "AD" or "CE" in year denotations), and finally some purely personal preferences, if you like. For practical reasons, though, most of the work revolves around language locales for now, though they may allow some variation.

Previously, different companies (and even different groups within one company), associations, groups of volunteers, and even individuals have decided on locale settings independently of each other—and without asking language authorities or representative groups of people using a language. Consequently, if you look at the different language versions of different programs, you can see incompatibilities and even errors. For example, language-dependent names for countries may vary within a language. For usability, it would be better if a U.K. citizen could see his country under the same name (and hence in the same place in alphabetic order) in country selection menus in different programs and services. Whether it is "United Kingdom" or "Great Britain" is less important from the practical point of view.

Some localization decisions in programs have been outright wrong, giving localization a somewhat bad reputation in some circles. Many people who do not speak English as their native language prefer an English version of a program to a poorly localized version. All too often, a "localized" version is actually a mixed-language version, perhaps even so that the program asks a question in the user's language but presents the options for an answer in English, or some commands in a menu in one language, others in another.

CLDR

The Common Locale Data Repository (CLDR) is about making user-oriented presentation of data easier, so that system designers and programmers can implement it easily. Ease of implementation is essential, since software vendors, still less individual people, cannot be expected to find out and implement all the possible conventions used in the hundreds of written languages of the world. Moreover, such conventions are sometimes debatable or subject to interpretation. Suppose you are designing programs that might be used throughout the world, with user interfaces in different languages. Would you like to take position on some heated question about the orthography or date format or names of countries in Swahili or Thai? You would probably prefer applying the rules decided by authorities and experts on the languages.

The general idea is to collect reliable data based on consensus about language-dependent conventions, present it in a rigorously defined (XML-based) format, and make it available worldwide. Ideally, the data is used when building general purpose subroutine libraries. Thus, a programmer need not know anything specific about the conventions, or even see them. She would just call, for example, a library routine to print a date, passed as a parameter in some standard format, according to the conventions of a language. The language would be specified by using a standardized language code, and it could be passed as a parameter to the output routine. Preferably, however, the routine would get the language code from user settings in the computer where the program runs. Of course, more primitive tools could be used, too. The mere availability of reliable data on cultural conventions on data presentation will help a lot, even if the information is implemented in programming "by hand"—i.e., by coding it separately for the supported languages.

At the cultural and social level, the CLDR approach makes it possible to support small languages and ethnic groups, even very small ones, at an acceptable cost. Once the data about the conventions of a language has been produced and stored in CLDR, there is no extra cost in supporting that language along with others, as regards the scope of CLDR. Of course, there would still be the cost of translating application-specific texts, such as command menus, instructions, and error message texts.

Dynamic adaptability to the user's locale is particularly important in modern online services, such as those based on the web services concept. When a request may come from any source, it is essential to try to recognize the user's preferred language and present the answer in the conventions of that language. This of course applies to situations where you communicate with a human user, rather than just a program. The localization is often best left to the user interface—e.g., so that in a server/client architecture, the server sends the response in internationalized format and the client presents it to the user according to the user's locale.

The CLDR activity was launched in 2004 by the Unicode Consortium, continuing the work of a joint effort by IBM, Sun, and OpenOffice.org. The activity has produced an extensive and growing database. The CLDR database is independent of the Unicode standard but related to it in many ways. Naturally, it uses Unicode as the character code, but many of the definitions in CLDR relate directly to the use of Unicode characters—e.g., the rules of using quotation marks in different languages and the language-specific collation rules that are to be superimposed on general Unicode rules. The main page of the CLDR activity is *http://www.unicode.org/cldr/*.

For discussion on CLDR, the public Unicode discussion list (email list), described at *http://www.unicode.org/consortium/distlist.html*, can be used. The list exists for all discussions related to the activities of the Unicode Consortium.

ICU is the best-known implementation of CLDR definitions, but a clear distinction should be made between them. CLDR specifies types of data that can be localized and specific values for such data in different locales. It does not prescribe any particular implementation. ICU, on the other hand, is a collection of software that implements the CLDR definitions, or part of it, among other things. It is quite possible to implement CLDR in other ways—e.g., using your own code that directly reads the CLDR data and converts it to suitable tables and algorithms. If you need or decide to implement just a small part of CLDR, you might even do it "by hand." As support to CLDR becomes more mature in software libraries, you will probably want to use their built-in CLDR support even for trivial tasks, just because it's easier.

CLDR versus Unix/Linux/POSIX locale concept

There have been some predecessors of CLDR, but their scope of application remained rather limited. In particular, although especially Unix and Linux systems have a "locale" concept, defined in the POSIX specifications and allowing user-selected presentation format for some data, it covers only a few features of presentation. CLDR is much wider, and growing even wider. Moreover, it is supported by major software companies, which have technological and economic motives for promoting and implementing the ideas. As an indication of this, they have permitted the creation of comparison tables, which compare CLDR definitions with the actual settings in software from different vendors.

Although CLDR owes much to the previous work, there will also be conflicts between old and new concepts and techniques. In particular, the POSIX-style locale concept involves *character code and encoding* in addition to language and country.

The POSIX specification has been merged into the Single Unix Specification, Version 3, by The Open Group, and it is available via *http://www.unix.org/version3/*. A POSIX locale contains the following categories, each identified with an environment variable:

LC_CTYPE
> Character classification and case conversion

LC_COLLATE
> Collation order

LC_MONETARY
> Monetary formatting

LC_NUMERIC
> Numeric formatting (other than monetary)

LC_TIME
> Date and time formats

LC_MESSAGES
> Formats of informative and diagnostic messages and interactive responses; in practice, strings that are to be interpreted as affirmative (yes) or negative (no) answers

Typically, the overall (POSIX) default values correspond to the locale "C" alias "POSIX," which is a programming-oriented locale, which in practice implies the English language. Setting the environment variable LC_ALL (e.g., with the shell command export LC_ALL=fr or setenv LC_ALL fr) is supposed to set all the above-mentioned variables to suitable values. In practice, the system-wide default for LC_CTYPE often carries the name of a *character encoding* (e.g., export LC_CTYPE=iso8859 -1, documented as "country setting"), as if encoding implied classification and conversion rules. Similarly, the available full locale names may carry the encoding, for example, en_GB.iso8859-1, en_US.UTF-8, etc.

Consider the following C program, which is very trivial: it simply prints the value "42.01" as formatted text. However, it has been localized in the POSIX sense. It calls the standard library routine setlocale in a manner that makes the program use the locale settings as defined by the environment variables. If the value of LC_ALL does not correspond to any locale known to the system, setlocale returns a null pointer, and our program recognizes this and issues an error message:

```
#include <stdio.h>
#include <locale.h>
int main() {
  if(!setlocale(LC_ALL, "")) {
    fprintf(stderr, "Unknown locale\n"); }
  printf("%6.2lf\n", 42.01);
  return 0; }
```

The following demonstration shows how the program (stored in *print.c*) is compiled with the gcc compiler and executed, then executed again after setting the locale (to French). Recompilation is not needed, since the locale selection takes place at runtime:

```
% gcc print.c
% ./a.out
 42.01
% setenv LC_ALL fr
% ./a.out
 42,01
%
```

Although this may look nice, localization has been rather problematic. The repertoire of available locales is usually rather limited, there can be errors in their values, and locale settings via environment variables might be used when they shouldn't. In testing the simple program, I made the mistake of having LC_ALL set to the value en (English) when trying to *compile* the program, and I got the error message "couldn't set locale correctly" from the compiler. Apparently, the compiler checked the locale settings, theoretically to adapt its own behavior to them, but did not recognize the locale name.

You can view the list of available locales with the locale -a command. The list may contain a mixture of primary language codes like "fr," language codes with country specifier like "fr_FR," and locale names that additionally contain the name of an encoding, such as "fr_FR.ISO8859-1." For some languages, there might be no simple, general locale like "fr" or "en."

 The repertoire of available locales in a system varies greatly. It may cause surprises. Even "en" for English might be missing.

Moreover, most users are probably unaware of the possibilities of setting the locale. Those who have tried to set the locale have often been disappointed with the effects. For example, you might expect that by doing the above in C, you would also make the standard isalpha function to work according to a localized definition of what is an alphabetic character, but this probably won't happen.

Using CLDR

Using software modules that output data in localized formats according to CLDR, a programmer can create programs that adapt to users' preferences in data presentation. Ideally, the programmer need not know the different conventions, though she needs to be aware of the fact that output formats vary. In particular, assumptions about any fixed or maximum length or character repertoire in, for example, date and time denotations should be avoided.

Do not localize everything. In the past, many mistakes have been made, for example, by writing numeric data to temporary files as formatted text. Suppose a number is written using an English-language locale as the string "1.234" (meaning a number somewhat larger than one). When the data is read by the same program in another environment, or just with a different locale setting, serious problems may arise. If the program uses a locale where the decimal separator is comma ",", it will fail to read "1.234" properly. An error might be reported or, worse still, just occur. The data might be read as "1234" for example, treating the period "." as a thousands separator.

Localize output presented to users, but not in the internal format inside a program or in interchange formats between programs.

Since CLDR is a relatively new invention, it will take time before you can use sufficiently high-level routines. The programming environment that can be expected to keep up with the development well is Java, since much of CLDR work adopts notations and definitions from the Java environment.

In the absence of library routines that print, say, a monetary amount according to each user's locale, you may need to write such routines yourself. You will probably want to deal with a few locales only, according to expected user base. Even in such somewhat boring work, CLDR can help you by specifying the exact format of output for the locales. If someone criticizes you for wrong output format for some locale, you can always say that you have been using the most up-to-date publicly collected information on it.

The CLDR data is primarily meant to be used in automatic data processing when a program generates menus, diagnostic messages, reports, tabulated data, date stamps, etc. It could also be used for data to be inserted into running text (paragraphs of normal text), though this involves many complications that are currently not addressed in CLDR, such as word inflection. As a large collection of information, CLDR can also be useful to translators, editors, and writers in "manual" work—e.g., in translating rarely used names of languages and in estimating what characters will probably be needed in texts in some language.

Internationalization and Localization

Before you can localize software reasonably well, it must be internationalized. The software must internally use data formats that can easily be mapped to various presentations. This typically means adherence to some published international standard or specification.

Moreover, the software must perform input and output operations by using subroutines that know how to find the current locale settings.

This mostly applies to output, since localization of input has not been addressed much yet. However, localization is important in menu-based input. For example, if the user is prompted to select a currency, typically from a short list, the currencies should usually be specified by names in the user's preferred language.

For example, localizable software would process monetary data in a standardized internal format, normally with the sum and the currency in separate fields, and always carrying the currency information, with no implied currency. Only on output (and input) should the monetary data be converted, via a general purpose routine, into a language-dependent format, such as "$42.50" or "42,50 $" or "42:50 dollar."

This approach avoids many character-level problems, since the internal data formats typically use a limited repertoire of characters only, often just ASCII. For example, monetary data would be represented as a combination of a number (represented as a binary integer or floating-point number, or perhaps as an ASCII string) and currency identifier (represented as a string of ASCII letters or as an integer). Only the output routine would need to deal with special currency symbols, digits of different scripts, etc.

 Localizable software uses universal, exact, and easily processable data formats internally. It converts to language-dependent format on output only.

Existing software that stores monetary data as strings like "$42.50" (to take a somewhat artificial example) might need considerable changes to become localizable. However, using a language-dependent format for the internal storage and processing of data does not as such prevent localization. You would just need to make sure that the format is well-defined and consistently used so that it can be converted to some international format that can be passed to a localized output routine. It would however be a real obstacle to localization, if the software has been coded to perform output at different places and directly using the internal format as the output format. In that case, it would need substantial modularization of output.

CLDR Description and Data

Currently CLDR contains definitions for data formats like the following:

- Names of languages (e.g., for use in language menus or bibliographic information)
- Names of scripts (such as "Latin," "Cyrillic," etc.)
- Names of countries and some other territories, such as continents
- Names of calendar systems (e.g. "Gregorian calendar")
- Names of time zones (e.g., "East European normal time")

- Different (short, medium, long) formats for dates (in different calendars)
- Formats for time of the day (e.g., "2 PM" versus "14.00")
- Format of decimal numbers (e.g., 2,50 versus 2.50) and percentages (e.g., 7% versus 7 %)
- Format of monetary data (e.g., €1.23 versus 1,23 €)
- Names of currencies (e.g., for use in explanations and menus)

Currently there is no data for localized names of characters, although there would surely be need for them, for example, in character maps, in some error messages, and in user interface components for asking "which character is this?" There have been some discussions on such data, but it would be a major effort to compose a consensus-based list of names for characters in some language, even if we limit ourselves to a small subset of Unicode.

The CLDR database uses an XML-based format called *Locale Data Markup Language* (LDML), which has been defined as Unicode Technical Standard #35 at *http://www.unicode.org/reports/tr35/*.

For quick access to files containing data for particular locales, use the index page *http://unicode.org/cldr/data/common/*. It is divided into directories:

collation
> Locale-specific exceptions and additions to Unicode collating order (which was described in Chapter 5)

main
> This contains most of the locale data—everything that has no specific directory

posix
> Locale settings for POSIX compatibility

supplemental
> Information that is needed for some formatting of data but is not itself localizable—e.g., information about the use of historical currencies

test
> Generated test data for checking implementations against CLDR (described in *http://unicode.org/cldr/data/common/test/readme.html*)

For example, most of the data for the French language locale (code: fr) is available at *http://unicode.org/cldr/data/common/main/fr.xml*. An extract of that data is shown in Figure 11-3, containing information about decimal and group (thousands) separator, currency format, and the start of data that contains French names for currencies. There is some additional data for country-specific French locales, for example, for Canadian (country code: CA) French at *http://unicode.org/cldr/data/common/main/fr_CA.xml*.

The data just mentioned is in LDML format, and if you access it with a web browser, you will see it as text with XML markup. Although it is readable to some extent, at least to people who have a basic knowledge of XML and who can guess the meanings of element

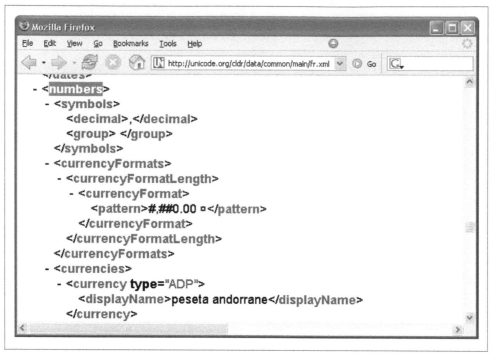

Figure 11-3. Extract of CLDR data for French, in XML format

and attribute names, it's really not for a common user. The data is also available in a more formatted and more readable form, though partly as very large documents, at *http://www.unicode.org/cldr/comparison_charts.html*, and specifically in the by-type chart index at *http://www.unicode.org/cldr/data/diff/by_type/index.html* illustrated in Figure 11-4. It shows different patterns for presentation of percentages (producing, for example, "42%", "%42", 42%, 42 %, etc.) and the codes of the languages for which they apply.

Problems with Aspects of Localization

As mentioned earlier in this chapter, locales are mostly about languages, not locality. However, the selection of a locale is very often presented to the user as a matter of choosing a country or area. Yet it is currently impossible to specify locale settings as applying to a country or other geographic area independently of language. Territory codes can only be used as a subcode after a language code.

This will hopefully be fixed somehow, making language and territory orthogonal aspects of "localeness." Few localization-relevant things can be reasonably described as belonging to a form of a language as spoken in a particular country, as opposed to the language in general. Such features include the different rules for quotation marks in U.S. English and British English. On the other hand, there are things that should depend on the geographic position alone. The default time zone might be one of them. For some large countries, the

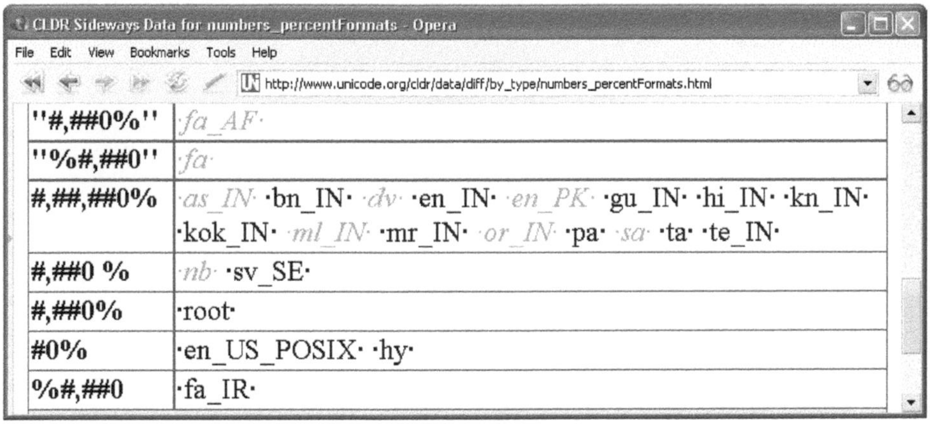
CLDR Sideways Data for numbers_percentFormats - Opera
File Edit View Bookmarks Tools Help
http://www.unicode.org/cldr/data/diff/by_type/numbers_percentFormats.html
"#,##0%" ·fa_AF·
"%#,##0" ·fa·
#,##,##0% ·as_IN· ·bn_IN· ·dv· ·en_IN· ·en_PK· ·gu_IN· ·hi_IN· ·kn_IN· ·kok_IN· ·ml_IN· ·mr_IN· ·or_IN· ·pa· ·sa· ·ta· ·te_IN·
#,##0 % ·nb· ·sv_SE·
#,##0% ·root·
#0% ·en_US_POSIX· ·hy·
%#,##0 ·fa_IR·

Figure 11-4. CLDR Sideways Data for percent formats

country code alone would not imply a meaningful default. The point is that the time zone is not derivable from language, even when a specific variant of language is specified.

Language selection menus often contain country-specific variants of languages for no good reason: the choice between them usually has no effect. The language forms could be different, but not in a manner that affects the behavior of programs. Spellchecks are probably the most common (potential) area where the country may matter. For example, Brazilian Portuguese has somewhat different spelling than Portuguese in Portugal.

Ideally, language codes such as en_GB and en_US should be kept separate from the territory setting. After all, an American living in the U.K. might prefer to see quotation marks used in the U.S. English style, yet see times displayed in the time zone used in Britain, even if the display format is in U.S. English style (assuming it differs from British English).

Some people prefer dates and times as 2005-09-15 and 23:54 (i.e., in ISO 8601 format), especially if they read texts in different languages. There is no locale that matches such preferences. It would be possible to define such a locale, of course, and distribute it for use by people who prefer such presentation. They would not need to understand how a locale definition is written in LDML. Naturally, this would work only in programs that allow the use of locale definitions outside a predefined set like CLDR. Even then, users would have the problem of combining their language preferences with the specific preferences they have selected. This will probably imply that good-quality implementations of CLDR-based localization will offer a way to *superimpose* locales: set a locale, and then set one or more other locales, which override some of the settings.

The conclusion is that whenever possible, language and country selection should be kept logically separate. Both of them should be derived from user-supplied data. They should affect different settings, such as date and number formats, in a manner that is overridable by the user.

Globalization is more than making things global. Adequately globalized software adapts to varying conditions of use, including the user's language, country, cultural habits, and personal preferences.

Tables for Writing Characters

This appendix consists of compact information on writing characters. The first three tables present some key sequences for writing some common characters in a few environments. The last table is different: it maps the Symbol font to Unicode.

In the first three tables, characters are classified logically, by meaning and usage, rather than by Unicode structure. Table A-1 contains Latin letters and their ligatures; Table A-2 is for Greek letters and punctuation; and Table A-3 has other commonly used characters. The columns in these tables are:

- A glyph of the character (in Times or Times New Roman font, if possible).
- A name of the character. Usually the Unicode name is used, but for brevity, some attributes have been omitted, when they can be inferred. Moreover, the name "guillemet" is used instead of "double angle quotation mark."
- The sequence of typing the character. This contains the Unicode number in hexadecimal. You can use the number to construct the character reference &#x*n*; that can be used in HTML and XML.
- The Alt-*n* sequence. This contains the Unicode number in decimal, except for numbers in the range 128–159, which are Windows Latin 1 codes. For numbers in the range 160–255, the sequences work in all Windows environments.
- A special way that *may* work in MS Word. This depends on Word version and settings as well as the keyboard. The information given mainly applies to English (U.S.) keyboards. For Greek letters, this column shows the key to be used on a qwerty keyboard when set in Greek mode.
- The entity reference in HTML, if available. Otherwise the (decimal) character reference, which can be used in HTML and in XML. Note that you can alternatively use a hexadecimal reference based on the number in column "Alt-X" (e.g., ¹).
- Notes, which refer to annotations after the tables. They may mention additional alternatives to produce the character, or comment on the usage of a character, or explain notations. Some notes just mention a language in which the character is used. This is meant to help in identifying the character, not to exclude use in other languages.

Table A-1. Latin letters and ligatures

	Name of character	Alt-X	Alt-*n*	Word	HTML	Notes
Á	A with acute	c1	0193	Ctrl-' A	&Aacute;	Note 1
Ă	A with breve	102	258		&#258;	
Â	A with circumflex	c2	0194	Ctrl-Shift-6 A	&Acirc;	Note 1
Ä	A with dieresis	c4	0196	Ctrl-Shift-; A	&Auml;	Note 1
À	A with grave	c0	0192	Ctrl-` A	&Agrave;	Note 1
Ā	A with macron	100	256		&#256;	
Ą	A with ogonek	104	260		&#260;	
Å	A with ring	c5	0197	Ctrl-Shift-2 A	&Aring;	Note 1
Ǻ	A with ring and acute	1fa	506		&#506;	
Ã	A with tilde	c3	0195	Ctrl-~ A	&Atilde;	Note 1
Æ	AE	c6	0198	Ctrl-Shift-7 A	&AElig;	Note 1
Ǽ	AE with acute	1fc	508		&#508;	
Ć	C with acute	106	262		&#262;	
Č	C with caron	10c	268		&#268;	
Ç	C with cedilla	c7	0199	Ctrl-, C	&Ccedil;	
Ĉ	C with circumflex	108	264		&#264;	
Ċ	C with dot above	10a	266		&#266;	
Ď	D with caron	10e	270		&#270;	
Đ	D with stroke	110	272		&#272;	Croatian
Ð	Eth	d0	0208	Ctrl-' D	&ETH;	Icelandic
É	E with acute	c9	0201	Ctrl-' E	&Eacute;	Note 1
Ĕ	E with breve	114	276		&#276;	
Ě	E with caron	11a	282		&#282;	
Ê	E with circumflex	ca	0202	Ctrl-Shift-6 E	&Ecirc;	Note 1
Ë	E with dieresis	cb	0203	Ctrl-Shift-; E	&Euml;	Note 1
Ė	E with dot above	116	278		&#278;	
È	E with grave	c8	0200	Ctrl-` E	&Egrave;	Note 1
Ē	E with macron	112	274		&#274;	
Ę	E with ogenek	118	280		&#280;	
Ğ	G with breve	11e	286		&#286;	
Ģ	G with cedilla	122	290		&#290;	

	Name of character	Alt-X	Alt-*n*	Word	HTML	Notes
Ĝ	G with circumflex	11c	284		&#284;	
Ġ	G with dot above	120	288		&#288;	
Ĥ	H with circumflex	124	292		&#292;	
Ħ	H with stroke	126	294		&#294;	Maltese
Í	I with acute	cd	0205	Ctrl-' I	&Iacute;	Note 1
Ĭ	I with breve	12c	300		&#300;	
Î	I with circumflex	ce	0206	Ctrl-Shift-6 I	&Icirc;	Note 1
Ï	I with dieresis	cf	0207	Ctrl-Shift-; I	&Iuml;	Note 1
İ	I with dot above	130	304		&#304;	
Ì	I with grave	cc	0204	Ctrl-` I	&Igrave;	Note 1
Ī	I with macron	12a	298		&#298;	
Į	I with ogonek	12e	302		&#302;	
Ĩ	I with tilde	128	296		&#296;	
IJ	ligature IJ	132	306		&#306;	Dutch
Ĵ	J with circumflex	134	308		&#308;	
Ķ	K with cedilla	136	310		&#310;	
Ĺ	L with acute	139	313		&#313;	
Ľ	L with caron	13d	317		&#317;	
Ļ	L with cedilla	13b	315		&#315;	
Ŀ	L with middle dot	13f	319		&#319;	
Ł	L with stroke	141	321		&#321;	Polish
Ń	N with acute	143	323		&#323;	
Ň	N with caron	147	327		&#327;	
Ņ	N with cedilla	145	325		&#325;	
Ñ	N with tilde	d1	0209	Ctrl-Shift-` N	&Ntilde;	Note 1
Ŋ	Eng	14a	330		&#330;	Sámi
Ó	O with acute	d3	0211	Ctrl-' O	&Oacute;	Note 1
Ŏ	O with breve	14e	334		&#334;	
Ô	O with circumflex	d4	0212	Ctrl-Shift-6 O	&Ocirc;	Note 1
Ö	O with dieresis	d6	0214	Ctrl-Shift-; O	&Ouml;	Note 1
Ő	O with double acute	150	336		&#336;	Hungarian
Ò	O with grave	d2	0210	Ctrl-` O	&Ograve;	Note 1
Ō	O with macron	14c	332		&#332;	

	Name of character	Alt-X	Alt-*n*	Word	HTML	Notes
Ø	O with oblique stroke	d8	0216	Ctrl-/ O	&Oslash;	Danish
Ǿ	O with stroke and acute	1fe	510		&#510;	
Õ	O with tilde	d5	0213	Ctrl-Shift-` O	&Otilde;	Note 1
Œ	ligature OE	152	0140	Ctrl-Shift-7 O	&OElig;	Note 1
Ŕ	R with acute	154	340		&#340;	
Ř	R with caron	158	344		&#344;	
Ŗ	R with cedilla	156	342		&#342;	
Ś	S with acute	15a	346		&#346;	
Š	S with caron	160	0160		&Scaron;	
Ş	S with cedilla	15e	350		&#350;	
Ŝ	S with circumflex	15c	348		&#348;	
Ť	T with caron	164	356		&#356;	
Ţ	T with cedilla	162	354		&#354;	
Ŧ	T with stroke	166	358		&#358;	Sámi
Þ	Thorn	de	0222		&THORN;	Icelandic
Ú	U with acute	da	0218	Ctrl-' U	&Uacute;	Note 1
Ŭ	U with breve	16c	364		&#364;	
Û	U with circumflex	db	0219	Ctrl-Shift-6 U	&Ucirc;	Note 1
Ü	U with dieresis	dc	0220	Ctrl-Shift-; U	&Uuml;	Note 1
Ű	U with double acute	170	368		&#368;	Hungarian
Ù	U with grave	d9	0217	Ctrl-` U	&Ugrave;	Note 1
Ū	U with macron	16a	362		&#362;	
Ų	U with ogonek	172	370		&#370;	
Ů	U with ring above	16e	366		&#366;	
Ũ	U with tilde	168	360		&#360;	
Ŵ	W with circumflex	174	372		&#372;	
Ý	Y with acute	dd	0221	Ctrl-' Y	&Yacute;	Note 1
Ŷ	Y with circumflex	176	374		&#374;	
Ÿ	Y with dieresis	178	376	Ctrl-Shift-; Y	&Yuml;	Note 1
Ź	Z with acute	179	377		&#377;	
Ž	Z with caron	17d	381		&#381;	
Ż	Z with dot above	17b	379		&#379;	

	Name of character	Alt-X	Alt-*n*	Word	HTML	Notes
á	a with acute	e1	0225	Ctrl-' a	&aacute;	Note 1
ă	a with breve	103	259		&#259;	
â	a with circumflex	e2	0226	Ctrl-Shift-6 a	&acirc;	Note 1
ä	a with dieresis	e4	0228	Ctrl-Shift-; a	&auml;	Note 1
à	a with grave	e0	0224	Ctrl-` a	&agrave;	Note 1
ā	a with macron	101	257		&#257;	
ą	a with ogonek	105	261		&#261;	
å	a with ring	e5	0229	Ctrl-Shift-2 a	&aring;	Note 1
ǻ	a with ring and acute	1fb	507		&#507;	
ã	a with tilde	e3	0227	Ctrl-Shift-` a	&atilde;	Note 1
æ	ae	e6	0230	Ctrl-Shift-6 a	&aelig;	Note 1
ǽ	ae with acute	1fd	509		&#509;	
ć	c with acute	107	263		&#263;	
č	c with caron	10d	269		&#269;	
ç	c with cedilla	e7	0231	Ctrl-, c	&ccedil;	
ĉ	c with circumflex	109	265		&#265;	
ċ	c with dot above	10b	267		&#267;	
ď	d with caron	10f	271		&#271;	
đ	d with stroke	111	273		&#273;	Croatian
ð	eth	f0	0240	Ctrl-' d	&eth;	Icelandic
é	e with acute	e9	0233	Ctrl-' e	&eacute;	Note 1
ĕ	e with breve	115	277		&#277;	
ě	e with caron	11b	283		&#283;	
ê	e with circumflex	ea	0234	Ctrl-Shift-6 e	&ecirc;	Note 1
ë	e with dieresis	eb	0235	Ctrl-Shift-; e	&euml;	Note 1
ė	e with dot above	117	279		&#279;	
è	e with grave	e8	0232	Ctrl-` e	&egrave;	Note 1
ē	e with macron	113	275		&#275;	
ę	e with ogenek	119	281		&#281;	
ƒ	f with hook	192	0131		&fnof;	Florin
ﬁ	ligature fi	fb01	64257		&#64257;	
ﬂ	ligature fl	fb02	64257		&#64257;	

Name of character		Alt-X	Alt-*n*	Word	HTML	Notes
ğ	g with breve	11f	287		&#287;	
ģ	g with cedilla	123	291		&#291;	
ĝ	g with circumflex	11d	285		&#285;	
ġ	g with dot above	121	289		&#289;	
ĥ	h with circumflex	125	293		&#293;	
ħ	h with stroke	127	295		&#295;	Maltese
í	i with acute	ed	237	Ctrl-' i	&iacute;	Note 1
ĭ	i with breve	12d	301		&#301;	
î	i with circumflex	ee	0238	Ctrl-Shift-6 i	&icirc;	Note 1
ï	i with dieresis	ef	0239	Ctrl-Shift-; i	&iuml;	Note 1
ì	i with grave	ec	0236	Ctrl-` i	&igrave;	Note 1
ī	i with macron	12b	299		&#299;	
į	i with ogonek	12f	303		&#303;	
ĩ	i with tilde	129	297		&#297;	
ı	dotless i	131	305		&#305;	
ij	ligature ij	133	307		&#307;	Dutch
ĵ	j with circumflex	135	309		&#309;	
ķ	k with cedilla	137	311		&#311;	
ĸ	kra	138	312		&#312;	Greenl.
ĺ	l with acute	13a	314		&#314;	
ľ	l with caron	13e	318		&#318;	
ļ	l with cedilla	13c	316		&#316;	
ŀ	l with middle dot	140	320		&#320;	
ł	l with stroke	142	322		&#322;	Polish
ʼn	n preceded by apostrophe	149	329		&#329;	Afrikaans
ń	n with acute	144	324		&#324;	
ň	n with caron	148	328		&#328;	
ņ	n with cedilla	146	326		&#326;	
ñ	n with tilde	f1	0241	Ctrl-Shift-` n	&ntilde;	Note 1
ŋ	eng	14b	331		&#331;	Sámi
ó	o with acute	f3	0243	Ctrl-' o	&oacute;	Note 1
ŏ	o with breve	14f	335		&#335;	

	Name of character	Alt-X	Alt-*n*	Word	HTML	Notes
ô	o with circumflex	f4	0244	Ctrl-Shift-6 o	&ocirc;	Note 1
ö	o with dieresis	f6	0246	Ctrl-Shift-; o	&ouml;	Note 1
ő	o with double acute	151	337		&#337;	Hungarian
ò	o with grave	f2	0242	Ctrl-` o	&ograve;	Note 1
ō	o with macron	14d	333		&#333;	
ø	o with stroke	f8	0248	Ctrl-/ o	&oslash;	Danish
ǿ	o with stroke and acute	1ff	511		&#511;	
õ	o with tilde	f5	0245	Ctrl-Shift-` o	&otilde;	Note 1
œ	ligature oe	153	0156	Ctrl-Shift-6 o	&oelig;	French
ŕ	r with acute	155	341		&#341;	
ř	r with caron	159	345		&#345;	
ŗ	r with cedilla	157	343		&#343;	
ś	s with acute	15b	347		&#347;	
š	s with caron	161	0154		&scaron;	
ş	s with cedilla	15f	351		&#351;	
ŝ	s with circumflex	15d	349		&#349;	
ſ	long s	17f	383		&#383;	Historical
ß	sharp s	df	0223	Ctrl-Shift-6 s	&szlig;	Note 1
ť	t with caron	165	357		&#357;	
ţ	t with cedilla	163	355		&#355;	
ŧ	t with stroke	167	359		&#359;	Sámi
þ	thorn	fe	0254		&thorn;	Icelandic
ú	u with acute	fa	0250	Ctrl-' u	&uacute;	Note 1
ŭ	u with breve	16d	365		&#365;	
û	u with circumflex	fb	0251	Ctrl-Shift-6 u	&ucirc;	Note 1
ü	u with dieresis	fc	0252	Ctrl-Shift-; u	&uuml;	Note 1
ű	u with double acute	171	369		&#369;	Hungarian
ù	u with grave	f9	0249	Ctrl-` u	&ugrave;	Note 1
ū	u with macron	16b	363		&#363;	
ų	u with ogonek	173	371		&#371;	
ů	u with ring above	16f	367		&#367;	
ũ	u with tilde	169	361		&#361;	

	Name of character	Alt-X	Alt-*n*	Word	HTML	Notes
ŵ	w with circumflex	175	373		&#373;	
ý	y with acute	fd	0253	Ctrl-' y	&yacute;	Note 1
ŷ	y with circumflex	177	375		&#375;	
ÿ	y with dieresis	ff	0255	Ctrl-Shift-; y	&yuml;	Note 1
ź	z with acute	17a	378		&#378;	
ž	z with caron	17e	382		&#382;	
ż	z with dot above	17c	380		&#380;	

Table A-2. Greek letters and tone marks

	Name of character	Alt-X	Alt-*n*	Word	HTML	Notes
΄	Greek tonos	384	900	;᾿	&#900;	Note 1
῞	Greek dialytika tonos	385	901	W᾿	&#901;	Note 1
Α	Alpha	391	913	A	&Alpha;	
Ά	Alpha with tonos	386	902	;A	&#902;	
Β	Beta	392	914	B	&Beta;	
Γ	Gamma	393	915	G	&Gamma;	
Δ	Delta	394	916	D	&Delta;	
Ε	Epsilon	395	917	E	&Epsilon;	
Έ	Epsilon with tonos	388	904	;E	&#904;	
Ζ	Zeta	396	918	Z	&Zeta;	
Η	Eta	397	919	H	&Eta;	
Ή	Eta with tonos	389	905	;H	&#905;	
Θ	Theta	398	920	U	&Theta;	
Ι	Iota	399	921	I	&Iota;	
Ϊ	Iota with dialytika	3aa	938	:I	&#938;	
Ί	Iota with tonos	38a	906	;I	&#906;	
Κ	Kappa	39a	922	K	&Kappa;	
Λ	Lamda	39b	923	L	&Lambda;	
Μ	Mu	39c	924	M	&Mu;	
Ν	Nu	39d	925	N	&Nu;	
Ξ	Xi	39e	926	J	&Xi;	
Ο	Omicron	39f	927	O	&Omicron;	
Ό	Omicron with tonos	38c	908	;O	&#908;	

	Name of character	Alt-X	Alt-*n*	Word	HTML	Notes
Π	Pi	3a0	928	P	&Pi;	≠ product
P	Rho	3a1	929	R	&Rho;	
Σ	Sigma	3a3	931	S	&Sigma;	≠ sum
T	Tau	3a4	932	T	&Tau;	
Υ	Upsilon	3a5	933	Y	&Upsilon;	
Ϋ	Upsilon with dialytika	3ab	939	:Y	&#939;	
Ύ	Upsilon with tonos	38e	910	;Y	&#910;	
ϒ	Upsilon with hook symbol	3d2	978		&upsih;	∉WGL4
Φ	Phi	3a6	934	F	&Phi;	
X	Chi	3a7	935	X	&Chi;	
Ψ	Psi	3a8	936	C	&Psi;	
Ω	Omega	3a9	937	V	&Omega;	≠ ohm
Ώ	Omega with tonos	38f	911	;V	&#911;	
α	alpha	3b1	945	a	&alpha;	
ά	alpha with tonos	3ac	940	;a	&#940;	
β	beta	3b2	946	b	&beta;	
γ	gamma	3b3	947	g	&gamma;	
δ	delta	3b4	948	d	&delta;	
ε	epsilon	3b5	949	e	&epsilon;	
έ	epsilon with tonos	3ad	941	;e	&#941;	
ζ	zeta	3b6	950	z	&zeta;	
η	eta	3b7	951	h	&eta;	
ή	eta with tonos	3ae	942	;h	&#942;	
θ	theta	3b8	952	u	&theta;	
ϑ	theta symbol	3d1	977		&thetasym;	∉WGL4
ι	iota	3b9	953	i	&iota;	
ϊ	iota with dialytika	3ca	970	:i	&#970;	
ΐ	iota with dialytika and tonos	390	912	Wi	&#912;	
ί	iota with tonos	3af	943	;i	&#943;	
κ	kappa	3ba	954	k	&kappa;	
λ	lamda	3bb	955	l	&lambda;	
μ	mu	3bc	956	m	&mu;	≠ micro
ν	nu	3bd	957	n	&nu;	

	Name of character	Alt-X	Alt-*n*	Word	HTML	Notes
ξ	xi	3be	958	j	&xi;	
ο	omicron	3bf	959	o	&omicron;	
ό	omicron with tonos	3cc	972	;o	&#972;	
π	pi	3c0	960	p	&pi;	
ϖ	pi symbol	3d6	982		&piv;	∉WGL4
ρ	rho	3c1	961	r	&rho;	
σ	sigma	3c3	963	s	&sigma;	
ς	final sigma	3c2	962	w	&sigmaf;	
τ	tau	3c4	964	t	&tau;	
υ	upsilon	3c5	965	y	&upsilon;	
ϋ	upsilon with dialytika	3cb	971	:y	&#971;	
ΰ	upsilon with dialytika and tonos	3b0	944	Wy	&#944;	
ύ	upsilon with tonos	3cd	973	;y	&#973;	
φ	phi	3c6	966	f	&phi;	
χ	chi	3c7	967	x	&chi;	
ψ	psi	3c8	968	c	&psi;	
ω	omega	3c9	969	v	&omega;	
ώ	omega with tonos	3ce	974	;v	&#974;	

Table A-3. Other commonly needed characters

	Name of character	Alt-X	Alt-*n*	Word	HTML	Notes
Superscripts						
¹	Superscript one	b9	0185		&sup1;	
²	Superscript two	b2	0178		&sup2:	
³	Superscript three	b3	0179		&sup3;	
Fractions						
½	One half	bd	0189	1/2	&frac12;	
¼	One quarter	bc	0188	1/4	&frac14;	
¾	Three quarters	be	0190	3/4	&frac34;	
⅛	One eighth	215b	8539		&#8539;	
⅜	Three eighths	215c	8540		&#8540;	
⅝	Five eighths	215d	8541		&#8541;	
⅞	Seven eighths	215e	8542		&#8542;	
/	Fraction slash	2044	8260		&frasl;	

	Name of character	Alt-X	Alt-*n*	Word	HTML	Notes
Presentational forms of Latin letters						
ª	Feminine ordinal indicator	aa	0170		&ordf;	Spanish
º	Masculine ordinal indicator	ba	0186		&ordm;	Spanish
ⁿ	Superscript n	207f	8319		&#8319;	
Letter-like symbols						
℅	Care of	2105	8453		&#8453;	
©	Copyright sign	a9	0169	(c)	&copy;	AltGr-c
℮	Estimated symbol	212e	8494		&#8494;	
µ	Micro sign	b5	0181	AltGr-m	&micro;	≠ mu
Ω	Ohm sign	2126	8486		&#8486;	≠ Omega
®	Registered sign	ae	0174	(r)	&reg;	AltGr-r
ℓ	Script small l	2113	8467		&#8467;	
™	Trademark sign	2122	0153	(tm)	&trade;	AltGr-t
℘	Script capital p	2118	8472		&weierp;	¢WGL4
ℑ	Black-letter capital I	2111	8465		&image;	¢WGL4
ℜ	Black-letter capital R	211c	8476		&real;	¢WGL4
ℵ	Alef symbol	2135	8501		&alefsym;	¢WGL4
Currency symbols						
¢	Cent sign	a2	0162	Ctrl-/ c	&cent;	
¤	Currency sign	a4	0164		&curren;	Generic
$	Dollar sign	24	036	$	&#36;	
€	Euro sign	20ac	0128	AltGr-e	&euro;	Note 2
₣	French franc sign	20a3	8355		&#8355;	Historical
₤	Lira sign	20a4	8356		&#8356;	Rare
₧	Peseta sign	20a7	8359		&#8359;	Historical
£	Pound sign	a3	0163		&pound;	
¥	Yen sign	a5	0165		&yen;	Also yuan
Quotation marks						
"	Quotation mark	22		" Ctrl-z	&quot;	ASCII
'	Apostrophe	27		' Ctrl-z	&apos;	ASCII
"	Left double quotation mark	201c	0147	Ctrl-` "	&ldquo;	Note 3

	Name of character	Alt-X	Alt-_n_	Word	HTML	Notes
"	Right double quotation mark	201d	0148	Ctrl-' "	&rdquo;	Note 3
'	Left single quotation mark	2018	0145	Ctrl-` '	&lsquo;	Note 3
'	Right single quotation mark	2019	0146	Ctrl-' '	&rsquo;	Note 3
«	Left-pointing guillemet	ab	0171	Ctrl-` <	&laquo;	Note 3
»	Right-pointing guillemet	bb	0187	Ctrl-` >	&raquo;	Note 3
‹	Left-pointing single angle quotation mark	2039	0139		&lsaquo;	
›	Right-pointing single angle quotation mark	203a	0155		&rsaquo;	
„	Double low-9 quotation mark	201e	0132		&bdquo;	Note 3
‚	Single low-9 quotation mark	201a	0130		&sbquo;	Note 3
'	Single high-reversed-9 quotation mark	201b	8219		&#8219;	

Hyphens

-	Hyphen-minus	2d	045	-	&#45;	ASCII
-	Hyphen	2010	8208		&#8208;	∉WGL4
	Soft hyphen	ad	0173		&shy;	Note 4
-	Nonbreaking hyphen	2011	8209		&#8209;	∉WGL4

Other punctuation marks

–	En dash	2013	0150	Ctrl-minus	&ndash;	Note 5
—	Em dash	2014	0151	AltGr-minus	&mdash;	Note 5
─	Horizontal bar	2015	8213		&#8213;	
…	Horizontal ellipsis	2026	0133	AltGr-.	&hellip;	
¿	Inverted question mark	bf	0191	AltGr-?	&iquest;	Note 6
¡	Inverted exclamation mark	a1	0161	AltGr-!	&iexcl;	Note 6
‼	Double exclamation mark	203c	8252		&#8252;	
·	Middle dot	b7	0183		&middot:	
·	Greek ano teleia	387	903		&#903;	Upper dot
•	Bullet	2022	0149		&bull;	

	Name of character	Alt-X	Alt-*n*	Word	HTML	Notes
〈	Left-pointing angle bracket	2329	9001		&lang;	∉WGL4
〉	Right-pointing angle bracket	2330	9002		&rang;	∉WGL4

Punctuation-like marks

	Name of character	Alt-X	Alt-*n*	Word	HTML	Notes
&	Ampersand	26	038	&	&amp;	
<	Less-than sign	3c	060	<	&lt;	
>	Greater-than sign	3e	062	>	&gt;	
_	Low line	5f	095	_	&#95;	
=	Double low line	2017	8215		&#8215;	
‾	Overline	203e	8254		&oline;	≠ macron
|	Vertical line	7c	0124	|	|	
¦	Broken bar	a6	0166		&brvbar;	
¶	Pilcrow sign	b6	0182	Insert →	&para;	
§	Section sign	a7	0167	Insert →	&sect;	
†	Dagger	2020	0134		&dagger;	
‡	Double dagger	2021	0135		&Dagger;	
@	Commercial at	40	064	@	&#64;	
\	Reverse solidus	5c	092	\	&#92;	
#	Number sign	23	035	#	&#35;	
‰	Per mille sign	2030	0137		&permil;	
°	Degree sign	b0	0176		&deg;	
′	Prime	2032	8242		&prime;	≠ '
″	Double prime	2033	8243		&Prime;	≠ "

Spacing diacritic marks and similar charcters

	Name of character	Alt-X	Alt-*n*	Word	HTML	Notes
´	Acute accent	b4	0180	´ ␣	&acute;	Note 7
˘	Breve	2d8	728		&#728;	
ˇ	Caron	2c7	711		&#711;	
¸	Cedilla	b8	0184	Ctrl-, ␣	&cedil;	
^	Circumflex accent	5e	094	^	&#94;	or: ^ ␣
¨	Dieresis	a8	0168	¨ ␣	&uml;	
˙	Dot above	2d9	729		&#729;	
˝	Double acute accent	2dd	733		&#733;	
`	Grave accent	60	096	`	&#96;	or: ` ␣

	Name of character	Alt-X	Alt-*n*	Word	HTML	Notes
‾	Macron	af	0175		`&macr;`	≠overline
ˆ	Modifier letter circumflex	2c6	710		`&circ;`	
ˉ	Modifier letter macron	2c9	713		`&#713;`	
˛	Ogonek	2db	731		`&#731;`	
˚	Ring above	2da	730		`&#730;`	
˜	Small tilde	2dc	0152		`&tilde;`	
~	Tilde	7e	0126	~	`&#126;`	or: ~ ʾ

Arrows

	Name of character	Alt-X	Alt-*n*	Word	HTML	Notes
←	Leftward arrow	2190	8592		`&larr;`	
↑	Upward arrow	2191	8593		`&uarr;`	
→	Rightward arrow	2192	8594		`&rarr;`	
↓	Downward arrow	2193	8595		`&darr;`	
↔	Left right arrow	2194	8596		`&harr;`	
↕	Up down arrow	2195	8597			
↨	Up down arrow with base	21a8	8616			
↵	Down and left arrow	21b5	8629		`&crarr;`	∉WGL4
⇐	Leftward double arrow	21d0	8656		`&lArr;`	∉WGL4
⇑	Upward double arrow	21d1	8657		`&uArr;`	∉WGL4
⇒	Rightward double arrow	21d2	8658		`&rArr;`	∉WGL4
⇓	Downward double arrow	21d3	8659		`&dArr;`	∉WGL4
⇔	Left right double arrow	21d4	8660		`&hArr;`	

Mathematical symbols

	Name of character	Alt-X	Alt-*n*	Word	HTML	Notes
≈	Almost equal to	2248	8776		`&asymp;`	
∠	Angle	2220	8736		`&ang;`	∉WGL4
≅	Approximately equal to	2245	8773		`&cong;`	∉WGL4
∗	Asterisk operator	2217	8727		`&lowast;`	∉WGL4
•	Bullet operator	2219	8729		`&#8729;`	
⊕	Circled plus	2295	8853		`&oplus;`	∉WGL4
⊗	Circled times	2297	8855		`&otimes;`	∉WGL4
÷	Division sign	f7	0247		`&divide;`	

	Name of character	Alt-X	Alt-n	Word	HTML	Notes
/	Division slash	2215	8725		&#8725;	
·	Dot operator	22c5	8901		&sdot;	∉WGL4
≥	Greater-than or equal to	2265	8805		&ge;	
≡	Identical to	2261	8801		&equiv;	
Δ	Increment	2206	8710		&#8710;	
∞	Infinity	221e	8734		&infin;	
∫	Integral	222b	8747		&int;	
⌈	Left ceiling	2308	8968		&lceil;	∉WGL4
⌊	Left floor	230a	8970		&lfloor;	∉WGL4
≤	Less-than or equal to	2264	8804		&le;	
∧	Logical and	2227	8743		&and;	∉WGL4
∨	Logical or	2228	8744		&or;	∉WGL4
−	Minus sign	2212	8722		&minus;	
×	Multiplication sign	d7	0215		&times;	
∇	Nabla	2207	8711		&nabla;	∉WGL4
∏	N-ary product	220f	8719		&prod;	
∑	N-ary summation	2211	8721		&sum;	
≠	Not equal to	2260	8800		&ne;	
¬	Not sign	ac	0172		&not;	
∂	Partial differential	2202	8706		&part;	
±	Plus-minus sign	b1	0177		&plusmn;	
∝	Proportional to	221d	8733		&prop;	∉WGL4
∟	Right angle	221f	8735		&#8735;	
⌉	Right ceiling	2309	8969		&rceil;	∉WGL4
⌋	Right floor	230b	8971		&rfloor;	∉WGL4
√	Square root	221a	8730		&radic;	
∴	Therefore	2234	8756		&there4;	∉WGL4
~	Tilde operator	223c	8764		&sim;	∉WGL4
⊥	Up tack	22a5	8869		&perp;	∉WGL4

Set theory symbols

	Name of character	Alt-X	Alt-n	Word	HTML	Notes
∋	Contains as member	220b	8715		&ni;	∉WGL4
∈	Element of	2208	8712		&isin;	∉WGL4

	Name of character	Alt-X	Alt-*n*	Word	HTML	Notes
∅	Empty set	2205	8709		&empty;	∉WGL4
∀	For all	2200	8704		&forall;	∉WGL4
∩	Intersection	2229	8745		&cap;	
∉	Not an element of	2209	8713		&notin;	∉WGL4
⊄	Not a subset of	2284	8836		&nsub;	∉WGL4
⊂	Subset of	2282	8834		&sub;	∉WGL4
⊆	Subset of or equal to	2286	8838		&sube;	∉WGL4
⊃	Superset of	2283	8835		&sup;	∉WGL4
⊇	Superset of or equal to	2287	8839		&supe;	∉WGL4
∃	There exists	2203	8707		&exist;	∉WGL4
∪	Union	222a	8746		&cup;	∉WGL4

Miscellaneous technical symbols

	Name of character	Alt-X	Alt-*n*	Word	HTML	Notes
⌂	House	2302	8962		&#8962;	
⌐	Reversed not sign	2310	8976		&#8976;	
⌠	Top half integral	2320	8992		&#8992;	
⌡	Bottom half integral	2321	8993		&#8993;	

Miscellaneous symbols

	Name of character	Alt-X	Alt-*n*	Word	HTML	Notes
☺	White smiling face	263a	9786		&#9786;	
☻	Black smiling face	263b	9787		&#9787;	
☼	White sun with rays	263c	9788		&#9788;	
♀	Female sign	2640	9792		&#9792;	
♂	Male sign	2642	9794		&#9794;	
♠	Black spade suit	2660	9824		&spades;	
♣	Black club suit	2663	9827		&clubs;	
♥	Black heart suit	2665	9829		&hearts;	
♦	Black diamond suit	2666	9830		&diams;	
♪	Eighth note	266a	9834		&#9834;	
♫	Beamed eighth notes	266b	9835		&#9835;	

Geometric shapes

	Name of character	Alt-X	Alt-*n*	Word	HTML	Notes
■	Black square	25a0	9632		&#9632;	
□	White square	25a1	9633		&#9633;	
▪	Black small square	25aa	9642		&#9642;	
▫	White small square	25ab	9643		&#9643;	

	Name of character	Alt-X	Alt-*n*	Word	HTML	Notes
▬	Black rectangle	25ac	9644		&#9644;	
▲	Black up-pointing triangle	25b2	9650		&#9650;	
►	Black right-pointing triangle	25b2	9658		&#9658;	
▼	Black down-point. triangle	25bc	9660		&#9660;	
◄	Black left-pointing triangle	25c4	9668		&#9668;	
◊	Lozenge	25ca	9674		&loz;	
○	White circle	25cb	9675		&#9675;	
●	Black circle	25cf	9679		&#9679;	
◘	Inverse bullet	25d8	9688		&#9688;	
◙	Inverse white circle	25d9	9689		&#9689;	
◦	White bullet	25e6	9702		&#9702;	

Spaces

	Space	20	032	⌴	&#32;	space bar
	No-break space	a0	0160	Ctrl-Shift-⌴		
	Em space	2003	8195	Insert →		∉WGL4
	En space	2002	8194	Insert →		∉WGL4
	Four-per-em space	2005	8197	Insert →	&#8197;	∉WGL4
	Thin space	2009	8201			∉WGL4

Invisible controls

	Zero width non-joiner	200c	8204		&zwnj;	∉WGL4
	Zero width joiner	200d	8205		&zwj;	∉WGL4
	Left-to-right mark	200e	8206		&lrm;	∉WGL4
	Right-to-left mark	200f	8207		&rlm;	∉WGL4

Additional Notes

The information on typing characters in Windows and in MS Word is not universal but depends on the keyboard, program settings, and language mode. When using Word, you can first try the method in column 5 ("Word") and if it does not work, resort to the more general methods, which are more difficult to remember.

The notation "Ctrl-Shift-6" means that you press down both the Ctrl key and the Shift key and, keeping them down, press the "6" key. On many European keyboards, Shift-6 is the ampersand &, so for them, the combination can be described as Ctrl-&. This is more mnemonic if you think about "Ctrl-& A" as "A & something." Similar notes apply to Ctrl-Shift-7 (often Ctrl-/) and Ctrl-Shift-; (often Ctrl-:).

The notation "Insert →" means that the character can be inserted via the command Insert → Symbol, selecting the Special Characters pane and clicking on the name.

Coverage

The table contains all WGL4 characters, *except*

- Most ASCII characters, which should not cause difficulties in typing
- Box drawing and block elements, which are rarely used nowadays
- Cyrillic letters, to save space

Note that WGL4 is the collection that you can more or less safely expect to be available in common fonts on Windows. The table contains some additional characters, too, but they have been annotated with "∉WGL4." In particular, all characters for which there are entities in HTML have been included.

Ordering

It is difficult to put a large character repertoire like this into an order that is convenient in practical use. The ordering used here is meant to be as intuitive as possible. In particular, the mutual of order of letters with diacritic marks (e.g., À, Á, Â etc.) is alphabetic by the Unicode name of the diacritic. This order is not the same as the collating order.

Specific Notes

Specific notes referred to in the tables are listed here:

1. The shortcuts that can be used to write letters with diacritic marks vary greatly between keyboards. On English (U.S.) keyboards, you use special characters together with the Ctrl key, as indicated in the table. For example, to write ü, you would write Ctrl-Shift-6 u. The notation Ctrl-Shift-; can be read as Ctrl-: too, on a keyboard where Shift-; produces the colon. Many European keyboards (as well the U.S. International keyboard settings) have a dead key for the same purpose, labeled with the dieresis symbol, ¨. On such a keyboard, you would simply type ¨u to produce ü. On the other hand, you might be able to use a method like Ctrl-: u on European keyboards, too, but the colon might be placed in the period "." key, so that technically you would need to use Ctrl-Shift-; u. Similarly, Ctrl-Shift-` corresponds to Ctrl-~, Ctrl-Shift-6 corresponds to Ctrl-^, Ctrl-Shift-7 corresponds to Ctrl-&, and Ctrl-Shift-2 corresponds to Ctrl-@.

2. The euro sign can usually be typed using the AltGr key (or the Alt and Ctrl keys), but there are differences between keyboard settings. Usually AltGr-E, AltGr-5, AltGr-U, or AltGr-ε works.

3. Quotation marks can usually be typed in MS Word just by pressing the " key, if Word has recognized or has been told the language of the text, so that it can convert ASCII quotation marks to language-specific characters. In that mode, to type the ASCII quotation mark or the ASCII apostrophe, first use the " or ' key, and then immediately press Ctrl-Z to undo the replacement that Word makes.

4. Soft hyphen is not widely supported. In particular, MS Word does not recognize it. You can insert a discretionary hyphen in MS Word by pressing Ctrl-hyphen, but this inserts a control character, not the Unicode soft hyphen.

5. In the notations for typing en dash and em dash, the word "minus" denotes the minus sign on the numeric keypad.

6. When the language has been set to Spanish, MS Word converts a leading question mark ? or exclamation mark ! into an inverted one (¿ or ¡).

Mapping from Symbol Font to Unicode

Table A-4 is different from the previous tables: it specifies how the use of Symbol font can be replaced by the use of Unicode characters. The characters can of course be entered in any suitable way, such as those given in the other tables. The Symbol font was discussed in Chapters 3 and 4. The font contains symbols that have no counterpart in Unicode, such as the Apple logo (on Mac), but most of the characters that you can fake using the Symbol font can be written as normal Unicode characters. Trivial mappings that map a character to itself have not been included in the table, causing some apparent holes.

The first column contains the internal code number (in hexadecimal) within the Symbol font, and the second column shows what happens if that number is interpreted as a Unicode (or as an ISO-8859-1) code number. Thus, if you are accustomed to writing the character ∀ (for all, U+2200) by setting the font to Symbol and typing ", then the row with " in the second column tells the Unicode identity of the character.

Table A-4. Mapping from Symbol font to Unicode

Symbol			Unicode number	Name
22	"	∀	U+2200	For all
24	$	∃	U+2203	There exists
27	'	∍	U+220D	Small contains as member
2A	*	∗	U+2217	Asterisk operator
2D	-	−	U+2212	Minus sign
40	@	≅	U+2245	Approximately equal to
41	A	Α	U+0391	Greek capital letter alpha
42	B	Β	U+0392	Greek capital letter beta
43	C	Χ	U+03A7	Greek capital letter chi
44	D	Δ	U+0394	Greek capital letter delta

Symbol			Unicode number	Name
45	E	E	U+0395	Greek capital letter epsilon
46	F	Φ	U+03A6	Greek capital letter phi
47	G	Γ	U+0393	Greek capital letter gamma
48	H	H	U+0397	Greek capital letter eta
49	I	I	U+0399	Greek capital letter iota
4A	J	ϑ	U+03D1	Greek theta symbol
4B	K	K	U+039A	Greek capital letter kappa
4C	L	Λ	U+039B	Greek capital letter lamda
4D	M	M	U+039C	Greek capital letter mu
4E	N	N	U+039D	Greek capital letter nu
4F	O	O	U+039F	Greek capital letter omicron
50	P	Π	U+03A0	Greek capital letter pi
51	Q	Θ	U+0398	Greek capital letter theta
52	R	P	U+03A1	Greek capital letter rho
53	S	Σ	U+03A3	Greek capital letter sigma
54	T	T	U+03A4	Greek capital letter tau
55	U	Y	U+03A5	Greek capital letter upsilon
56	V	ς	U+03C2	Greek small letter final sigma
57	W	Ω	U+03A9	Greek capital letter omega
58	X	Ξ	U+039E	Greek capital letter xi
59	Y	Ψ	U+03A8	Greek capital letter psi
5A	Z	Z	U+0396	Greek capital letter zeta
5C	\	∴	U+2234	Therefore
5E	^	⊥	U+22A5	Up tack
61	a	α	U+03B1	Greek small letter alpha
62	b	β	U+03B2	Greek small letter beta
63	c	χ	U+03C7	Greek small letter chi
64	d	δ	U+03B4	Greek small letter delta
65	e	ε	U+03B5	Greek small letter epsilon
66	f	φ	U+03C6	Greek small letter phi
67	g	γ	U+03B3	Greek small letter gamma
68	h	η	U+03B7	Greek small letter eta
69	i	ι	U+03B9	Greek small letter iota
6A	j	ϕ	U+03D5	Greek phi symbol
6B	k	κ	U+03BA	Greek small letter kappa

Symbol			Unicode number	Name
6C	l	λ	U+03BB	Greek small letter lamda
6D	m	μ	U+03BC	Greek small letter mu
6E	n	ν	U+03BD	Greek small letter nu
6F	o	o	U+03BF	Greek small letter omicron
70	p	π	U+03C0	Greek small letter pi
71	q	θ	U+03B8	Greek small letter theta
72	r	ρ	U+03C1	Greek small letter rho
73	s	σ	U+03C3	Greek small letter sigma
74	t	τ	U+03C4	Greek small letter tau
75	u	υ	U+03C5	Greek small letter upsilon
76	v	ϖ	U+03D6	Greek pi symbol
77	w	ω	U+03C9	Greek small letter omega
78	x	ξ	U+03BE	Greek small letter xi
79	y	ψ	U+03C8	Greek small letter psi
7A	z	ζ	U+03B6	Greek small letter zeta
7E	~	~	U+223C	Tilde operator
A0		€	U+20AC	Euro sign
A1	¡	ϒ	U+03D2	Greek upsilon with hook symbol
A2	¢	′	U+2032	Prime
A3	£	≤	U+2264	Less-than or equal to
A4	¤	⁄	U+2044	Fraction slash
A5	¥	∞	U+221E	Infinity
A6	¦	ƒ	U+0192	Latin small letter f with hook
A7	§	♣	U+2663	Black club suit
A8	¨	♦	U+2666	Black diamond suit
A9	©	♥	U+2665	Black heart suit
AA	ª	♠	U+2660	Black spade suit
AB	«	↔	U+2194	Left right arrow
AC	¬	←	U+2190	Leftward arrow
AD		↑	U+2191	Upward arrow
AE	®	→	U+2192	Rightward arrow
AF	¯	↓	U+2193	Downward arrow
B2	²	″	U+2033	Double prime
B3	³	≥	U+2265	Greater-than or equal to
B4	´	×	U+00D7	Multiplication sign

Symbol			Unicode number	Name
B5	µ	∝	U+221D	Proportional to
B6	¶	∂	U+2202	Partial differential
B7	·	•	U+2022	Bullet
B8	¸	÷	U+00F7	Division sign
B9	¹	≠	U+2260	Not equal to
BA	º	≡	U+2261	Identical to
BB	»	≈	U+2248	Almost equal to
BC	¼	…	U+2026	Horizontal ellipsis
BD	½	|	U+23D0	Vertical line extension
BE	¾	—	U+23AF	Horizontal line extension
BF	¿	↵	U+21B5	Downward arrow with corner leftward
C0	À	ℵ	U+2135	Alef symbol
C1	Á	ℑ	U+2111	Black-letter capital i
C2	Â	ℜ	U+211C	Black-letter capital r
C3	Ã	℘	U+2118	Script capital p
C4	Ä	⊗	U+2297	Circled times
C5	Å	⊕	U+2295	Circled plus
C6	Æ	∅	U+2205	Empty set
C7	Ç	∩	U+2229	Intersection
C8	È	∪	U+222A	Union
C9	É	⊃	U+2283	Superset of
CA	Ê	⊇	U+2287	Superset of or equal to
CB	Ë	⊄	U+2284	Not a subset of
CC	Ì	⊂	U+2282	Subset of
CD	Í	⊆	U+2286	Subset of or equal to
CE	Î	∈	U+2208	Element of
CF	Ï	∉	U+2209	Not an element of
D0	Ð	∠	U+2220	Angle
D1	Ñ	∇	U+2207	Nabla
D2	Ò	®	U+00AE	Registered sign *in serif font*
D3	Ó	©	U+00A9	Copyright sign *in serif font*
D4	Ô	™	U+2122	Trademark sign *in serif font*
D5	Õ	∏	U+220F	N-ary product
D6	Ö	√	U+221A	Square root
D7	×	·	U+22C5	Dot operator

Symbol			Unicode number	Name
D8	Ø	¬	U+00AC	Not sign
D9	Ù	∧	U+2227	Logical and
DA	Ú	∨	U+2228	Logical or
DB	Û	⇔	U+21D4	Left right double arrow
DC	Ü	⇐	U+21D0	Leftward double arrow
DD	Ý	⇑	U+21D1	Upward double arrow
DE	Þ	⇒	U+21D2	Rightward double arrow
DF	ß	⇓	U+21D3	Downward double arrow
E0	à	◦	U+22C4	Diamond operator
E1	á	〈	U+3008	Left angle bracket
E2	â	®	U+00AE	Registered sign *in sans serif font*
E3	ã	©	U+00A9	Copyright sign *in sans serif font*
E4	ä	™	U+2122	Trademark sign *in sans serif font*
E5	å	Σ	U+2211	N-ary summation
E6	æ	⎛	U+239B	Left parenthesis upper hook
E7	ç	⎜	U+239C	Left parenthesis extension
E8	è	⎝	U+239D	Left parenthesis lower hook
E9	é	⎡	U+23A1	Left square bracket upper corner
EA	ê	⎢	U+23A2	Left square bracket extension
EB	ë	⎣	U+23A3	Left square bracket lower corner
EC	ì	⎧	U+23A7	Left curly bracket upper hook
ED	í	⎨	U+23A8	Left curly bracket middle piece
EE	î	⎩	U+23A9	Left curly bracket lower hook
EF	ï	⎪	U+23AA	Curly bracket extension
F1	ñ	〉	U+3009	Right angle bracket
F2	ò	∫	U+222B	Integral
F3	ó	⌠	U+2320	Top half integral
F4	ô	⎮	U+23AE	Integral extension
F5	õ	⌡	U+2321	Bottom half integral
F6	ö	⎞	U+239E	Right parenthesis upper hook
F7	÷	⎟	U+239F	Right parenthesis extension
F8	ø	⎠	U+23A0	Right parenthesis lower hook
F9	ù	⎤	U+23A4	Right square bracket upper corner
FA	ú	⎥	U+23A5	Right square bracket extension
FB	û	⎦	U+23A6	Right square bracket lower corner

Symbol			Unicode number	Name
FC	ü	⎫	U+23AB	Right curly bracket upper hook
FD	ý	⎬	U+23AC	Right curly bracket middle piece
FE	þ	⎭	U+23AD	Right curly bracket lower hook

Index

We'd like to hear your suggestions for improving our indexes. Send email to *index@oreilly.com*.

vs. single quotation mark, 418
appearance of characters, 9
application dependent, using virtual keys, 80
application media type, 494
Application Programming Interface (API), 554
application type, 483
ar (Arabic) ISO 639-1 code, 364
Arab (Arabic) script code, 336
Arabic digits (0–9), 375
Arabic language
    encodings, 148
    ISO 639-1 code, 364
    long and short codes for, 336
Arabic presentation forms, 476
ArabicShaping.txt file, 217
Armenian encodings, 148
Armenian scripts, 402
Armn (Armenian) script code, 336
arrows (← →), 13
ASCII (American Standard Code for Information
        Interchange), 37, 45, 117, 374–393
    Internet and, 505
    storage requirements and, 318
ASCII apostrophe, 377
ASCII Hex Digit, 215
ASCII quotation mark ("), 384
assigned code points, 177
asterisk (*), 377
at sign (@) (see commercial at)
atomic (units of text), 8, 12
attributes (HTML/XML), 360
audio media type, 494
authoring software, 506
auto-synchronization, 295
AutoCorrect (MS Word), 94
auxiliary characters data fields, 343
auxiliary keys, 74
azerty keyboard, 349

B

B (paragraph separator) Bidi Class value, 260
B encoding, 530
B2 LineBreak property value, 271
BA LineBreak property value, 271
BabelPad, 111
backquote (`) (see grave accent)
backslash (\), 374, 386
    (see also reverse solidus)
    CSS, uses for, 544

escape notations and, 537
backspace (BS) character, 392
backtick (`) (see grave accent)
Bali script code, 336
Baltic encodings, 148
bar (|), 389
base characters, 224
Base64, 304, 306, 498
basic characters (exemplarCharacters) data
        fields, 343
Basic Latin, 37, 173, 298, 374–393
    illogical division into blocks and, 205
    invariance of, 240
    rows and blocks, 173
    structure of database files and, 222
    vs. ISO-8859-1, 299
Basic Multilingual Plane (BMP), 139, 160, 171,
        207, 296
    CESU-8 encoding, 305
    noncharacter code points, 176
    storage requirements and, 318
Basque language, 346
Batk script code, 336
BB LineBreak property value, 271
bc (Bidi Class), 215
BCP (Best Current Practice), 319
BE (big-endian), 300
BEL (bell), 392
Beng (Bengali) script code, 336
Best Current Practice (BCP), 319
Bidi C property, 215
Bidi Class, 215
BiDi class, directionality property values, 260
Bidi M property, 215
Bidi Mirrored, 215
Bidi Mirroring Glyph, 215
BidiMirroring.txt, 215
bidirectionality, 259, 286
Bido Class, mirroring, 262
big-endian (BE), 300
Big5 encoding for Chinese, 141
Big5-HKSCS encoding for Chinese, 141
binary collations, 306
binary Content-Transfer-Encoding value, 498
Binary Ordered Compression for Unicode
        (BOCU-1), 305
BIPM (Bureau International des Poids et
        Mesures), 430
bit, 46

bitmap fonts, 33
BK * LineBreak property value, 271
blanked (ignorable) settings for collation
        elements, 255
Blis script code, 336
blk (Block), 215
blocked character, 241
blocks, 172, 215, 434
    illogical division into, 205
    internal structure of, 174–176
Blocks.txt file, 215
bmg (Bidi Mirroring Glyph), 215
BMP (Basic Multilingual Plane), 139, 160, 171,
        207, 296
    CESU-8 encoding and, 305
    noncharacter code points, 176
    storage requirements and, 318
BN (boundary neutral) Bidi Class value, 260
BOCU-1 (Binary Ordered Compression for
        Unicode), 305
bold type face, 32, 461
BOM (byte order mark), 301, 511
Bopo (Bopomofo) script code, 336

 tag (HTML), 469
braces ({ }), 376
Brah script code, 336
Brai (Braille) script code, 336
Breton language, 346
British (U.K.) keyboards, 76
broken bar (¦), 399
browsers, 361
    directionality and, 263
    encodings, viewing, 54
    entity references and, 109
    font support for, 58
    HTTP headers and, 508
    language negotiation and, 523
    languages, setting preferences for, 329
    settings, 64
BS (backspace) character, 392
Bugi script code, 336
Buhd script code, 336
Bureau International des Poids et Measures
        (BIPM), 430
button-like symbols, 456–457
buttons for character input, 578
byte order, 300–303
byte order mark (BOM), 511
bytes, 4, 46

C

C (Common) rule, 246
C programming language, 306, 377, 547
    escape notations and, 537
        Unicode, 551
    wide characters and, 553
C0/C1 controls, 389–393
    HTML characters, 540
    XML characters, 540
calendar subtype, 484
CAN (cancel) character, 392
Canadian Multilingual keyboards, 76
Canonical Combining Class (ccc), 215, 232,
        241
canonical decomposable, 234
canonical decompositions, 231–234
canonical equivalence, 99, 224, 228
canonical mappings, 226, 227
Cans script code, 336
capital letters, 244
caret (^) (see circumflex)
carriage return (CR), 390, 392, 426
Cascading Style Sheets (CSS) (see CSS)
Case Charts, 247
case folding, 215, 246, 588
    case mappings and, 245
    vs. normalization, 238
case mappings, 245
case ordering, collating, 253
case properties, 244–248
case sensitivity, 585
CaseFolding.txt, 220, 246
Catalan language, 346
catalog, 215
catenation operator (.), 557
CB * (Contingent Break Opportunity) LineBreak
        property value, 271
Cc General Category value, 212
ccc (Canonical Combining Class), 215, 232,
        241
CE (Composition Exclusion), 215, 242
cent sign (¢), 396, 435
Central European encodings, 148
CESU-8 (Compatibility Encoding Scheme for
        UTF-16: 8-bit), 304, 305
cf (Case Folding), 215
Cf General Category value, 212
CGI (Common Gateway Interface), 579
CGI scripts, 526

insertion menu in, 81
Unicode, sending, 54
MS DOS (see DOS)
MS Office, 58, 61
MS Word (see Microsoft Word)
MSB (most significant bit), 46
multi-octet encoding, 48
Multibyte Character Sets (MBCS), 555
multilingual applications, 7
multilingual web sites, 515–527
multipart media type, 494
multiple uses (semantics) of characters, 374
multiplication sign (×), 274, 398, 431
Multipurpose Internet Mail Extensions (see
        MIME)
multiviews method (Apache), 522
Mymr script code, 337

N

na (Name) property, 218
na1 (Unicode 1 Name), 218
NAK (negative acknowledge) character, 392
Nameprep algorithm, 532
names (Unicode characters), 165–167
<narrow> tag, 231, 476
narrow no-break space (U+202F), 415, 476
national variants of ASCII, 120
NChar (Noncharacter Code Point), 218
Nd General Category value, 212
negative acknowledge (NAK) character, 392
negative kerning, 269
negative transfer, 545
NEL (next line), 426
Netscape, 558
neutral directionality, 261
next line (NEL), 426
NFC (Normalization Form C), 238
    W3C normalization and, 243
NFC QC (NFC Quick Check), 218
NFD (Normalization Form D), 238, 240
NFD QC (NFD Quick Check), 218
NFDK (Normalization Form KD), 240
NFKC (Normalization Form KC), 238, 240,
        242
NFKC QC (NFKC Quick Check), 218
NFKD (Normalization Form KD), 238
NFKD QC (NFKD Quick Check), 218
Nkoo script code, 337
nl (Dutch) ISO 639-1 code, 364

NL (Next Line) LineBreak property value, 271
Nl General Category value, 212
No (General Category value), 212
no-break space (U+00A0), 122, 265, 400, 412,
        476
<noBreak> tag, 231, 476
non-ASCII characters, 530
    programming languages and, 536
non-breaking characters, 476
non-breaking hyphen (U+2011) character, 265,
        421, 449, 476
non-collapsing (space characters), 413
non-ignorable setting for collation elements,
        255
non-overridable properties (normative), 222
non-starter decomposition characters, 242
Noncharacter Code Point (NChar), 218
noncharacter code points, 176–178
normal (non-compatibility) characters, 234
normal (regular) type face, 32
normal form, 237
Normal.dot file, 97
normalization, 237–244, 588
normalization forms, 286
NormalizationCorrections.txt, 216
normative properties, 209, 215, 221
normative references, 286
Norwegian language, 346
not sign (¬), 398
notations, 7, 168
Notepad (Windows), 44, 71, 447
NS (Non Starter) LineBreak property value,
        271
NSM (non-spacing mark) Bidi Class value, 260
nt (Numeric Type), 218
NU (Numeric) LineBreak property value, 271
NUL byte (zero byte) convention, 550–551
NUL character, 306, 392
null pointer, 550
number forms block, 429
number sign (#), 374, 383
numbering characters, 39
numbers, 17, 164
    as indexes, 41
numeric character references, 109
Numeric Type (nt), 218
Numeric Value (nv), 219
numero sign (№), 411
nv (Numeric Value), 219

O

O with a stroke (Ø, ø), 395
OAlpha (Other Alphabetic), 219
objects (Java), 561
obsolete characters, 181
octet, 4, 66
    UTF-8 ranges, 299
octet sequences, 43
ODI (Other Default Ignorable Code Point), 219
OE (Outlook Express), 54, 146
    non-ASCII characters and, 530
OEM (original equipment manufacturer) code
        pages, 86, 128
offline data, 147
Ogam script code, 337
OGr Ext (Other Grapheme Extend), 219
OIDC (Other ID Continue), 219
OIDS (Other ID Start), 219
OLower (Other Lowercase), 219
OMath (Other Math), 219
ON (other neutrals) Bidi Class value, 260
OP (Opening Punctuation) LineBreak property
        value, 271
open collections, 36
OpenType, 33, 368
Opera browser, 55
Optional Hyphen, 83
original equipment manufacturer (OEM) code
        pages, 86, 128
Orkh script code, 338
orthography, 371
Orya (Orlya) script code, 338
Osma (Osmanya) script code, 338
Other Alphabetic (OAlpha), 219
Other Default Ignorable Code Point (ODI), 219
Other Grapheme Extend (OGr Ext), 219
Other ID Continue (OIDC), 219
Other ID Start (OIDS), 219
Other Lowercase (OLower), 219
Other Math (OMath), 219
Other Uppercase (OUpper), 219
OUpper (Other Uppercase), 219
Outlook Express (OE), 54, 146
    non-ASCII characters and, 530
overlined text, 461
override characters, 261

P

<p> tag (HTML), 469
pair table for line breaking, 278
PanEuropean character set, 36
paragraph breaks (¶), 83
paragraph separator (B) Bidi Class value, 260
paragraph separator (PS), 426, 469
parentheses (()), 376
parenthesized letters, 475
parenthesized numbers, 475
parenthesized symbols, 476
parityfec subtype, 485
paste (Ctrl-V), 91
Pat Syn (Pattern Syntax), 219
Pat WS (Pattern White Space), 219
pattern characters, 586
pattern syntax, 592
Pattern Syntax Characters, 586
Pattern Whitespace Characters, 587
patterns, 585
Pc General Category value, 212
Pd General Category value, 212
PDF (pop directional format) Bidi Class value,
        260
PDF (Portable Document Format), 45
Pe General Category value, 212
per mille sign (‰), 384
percent sign (%), 384
period (.) (see full stop)
Perl, 526, 556–558
    I/O, 574
    regular expressions and, 593
Perm (Old Permic) script code, 338
Pf General Category value, 212
Phag script code, 338
Phnx script code, 338
phonemes, 403
phonetic characters, 435
phonetic transcription, 355
PHP, 560
physical records (lines), 425
physical symbols, 397–398
Pi General Category value, 212
pilcrow sign (¶), 400
pipe (|), 144, 389
Pird script code, 338
pl (Polish) ISO 639-1 code, 365
plain text, 44, 193, 446, 482
    database files and, 222

About the Author

Jukka K. Korpela is a consultant who specializes in character codes, localization, orthography, usability, and accessibility. After graduating from the University of Helsinki, he worked at Helsinki University of Technology and taught in different institutions. Later he worked on localization and accessibility issues at TIEKE before becoming a full-time author and consultant.

Colophon

The animal on the cover of *Unicode Explained* is a long-tailed glossy starling (*Lamprotornis caudatus*). So named because of its lustrous plumage, this bird is indigenous to tropical parts of Africa, stretching from Senegal to Sudan. Glossy starlings are a common sight in that part of the world, and the bird's harsh, noisy call makes it difficult to miss.

Long-tailed glossy starlings spend most of their time in areas of open woodland, feeding on a mix of fruit and insects. Nests are normally built in a hole in a tree trunk, and a female starling will usually lay two to four eggs at a time. The feathers on young glossy-tailed starlings are dull brown and are not nearly as bright as adult feathers. Starlings grow to be about 21 inches, 13 of which is their long, striking tail.

The cover image is from the Dover Pictorial Archive. The cover font is Adobe ITC Garamond. The text font is Times New Roman; the heading font is Adobe Myriad Condensed; the table font is Arial Unicode MS; and the code font is LucasFont's TheSans Mono Condensed. Special characters that don't exist in the main body font are primarily in Arial Unicode MS. However, some special characters required particular fonts: Everson Mono Unicode, Microsoft Times New Roman, Microsoft Wingdings, Georgia, Symbol, Tahoma, and Verdana.

Get even more for your money.

Join the O'Reilly Community, and register the O'Reilly books you own. It's free, and you'll get:

- $4.99 ebook upgrade offer
- 40% upgrade offer on O'Reilly print books
- Membership discounts on books and events
- Free lifetime updates to ebooks and videos
- Multiple ebook formats, DRM FREE
- Participation in the O'Reilly community
- Newsletters
- Account management
- 100% Satisfaction Guarantee

Signing up is easy:

1. **Go to: oreilly.com/go/register**
2. **Create an O'Reilly login.**
3. **Provide your address.**
4. **Register your books.**

Note: English-language books only

To order books online:

oreilly.com/store

For questions about products or an order:

orders@oreilly.com

To sign up to get topic-specific email announcements and/or news about upcoming books, conferences, special offers, and new technologies:

elists@oreilly.com

For technical questions about book content:

booktech@oreilly.com

To submit new book proposals to our editors:

proposals@oreilly.com

O'Reilly books are available in multiple DRM-free ebook formats. For more information:

oreilly.com/ebooks

O'REILLY®

Spreading the knowledge of innovators   oreilly.com

Have it your way.

Milton Keynes UK
Ingram Content Group UK Ltd.
UKHW051008131024
449552UK00007B/135